外池滋生教授近影

In Untiring Pursuit of
Better Alternatives

より良き代案を
絶えず求めて

In Untiring Pursuit of Better Alternatives

より良き代案を絶えず求めて

江頭浩樹・北原久嗣・中澤和夫・野村忠央
大石正幸・西前　明・鈴木泉子 ［編］

開拓社

は　し　が　き

　本書は，青山学院大学教授外池滋生先生が2015年3月31日を以て，定年退職をお迎えになるのを祝し，授業や研究会を通して先生の教えを受けた者と先生と交友のある内外の研究者48名が，それぞれの研究論文を寄稿して編まれた記念論文集である．本書の書名『より良き代案を絶えず求めて』は外池先生の研究姿勢を示すもので，本論文集には先生のそのような姿勢に影響を受けた寄稿者による直近の研究を一歩進めた諸論文と，先生のこれまでの研究人生を振り返られた特別寄稿論文で構成されている．

　外池滋生先生は，1971年，東京都立大学大学院修士課程を修了後，同大学大学院博士課程に進学された．その後，1973年，ハワイ大学大学院言語学科に入学され，1979年5月，日本語の補文構造に関する博士学位論文によりPh.D.を取得された．またその間，1976年4月に明治学院大学文学部英文学科に職を得られ，2002年3月までの26年間，教鞭を取られた．また，明治学院大学在職中の1990-1992年には，フルブライト上級研究員としてMIT客員研究員も務められた．その後，2002年4月に青山学院大学文学部英米文学科に異動され，現在に至っておられる．

　私たちは「より良き代案を絶えず求める」先生の研究姿勢に，様々な場面において接してきた．先生は言語研究を始められた早い時期より，英語の分析と同様に日本語の分析を行ってこられ，生成文法理論の発展と共に，常に新たな日本語の分析を示されてきた．直近の研究では，日本語の語順そして疑問文の派生，構造に関して，より包括的な新たな代案を提案されている（「私の研究遍歴」を参照）．

　また，1993年に『英語青年』に掲載された論文，「ミニマリスト・プログラム：諸問題と展望 (7) 今後の展望—AGRの廃止をめぐって」も印象的である．当時，AGRという機能範疇を想定し分析することは当然のことで，AGRの存在理由を疑問視する研究者はほとんどいなかった．しかし，その数年後，AGRがその存在理由が疑われ廃止されることになることは多くの研究者の知るところである．これらのことは，「より良き代案を絶えず求める」先生の研究姿勢を考えると，当然のことなのかもしれない．

　私たちは，そのような先生の研究姿勢に，先生が週に1回開催されている

読書会においても，直接，接することができる．この読書会は長い歴史を持つもので（野村氏による「外池先生との思い出」を参照），先生の本務校の学生や教員のみならず，他大学の院生や研究者，そして言語学に関心がある社会人にも広く門戸が開かれている．この読書会をきっかけに，国内外の大学院へ進学し研究者の道を歩み始めた人，学位論文を書き上げた人——そういった人々にとっては，この読書会はかけがえのない存在である．青山学院大学を退職された後も，週に一度，読書会を続けていく意向を示された先生には感謝するばかりである．

外池先生は2015年2月24日に68歳の誕生日を迎えられ，同年3月を以て青山学院大学を退職されるが，学会や読書会などを通して，私たちはまだまだ多くのことを先生から学びたいと思っている．そして，私達自身が，先生のように「より良き代案を絶えず求めて」言語研究を続けていきたいと切望している．

最後に，特別寄稿論文の依頼を快く受けて下さった外池先生，そして招待執筆に応じて下さった寄稿者の方々に感謝の意を表しておきたい．

本書を外池先生と長年にわたって先生を支えて共に歩んでこられた奥様にお贈りしたい．

　　2014年　晩秋

　　　　　　　　　　　　江頭浩樹・北原久嗣・中澤和夫・野村忠央
　　　　　　　　　　　　大石正幸・西前　明・鈴木泉子

目　次

はしがき　v

〈第 I 部〉

Josef Bayer
A Note on Possessor Agreement ……………………………………… 2

Hubert Haider
On the Comparative Syntax of OV-Languages—Relating Unrelated Languages ………………………………………………………… 12

今井邦彦　Kunihiko Imai
認知語用論から見た英語のイントネーション
(English Intonation as It Is Viewed from Cognitive Pragmatics) ……… 26

金水　敏　Satoshi Kinsui
古代日本語の主格・対格の語順について
(Word Order of Nominative and Accusative Noun Phrases in Old Japanese) …… 37

久野　暲　Susumu Kuno
Sluicing と「島」の制約
(Sluicing and Island Constraints) ………………………………… 46

中島平三　Heizo Nakajima
Unpassivizable Transitive Verbs and Minimality ……………………… 56

西山佑司　Yuji Nishiyama
　属格名詞句の分離可能性について
　(Extraction of NP₁ from 'NP₁ no NP₂' in Japanese) ·· 68

大塚祐子　Yuko Otsuka
　On Tagalog Relative Clauses ·· 78

Henk C. van Riemsdijk
　Jeopardy ·· 88

Donald L. Smith
　Are World Englishes Movable: The Case of Asian Englishes ··············· 98

山内一芳　Kazuyoshi Yamanouchi
　パリ詩篇散文訳と King Alfred
　(The Authorship of the Prose Psalms in the Paris Psalter) ··················· 109

〈第 II 部〉

秋元実治　Minoji Akimoto
　'Be going to' 再考
　('Be going to' Reconsidered) ·· 120

阿部　潤　Jun Abe
　No Reconstruction Approach to A-Chains ······································ 130

坂野　収　Osamu Banno
　「ガ／ノ」交替現象についての一考察——中古・現代コーパスを対照して——
　(On *Ga/No* Conversion: A Diachronic Corpus-based Study) ··················· 140

江頭浩樹　Hiroki Egashira
　主語からの *Wh* 移動の可能性について
　(On the Possibility of *Wh*-extraction from Subjects) ························ 150

遠藤喜雄　Yoshio Endo
　ことばに見る対称性：サリンジャー・村上春樹・川端康成のカートグラフィー
　(Symmetry in Language: A Cartographic Approach to J. D. Salinger, Haruki Murakami and Yasunari Kawabata) ……………………………………………… 160

保阪靖人　Yasuhito Hosaka
　ドイツ語における非能格動詞の非対格化
　(The Unaccusative Usage of Unergative Verbs in German) ……………… 170

伊藤達也　Tatsuya Ito
　Eタイプ代名詞と「その」
　(E-type Pronouns and *Sono*) …………………………………………………… 179

泉谷双藏　Matazo Izutani
　Tangled Up in HOME—A Functional Approach— ……………………… 188

川島るり子・北原久嗣　Ruriko Kawashima and Hisatsugu Kitahara
　On the Core Ideas of Generative Grammar—Then and Now …………… 198

木口寛久　Hirohisa Kiguchi
　A Note on Binding Phenomena in Null Operator Constructions ………… 209

小泉政利　Masatoshi Koizumi
　言語の語順と思考の順序——インターフェイス条件の実証的研究にむけて——
　(Order in Language and Thought) ……………………………………………… 219

Eric McCready
　Syntax for Semantics: An Assessment ………………………………………… 229

森川正博　Masahiro Morikawa
　「腑に落ちない」の二重性が'腑に落ちる'今日
　('*Fu-ni ochi-nai*' and Its Lexical and Syntactic Structure) ………………… 237

森田千草　Chigusa Morita
　A Note on *Teki*-modifiers in Japanese ………………………………… 247

中栄欽一　Kinichi Nakae
　数量詞の逆スコープ解釈
　(Inverse Scope Interpretation of Quantifiers) ……………………………… 257

中澤和夫　Kazuo Nakazawa
　統語的機能構造について
　(On the Notion Syntactic Functional Structure) …………………………… 267

根本貴行　Takayuki Nemoto
　文法の発達過程における削除現象
　(Deletion Operation in the Process of Language Acquisition) …………… 279

野地美幸　Miyuki Noji
　The Acquisition of Inversion in Non-Subject *Wh*-Questions by Japanese Learners of English: An Asymmetry between *Why* and Argument *Wh*-Questions …………………………………………………………… 288

野村美由紀　Miyuki Nomura
　On Relatives ……………………………………………………………… 299

野村忠央　Tadao Nomura
　beware の用法及び活用体系に基づく定形性の概念について
　(On the Notion of Finiteness Based on the Uses and the Paradigm of *Beware*)
　……………………………………………………………………………… 310

大石正幸　Masayuki Oishi
　The Hunt for a Label …………………………………………………… 322

岡　俊房　Toshifusa Oka
　A Minimalist Sketch of Some Correlations between Word Order and Case ………………………………………………………………………… 335

Peter Robinson
  Second Language Acquisition Research and Syllabus Design: The Cognition Hypothesis and Task Sequencing ········· 346

佐野哲也　Tetsuya Sano
  Another Argument for the Sentential Scope Analysis of a Focus Marker in Child Languages ········· 357

西前　明　Akira Saizen
  tough 構文の派生について
  (On the Derivation of *Tough*-Constructions) ········· 368

瀬田幸人　Yukito Seta
  英語の複合名詞再考——概念結合の観点から——
  (Revisit of English Compound Nouns—From the Viewpoint of the Association of Concepts) ········· 376

島田　守　Mamoru Shimada
  可能性を表す can, may と必然性を表す must について
  (*Can* and *May* Expressing Possibility and *Must* Expressing Necessity) ········· 385

鈴木泉子　Motoko Suzuki
  ヲ格を伴う移動動詞について
  (Verbs of Motion with an Accusative Argument) ········· 394

高橋洋平　Yohei Takahashi
  空所欠落関係節の移動分析
  (Movement Analysis of Gapless Relatives in Japanese) ········· 404

高見健一　Ken-ichi Takami
  二重目的語／与格構文と「所有」の意味
  (The Double Object/Dative Constructions and the Meaning of "Possession") ········· 413

Christopher Tancredi
　　Anaphora, Deaccenting and Context Incrementation ⋯⋯⋯⋯⋯ 423

豊島孝之　Takashi Toyoshima
　　Unified Merge into Multidominance ⋯⋯⋯⋯⋯⋯⋯⋯⋯⋯⋯⋯ 435

塚田雅也　Masaya Tsukada
　　文型と項構造に関する一考察
　　(Issues on Sentence Patterns and Argument Structures) ⋯⋯⋯⋯⋯ 446

上田　功　Isao Ueda
　　機能性構音障害の音韻体系は「自然」なのか？
　　(Are Functionally-disordered Systems of Children "Natural"?) ⋯⋯⋯ 453

宇佐美文雄　Fumio Usami
　　head-lastへの語順変化は下降リズムが要因
　　(Head-last Syntax Goes with Falling Rhythm) ⋯⋯⋯⋯⋯⋯⋯⋯ 462

吉田方哉　Masaya Yoshida
　　Wh-movement out of DP and Intervention Effect ⋯⋯⋯⋯⋯⋯⋯ 474

遊佐典昭　Noriaki Yusa
　　カクチケル語から見た日本人英語学習者の空主語現象
　　(Null Subjects in Japanese Learners of English: A View from Kaqchikel) ⋯⋯ 481

外池滋生教授　略歴 ⋯⋯⋯⋯⋯⋯⋯⋯⋯⋯⋯⋯⋯⋯⋯⋯⋯⋯ 491
外池滋生教授　業績一覧 ⋯⋯⋯⋯⋯⋯⋯⋯⋯⋯⋯⋯⋯⋯⋯⋯ 493
私の研究遍歴―君子豹変― ⋯⋯⋯⋯⋯ 外池滋生 ⋯⋯⋯⋯⋯⋯ 507
外池先生との思い出 ⋯⋯⋯⋯⋯⋯⋯⋯ 野村忠央 ⋯⋯⋯⋯⋯⋯ 534
執筆者一覧 ⋯⋯⋯⋯⋯⋯⋯⋯⋯⋯⋯⋯⋯⋯⋯⋯⋯⋯⋯⋯⋯ 545

〈第Ⅰ部〉

A Note on Possessor Agreement*

Josef Bayer

University of Konstanz

1. Introduction

Since the seminal work of Abney (1987) and its introduction of the DP-hypothesis much progress has been made in the understanding of the structure of nominal phrases. Given the complementary distribution of the possessor phrase and the determiner—*Mary's book* or *the book of Mary* but not **Mary's the book*—it seems attractive to argue that the Saxon genitive *-s* occupies the same position as the determiner, namely the D-position. The question is then how to analyze possessive pronouns as in *her books*. Is *her* a D-head? Or is it a phrase in SpecDP with an associated zero D-head? I want to add some remarks about this question that arise from a comparison between English and German, and in particular from the question of the possessor's agreement with N(P).

2. A significant Difference between English and German

As has been noticed at least since Haider (1988), German shows the following contrast.

(1) a. All-e   ihr-e   Büch-er   sind   nass   geworden
       all-PL her-PL book-PL   are   wet   become
       'All her books got wet'

---

* The idea for this squib came from a seminar on the syntax of Germanic DPs that I taught in the winter term 2012-2013. My students may not have been aware of the fact that I learned from their questions. Thanks to Ellen Brandner and to Henk van Riemsdijk for communication.

b. *All-e   Maria-s   Büch-er   sind   nass   geworden[1]
   all-PL   Maria's   book-PL   are   wet   become
   'All Maria's books got wet'

Notably, this contrast is absent in English

(2) a. All her books got wet
    b. All Mary's books got wet

English and German look the same with pronominal possessors but different with nominal possessors. Where does this difference come from?

3. Agreement

Consider now the following German "possessor doubling" construction that differs formally but not semantically from the one in (1b).

(3) All-e   de -r   Maria ihr-e   Büch-er   sind   nass   geworden
     all-PL   the-DAT   Maria her-PL   book-PL   are   wet   become
     'All Maria's books got wet'

This construction is historically older than the Saxon genitive and survives especially in Southern German dialects but also in all kinds of spoken varieties. The name *Maria* appears decorated with the definite determiner *der*. The fact that this determiner can hardly be dispensed with may have to do with the fact that the possessor here is in dative Case, and that there are strong reasons in German to license dative Case by means of overt morphology.[2] Since proper names have given up overt Case morphology, assistance from outside is called for. Since pronouns and determiners etc. retain overt Case in the language, this assistance comes from the determiner. Assume now—following standard proposals about the German DP—that in the

---

[1] Notice that the examples in (1) can also appear with the plural –*e* lacking: *All Marias Bücher* .... The reason seems to be a mainly phonological one. There is a rule of schwa-deletion which might kill the final vowel. The issue is not trivial as seen by the deviance of missing-*e* in *all*(-e) Bücher von Maria* (all-(PL) books of Maria). I have to leave this issue aside.

[2] Various argument for that can, for example, be found in Bayer, Bader and Meng (2001).

possessor doubling construction the dative possessor *der Maria* is in the specifier of the DP headed by the possessive pronoun *ihre* (her-NOM,PL): [$_{DP}$ [$_{DP\text{-}DAT}$ *der Maria*] [$_{D'}$ *ihre* [$_{NP}$ *Bücher*]]]. The example looks exactly like the grammatical version in (1a), the only difference being the presence of the doubling DP in SpecDP. Compare now (4a) and (4b), where agreement in terms of Case and phi-features appears in bold-face.

(4) a. all-**e** ([der Maria]) ihr-**e** Büch-**er**
    b. *alle-**e** Marias Büch-**er**

This representation, I would like to argue, paves the way to understanding the contrast between German (1b) and English (2b). Two ingredients are required for the explanation: (i) pre-nominal agreement must be contiguous, i.e. there is something like an uninterrupted "agreement chain."[3] (ii) the Saxon genitive fails to agree. If this is the case, Q, Poss-pronoun and N agree in (1a) and (3) whereas Q and N fail to agree in (1b). As seen in (5b), there is intervention by the non-agreeing possessor *Marias*.

(5) a. all-**e** ([der Maria]) ihr-e   Büch-**er**
        +AGR   +AGR   +AGR
    b. *alle-**e**   Marias   Büch-**er**
        +AGR   −AGR   +AGR

What does this proposal say about English? The only logically sound consequence can be that (i) is trivialized by the fact that there is no agreement. If so, Q, N_{Gen} and N, "agree" in the sense that they all lack agreement features. This seems to be reasonable. There is no overt agreement in the pre-N domain in English whereas there is obligatory agreement in German. Is there "abstract" agreement in English with the Saxon genitive morpheme *-s* in an agreeing D-position? If this were the case, why would the same not hold in German?

Proposals about the syntactic structure of possessors are often and, in fact, should be guided by a hypothesis of maximal uniformity. Like any hypothesis, however, they must be open to falsification. According to Roehrs

---

[3] I believe it was in early work by Sue Olsen that I came across the useful term "Kongruenzkette" (agreement chain).

(2013), Krause (1999: 203) suggests that -*s* and possessive pronouns are allomorphs. This can well be the case but only as long as their semantic side and their internal distribution is considered. Morphologically they appear to be rather different. Roehrs (2013: 56) suggests for German a uniform structure as in (6) in which the functional exponent of the possessor is the morpheme -*s* throughout. It appears separated from the determiner and assigns Case to the lexical possessor that appears in (6a, c).[4]

(6) a. [$_{FP}$ Peter s-] [$_D$ ein] Buch   *Peter his book*
   b. [$_{FP}$ pro s-] [$_D$ ein] Buch   *his book*
   c. [$_{FP}$ Peter 's] [$_D$ ∅] Buch   *Peter's book*
   d. *[$_{FP}$ pro 's] [$_D$ ∅] Buch   *'s book*

The proposal is developed in such a way that there is underlyingly a generalized poss-head -*s* which then moves into the head position of FP. Although Roehrs does not say much about agreement, it seems to be implicitly assumed that the poss-head agrees with (the extended) N(P),[5] and that divergences from the underlying structure hold only on the surface. Of course, it depends on which properties of grammar one would relegate to the "surface". To me it seems that the difference between possessors with -*s* in English and in German signal a rather robust typological split between these historically closely related languages. As I will argue on the basis of further examples below, this split suggests that (2b), *All Mary's books got wet*, is fine because English lacks pre-nominal agreement altogether. German, on the other side, insists on pre-nominal agreement. The remarkable property

---

[4] FP stands for a functional projection. In (6a), the idea is that the separated -s assigns dative Case to *Peter*. As I said in note 2, according to my own intuitions an overt determiner would be required here: *dem Peter sein* ....

[5] He makes an exception though for Norwegian *hans* (his) which is said (p.86) to be uninflected.
According to Georgi and Salzmann (2010), Krause (1999) proposes that in the Saxon genitive construction –s assigns dative Case to the possessor:
   (i)   [[$_{DP}$ *Peter*$_{DAT}$] *s*]
But in this case we have to ask why (ii) is ungrammatical.
   (ii) *[[$_{DP}$ *dem Peter*$_{DAT}$] *s*]
If the -*s* is essentially the same as the possessive pronoun, it becomes difficult to account for the difference between (1b) and (3).

of German is then that with the adoption of the Saxon genitive its grammar has integrated a non-agreeing possessor. If this is correct, the descriptive generalization is as in (7).

(7) Generalization about prenominal agreement

	Q	D	A	-s
English	–	–	–	–
German	+	+	+	–

The examples with *all* are by no means isolated. Here are some with *every* and *some*.

(8) a. People put at *every John's gate* a decorated Christmas tree.
    http://www.exploringromania.com/saint-john-day.html   26.03.2013
  b. *Some John's most personal songs* were on his first album after the Beatles
    http://www.richmond.com.mx/microsites/readers/pdfs/MEDL4_3_FILE.pdf
                                                              26.03.2013

Any such examples are inconceivable in German. If in German the Q-head is followed by a Poss-DP, this DP is normally in a PP.

(9) a. Die Leute   stellen vor   jedes von Johns   Toren einen ...
       the people put   in-front-of every of   John's gates a
  b. Einige von   Johns   persönlichsten Liedern waren ...
     some   of   John's   most.personal   songs   were ...

With possessive pronominals it would be a genitive construction as in (10).

(10) Einige sein-er   persönlichst-en   Lied-er   waren ...
     some   his-GEN.PL   most.personal-GEN.PL   song-GEN.PL   were ...

There are speakers who do not use the genitive any longer. They produce data like the following.

(11) a. Jede-r   mein   Schritt   führt in die Hölle
       every-NOM.SG my-NOM.SG step-NOM.SG leads in the hell
       'Every step of mine leads to hell'
       http://forum.gofeminin.de/forum/carriere1/__f3336_carriere1-Warum.html
                                                                    26.03.2013

   b. Und einig-e   mein-e   Freund-e   haben
      and some-NOM.PL my-NOM.PL friend-NOM.PL have
      sogar geweint ...
      even cried ...
      'and some of my friends even cried'
      http://stubb.org/wp-content/uploads/2012/02/wahlen-erfahrungsbericht-nr-1.pdf
                                                                    26.03.2013

The interesting thing is that even under such conditions of loss of Case pre-nominal agreement remains as solid as ever.

The following data from English appear to be exceptional. Possessor and quantifier are inverted.

(12) a. Larry only likes girls who hang on his every word
       http://idioms.thefreedictionary.com/hang+on+every+word   17.12.2013
   b. John's every word seems to contain pearls of wisdom
       http://www.awakin.org/forest/index.php?pg=profile&cid=38&sid=11568
                                                                    17.12.2013

One can conclude from this that quantifier and possessor are equal with respect to agreement, no matter whether the possessor is a pronoun or a DP marked with the Saxon genitive -*s*.

4. Beyond Possessors

As one would expect, the findings about agreeing and non agreeing possessors are not an isolated fact. There are various cases that show that German insists on pre-nominal agreement whereas this is not an issue in English at all. Take the particle *only* and its correspondent *nur* in German. As the category 'particle' suggests, it cannot be inflected. In both languages it can appear in the leftmost position of DP where some researchers analyze them as adverbs and others as syncategorematic heads.

(13) a. Only the rain disturbs me
     b. Nur der Regen stört mich

Non-agreement in a pre-DP position, even if this position is part of DP, does not affect the generalization. The question is what happens when *only/nur* become part of the agreement chain. Here the languages diverge sharply.⁶

(14) a. The only real friend he has is George
     b. *Der nur   echte Freund, den   er hat, ist George
         the only real friend whom he has is George

The fact that *only* cannot be inflected does not hamper its role as a pre-nominal modifier or operator in English. German can only resort to lexical options which are semantically equivalent but are adjectival and can as such be inflected. Consider the adjective *einzig* (single).

(15) De-r   einzig-e   echt-e   Freund, den   er hat, ist George
     the-AGR single-AGR   real-AGR   friend   whom   he has is George

The same is true for pairs like *The very idea makes me shiver* versus *Der {bloss-e/*bloss} Gedanke macht mich zittern*. *Very* does not and cannot agree, *bloss* can agree and it must agree for the German construction to converge.

Before I conclude, let me add that agreement in DP is slightly more complex than shown so far. As van Riemsdijk (1998) has shown on the basis of Dutch data, agreement needs to be signaled at the right edge of AP.⁷ A

---

⁶ Notice that *nur* does appear inside DP.
 (i) Sein-e nur wenig-en Freund-e sind gekommen
     his-PL only few-PL   friend-PL are come
 'His friend, which were no more than few, have come'
Since *nur* has only scope over the quantifier, it is part of the agreeing QP *wenige* and does not interfere with the agreement between the three categories which are linked in (i) in an uninterrupted chain of agreement. This is different from (14) where *only/nur* takes scope over the next two words that follow it.

⁷ In the generative literature this has become known as the HEAD FINAL FILTER, cf. Escribano (2004).

post-adjectival adverb disrupts the agreement process although the adverb *genug* is contained in the AP *groß genug* and is therefore not a non-agreeing intervener between D, AP and NP.

(16) a. ein genug groß **-er** Teller
 a enough big -AGR plate
 b. *ein groß-**er** genug Teller

Witness now that the order Adv < A can be inverted and is even preferred in inverted order in predicative or adverbial usage as seen in (17).

(17) a. Der Teller ist groß genug
 the plate is big enough
 'The plate is big enough'
 b. Hans lief nicht schnell genug
 Hans ran not fast enough
 'Hans didn't run fast enough'

As van Riemsdijk observes, speakers who continue to use the order A < Adv frequently "repair" this order by simply inflecting the adverb.

(18) %ein groß genug-**er** Teller

For English, in contrast, there is no question that (19) is a completely legitimate output. Agreement plays no role.

(19) a big enough plate

A can be expected from this, English abounds with prenominal modifiers which lack the right-edge designation of adjectives altogether.

(20) a. a tongue-in-cheek remark (Escribano (2004: 26))
 b. a wrong in my opinion view (personal observation)

If so, one could expect all kinds of interventions between A and N in English, e.g. *the tired after the long walk people*. These are for sure dispreferred in comparison with *the people tired from the long walk*. My guess is that there are factors involved which are independent of agreement proper, perhaps preferences in phonological phrasing. I refer interested readers to

Biberauer et al.'s (2008, 2014) discussion of the so-called Final-Over-Final Constraint.[8]

5. Conclusion

English and German are, although historically closely related, typologically rather different languages. In English, the lack of agreement in DP leads to significant deviations from German (and certainly also from the predecessors of modern English). It is tempting to speak of a parametric alternation. Interestingly, however, one can see that the agreement system can be disrupted. The adoption of the Saxon genitive into the grammar of German has obviously lead to a small lacuna which the system somehow has to cope with. Possessors which are marked with the Saxon -s genitive are relegated to the DP's left edge, which as we have seen, is allowed to contain material that does not participate in agreement. If so, we can explain the deviance of (1b), *alle Marias Bücher. It is not really clear how one should exclude the order that does not interfere with agreement, namely *Marias alle Bücher. An explanation of this, related to the rare English examples in (12), must obviously come from a different angle. Notice that the quantifier beid- (both) is restricted like all- (all) in (1b) but allows the Saxon possessor in first position.

(21) a. *Beid-e   Marias   Büch-er   sind   nass   geworden
        both-PL   Maria's   book-PL   are   wet   become
     b. Marias   beid-e   Büch-er   sind   nass   geworden
        Maria's   both-PL   book-PL   are   wet   become
        'Both Maria's books got wet'

---

[8] This constraint, abbreviated as FOFC, is formulated in the form of a filter: *[γP [αP αβ] γ]. It rules out the example in (i) whose relevant structure is as in (ii).
  (i) *John is a proud of his son man
  (ii) ... [γP [αP proud of his son] man].

References

Abney, Steven (1987) *The English Noun Phrase in Its Sentential Aspect*, Doctoral dissertation, MIT.

Bayer, Josef, Markus Bader and Michael Meng (2001) "Morphological Underspecification Meets Oblique Case. Syntactic and Processing Effects in German," *Lingua* 111, 465-514.

Biberauer, Theresa, Anders Holmberg and Ian Roberts (2008) "Structure and Linearization In Disharmonic Word Orders," *Proceedings of WCCFL* 26, 96-104.

Biberauer, Theresa, Anders Holmberg and Ian Roberts (2014) "A Syntactic Universal and Its Consequences," Linguistic Inquiry 45, 169-225.

Escribano, José Luis González (2004) "Head-final Effects and the Nature of Modification," *Journal of Linguistics* 40, 1-43.

Georgi, Doreen and Martin Salzmann (2010) "Unifying Double Agreement and Possessor Agreement," handout, *4th European Dialect Syntax Meeting*, Donostia, San Sebastián, June 21st 2010.

Haider, Hubert (1988) "Die Struktur der deutschen Nominalphrase," *Zeitschrift für Sprachwissenschaft* 7, 32-57.

Krause, Cornelia (1999) "Two Notes on Prenominal Possessors in German," *MIT Working Papers in Linguistics* 33, 191-217.

Roehrs, Dorian (2013) "Possessives as Extended Projections," *Working Papers in Scandinavian Syntax* 91, 37-112.

van Riemsdijk, Henk (1998) "Head Movement and Adjacency," *Natural Language and Linguistic Theory* 16, 633-678.

On the Comparative Syntax of OV-Languages
—Relating Unrelated Languages

Hubert Haider
University of Salzburg

1. Introduction

Title and plot of this paper refer to Tonoike (1991). In this paper, he intends to demonstrate how close the structural parallels between the organization of phrase and clause structure seem to be between Japanese and English, modulo the head-final versus head-initial positioning of the heads in Japanese and English, respectively. The phrasal architectures are assumed to be identical in their hierarchical organization. It is only the relative order of heads and complements that differs. In other words, in English, lexical as well as functional heads precede while in Japanese they arguably follow their dependants. As a consequence, functional extensions of lexical phrases – in particular the functional extensions of VP that constitute the structure of a clause – are assumed to be left-branching structures in Japanese, in contrast to the right-branching organization in English.

However, if head-complement order is the major difference, this should also be the source of the systematic structural differences between a language like English and a language like Japanese. The two languages are representative of two language types, namely the SVO and the SOV organization of clauses. The numerous syntactic differences are not language specific; they reflect general properties of OV vs. VO languages. SVO languages share properties that are systematically absent in SVO languages and vice versa. What is the source of these systematic differences?

In this paper, Japanese and German will be adduced as representative cases of languages with an OV organization of clause structure. It will be shown that the head-final organization of clause structure is the syntactic source of at least the following list of differences (for a more extensive set of contrastive properties see Haider (2010: 11; 2013: 130-132). This brief list is not exhaustive, of course, but it is sufficient for making the point.[1] OV languages share these properties; in VO languages they are absent. This calls for a principled explanation. If the phrase structures were basically homomorphic, the syntactic properties of these languages should be alike, too. The directionality of the head of the phrase will turn out to be the crucial source of the differences.

- scrambling: OV yes; VO no
- non-compact sequencing of arguments in OV, but not in VO
- compact V-clusters in OV, inducing clause-union properties
- no functional subject position in OV and therefore no subject expletives in constructions without a subject argument
- nominalization of sequences of verbs (*verb cluster nominalization*)

2. SOV Properties, Exemplified by Japanese and German

OV languages reveal *scrambling phenomena*, VO languages do not.[2] Scrambling means linearization variation among nominal arguments, provided their relational grammatical status is marked distinctively (e.g. distinct case marking, distinct marking by postpositions, or distinct cross-referencing by means of agreement). As is well-known, Japanese and German allow for scrambling, but in English, scrambling is ungrammatical, even for relationally clearly identifiable items like the PP object in (1b, c):

(1) a. They will bring a box to you
    b. *They will bring [to you]$_i$ a box e$_i$

---

[1] This list does not contain SOV properties that are absent in Japanese for principal reasons. In particular, it does not contain movement-related constructions (e.g. the absence of a 'superiority' constraint in OV) since Japanese does not employ wh-movement operations (like wh-movement for question formation and relative clauses, or fronting into spec-positions, as in V2-constructions in German).

[2] I am aware that scrambling is a typical property of Slavic languages and that these languages are customarily filed as SVO. This attribution is empirically inadequate, however. Slavic languages do not share the typical SVO correlates. They are representative of a hitherto overlooked third type (see Haider and Szucsich (in press)).

c. *They will [to you]_i bring a box e_i

Dutch shares the absence of morphological case marking with English. Dutch is OV, however, and so it allows scrambling of prepositional objects (Geerts et al. (1984: 989f.)). (2) contrasts with (1b). In other words, Dutch scrambles; English does not.

(2) Toen   hebben de   autoriteiten [aan de moeder]_i het kind e_i
     then   have   the authorities   to the mother   the child
     teruggegeven
     back-given

The ungrammaticality of scrambling and the *compactness* of the sequence of nominal objects are instances of the very same restriction. In English, the sequence of the main verb and its objects is compact in the sense that intervening adverbials are ungrammatical:

(3) a. She hugged (*gently) her daughter
    b. She gave her daughter (*gently) a hug

In OV languages, adverbials may intervene[3] freely, both in Japanese and in German.

(4) a. Sie hat ein   Kind (sanft)   umarmt
       she has a   child (gently) embraced
    b. Sie hat einem Kind (sanft)   die Augen aufgemacht
       she has a   child (gently) the eyes   opened

Adverbials are interveners and so are scrambled items. This (at least partially) explains why these two properties are strictly correlated. What rules out the former, rules out the latter in VO.

Compactness is also at issue with sequences of verbs, that is, the main verb plus (quasi)-auxiliaries. In the case of verbs, compactness is a property of the clause-*final* sequence of verbs in a simple clause in OV languages.

---

[3] The object in (4) is not scrambled. It is indefinite and retains its existentially quantified interpretation.

For head-initial sequences, there is no compactness restriction, as the following English example from Quirk et al. (1986: 495 § 8.20) demonstrates:

(5) The new theory *certainly* may *possibly* have *indeed* been *badly* formulated

In VO, even in 'restructuring' constructions (as familiar from Italian and other Romance languages), adverbs may be placed between any two of the verbs:

(6) a. Maria lo$_i$ vuole poter (*immediatamente*) comprare e$_i$
Maria it$_{cl\text{-}acc}$ wants be-able (immediately) buy
'Pia wants to be able to buy it (immediately)'
b. Maria lo$_i$ vuole (*immediatamente*) poter comprare e$_i$

In German or Dutch, however, and in fact in any other OV clause structure, the sequence of clause final verbs does not tolerate any intervening material (except for particles of particle verbs), as (7b, c) illustrate.

(7) a. V°(*X) V°(*Y) V°
b. *dass er gesprochen *mit der Frau* haben muss
that he spoken with the woman have must
c. *dass er gesprochen haben *mit der Frau* muss
d. [Gesprochen mit der Frau]$_i$ muss er e$_i$ haben
e. [Gesprochen haben mit der Frau]$_i$ muss er e$_i$

VPs are extraposition sites in German, as the topicalized VPs in (7d, e) exemplify. The PP may be extraposed within the VP. In this case, it follows the head verb. However, reconstructing the topicalized VP into its base position would be ungrammatical (7b, c). Let me point out in passing that this fact is detrimental for a copy theory of movement, too.

The source of this syntactic behavior is 'verb clustering.' This is a phenomenon of OV languages. In head-final languages, complex head-final V-projections would be center-embedding structures. V-clustering is a grammatical means of avoiding stacked, center-embedded V-projections in simple clauses (8a). Instead of stacking VPs, the main verb and the (quasi)-auxiliaries are joined in a head-to-head adjunction structure, that is, a verbal cluster (8b). For Japanese, Saito and Hoshi (1998) argue that 'restructuring' involves complex predicate formation via direct merger of the verbs (see also Miyagawa (1987), Takahashi (2012)). For German and Dutch, the same conclusion is defended in Haider (1994, 2010). Compactness is an immediate consequence of clustering. As head-to-head adjunction structures, verb clusters do not provide any room for intervening phrasal material.

(8) a. *... [[[XP V_1]$_{VP}$ V_2]$_{VP}$ V_3]$_{VP}$
  b. ... [XP [[V_1 V_2]$_{V°}$ V_3]$_{V°}$]$_{VP}$

The bracketing notation betrays the offending property of (8a) in comparison to (8b) by its accumulation of brackets at the beginning. In (8a), the lowest VP is the most deeply embedded recursive domain. Verb clustering replaces stacked VPs by a single VP with stacked verbal heads. The verbal cluster is a local domain that does not provide any room for phrasal recursion. In short, this is the reason why the grammar of OV languages provides clustering. Clustering is parser-friendly and the clustering property of OV languages is a consequence of grammar-parser co-evolution in terms of the cognitive evolution between grammars a cognitive structures and the parser as part of the selecting environment (see Haider (2013: ch. 2); Haider (in press)).

Let us turn now to THE characteristic property of the SVO clausal architecture, namely the obligatory functional subject position preceding the VP.[4] Its grammatical raison d'être is the head-initial structure of the VP. In clauses with a head-final VP the grammatical trigger for projecting this functional layer is not operative (see section 3):

(9) a. [$_{VP}$ Subj. [V° Obj.]]   SVO
  b. [$_{VP}$ Subj. [Obj. V°]]   SOV
  c. [... [$_{FP}$ Subj$_i$ [F° [$_{VP}$ e$_i$ [$_{V'}$ V°→ ......]]]]]   SVO
  d. [................ [$_{VP}$ Subj [$_{V'}$... ←V°]]]   SOV

In a head-initial VP of the SVO-type, there is a single argument, namely the subject, which precedes the verb (9a). All the other arguments follow. In

---

[4] Originally, Chomsky (1981: 40) correctly associated this property with "English and similar languages." Later, it was mistakenly elevated to the rank of a universal property of clause structure and named EPP.

OV, every argument precedes the verbal head (9b). So, SVO singles out the highest argument already in the VP by placing it outside the domain of the object arguments. Given that the serialization of the objects relative to the verb is triggered by a directionality property of the head, the subject is not within the directionality domain of the verb in VO languages, but in OV languages it is. This is an essential grammatical difference. In VO, a functional head preceding the VP provides the directional license by a head and it provides a spec-position, too (9c). This is the source of the EPP property of SVO languages. The EPP property known from SVO languages is absent in OV languages (9d).

Expletive subjects are an immediate reflex of the obligatory functional subject position in SVO languages. Their systematic absence in OV languages proves the point. Since there is no obligatory functional subject position, there is no room for an expletive subject, and there is no need for explaining them away.

In Japanese, the absence of subject expletives could be explained away by reference to the null-subject property of Japanese which in fact is a null-topic property. Japanese is a topic-prominent language. Consequently, it permits null-topics, both for subjects as well as for objects. But, expletive subjects do not qualify as topics. So, topic-drop would not apply. An expletive subject is not employed in a clause without a subject argument, neither in Japanese nor in German (10):

(10) a. Es   wurde nicht gekämpft
         EXPL   was   not   fought
     b. dass (*es)   nicht gekämpft wurde
         that   EXPL   not   fought   was

In (10a), there is an expletive in the clause-initial position, but this is not a subject expletive. It is the expletive in the obligatory clause-initial spec-position of a German declarative clause. The expletive in (10b) would be the subject expletive and it is ungrammatical. Again, one ought to resist the temptation of explaining it away by allusion to a potential variety of pro-drop.

First, and in general, the explanatory gain would be nil if one insisted that each and every OV language is a semi-pro drop language simply because they all lack an expletive subject in clauses without a subject argument.

Second, and in particular, German is not semi-pro drop in other contexts. For instance, the subject expletive is mandatory in middle constructions of intransitive verbs (11) while in extraposition constructions, the "es" may be present or absent, both for subjects (12a) and objects (12b), with different syntactic effects, though.[5]

(11)   Hier sitzt *(es) sich   bequem
       here sits   (it)   itself comfortably
       'Here, one sits comfortably'

(12) a. Mich hätte (es) interessiert, ob   das stimmt
        me   had   (it) interested,   whether this correct-is
     b. Er hat (es) bestätigt,   dass das stimmt
        he has (it) confirmed   that this correct-is

For German subjectless passives, there is no choice, however. An expletive would turn the sentence ungrammatical (10b). There is, of course, independent and confirming evidence for VP-internal subjects in SOV. Since Japanese does not employ fronting operations to a clause-initial spec-position, the evidence is adduced from German. For example, a transitive subject may be part of a topicalized VP (13) in German.

(13)   [Der Mut   verlassen]$_{VP}$ hat den Mann   schon oft
       [the courage$_{Nom}$ left]   has the man$_{Acc}$ already often

Another clear case of contrast between OV and VO is the principal permeability of subject clauses for extractions in SOV languages, in contrast to SVO languages. In (14), the wh-item is extracted out of the infinitival subject clause of a transitive verb (Haider (2010: 201, 155)); in (15) out of a scrambled object clause.

(14)   [Wen]$_i$ würde   [dorthin e$_i$ begleiten zu dürfen]   dich mehr
       whom   would   [thither   escort   to be-allowed-to] you   more

---

[5] In the presence of "es", the extraposed clause is an opaque domain for extraction. Extraction is ungrammatical. If it is absent, extraction is grammatical. This indicates that there is no null pronoun instead of "es". It would block extraction just like the overt pronoun does.

freuen, sie oder ihn?
please, her or him?
'whom would it please you more to be allowed to escort, her or him?'

(15) [Wen]$_i$ hat (denn) [e$_i$ damit zu attackieren] jemand versucht?
     whom has (PARTICLE) [with-it to attack] somebody tried

Independent evidence for the existence of verb clusters in OV comes from deverbal nominalization. This construction is not admissible in VO languages simply because there is no base for this kind of nominalization since VO languages do not cluster verbs. Here are some specimens collected in web searches (16a–c):

(16) a. das [*Liegen-Lassen*]$_{N°}$ von Gegenständen auf der Fahrbahn
       the [lie (about) let] of objects on the roadway
    b. das [*Ertragen-Müssen*]$_{N°}$ von Schmerz
       the [bear must] of pain ('the state of having to bear pain')
    c. das [*Verstehen-Wollen*] des Anderen
       the understand-want (of) the$_{Gen}$ other
    d. das [*Gesehen-Werden-Wollen*]$_{N°}$ des Franz Müntefering
       the seen-be-want] (of) the $_{Gen.}$ Franz Müntefering

German NPs are head-initial, VPs are head-final. So it is easy to inspect the effect of nominalizing. The preverbal objects of the VP (17) are turned into nominal objects in the NPs in (16). Direct objects of the verb become genitive objects (16c) or prepositional objects (16a, b) in the NP. The genitive in (16d) is a subject-related genitive (as in: *Wile's proof of the theorem*).

(17) a. [Gegenstände$_{Acc}$ auf der Fahrbahn [*liegen*$_{V°}$ *lassen*$_{V°}$]$_{V°}$]$_{VP}$
    b. [Schmerz$_{Acc}$ [*ertragen*$_{V°}$ *müssen*$_{V°}$]$_{V°}$]$_{VP}$
    c. [den Anderen$_{Acc}$ [*verstehen*$_{V°}$ *wollen*$_{V°}$]$_{V°}$]$_{VP}$
    d. [[*gesehen*$_{V°}$ *werden*$_{V°}$ *wollen*$_{V°}$]$_{V°}$]$_{VP}$

Crucially, nominalization applies to zero level items. A cluster of verbs is the result of head-to-head adjunction and hence it counts as a (complex) zero level category. In VO, however, the corresponding verbs are the heads of stacked VPs; hence they are part of phrase level categories. So there is no way of joining verbs into a verb cluster for providing the necessary base of a deverbal nominalization in an SVO language:

(18) a. *the *let-go-skiing*
 b. *the *letting-go skiing*
 c. *the *letting-going skiing*

Cluster nominalization must not be confused with phrasal nominalizations as in the case of combining a VP with an article or a possessive, as in (19). In this case, the internal structure remains unaffected. It remains a VP.

(19) [das$_{D°}$ [dauernde [den Anderen verstehen wollen]$_{VP}$]$_{DP}$
 the [permanent [the other-one understand want]]

The essential difference is easy to isolate in German. In the nominalized form (16c, d), a nominal argument follows the head and bears genitive case, since NPs are head-initial and the objects of nouns are marked with genitive. In the VP (17c; 19), the object is marked accusative and it precedes the verbal head(s). In Japanese, the difference is less obvious, since NP and VP are both head-final. But case reflects the difference between a V-dependent argument (accusative (20a)) and an argument of a nominalized verb cluster (genitive (20b)).[6]

(20) a. [tegami-wo [kak-i-wasure]-ru/ta]$_{VP}$
   letter-Acc [write-inf-forget]-Present/Past
 b. [[tegami-no/*-wo [kak-i-wasure]]-wa$_{Nom}$]$_{NP}$
   letter-Gen/*-Acc write forget
        ('the forgetting of the writing of a letter')

3. Explaining the OV Syndrome

An in-depth exposition can be found in Haider (2010: ch. 1) and Haider (2013: ch. 3 and 5). The core theoretical assumptions are the following:

---

[6] I gratefully acknowledge that these examples were kindly provided to me by Masayuki Oishi (p.c.).

(21) i. Phrases are endocentric and universally *right-branching*.[7]
ii. A dependent phrase is licensed[8] by the head in the *canonical direction*.

Compactness, strict word order and the *need for a functional head* that relates to the subject in VO languages are properties that follow immediately from clause (21ii), as will be shown. Let me emphasize that the *very same* principle, applied under different directionality produces the different outcomes for OV and VO.

According to (21i) the universal structural grid of a single phrase is that of (22a) but not (22b). (22a) offers two alternative foot positions for a head, namely x or y.

(22) a. ... [... [... [x y]]]
b. *[[[x y] ...] ...] ...

The value for the canonical licensing direction is parametrical, that is, it is either progressive ("→") or regressive ("←"). The two implementations in (23) illustrate the directionality difference in the sub-tree that contains the head.

(23) a. ... [... [... [ZP ←V°]]]   OV
b. ... [... [... [V°→ ZP]]]   VO

The crucial differences between OV (23a) and VO (23b) become 'visible' when the phrase becomes more complex (24). In OV (23a), the canonical direction of licensing is congruent with the direction of merger. In (23b), however, the canonical direction is opposite to the universal direction of merger. This is the source of VP-shell formation which in turn is the source of compactness:

(24) a. ... [YP [$_{V'}$ V°→ ZP]]
b. ... [V$_i$ → [YP [$_{V'}$ e$_i$ → ZP]]]

When a second object is merged in VO (24a), its position is not in the

---

[7] In other words, the direction of merger *within* a phrase is universally to the left.
[8] A head *h* licenses a dependent phrase $P \equiv_{Def.}$ (a projection of) *h* and *P minimally* and *mutually c-command* each other (Haider (2010: 29)).

directionality domain of the head. Hence the head is re-instantiated (24b). This amounts to the formation of a VP shell. A shell is necessarily compact because of the minimality requirement of the licensing condition (see fn. 7). Any intervening phrase would destroy the relation of *minimal* c-command between the verb and YP, or between YP and the trace of the verb. Since this is the core of the licensing relation, interveners are excluded from complex head-initial phrases.

In OV, the situation is different, since the canonical directionality of licensing is congruent with the directionality of merger:

(25) a. ... [... [YP ← [$_{V'}$ ZP ←V°]]]
 b. ... [... [YP ← [Adv-P ← [$_{V'}$ ZP ←V°]]]]

In (25a), V′ as a projection of the head is a licit licenser for YP, but not in (24b) for the simple reason, that the canonical directionality domain of V′ includes YP in (25a), but not in (24b). Consequently, the OV structure tolerates interveners (26a), but the VO structure does not (26b, c). An Adverb, for instance, as an adjunct to V′ would not interfere with minimality, since there is always a sister node for the next higher argument (viz. YP) that is a projection of the head with the required directionality.

This is the essential difference between VO and OV. In OV, the projection nodes are potential licensing nodes, in VO they are not, because of the directionality mismatch. In VO, the only licensing element is the head, and therefore it must be re-instantiated, whence the shell structure of complex head-initial phrases. This explains compactness of VO structure and the incompatibility with scrambling.

(26) a. [$_{V'}$ YP ← [$_{V'}$ *Adv* ← [$_{V'}$ ZP ↔V°]]]
 b. *[$_{V'}$ $V_i°$→ [$_{V'}$ Adv YP [$_{V'}$ [$_{V'}$ e_i ↔ ZP]]]]
 c. *[$_{V'}$ $V_i°$→ [$_{V'}$ YP [$_{V'}$ Adv [$_{V'}$ e_i ↔ ZP]]]]

In (26b), the adverb would destroy the minimal c-command relation between V and YP. In (26c), the adverb prevents YP from minimally c-commanding the empty verb position, which is required for mutual c-command between V and YP. In each case, *minimal & mutual* c-command is violated.

Note that in (26), the crucial property of the adverb is its status as an *in-*

tervening element. The very same intervener status blocks scrambling. If an argument is scrambled, this means it is adjoined higher up. This turns the scrambled item into the same kind of intervener element as an adverb. Thus, compactness and the ban against scrambling are just two sides of the same medal.

The directionality mismatch is the trigger of the 'EPP' property of SVO structures. In SVO, the highest argument in the VP is outside the directionality domain of the verbal head (27a). Therefore, a functional head provides the directional licensing (27b). This functional projection establishes the functional subject position typical for SVO languages. In OV, all arguments of a verb are within its directionality domain, whence the absence of this functional projection in OV.

(27) a. .... [$_{VP}$ XP [V_i → [YP [$_{V'}$ e_i → ZP]]]]
 b. [$_{FP}$ XP$_j$ [$_{F'}$ F°→ [$_{VP}$ e_j [V_i → [YP [$_{V'}$ e_i → ZP]]]]]]

Verb clustering is related to the right-branching constraint (clause i.), too. Stacking VPs in OV produces left-branching structures. Cluster-formation avoids the stacking of VPs in favor of a single VP with a verb cluster.

4. Summary

Uniform principles – directional licensing (21ii) in universally right-branching phrases (21i) – produce two distinct sets of syntactic properties when applied to parametrically instantiated phrase structures, that is, to head-initial (VO) versus head-final (OV) phrases.

In OV, the direction of licensing matches the direction of merger. Hence, the head as well as any of its projection nodes are potential licensing nodes. In head-initial phrases, however, the direction of licensing is the opposite of the direction of merger. So, directional licensing depends only on the head of the phrase. Consequently, complex head-initial phrases display a shell structure. The head must be re-instantiated in order to be able to directionally license its complements. In OV, directional licensing is accomplished by the projection node that happens to be the sister node of a merged phrase.

The shell-structure plus the minimal c-command requirement for licensing amount to the grammatical causality for the typical restrictions of head-initial phrases, namely compactness and rigid order. For head-final phrases, these restrictions do not come up.

However, there are restrictions for head-final phrases—in particular for head-final VPs—that are absent in VO settings. These restrictions are the restrictions that apply to verbal clusters. Verbal clustering is a means of avoiding left-branching VP stacks, that is, stacked, center-embedded VPs. In head-initial languages, VP stacks are right-branching. Hence there is no need for providing an alternative to center-embedding. So, verbal clustering is not at issue in VO grammars.

Japanese, as a consistently head-final language, and German, as a mixed head-final language (i.e. head-final VP, head-initial NP), share the syntactic properties of head-final phrase structures for verbal projections and a sentence structure that is based on this type of VP. They contrast systematically with consistently head-initial languages like English.

References

Chomsky, Noam (1981) *Lectures on Government and Binding*, Foris, Dordrecht.
Geerts, Guido, Walter Haeseryn, Jaap de Rooij and Maarten C. van den Toorn (1984) *Algemene Nederlandse Spraakkunst*, Wolters-Noordhoff, Groningen.
Haider, Hubert (1994) "Fakultativ kohärente Infinitkonstruktionen im Deutschen," *Zur Satzwertigkeit von Infinitiven und Small Clauses*, ed. by Anita Steube and Gerhild Zybatow, 75-106, Niemeyer, Tübingen.
Haider, Hubert (2010) *The Syntax of German*, Cambridge University Press, Cambridge.
Haider, Hubert (2013) *Symmetry Breaking in Syntax*, Cambridge University Press, Cambridge.
Haider, Hubert (in press) "'Intelligent Design' of Grammars—a Result of Cognitive Evolution," *System, Usage and Society*, ed. by Aria Adli, Marco García García and Göz Kaufmann, de Gruyter, Berlin & New York.
Haider, Hubert and Luka Szucsich (in press) "Scrambling and V-positioning in Slavic Languages—Exeptionally VO or Regular T3?" *The German Middle Field in a Comparative and Diachronic Perspective*, ed. by Roland Hinterhölzl, Kristine Bentzen, Augustin Speyer and Luka Szucsich, Mouton de Gruyter, Berlin.
Miygawa, Shigeru (1987) "Restructuring in Japanese," *Issues in Japanese Linguistics*, ed. by Takashi Imai and Mamoru Saito, 273-300, Foris, Dordrecht.

Quirk, Randolph, Sidney Greenbaum, Geoffrey N. Leech and Jan Svartvik (1986) *A Comprehensive Grammar of the English Language*, 4th ed., Longman, London.

Saito, Mamoru and Hajime Hoshi (1998) "Controling Complex Predicates," *Report of the Special Research Project for the Typological Investigation of Languages and Cultures of the East and West*, 15–46, University of Tsukuba.

Takahashi, Masahiko (2012) "On Restructuring Infinitives in Japanese: Adjunction, Clausal Architecture, and Phases," *Lingua* 122, 1569–1595.

Tonoike, Shigeo (1991) "The Comparative Syntax of English and Japanese: Relating Unrelated Languages," *Current English Linguistics in Japan*, ed. by Heizo Nakajima, 455–506, Mouton de Gruyter, Berlin.

ID認知語用論から見た英語のイントネーション

今井　邦彦
東京都立大学名誉教授

1. はじめに

　Imai (1998) には「英語のピッチアクセントはその発話の関連性 (relevance) を示す」という趣旨のことが記されている．ピッチアクセントの適切な組み合わせであるイントネーションも（それが聞き手ないし第三者の口真似でない限り）まさしく関連性の表示である．今井 (2007) ではこの書が発音習得教本であることを考慮して関連性理論を表には出さなかったものの，同書のイントネーション記述の根本的背景は関連性理論である．
　本論文では，今井 (2001)，今井・西山 (2012) が展開している認知語用論[1]（＝関連性理論）と英語イントネーションとの関係を更に明らかに示したい．

2. 概念的符号化と手続き的符号化

　古くからの意味理論では，語や句はすべて概念を符号化したものであるかのように漠然と考えられていた．確かに「猫」，「美しい」，「尊敬に価する」などの語句は「概念的符号化 (conceptual encoding)」を受けた語句である．しかし関連性理論は，語句の中には，その発話の意味をどのように解釈するべきかを規制・誘導する機能を持つもの，つまり，発話解釈の「道しるべ」の役割を果たすものがあることを明らかにした．[2] これらは「手続き的符号化 (procedural encoding)」を受けた語句であり，(1) の斜体部にその例を見る．

---

[1] 関連性理論がそれ自身を Cognitive Pragmatics と呼び始めたのは比較的新しいことである．この時期にはすでに認知言語学 (cognitive linguistics) という，関連性理論とは全く異質な学説が勢いを得ていた．両者を混同することにないよう注意したい．
[2] 先鞭をつけたのは，Blakemore (1987) である．

(1) a. He'll be all right. *After all,* he's a grown-up man.
　　b. Ali Baba was poor, *but* his brother was rich.
　　c. *Well*, shall we start the ball rolling?
　　d. *So* you've been drinking again!

　(1a) の after all はその後に来る文が第1文の主張の理由付けであるものとして解釈が行われることを要請し，(1b) の but は，第1文が述べていることと第2文のそれとの間に何らかの対照があるとして解釈されることを要請し，(1c) の well は聞き手の考え（この場合は「まだ本題に入らず，雑談を続けていい」という気持ち）に終止符を打つことを要請し，(1d) の so はそれに続く文内容が，聞き手の息の熟柿臭さとか呂律の怪しさを根拠とした結論であることを示している．なお (1c, d) からは，手続き的符号化を受けた語が，必ずしも先行する発話を必要とはしていないことが理解される．

　これらの手続き的符号化語句は，必ずしも使用されなくとも，その発話が，聞き手の推論により，正しく解釈されることが多いが，使用されれば聞き手の理解のためのコストはその分軽減されることになると言える．

3. 語用論過程

　符号化された語を用いた言語形式の使用，つまり発話の構成は，話し手の行う行為である．これに対して，言語形式を手掛かりの1つとして，推論を用いて話し手の意図する意味を解釈・理解するのは聞き手の役目である．

　語用論過程は，聞き手が話し手の発話の明意（explicature）を同定する推論過程であり，次の4種を数える．

曖昧性除去 (disambiguation)

　(2)　He went to the bank.

の bank 部分について，「銀行・土手」のどちらが話し手の意図する意味であるかを聞き手が推論により判定するのが「曖昧性除去」の例である．

飽和 (saturation)

　「彼，これ，昨日，あそこ」等の直示的表現が具体的に誰，何，何時(いつ)，何処(どこ)を指しているかを明らかにするのが「飽和」である．この過程にはもう1つ役割がある．(3) を例に取れば，[ ] に囲まれた「言語形式上本来存在するが，

表現されていない要素」を補う役割である．

(3) a. リニア新幹線の方がずっと速いよ．［何よりも？］
    b. 大好きよ．［誰が何／誰を？］
    c. 太郎は若すぎる．［何をするために？］

(3a) の［　］内が，たとえば「フランスの TGV よりも」と解されるならば，それは飽和がもたらした解釈である．

アドホック概念構築 (ad hoc concept construction)

(4) a. 正月には飲みすぎた．
    b. この塩焼き，生(なま)だぜ．
    c. 花子の顔は正三角形だ．

(4a) では「飲む」の対象がアルコール飲料に限定されており，この動詞の意味が狭隘化されている．(4b) では「生」が「一切加熱されていない」よりも意味を拡張して使われている．(4c) では「正三角形」が「正三角形に似た形」という，やはり意味を広げた形で使われている．これらは，語句がアドホック概念 (ad hoc concept) で用いられている例である．

自由補強 (free enrichment)

(5) a. You're not going to die.
    b. Sheila hit Ron and he walked out on her.
    c. I've eaten breakfast.

(5) からは，自由補強によりたとえば (5′) が得られる．

(5′) a. You're not going to die *from that cut*.
     b. Sheila hit Ron, *and then, as a result*, he walked out on her.
     c. I've eaten breakfast *this morning*.

(5a) は，指先にちょっとした擦り傷ができただけで泣き叫んでいる子に言われたのだとしよう．その解釈である (5′a) の斜体部は自由補強によって補足的に解釈された要素である．(5b) で and より前の部分は後の部分より時間的に先に起こり，前者は後者の原因である，と解釈できる．その解釈を表した (5′b) の斜体部も，自由補強によりもたらされたものである．(5c) が 30 年前の朝食などではなく，「その日の」朝食をとった，という解釈を表した (5′c)

の斜体部は，これまた自由補強により補われたものである．

4. ピッチアクセント

英語のピッチアクセントはまず下降調 (Fall) と上昇調 (Rise) に分かれ，それぞれの出発点が高いか低いか[3]によって4種を数える．さらに高い下降調と低い上昇調がこの順で組み合わされた下降上昇調，低い上昇調と高い下降調がこの順に組み合わされた上昇下降調が1種ずつある．これに加えて高い下降調が「弱化」[4]した高い平板調と，低い上昇調が弱化した低い平板調が1種ずつあり，計8種となる．この8種のピッチアクセントの名称と，それを表す記号とを示すと，(6) となる．

(6) a. 「低下降調 (Low Fall)」　　　[ˎ]
    b. 「高下降調 (High Fall)」　　　[ˋ]
    c. 「低上昇調 (Low Rise)」　　　[ˏ]
    d. 「高上昇調 (High Rise)」　　　[ˊ]
    e. 「下降上昇調 (Fall-Rise)」　　[ˇ]
    f. 「上昇下降調 (Rise-Fall)」　　[ˆ]
    g. 「低平板調 (Low Level)」　　　[ˌ]
    h. 「高平板調 (High Level)」　　 [ˈ]

(6a-f) は発話の最後のストレスのある音節に与えられることが多いため，伝統的音声学では「核 (nuclear tones; nuclei)」と呼ばれ，(6g-h) は核より前の所謂 pre-nuclear tunes に用いられる．

5. イントネーションが表すこと

説明の都合上，上昇調の"意味"から始めると，それは「判断保留」である．何に関する判断保留か？（以下の例文では，< >内は先行する発話とする．）

(7) a. <I'll give him the sack.> You ˌcan't do ˏthat.
    b. ˈSleep ˏtight.

---

[3] 「高」と「低」の意味の差については，今井 (2007: 181ff.) を見ること．
[4] このタイプの弱化，および平板調の"意味"については今井 (2007: 175ff.) を見ること．

c. <Which city is the state capital of California?> San Fran ´cisco.

　(7a) の < > 内がワンマン社長，後続する発話がヒラトリのものとしよう．ヒラトリ氏は社長の意見に反対しているわけだが，これをもし下降調で言ったらば，自分の首も危なくなる．そこで上昇調によって「自分が反対意見を言うことの是非」についての判断保留をいわば修辞的に示し「お言葉を返すようで申し訳ありませんが」という態度を表現しているわけである．

　(7b) は命令文である．命令文は基本的に聞き手に何かを強いる文型だ．しかしこの発話は，修辞的判断保留の使用によって，強要ではなく，「よく眠れますように」という優しい祈願となっている．

　(7c) の < > 内のクイズへの正答はむろん Sacramento である．San Francisco と答えてしまったこの人は，自信がないので，「自分の答えの正しさ」に対する判断保留を示すために上昇調を使っているのである．

　次に下降調の "意味" を見よう．それは「判断保留の不在」である．

　(8) a. <I'll sock him on the jaw.> You 'can't do `that. You'd be arrested for an act of violence.
　　　b. 'Are you 'quite `sure?
　　　c. <'Bill is 'well-`read.> 'Bill is 'well-`read indeed. He's even heard of Shakespeare.

　(8a) の You can't … 以下の発話をしている人は，< > 内の発話の話し手と同等かそれより目上の人物としよう．(7a) の場合と違って遠慮の必要はないから，下降調を使って「判断保留の不在」を示すわけである．

　(8b) は疑問文である．疑問文が 'Have you got the ‚time? とか 'Could you do me a ‚favour? のような丁寧な質問ないし依頼であるならば，示したように上昇調の使用によって自分が質問ないし依頼を行う権利への判断保留を示し，「お手間を取らせて申し訳ありませんが」とでもいうべき態度の表明を行う．しかし (8b) は充分な証拠や論拠を示さずに話し手を非難する相手に対する詰問である．判断保留不在を示すことによって「これは私が当然の権利の下に行っている質問である」という態度が表明されている．

　(8c) の < > 内はビルが本当に多読博識であると考えている人の発話である．そこに何の判断保留がないため，下降調が使われている．< > より後の発話は，ビルが多読博識であると信じるなどとは愚の骨頂だと見ている人の発話だ．そのことは He's even heard of Shakespeare. という嘲笑的な言葉にも

現れている．ではなぜこの人の Bill is well-read indeed. は＜　＞内の発話と同じく下降調で言われているのか？　それは前者が後者の口真似（echo）だからである．ここでもし上昇調を使ってしまえば，皮肉ではなくなってしまう．

次は下降上昇調に移ろう．(9) に例を挙げる．

(9) a. You have `lovely ˇeyes.
　　b. He `doesn't `lend his books to ˇanybody.
　　c. ＜娘：What a 'lovely ˌswimsuit!＞
　　　　父親：What a `lovely ˇhandkerchief!

上昇調が判断保留を示し，下降調がその不在を示すものであるならば，上昇下降調・下降上昇調とは矛盾ではないか，という疑問が起こるかもしれない．しかしそれは当たっていない．下降部分と上昇部分の対象が異なるからである．
(9a) では下降部分は「君の眼は綺麗だ」という命題が対象になっており，これについては判断保留がないことを示している．上昇部分は「眼」から連想される鼻，口等の顔の造作や体形などが lovely であるかどうかについての判断保留を示している（つまり，言外に造作や体形をけなしている）わけである．日本語に意訳すれば，「君は眼は綺麗なんだがねえ ...」ということになろう．
(9b) についても，下降部分は He doesn't lend his books to anybody. という命題を対象とし，この対象に関する判断保留がないことを示しており，上昇部分は not+anybody が文字通り nobody であるという解釈に判断保留をしている．そこで (9b) を日本語にすれば「彼は誰にでも本を貸すわけではない（人を選んで貸す）」となるのである．

(9c) の娘はビキニか何かを店のウィンドウで見て本気で（つまり，判断保留なしに）「素敵だ」と言っているのだが，父親の発話は，説明的訳を先に挙げれば，「あんなに少しの布しか使っていない水着じゃあ，ハンカチを着ているようなもんだぜ」とでもなろう．下降調は件の水着を比喩的に「ハンカチだ」と言っている部分を対象とし，上昇調は娘へのたしなめの言葉を和らげるための判断保留の役割を果たしている．

上昇下降調について見てみよう．(10) が例である．

(10) a. ＜Would you lend me a hand?＞ You're a ^nuisance.
　　　b. ＜Would you lend me a hand?＞ I'd be de^lighted to.
　　　c. ＜As a matter of fact, I hate this job.＞ ^Tell them you hate it.

上昇下降調の下降部分は，(10a, b, c) いずれの場合も，文が持つ意味——それ

ぞれ「君は迷惑をかける奴だ」「喜んで致しますよ」「その仕事がいやだって連中に言ってやりなさい」——について話し手が何の判断保留も持たないことを表す．一方，上昇部分は相手が前提的に抱いていると見られる考え・態度に対する幾分の驚きを持った判断保留（否定に近い）を示している．(10′) に (10a, b, c) 各々について，判断保留の対象を [ ] 内に，それを盛り込んだ意訳を 〈 〉 内に示す．

(10′) a. ［相手が話し手への依頼を当然のこととしている態度］
〈また他人(ひと)頼みか？迷惑な奴だ．少しは自立心を持てよ．〉
b ［相手がこちらに遠慮すべき立場にいるとする考え］
〈御依頼を受けなくたって，貴女のためなら何でも致しますよ．〉
c. ［仕事を命じた人に不平は言えないと決めている相手の考え］
〈遠慮することはない．堂々と文句を言ってやれよ．〉

6. イントネーション解釈は語用論過程のどれに相当するか？

　判断保留も，判断保留不在も，その対象は千差万別である．したがって何が対象であるかを同定することは，bank が持つ有限数の意味からいずれかを選択するのとは異なる．イントネーション解釈は，したがって，「曖昧性除去」ではない．

　イントネーションの"意味"には，直示的な表現の指示対象を明らかにしたり，「言語形式上本来存在するが，表現されていない要素」を補ったりする機能はない．よってイントネーション解釈は「飽和」であるとは言えない．[5]

　「アドホック概念構築」は，ある語や句の概念的意味を，より狭く，あるいはより広く解釈することであるが，イントネーションにはそうした機能がないので，イントネーション解釈はアドホック概念構築にも当てはまらない．

　語用論過程のうち，イントネーション解釈に相当しそうに思えるのは「自由補強」である．(7a-c) の，イントネーションを考慮した解釈は，(7′a-c) のように表すことができる．

---

[5] John hit Bill, and then ʹhe hit ˋhim. において，アクセントゆえに he が Bill, him が John を指すことが明らかになるとする説があるが，この，native speakers の中にも異論を持つ人がいる1例を以てイントネーション解釈が飽和であることの根拠とするのは些か無理である．

(7′) a. *I hate myself saying this, but* you can't do that.
　　b. *I sincerely hope that you will* sleep tight.
　　c. *I **think** it is* San Francisco, *though I'm not at all sure if this answer is correct.*

これらの斜体部は，(5) の各文に自由補強によって付加された斜体部と同種の原因と同種の効果を以て与えられたものと考えられる.

　(8a, b) についても，その解釈は (8′a, b) として示すことができる.

(8′) a. *I strongly urge that you refrain* from doing that.
　　b. *The question is,* whether you are quite sure!

ここでも，斜体部は自由補強によってもたらされたものと考えられる.

　(8c) の 'Bill is 'well-ˋread indeed. は幾分特殊である. これは表出命題ではあるが，明意ではない.[6] 言い換えれば発話のこの部分は相手の発話をオウム返しにしたもので，「言及されてはいるが，意味されてはいない」部分なのである.

　(9) の解釈は，(9′) のように spell out できよう.

(9′) a. I admit that your eyes are lovely, *but I reserve judgement on other features of yours.*
　　b. He lends his books *not to everybody: he's choosy about people he lends his books to.*
　　c. *That garment is more like a handkerchief than a swimsuit, if you don't mind my saying so.*

この場合も斜体部は自由補強によって供給された部分と言えよう.

　今度は (10) について考えよう. 解釈は (10′) と考えられる.

(10′) a. *It goes without saying that* you're a nuisance.
　　 b. *Needless to say,* I'd be delighted to.
　　 c. *Obviously, you ought to* tell them you hate it.

これらの例でも，斜体部は自由補強によってもたらされた要素である.

---

[6] 表出命題と明意の違いについては，今井 (2005) や今井・西山 (2012) を見よ.

7. 暗 意

語用論による発話解釈は，語用論的過程という柱に加え，もう1本の柱として「暗意 (implicature)」の獲得という柱から成る．(11a-c) の < > 部分に対する返答からはそれぞれ (11'a-c) という暗意が得られる．

(11) a. <Have you read John's new book?> I don't read what hacks write.
　　b. <May I have a word with you?> I have my hands full right now.
　　c. <Is Jane a good cook?> She's English.
(11') a. I haven't read John's new book.
　　b. I haven't got time to talk with you right now.
　　c. Jane is a bad cook.

8. 自由補強と暗意獲得

4種の語用論過程の中で，自由補強は言語形式から最も遠い過程であると言える．曖昧性除去は語句に符号化されている有限個の概念の中から1つを選ぶ過程だから，言語形式に強く依存している．飽和は，直示的な表現の指示対象を明らかにしたり，言語形式上本来存在するが，表現されていない要素を補う過程だから，やはり言語形式に密着している．アドホック概念構築も，語句に符号化されている概念を狭隘化したり，拡大したりして使用するのだから，やはり言語形式に依存している．

上記3種に比べると，自由補強の言語形式への依存度は低い．飽和の場合も表面に表れていない言語形式が補われるが，それは文法上本来あるべきタイプの言語形式である．(3a) を例に取れば，「... の方が速い」という語句には文法上「～よりも」という語句が文法上本来伴われなければならない．それは英語の is faster の後には than ～ が本来的に文法上伴われなければならないのと同じである．それに対して自由補強では，(5a) を例に取れば，死には必ず死因があるわけだが，それは理論上の，あるいは生物学上の必然性であって，日本語の「死ぬ」にも英語の die にも，死因をあらわす語句は，文法上は必須のものとして伴われていない．少し古い生成文法の用語を用いるなら，「死ぬ」も die も死因をあらわす語句によって下位範疇化 (subcategorize) されていないのである．つまり自由補強は下位範疇化の資格を持たない語句が補われる，

という点で，飽和の場合よりも言語形式への依存度が低いのである．

では暗意の言語形式依存度はどうか？　少なくとも (11) のような例を見る限り，それは自由補強の言語形式依存度よりもさらに低い．自由補強で得られた解釈には，(5) と (5′) を比べれば判る通り，解釈前の言語形式が解釈後も残っているが，(11) の ＜　＞ より後の発話と，(11′) に示された解釈を比べると，前者の言語形式が後者には全く使われていないことが判る．つまり自由補強は語用論過程の中でこそ言語形式に対する依存度が低いが，それでも幾分かの依存度を有しているのに対し，暗意は，その獲得の源泉となる発話その他から「推論のみによって得られる」ものである（これが関連性理論による主張である）ことの証拠と言えよう．

翻って，イントネーションを手掛かりとする自由補強・暗意獲得の差を見てみよう．(7) の言語形式は確かに (7′) の中に生きている．しかし (9)，(9′) を比較してみると，前者の言語形式が後者に残っているとはいえ，後者には前者の言語形式に依存しない部分があまりにも多いと感ぜられないだろうか？ (9′a) の *but I reserve judgement on other features of yours*，(9′b) の *he's choosy about people he lends his books to* という部分，さらに (9′c) の全文は，むしろ暗意と言っていいほど (9c) の言語形式から離れているのではないか？

O'Connor and Arnold (1973) は次の 2 文の 'intonation pattern' の "意味" を protesting, challenging, censorious 等の言葉で表している．

(12) a.　<May I have some more trifle?>　You've ˆeaten it all.
　　　b.　<Would you mind lending me a hand?>　You're a ˆnuisance.

これを敷衍すれば，(12a, b) はそれぞれ (12′a, b) という暗意を持つことになる．

(12′) a.　It's YOUR fault that there's no more trifle left.
　　　b.　It's time you learned to do things by yourself.

このことはイントネーションを対象に含ませつつ発話解釈を行う場合，自由補強によって得られる解釈と暗意の区別が難しいことを示している．言い換えれば，明意と暗意の差が，少なくともイントネーションを考慮に入れる場合，再考の余地があるかもしれないということである．さらに，自由補強と高次明意 (higher-level explicature) の異同も問題となるが，これは紙数からして宿題とするほかない．

関連性理論の根幹に関わることではないが，この理論の細部に亘る交通整理が必要であろう．そう考えるとこの最終節は，Imai (1998) のそれと同じく，Some residual problems と題されてもよかったかもしれない．

参考文献

Blakemore, Diane (1987) *Semantic Constraints on Relevance*, Blackwell, Oxford.

Carston, Robyn (2002) *Thoughts and Utterances: The Pragmatics of Explicit Communication*, Blackwell, Oxford.［内田聖二ほか（訳）『思考と発話——明示的伝達の語用論』，2008，研究社，東京.］

Imai, Kunihiko (1998) "Intonation and Relevance," *Relevance Theory: Applications and Implications*, ed. by Robyn Carston and Seiji Uchida, 69-86, John Benjamins, Amsterdam.

今井邦彦 (2001)『語用論への招待』大修館書店，東京.

今井邦彦 (2005)「語用論」『言語の事典』，中島平三（編），109-143，朝倉書店，東京.

今井邦彦 (2007)『ファンダメンタル音声学』ひつじ書房，東京.

今井邦彦・西山佑司 (2012)『ことばの意味とはなんだろう——意味論と語用論の役割』岩波書店，東京.

O'Connor, Joseph D. and Gordon F. Arnold (1961, 1973^2) *Intonation of Colloquial English*, Longman, London.［片山嘉雄ほか（訳）『イギリス英語のイントネーション』，1994，南雲堂，東京.］

Sperber, Dan and Deirdre Wilson (1995) *Relevance: Communication and Cognition*, 2nd ed., Blackwell, Oxford.［内田聖二ほか（訳）『関連性——伝達と認知』（第2版），1999，研究社，東京.］

古代日本語の主格・対格の語順について*

金水　敏
大阪大学

1. はじめに

　古代日本語の格成分や「係り句」(名詞句＋係助詞) の語順について，主に統語論や類型論の立場から注目が集まっている．例えば，野村剛史 (2002, 2011) 他によれば，係り句「～か」「～ぞ」「～や」と，格助詞「が」が付加された主格名詞句「～が」の語順は，おおむね「係り句…～が…動詞」という語順として現れ，例外は極めて少ない．この現象を捉えて，古代日本語に wh 移動があったという説が登場し，またそれに対する反論もいくつか発表されるなど，学界を大いに刺激した (Watanabe (2002)，外池 (2002)，菊田 (2005) 等)．さらに，上代日本語，あるいはそれ以前の日本語の格配置 (alignment) を巡る議論も活発である (Vovin (1997)，竹内 (2002, 2008)，Yanagida (2006)，柳田 (2007)，Kuroda (2007)，Yanagida and Whitman (2009)，菊田 (2012) 等)．

　さて，いずれの場合にしても，議論の基本的な土台となる，現存資料の調査が正確でなければならないことは言を俟たない．この点について，筆者がかつて不十分な調査により誤った結論を導いた事例を示し，これを新しい調査によって訂正したい．また，このような歴史統語論の研究ツールとして，コーパスが有用であることも示したい．

　＊ 歴史統語論の可能性を早くからお示し下さった外池滋生先生に感謝の意を表し，この論文を捧げます．
　また，上代日本語コーパスの利用をご許可くださった Bjarke Frellesvig 氏はじめ開発チームと，スクリプトによる検索のご協力を賜った Kerri Russell 氏に感謝を申し上げます．

2. ノ・ガ主格とヲ対格

　金水（2002b）では、『万葉集』を調査し、助詞「の・が」を持つ主格名詞句と助詞「を」を持つ対格名詞句が一文に共起する場合、対格名詞句が主格助詞に先行するということを述べた（これを、ヲ＞ガと表示することとする）（同じような仮説は、Yanagida（2006）でも独立に採用されている）。しかし結論から言えば、これは誤りであった。明らかな反例を見落としていたと言わざるを得ない。新しい調査結果を示す前に、上代日本語の主格・対格名詞句の現れ方について説明しておきたい。

　まず主格名詞句は、名詞句が裸で現れる場合（これを「ゼロ主格」と呼ぶ）と、助詞「の」または「が」で表示する場合とがある（これを「ノ・ガ主格」と呼び、「ノ・ガ」と略称する）。「の」と「が」には使い分けがあると言われるが、この点については本稿では立ち入らない（野村（1993a, 1993b, 2011）等を参照）。ゼロ主格には特に条件はないが、ノ・ガ主格には生起する環境に制約がある。即ち、述語が連体形で終止する節（連体修飾節、準体節、ゾ・ヤ・カによる係り結びの結び句）および、「〜已然形＋ば」「〜未然形＋ば」など、既定・未定順接条件節の中の主格名詞句に限られる。

　対格名詞句は、名詞句が裸で現れる場合（これを「ゼロ対格」と呼ぶ）と、助詞「を」で表示する場合とがある（これを「ヲ対格」と呼び、「ヲ」と略称する）。

　他動詞構文では主格と対格の名詞句が現れるが、名詞句そのものが省略され得る（φで表す）ので、語順は別として次のような組み合わせがあり得ることになる。

　　（ノ・ガ, ヲ）（ノ・ガ, ゼロ対格）（ゼロ主格, ヲ）（ゼロ主格, ゼロ対格）
　　（φ, ヲ）（ノ・ガ, φ）（ゼロ主格, φ）（φ, ゼロ対格）（φ, φ）

　ここで、（ノ・ガ, ヲ）の組み合わせについて、語順を調査した結果を示すこととする。なお、調査のためにはOxford古代日本語コーパスを利用し、Kerri Russell氏が書いたスクリプトによって得られたリストを利用したことを付記しておく。本コーパスの典拠は以下の通りである。

　　　古事記歌謡　　　土橋寛・小西甚一（校注）（1957）『古代歌謡集』日本古
　　　　　　　　　　　典文学大系，岩波書店．
　　　日本書紀歌謡　　土橋寛・小西甚一（校注）（1957）『古代歌謡集』日本古

	典文学大系，岩波書店．
万葉集	高木市之助・五味智英・大野晋（校注）（1957-62）『万葉集一～四』日本古典文学大系，岩波書店．

3. 助詞の表記

さて，上代文献はすべて漢字によって表記されているが，ガ主格，ヲ対格でも次のような表記上の違いがある．

1. 助詞「の・が」「を」が表音表記（仮名）で表記されている．
2. 助詞「の・が」「を」が「之」「矣」等の漢字によって表意的に表記されている．
3. 助詞「の・が」「を」は表記されておらず，音数律や類歌の参照等によって読み添えられている．

それぞれについて注記しておく．古事記歌謡，日本書紀歌謡は一字一音の万葉仮名で書かれているが，万葉集は様々な表記が混在している．例えば動詞「ゐる」を「為留」と表音表記＝万葉仮名で書く場合もあれば，「居」と正訓字で書く場合もある．前者は確かに「ゐる」と読めるが，後者はいわば解釈によるので，「ゐる」なのか「をり（をる）」なのか確定できないこともある．助詞に関して言うと，表音表記では「の」は「乃」「能」，「が」は「我」「賀」「餓」「何」，「を」は「乎」「袁」「烏」「口リ」（口偏に「リ」）などの漢字が当てられる．一方で，「の」「が」に「之」，「を」に「矣」が当てられる場合があるが，これらは表音表記ではなく，助字を助詞の表記に応用している点で，表意表記の一種であると考えられる．特に「之」は「の」と読むべきか「が」と読むべきか，その字単独では決められない．さらに，助詞の場合はそもそも表記されない場合がある．つまり「吾」とのみ書いてあって，「我が」と読む場合がある．これは漢文訓読のように，原文に書かれていない助詞を「読み添え」るのである．これも解釈の結果出てくる読みで，一次資料としては扱えない．例えば「吾越来者」（万葉集 8 巻 1428 番）は，「わがこえくれば」とも読めるが，「われこえくれば」と読む可能性を，この例だけからは排除できない．このように，用例として確かなのはむろん 1 のみで，2, 3 は参考程度にとどめるしかない．しかし，2, 3 であっても類例として参照すべき場合もあることは言うまでもない．

4. 用例の検討

では，一文中にノ・ガ主格とヲ対格がともに現れている用例がどれくらいあるか，実数で示そう．表1は「ヲ＞ガ」の語順で現れているもの，表2は「ガ＞ヲ」で現れているものである．

表1　上代資料「ヲ＞ノ・ガ」

	ノ・ガ表音	ノ・ガ「之」等表意	ノ・ガ読添え
ヲ表音	20	11	18
ヲ「矣」等表意			2
ヲ読添え		1	3

表2　上代資料「ノ・ガ＞ヲ」

	ノ・ガ表音	ノ・ガ「之」等表意	ノ・ガ読添え
ヲ表音	10	4	1
ヲ「矣」等表意			
ヲ読添え	2	2	1

いずれも，先に示した助詞の表記形式に分類してしめしている．「ノ・ガ表音」と「ヲ表音」の交差したところに「20」とあるのは，ノ・ガ，ヲがいずれも表音表記されている例が20例あるという意味である．他の項目も同様である．

では，表音表記されたものを中心に，実例を示そう．まず，「ヲ＞ガ」の例である．類歌は適宜省略している．

(1) しなだふゆ佐佐那美路を（佐佐那美遅袁）すくすくと我が行ませばや（和賀伊麻勢婆夜）　　　　　　　　　　　　　　（古事記歌謡42）
(2) つぎねふや山代河を（夜麻斯呂賀波袁）河上り我が上れば（和賀能煩禮婆）　　　　　　　　　　　　　　　　　　　　（古事記歌謡57）
(3) つぎねふ山背河を（揶莽之呂餓波烏）宮のぼり我がのぼれば（和餓能朋例瓊）　　　　　　　　　　　　　　　　　　　（日本書紀歌謡5）
(4) あずの上に駒を繋ぎて危ほかど人妻子ろを（比等豆麻古呂乎）息に我がする（伊吉尓和我須流）　　　　（万葉集14巻3539番〈東国歌〉）
(5) 佐保川に凍りわたれる薄ら氷の薄き心を（宇須伎許己呂乎）我が思は

(6) 韓衣裾のうち交へ逢はねども異しき心を（家思吉己許呂乎）我が思は
なくに（安我毛波奈久尓）　　　　　　（万葉集 14 巻 3482 番）

(7) 家島は名にこそありけれ海原を（宇奈波良乎）我が恋ひ来つる（安我
古非伎都流）妹もあらなくに　　　　　（万葉集 15 巻 3718 番）

(8) 我が背子を（和我勢兒乎）吾が松原よ（安我松原欲）見わたせば海人娘
子ども玉藻刈る見ゆ　　　　　　　　　（万葉集 17 巻 3890 番）

(9) 庭に降る雪は千重敷くしかのみに思ひて君を（於母比氏伎美乎）我が
待たなくに（安我麻多奈久尓）　　　　（万葉集 17 巻 3960 番）

(10) 我が宿の花橘を（花橘乎）花ごめに玉にぞ我が貫く（多麻尓曽安我奴
久）待たば苦しみ　　　　　　　　　　（万葉集 17 巻 3998 番）

(11) 印南野の赤ら柏は時はあれど君を我が思ふ（伎美乎安我毛布）時はさ
ねなし　　　　　　　　　　　　　　　（万葉集 20 巻 4301 番）

(12) 薪伐る鎌倉山の木垂る木を（許太流木乎）松と汝が言はば（麻都等奈
我伊波婆）恋ひつつやあらむ　　　　　（万葉集 14 巻 3433 番）

(13) 旅にあれど夜は火灯し居る我れを（乎流和礼乎）闇にや妹が（也未尓
也伊毛我）恋ひつつあるらむ　　　　　（万葉集 15 巻 3669 番）

(14) あやめぐさ 花橘を（花橘乎）娘子らが（[女+感]嬬良我）玉貫くまで
に　　　　　　　　　　　　　　　　　（万葉集 19 巻 4166 番）

(15) しばしばもみ放けむ山を（見放武八万雄）情なく雲の（雲乃）隠さふべ
しや　　　　　　　　　　　　　　　　（万葉集 1 巻 17 番）

次に，「ノ・ガ＞ヲ」の例を示す．

(16) 家人の使ひにあらし春雨の（春雨乃）避くれど我れを（与久列杼吾等
乎）濡らさく思へば　　　　　　　　　（万葉集 09 巻 1697 番）

(17) 岩田野に宿りする君家人の（伊敝妣等乃）いづらと我れを（伊豆良等
和礼乎）問はばいかに言はむ　　　　　（万葉集 15 巻 3689 番）

(18) いかにある布勢の浦ぞもここだくに君が見せむと（吉民我弥世武等）
我れを留むる（和礼乎等登牟流）　　　（万葉集 18 巻 4036 番）

(19) 松の木の並みたる見れば家人の（伊波妣等乃）我れを見送ると（和例
乎美於久流等）立たりしもころ　　　　（万葉集 20 巻 4375 番〈防人歌〉）

(20) なにしかも我が大君の（吾王能）立たせば玉藻のもころ臥やせば川藻
のごとく靡かひし宜しき君が朝宮を（朝宮乎）忘れたまふや

　　　　　　　　　　　　　　　　　　（万葉集 2 巻 196 番）

(21) 山の名と言ひ継げとかも佐用姫が（佐用比賣何）この山の上に領巾を振りけむ（必例遠布利家牟）　　　　　　　　（万葉集 5 巻 872 番）
(22) しかれども我が大君の（吾大王乃）諸人を（毛呂比登乎）誘ひたまひよきことを（善事乎）始めたまひて　　　（万葉集 18 巻 4094 番）
(23) 大伴の遠つ神祖の（遠都神祖乃）その名をば（其名乎婆）大久米主と負ひ持ちて　　　　　　　　　　　　　（万葉集 18 巻 4094 番）

　以上の例に基づいて，上代日本語のノ・ガ主格とヲ対格の語順について考察するならば，確かに「ヲ＞ノ・ガ」という用例が多数を占めるが，しかし「ノ・ガ＞ヲ」も無視できない用例が存在すると言わざるをえない．(18)，(20) は，主格名詞句と対格名詞句の間に節が挟まっていて，主格名詞句は従属節と主節の両方に対して主格として解釈できるので，そのためにこのような語順になっているのだと言えるが，そのような例ばかりではないことは明らかである．

5. ノ・ガ主格，ヲ対格の分布の特徴

　では，上代日本語の主格・対格名詞句について何らかの特徴がないのかと言えば，そうとも言えない．「ヲ＞ノ・ガ」としたが，用例を見ても分かるように，実はこの語順では「が」が圧倒的に多い．確例の 20 例中実に 19 例が「が」であり，しかもそのうちの 16 例は「我が（わが・あが）」である．上代資料には，「我が（動詞）」という表現が非常に多いと言える．逆に，「ノ・ガ＞ヲ」の語順を持つ用例では，音声表記の確例に限って言うと，「の」が 8 例，「が」が 2 例と，「の」が優勢である．またこの「が」の例に「我が」は含まれない．つまり，主格「我が」は動詞に近接して用いることを原則とする（隣接とまでは言えない）．実は，「の」「が」読み添えの例には「我が」が大変多いのであるが，これは「われ（吾）＋動詞」とあったら「我が」に決まっているから，助詞を表記しない，ということが背景にありそうだ．この「我が」が持つ動詞に近接する性質は平安時代でも変わらないようであるが，用例数において主格「我が」を多用するという傾向は平安時代以降は見られない（平安時代の仮名作品 10 作品を集めた国立国語研究所「古典日本語コーパス」で，「我が（動詞）」という語列の用例数は 82 例に留まる）．これが，何らかの統語論的な現象なのか，あるいは作歌上の修辞論的な現象なのかは，今のところ分からない．
　さらに，係助詞との関連で，ノ・ガ主格とヲ対格には興味深い分布の違いがある．野村（2002, 2011）その他によれば，係助詞「ぞ」「か」「や」の付いた

係り句とノ・ガ主格の語順を見ると，上代文献では「係り句＞ノ・ガ主格」となり，その例外は極めて少ないと言う（この点については論者も確認し，例外はほぼゼロと言えることが分かった）．では，これに対してヲ対格はどのような分布を示すかというと，極めて自由度が高いのである．次の模式図を見られたい．

```
___係り句___ノ・ガ主格___動詞
 ①     ②    ③        ④
```

この図において，ヲ対格は①～④のどの位置にも現れることができる．②は，ヲ対格自身に係助詞が付加される場合である．それぞれについて例を示しておく．なお，ここでの例示は音声表記のみには限定しないことにする．

(24) 旅にあれど夜は火灯し居る我れを（乎流和礼乎）闇にや妹が（也未尓也伊毛我）恋ひつつあるらむ　　　（万葉集15巻3669番）（①の例）

(25) 紫の糸をぞ我が搓る（絲乎曽吾搓）あしひきの山橘を貫かむと思ひて
　　　　　　　　　　　　　　　　　　　　（万葉集7巻1340番）（②の例）

(26) 天の川川門八十ありいづくにか（何尓可）君がみ舟を（君之三船乎）我が待ち居らむ（吾待将居）　　　（万葉集10巻2082番）（③の例）

(27) 秋の田の穂田の刈りばかか寄りあはばそこもか人の（彼所毛加人之）我を言成さむ（吾乎事将成）　　　（万葉集4巻512番）（④の例）

これは，ノ・ガ主格が厳密にCPないしTPの中に留まるのに対し，ヲ対格は「を」を持ったまま係助詞を付加されて焦点化されたり（②），さらに「を」を持ったまま主題化されて左方移動されたり（①）することを表すのだろう．詳細については，今後の研究にゆだねたい．

6. さいごに

今後も，日本語の歴史統語論はさらに活発化していくものと思われる．繰り返しになるが，その基礎作業となるのは現存資料の緻密な分析である．そのためにも高度な統語構造情報を埋め込んだ，「上代日本語コーパス」のような大規模コーパスが重要性を増していくことであろう．

参考文献

菊田千春（2005）「格助詞の体系化と語順制約—最適性理論からの上代 wh- 移動再考」 *JELS* 22: *Papers from the Twenty-Second National Conference of the English Linguistic Society of Japan*, 41-50.
菊田千春（2012）「上代日本語のガ格について—活格説の問題点」『同志社大学英語英文学研究』89号, 89-123.
金水　敏（2002a）「日本語文法の歴史的研究における理論と記述」『日本語文法』2巻2号, 81-94, くろしお出版.
金水　敏（2002b）「現代日本語文法の歴史的基盤」2002年度日本言語学会夏期講座「日本語文法上級」教材.
Kuroda, S.-Y. (2007) "On the Syntax of Old Japanese," *Current Issues in the History and Structure of Japanese*, ed. by B. Frellesvig, J. C. Smith and M. Shibatani, 263-318, Kurosio, Tokyo.
野村剛史（1993a）「上代のノとガについて（上）」『国語国文』62巻2号, 1-17.
野村剛史（1993b）「上代のノとガについて（下）」『国語国文』62巻3号, 30-49.
野村剛史（2002）「連体形による係り結びの展開」『日本語学と日本語教育』, 上田博人（編）, 11-37, 東京大学出版会, 東京.
野村剛史（2011）『話し言葉の日本史』吉川弘文館, 東京.
竹内史郎（2002）「古代日本語の主節の無助詞名詞句—活格性との関わりから—」 http://www.ninjal.ac.jp/event/specialists/project-meeting/files/JCLWorkshop_no1_papers/JCLWorkshop2012_04.pdf
竹内史郎（2008）「古代日本語の格助詞ヲの標示域とその変化」『国語と国文学』85巻4号, 50-63.
外池滋生（2002）「上代日本語に左方wh移動はあったか？」『言語』31巻3号, 86-91.
Vovin, A. (1997) "On the Syntactic Typology of Old Japanese," *Journal of East Asian Linguistics* 6, 273-290.
Watanabe, A. (2002) "The Loss of Overt Wh-movement in Old Japanese," *Syntactic Effects of Morphological Change*, ed. by D. W. Lightfoot, 179-195, Oxford University Press, Oxford.
Whitman, J. and Y. Yanagida (2012) "The Formal Syntax of Alignment Change," *Parameter Theory & Linguistic Change*, ed. by Charlotte Galves, Sonia Cyrino, Ruth Lopes, Filomena Sandalo and Juanita Avelar, 177-195, Oxford University Press, Oxford.
Yanagida, Y. (2006) "Word Order and Clause Structure in Early Old Japanese," *Journal of East Asian Linguistics* 15, 37-67.
柳田優子（2007）「上代語の能格性について」『日本語の主文現象—統語構造とモダリティ』, 長谷川信子(編), 147-188, ひつじ書房, 東京.
Yanagida, Y. and J. Whitman (2009) "Alignment and Word Order in Old Japanese,"

Journal of East Asian Linguistics 18, 101–144.

上代日本語コーパス：
Frellesvig, Bjarke, Horn, Stephen Wright, Russell, Kerri L., and Sells, Peter. *The Oxford Corpus of Old Japanese.*
http://vsarpj.orinst.ox.ac.uk/corpus/ojcorpus.html

　付記：　本稿の初稿を John Whitman 氏，柳田優子氏に見ていただいたところ，お二人から論文 Whitman and Yanagida（2012），Yanagida（2006），Yanagida and Whitman（2009）をご教示いただいたうえ，懇切なるコメントをいただいた．お二人の趣旨で著者と大きく異なる点は，「ノ・ガ」を一括りにせず，機能の異なる別個の助詞と見ている点で，評価に値する見解であると考えられる．今後の論考ではぜひこの説を踏まえて考えていきたい．また個々の用例の解釈についてもご意見を頂戴したところがある．一部はご批判を受け入れ，著者の解釈を変更したが，意見を異にする部分もあったことを附言しておく．いずれにせよ，お二人には改めて深い感謝を捧げたい．

Sluicing と「島」の制約*

久野　暲
ハーバード大学名誉教授

1. はじめに

　本稿では，第2節で，「島」(island) に埋め込まれた潜在的語句を先行詞とする Sluicing-文は，「島」の制約の適用を受けるという Chung, Ladusaw and McCloskey (1995)（以降，CLM (1995)）の仮説が維持できないことを示し，「島の制約」に代わるものとして，Wh-句の潜在的先行詞 (implicit antecedent) が聞き手の意識の中で活性化されていなければならない，という非構文法的制約を提案する．第3節では，3.1節で Sluicing が構文法的な「否定の島」制約を受けるという主張，3.2節で多重 Wh-否定疑問文で，否定辞が Wh-句の文頭移動をブロックする構文法的バリアーの機能を果たすという主張，を検討して，いずれの主張も維持できないことを示す．

2. 潜在的語句を先行詞とする Sluicing と「島」の制約

2.1. Chung, Ladusaw and McCloskey (1995) (CLM (1995)) の仮説
次の二つの文を参照されたい．

　　(1) a.　Somebody just left—guess who just left.　　(Ross (1969: (1a)))
　　　　b.　Somebody just left—guess who.　　　　　　(Ross (1969: (2a)))

(1a) と (1b) は，同じ意味を表わす．(1a) は省略のない完全な Wh-疑問節を埋め込み構造としているが，(1b) は，Wh-句のみを埋め込み構造としている．Ross (1969) は，(1b) が (1a) の構造から，Wh-句のみを残して，疑問節の

---

　* 本稿の内容に関し，高見健一氏（学習院大学）から有益なコメントを数多くいただいた．ここに記して感謝申し上げる．

残りのすべてを省略して派生するものと仮定し,この派生規則を Sluicing と名づけた.(1a, b) の前半節の somebody は後半節の Wh-句に対応する.前半節のこのような語句を「Wh-句の先行詞」と呼ぶ.

　Ross は,Wh-句の先行詞が「島」に埋め込まれている場合,Sluicing が「島の効果」(island effects) を弱めることを示した.

(2) a. *She kissed [$_{ISLAND}$ a man who bit one of my friends], but Tom doesn't realize [which one of my friends]$_i$ she kissed [$_{ISLAND}$ a man who bit e$_i$]. (Ross (1969: 72a)))
　　b. ?She kissed [$_{ISLAND}$ a man who bit one of my friends], but Tom doesn't realize which one of my friends. (Ross (1969: (72b)))

(2a) は,「島の制約」(island constraints) の一つである「複合名詞句制約」(Complex NP Constraint) に違反しているので,不適格文である.Ross はそれに対応する Sluicing-文 (2b) の適格度を "?" と表記しているが,Sluicing 研究に携わる言語学者一般は,(2b) パターンの文を適格文と判断している.

　(1b) と (2b) は,Wh-句の先行詞 somebody, one of my friends が前半節に顕在する Sluicing-文である.それに対して,(3b) は,Wh-句の先行詞が潜在する Sluicing-文である.

(3) a. He is writing, but you can't imagine what/where/why he is writing.
　　b. He is writing, but you can't imagine what/where/why.
(Ross (1969: (2c)))

(3b) の前半節には,Wh-句 what, where, why に対応する (writing) something, at some place, for some reason のような語句が現れていない.このパターンの Sluicing-文を「潜在的先行詞 (implicit antecedent) を持つ Sluicing-文」と呼ぶ.

　CLM は,例えば (4) をあげて,潜在的先行詞が前半節の「島」の中に埋め込まれている Sluicing-文は構文法的に不適格な文である,と主張している.

(4) *Tony sent Mo a picture that he painted, but it's not clear with what.
(CLM (1995: (102f))) (* は CLM の適格性判断)

CLM は,なぜ「島」に埋め込まれた顕在的語句を先行詞とする Sluicing-文 (例えば (2b)) が適格で,「島」に埋め込まれた潜在的語句を先行詞とする

Sluicing-文（例えば（4））が不適格であるかを説明するために，この二つの構文に，全く異なる派生過程を想定している．顕在的先行詞をもつ構文の派生過程には，「島の制約」の違反がないが，潜在的先行詞をもつ構文の派生過程には，「島の制約」の違反がある，という仮説である．本稿第2節の目的は，CLMの仮説の基となっている前提——(4)が構文的理由によって不適格である，という前提——が成り立たないことを示すことにある．

2.2. Sluicing-文の適格度判断の流動性

英語のネイティブスピーカーの多くは，(4) が不適格文であるという CLM の判断に同意するが，筆者のネイティブスピーカー・コンサルタントの一人を含めて，(4) を適格文と判断する人もいる．さらに，(4) の with what を with what kind of brushes に置き換えると，この文を，適格，あるいは，"?" の文と判断する人の数が増える．

(5) ?Tony sent Mo a picture that he painted, but it's not clear with what kind of brushes.　　　　　(Kuno and Kim (to appear: (6)))

この事実は，(4) の「不適格度」が with what が何を意味するか不確定であることに多分に起因することを示しているものと考えられる．With は，絵を描くというコンテキストのもとでも，道具，媒介，付帯状況など，多様の意味を表わし得る．聞き手は，話し手が一体何についての質問をしているのか決めかねて，不適格文という判断をするものと推察できる．他方 (5) では，with what kind of brushes が，絵を描くときの道具についての質問と直ちに解釈できるので，with what と比べて，適格度がはるかに上がるものと考えられる．それでもこの文を "?" と判断する話し手は，どうして，突拍子に，絵を描くときの筆の種類が問題となっているのか，という疑問から，この文を不自然な文と判断しているものと推察できる．その証拠に，先行文脈で絵を描くときの筆の種類が問題となっていることを明らかにすれば，(5) が適格度の高い文となるからである．

(6) (Tony has been painting with two kinds of brushes—badger-hair brushes and horse-hair brushes.) √Yesterday, he showed Mary a picture that he had just painted, but he didn't tell her with which kind of brushes.　　　　　(Kim and Kuno (2013: (7)))

(6) が適格文であるという事実は，「島」に埋め込まれた潜在的語句を先行詞

とする Sluicing-文は，先行詞が聞き手の意識の中で活性化されていれば適格文となることを示している．

次に「島」が疑問節の場合の例文を示しておく．

(7) a. *Sandy was trying to work out which students would speak, but she refused to say {who to/to who(m)}. (CLM (1995: (102a)))
   b. (Sandy plans to have a Chinese drill session in which each of her designated students will introduce himself/herself to some other student, who in turn will summarize what (s)he has heard and tell it to the class.) √She is working out which students will make self-introductory statements, but she hasn't even started thinking about who to. (Kim and Kuno (2013: (4d)))

(7a) の前半節を聞くと，聞き手は，学生のクラス発表を頭に思い浮かべる．クラス発表は，通常（先生と）クラスの学生全体を相手とするものであるから，後半節の Wh-句に必要な潜在的先行詞 to someone あるいは to some other student を聞き手の意識の中に活性化させない．(7a) が不適格なのはこの理由による．他方，(7b) の先行文脈は，先生 Sandy に指名された学生の一人一人が誰か他の学生に対して自己紹介し，その学生がクラス全体に，自己紹介の内容を伝えるという特殊なクラス発表の設定を記述しているので，Wh-句の潜在的先行詞 to someone が聞き手の意識の中で活性化される．(7b) が適格文であるのは，この理由による．

(6), (7b) は，Sluicing-文に先行する文脈で，島に埋め込まれた Wh-句の潜在的先行詞が聞き手の意識にのぼるケースであるが，次の文は，先行文脈の助けを受けないで潜在的先行詞の活性化が起きる例である．

(8) a. √Mary met a man who claimed he could turn copper into gold, but she couldn't find out from him with what kind of technique.
   (Kim and Kuno (2013: (16a)))
   b. √I've heard about a mathematician who has proved Fermat's Last Theorem—I want to find out from him how. (ibid.: (16c))

錬金術に成功したと主張する男の話を聞けば，一体どういう方法で成功したと主張しているのか，ということが意識にのぼる．従って，(8a) では，Sluicing の前半節の中の he could turn copper into gold が，潜在的先行詞 with a certain technique を聞き手の意識の中で活性化させる．(8b) のフェルマーの

最終定理を証明した数学者についての文も同様である．これらの文も，CLMの仮説の予測に反して，適格文である．[1] 島の中に埋め込まれた潜在的語句を先行詞とする Sluicing-文は島の制約を受けないと仮定し，先行詞の活性化をフィルターとして，CLM の例 (4)，(7a) などを不適格文としてふるい落とすというのが妥当な解決策だと思われる．顕在する先行詞は，島の中に埋め込まれているか否かにかかわらず聞き手の意識の中で活性化されると予測できるから，意識活性化制約は，次のようにジェネラライズすることができる．

(9) Sluicing-文に課される Wh-句の先行詞の「意識活性化」制約：
    a. Sluicing-文は，Wh-句の先行詞が聞き手の意識の中で活性化されているときにのみ，適格文となる．
    b. 島に埋め込まれている潜在的先行詞の活性化は，先行文脈による活性化（例：(6), (7b)），前半節内の辞書項目による活性化（例：(8a, b)），あるいは，後半節での潜在的先行詞の特定化（例：(5)）に頼らなければならない．

3. 否定辞は「否定の島」，「移動のバリアー」を形成するか？

Sluicing が「否定の島」の制約を受けるという主張や，多重 Wh-疑問文で，主語位置の Wh-句を越えて Wh-句が文頭移動を受ける場合，否定辞がバリアーとなってその移動をブロックする，という主張がなされている．本節では，この二つの主張が維持できるかどうかを考察する．

---

[1] CLM の仮説の反例として Culicover and Jackendoff (2005: 258) は次の3文を含む4例をあげている（4つ目の例文は (ii) と重複するので省略する）．
  (i) Bob found a plumber who fixed the sink, but I'm not sure with what.
  (ii) A: Does eating at a baseball game interest you?
       B: Depends on what.
  (iii) Tony sent Mo a picture that he says he painted, but I can't imagine with what, given that Tony can't afford brushes.
Culicover and Jackendoff は，なぜ上の文が適格文かの説明を提供していない．(i)-(iii) が適格文と判断される理由は，次の通りである．一般の聞き手にとって，配管工がどんな道具を使って台所の流しを修理するかは，画家がどんな筆を使って絵を描くかよりはるかに大きい関心事である．よって，(i) の前半節が聞き手の意識の中で道具の解釈での (with) something を活性化させる蓋然性は，CLM の不適格文 (4) の場合よりはるかに高い．(ii) の前半節の動詞 eat は，潜在的目的語を極めて活性化しやすい動詞である．(iii) は，後半節が Wh-句の潜在的先行詞の種類を特定するケースである．

3.1. Sluicing と否定の島

Sluicing 一般が「否定の島」の制約を受けるという主張は，次のような文の不適格性に基づいている．

(10) a. *Nigel never hunts, but I don't remember what.　　(Albert (1993))
　　 b. *No one drank, but I can't say what kind of wine.　　(ibid.)
　　 c. *Nobody went out for dinner, but I don't remember to which restaurant.　　(Romero (1998: 59))

しかし，これらの文は，Sluicing が「否定の島」の制約を受けることの証拠にはならない．なぜなら，これらの文の不適格性は，文の前半節と後半節との間に意味の矛盾があるからである．例えば (10a) の前半節は，Nigel は狩をしないと述べているのであるから捕獲するものは何もないことを含意する．何もないものが何であるか覚えていないという後半節は，意味をなさない．

次の文の適格性は，仮に Sluicing に「否定の島」の制約を認めるとしても，否定辞が構文法的否定辞ではなくて，意味的否定辞（意味の上で潜在的先行詞が指すものが存在することを否定する辞）であることを示す．

(11) a. John said that he wouldn't mind going out for dinner, but he didn't say to what kind of restaurant.
　　　　　　　　　　　　　　　　　　(Kim and Kuno (2013: (27a)))
　　 b. John said that he hadn't been able to stop reading at dinner time, but he didn't say what kind of books.　　(ibid.: (27b))

(11a, b) が適格なのは，その前半節が，ジョンが夕食を食べに行ってもよいと思っているレストランが存在することを暗意し，ジョンが夕食時に読むことをやめられない読み物が存在することを含意しているからである．従って，(11a, b) の否定辞は，上で述べた意味での否定辞ではない．

さて，次の3つの文を参照されたい．

(12) a. I remember she wants to hire someone who works on GREEK, but I don't remember which OTHER language.
　　　　　　　　　　　　　　　　　　(Fukaya (2012: (85a)))
　　 b. *I remember she didn't want to hire someone who works on GREEK, but I don't remember which OTHER language.
　　 c. (Abby thought that the department shouldn't hire anyone who

works on languages that are already well covered by the faculty members.) √She didn't want to hire someone who works on Greek, but I don't remember which other language.

(12a) は Merchant (2001) が Contrast Sluicing と名付けた Sluicing-文である．(12a) は適格文であるが，その埋め込み文が否定形になっている (12b) は，不適格文である．この事実は，Sluicing が「否定の島」の制約に従う，という仮説を支持するかのように見えるが，(12c) が適格であるという事実は，事態がそれほど単純ではないことを示している．一体どうして，(12c) の適格性が生じるのであろうか．

　肯定陳述は無標陳述であり，否定表現は有標陳述である．肯定陳述は，文脈のない状況で，予想される陳述であり，否定陳述は，文脈のない状況で，予想されていない陳述である．(12a) が適格で，(12b) が不適格である，という事実は，Contrast Sluicing-文の先行詞が島を含む無標陳述の中に埋め込まれていれば適格文ができ，有標陳述の中に埋め込まれていれば，不適格文ができることを示している．他方，(12c) では，先行文脈で，既存の教授メンバーの守備範囲と重複する言語を守備範囲とする応募者は，採用するべきでない，という否定陳述が Abby の意見として，提出されている．したがって，続く文章が否定陳述であることが，予測され得る．否定陳述が予測される状況では，否定陳述は，もはや有標陳述ではなく，無標陳述である．したがって，(12c) は適格文と判断される，というのが (12c) が適格文であることの私の説明である．この観察から，次の仮説をたてることができる．

(13) 否定辞の「否定の島」形成機能の中性化：否定陳述が予測される文脈では，否定辞は，「否定の島」形成の機能を失う．（否定辞は肯定陳述が予測される文脈でのみ，「否定の島」を形成する機能をもつ．）

3.2. 移動規則と否定辞のバリアー機能

　Beck (1996) は (14a) のような文の適格性と，(14b) のような文の不適格性に基づいて，否定辞が，Wh-移動のバリアーを形成すると仮定した．

(14) a.　Which book did which boy buy?　　　　　　(Beck (1996))
　　　b. ??Which book didn't which boy buy?　　　　　　(ibid.)

次の (15a, b) は，(14a, b) のような主語と目的語の位置に Wh-句を持った疑問文を埋め込み文としたものである．

(15) a. Tell me which assignments which of you want to work on.
　　 b. ??Tell me which assignments which of you don't want to work on.

ところが，次に示す（16a）は，括弧に入れて示した先行文脈を除けば，不適格な（15b）とまったく同じ文であるにもかかわらずまったく問題のない適格文であり，（16b）の後半節も，（15b）とまったく同じ文であるにもかかわらずまったく問題のない適格文である．

(16) a. (I hear that some of you don't want to work on some of the assignments.) √Tell me which assignments which of you don't want to work on.
　　 b. √Tell me which assignments which of you want to work on and which assignments which of you don't want to work on.

この一見不可思議な現象は，（13）の否定辞の「否定の島」形成機能の中性化と類似した規則で説明できる．（16a）は，先行文脈で否定状況が設定されることによって，次に現れる陳述が否定陳述であることが予測されるので，否定疑問文が無標疑問文となり，否定辞が，そのバリアー機能を失う．同様，（16b）では，後半疑問文が，前半肯定埋め込み疑問文に対立するものとして，否定疑問文であろう，という予測が可能なため，この予測の中で，否定疑問文が無標疑問文となるものと考えられる．

　以上の考察から，（13）の否定辞の「否定の島」形成機能の中性化規則を次のようにジェネラライズすることができる．

(17)　否定辞は，肯定陳述が予測される文脈では有標で「否定の島」および「移動のバリアー」を形成する機能を持つが，否定陳述が予測される文脈では，無標となり，「否定の島」および移動のバリアーを形成する機能を失う．[2]

(12c) のような Sluicing-文や（16a, b）のような Wh-句移動文が「否定陳述が予測される文脈」に現れているか否かをその文脈から構文法的分析手順によってのみ判定することは至難の業である．また，「否定陳述が予測される文脈」が言語化されず，話し手と聞き手の間の暗黙の了解事項になっている場合（例

---

　[2] 否定辞が非指示 (non-referential) 表現と付加詞 (adjunct) の文頭移動に対するバリアーの機能を持つという Rizzi (1990) の主張が維持できないことについては，Kuno and Takami (1997) を参照．

えば，The doctor told me what I shouldn't eat or drink until my heartburn is completely gone.) もある． これらの事実と，(10a) (=*Nigel never hunts, but I don't remember what.) が不適格文である理由，(11a) (=John said that he wouldn't mind going out for dinner, but he didn't say to what kind of restaurant.) が適格文である理由，を兼ね合わせると，「否定の島」制約は，構文法的制約ではなくて，意味的・機能的制約であるという結論になる．

4. おわりに

本稿では，第2節で，潜在的語句を先行詞とする Sluicing は，「島の制約」を受けるという CLM（1995）の主張が維持できないことを示し，この構文法的制約を排除して，聞き手の意識の中で先行詞が活性化されていることを，Sluicing-文が適格であるための条件として提案した．また，第3節で，否定辞が「否定の島」を形成するという構文法的主張と，否定辞が「移動のバリアー」を形成するという構文法的主張が，いずれも維持できないことを示した．

参考文献

Albert, Chris (1993) "Sluicing and Weak Islands," ms., University of California, Santa Cruz.

Beck, Sigrid (1996) "Quantified Structures as Barriers for LF Movement," *Natural Language Semantics* 4, 1-56.

Chung, Sandra, William Ladusaw and James McCloskey (1995) "Sluicing and Logical Form," *Natural Language Semantics* 3, 239-282.

Culicover, Peter W. and Ray Jackendoff (2005) *Simpler Syntax*, Oxford University, Oxford.

Fukaya, Teruhiko (2012) "Island-Sensitivity in Japanese Sluicing and Some Implications," *Sluicing: Cross-Linguistic Perspectives*, ed. by Jason Merchant and Andrew Simpson, 123-163, Oxford University, Oxford.

Kim, Soo-Yeon and Susumu Kuno (2013) "A Note on Sluicing with Implicit Indefinite Correlates," *Natural Language Semantics* 21, 315-332.

Kuno, Susumu and Soo-Yeon Kim (to appear) "How Much Do Islands Matter in Sluicing?" *Proceedings of the 9th Workshop on Altaic Formal Linguistics (WAFL 9)*, MIT, Cambridge, MA.

Kuno, Susumu and Ken-ichi Takami (1997) "Remarks on Negative Islands," *Linguis-

tic Inquiry 28, 553-576.

Merchant, Jason (2001) *The Syntax of Silence: Sluicing, Islands, and the Theory of Ellipsis*, Oxford University Press, Oxford.

Rizzi, Luigi (1990) *Relativized Minimality*, MIT Press, Cambridge, MA.

Romero, Maribel (1998) *Focus and Reconstruction Effects in* Wh-*Phrases*, Doctoral dissertation, University of Massachusetts at Amherst.

Ross, John R. (1969) "Guess Who?" *CLS* 5, 252-286.

Unpassivizable Transitive Verbs and the Minimality*

Heizo Nakajima

Gakushuin University

1. Introduction

Since the early days of generative grammar, it has been widely noticed and discussed that some transitive verbs cannot be passivized, as demonstrated in (1)-(3):

(1) a. This evolutionary theory resembles the Principles-and-Parameter approach to language acquisition.
   b. *The Principles-and-Parameter approach to language acquisition is resembled by this evolutionary theory.
(2) a. The visitor's name eluded my memory.
   b. *My memory was eluded by the visitor's name.
(3) a. The new suit fits the man.
   b. *The man is fitted by the new suit.

Examples of unpassivizable transitive verbs, which will be henceforth referred to as *resemble*-verbs, are illustrated in (4):

(4) Symmetrical verbs: *resemble, marry, meet, equal,* ...
   Measure verbs: *cost, weigh, measure, last,* ...
   Suit-verbs: *suit, fit,* ...

---

* I am grateful to Shigeo Tonoike for his longtime friendship for, and consistent encouragement to, me since our graduate student days. My thanks also go to Lyle Jenkins, Masayuki Ike-uchi, Koji Fujita, Masanobu Ueda, Kaneaki Arimura, Minoru Fukuda, Norio Suzuki, Takamichi Aki, Shinsuke Honma, and Alison Stewart, for their useful comments and suggestions on earlier versions of the paper. Parts of the earlier versions of this paper were presented at Konan University, Niigata University, and the special workshop at the 30th anniversary of the English Linguistic Society of Japan.

Spatial verbs: *elude, escape, depart*; *enter, approach, near, turn*,[1]...

(We will turn to another class of unpassivizable verbs, Possession verbs, such as *have* and *lack*, in section 2.5.)

As *resemble*-verbs take exactly the same syntactic structures in relevant respects as most other transitive verbs which can be passivized, few syntactic proposals thus far seem to have sufficiently succeeded in accounting for their unpassivizability in *principled* ways.

In this paper, the next section, Section 2, argues that though the verbs in (4) are apparently transitive ones, they are actually unaccusative intransitive ones with underlying structures in which the surface subject is in the "object" position, and the surface object is the object of a preposition rather than of a verb. Section 3 maintains that the unpassivizability of unaccusative verbs including the *resemble*-verbs can be attributed to the Minimality Principle (Rizzi (1990)), a candidate for a third factor principle in the sense of Chomsky (2005).

2. *Resemble*-Verbs as Unaccusatives

A very obvious semantic or thematic property common to the *resemble*-verbs in (4) is that the θ-role of their subjects is Theme, as is clear from the (a)-sentences in (1)-(3).[2] This thematic property is supposed to have led Jackendoff (1972) to propose the Thematic Hierarchy Condition on Passivization, to the effect that the passive *by*-phrase must be higher on the Thematic Hierarchy than the derived subject, in conjunction with the assumption that Theme is the lowest on the Thematic Hierarchy. The *by*-

---

[1] The verbs on the right of the semicolon resists passivization when they express "a purely spatial or existential relationship" (Bolinger (1975: 68)) rather than a volitional activity of the subject. Compare the (a)-sentences expressing volitional activities with the (b)-sentences expressing spatial relations:
 (i) a. I was approached by the stranger.
    b. *I was approached by the train.
 (ii) a. The store was entered by the two thieves.
    b. *The store was entered by the two customers.

[2] On the basis of this fact, Lødrup (2000) proposes that (un)passivizability be thematically defined with recourse to the θ-role of Theme.

phrase in passive sentences with *resemble*-verbs, being Theme, is the lowest on the Thematic Hierarchy and is never higher than the derived subject whatever its θ-role is; hence, always in violation of the Thematic Hierarchy Condition on Passivization.[3]

The thematic property of the *resemble*-verbs' subjects being Theme suggests, especially given the UTAH of Baker (1988), that the subjects are not "genuine" but "surface" subjects which have moved to the subject position from some other positions. Since the Theme phrases such as the objects of transitive verbs as in *John kicked the ball* or the surface subjects of unaccusatives as in *The ball fell on the floor* are generally regarded as objects in underlying structures, the surface subjects of the *resemble*-verbs can also be reasonably assumed to be in the object position in underlying structures. The underlying status of the subjects of the *resemble*-verbs as objects is the same as that of unaccusative verbs. In what follows, I will argue that *resemble*-verbs are unaccusative, by illustrating that they lack an external argument, their subjects have moved from the underlying object position, and their objects are not of verbs, but of prepositions.

2.1. Absence of External Argument

First of all, *resemble*-verbs are similar to unaccusatives in that neither of them can derive "agentive" *er*-nominals:

(5) a. *appearer, *occurrer, *happener, *emerger, *remainer, *exister, ...
(Rappaport Hovav and Levin (1988))
b. *resembler, *meeter, *coster, *weigher, *approacher, *eluder, ...

The term *agentive nominals* is not adequate because the *er*-nominlas are possible not only with verbs with Agent but also with those with such θ-roles as Instrument, Experiencer, or Goal, as shown in (6):

(6) [Agent] watcher, kicker, pitcher, listener, looker, talker, ...
[Instrument] opener, washer, cleaner, cutter, ...

---

[3] An inadequacy of the Thematic Hierarchy Condition immediately becomes obvious from the passive sentences containing another class of unpassivizable verbs, Possession verbs such as *have*, *lack*, or *house*, which take Locative as the subject, and Theme as the object. See section 2.5.

[Experiencer] believer, knower, liker, hearer, seer, ...
[Goal] receiver, buyer, ...

The verbs from which the *er*-nominals in (6) are derived are common in that they all take external arguments. It can be supposed, then, that the affix *-er* in the *er*-nominals is the morphological realization of the external argument. The impossibility of the *er*-nonimals in (5b), as well as those in (5a), strongly suggests that the *resemble*-verbs do not have an external argument.

Secondly, the *resemble*-verbs in (8) and the unaccusatives in (9) do not appear in the *Do* pseudo-cleft sentence, schematized in (7), whose *what*-clause contains the subject NP and the verb *do* and whose focus position is composed of VP.

(7) [What NP do] is [$_{VP}$ V ....]
(8) a. *What John does is resemble Tom.
 b. *What the imported car does is cost more than 50,000 dollars.
 c. *What his name did was elude my memory.
(9) a. *What the sun did was rise above the horizon.
 b. *What the riot did was happen in the center of the city.
 c. *What the window did was break last night.

The θ-role of the subject of a verb in the focus position of the *Do* pseudo-cleft sentence is not restricted to Agent, but can be such θ-roles as Experiencer (10a, b), Instrument (10c), or Goal (10d), all of which have been shown above to allow for the *er*-nominals:

(10) a. What a good point guard does is know when to pass the ball...for the good of the team .... so the team can win.
   (http://www.huffingtonpost.com/social/Luv2Purple)
 b. What I did was like a Bob Dylan protest song.
 c. ... what stents do is open up the coronary arteries to allow greater blood flow/oxygen to the heart muscle.
   (www.ptca.org/forumtopics/topic049.html)
 d. What you are required to do is receive enough instruction to take and pass the oral and flight-tests which will be conducted ...
   (www.sportpilot.org/learntofly/articles/questions.html)

It can be supposed, then, that verbs may occur in the *Do* pseudo-cleft sentences insofar as they have external arguments. Notice that the verb *do* in the *what*-clause in (7) is not an auxiliary, but the main verb meaning the performance of activity, and therefore, its subject NP is necessarily an external argument. The *Do* pseudo-cleft sentences may be understood as the construction in which one sentence is cloven into an external argument on one hand and a verb plus internal arguments and some others on the other. Given this, the impossibility for the *resemble*-verbs to occur in the *Do* pseudo-cleft sentences in (8) also shows that they lack an external argument.

2.2. Movement to Subject Position

Thirdly, *resemble*-verbs as well as unaccusative ones cannot be felicitously followed by the reflexive pronouns coreferential with the subject NPs. The sentences with the *resemble*-verbs in (11) and those with the unaccusatives in (12) are all semantically anomalous. For example, a train can approach other things or places, but not itself. Similarly, a stone can fall on some other things, but not on itself.

(11) a. #The train approached itself.
 b. #Mary married herself.
 c. #The jacket fits itself.
 d. #The memory eluded itself.
(12) a. #The stone fell on itself.
 b. #She appeared before herself.
 c. #The sun rose above itself.

Such semantic anomaly as the one in (11) and (12) reminds us of the classical "cross-over" phenomena in simple sentences discussed in Postal (1971). The simple sentences involving the reflexives coreferential with the subjects are semantically unproblematic in the active voice, but anomalous in the passive voice:

(13) a. John respects himself.
 b. #John is respected by himself.
(14) a. Mary talked to herself.
 b. #Mary was talked to by herself.

The semantic anomaly in the passive (b)-sentences of (13)-(14) can be easily accounted for by the semantic interpretation principle, the Binding Principle (A), which requires the local binding of anaphors (Chomsky (1981)), on the assumption that a trace is left between the surface subject and the reflexive; the reflexive is not locally bound by the subject because of the existence of the traces left by the subjects. The anomaly in the sentences with unaccusatives in (12) can also be accounted for in the same way; the movement of the surface subject NP leaves a trace in the object position, which serves to block the local binding of the reflexive by the subject NP.

The anomaly in the sentences with the *resemble*-verbs in (11) will also be accounted for in the same way if the surface subject is only assumed to have moved from the object to the subject position, leaving a trace between them.

2.3. Objecthood of Surface Subjects

In nominals, the preposition *of* is inserted before object NPs, for the head Ns do not assign Case to the following object NPs, and instead the semantically vacuous proposition *of* serves as the Case-assigner to the following object NPs:

(15) a. their destruction *of* the city
 b. his translation *of* Chomsky's book
 c. our support *of* the victims

The preposition *of* also appears before the surface subjects of unaccusatives, as is expected, since they are assumed to occupy the object position in underling structures (the examples in (16) are taken from Postal (2010)):

(16) a. the arrival *of* a bunch of drunks
 b. the occurrence *of* an earthquake
 c. the existence *of* such weapons

Interestingly, the same thing holds true of the surface subjects of the *resemble*-verbs (the examples of (17c, d) are provided by Alison Stewart (p.c.)):

(17) a. the resemblance *of* a cloud to a weasel
 b. the marriage *of* HRH Prince William of Wales to Miss Catherine

Middleton

c. The weight *of* the steel helmet at 50 pounds (was more than the soldier could bear for longer than a few hours.)

d. The cost *of* the imported car at $1,000,000 (was twice as high as the most expensive domestically produced car.)

All the facts above lead us to conclude that the *resemble*-verbs are unaccusatives, and their surface subjects are objects in underlying structures and move to the position where they are in surface structures.

2.4. Surface Objects as Objects of Prepositions

Now that the surface subjects of the *resemble*-verbs occupy the object position in underlying structures, the next question to be asked is where their "surface objects" are in underlying structures.

A crucial clue to this question has already been provided by the nominals in (17), repeated here as (18), with the prepositions before the surface objects highlighted by italics:

(18) a. the resemblance of a cloud *to* a weasel
    b. the marriage of HRH Prince William of Wales *to* Miss Catherine Middleton
    c. the weight of the steel helmet *at* 50 pounds (was more than the soldier could bear for longer than a few hours.)
    d. The cost of the imported car *at* $1,000,000 (was twice as high as the most expensive domestically produced car.)

In the nominals in (18), the surface objects are preceded not by *of*, but by some other prepositions such as *to* or *at*. It can be safely assumed, then, that in verb phrases, the surface objects of the *resemble*-verbs are not genuine objects, but are objects of "null" prepositions corresponding to those prepositions.[4]

To put the arguments in sections 2.1 through 2.4 together, the underlying

---

[4] The assumption of the null preposition before the surface object is along the same line with Landau (2010), who assumes null prepositions before the objects of his "class-II" psych-verbs. Some dative prepositions could be assumed to become null immediately after V, as in the case of double object constructions.

structure of a *resemble*-verb will be something like (19):

(19) ___ [$_{VP}$ resemble [$_{NP}$ John] [$_{PP}$ P$_\emptyset$ his father]]

The structure in (19) is exactly the same as the underlying structure of an unaccusatve in (20) in relevant respects; the external argument position is vacant, the surface subject is in the object position, and the surface object is the object of a preposition:[5]

(20) ___ [$_{VP}$ happen [$_{NP}$ the accident] [$_{PP}$ to John]]

Note that the assumption that some unpassivizable transitives verbs are unaccusatives to use the terms here is not totally novel, but has been sporadically claimed by some people without detailed argument. See, for example, Perlmutter and Postal (1984), Belletti and Rizzi (1988), Levin and Rappaport Hovav (1995), Pesetsky (1995), Blevins (2003), Landau (2010), and Randall (2010).

2.5. Possession Verbs

Before closing this section, we briefly touch on another class of unpassivizable transitive verbs, namely, Possession verbs, such as *have*, *lack*, *contain*, *sleep*, or *house*:

(21) a. *Many books are had by John.
b. *Moral is lacked by those young people.
c. *Five people are slept by this room.

The Possession verbs are thematically different from the *resemble*-verbs in that in the active voice, the surface subjects are Locative rather than Theme, and the surface objects are Theme rather than Locative. In the light of this thematic relations, Ross (1967)'s idea that the sentence with the verb *have* in (22b) is derived from the existential sentence in (22a) proves to be sug-

---

[5] It is controversial whether the PPs following unaccusatives are complements or adjuncts. What is certain is that unaccusative verbs of existence/appearance, such as *exist*, *remain*, *appear*, or *occur*, require Locative or Goal PPs which express the places where Theme exists or appears. Unaccusative verbs of change of location, such as *slide*, *arise*, or *fall*, also seem to require Goal PPs, which therefore are complements rather than adjuncts of the verbs.

gestive of the underlying structures of Possession verbs (see also Bolinger (1975: 70), who states that sentences with the Possession verbs mostly can be paraphrased by the existential sentences or by the copular *be* with spatial prepositions):

(22) a. There are many pictures in his book.
     b. His book has many pictures.

Though such an expressively strong rule as the one relating (22a) and (22b) is not admitted in these days, it could be supposed that the Possession verbs, just like the unaccusative *be* in (22a), do not have an external argument, and a Locative phrase moves to the subject position in a fashion similar to the way that a Locative phrase moves to the subject position in the Locative Inversion. If so, the Possession verbs, as well as the *resemble*-verbs, do not have an external argument.

3. Unpassivizability as Minimality Violation

The assumption of the *resemble*-verbs as unaccusatives opens a way to account for their unpassivizability in a *principled* way. The passive morphology will accomplish two major things. One is to demote the highest argument (an external argument if present, and a direct internal argument if an external argument is absent) into the *by*-phrase,[6] and the other is to absorb Structural Case (Chomsky (1981)), and consequently, to promote the Case-absorbed NP to the surface subject. We assume, along with Anagnostopoulou (2003: 62), that Structural Case is assigned not only by verbs, but also by prepositions, especially in languages showing preposition-stranding and formation of pseudo-passives. Then, the objects of prepositions as well as those of verbs can be targets of Case-absorption in English, and consequently targets of the promotion (NP-Movement) to a subject.

---

[6] See Jaegglie (1986: 612). This definition of demotion will readily rule out the passivization of the Possession verbs discussed in 2.5, whose surface subjects are not the direct internal, but the indirect internal argument; the passivization demotes the lower argument of the two internal arguments, contra to the definition.

(23) ___ be V$_{unacc}$-en ... NP$_1$ ... P NP$_2$ ...

In (23), NP$_1$ cannot move to the subject position because it is the highest argument of unaccusatives (the direct internal argument) and will become the *by*-phrase. Thanks to the intervention of NP$_1$, the NP-movement of NP$_2$ to the subject position induces the violation of the Minimality Principle (Rizzi (1990)),[7] a very promising candidate for a third factor principle in the sense of Chomsky (2005) (see Hornstein (2009), Chomsky (2010), Jenkins (2011), and Boeckx (2011)). In this way, the unpassivizability of unaccusatives including the *resemble*-verbs discussed in section 2 can be attributed to the Minimality rather than to the descriptive generalization that passivization undergoes the suppression of an external argument, which is absent in unaccusatives.

The account in terms of the Minimality might pose a problem for the representative type of passive sentences, namely, those with an external argument. An external argument is demoted to the *by*-phrase and intervenes between the object position and the surface subject position; because of this intervention, the object movement to the subject position would bring about the Minimality violation. Belletti and Rizzi (2013) attempt to overcome this problem with a recourse to Collin's (2005) *smuggling*, which extracts the VP containing the V and the object and excluding the external argument (EA) from the vP containing the EA (i.e. the *by*-phrase), and adjoins the VP to the left of the vP, as is shown in (24). The object movement from the fronted VP$_i$ does not evoke the Minimality violation:

(24) ___ be [$_{VPi}$ V Object] [$_{vP}$ by EA t_i]
　　　↑　NP movement　　↑　smuggling

The unaccusatives, in contrast, do not have the vP, and the direct internal argument, which becomes the *by*-phrase, and the NP to be moved (i.e., the

---

[7] The original version of the Minimality in Rizzi (1990) is designed to be the condition on the choice of a "landing site" for elements to be moved. I take the Minimality here, along with Belletti and Rizzi (2013), to be the condition on the choice of an element to be moved to a given landing site, also. The Minimality Principle essentially requires the shortest movement.

object of a preposition) are always in the same VP (see (20)). The movement of the NP out of the VP cannot but cross over the intervening by-phrase, hence, always in violation of the Minimlaity, as is claimed above.

References

Anagnostopoulou, Elena (2003) *The Syntax of Ditransitives*, Mouton de Gruyter, Berlin and New York.
Baker, Mark C. (1988) *Incorporation: A Theory of Grammatical Function Changing*, University of Chicago Press, Chicago.
Belletti, Adriana and Luigi Rizzi (1988) "Psych-Verbs and θ-Theory," *Natural Language and Linguistic Theory* 6, 291-352.
Belletti, Adriana and Luigi Rizzi (2013) "Ways of Avoiding Intervention: Some Thoughts on the Development of Object Relatives, Passive, and Control," *Rich Languages from Poor Inputs*, ed. by Massimo Piattelli-Palmarini and Robert Berwick, 115-126, Oxford University Press, Oxford.
Blevins, James (2003) "Passives and Impersonals," *Journal of Linguistics* 39, 473-520.
Boeckx, Cedric (2011) "Approaching Parameters from Below," *The Biolinguistic Enterprise; New Perspectives on the Evolution and Nature of the Human Language Faculty*, ed. by Anna Maria Di Sciullo and Cedric Boeckx, 205-221, Oxford University Press, Oxford.
Bolinger, Dwight L. (1975) "On the Passive in English," *The First LACUS Forum*, ed. by Adam Makkai and Valerie Makkai, 57-80, Hornbeam Press, Columbia.
Chomsky, Noam (1981) *Lectures on Government and Binding*, Foris, Dordrecht.
Chomsky, Noam (2005) "Three Factors in Language Design," *Linguistic Inquiry* 36, 1-22.
Chomsky, Noam (2010) "Some Simple Evo Devo Theses: How True Might They Be for Language," *The Evolution of Human Language*, ed. by Richard Larson, Viviane Deprez and Hiroko Yamakido, 45-62, Cambridge University Press, Cambridge.
Collins, Chris (2005) "A Smuggling Approach to Passive in English," *Syntax* 8, 81-120.
Hornstein, Norbert (2009) *A Theory of Syntax: Minimal Operations and Universal Grammar*, Cambridge University Press, Cambridge.
Jaeggli, Osvaldo (1986) "Passive," *Linguistic Inquiry* 17, 587-622.
Jackendoff, Ray S. (1972) *Semantic Interpretation in Generative Grammar*, MIT Press, Cambridge, MA.

Jenkins, Lyle (2011) "The Three Design Factors in Evolution and Variation," *The Biolinguistic Enterprise; New Perspectives on the Evolution and Nature of the Human Language Faculty*, ed. by Anna Maria Di Sciullo and Cedric Boeckx, 169-179, Oxford University Press, Oxford.

Landau, Idan (2010) *The Locative Syntax of Experiencers*, MIT Press, Cambridge, MA.

Lødrup, Helge (2000) "Exceptions to the Norwegian Passive: Unaccusativity, Aspect and Thematic Roles," *Norsk Lingvistisk Tidsskrift* 1, 37-54.

Perlmutter, David M. and Paul Postal (1984) "The 1-Advancement Exclusiveness Law," *Studies in Relational Grammar 2*, ed. by David M. Perlmutter and Carol Rosen, 81-125, University of Chicago Press, Chicago.

Pesetsky, David Michael (1995) *Zero Syntax: Experiencers and Cascades*, MIT Press, Cambridge, MA.

Postal, Paul M. (1971) *Cross-over Phenomena*, Holt, Rinehart & Winston, New York.

Postal, Paul M. (2010) *Edge-Based Clausal Syntax: A Study of (Mostly) English Object Structure*, MIT Press, Cambridge, MA.

Randall, Janet H. (2010) *Linking: Geometry of Argument Structure*, Sringer, Dordrecht.

Rappaport Hovav, Malka and Beth Levin (1992) "*-Er* Nominals: Implications for the Theory of Argument Structure," *Syntax and Semantics 26: Syntax and Lexicon*, ed. by Tim Stowell and Eric Wehrli, 127-153, Academic Press, San Diego.

Rizzi, Luigi (1990) *Relativized Minimality*, MIT Press, Cambridge, MA.

Ross, John Robert (1967) *Constraints on Variables in Syntax*, Doctoral dissertation, MIT.

属格名詞句の分離可能性について

西山　佑司

慶應義塾大学

1. はじめに

(1a) と (1b) の間に密接な関係があることは明白である．

(1) a. [田中先生の息子] が家出した．（述定）
　　b. [息子が家出した] 田中先生　（装定）

(1b) の主名詞「田中先生」は「息子」との間に，「田中先生の息子」という所有関係を結んでいると考えられる．そこから，(1b) の基礎には (1a) があり，(1a) の属格名詞句「田中先生の息子」の「田中先生」を分離し，それを主名詞にすることによって連体修飾節表現 (1b) を構築できるように思われる．(1b) のような連体修飾節表現を「装定」，装定の基礎となる (1a) のような文を「述定」と呼ぶ．(2), (3) の対も同様である．

(2) a. [村の村長] が汚職で逮捕された．（述定）
　　b. [村長が汚職で逮捕された] 村　（装定）
(3) a. [車のエンジン] が壊れた．（述定）
　　b. [エンジンが壊れた] 車　（装定）

(1a), (2a), (3a) の [NP_1 の NP_2] はいずれも主語位置にあったが，(4) のように目的語位置にある属格名詞句 [NP_1 の NP_2] からも NP_1 の分離は可能であるように思われる (cf. 菊地 (1995: 43))．

(4) a. 田中教授が [花子の卒業論文] を指導した．（述定）
　　b. [田中教授が卒業論文を指導した] 花子　（装定）

このように，各 (a) を述定とし，そこから対応する装定 (b) を構築できるとする見解の背後には，(5) のような仮説がある．

(5) 属格名詞句 [NP₁ の NP₂] を含む文を基礎にして，NP₁ をその名詞句から抜き出し，それを主要語とする連体修飾節表現を構築できる．

本稿ではこの仮説の妥当性を検討し，この仮説には問題があること，(1b)，(2b)，(3b)，(4b) のような装定に対応する述定形式は，(1a)，(2a)，(3a)，(4a) とは別の形に求めるべきであることを論じる．

2. 属格名詞句分離の仮説

よく知られているように，久野（1973: 41）は次のような「主語化」および「主題化」操作を提案した．

(6) 主語化：文頭の「名詞句＋ノ」を「名詞句＋ガ」に変えて，その文の新しい主語とせよ．
(7) 主題化：文中の「名詞句＋助詞」に「ハ」を附して文頭に移動せよ．

日本語学では，(8) で代表される「A は B が C（だ）」構文について，久野の仮説に従い，(9a) における「象の鼻」から「象」を抜きだして派生するという分析が広く採用されてきた (cf. 野田 (1996)，菊地 (1995)，長谷川 (2011))．

(8) 象は鼻が長い．
(9) a. [象の鼻] が長い．
  b. 象が，鼻が長い．（主語化）
  c. 象は，鼻が長い．（主題化）

もちろん，久野 (1973: 162) が指摘しているように，あらゆる「A は B が C（だ）」について，「A の B が C（だ）」が対応しているわけではない．例えば，(10c) に対応して (10a) をつくったとしてもそれは非文法的になるだけである．

(10) a. *[魚の鯛] がいい．
  b. *魚が，鯛がいい．（主語化）
  c. 魚は，鯛がいい．（主題化）

久野は (9c) と (10c) をいかに区別するかについてはなにも説明していないが，すくなくとも (8) のようなタイプの「A は B が C（だ）」構文については (9) のような派生の存在を主張しているわけである．（久野の例文は (8) と実

質的に同じ「日本は男性が短命です」である．）長谷川（2011: 88-89）は，久野の言う主語化・主題化における属格名詞句の分離現象は，日本語に特有な現象ではあるが，[NP$_1$ の NP$_2$] が主語の位置にあるときだけではなく，次例の如く，主語以外の位置（例えば目的語など）からも可能であると主張する．

(11) a. 花子が [太郎の頭] をたたいた．
  b. 花子が頭をたたいたのは太郎だ．（分裂文）
(12) a. 誰かが [太郎の足] を踏んだ．
  b. 太郎が（誰かに）足を踏まれた．（所有受動文）

そこから長谷川（2011: 89）は久野の主語化・主題化規則をも包括する，より一般的な規則として (13) を提案する．

(13) 所有者分離規則
   名詞句内の「ノ」格（属格）要素は，その名詞句から構造的に分離し，文の構成要素となる．

実際，(13) の規則が与えられれば，(9c), (11b), (12b) は対応する (9a), (11a), (12a) から派生したものであることが統一的に説明できるばかりでなく，(1b), (2b), (3b), (4b) のような装定についても対応する (1a), (2a), (3a), (4a) のような述定形式から派生したものであることが統一的に説明できそうである．では，(13) は本当に妥当であろうか．以下，この問題を検討する．

3. 属格名詞句分離の仮説に対する反例

文中の [NP$_1$ の NP$_2$] における NP$_1$ を無制限に抜き出すことができないことは明らかである．とくに，[NP$_1$ の NP$_2$] が主語以外の位置にある場合は，NP$_1$ の分離は一般に難しい．

(14) a. 太郎が [その女性の本] を読んだ．
  b.?その女性$_i$は，太郎が (e$_i$ の) 本を読んだ．（主題化）
  c.?[太郎が [(e$_i$ の) 本] を読んだ] その女性$_i$（関係節化）
(15) a. [太郎の部屋] で，花子が倒れた．
  b.*太郎$_i$は，(e$_i$ の) 部屋で，花子が倒れた．（主題化）
  c.*[(e$_i$ の) 部屋で，花子が倒れた] 太郎$_i$（関係節化）

(16) a. 太郎が [北海道の画家] に手紙を書いた．
   b. *北海道$_i$ は，太郎が [(e_i の) 画家] に手紙を書いた．（主題化）
   c. *[太郎が [(e_i の) 画家] に手紙を書いた] 北海道$_i$ （関係節化）

ただし，[NP$_1$ の NP$_2$] における NP$_1$ と NP$_2$ の関係が西川 (2013) の言うタイプ F の場合，つまり NP$_2$ が譲渡不可能名詞で，NP$_1$ が NP$_2$ の基体を具現化する機能を果たす「基体表現」である場合は，[NP$_1$ の NP$_2$] が主語以外の位置にあっても NP$_1$ の分離は可能であると思われる．

(17) a. 太郎が 315 号室の床を掃除した．
   b. 315 号室$_i$ は，太郎が (e_i の) 床を掃除した．（主題化）
   c. [太郎が (e_i の) 床を掃除した] 315 号室$_i$ （関係節化）
(18) a. あの家の屋根裏部屋で沢山のネズミが出た．
   b. あの家$_i$ は，(e_i の) 屋根裏部屋で沢山のネズミが出た．（主題化）
   c. [(e_i の) 屋根裏部屋で沢山のネズミが出た] あの家$_i$ （関係節化）

「315 号室の床」「あの家の屋根裏部屋」はタイプ F の関係にある．一方 [NP$_1$ の NP$_2$] がタイプ F 以外の場合，例えば，西山 (2003) の言うタイプ D の場合，[NP$_1$ の NP$_2$] が主語の位置に現れる場合とそれ以外の位置に現れる場合には容認可能性に差がある．(19) と (20) を比較してみよう．

(19) a. [画家の妻] が太郎にぶたれた．
   b. 画家$_i$ は，(e_i の) 妻が太郎にぶたれた．（主題化）
   c. [[(e_i の) 妻が太郎にぶたれた] 画家$_i$ （関係節化）
(20) a. 太郎が [画家の妻] をぶった．
   b. ?画家$_i$ は，太郎が (e_i の) 妻をぶった．（主題化）
   c. ?[太郎が [(e_i の) 妻をぶった] 画家$_i$ （関係節化）

そこからひとまず (21) のような仮説をたてることができるかもしれない．

(21) a. [NP$_1$ の NP$_2$] が主語の場合，NP$_1$ の分離は可能である．
   b. [NP$_1$ の NP$_2$] が主語以外の場合，[NP$_1$ の NP$_2$] がタイプ F のときに限り NP$_1$ は分離可能である．

(21) はデータの単なる整理以上のものではないが，これにも問題がある．とくに，(21a) に対してはすぐ反例が出てくる．(22) と (23) を比較しよう．

(22) a. [田中先生のネクタイ] が曲がっている．

  b. 田中先生は，ネクタイが曲がっている．（主題化）
  c. [ネクタイが曲がっている] 田中先生　（関係節化）
(23) a. [森英恵のネクタイ] が曲がっている．
  b.?森英恵は，ネクタイが曲がっている．（主題化）
  c.?[ネクタイが曲がっている] 森英恵　（関係節化）

　(22a) の「田中先生のネクタイ」，(23a) の「森英恵のネクタイ」はいずれも西山（2003）で言うタイプ A の [NP_1 の NP_2] であり，NP_1 と NP_2 の具体的な関係は語用論的に決まる．今，(22a) の「田中先生のネクタイ」を《田中先生が締めているネクタイ》と読んだ場合，その意味は (22b)，(22c) においても維持できるであろう．一方，(23a) の「森英恵のネクタイ」を《森英恵がデザインしたネクタイ》と読んだとしよう．あるひとの締めた，森英恵がデザインしたネクタイが曲がっているとき，その意味は (23b)，(23c) において維持されないのである．以上の観察は，[NP_1 の NP_2] が主語の位置にあっても，NP_1 と NP_2 の関係がタイプ A の場合は，NP_1 を分離できるか否かをコントロールする要因に語用論も関与することを示している．しかし，一般に，述定形式から装定をつくるとき，その可否に語用論的要因が関与するというのは，属格名詞句 [NP_1 の NP_2] 以外では通常考えられないことである．

　さらに注意すべきことは，属格名詞句 [NP_1 の NP_2] を含む述定形式をもとに，主題化が可能か否かという事実と，述定形式をもとに連体修飾化が可能か否かという事実とは連動するという点である．そのことは，(14)，(15)，(16)，(20)，(23) における主題化文 (b) と連体修飾表現 (c) との対を見れば明らかであろう．いずれも容認可能性が低いのである．一方，(17)，(18)，(19)，(22) における主題化文 (b) は容認可能であるが，対応する連体修飾節表現 (c) もやはり容認可能なのである．このことを (24) についていえば，(25a) が可能であるということと，(25b) が可能であるということはつねに連動するということである．この事実は，「関係節化される名詞句は，関係節中の主題である」とする久野（1973: 158-170）の仮説とも整合的である．

(24) [象の鼻] が長い．(=(9a))
(25) a. 象は鼻が長い．(=(8))
  b. 鼻が長い象　（装定）

　そこで次節では，久野（1973），菊地（1995），野田（1996），長谷川（2011）で当然のこととして仮定されている見解，つまり，(25a) は (24) における

「象」を抜き出して主題化した結果であるとする見解の妥当性について検討する．

4. 属格名詞句の分離と主題化操作

西川（2013: 168-170）は，(24) のような「象の鼻」を含む文から「象」を分離して (25a) を派生するという広く受け入れられている見解に対して次のような反論をしている．(26) は明らかに「象は鼻が長い」構文の変種である．

(26) ある象は鼻だけでなく尻尾も長い．

では，(26) は，主題化以前の基底形としていかなるものを想定すべきであろうか．(25a) を (24) から主題化によって派生する操作と並行的にこの問題を考えるならば，(26) の主題化以前の基底形は (27) のいずれかとなるであろう．

(27) a. ある象の鼻だけでなく尻尾も長い（こと）
    b. ある象の鼻だけでなくある象の尻尾も長い（こと）

しかし (27) のいずれも (26) の基底形とみなすわけにはいかない．なぜなら (26) では，「鼻」と「尻尾」の持ち主は同一の象であるが，(27) のいずれにおいてもその意味を読みとることができないからである．(27a) の「鼻」の持ち主はある象であるが，「尻尾」の持ち主はキリンでも熊でも可能なのである．また，(27b) の「鼻」の持ち主も「尻尾」の持ち主もある象ではあるが，同一の象であることが保証されていない．したがって，(26) の基底形として (27) のいずれも妥当ではない．実際，(26) の主題化以前の基底形は設定できないのである．基本的に同じ「象は鼻が長い」構文でありながら，(25a) には基底形があるが，(26) には基底形がないという分析は，一般性を欠く分析であると言わざるをえない．そこから西川 (2013) は，(24) から (25a) への主題化を認めず，(25a) は基底生成され，その意味構造は (28) のようなものであるとする．

(28) [$_S$ 象$_i$ は [$_S$ α_i の鼻ハ長い]]

つまり，「象は鼻が長い」という構文は，象に「鼻ハ長い」という属性を帰しているという点で措定文である．ところが「鼻ハ長い」それ自体も措定文である．ただ，(25a) においては「鼻は」ではなくて「鼻が」になっているのは，根文

(root sentence) の「ハ」は埋め込み文中では「ガ」に変わるからである．結局，「象は鼻が長い」は措定内蔵措定文という点で二重コピュラ文であるということになる．なお，「鼻」に変項 α が付随すること，α と「鼻」との関係はタイプ F の [NP$_1$ の NP$_2$] であること，さらに「象」と変項 α との間に束縛関係があることに注意しよう．

5. 「鼻が長い象」に対応する述定形式は何か？

ここで，装定形式 (29) を検討しよう．

(29)　鼻が長い象（=(25b)）

通説では (29) は，基底形 (30a) における「象の鼻」から「象」を分離し，それを主名詞にすることによって得られた連体修飾節表現（装定）とみなされている．この立場では，(29) の論理形式は (30b) ということになる．

(30) a. [象の鼻] が長い．（=(24)）
　　 b. [[e$_i$ の鼻] が長い] 象$_i$

しかし，(29) に対してはその基底形を (30a) ではなく (31a) とし，(29) は (31a) の主語「象」を抜き出した結果得られた装定であるとみなす見解も可能である．この立場では，(29) の論理形式は (31b) ということになる．

(31) a. 象$_i$ は，α_i の鼻が長い．
　　 b. [e$_i$ は，α_i の鼻が長い] 象$_i$

(29) の述定形を (31a) に求める仮説を「主語の（連体修飾節の）主名詞への移動説」と呼ぶことにしよう．この説と，(29) の述定形を (30a) に求める「属格からの分離説」のいずれの見解が正しいかを見るために次の例を見よう．

(32)　[鼻だけでなく尻尾も長い] 何頭かの象

(32) は (29) の変種とでもいうべき装定（連体修飾節表現）である．この装定に対応する述定形式は (33) のいずれでもなく，(34) である．

(33) a. 何頭かの象の鼻だけでなく尻尾も長い（こと）
　　 b. 何頭かの象の鼻だけでなく何頭かの尻尾も長い（こと）
(34)　何頭かの象は鼻だけでなく尻尾も長い．

なぜなら，(32) では，鼻の持ち主と尻尾の持ち主が同一個体であることが保証されているのに対して，(33) のいずれにおいても，鼻の持ち主と尻尾の持ち主が同一個体であることが保証されていないからである．一方，(34) ではその点が保証されている．装定と対応する述定形は基本的意味を共有するはずである．したがって，装定 (32) に対応する述定形は (33) ではなく (34) とみなすべきであろう．(32) は (29) と同じタイプの装定である以上，(29) についても対応する述定形は (30a) ではなく (31a) とみなさざるをえない．つまり，(29) を，(30a) から属格「象」が抜き出された結果と考える必要はなく，(31a) から主語「象」が抜き出された結果と考えるべきなのである．同様に，装定 (35) に対応する述定形は (36a) ではなく (37a) とみなすべきである．つまり，(35) の論理形式は (36b) ではなく，(37b) なのである．

(35) 父親が医者である少年
(36) a. [少年の父親] が医者だ．
  b. [[e$_i$ の父親] が医者である] 少年 $_i$
(37) a. 少年 $_i$ は，α$_i$ の父親が医者だ．
  b. [e$_i$ は，α$_i$ の父親が医者である] 少年 $_i$

ここで，冒頭の (1a) と (1b) の対を検討しよう．これまで，連体修飾節の主動詞がコピュラである装定を扱ってきたが，(1b) では主動詞が「家出した」のごとくコピュラ以外の動詞である．通説では (1b) は，対応する述定を (1a) とみなし，そこから「田中先生」を抜き出した結果であると考えられている．しかしこの分析には問題がある．(38) は (1b) の変種というべき連体修飾節表現 (装定) である．では，(38) に対応する述定は何であろうか．

(38) [息子ばかりでなく娘も家出した] 何人かの先生
(39) a. 何人かの先生の息子ばかりでなく娘も家出した．
  b. 息子ばかりでなく何人かの先生の娘も家出した．
  c. 何人かの先生の息子ばかりでなく，何人かの先生の娘も家出した．
(40) 何人かの先生は，息子ばかりでなく娘も家出した．

(38) に対応する述定は (39) ではない．(38) では，娘の親と息子の親が同一の先生であることが保証されているのに対して，(39) のいずれにおいてもその保証がないからである．一方，(40) ではその点が保証されている．したがって装定 (38) に対応する述定は (40) であると考えるべきである．ここでも「属格からの分離説」ではなく「主語の主名詞への移動説」の方が正しいこ

とが分かる．

　第3節で，データを見るかぎり，[NP$_1$ の NP$_2$] を含む述定形をもとに，主題化が可能か否かという事実と，[NP$_1$ の NP$_2$] を含む述定形に対応する装定が可能か否かという事実とは連動するという点を指摘した．「主語の主名詞への移動説」の立場ではこのデータは自然に説明できる．われわれの立場では，[NP$_1$ の NP$_2$] を含む文を基礎にした NP$_1$ の主題化も，装定化も認めない．むしろ，「鼻が長い象」の派生を，「象の鼻が長い」を基底とするのではなく，「象は鼻が長い」から「象」が抜き出されたと考えるのである．したがって，「鼻が長い象」の文法性は「象は鼻が長い」の文法性に依拠するのは当然である．

　さらに，(41) のような [NP$_1$ の NP$_2$] を含む文を基礎にして，NP$_1$ を主名詞とした装定 (42) を作ることは不可能であるが，(5) や (13) のような「属格からの分離説」ではこれを原理的に阻止できない点に注意しよう．

(41)　[病気の息子] が家出した．
(42)　*[息子が家出した] 病気

一方，「主語の主名詞への移動説」の立場ではこの事実は説明できる．もし (42) が可能だとするならば，対応する述定形は (43) のようなものでなければならない．

(43)　*病気$_i$ は，(α_i の) 息子が家出した．

(41) における [病気の息子] は西山 (2003) の言うタイプ B の [NP$_1$ の NP$_2$] であり，「病気」は叙述名詞句である．叙述名詞句は主題の位置に来ることはできないため，(43) は非文である．(43) が非文である以上，対応する装定 (42) は非文法的であるのは当然である．

6. おわりに

　われわれは，属格名詞句 [NP$_1$ の NP$_2$] から NP$_1$ を分離して NP$_1$ を主題にしたり，NP$_1$ を主名詞とする連体修飾表現を構築できるとする通説には問題があることを指摘した．さらに，NP$_1$ を主名詞とする連体修飾表現の基底には NP$_1$ を主語とする文があること，NP$_2$ には変項 α が付随していること，そして NP$_1$ は変項 α を束縛していることを主張した．もしこの議論が正しいならば，仮説 (5) およびそれを一般化した (13) は妥当でないと結論づけざるをえない．

参考文献

菊地康人（1995）「「は」構文の概観」『日本語の主題と取り立て』，益岡隆志・野田尚史・沼田善子（編），37-69，くろしお出版，東京．

長谷川信子（2011）「「所有者分離」と文構造—主語化からの発展」『70年代生成文法再認識』，長谷川信子（編），85-121，開拓社，東京．

久野 暲（1973）『日本文法研究』大修館書店，東京．

西川賢哉（2013）「二重コピュラ文としての「AはBがC（だ）」構文」『名詞句の世界—その意味と解釈の神秘に迫る』，西山佑司（編），167-211，ひつじ書房，東京．

西山佑司（2003）『日本語名詞句の意味論と語用論—指示的名詞句と非指示的名詞句』ひつじ書房，東京．

野田尚史（1996）『「は」と「が」』くろしお出版，東京．

On Tagalog Relative Clauses

Yuko Otsuka

University of Hawai'i at Mānoa

1. Introduction

Kayne's (1994) approach to relativization has created some active debate in the literature (Borsley (1997), Bianchi (2000), Aldridge (2003) among others). Tonoike (2008), for example, adopts Kayne's proposal that relativization involves movement of a DP rather than that of an operator, but maintains, contra Kayne, that relative clauses is an adjunct to DP. Otsuka and Tonoike (2013) advocate for Tonoike's (2008) approach by drawing on Tagalog free relative data. This paper examines headed relatives (both head-initial and head-final) in Tagalog and shows that Tonoike's approach provides a more elegant account of relativization in Tagalog than Kayne's. The present study also puts forward a novel analysis of the item conventionally called "linker" in the Tagalog linguistic literature as (at least historically) an allomorph of the determiner *ang*.

2. Movement Approach to Relativization

Traditional analysis of relativization assumes (a) that a relative clause is a CP adjunct; and (b) that relativization involves movement of a *wh*-operator (OP) to [Spec, CP]. In contrast, Kayne (1994) proposes (a) a relative clause is a complement of D; and (b) relativization involves movement of a NP to [Spec, CP]. This is illustrated in (1) below. Angular brackets < > indicates a copy of the moved item.

(1)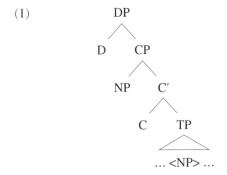

Such a derivation accounts for relative clauses without a relative pronoun such as *that*-relatives in English: [$_{DP}$ *the* [$_{CP}$ *man* [$_{C'}$ *that* [$_{TP}$ <man> *came*]]]]. This NP movement approach provides a straightforward account for coreference between the head noun and the gap in the relative clause. The OP movement analysis requires a special operation of coindexation/predication. As for relative clauses with a relative pronoun, e.g., *the man who came*, Kayne's analysis relies on two additional assumptions: (a) the relevant argument is generated as a DP whose head is a relative pronoun; and (b) there is an additional movement of the NP to the [Spec, DP] of the moved DP.

(2)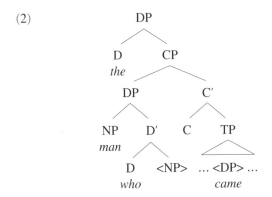

Tonoike (2008) adopts Kayne's proposal that relativization involves movement of a DP rather than OP, but diverges from Kayne by claiming that relative clauses are in fact adjuncts. Tonoike thus proposes additional two operations: (a) DP extraction, by which a DP is extracted from the existing syntactic object to become an independent syntactic object (as an instance of the generalized version of Nunes' (2004) sideward movement); and (b) CP adjunction, by which the relative CP is adjoined to the extracted DP. This analysis is illustrated in (3). It is also assumed that each movement of DP leaves a copy of D alone, whose identity captures coreference. When the DP is extracted by means of sideward movement, the D's valued phi- and Case features are left behind with the copy in [Spec, CP], which are then realized as a relative pronoun if pronounced. This in turn explains why certain relative pronouns are inflected for Case that was assigned to the base position (e.g. *who* vs. *whom*). The sideward moved DP has no specific values on D other than the categorial feature [D]. Its Case feature will be determined when it is merged in the matrix clause.

(3)

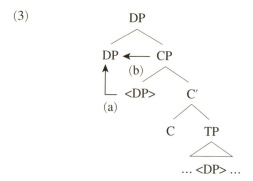

Tonike's model has several advantages over Kayne's. First, it correctly captures the fact that relative clauses behave like adjuncts, or at least differently from complements. Consider, for example, the binding contrast observed by Van Riemsdijk and Williams (1981) and Freidin (1986), as illustrated in (4).

(4) a. Which claim [that John$_i$ was guilty] was he$_{*i/j}$ willing to discuss?
    b. Which claim [that John$_i$ made] was he$_{i/j}$ willing to discuss?

Second, it nicely accounts for the derivation of relative pronoun (as a spell out of a copy of D) without postulating an unusual operation such as DP-internal movement of NP to [Spec, DP]. Third, in this model, CP alone forms a constituent independent of the head noun, while in Kayne's model, it isn't.

3. Tagalog Pseudo-Cleft Constructions

Otsuka and Tonoike (2013) (henceforth O&T) apply this alternative model of relativization to the analysis of Tagalog pseudo-cleft constructions. Tagalog is a predicate-initial language, in which the syntactically prominent argument is marked by a definite determiner *ang*.[1] Argument *wh*-questions in Tagalog are pseudo-cleft constructions in which the subject is a free relative. O&T argue that in Tagalog argument *wh*-questions, the relevant argument is generated only as D rather than DP. This D undergoes movement to [Spec, CP] first, then sideward movement, and is subsequently adjoined by the CP in which it originates. This is illustrated in (5).[2]

(5) [$_{DP\_PRED}$ ano] [$_{DP\_SUBJ}$ [$_D$ ang] [$_{CP}$ <ang> [$_{C'}$ binili <ang> ni
     what   DEF   buy.PERF   DET
Maria]]]?
Maria
'What did Maria buy?' (lit. 'what is the (thing) that Maria bought?')

In O&T's analysis, *ang* is regarded as a definite determiner with an uninterpretable focus feature [*u*Foc] and the relative C is assumed to have a focus feature value as well as an EPP feature. Agree between *ang* and relative C licenses movement of *ang* to [Spec, CP]. Tagalog is known for its "subject" only constraint on relativization (Schachter (1976) among many others): only *ang*-marked NP can be relativized. O&T's analysis nicely accounts for this language-specific constraint: only those DPs with [*u*Foc] may Agree with C.

Turning to Kayne's approach, there are two possible analyses of the relevant construction. One assumes *ang* to be the head of a DP inside the rela-

---

[1] Analysis of Tagalog verbal constructions is a point of contention in the literature, but in the interest of space, the full range of analyses cannot be discussed here. Tagalog data are presented in a simplified manner, glossing over the complexity of verbal inflection and its relationship with the *ang*-marked DP. The particle *ang* is treated as a definite determiner (Otsuka and Tonoike (2013)) and only the aspect of the verb is indicated in the interlinear gloss.

[2] Abbreviations: DEF = definite, DET = determiner, LNK = linker, PERF = perfective, SG = singular, 1 = first person.

tive clause (6a). In this analysis, the head of the matrix DP is taken to be phonetically null (indicated as D in (6a)). The other assumes *ang* is the head of the larger DP that takes a CP-complement (6b).

(6) a. [$_D$ D [$_{CP}$ [$_{DP}$ $_{NP}$Ø [$_{D'}$ ang <$_{NP}$Ø>]] [$_{C'}$ binili   <ang $_{NP}$Ø>
                           DEF   BUY.PERF
       ni   Maria]]]
       DET Maria

    b. [$_D$ ang [$_{CP}$ [$_{NP}$ Ø] [$_{C'}$ binili   <$_{NP}$Ø> ni   Maria]]]
         DEF   BUY.PERF   DET Maria

(6a) is incompatible with the general constraint in Tagalog that NPs must be marked by an overt determiner.[3] (6b) faces another kind of problem, that is, the alleged NP undergoing movement to [Spec, CP] is phonetically null. Though Tagalog does permit null NPs such as discourse topic drop, the nature of this null N is questionable. More importantly, this analysis fails to account for the subject-only constraint on relativization. If the moved NP lacks the DP layer, and hence *ang*, we would expect any argument to undergo relativization. Thus, Kayne's model of relativization cannot provide sufficient account for Tagalog free relatives.

4. Headed Relatives in Tagalog

O&T's analysis of Tagalog free relatives is repeated in (7a). If we apply the same derivation to headed relatives such as 'the book which Maria bought' in Tagalog, we would expect (7b), with the surface form *ang libro [binili ni Maria]*.

(7) a. [$_D$ [$_D$ ang] [$_{CP}$ <ang> [$_{C'}$ binili <ang> ni   Maria]]]
            DEF   buy.PERF   DET Maria
       'the (thing which) Maria bought'

---

[3] Except in existential constructions, constructions in recent perfective aspect, and constructions with perception verbs (Schachter and Otanes (1972), Otsuka and Tonoike (2013)).

b. [_DP ang libro] [_CP <ang> [_C' binili   <ang> ni   Maria]]
     DEF book   buy.PERF   DET Maria
     'the book Maria bought'

However, (7b) is not the actual form. In headed relatives, a linker *na/ng* (phonologically conditioned allomorphs) appears between the head noun and the relative clause, as shown in (8a). Furthermore, the head noun and the relative clause can switch their positions, as in (8b).[4]

(8) a. (ang) libro=**ng**   [binili   ni   Maria]
         DEF   book=LNK buy.PERF DET Maria
         'the book Maria bought'
   b. (ang) [binili   ni   Maria]=**ng** libro
         DEF   PERF.buy DET Maria=LNK book
         'the book Maria bought'

Adopting Kayne's approach to relativization, Aldridge (2003) proposes the following analysis of Tagalog headed relative clauses. Head-initial relatives are derived by means of NP movement to [Spec, CP] (9a). Aldridge proposes subsequent remnant TP movement to [Spec, DP] to derive head-final relative clauses (9b).

(9) a. [_DP [_CP book [_TP Maria bought t_book]]]
   b. [_DP [_TP Maria bought t_book] [_D' [_CP book [_C' t_TP]]]]

In addition to the lack of clear theoretical motivation for the optional remnant TP movement, Aldridge's analysis has two problems. First, it does not explain the categorial status as well as the structural position of the linker. In (8a), the linker *ng* occurs below [Spec, CP] and above TP. One may hypothesize that it is a complementizer, as it so happens that sentential complements of verbs such as *think* are introduced by a homophonous item, *ng/na* (even showing the same allomorphs). However, this hypothesis fails to account for the position of the linker in (8b), which precedes the head noun in [Spec, CP]. If the linker is C, we would expect the order *binili ni Maria*

---

[4] Head-internal relatives also exist: e.g., *bilini-ng libro ni Maria*. Due to the space limitation, I exclude them from the present discussion, however (see Aldridge (2004) for an analysis of head-internal relatives in Tagalog).

libro-ng. Also, it fails to account for the lack of the linker in free relatives such as (5). The second problem is the position of the determiner in (8b). If the structure in (9b) is correct, this D is located below the TP which has undergone movement to [Spec, DP]. Thus, the predicted linear order would be *[binili ni Maria] ang libro* (ignoring the linker) instead of the actual *ang [binili ni Maria]-ng libro*. In the next section, it will be shown how Tonoike's approach can account for the headed relatives in Tagalog.

5. Alternative Analysis of Tagalog Headed Relatives

To recap, a satisfactory analysis of Tagalog headed relatives must account for three facts: (a) the position and categorial status of the linker; (b) its obligatory presence in headed relatives and obligatory absence in free relatives; and (c) head-final relatives. The present study proposes that headed relatives in Tagalog at least historically involve relativization of nominal constructions in which the predicate DP is a free relative. Consider the nominal construction in (10a), whose structure is represented in (10b).

(10) a. ang libro ang bilini=ko
DEF book DEF buy.PERF=1.SG
'The one I bought was the book.'

b. [$_{DP\_PRED}$ ang libro] [$_{DP\_SUB}$ [$_D$ ang] [$_{CP}$ <ang> [$_{C'}$ binili=ko <ang>]]]
DEF book   DEF   buy.PERF=1.SG

Suppose relativization applies to (10b) in the fashion proposed by Tonoike (2008): the subject DP undergoes first raising to [Spec, CP], then sideward movement, followed by adjunction of CP. This would derive the structure in (11) (the internal structure of the predicate DP is omitted).

(11)   [$_{DP}$ [$_{DP}$ (ang) [$_{CP}$ blinili=ko]] [$_{CP}$ <ang> [$_{TP}$ [$_{DP\_PRED}$ ang libro] <ang>]]]

'the one I bought which was the book'

The linear sequence of this awkward double relative construction is identical to a verbal construction: *bilini-ko ang libro* 'I bought the book'. I propose that the need to disambiguate these two constructions (relative clause vs. verbal construction) led to the replacement of *ang* in (11) with *ng*. When this replacement took place historically, this gave rise to an allomorph of *ang* which marks the predicate DP in a relative clause. The distribution of allomorphs of *ang* can be formally understood as realization of the clause-type feature on C on D. When its value is [Rel(ative)], it is spelled out as *ng*. I assume that the head of the predicate DP, being a predicate, agrees with T and C (transitively through T).[5]

Head-initial relatives can be derived in a similar fashion; only, the subject and predicate DPs are switched, as shown in (12). The replacement of *ang* with *ng* is also necessary here, as the linear sequence of the resulting head-initial relative is identical to a nominal construction: *ang libro ang binili=ko* 'what I bought was the book.'

(12) a. [$_{DP\_PRED}$ ang binili=ko]   [$_{DP\_SUBJ}$ ang libro]
    DET buy.PERF=1.SG   DEF book
    'The book is the one I bought.'
  b. [$_{DP}$ [$_{DP\_SUBJ}$ (ang) libro] [$_{CP}$ <ang> [$_{TP}$ [$_{DP\_PRED}$ ang binili=ko] <ang>]]]
  c. [$_{DP}$ [$_{DP\_SUBJ}$ (ang) libro] [$_{CP}$ <ang> [$_{TP}$ [$_{DP\_PRED}$ **ng** binili=ko] <ang>]]]
    'the book which is the one I bought'

Finally, this analysis also accounts for the lack of the linker in free relatives. Free relatives such as one given in (13) do not contain a predicate DP marked by *ang*, since the relative clause is a verbal construction. In fact, the relative clause does not contain any *ang*, since the sole *ang*-marked DP is the one undergoing movement to [Spec, CP]. Therefore, there is no need or possibility for *ng* to arise to replace *ang*.

(13) [$_{DP}$ [$_D$ ang] [$_{CP}$ <ang> [$_{TP}$ binili=ko   <ang>]]]
    DEF   BUY.PERF=1.SG
    'the (thing which) I bought'

There is, however, an apparent problem with the present proposal: the

---

[5] A third alternative approach to head-final relatives would be to claim that adjuncts can freely merge on either side of the head. This would also leave the position (and the status) of the linker unexplained, however.

structure in (12a) is synchronically considered ungrammatical (Schachter and Otanes (1972: 530)). It is reasonable to assume that nominal constructions like (12a) historically existed (Starosta et al. (1982); Kauman (2009a, b)). According to Starosta et al. (1982), such constructions were reanalyzed as verbal constructions, giving rise to the synchronic *bilini-ko ang libro* 'I bought *the book*', in which 'the book' is in focus. This essentially is semantically identical to 'the book is what I bought', the intended meaning of (12a). It is thus reasonable to conjecture that (12a) is synchronically generable, but that it is blocked because of the corresponding verbal construction.[6]

6. Conclusion

The present study has shown that relative clauses in Tagalog are better accounted for by Tonoike's (2008) approach to relativization than Kayne's (1994). It has also put forward a proposal that the linker *ng/na* which appears in Tagalog headed relatives should be regarded as an allomorph of the definite article *ang*, which marks the predicate DP in a relative clause. This analysis provides a simpler account for the derivation of head-final relatives than the remnant TP analysis proposed by Aldridge (2003). It should be noted the linker *ng/na* appears to mark noun modifiers of any type, including adjectives and numerals, and that these modifiers can also occur before or after the noun that is modified: *dalawa-ng libro* vs. *libro-ng dalawa* for 'two books', *mabuti-ng tao* vs. *tao-ng mabuti* for 'good person'. In the present analysis, these modifier-noun constructions are also treated as relative clauses: e.g., 'the books that are two', 'the person who is the good one', in which the predicate DP is marked by an allomorph *ng/na* of the definite determiner *ang*.

---

[6] Alternatively, one may hypothesize that as a result of this nominal-to-verbal reanalysis, head-initial relatives have also undergone reanalysis: the relative clause as a verbal construction with *ng* being a complementizer, as illustrated in (i). If that is the case, *ng* in head-initial relatives and the one in head-final relatives should be regarded synchronically as separate items, complementizer and an allomorph of *ang*, respectively.

(i) [$_{DP}$ (ang) libro] [$_{CP}$ <ang> [$_{C'}$ ng [$_{TP}$ binili=ko <ang>]]]

References

Aldridge, Edith (2003) "Remnant Movement in Tagalog Relative Clause Formation," *Linguistic Inquiry* 34, 631-640.

Aldridge, Edith (2004) "Internally Headed Relative Clauses in Austronesian Languages," *Language and Linguistics* 5, 99-129.

Bianchi, Valentina (2000) "The Raising Analysis of Relative Clauses: A Reply to Borsley," *Linguistic Inquiry* 31, 123-140.

Borsley, Robert (1997) "Relative Clauses and the Theory of Phrase Structure," *Linguistic Inquiry* 28, 629-647.

Freidin, Robert (1986) "Fundamental Issues in the Theory of Binding," *Studies in the Acquisition of Anaphora*, ed. by Barbara Lust, 151-188, Reidel, Dordrecht.

Kaufman, Daniel (1992a) "Austronesian Nominalism and Its Consequences: A Tagalog Case Study," *Theoretical Linguistics*: 1-49

Kaufman, Daniel (1992b) "Austronesian Typology and the Nominalist Hypothesis," *Austronesian Histrorical Linguistics and Calture History: A Festschrift for Robert Blust*, ed. by Alexander Adelarr and Andrew Pawley, 197-226, Pacific Linguistics 601, Pacific Linguistics, Canberra.

Kayne, Richard (1994) *The Antisymmetry of Syntax*, MIT Press, Cambridge, MA.

Lebeaux, David (1988) *Language Acquisition and the Form of The Grammar*, Doctoral dissertation, University of Massachusetts, Amherst.

Nunes, Jairo (2004) *Linearization of Chains and Sideward Movement*, MIT Press, Cambridge, MA.

Otsuka, Yuko and Shigeo Tonoike (2013) "The Role of Determiners in the Probe-Goal System: Verbal Morphology and *Wh*-Extraction in Tagalog," unpublished manuscript, University of Hawai'i.

van Riemsdijk, Henk and Edwin Williams (1981) "NP-Structure," *The Linguistic Review* 1, 171-217.

Schachter, Paul (1976) "The Subject in Philippine Languages: Topic, Actor, Actor-Topic or None of the above," *Subject and topic*, ed. by Charles N. Li, 491-518, Acadmic Press, New York.

Schachter, Paul and Fe Otanes (1972) *Tagalog Reference Grammar*, Berkeley, University of California Press.

Starosta, Stanley, Andrew Pawley, and Lawrence Reid (1982) "The Evolution of Focus in Austronesian," *Papers from the Third International Conference on Austronesian Linguistics 1: Tracking the Travellers*, ed. by Amran Halim, Lois Carrington, and S. A. Wurm, 145-170, Pacific Linguistics, Canberra.

Tonoike, Shigeo (2008) "DP Movement Analysis of Relativization," unpublished manuscript, Honolulu, University of Hawai'i.

Jeopardy

Henk C. van Riemsdijk

Annesso Cartesiano, Arezzo; formerly Tilburg University

1. Introduction

On March 30 1964 NBC started a new quiz show that was to become one of the most popular shows on American TV. The show was based on a very simple idea. Instead of the host asking questions that the participants are asked to answer, in this show things are the other way round. The host presents an answer and the participants' task is figuring out what the question must have been. Accordingly, this show was called "What's the Question?" A simple example would be this:

Answer: 5280
Question: How many feet are there in a mile?

In 1983 the show was renamed "Jeopardy," whence the title of this little essay, but the overall principle of the show remained the same.

I have chosen this title in direct reference to the notion of inverted question-answer systems as represented by these shows. The reason is that I have come to believe that the notion of 'question' has undergone a quite remarkable transformation, at least in the way it is used by current researchers in the field of modern linguistics. Indeed, my impression is that in the present day linguistics scene people hardly dare ask linguistic questions to which they do not have already a substantive chunk of the answer. Putting it differently, it appears to me that linguists these days shy away from asking questions that are interesting, perhaps far-reaching, perhaps even very important, but that they do not have the foggiest idea of how to answer.

My purpose in this essay is to make this point and to urge my fellow linguists to be both bolder and ambitious in formulating questions as well as more modest about the chance that they could provide an answer in foreseeable time.

My dear Shigeo, as you are a fervent golf player you must have often been in the situation that you (or a fellow player) hit a ball really hard and the ball ends up somewhere behind some elevation in the rough between a bunch of tall trees. So you go searching for it. In Jeopardy golf you would go wandering in the far corners of the golf course, among the tall trees in the rough, where you would be likely to find the odd hidden, disappeared golf ball. Jeopardy would tell you to try to figure out where it might have come from. An idea for your next trip to Hawaii perhaps?

2. Some Recent History

The most important questions that have guided research in linguistics over the past decadeds are the three questions that Chomsky formulated in Chomsky (1985: 131):

1. What constitutes knowledge of language?
2. How is knowledge of language acquired?
3. How is knowledge of language put to use?

Most practitioners of the field would readily agree with Chomsky that in order to answer question 2, we need to know a lot more about the answer to question 1, though specific research in the domain of language acquisition studies is surely also required. And as far as question 3 is concerned, it is certainly not impossible to study issues of pragmatics and spoken language etc., but most would agree that the fundamental answers which would include drawing extensive inferences from preceding text and knowledge of the world would be probably in the realm of mysteries rather than problems.

One might argue that the above questions 1 and 2 together constitute a serious longterm challenge that will dominate the research agenda of linguistics for decades if not centuries to come.

In recent years perhaps the most important shift in our perception is the idea that there are not two fundamental factors determining the build-up and acquisition of linguistic knowledge, viz. external experience and the biological endowment of humans ("universals"), but that there is a third type of factor, equally important, that should also be taken into consideration: laws of nature, i.e. design principles determining the structure and properties of biological organisms. (Chomsky (2005).)

It is within this overall framework of 'big questions' that linguistic research is carried out. But these questions define goals that are so ambitious and distant that they do not really guide every-day normal science.

This does not mean, however, that it is not possible to wonder about other questions, at any level of generality, that we might carry around with us, be it consciously or unconsciously. In particular, it is interesting to see if questions of a more specific kind could be formulated that could, as it were, fill in in greater detail, the research agenda that Chomsky's three questions provided the contours of.

Such a filling in of the contours of a far reaching research agenda had, most famously, been undertaken for Mathematics at a Paris conference in 1900, see Hilbert (1902). Today, 114 years later, 11 of the 23 problems that Hilbert formulated are considered resolved, four remain unsolved, and the remaining 8 are either partly resolved or the solution proposed for them remains controversial.

This is the idea that Hubert Haider had in mind when he asked me to join a project of his. This project was to formulate Problems (in Hilbert's terms) that, at various levels of generality, would define a rich research agenda for linguistics. This we set out to do, asking around 150 peers to come up with Hilbert-style problems. So far, it is fair to say, our project has failed miserably. The input has been very low, and many of the questions/problems submitted can hardly be classified as questions because, in a sense they start with the answer.[1]

This is why I have called this essay 'Jeopardy.' Many took some problem on which they were currently working and which they had, in their own mind, solved to a certain extent. (This extent could well reach about 80%

---

[1] A conference that started from similar premises including the guiding role of Hilbert was organized in Pavia by Andrea Moro and his co-workers in November 2013. While the discussions were quite interesting, my overall conclusions were the same: if we want to achieve a detailed and rich research agenda for linguistics, there is a lot of work to do. Some of the discussion around our Questions project can now also be found on Norbert Hornstein's 'Faculty of Language' Blog: http://facultyoflanguage.blogspot.it

in a number of cases). The question that that article was supposed to solve would be formulated as the central problem. The (partial) solution to that problem would be summarized, and the remaining open questions are supposed to set the research agenda. Mostly this would be the contributor's own research agenda, and the implicitly envisaged time it would take to solve the remaining issues would be measurable more in terms of months than in years, let alone decades.

I am therefore led to the conclusion that the way many linguists work is by taking some idea that they like. Consider it a solution to something, and then go hunt for the question that that idea could be the solution of. In other words: "What's the question?" Or, indeed, Jeopardy. And it seems to me that there is indeed a serious danger if we plan our research activities in this way.

We, Haider and myself, feel very strongly, therefore, that the art of asking real long term questions that can help define the research agenda for linguistics must be rediscovered or, more likely, discovered. And we are determined to try and engage the linguistic community in the quest for significant hard and longterm research questions.

Interesting questions arise as to why it seems to be so difficult to formulate Hilbert-style problems for linguistics. Part of the answer is undoubtedly tied to the fact that mathematics as a formal discipline has had a much longer history. Another factor may well be that at some point during the second half of the 1980s the consensus about some major basic notions and the sense of common purpose that had been at its peak after the publication of Chomsky's (1981) *Lectures on Government and Binding* (see also Chomsky (1982)) started to dissolve. Without a common conceptual basis, it is difficult to formulate cogent questions. This is particularly detrimental when those questions are intended to be part of the research agenda for a substantial percentage of the researchers in the field and for at least several decades into the future.[2]

Let me, despite these difficulties, sketch, by way of illustration, two ques-

---

[2] Indeed, the conference mentioned in the first note was primarily intended to investigate the chances for reestablishing a foundation of common tenets for modern generative linguistics.

tions that have bothered me for quite some time and to which I cannot even begin to discern a path towards a possible answer.

4. Two Examples

4.1. Why Are There No Inverse Resultatives?

Many languages have resultative constructions of the type (1).

(1) John hammered the metal flat

In (1) the initial state of the metal is that of being "not flat." The exact shape that the metal is in before the hammering is not specified. After the hammering the metal is flat. Therefore we say that the metal being flat is the result of the hammering of the metal. That is, the small clause predicate 'flat' is the resultative predicate.

Strangely enough there do not seem to be any languages in which it is possible, by means of a similarly simple structure, to express the opposite type of meaning, the meaning in which the small clause predicate denotes the initial state and the result of the verb is the negation of the small clause predicate. An example might be like this:

(2) John kicked the ball round

This example might be taken to mean that the ball is round in its initial state and that the result of the kicking is that the ball is "not round," where the actual shape it has as the result of the kicking is not specified.

Such a construction, which we might call the 'inverse resultative' does not exist in English and, as far as I am aware does not exist in any language.

The question thus is twofold:

    A. Is the empirical generalization that there are no natural languages with inverse resultatives correct?

    B. If this generalization is correct, why?

My best guess is that the answer to B must be somehow related to the fact that constructions involving SOURCE and constructions involving GOAL are not symmetrical but, in fact, rather different in several ways, see Van Riemsdijk (2012). How this asymmetry between source and goal could be used to explain the inexistence of inverse resultatives, however, is entirely unclear to me.

4.2. Forces of Nature and Parameters

It has become popular in the course of the last decade to attribute certain properties of natural language to a "third factor" (in addition to innate principles of Universal Grammar and properties due to experience), viz. general principles of physical/biological design, cf. Chomsky (2005). Indeed, many "forces" active in grammar do appear to constitute linguistic reflexes of forces of nature. Take, for example, the forces of Attraction and Repulsion. In nature these are found everywhere, magnetism being only one of many manifestations, cf. Winslow (1869) for an early discussion. In linguistics we may think of various kinds of identity avoidance (from haplology to more abstract principles like the OCP) and their inverse such as reduplication, copying and many others cf. Van Riemsdijk (2008) What is bothersome, from the perspective of general principles of design or forces of nature is that, as far as we can, at this point, determine, attraction and repulsion are competing forces and, what is worse, both seem to be heavily parametrized. The Doubly Filled Comp filter, for example, undeniably an instance of identity avoidance, that is, repulsion, clearly works differently (more strongly or more weakly) in different languages. Is this a paradox?

The phenomena that correspond to attraction and repulsion in linguistics can be subsumed largely under the notions 'identity creation' and 'identity avoidance.' The most obvious candidates for identity creations are reduplication, cf. Raimy (2011 and references cited there) and copying. The antithesis is identity avoidance, which is well known from virtually all domains of grammar, such as haplology in phonology, morphology and syntax. A sequence of two phonologically identical clitics, for example, is often avoided. And the grammar finds various ways of avoiding the (juxtaposition of) two identical elements. Take for example the fact that Italian has two clitics [si], one reflexive and one impersonal. Thus one would expect (3):

(3) *In Italia si   si munisce di scontrino   prima di   ordinare
     in Italy one   oneself   provides with receipt before ordering

il caffè
the coffee

However (3) is ungrammatical, due to the repetition of two identical clitics. Instead, 'si si' has to be replaced by 'ci si,' a case of dissimilation. Another typical way in which offending cases of identity, often abbreviated as *XX, are rectified is by deletion of one of the two. This is what Spanish does in the case corresponding to (3).

Sometimes, *XX seems to manifest itself in more obscure, more abstract ways. Take, for example, the fact that many languages exhibit so-called Doubly Filled COMP filter (DFC) effects, see Chomsky and Lasnik (1977) A typical example is English (4).

(4) *the man who that I saw/√the man who I saw/√the man that I saw

Apparently a filled Spec,CP does not go together with a lexically realized complementizer. But note that fronted finite verbs in V2 languages are in complementary distribution with complementizers. Let us assume for simplicity's sake that the fronted V is in C°. Standard German is like English in that it obeys the DFC, and it is a V2 language. However V2 never produces a DFC effect. If we assume that complementizers are nominal or prepositional, as seems reasonable, we may say that the DFC effect obtains between elements that are [–V] but not between an element that is [+V] (such as the fronted verb) and another element that is [–V] (such as the *wh*-word in Spec,CP. Hence the offending identity is not phonological but at the level of categorial features.

Some very general principles that have been proposed in the literature may be reducible to, or interpreted as instances of, identity avoidance. Take various proposals of intervention constraints such as Relativized Minimality (cf. Rizzi (1990)) or the Head Movement Constraint (cf. Travis (1984)). Such constraints can be conceptualized as movement of some element along a path on which it encounters some element that is sufficiently similar (i.e. partly identical) to itself. In that virtual intermediate position on the path, we have an identity avoidance situation that can be made responsible for the blocking effect. See Wilkins (1977) and Van Riemsdijk (1982) for some early ideas along these lines.

Consider finally the concept of feature checking. On the standard interpretation some element carrying a feature F moves to (or is attracted by) some position that also has the same feature. The checking done, the feature is deleted. This process has been likened to the interaction between viruses and their hosts in immunology see Piattelli-Palmarini and Uriagereka (2004). Other metaphors that have been suggested include covalent bonding in chemistry and magnetism, whence attraction and repulsion, cf. Van Riemsdijk (2008). For more examples, ideas and discussion of identity creation and avoidance, see Nasukawa and Van Riemsdijk (2014).

If we deem the high incidence of phenomena in natural languages that evidence identity creating or identity avoiding effects significant enough to suspect that highly general principles are at work, it is plausible to conclude that general principles determining the design of the physical world and thereby of biological organisms are involved, in other words, laws of nature. Laws of nature are, however, considered to be exceptionless. What we know about identity creation and identity avoidance in Linguistics, however, strongly suggests that there is considerable variety within and among languages. The DFC holds in some languages but not in others, identity is sometimes determined by phonetic or phonological factors, but sometimes by grammatical features of some kind, identity may be partial or full, and so on and so forth. Putting it differently, it appears as if forces of nature at play in natural language grammars are highly parametrized. For a philosophical discussion of this kind of problem, see Hall (2009). This problem may simply reflect our limited understanding of what is going on, but it may also point to some more fundamental property of language design. This, then, is the question.

5. Conclusion

In this short essay I have tried to discuss some of the factors that make it very hard and perhaps impossible to formulate a set of 'problems' in the sense of Hilbert for current linguistic theorizing. It would be easy to end up being defeatist about this conclusion, but I have also tried to suggest some examples that are intended to show that it is not impossible to formulate some 'real' questions (as opposed to the pseudo-questions that I referred to in section 2 above).[3]

References

Chomsky, Noam (1981) *Lectures on Government and Binding*, Foris, Dordrecht.
Chomsky, Noam (1982) *The generative Enterprise: A Discussion with Riny Huybregts and Henk van Riemsdijk*, Foris, Dordrecht.
Chomsky, Noam (1985) *Knowledge of Language: Its Nature, Origins, and Use*, Praeger, New York.
Chomsky, Noam (2005) "Three Factors in Language Design," *Linguistic Inquiry* 36, 1-22.
Chomsky, Noam and Howard Lasnik (1977) "Filters and Control," *Linguistic Inquiry* 8, 425-504.
Hall, Ned (2009) "Humean Reductionism about Laws of Nature," unpublished manuscript, Harvard University.
Hilbert, David (1902) "Mathematical Problems," *Bulletin of the American Mathematical Society* 8, 437-479.
Nasukawa, Kuniya and Henk C. van Riemsdijk, eds. (2014) *Identity Relations in Grammar*, Mouton de Gruyter, Berlin.
Piattelli-Palmarini, Massimo and Juan Uriagereka (2004) "The Immune Syntax: The Evolution of the Language Virus," *Variation and Universals in Biolinguistics*, ed. by Lyle Jenkins, 342-377, Elsevier, London.
Raimy, Eric (2011), "Reduplication," *The Blackwell Companion to Phonology* 4, ed. by Marc van Oostendorp et al., 2383-2413, Wiley-Blackwell, Oxford.
Riemsdijk, Henk C. van (1982) "Locality Principles in Syntax and Phonology," *Linguistics in the Morning Calm*, ed. by The Linguistic Society of Korea, 693-708, Hanshin, Seoul.
Riemsdijk, Henk C. van (2008) "Identity Avoidance: OCP-effects in Swiss Relatives," *Foundational Issues in Linguistic Theory. Essays in Honor of Jean-Roger Vergnaud*, ed. by Robert Freidin, Carlos P. Otero and Maria Luisa Zubizarreta, 227-250, MIT Press, Cambridge, MA.
Riemsdijk, Henk C. van (2012) "Discerning Default Datives: Some Properties of the Dative Case in German," *Discourse and Grammar*, ed. by Günther Grewendorf and Thomas Ede Zimmermann, 247-287, Mouton de Gruyter, Berlin.
Rizzi, Luigi (1990) *Relativized Minimality*, MIT Press, Cambridge, MA.

---

[3] Many thanks are due to Hubert Haider to whose invitation to join his Questions project I owe many of the ideas and speculations presented in the above pages.

Travis, Lisa (1984) *Parameters and the Effects Of Word Order Variation*, Doctoral dissertation, MIT.

Wilkins, Wendy (1977) "The Variable Interpretation Convention: A Condition of Variables in Syntactic Transformations," Doctoral dissertation, UCLA, California. [Published in 1979 by the Indiana University Linguistics Club.]

Winslow, Charles Frederick (1869) *Force and Nature. Attraction and Repulsion: The Radical Principles of Energy, Discussed in Their Relations to Physical and Morphological Developments*, J. B. Lippincott & Co., Philadelphia. (Facsimile edition by the University of Michigan Library.)

Are World Englishes Movable: The Case of Asian Englishes

Donald L. Smith

The University of North Georgia

1. Questions We Might Ask about Asian Englishes[1]

The phenomenon of the globalization of English has given birth to the concept of World Englishes and forums for research in this newly defined field of sociolinguistic research are represented in the journal *World Englishes*[2] and organizations such as the International Association for World Englishes. Subsequently, we have the journal *Asian Englishes: An International Journal of the Sociolinguistics of English in Asia/Pacific*[3] and the sponsoring organization, the National Conference of the Japanese Association for Asian Englishes as well as numerous other regional associations that focus on varieties of English and issues relating to English and English education throughout Asia. What has not received much attention as yet is the influence of or even the spread of Asian Englishes out of Asia to other parts of the world. I would like to address this issue in this note on the movement of Asian Englishes to the West and its possible new role from being a variety of English to being a socio-dialect of English.

---

[1] This paper is a commentary, mostly based on my own observations on the recent increase in the number of immigrants arriving in North America and the possible influence of Asian Englishes on the languages of North America. It remains to be seen what the possible imprint on language use in North America might be, although changes can be seen in popular culture and in businesses fostered by Asians who are making their new home this side of the Pacific. Thanks for the inspiration to look into these fascinating influences on language use and for sharing the joy of linguistics with me go to my friend and colleague, Shigeo Tonoike.

[2] *World Englishes* is published by Blackwell Publishers, Oxford UK & Cambridge USA.

[3] *Asian Englishes* was published by ALC Press Inc., Tokyo, Japan. It is now published by Taylor and Francis Group, London, GB.

When we speak of new varieties of English, the implication is that they are, in fact, new distinct languages that can stand alone in the sense that American English and British English are distinct from one another. If so, we should be able to consider them as we do all living languages in the context of time and space.

Languages, of course, have no boundaries. They respect no boundaries and they are born and grow, evolve, expand, develop, change, blend, divide, diversify, and often age and die. Languages, like the people who use them can thrive and prosper on earth and then disappear, often without a trace. Languages have families, descendants, and when remembered or studied after they are no longer in use, they become dead languages.

Languages are acquired or learned and an individual will normally have at least one language he or she can call a first language, but many individuals will learn additional languages presumably without limit except for the limitations of time and space. Also, there are limitations in terms of age in language learners and the critical period, after which language acquisition becomes less instinctive and native competency in a new language without considerable conscious effort will become unlikely. Hence, we have the distinction between a native language and a second or learned language. Asian Englishes may fall somewhere between the two poles.

2. The Immigration of Asians to North America

North America, especially the United States, has been known as the melting pot of the world. People from all over the world have come and settled in this part of the world to eventually blend in and become natives of the regions they have come to know as home. Different periods have seen the influx of peoples from many different parts of the world. Most recently, we have seen an especially big influx of Hispanic immigrants and Asian immigrants. Although Hispanic immigrants have received much attention in the past few years, we note that the rate of Asian immigration now exceeds that of all other groups, including the Hispanic immigrants, particularly on the West Coast, but also to other parts of the Unites States, including my own part of the country, Atlanta and the surrounding area.

Georgia is perhaps typical of many other states where we have seen the recent immigration of people from various parts of Asia. In the northeast sector of Atlanta, there has been a very conspicuous influx of Asians to the extent that the Chambly Tucker area has been dubbed Chambodia. Cambodians are not the only group represented. The area is dotted with Korean stores and churches, one of which is next to a Thai temple and monastery, and the local Buford Farmers' Market, which is like a mini-UN, catering to Asians from all parts of Asia as well as the Latino population. The fresh fish section of the market, where scores of customers have to take numbers to await their turns, features bins of seafood from all over the world and would rival any retail fish market in Tokyo or Taipei. In addition to the Farmers' Market, there are several Asian supermarkets including the Hong Kong Supermarket in Hong Kong Square (http://www.hongkongmkt.net) and three Korean Super H-mart stores (http://www.hmart.com) in the area, and innumerable stores that cater to Asians, often catering to particular Asian ethnicities such Thais, Filipinos, and Vietnamese. In the nearby town of Winder, there are two Hmong food stores. Northeast of Atlanta, around Alto and Cornelia, there is a community of Laotians large enough to support two local Buddhist temples. The schools in the area have many Asian American children and young adults in attendance, many of whom were born in the U.S., but still require training in English, ESL, to augment their English language skills, especially in reading and writing for academic purposes.

In an article in *The New York Times*, 'New Suburban Dream Born of Asia and Southern California,' Jenifer Medina (2013) observes that, "Much of the current immigration debate in Congress has focused on Hispanics, and California has for decades been viewed as the focal point of that migration. But in cities in the San Gabriel Valley—as well as in Orange County and in Silicon Valley in Northern California—Asian immigrants have become a dominant cultural force in places that were once largely white or Hispanic." In the same article, Medina quotes Hans Johnson, a demographer at the Public Policy Institute of California, who observes in reference to Asian immigration, that "There are astonishing changes in working-class towns and old, established wealthy cities." The article goes on to point out that many of the immigrants "come here from China and Taiwan, where they were part of a highly and affluent population. They have eagerly bought property in places like San Marino, where the median income is nearly double of that of Beverly Hills and is home to one of the highest performing school districts in the state." Interestingly, the immigrant population is bringing along cultural changes as well, reflected, for example, in the popularity of hangouts where, as Medina reports, "People here think it's normal, hanging out to drink boba all day long."

Boba tea shops, also called bubble tea shops, may actually be symbolic and symptomatic of a change in the culture of areas where there are a significant number of young, often born in America, Asians, who prefer spending their free time, in the words of the Fung brothers' hip-hop videos, celebrating "what they termed the "boba life," to embrace the area where, as their lyrics explain, 'kids drink more milk tea than liquor.'" (Medina (2013))

The popularity of boba tea is nothing to be ignored. It may in fact represent one aspect of a new Asian-American identity in Asian-American communities that is especially apparent in the rise of one of the largest and most successful chains of snack and tapioca milk tea shops in the world, Quickly. Quickly is described in Wikipedia as follows:

(1) Quickly (Chinese: 快可立 ; pinyin: *Kuàikělì*) is one of the largest tapioca milk tea franchises in the world, with over 2000 locations in Africa, Asia, Europe and North America. Quickly is the brand name of Kuai Ke Li Enterprise Co. Ltd., which was founded by Nancy Yang in Taiwan and started franchising.

It is further pointed out in the same entry that:

(2) Quickly Corporation was founded in California and started its trademark licensing program at the same time. Quickly began marketing themselves as a New Generation Asian Fusion-style cafe in the USA, as opposed to just a tapioca drink shop. Most locations offer free Wi-Fi internet access. (http://en.wikipedia.org/wiki/Quickly)

Without question, the Quickly franchise is an Asian-American icon, and it attracts mainly Asian-American patrons. This is easily seen in the many blogs for Quickly shops on Yelp.com, a site designed to "help people find great local business." (http://www.yelp.com) The name of the chain, Quickly itself, may be a cute name, but it caught my attention because it is very unusual to adopt an adverb as a name for a business. I have found no business named with adverbs such as 'Cheaply' or 'Carefully' or 'Sincerely,' etc., even though these might be qualities that would sell. I did find reference to a German moped, the NSU Quickly, manufactured by NSU Motorenwerke AG of Germany from 1953 to 1963. The name in Chinese script is pronounced like the English word 'quickly' with characters that indicate the concept 'fast,' so it is most likely that the source of the name of the store is the English word 'Quickly,' and the name has subsequently been rendered unmodified in numerous languages. The Quickly cup bears the English name of the store in Japanese, Korean, Thai and English script in addition to Chinese. In Spanish, the store is named Enérgetico. The popularity of Quickly speaks well for the Asian American identity of the young Asian Americans who patronize their shops, but looking through the many many blogs where customers have expressed their evaluations of the offerings and service of the shops they have visited, I have found virtually no linguistic evidence of any carryover into their English from any Asian variety of English that they might have carried over from their Asian heritage. I did find evidence of the Asian American identity that many maintain along with mention of the names of Asian foods and drinks, some of which have not made it into 'the dictionary,' i.e. the generally accepted American English lexicon. Following are a few excerpts found on reviews on Yelp with no specific reference for the sake of privacy.

(3) a. Ironically, the only thing of the menu I don't like is their boba. I get the lychee slush (with lychee chunks in it that really make the drink) and fried tofu as a snack every time. The service sucks unless you speak Chinese and is slow no matter what. Great for when I have that craving, but I'll go elsewhere if I want boba.
b. Really bad experience! The milk tea spilled everywhere, made my hands sticky. I was thirsty but cold, so I ordered hot boba milk tea. But when I got the beverage I totally couldn't drink, because it's too "hot" to drink ....
c. Minus two stars because if this is tapioca done Quickly then I would hate to see their sister restaurant Slowly open up. How-

ever, pretty consistently good tapioca (which I judge very scientifically based on flavor, texture, and chewy-to-smooshy ratio) — the only thing this Quickly lacks is the murasaki imo slushy that they offer at the Naha, Okinawa shop.

d. How can I express my feelings for taro milk tea in words? Taro milk tea is like the essence of oreos, all filtered and purified into purple bliss. It is the only thing left in this world sugary enough to put me into that bouncing off the walls state. It is really my drug, sorry, beverage, of choice. I like this Quickly because it is not the one on Durant. That whole area annoys me since I left the dorms. Also, the guy working there last night was cool, because he joined me in a double take when my uneducated-on-boba drinks boyfriend asked for apple jelly in a taro milk tea. You just don't mess with the unusual drink additives.

e. I went here two times already when I was visiting my friends. I think I'm gonna become a regular like every week! I love their 2 for $3 deals, TOTALLY WORTH IT! Their drinks are soooo much cheaper than other places (Cha Time!!!!). Bubble tea, Thai Tea, Jasmine Green Tea (wasn't a big fan until I tried theirs) and the Mango Green Tea is delishhhh. They look like they have good deals on the food too. $6 for Bento Box?

f. I would first like to say how thankful I am that Atlanta *finally* has a shop dedicated to the making of bubble tea. While I'd love for it to be more in town, I'll take what I can get and dream of the days when boba is like froyo and you can get it on every corner. Quickly's bubble tea is good. It's not the best I've had, but it's far and away better than most I've had here in Atlanta. Especially if you take in to account their range of flavors. And the non-slushiness. The balls are always perfectly cooked and nice and chewy: some of the best balls around (yes, that's what she said). The shopkeeps are quite friendly and happy to help you make a decision from the lengthy menu. On my first visit, my whiteness led the shopkeep in to thinking I was a bubble tea virgin and she explained everything in great detail, slowly and clearly. While I obviously didn't need the lesson, I appreciated the thought. Oh, and while not on the menu, their little fried chicken bits are pretty impressive. You know, for not being made at an actual restaurant.

g. I lived in China for a year and would always get bubble tea on my way home from one of the many cute little bubble tea cafes. Quickly is JUST LIKE those places; cute atmosphere, big selection of drinks, and cheap. I really like the green tea slushie and the plain old classic green tea with tapioca pearls (these are the "bubbles"). Come here for an authentic tasty bubble tea experience.

h. Taiwanese chicken nuggets and squid balls to accompany my bubble layer milk or thai tea? fook yes! I like this place, it's fast, easy on the wallet and opens till late. Sometimes as an indian, i look out of place here ... but whatever.

i. My experience summed up to three letters: MEH. 2 stars, yo. (http://www.yelp.com)

The popularity of bubble tea shops is reflected in the climax of a popular award winning animated novel by Gene Luen Yang (2006), *American Born Chinese*. The story is about a young ABC, (pronounced as in the alphabet and meaning American Born Chinese) and his struggles to make friends and be accepted in school. His teacher introduces Jin Wang as "Jing Jang" as "all the way from China," although he is actually an ABC and is from Chinatown in "San Francisco." Another character in the story is his counterpart, Wei-Chen Sun, who is introduced as Chei-chen-Chun, a FOB (pronounced [fa:b], meaning Fresh Off the Boat) who is introduced as "all the way from China," to which he counters "Taiwan." Wei-Chen chooses to speak to Jin in Chinese (indicated by brackets around English translations of his utterances), but Jin insists that he speak English.

(4) <Sorry to bother you, but you're Chinese, aren't you?>
You're in AMERICA. Speak ENGLISH.
Eh… you-you- chinese person?
Yes.

(Yang (2006: 37-40))

Later they become friends and converse in Chinese, rendered in English with brackets. When Wei Chin speaks English his English shows some differences from standard English, mostly lacking tense marking and number agreement such as might be found in Chinese English.

(5) He treat me like a little brother, show me how things work in America. He help me with mi English. He teach me hip English phrase Like "Don't have a cow, man" and "word of your—" No, No … "word to your mother." Ha Ha. He take me to McDonald's and buy me french fries. (Yang (2006: 102))

This is a rather complex story, mostly about Jin's struggle with his identity, and he is sometimes portrayed as Danny with light hair, upset by the appearance of a cousin, Chin Kee from China, who is portrayed or rather illustrated as a stereotypical buck-toothed Chinese cartoon character in traditional Chinese clothing, arms folded in front with his hair in a single braid in back. Chin Kee speaks some form of fractured English beginning with the greeting, "HARRO AMELLICA." He shows no inclination to approximate any variety of English at all, and will not leave Jin (Danny) alone.

(6) Sirry cousin Da-Nee. Chin-Kee ruv Amellica.
Chin-Kee rive for Amellica.
Chin-Kee come visit evely year. Forever. (Yang (2006: 211))

It turns out that Chin-Kee is actually the mythological Monkey King who also has own identity problems, since he cannot accept the fact that he is a monkey. In the end, he accepts his identity as a monkey and in the process reverts to regular English. The identity crisis for Jin Wang is settled as well in the end, and he transforms from being Danny to the ABC that he is when he sits down for a cup of pearl milk tea with Wei-Chen. Wei-Chen converses from this point on in Chinese and promises to take Jin to …

(7) "<….a little hole in the wall place just down the street from here. Best pearl milk tea you've ever tasted>," to which Jin replies, "That'd be cool." (Yang (2006: 232))

All of the characters have come together to accept themselves for who they are.

3. Concluding Remarks

The recent influx of Asians to North America is, of course, not the first wave of Asians to the continent. Chinese and Japanese immigrants in particular, have arrived at different times, mostly as laborers. The Chinese first came to build the Union Pacific Railroad in the nineteenth century (Chang (1994)), and the Japanese, too, came to work on the plantations in Hawaii, and as laborers at various times when Asians were not blocked from immigration by law. The recent wave of Asian immigrants to North America comprises a complete spectrum of people from many different parts of Asia, ranging from people of means, scientists, people in business, educators, etc., to people looking for new opportunities and even groups of refugees escaping difficult situations at home.

In many ways, this is the story of immigration as it has always been. At the same time, there are some differences in that some of the groups of people come as people who speak established varieties of English who are now ready to assimilate into a larger community of speakers of another variety of English. The question is to what extent might this phenomenon bring changes to the American vernacular. I do not think we are in a position to offer a definitive answer to this question, but I think we can say that it is possible that we will see some influences on regional varieties of American English, particularly in the lexicon and idiomatic usage. At the same time, I think it is already pretty clear that succeeding generations of the Asian children raised in North America will assimilate and the vestiges of their Asian varieties of English will be greatly diluted.

The first Quickly cup I used had the following messages printed on it.

(8) Please beware if using cup for hot drinks to avoid being burnt.
Please be Cautious when drinking to avoid choking.

The next time I had a cup of bubble tea, this somewhat ornate messages had been replaced by a simpler message on the lid, I suspect in response to some raised eyebrows caused by the original detailed message around the rim.

(9) Caution: The Contents Are Hot.

The only final step that might be taken would be to change this warning to that used by a simpler more direct one on containers of probably the most popular American fast food company in the business, to read:

(10) CAUTION HOT!

Something may have been lost in the process of simplifications, but this exercise in minimalism reminds me of one of the tasks I undertake as one of the editors of the journal *Asian Englishes*. Since many of the papers accepted are written by Asian scholars, I find myself 'editing' the papers to fit into what we might call 'conventional academic English' as it is used in general by other scholars in the field of linguistics, i.e., what we might call the 'conventional idiom of academic English' used by the almighty 'native speaker.' When I was teaching in Japan, I was often asked to help authors by providing what is called "a native speaker check." In a sense, it seems almost hypocritical that I should be asked to edit the language used by scholars who are competent speakers and writers of English, albeit perhaps different varieties of English, to ready their papers for publication in the journal, *Asian Englishes*.

However, I do not think there is any need to be apologetic, although I do hesitate to use the word "correction" for the "changes I suggest." After all, academic English is yet another variety of English that, however hard to describe, is a standard that scholars in the academic world have come to expect. So, for example, in editing a paper, I do not hesitate to recommend changes in number and agreement and in definite vs. indefinite articles and in word choice, although at the same time I am happy to accomodate if the author chooses to argue for an Asian way of saying things. For terminology, I have to follow established norms. In terms of word choice or word usage, I try to limit suggested changes to a more common idiom or changes in the use of discourse markers where misunderstanding might arise. To cite only one example, while researchers might report that a study *revealed* certain facts, I have suggested that they should not say in a review that the researchers themselves *revealed* certain facts, unless they want to imply that they had been withholding information up to a certain point. Often as not in editing, I am not "correcting" errors in English, but rather, I am fussing over word order or word choice or fixing unintended inferences in English expressions that are otherwise perfectly clear and easy to understand in the original. In such cases, if it could be arranged, I would rather suggest that we sit down for a cup of iced Thai Bubble Tea with a good portion of soft tapioca pearls at the bottom and then work on the fine-tuning of the wording of a nice research report for consumption in academic circles across multiple varieties of English.

References

Chang, Iris (1994) *The Chinese in America: A Narrative History*, Penguin Books, New York.

Medina, Jennifer (2013) "New Suburban Dream Born of Asia and Southern California," *New York Times*, April 28, 1913.

Yang, Gene Luen (2006) *American Born Chinese*, An Inprint of Macmillan, New York.

パリ詩篇散文訳と King Alfred

山内　一芳

東京都立大学名誉教授

1. 序

　11世紀半ばに書かれた Paris Psalter(Bibliothèque Nationale Paris fonds Latin 8824) には，古英語の散文訳（詩篇1-50:8）と韻文訳（詩篇51:7-150:3) が含まれている。このパリ詩篇散文訳が，突如，注目されることになったのは，1885年，R. P. Wülker が発表した King Alfred 訳者説であった．Wülker は，パリ詩篇の散文訳は，12世紀の歴史家 William of Malmesbury が『英国王列伝』(*De Gentis Regum*) の中で，アルフレッド王が死の直前まで行っていたと伝えている未完の詩篇訳である可能性を指摘以来，19世紀末から今日まで100年余りの間，アルフレッド作者説の是非をめぐって，数多くの議論が展開されてきた．

　アルフレッド王は，古英語訳の『牧夫の心得』の序文で，人々が知る必要のあるラテン語の書物を自国語に翻訳することの重要性を説き，「様々な多くの国事の中で，『パストラリス』（司教教書）を時には一語一語，時には意味に応じて，大司教のプレイムンド，司教のアッサー，司祭のグリムバルド，ジョンから学んだように，英語に訳し始めた．」と述べているが，[1] すべての人が必要としていた書物とは何であったのか，王が翻訳した作品は何であったのかについては言及されていない．アルフレッド王は，どのような書物を翻訳したのか？　また，翻訳に関わったとすれば，どのように関与したのか？　20世紀のアルフレッド研究は，この 'Alfredian canon' の解明が主要なテーマであったと言うことができるだろう．古英語の方言，語彙の研究が進展するにしたがって，この状況は，次第に明らかにされていった．中でも，1960年代から80

---

[1] Simon Keynes & Michael Lapidge (1983) *Alfred the Great: Asser's Life of King Alfred and other Contemporary Sources*, 125, London.

年代にかけて発表された Dorothy Whitelock, Janet Bately を中心とする研究によって，それまでアルフレッド王の訳とされていたグレゴリー大教皇の『対話』，ビードの『英国民教会史』，オロシウスの『異教徒との戦いの歴史』が除かれ，新たに，パリ詩篇散文訳が加えられて，'Alfredian canon' は，グレゴリー大教皇の『牧夫の心得』，ボエシウスの『哲学の慰め』，オーガスティンの『独白録』，『パリ詩篇散文訳』の4作品であるというのが，今日の一般的な見解である．

パリ詩篇散文訳は，1982年，J. M. Bately が "Lexical Evidence for the Authorship of the Prose Psalms in the Paris Psalter" を発表して，アルフレッド作者説は，確定的になった感が強い．[2] Simon Keynes & Michael Lapidge, Alan Frantzen, Patrick O'Neill, Robert Stanton など多くの研究者は，Bately の見解を支持し，2001年に出版された O'Neill によるパリ詩篇散文訳の校訂本 *King Alfred's Old English Prose Translation of the First Fifty Psalms* も，その表題にあるように，King Alfred 作者説に肯定的な見解を示している．[3] しかしながら，2007年になって，これまでの考え方に対して，疑問を提起する論文があらわれた．Malcolm Godden の "Did Alfred Write Anything?" である．[4] Godden は，パリ詩篇散文訳には，その明確な証拠はないとして，『牧夫の心得』，『哲学の慰め』，『独白』を含め，アルフレッド説に再検討の必要を主張している．2009年，Bately は "Did King Alfred Actually Translate Anything? The Integrity of the Alfredian Canon Revisited" において，これに反論をしているが，Godden の疑問に十分応えるものとなっていない．[5] 「パリ詩篇散文訳の訳者は，誰か？」という問題は，今なお，検証が求められている課題である．

本稿では，パリ詩篇散文訳のアルフレッド作者説について，これまでの主要な議論を概観し，Godden と Bately の対立する問題点について考えてみたい．

---

[2] Janet M. Bately (1982) "Lexical Evidence for the Authorship of the Prose Psalms in the Paris Psalter" 69-95, *Anglo-Saxon England* 10.

[3] Keynes & Lapidge (1983); Alan J. Frantzen (1986), *King Alfred*, Twayne's English Authors Series 425, Boston; Patrick O'Neill, (2001) *King Alfred's Old English Prose Translation of the First Fifty Psalms*, The Medieval Academy of America, Cambridge, Massachusetts; Robert Stanton (2002), *The Culture of Translation in Anglo-Saxon England*, Cambridge.

[4] Malcolm Godden (2007) "Did Alfred Write Anything?", 1-23, *Medium Ævum* 76.1.

[5] Janet M. Bately (2009) "Did King Alfred Actually Translate Anything? The Integrity of the Alfredian Canon Revisited" 189-215, *Medium Ævum* 78.2.

2. William of Malmesbury と Richard P. Wülker

アルフレッド王の名前は，詩篇の訳者として，12世紀の歴史家 William of Malmesbury (c.1095-c.1143) の『英国列王伝』にあらわれる．William of Malmesbury は，この中で，アルフレッドが翻訳した書物として，オロシウスの『異教徒との戦いの歴史』，グレゴリウスの『牧夫の心得』，ビードの『英国教会史』，ボエティウスの『哲学の慰め』，アルフレッド王のハンドブック（「エンキリディオン」(Enchiridion)）を挙げ，詩篇について，「彼（アルフレッド王）は，詩篇を翻訳し始めたが，最初の部分 (1-50) をもう少しのところで訳し終わろうとした時に，生涯を終えた．」と，次のように記している．

> Psaterium transferre aggressus, uix prima parte expllicata uiuenndi finem fecit. (He began to translate the Psalter, but reached the end of his life when he had barely completed the first part.)[6]

1885年，Richard P. Wülker によって，パリ詩篇の散文訳が，アルフレッド王が死の直前まで訳していたと William of Malemesbury が伝えた詩篇であることが発表された．

Wülker は，『アングロ・サクソン文学史概説』(*Grundriss zur Geschichte der angelsächsischen Literatur*) の §500 Ælfred's Psalmenübertragung において，William of Malemesbury の『英国王列伝』の上記の一節を挙げ，アルフレッド王が，パリ詩篇の散文訳の訳者であると推定している．[7] これが，アルフレッド作者説の発端となった．

3. 19世紀末

1889年，J. Wichmann は "König Aelfred's angelsächsische Übertragung der Psalmen I-LI excl.," を発表した．[8] C. W. M. Grein の *Sprachschatz der angelsäshsischen Dichter* と Joseph Bosworth の *An Anglo-Saxon Dictionary* に基づいて，『牧者の心得』と詩篇散文訳の (1) 音韻，語形，語彙，(2) 翻訳

---

[6] William Stubbs, ed., (1887) *Willelmi Malmesbiriensis Monachi De Gestis Regum*, 1:132.
[7] *Grundriss zur Geschichte der angelsächsischen Literatur*, Leipzig (1885), §§ 500-1, 435-6.
[8] "König Aelfred's angelsächsische Übertragung der Psalmen I-LI exc.," (1889), 39-96, *Anglia* 11.

方法，(3) 詩篇の訳文の比較を行ない，Wülker のアルフレッド訳者説を支持した．これに対し，1894年，Bruce, J. Douglas はアルフレッド訳者説を批判し，"The Anglo-Saxon Version of the Book of Psalms Commonly Known as the Paris Psalter" において，聖職者でなければ聖書釈義のコメンタリ——を詩篇散文訳に組み入れることは不可能であると述べている．[9] 1898年，A. S. Cook は *Biblical Quotations in Old English Prose Writers* において，アルフレッド王は聖職者の協力を得て翻訳したと，Bruce に反論した．[10] 詩篇散文訳と『牧夫の心得』，『英国教会史』に現れる詩篇訳部分を比較し，詩篇散文訳と『牧夫の心得』の類似性を指摘している．詩篇訳すべてが王によるものかどうかについては明らかにしていない．

4. 20世紀後半

1950年に発表された J. I'A Bromwich の論文 "Who was the Translator of the Prose Portion of the Paris Psalter?" によって，アルフレッド作者説が提起され，この後，訳者の問題が，本格的に再開されることとなった．[11] J. I'A Bromwich (1950), Kenneth Sisam & Celia Sisam (1956), J. M. Bately (1982) の見解を示す．

Bromwich は，詩篇散文訳と『哲学の慰め』，『牧夫の心得』の語彙，文体，統語の類似性を示す多くの例を挙げて，この三つの翻訳はいずれも，アルフレッド王によるものであると次のように述べて，アルフレッドが訳者であることを明言している．

> ... this will not materially alter the fact that the vocabulary, phraseology and syntax of the prose portion of the Paris Psalter are substantially those of the Old English versions of the *De Consolatione Philosophiae* and the *Cura Pastolalis*.[12]
>
> The boldest and simplest explanation is that King Alfred has just as good a claim to the translation of the Paris Psalter as he has to the *Cura*

---

[9] "The Anglo-Saxon Version of the Book of Psalms Commonly Known as the Paris Psalter", (1894), 43-164, *PMLA* 9.

[10] *Biblical Quotations in Old English Prose Writers*, (1898) xl, London

[11] "Who was the Translator of the Prose Portion of the Paris Psalter?" (1950), 289-303, *The Early Cultures of North-West Europe*, ed. Sir Cyril Fox and Bruce Dickins, Cambridge.

[12] *Ibid.*, 301.

Pastoralis and the *Boethius*.[13]

Kenneth Sisam & Celia Sisam は, 1956年に出版された *The Paris Psalter* の *Facsimile* の序文で,「詩篇散文訳と『牧夫の心得』,『哲学の慰め』の語句の類似性は, Bromwich が言うほど顕著なものではなく, 相違点を慎重に考慮しなければならない. 散文訳の言語は, Ælfric, Wulfstan よりも『哲学の慰め』に近く, アルフレッドの作品グループとは矛盾するものではない.」と述べて, アルフレッド作者説を否定せず, 司教, 聖職者の協力を得て翻訳されたという見解を示している.[14] その後, Dorothy Whitelock (1966),[15] Patrick O'Neill (1980), Allan Franzen (1986) など, アルフレッドの可能性を示唆する傾向が強まっていく中で, Janet Bately が発表した "Lexical evidence for the Authorship of the prose psalms in the Paris Psalter" (1982) は, アルフレッド作者説を強く支持し, その後の研究に大きな影響を与えた. Bately は,『散文詩篇』とアルフレッド訳ではない作品の語彙的相異を精査し,『英国民教会史』, ウェルフェルス訳の『グレゴリウスの対話』,『ヴェスパージアン詩篇』,『ウェストサクソン福音書』との訳語の相異が著しいと述べて, *infirmitas*, *iniquitas*, *tribulation* など任意に抽出した16語の訳語を検証する. 次に,『散文詩篇』とアルフレッド訳とされる作品の語彙的一致を精査し, 変異形の例 (variants) を考察した後,『詩篇散文訳』の言語と文体の類似性を立証すべく, 数多くの一致点 (correspondences) に言及している。そして, 結論で, この翻訳の背後には, 一つの精神が働いている, それは, アルフレッド王の精神であると, その確信を力強く, 次のように述べている.

> I am convinced that behind the translations, or rather renderings, of *CP*, *Bo*, *Solil* and *Ps*(*P*) there was one mind at work (though probably never entirely on its own). Given the claims made by prefaces, scribes, Asser and William of Malmesbury, and give the absence of any evidence to the contrary, it is reasonable to conclude that that mind was King Alfred's.[16]

---

[13] *Ibid.*, 303.

[14] Bertram Colgrave et al., *The Paris Psalter* (*MS. Bibliothéque Nationale Fonds Latin 8824*), Early English Manuscripts in Facsimile 8, Copenhagen (1956), 16.

[15] "The Prose of Alfred's Reign" (1966), 67-103, E. G. Stanley, ed., *Continuation and Beginning*, London.

[16] Bately (1982), 94-5. なお, 最後の注で, 次のように付記している. I have heard it

5. 21世紀はじめ

今世紀に入って、アルフレッド作者説は、Patrick O'Neill (2001), Robert Stanton (2002), David Pratt (2007)[17] などが支持しているが、近年 Malcolm Godden (2007), Michael Treschow, Pramjit Gill & Tim B. Swarts (2007)[18] によって、強い疑問が提出されている。以下 O'Neill (2001), Godden (2007), Bately (2009) の見解を示す。

O'Neill は、*King Alfred's Old English Prose Translation of the First Fifty Psalms* の第6章 Authorship において、Alfred canon との翻訳方法、言語、文体の数多くの類似性を指摘している。O'Neill は、アルフレッド作品、特に『牧夫の心得』と共通する詩篇翻訳の類似点、相異点の綿密な検証を行なって、その分析の結果を、次のようにまとめている。

> The agreements between *Ps*(*P*) and Alfred's works in ideas, in the phrasing of these ideas, and in idiosyncracies of translation are best explained by common authorship. ... When to these fundamental agreements are added many other types of evidence (especially that of word choice), which, despite their disparate nature, harmonize as to time, place, or person, the only reasonable conclusion is that Alfred was the author of *Ps*(*P*).[19]

そして、パリ詩篇散文訳にアルフレッド王が着手した動機、理由を次のように述べて、アルフレッド作者説の可能性を強く支持している。

As attested by Asser, his biographer and confident, Alfred had a special

---

suggested that King Alfred's involvement in 'his' translations was possibly purely nominal. Lexical studies cannot, of course, either prove or disprove that theory. But, if Alfred's authorship were to be rejected on nonlinguistic grounds, the linguistic evidence is still that overall responsibility rested with one man. これは、Godden (2007) と Bately (2009) の論争を考える上で、重要な言及である。アルフレッドの翻訳が、名目上のものではないかとする、『牧夫の心得』、『哲学の慰め』、『独白』に付けられた序文の Godden の見解と、言語、文体の証拠からは、一人の人物、すなわち、アルフレッド王の責任において翻訳が行われたことを示唆する Bately の見解の相違を明確に表しているからである。

[17] David Pratt (2007), *The Political Thought of King Alfred thee Great,* Cambridge.

[18] "King Alfred's Scholarly Writings and the Authorship of the First Fifty Prose Psalms", *Heroic Age* 18.

[19] O'Neill (2001), 94-5.

devotion to the psalms, reciting them daily. In sum, there weighty reasons, public and private, why Alfred would have undertaken the translation that has survived as the first fifty prose Psalms in the Paris Psalter.[20]

　Malcolm Godden は，2007 年に発表した 'Did King Alfred Write Anything?' において，「ほんとうに，アルフレッド王が，『牧夫の心得』，『哲学の慰め』，『独白』，『詩篇散文訳』を書いたのだろうか？」と問う．第一の疑問は，アルフレッド王の翻訳能力の問題であり，第二の疑問は，アルフレッド作者説を裏付ける証拠の信頼性の問題である．Godden は，「アルフレッド王が，ラテン語の翻訳，適用，拡大を行う時間と知的能力を持っていた．」とする提案は，保留がなければならないと述べて，その理由を以下のように説明する．アルフレッドの翻訳計画は，アッサーが『アルフレッド大王伝』を書き終えた 893 年から，王の死んだ 899 年の間に遂行されたと想定されているが，最初の 3 年は，ヴァイキング軍と戦っていたきわめて困難な時期であり，王位に就いた 22 歳の時にはラテン語の知識を持っておらず，39 歳の時までラテン語を学んだことがなかった．アルフレッド作者説に論拠を与えている William of Malmesbury の挙げた翻訳リストは，現在考えられている作品とは一致していない．王自身が翻訳したと主張する『牧夫の心得』，『哲学の慰め』，『独白』の序文は，程度の差があるが，信頼性に問題があり，『独白』，『哲学の慰め』の翻訳を実際に行うためには，幅広い読書，言語能力，学問的信頼が不可欠で，特に『哲学の慰め』の場合は，作品全体をよく理解した上で，パッセージ一つ一つを自国語のふさわしい表現にし，さらに，根本的な書直し，短縮といった再構成が求められ，古英語のテクストの前後参照も十分に行わなければならない．言語・文体の類似性から，アルフレッド作者説の証拠を示そうとする考え方は，関連するテクストが，同じ作者によるものである可能性を証明するにすぎず，作者が王であったことにはならない．4 つの作品に，同じ「精神」が働いているとする Bately の議論は，「証拠がほとんど与えられておらず，立証するには，あまりにも漠然としすぎている．」と批判し，これまで，多くの人たちは類似点を求めすぎたのではないかと指摘する．結論として，「『牧夫の心得』の序文とテクストは，彼の権威で発表されたものであって，『牧夫の心得』と『独白』の翻訳は，王とまったく関係がなく，彼の死後に，王のものとされたものである．詩篇散文訳は，序文もアルフレッド王に関連する記述も

---

[20] *Ibid.*, 95-6.

なく，作者につながる証拠はない.」と明言している.

> The preface and text of the *Pastoral Care* were done by another and issued with his authorization. The translations of the *Consolation* and *Soliloquies* probably had no direct connection with the king at all but were attributed to him after his lifetime. ... On the Psalms there is no real evidence for authorship.[21]

Janet M. Bately は，2009 年 "Did King Alfred Actually Translate Anything? The Integrity of the Alfredian Canon Revisited" において，(1) 翻訳を行なうアルフレッドの能力，(2) 詩篇散文訳を含む4作品の証拠の信頼性の2点について，Godden に反論をしている．(1) については，『アルフレッド大王伝』の87節,「同じ年（887年），しばしば言及したアングロ・サクソン人の王アルフレッドは，聖なる霊感によって，まさに同じ日に，はじめて読書し翻訳し始めた.」の記述を挙げて，これは「この時期に，アルフレッドが，ラテン語の書物の翻訳を，全ての人の教育のために行う計画に熱心に取り組もうとしていたであろう.」とする Keyns and Lapidge の説明に従って，アルフレッドの翻訳能力を信頼する立場を取っている．(2) に関連して，Godden が疑義を示した序文の問題については，王自らが訳したとする『牧夫の心得』の序文に異論を唱えていない．Bately が，特に反論の対象としているのは，Alfredian canon における言語・文体の統合性の問題である．

> On the other hand, there is Godden's article 'Did King Alfred write anything?' which in support of his doubts about Alfred's authorship, quotes figures from studies by Elizabeth Liggins and myself that, in his words, reveal 'startling', 'remarkable', and 'radical' differences between individual members of the canon in their linguistic and stylistic choices, and by implication serve to cast serious doubt upon the integrity of the canon and – again the right of *Psalms* to membership of it.[22]

Godden が指摘した言語の相違点に対するこの疑問に，文脈を厳密に検討する必要があると述べ，'rejoicing,' 'answering' を表す動詞の使い方，'tid' 'time' を表す語の具体例を示して，同一の作者の可能性を否定するものとは

---

[21] Godden (2007), 18.
[22] Bately (2009), 191-2.

ならないと指摘している．

> As it is, in all three texts it is *tid* that is the preferred form. And in these circumstances, I would argue that, as with the verbs of answering, the 'remarkable disagreement' noted by Godden cannot be said to gainsay the possibility of common authorship.[23]

そして，Bately はパリ詩篇の散文訳を含む4作品の精神が，アルフレッド王のものであると主張して，この論文の結論としている．

> Indeed I have not been persuaded by any of the argument in Godden and Treschow et al.'s papers to change my opinion that 'behind the translations, or rather renderings, of [*Pastoral Care*, *Consolation*, *Soliloquies*] and [*Psalms*] there was one mind at work (though probably never entirely on its own),' and given the existence in ninth-century manuscripts of a first-person prefatory letter by the king himself, claiming authorship of *Pastoral Care*, I continue to maintain that 'it is reasonable to conclude that that mind was King Alfred's'.[24]

6. 結び

これまで，パリ詩篇散文訳のアルフレッド作者説をめぐって，19世紀末，20世紀半ば，21世紀初めの主要な議論を見てきた．19世紀末に現れた見解は，いずれも 'Alfredian canon' の定義が確立していなかったことに加えて，詩篇散文訳との比較は翻訳方法と訳語が中心で，ラテン語の原典との検討が十分とは言えなかった．20世紀半ばになって，Bromwich の論文が契機となり，アルフレッド作者説は大きく進展し，その根拠は 'Alfredian canon' とされる4作品に見られる言語・文体の類似性に求められることになった．Bately (1982) が起点となって，アルフレッド作者説は有力になるが，Bately も認めるように，言語・文体を含めた訳語と翻訳方法という内的証拠だけでは，限界があり，Bately の立場からは，パリ詩篇散文訳の背後には，アルフレッド王の精神が反映しているという結論にせざるを得ないであろう．4作品間の内的

---

[23] *Ibid.*, 204.
[24] *Ibid.*, 208.

証拠だけでなく，Godden（2007）が取り上げたように，アルフレッドを取り巻く歴史的資料の分析と評価という，いわば，外的証拠の信頼性を再検討する必要がある．実のところ，作品相互の内的証拠について，まだ未解決の多くの問題が残されている．これまで，'Alfredian canon'とされてきた作品のうち，翻訳をする上でもっとも複雑で，ラテン語の素養及びラテン語原典の深い理解が必要される『哲学の慰め』は，Godden 教授が中心となって，2002年から2007年にかけて行われた The Alfredian Project の成果として，2009年に出版された The Old English Boethius には，その写本，散文訳，韻文訳，Authorship，ラテン原典とテクスト，コメンタリーを含む最新の情報と見解が明らかにされている．[25] 訳語、翻訳方法という範囲の比較だけでなく，当然のことながら，テクストをゆっくり，しかも，しっかりと読み込むという極めて基本的な作業によって，アルフレッド作者説は考察されなければならない．この意味で，Godden（2007）の問題提起の意義は非常に大きい．これからは，'Alfred canon'とともに，アルフレッド作者説は，外的証拠とともに，ラテン語原典と古英語散文訳のこれまで以上の周到な検証が求められていると言うことができる．

---

[25] Malcolm Godden and Susan Irvine eds., (2009), *The Old English Boethius: An Edition of the Old English Versions of Boethius's De Consolatione Philosophiae*, vols. 1.2, Oxford.

〈第 II 部〉

'Be going to' 再考*

秋元　実治

青山学院大学名誉教授

1. はじめに

'Be going to' の発達に関わる研究は最近文法化，特に構文化との関係で論じられることが多い．主な研究として次のようなものがある．Danchev and Kytö (1994), Chafe (2002, 2008), Hopper and Traugott (2003), Bybee (2010), Boye and Harder (2012), Traugott and Trousdale (2013), Traugott (forthcoming) など．[1]

本稿の目的は確実なデータに基づいて，'be going to' に関わる問題の幾つかについて再考することである．それらの問題としては，

① 'Be going to' はどのような変化を経て未来を表す助動詞に発達したか．
② 'Be going to' はいつ頃から助動詞として確立したか．
③ 'Be going to' と主観化の関係．

以下の議論において，Archer Corpus[2] を基に上記の問題について検討する．

2. 先行研究

紙面の制約上，Danchev and Kytö (1994) と Traugott (forthcoming) を主

---

* Archer Corpus に関して，その使用便宜を図ってくれた Merja Kytö 氏に感謝申し上げる．

[1] 'Be going to' に関する研究に関しては，現代英語では特に 'will' との競合において論ぜられることが多い．主な研究としては Nicolle (1998), Brisard (2001), Szmercanyi (2003), Cacollos and Walker (2009) など．

[2] Archer Corpus に関しては，Biber et al. (1994) 参照．なお，今回の調査では，'be going to' のみを扱った．

としてとりあげる.

　Danchev and Kytö (1994) は Helsinki Corpus, シェイクスピアコーパスなどを基に, 17 世紀中ごろまでの 'be going to' の発達過程を調査している. そこではいわゆる意味特性として, movement, futurity, intention, aspectuality 及び expressivity を設定しており, 初期の例では, movement が主であるが, 徐々に intention, futurity が強まっていく過程を例証している. 初期の例（15世紀）はラテン語やフランス語からの翻訳のためオリジナルが翻訳の過程で英語に影響を与えていることが考えられる. 16 世紀後半から 17 世紀にいたる例においては, 文字通りの意味（= movement）が強いが, intention の意味も感じられるようになった. また 'be going to' の文法化のプロセスについても論じられている. 文法化は二項的なものではなく, 段階的なものとして捉えられており, 次の 3 つの基準をあげている:

① 文字通りの意味（= movement）とそれ以外の意味との割合,
② 'Be going to + V' に見られる結合動詞の種類. 種々の動詞が 17 世紀後半に結びつくようになる.
③ 言語横断的な観点. 運動を表す go が未来時制を表すようになるのは多くの言語にみられる.

結論として,

① 'Be going to + infinitive' の未来時制は一般的に考えられるより早く, 17 世紀中頃以前である.
② 'Be going to' の変化の原因には内的, 外的要因が組み合わさって作用している.

Hopper and Traugott (2003: 93) によると, 'be going to' の助動詞化はステージ I では to 不定詞は目的節を表しており, ステージ II では再分析及びメトニミーにより, 'be going to' が一つになり, ステージ III では類推及びメタファーにより, 動的動詞から状態動詞にまで拡大していったとされる. 通時的構文文法（diachronic construction grammar）からの説明として, Traugott (forthcoming) は構文化（constructionalization）を語彙的構文化（lexical constructionalization）と文法的構文化（grammatical constructionalization）に分け, 後者に関しては, "... the creation of new signs that are primarily procedural" (p. 5) と述べ, さらに "procedural" に関しては, 以下のように説明している:

"Procedural meaning is abstract meaning that signals linguistic relations … Linguistic relations include indexical and information-structure marking (topic, definiteness, etc.), argument-structure marking (case), and marking temporal phase (aspect), or of relationship to time of speaking [tense]." (p. 6)

さらに, grammatical constructionalization には① increase in schematicity (抽象度が高まること), ② increase in productivity (新しいタイプの構文が出てきたり, 'host' クラスが伸張すること), そして③ decrease in compositionality (意味の解読性が下がること) の特徴をあげている (p. 7). 以下の 'be going to' の説明はこの 'grammatical constructionalization' に基づいている.

その説明によれば, 'be going to' は元々語彙的 'go' と a set of constructions' として, 'purpose', 'preprogressive' そして 'passive (optional)' から成る 'a set of constructions' を統合した形でのいわば 'micro-construction' を構成することになる. この構文の意味拡大 (17世紀ごろ) が 'intention' の意味を誘発し, これら purpose/preprogress/passive (optional) (これらを direct critical context と呼ぶ) 及び一方では 'be to' や 'have to' といった peripheral set (これらを indirect context と呼ぶ) により, 未来の意味が発生した (18世紀ごろ). さらに19世紀ごろには無生物主語の構文が, そして20世紀には there-raising 構文が発達した. 加えて, be going to は未来をあらわす 'semi-auxiliary' に発達し, 現代英語では will と競合するようになっていると述べている.

'Passive' の要素が必要なのは, 次例にみられるように, be going to が未来の意味を持つためには主語の動作性を弱める必要があるからである:

(1) Ther passed a theef byfore aleexandre that **was going to** be hanged whiche saide there passed a thief before Alexander who was going to be hanged who said
  'a thief who was going to be hanged passed before Alexander and said'
  (1477 Mubashshir ibn Fatik, Abu al-Wafa', 11th C; *Dictes or sayengis of the philosophhres* [LION EEBO; Traugott forthcoming])

Danchev and Kytö (1994), Hopper and Traugott (2003), Traugott (forthcoming) を総合すると, 以下のようなシナリオが考えられる:

表1：Be going to の助動詞化

```
15th         16th         17th         18th         19th         20th
movement     movement     intention   ⎫
             ⎧ intention ⎬ ⎧ future   ⎭
                                    AUXILIARIZATION ─────▶
```

すなわち，助動詞化したのは 18 世紀前ごろと考えられるが，それが定着するのはさらに後であると思われる．

3. Archer Corpus からの考察

3.1. 'Be going to' の頻度的変遷

'Be going to' の頻度を 50 年ごとに区分して示したのが次表である：

表2：Be going to の頻度

1650-99	1700-49	1750-1799	1800-49	1850-99	1900-49	1950-90
5	12	22	22	72	56	174
(2.5)*	(6)	(11)	(11)	(36)	(28)	(87)

* occurrences per 10,000 words

それをグラフで示すと以下のようになる：

図1：Be going to の頻度の変遷

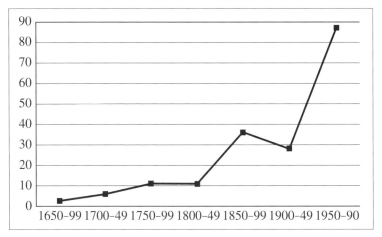

以下にいくつかの例をあげる．

(2) … all his other inward parts not much disaffected, except the Liver; which now I *am going to* describe to you. (1685 brow. m1)

(3) Just as I *was going to* take Horse for Kelston … Sevant came, to have me go to Mrs. Edith who was very Sick. (1722 clav. J2)

(4) I *am* not *going to* inflict a long letter upon you. (1842 dick. x5)

(5) Clearly we *are* not *going to* gain ground so cheaply as yesterday.
(1915 hami. j8)

(6) When I rang up Roy I found that he *was going to* spend it at his cottage in the Hendreds … (1968 cros. j9)

3.2. Be going to + 動詞の種類

'Be going to' が助動詞として発達するためには，動詞の種類を広げる必要がある (host の拡大)．すなわち，行為動詞から状態動詞への移行である．[3] Hopper and Traugott (2003: 69) では Stage III として，'be going to like' を analogy の例としてあげているが，いつ頃であるのかは言っていない．Archer Corpus によれば，まず，状態動詞と共に使われる 'be going to' の例は，1850 年以降であり，1900 年以降になると，be (30), have (10), like (2) と状態動詞と共に使われる例が見られる．It + be going to は 1850 年以降に見られるが，there との使用は 1950 年以降 2 例見られる．なお，'do' との共起も 1900 年以降 17 例見られる．

以上のことを考え合わせると，'be going to' の助動詞化の定着は 19 世紀中ごろと考えるのが妥当であろう．以下はそれらの例である．

(7) "This is for the last, Mr. Dodgson, because I'*m going to be* sixteen next month!" (1881 carl. x6)

(8) Now listen to me carefully, because you'*re* not *going to like* what I say, some of you! (1962 walk.h0)

(9) I think I'*m going to die*. (1967 chee. f0a)

(10) "At dinner I was busy in thinking what it was you had to disclose. I will not fatigue you with my guesses. They would be impertinent,

---

[3] 動詞の意味分類に関しては，Quirk et al. (1985: 201) 参照．そこでは動詞を stative と dynamic に分け，さらに stative を quality, state, stance に下位区分している．

as long as the truth *is going to be* disclosed. (1799 brow. f4)

(11) "*There's going to be* a day of reckoning ..!" (1976 coov. f0a)

(12) "So then, my dear, I find we *are going to have* a story of one of your namesakes." (1723 blac. f2)

(13) I've got an order to deliver and it is a very delicate one and I don't know how *it is going to be* received. (1899 hern. d7)

4. FLOB Corpus との比較

FLOB Corpus[4] において, 'be going to' に続く動詞を頻度順にあげると次のようになる: have (to) (16), do (14), be (8), make (6), take (6), tell (6), ask (5), say (4). 以下に例をあげる:

(14) "If we'*re going to* have a permanent refugee problem then it's going to be worse, a lot worse than expected," ... (Press: Reportage)

(15) Now what *am* I *going to* do? (Mystery and Detective Fiction)

(16) "You'*re going to* be on location in Tunisia next month," Tommy said. (Adventure and Western)

(17) "Anyone who doesn't make it through this soon, *isn't going to* make it at all." (Science Fiction)

(18) "Because I've had about all I'*m going to* take from you for one evening." (Romance and Love Story)

(19) "The story I *was going to* tell you was of a wronged woman." (Romance and Love Story)

(20) He cast her an appealing glance, and she knew whatever he *was going to* ask, she would be unable to refuse him. (Romance and Love Story)

(21) "No one *is going to* say there will never be another one." (Press: Reportage)

Archer Corpus (1900 以降) では, be (30), do (17), have (10), get (7), make (6), say (6) と続き, ask, tell は見当たらなかった.

---

[4] FLOB Corpus に関しては, Mair (2006) 参照.

5. 'Be going to' と主観化

　Langacker (1998: 76, 79) は主観化を "a gradual process of progressive attenuation" と述べ、"be going to" の主観化への例として、次のような例をあげている。なお、注意すべきは、以下の文法化及び主観化過程において、"go" だけでなく、"be going to" 全体がその過程に関わるということである。

(22) He *was going to* mail the letter but never reached the postoffice.
(23) He *was going to* mail the letter but never got around to it.
(24) If he's not careful he*'s going to* tumble over the rail.
(25) Something bad *is going to* happen – I just knew it.
(26) It*'s going to* be summer before long.

　(22) において "be going to" は移動の意味で、主語の意志がその行為を行なううえで強い。(23) は移動の意味が弱まっているが、不定詞以下の行為を行なううえで依然意志が働いている。ただし (22) に比べて、主語の役割が少し低下する。(24) では不定詞の行為を行なううえで主語の意志がなくなったと考えられるが、その行為を行なううえでの責任はあると考えられる。また主語の影響の範囲内にある（例えば、不注意）ことが感じられる。(25) は本来の出来事を実現させるうえで、主語はなんら責任がない。(26) においては、主語は付随する移動能力、意志性、責任といったものは失われ、その分話者の主観的見方が目立つようになる。

　上記のプロセスはデータ上も裏付けられる。
　非人称 "it + be going to" や "there + be going to" は Archer Corpus において 19 世紀以降使われるようになり、FLOB Corpus においては、人称主語 vs. 非人称主語の比率は 8：2 にまで広がっていく。以下はその例である。

(27) *Is* it *going to* rain? Unless it*'s going to* snow. (1954 park.d0)[AC]
(28) There*'s going to* be a day of reckoning …! (1976 coov.f0a)[AC]
(29) "You can get down now," Sarah called. It *was going to* be easier said than done. (Romance and Love Story){FLOB}
(30) We don't know yet what kind of a mess Talley is in, nor if there*'s going to* be a criminal charge. (Adventure and Western)[FLOB]

　上の例からも分かるように、Traugott (2010: 35) の言う "meanings are recruited by the speaker to encode and regulate attitudes and beliefs (subjectification)"というプロセスが 'be going to' においても進行していることが分かる.

なお，Cacoullos and Walker (2009: 346) においても，'be going to' は 'I think や 'I don't know' の補文において 'be going to' が好まれる（データは Canadian English）ことは主観性を反映しているのではないかと述べている.

6. おわりに

'Be going to' の発達過程を Archer Corpus を基に考察してきたわけであるが 'be going to' は 1800 年以降頻繁に使われるようになり，19 世紀後半には助動詞化したと考えられる．今後の課題として以下のような問題点を指摘できよう.

1. 'Be going to' の発達原因．本稿でも内的・外的要因を述べたが，他のいわゆる 'emerging modals' (Krug (2000)) との競合や進行形の発達などを吟味する必要があろう.
2. 現代英語に近づくにつれて，人称主語から非人称主語を取る傾向が強まってきており，これは Langcker (1998) や Traugott (2010) のいうところの主観化が進んだということであるが，この主観化の意味は 'epistemic' な意味の発達と理解してよいものであろうか．もしそうなら，'may' や 'must' の発達と同じものになろう.
3. 'Be going to' の起源について触れる余裕はなかったが，Garrett (2012) の OED (*s.v. go* 34.a.) に求める案は興味深く，再考に値すると考えられる.

コーパス

Archer = A Representative Corpus of Historical English Registers (1.7 million words)
FLOB = Freiburg-Lancaster-Oslo-Bergen Corpus (one million words, available in ICAME CD-ROM)

参考文献

Biber Douglas, Edward Finegan and Dwight Atkinson (1994) "ARCHER and Its Challenges: Compiling and Exploring a Representative Corpus of Historical English Registers," *Creating and Using English Language Corpora: Papers from the Fourteenth International Conference on English Language Research on Computerized Corpora, Zurich 1993,* ed. by Udo Fries, Grunnel Tottie and Peter Schneider, 1-13, Rodopi, Amsterdam-Atlanta.

Brisard, Frank (2001) "*Be going to*: An Exercise in Grounding," *Journal of Linguistics* 37, 251-285.

Boyer, Kasper and Peter Harder (2012) "A Usage-Based Theory of Grammatical Status and Grammaticalization," *Language* 88, 1-44.

Bybee, Joan (2010) *Language, Usage and Cognition*, Cambridge University Press, Cambridge.

Cacoullos, Rena T. and James A. Walker (2009) "The Present of the English Future: Grammatical Variation and Collocations in Discourse," *Language* 85, 321-354.

Chafe, Wallace (2002) "Putting Grammaticalization in Its Place," *New Reflections on Grammaticalization*, ed. by Ilse Wischer and Gabrielle Diewald, 395-412, John Benjamins, Amsterdam/Philadelphia.

Danchev, Andrei and Merja Kytö (1994) "The Construction b*e going to + infinitive* in Early Modern English," *Studies in Early Modern English*, ed. by Dieter Kastrovsky, 59-77, Mouton de Gruyter, Berlin/New York.

Garrett, Andrew (2012) "The Historical Syntax Problem: Reanalysis and Directionality," *Grammatical Change: Origins, Nature, Outcomes,* ed. by D. Jonas, J. Whitman and A. Garrett, 52-72, Oxford University Press, Oxford.

Hopper, Paul J. and Elizabeth C. Traugott (2003) *Grammaticalization*, 2nd ed., Cambridge University Press, Cambridge.

Krug, Manfred G. (2000) *Emerging English Modals: A Corpus-Based Study of Grammaticalization*, Mouton de Gruyter, Berlin/New York.

Langacker, Ronald W. (1998) "On Subjectification and Grammaticalization," *Discourse and Cognition: Bridging the Gap*, ed. by Jean-Pierre Koening, 71-89, CSLI Publications, Stanford.

Mair, Christian (2006) *Twenty-Century English: History, Variation and Standardization*, Cambridge University Press, Cambridge.

Nicolle, Steve (1998) "Be going to and Will: A Monosemous Account," *English Language and Linguistics* 2, 223-243.

Quirk, Randolph, Sidney Greenbaum, Geoffrey Leech and Jan Svartvik (1985) *A Comprehensive Grammar of the English Language*, Longman, London.

Szmercsanyi, Benedikt (2003) "Be going to versus Will/Shall: Does Syntax Matter?" *Journal of English Linguistics* 31, 295-323.

Traugott, Elizabeth C. (2010) "(Inter)subjectivity and (Inter)subjectification: A Reassessment," *Subjectification, Intersubjectification and Grammaticalization.* ed. by Kristin Davidse, Lieven Vandelanotte and Hubert Cuyckens, 29-71, De Gruyter

Mouton, Berlin/New York.
Traugott, Elizabeth C. (forthcoming) "Toward a Coherent Account of Grammatical Constructionalization," *Historical Construction Grammar*, ed. by Jóhanna Barðdal, Spike Gildea, Elena Smirnova and Lotte Sommerer, John Benjamins, Amsterdam.
Traugott, Elizabeth C. and Graeme Trousdale (2013) *Constructionalization and Constructional Changes*, Oxford University Press, Oxford.

No Reconstruction Approach to A-Chains*

Jun Abe
Tohoku Gakuin University

In this paper, we consider the phenomenon of reconstruction that shows different patterns with respect to what is licensed through reconstruction in A-chains. We aim to give explanations to these patterns of reconstruction under a movement theory of anaphora of the sort developed by Abe (2014), which will provide a new perspective to approaching the present task. In so doing, we argue against a recent approach to the reconstruction phenomenon taken by Lebeaux (2009) and instead give support to Chomsky's (1995) position that A-movement does not reconstruct.

Chomsky (1995) claims that "the phenomenon [= reconstruction] is a consequence of the formation of operator-variable constructions driven by FI, a process that may (or sometimes must) leave part of the trace—a copy of the moved element—intact at LF, deleting only its operator part." (p. 326) A significant consequence of this claim is that no reconstruction should take place in A-chains, since A-chains have no direct relevance for the formation of operator-variable constructions. Chomsky then provides the following examples as empirical support for this claim:

(1) *John$_1$ expected him$_1$ to seem to me to be intelligent.
(2) a. (It seems that) everyone isn't there yet.
    b. I expected everyone not to be there yet.
    c. Everyone seems not to be there yet.

---

* I am glad to contribute this paper to a festschrift for Shigeo Tonoike, who has been one of the respectable scholars in our field with great enthusiasm for pursuing his research in a unique way.

The ungrammaticality of (1) immediately follows as a Condition B violation on the assumption that the pronoun *him* is not reconstructed to any other position to obviate the violation. (2) demonstrates the presence/absence of "lowering effects" of a quantifier like *everyone*, and Chomsky observes that "negation can have wide scope over the quantifier in [2a], and it seems in [2b] but not in [2c]." (p. 327) The fact that *everyone* cannot take scope under negation in (2c) clearly indicates that no reconstruction takes place in A-chains.

Lasnik (1999) provides further data that support Chomsky's (1995) claim:

(3) a. No large Mersenne number was proven to be prime.
 b. No one is certain to solve the problem.
 c. Every coin is 3% likely to land heads.

These sentences do not have the readings that can be paraphrased as the following:

(4) a. It was proven that no large Mersenne number is prime.
 b. It is certain that no one will solve the problem.
 c. It is 3% likely that every coin will land heads.

This indicates that the head member of an A-chain does not reconstruct. The only exception to this pattern of facts, noted by Lasnik (1999), comes from those data that involve A-movement of indefinites, such as the following:

(5) Some politician is likely to address John's constituency.

It has been well known since May (1977) that this sentence is two-ways ambiguous and that the ambiguity should arise from whether *some politician* is reconstructed into its original position, taking scope under *likely*. But the following example, taken from Jackendoff (1972), casts doubt on such an analysis:

(6) A catastrophe is quite likely in California. (Jackendoff (1972: 297))

This is because (6) is two-ways ambiguous in the same way as (5) but it is a simplex sentence so that there is no place for *a catastrophe* to reconstruct into under *likely*.

On the other hand, there are cases that appear to show that reconstruction does take place in A-chains, which is concerned with Condition A licensing, as illustrated below:

(7) Replicants of themselves seemed to the boys to be ugly.

(Belletti and Rizzi (1988: 316))

Here it would be necessary, under the traditional binding theory, for the whole subject to be reconstructed into the embedded clause, so that *themselves* could be bound by its antecedent *the boys*. For such a fact, Lasnik (1999) makes the following suggestion:

"A-movement Condition A reconstruction … might be treated in a similar on-line fashion, as proposed by Belletti and Rizzi. This makes sense if satisfaction of Condition A involves a formal feature …" (p. 211)   On the other hand, "determination of scope is not satisfaction of a formal feature, but a matter of interpretation at the interface." (p. 156)

Following this suggestion, Abe (2014) claims that cases of A-movement Condition A reconstruction are accommodated by the movement theory of anaphora in which he assumes the following:

(8) Pro undergoes Move to establish an anaphoric relation.

Under this theory, (7) will be derived in the following way:

(9) a. ___ seemed to ___ to [replicants of pro be ugly]
    b. ___ seemed to pro to [replicants of pro be ugly]
    c. ___ seemed to the boys to [replicants of themselves be ugly]
    d. replicants of themselves seemed to the boys [$_{TP}$ <replicants of themselves> to [<replicants of themselves> be ugly]]

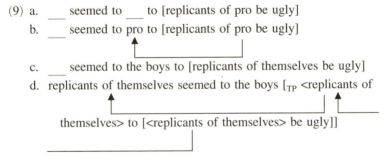

As shown in (9a), pro is merged into the complement position of *replicants of*. Then it undergoes movement to the complement position of *to*, as in (9b), and the bottom copy of pro is replaced by *themselves*. After the top copy of pro is replaced by *the boys*, we obtain (9c). Finally, the embedded subject *replicants of themselves* undergoes successive-cyclic A-movement to the matrix Spec-TP, as shown in (9d). In this way, we can account for an apparent reconstruction effect of Condition A by way of the "on-line" licensing that is made possible under the movement approach to anaphora.

Lebeaux (2009) provides further apparent evidence for reconstruction in A-chains, which has to do with so-called quantifier lowering discussed around (5). He provides the following pair:

(10) a. Two women seem *t* to be expected *t* to dance with every senator.
 b. Two women seem to each other *t* to be expected *t* to dance with every senator. (Lebeaux (2009: xiii))

(10a) is two ways ambiguous with respect to the scope relation between the expressions *two* ___ and *every* ___. According to Lebeaux's (2009) theory of reconstruction, this fact is captured if the lowest copy of the A-moved phrase is retained, as shown below:

(11) [$_{TP}$ <two women> seem [$_{TP}$ <two women> to be expected [$_{TP}$ <two women> to [$_{vP}$ <two women> dance with every senator]]]]

Given this representation, the scope ambiguity observed in (10a) is captured in the same way as that observed in the following simple sentence:

(12) Two women danced with every senator.

Interestingly, (10a) contrasts sharply with (10b), in which *to each other* is added as the experiencer phrase of *seem*, in that the latter has only the reading in which *two women* scopes over *every senator*. In this case, *two women* serves as the antecedent of *each other* in the matrix subject position. Hence it looks as if this quantifier were "trapped" in that position and prevented from being lowered to the most embedded clause. This would result in producing only the reading in which this quantifier takes scope over *every senator*. Lebeaux thus names this effect "trapping effect." In order to capture this effect, Lebeaux (2009) proposes what he calls the Single Tree Condition, which is given below:

(13)　*Rule for a candidate set at LF (A-chains)*
　　　Erase all members of a candidate set, except one.

(Lebeaux (2009: 13))

In the case of (10b), we need to retain the highest copy of the A-moved phrase to license *each other*, as shown below:

(14)　[$_{TP}$ <two women> seem to each other [$_{TP}$ <s>two women</s>> to be expected [$_{TP}$ <s>two women</s>> to [$_{vP}$ <s>two women</s>> dance with every senator]]]]

According to the Single Tree Condition, all the other members of *two women* must be erased, as indicated in (14). Since the retained copy belongs to a clause that is higher than the one to which *every senator* belongs, the former must take scope over the latter. Note that if more than one copy of a chain were available for interpretation at LF, then such a trapping effect would not be captured.

Under the present approach, according to which no reconstruction process is admitted, we would not expect any contrast for such a pair as given in (10). We might claim that the scope ambiguity observed in (10a) should be captured as a result of the scope interaction between the pronounced copies of the involved quantifiers; thus, the pronounced copy of *two women* in the matrix Spec-TP should be able to take scope under *every senator*. We would then need to claim that such a scope interaction is somehow prohibited when the pronounced copy of *two women* serves as the antecedent of an anaphor. All of these claims seem to defy any reasonable explanation. Lebeaux (2009) provides more evidence for the reconstruction approach according to which such a scope interaction as found in (10) is due to the fact that the quantifier phrase that has undergone A-movement retains its copy in the original position, as shown in (11), the position in which it becomes a clause-mate with the other quantifier phrase. This has to do with such an example as the following:

(15)　Mary seems to two women *t* to be expected *t* to dance with every senator.

(Lebeaux (2009: 7))

Lebeaux observes that in (15), only one scope ordering is possible, namely, the one according to which *two women* takes scope over *every senator*. Crucially, this sentence does no have the reading that arises from the opposite scope ordering. This will receive an immediate explanation if we assume that scoping out of a lower quantifier over a higher one takes place only if both quantifiers are clause-mates at some stage of the derivation, since there is no stage of the derivation of (15) at which *two women* and *every senator* become clause-mates. This in turn argues strongly against the no reconstruction approach to such a scope interaction as observed in (10a).

First of all, it is not clear whether the trapping effect, as observed in (10), actually has to do with the possibility of reconstruction under the Single Tree Condition. In fact, Tanaka et al. (2011) provide data that seem to run counter to this claim:

(16) a. Some girl kissed every boy. ($\forall><\exists$)
    b. Some girl$_1$ kissed every boy on her$_1$ birthday. ($\exists>\forall$, *$\forall>\exists$)

They observe that even though scoping out of *every boy* over *some girl* is possible in (16a), it becomes impossible when the higher quantifier *some girl* binds a pronoun, as shown in (16b). This looks like showing that the trapping effect occurs even with a simplex sentence. Whatever the reason is, it strongly suggests that such a trapping effect as observed in (10b) has no direct relevance for the possibility of reconstruction.

Further, there is evidence that the Single Tree Condition is too strong in that anaphors show no trapping effect, as Lebeaux himself notes:

(17) John seemed to himself *t* to like himself. (Lebeaux (2009: 87))

In order to license the first occurrence of *himself*, we would have to retain the upper copy of the chain (*John, t*), but the Single Tree Condition would then require that only this copy should be retained, which would thus leave the second occurrence of *himself* unlicensed. The grammaticality of (17) then indicates that the Single Tree Condition is too strong. Lebeaux (2009) stipulates that "[i]f it [= A-reconstruction] does not occur, what is in the trace sites are the bound ϕ-features," (p. 13) which serve to license anaphors, but this stipulation simply undermines the effects of the Single Tree Condition.

Under the present movement theory of anaphora, there is no problem in deriving such a sentence as (17) that involves more than one occurrence of an anaphor being licensed by a single antecedent. This sentence is derived in the following way:

(18) a. __ seemed to pro to [__ like pro]
b. __ seemed to pro to [pro like himself]

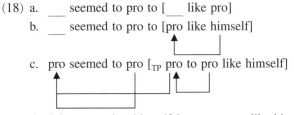

c. pro seemed to pro [$_{TP}$ pro to pro like himself]

d. John seemed to himself [$_{TP}$ pro to pro like himself]

In (18b), the pro that is merged into the complement position of *like* undergoes Move to the subject position of this predicate, and the bottom copy of pro is replaced by *himself*. Then, it undergoes successive-cyclic A-movement to the matrix Spec-TP and at the same time, it undergoes Across-the-Board (ATB) movement with the pro that is merged into the complement position of *to* in the final step of the successive-cyclic movement, as shown in (18c). Finally, *himself* is overlaid onto the pro in the complement position of *to* and *John* onto the top copy of pro, giving rise to the correct final output given in (18d). Thus, the present movement theory of anaphora properly captures the fact that more than one anaphoric relation can be established with a single antecedent, unlike what would be expected by the Single Tree Condition.

As for the contrast between (10a) and (15), I agree with Lebeaux (2009) on his claim that clause-mate is a key condition on scoping out of a lower quantifier over a higher one. I then suggest that scope interaction among QPs is also licensed derivationally, just like anaphoric relations. Following the idea of Chierchia (1993) about the scope interaction between a universal quantifier and a *wh*-phrase, let us assume the following:

(19) A QP_1 under the scope of another QP_2 is analyzed as a function that takes the value of QP_2 and returns a value from the set whose domain is determined by QP_1.

Under this hypothesis, the wide scope reading of *every boy* in such a sentence as (20a) is represented as in (20b):

(20) a. Every boy likes a girl.
 b. $\forall x$, x a boy, x likes $F(x)$

This characterization of scope interaction implies that a QP_1 under the scope of another QP_2 is dependent upon the latter in the sense that it contains a variable bound by QP_2. I then propose the following:

(21) The scope relation between QP_1 and QP_2 is established via Move.

Under the assumption that this scope relation is also mediated by pro-movement, the wide scope reading of *every boy* in (20a) is obtained from the following derivation:

(22) a. ___ likes [$_{DP}$ pro a girl]
 b. pro likes [$_{DP}$ pro a girl]
 c. every boy likes [$_{DP}$ pro a girl]

Pro is inserted into the DP *a girl* to function as a variable bound by another QP, as in (22a), and then moves to the subject position, as in (22b). After it is replaced by *every boy*, as in (22c), its bottom copy serves as a variable to which the function denoted by *a girl* applies to return a value that is among the *girl*-set determined by that function. This amounts to representing the wide scope reading of *every boy*.

Let us now consider a case where a lower QP takes scope over a higher one, as in (12). One apparent difficulty in applying the above analysis to such a case comes from the fact that the pro-movement involved in such a case seems downward. Here I follow Huang (1982) and Abe (2002) in their claim that in such a case, the lower QP undergoes rightward movement to a position from which it can c-command the other QP. Thus, the wide scope reading of *every senator* in (12) will be obtained from the following derivation:

(23) a. Past [$_{vP}$ [$_{DP}$ pro two women] dance with pro]
 b. Past [$_{vP}$ [$_{vP}$ [$_{DP}$ pro two women] dance with pro] pro]
 c. Past [$_{vP}$ [$_{vP}$ [$_{DP}$ pro two women] dance with pro] every senator]
 d. [$_{TP}$ [$_{DP}$ pro two women] Past [$_{vP}$ [$_{vP}$ <[$_{DP}$ pro two women]> dance

with pro] every senator]]

At the stage of (23b), the pro that occupies the complement position of *with* undergoes rightward movement to adjoin to *v*P. This movement takes place in an ATB-fashion with the pro inserted in the DP *two women*. The movement of the latter pro establishes the scope relation between *every senator* and *two women*. This analysis carries over to such a raising case as (10a), in which the relevant scope relation between *every senator* and *two women* is established in exactly the same way as given in (23) before *two women* undergoes successive-cyclic A-movement to the matrix Spec-TP. Further, the fact that the wide scope reading of *every senator* is unavailable in (15) falls into place under the present analysis, since there is no stage of the derivation of this sentence at which the pro inserted into the DP *two women* could possibly move to the position occupied by *every senator*.

To recapitulate, given the present movement theory of anaphora, we can maintain the no reconstruction approach to A-chains, advocated by Chomsky (1995). Under this approach, there is no need for any reconstruction process or any equivalent operation for A-chains in terms of Copy and Delete with the further assumption that only one copy survives deletion in accordance with the Single Tree Condition, advocated by Lebeaux (2009). This approach thus assumes that the pronounced copy of an A-chain is active for LF interpretation, a condition that Abe (2012) calls P-L Match Condition (see Bobaljik 2002 for a similar claim.). This condition properly accounts for the scope facts given in (2) and (3).

References

Abe, Jun (2002) "On the Displacement Property of Language and Minimality," ms., Tohoku Gakuin University.
Abe, Jun (2012) "String-Vacuity and LF Interpretation in A-Chains: Cases of ECM and Nominative-Genitive Conversion," ms., Tohoku Gakuin University.
Abe, Jun (2014) *A Movement Theory of Anaphora*, de Gruyter Mouton, Berlin.
Belletti, Adriana and Luigi Rizzi (1988) "Psych-Verbs and θ-Theory," *Natural Language and Linguistic Theory* 6, 291-352.
Bobaljik, Jonathan David (2002) "A-Chains at the PF Interface: Copies and 'Covert' Movement," *Natural Language and Linguistic Theory* 20, 197-267.

Chierchia, Gennaro (1993) "Questions with Quantifiers," *Natural Language Semantics* 1, 181-234.

Chomsky, Noam (1995) "Categories and Transformations," *The Minimalist Program*, by Noam Chomsky, 219-394, MIT Press, Cambridge, MA.

Huang, C.-T. James (1982) *Logical Relations in Chinese and the Theory of Grammar*, Doctoral dissertation, MIT.

Jackendoff, Ray S. (1972) *Semantic Interpretation in Generative Grammar*, MIT Press, Cambridge, MA.

Lasnik, Howard (1999) "Chains of Arguments," *Working Minimalism*, ed. by Samuel David Epstein and Norbert Hornstein, 189-215, MIT Press, Cambridge, MA.

Lebeaux, David (2009) *Where Does Binding Theory Apply?*, MIT Press, Cambridge, MA.

May, Robert (1977) *The Grammar of Quantification*, Doctoral dissertation, MIT.

Tanaka, Hidekazu, George Tsoulas and Norman Yeo (2011) "(Quantificational) Objects on the Edge," talk given at Nanzan University in December, 2011.

「ガ／ノ」交替現象についての一考察*
——中古・現代コーパスを対照して——

坂野　収

青山学院大学

1. はじめに

　三上（1953）以来，「ガ／ノ」交替について，さまざま議論されてきた．[1] しかし，現代語中心で，内省に基づく議論が主であった．幸いにして，充実されつつある通時コーパスが利用できるようになった[2]ので，可能な限りコーパスを利用して検討した．その結果，次のような知見が得られた．

① 　中古語（平安時代）の主語の格表示は，基本的にはゼロ格（φ）であるが，連体修飾節等の特殊環境では，「ガ」または「ノ」が用いられることがある．これら「ガ・ノ」の格は属格である．

② 　中古語の主語表示における「ゼロ格（φ）／ガ・ノ」交替と，現代語における「ガ／ノ」交替は，共に「主格／属格」交替であり，同一現象である．

③ 　中古と現代とで，属格主語の出現する比率も環境も同等である．このことは，格交替の統語的メカニズムについても通時的変化はないことを示している．もっぱら，連体形で結ばれた節内で生ずる現象である．

＊ 本稿は，国立国語研究所主催の「第4回コーパス日本語学ワークショップ」（2013/09/06）における発表内容を修正のうえ，その骨子をまとめたものである．内容に関して，青山学院大学の外池滋生教授，近藤泰弘教授，ならびに共に学ぶ諸氏から貴重なご意見を賜った．記して感謝申し上げる．

[1] Harada (1971), Miyagawa (1993), Watanabe (1994), Hiraiwa (2001) など．

[2] 国立国語コーパス開発センターのWEBサイト参照．
　　（http://www.ninjal.ac.jp/corpus_center/）

本稿で利用したコーパスは，「日本語歴史コーパス（平安時代編：先行公開版）」(http://www.ninjal.ac.jp/corpus_center/chj/) と「現代日本語書き言葉均衡コーパス」(http://www.ninjal.ac.jp/corpus_center/bccwj/) である．

④ 現代語における，属格主語の生起に対する制約は，統語的なものでなく，認知的なものと考えられる．

2. 中古語の「主格／属格」交替

中古語においても，例文（1）のように，鉤括弧内の連体形述部で結ばれた節（以降，連体形節と呼ぶ）では，各々のペアーで示すように，主語の格表示における「ゼロ格（φ）／ガ・ノ」交替がみられることはよく知られた事実である．この格交替は「主格／属格」交替であろうか．

(1) a.　花すすき [君φなき] 庭に群れたちて　　　　　　　　（古今和歌集）
　　 a′.　[鏡にて影見し君がなき] ぞ悲しき　　　　　　　　　（大和物語）
　　 b.　[梅の香φをかしき] を見出してものしたまふ　　　　（源氏物語）
　　 b′.　[菊の花のうつろへる] を折りて，男のもとへやる　（伊勢物語）

2.1. 属格による主語表示

「梅の香」「わが君」などの「ガ・ノ」は属格（いわゆる所有格）といわれている．(1a′, b′) のような主語表示の場合の格種類は何であろうか．

本来の属格として用いられている場合と，主語表示に使われている時とで，上に付く名詞類（上接語）の分布はどの様であるかを，中古語コーパスによって検索した．結果を図形化したものを図1，2に示す．

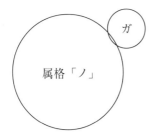

図1　属格表示での上接語分布　　図2　主語表示での上接語分布

図1は，属格として用いられた場合の，「ガ」と「ノ」の上接語分布の概要を図形で示したものである．円形の内部が各上接語の集合を表している．共通

(交わり) 部分は非常に小さく，ほぼ相補分布をしている．[3] 図2では，主語表示の場合の上接語の分布を，属格表示の分布に関連づけて表示した (着色部分). 完全に，属格表示の場合の部分集合をなしている．

この結果と，「ガ・ノ」による主語表示は連体形節にしか現れない[4]ことから，これらの表示格は属格とみて差支えない (cf. Frellesvig (2010: 127))．以降，属格表示された主語を属格主語と称する．

2.2. 中古語の格交替

(1a, b) における主語のゼロ格「ϕ」は何であろうか．中古語の平叙文 (終止形終止文) の主語は「ゼロ格」表示である (金水・他 (2011: 95)，Frellesvig (2010: 129))．現代語の平叙文で主語表示の「ガ」を主格としているのと同じ意味で，中古語の主語表示の「ゼロ格」を主格と認定するのが妥当である．従って (1) に示した格交替は「主格／属格」交替であり，現代語と同じ現象である．

3. 現代語の格交替

現代語では，(2) に示すように，連体修飾節や補足節[5]などにおいて，「主格／属格」交替 (あるいは「ガ／ノ」交替) が現れる．

(2) a. [山田が／の買った] 本　　　　　　　　　　　　(連体修飾節)
　　b. [秋刀魚が／の焼ける] 匂い　　　　　　　　　　(連体修飾節)
　　c. [山田が／の来たの] を思い出した．　　　　　　(補足節)
　　d. [リンゴが／の皿の上にあったの] を食べた．　　(補足節)

(1) と (2) を比較して分かるように，属格主語が生ずるのは連体修飾節，補足節など，すべて連体形節であり，中古語も現代語も同じである．

---

[3] データの詳細は坂野 (2013) を参照されたい．分布の内容について (cf. 野村 (2011: 75-76) など) は本稿の目的とは関係ないので立ち入らない．

[4] 中古においては，已然形や「未然形＋ば」で結ばれた節でも属格主語が現れる．これらは，連体形と同源，あるいは「連体形＋α」と考えられる (早田 (2010)，金水・他 (2011: 87))．また，現代語では，これらが存在しないこともあり，対照分析のターゲットとしては，連体形節に焦点を絞った．

[5] 連体形＋「の」で結ばれた「ノ型準体句」とも呼ばれている．古典語のそれは「ゼロ型準体句」である．共に連体形述部で結ばれた連体形節である．

4. 中古語と現代語における属格主語の出現割合

中古語と現代語の連体形節における，主格主語と属格主語の現れる比率をコーパスで調査した結果を図3に示す．出現比率を横棒で表してある．

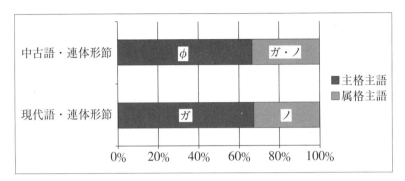

図3　中古語・現代語の主格主語と属格主語の出現比率

重要なことは，「主格／属格」交替現象において，属格主語の現れる比率には，中古語と現代語で，ほとんど差がないことである．ただし，一定範囲，一定条件での検索[6]であることから，図3の数値は，概略傾向を示す値であると認識されたい．

5. 属格主語が生ずる環境

現代語においても，平叙文，疑問文，そして命令文などには，属格主語は現れない．属格主語が現れる典型的な例は，(1) や (2) で述べたような，連体修飾節や補足節であるが，(3) に示すように，副詞節等にも現れる．これも，中古と現代で同じである．

(3) a.　[中将のなき] をりに見すれば，心憂しと思へど　　　　（源氏物語）
　　a'.　[御都合のよろしい] おりに，お訪ねするつもりです．（大西 (2003)）
　　b.　[月の傾く] まであばらなる板敷に臥せりてよめる　　（古今和歌集）
　　b'.　[彼女の帰宅する] までに，決着をつけておきたかった．
　　　　　　　　　　　　　　　　　　　　　　　　　　　　（折原 (1992)）

---

[6] 検索は，随意に格交替が可能と思われる，主語と述語の間に介在がない単純な文脈に限定した（具体的検索条件等は，坂野 (2013: 180) を参照されたい）．

c. [日のかさなる]ままにいみじくなむ (落窪物語)
c'. [犯人のいう]ままに動いた. (木谷 (2004))
d. かならずしも [我が思ふ] にかなわねど (源氏物語)
d'. [私の思う] に，これは芸術的衝動というよりも (澁澤 (2003))

従来から，属格主語が現れる説明の一つとして，名詞的主要部（先行詞）の存在を仮定してきた．しかし，(3c-d')のように，名詞的主要部がなくても属格主語が現れる．属格主語が生ずるためには，連体形述部で結ばれた連体形節そのものの存在が基本的に重要である．

6. 属格主語が生ずるメカニズム

6.1. 先行研究概観

属格主語に関する先行研究は，ほぼ三分類できる．Miyagawa (1993) を主とした DP 仮説, Watanabe (1994) の WH-agree 仮説, そして Hiraiwa (2001) の連体形認可仮説である．詳細は省き，概念のみ説明する．

DP 仮説は，連体修飾節をその典型として，先行詞 (DP) の存在を前提とし，LF（論理形式）において，節内の主語が DP の指定部に移動して属格が認可されるという主張である．前節で述べたように，先行詞の存在が必須の条件ではないので，この仮説には不備がある．

WH-agree 仮説では，属格主語が生ずるのは WH-domain においてであり，WH-agree システムにより属格が認可されると主張する．WH-domain が前提ならば，普通の WH 疑問文で属格主語が生じないのは説明できない．

最後は連体形認可仮説であるが，Hiraiwa は述部連体形のみが属格主語の認可に関与すると述べている．しかし，独立用法（または，結びとして）の連体形と接続用法の連体形との区別[7]がついていないために，例えば「山田が／*の来るはずだ」のような，いわゆる体言締め文（角田 (1996)）では，連体形「来る」が存在するにも拘わらず，属格主語が許されない[8]ことを説明できない．

---

[7] 金水・他 (2011: 79-83) に活用の独立用法，接続用法の解説がある．本稿では，6.2 項で述べるように，節 (CP) の主要部 C により認可される活用形を独立用法の活用形と考える．

[8] 「山田*の来るはずだ」の文では，「来るはずだ」が複合述部をなす平叙文である．連体形「来る」は，単に「はず」につながる接続用法の連体形である．一方「[山田が／の来る] はずがない」では，「はず」を修飾する連体形節（「来る」は独立用法の連体形）内であるから属格主語が認可される．

このように，いずれの理論も十全とは言い難い．そこで，以下述べるような節タイプとしての連体形節における属格付与を提案する．

6.2. 属格付与メカニズムの説明

前節で述べた連体形節は，従来から，体言相当の名詞性を帯びた節とされてきたが，節タイプ[9]としての扱いはされてこなかった．本稿では，これを独立した節タイプの一つと認め，この連体形節の存在のみが，属格主語が生ずる必要十分条件であると主張する．以下，属格主語の派生をミニマリスト生成論の立場で説明する．

文（節）は，項構造を派生する vP（動詞句）相と，その上部に位置し表現形式を決める CP 相から構成される．CP 相の主要部 C が節タイプを決める素性（Illocutionary force ＝発話内力）を持っているとされている（cf. Radford (1997: 148, 511)）．日本語においては，節タイプと述部活用形は密接な関係にあり，主要部 C は述部の活用形も決定する力を持つと考える．

終止形節である平叙文と比較して，連体形節の派生の概要を説明する．図4は平叙文の基本的な節構造，図5は連体形節のそれである．

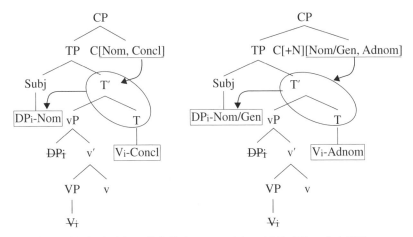

図4　終止形節（平叙文）の基本構造　　図5　連体形節の基本構造

図4に於いて，平叙文 CP の主要部 C(補文標識) は無標であって，主語に

---

[9] 節タイプ（あるいは「節ムード」）とは，平叙文（Declaratives），疑問文（Interrogatives），命令文（Imperatives）などを言う（cf. Narrog (2009: 135-158)）．

主格を，述部に終止形を認可する素性 [Nom,Concl] を持ち，時制句（TP）の主要部 T を介して，TP 指定部に繰り上がった主語（DP_i）に主格（Nominative）を与えると同時に，主要部 T に移動した述語（V_i）の活用形として終止形（Conclusive）を認可する．

一方図 5 では，名詞素性 [+N] を持つ主要部 C が選択されている．[+N] 素性を持つ節主要部（C[+N]）には，[Nom/Gen, Adnom] 素性が与えられているとする．それが TP の主要部 T を経由して，主語に主格または属格（Nominative/Genitive）を与え，述語には連体形（Adnominal）を認可して連体形節を派生させる（時制素性 [Tns] はどちらにも共通にあるので省略した）．

このように，派生の段階で，節主要部として名詞素性 [+N] を持つ主要部 C が選択されれば，その節（CP）は連体形節になり，属格主語の出現が可能となる．

現代語の補足節では，補文標識 C に「の」の存在が一般的である．これは [+N] 素性の音声化とも考えられる．[10] ただし，この「の」の顕在化の理由や経緯には諸説あるが，未解決の問題である．

7. 付随する問題

7.1. 主格目的語

属格付与の特殊な場合として，(4) のような状態動詞による連体形節において，主語と目的語の格表示に関し，「主格／属格」四通りの組合せが考えられる．

(4) a. [山田 が 英語 が／？の できる] こと
　　b.??[山田 の 英語 が／の できる] こと

内省としては，(4a) は許容の範囲にあるが，(4b) の許容性については意見が分かれるところである．各組合せに対する，コーパスでの検索結果を (5) に示す．

(5) a. [彼が気が済む] までゲームをやっている． 　　(浦賀 (2001))
　　a'. [俺が関心があるの] は，誤診だけだ． 　　(北方 (2001))
　　b. [彼が人気のある] わけがわかるような気がした． (立木 (1992))

---

[10] 外池滋生（私信）による．

b'. [一介の中将くらいが歯の立つ] 相手ではない． （水沢 (1991)）
c. [私の気の済む] ようにさせて． （小林 (1998)）
c'. [浪人兵法者の歯の立つ] ような手合いではない． （司馬 (2003)）

「が〜が」「が〜の」そして「の〜の」の組合せの例は容易に見つけられるが，残念ながら，「の〜が」の組合せが見つかっていない（内省では十分に可能と思われるが）．[[NP の] [NP が] VP] なる組合せは，[[NP の NP] が VP] の読みが最優先される解析上 (parsing) の制約により実例が稀少だけで，統語上の制約とは考えられない．

結論として，格表示の四通りの組合せに関しては，統語的には随意に選択できると考える．しかし「の〜が」の組合せは，認知（解析）上の制約があり，実際の発話では殆ど現れないと思われる．

状態動詞のような自動詞からの格付与は考えられないので，主語と目的語へ，四通りの組み合わせの格付与が随意にできることは，主格／属格の認可元が一元的であることを示している．[Nom/Gen, Adnom] 素性が与えられた連体形節主要部 C[+N] のみが格付与の源であるという主張を裏付けている．

7.2. 他動性制約

現代語では，(6) のように，属格主語と対格目的語とが共存できないと言われている．Watanabe (1994), Hiraiwa (2001) などは，対格目的語が主語の属格表示を抑制する制約（他動性制約：Transitivity Restriction）があるという記述的一般化を提示している．

(6) a. [山田が／*の本を買った] 店
    b. [本を山田が／*の買った] 店

中古・現代コーパスでの検索結果を (7) に示す．(7a) 以外は，中古語からの例文である．

(7) a. 秋田市では，[博士を蝶の取り巻く] こと，大略斯の通りであった．
        （泉 (2004)）
    b. [かじけたる女の童を得たるな] なり （源氏物語）
    c. [朱買臣が妻を教えけむ] 年には （枕草子）
    d. 隣の家より，[風の雪を吹き越しける] を見て （古今和歌集）

確かに，現代語では，対格目的語が介在する例文を見つけるのは困難で，倒

置文一例（7a）だけであるが，中古語では容易に探し出せる（7b, c, d）．従って，統語的制約ではなく，認知（解析）上の制約であると考えることができる．この事実も，属格主語が生ずるのは，連体形節そのものが関与するだけであるという本稿の主張を支持するものである．

8. おわりに

中古語と現代語のコーパスを使った対照分析と，内省だけに頼らない用例検索により，次のことを主張した．

① 連体形節における，「主格／属格」交替現象の本質は，中古と現代とでは何の変化も生じていない．従って，現象が生ずる統語的メカニズムも同じである．
② 格交替は，名詞素性をもつ連体形節そのものの機能に由来する現象である．すなわち，連体形節の主要部 C がもつ「主格／属格」付与素性によるものである．
③ 主語と述語との間の，目的語などの介在物も，属格主語の派生を妨げるものではない．妨げがあるのは，認知的（解析上の）条件である．

ただし，属格による主語表示への認知的制約条件については更なる検討が必要である．今後の課題としたい．

このような結果が得られたのも，身近に利用できたコーパスのお陰である．通時コーパスの更なる充実を期待する．

参考文献

坂野収（2013）「「ガ／ノ」交替現象についての一考察」第 4 回コーパス日本語ワークショップ予稿集，177-186，国立国語研究所．
　　(www.ninjal.ac.jp/event/specialists/project-meeting/m-2013/jclws04/)
Frellesvig, Bjarke (2010) *A History of the Japanese Language*, Cambridge University Press, Cambridge.
Harada, Shinichi (1971) "Ga-No Conversion and Idiolectal Variations in Japanese," 『言語研究』第 60 号，25-38．
早田輝洋（2010）「上代語の動詞活用について」『水門——言葉と歴史』第 22 号，1-29，水門の会．
Hiraiwa, Ken (2001) "On Nominative-Genitive Conversion," *A View from Building*

E39, MITWPL#39, 65-123, MITWPL, Cambridge, MA.
金水敏・高山善行・衣畑智秀・岡崎友子（2011）『シリーズ日本語史3 文法史』岩波書店，東京．
三上卓（1953）『現代語法序説』刀江書院（復刊（1972）くろしお出版），東京．
Miyagawa, Shigeru (1993) "Case-Checking and Minimal Link Condition," *Papers on Case and Agreement*, MITWPL#19, 213-254, MITWPL, Cambridge, MA.
Narrog, Heiko (2009) *Modality of Japanese,* John Benjamin, Amsterdam.
野村剛史（2011）『話言葉の日本史』吉川弘文館，東京．
Radford, Andrew (1997) *Syntactic Theory and the Structure of English*, Cambridge University Press, Cambridge.
角田太作（1996）「体言締め文」『日本語文法の諸問題』，鈴木泰・角田太作（編），139-161，ひつじ書房，東京．
Watanabe, Akira (1994) "A Cross-Linguistic Perspective on Japanese Nominative-Genitive Conversion and Its Implications for Japanese Syntax," *Current Topics in English and Japanese*, ed. by Masaru Nakamura, 341-369, Hituzi Syobo, Tokyo.

例文出典（引用順）

大西巨人（2003）『三位一体の神話』光文社．
折原一（1992）『灰色の仮面』講談社．
木谷恭介（2004）『瀬戸大橋殺人海峡』桃園書房．
澁澤龍彦（2003）『イコノエロティシズム』河出書房新社．
浦賀和宏（2001）『記憶の果て』講談社．
北方謙三（2001）『小説現代』第35号，14，講談社．
立木ありあ（1992）『恋愛の市場心理』講談社．
水沢蝶児（1991）『獅子と薔薇の銀河』朝日ソノラマ．
小林光恵（1998）『ぽけナース』メディアワークス．
司馬遼太郎（2003）『大盗禅師』文藝春秋社．
泉鏡花（2004）『新編泉鏡花集』岩波書店．

主語からの *Wh* 移動の可能性について

江頭　浩樹

大妻女子大学

1. はじめに

生成文法理論の誕生以来，(1) に見られる主語からの要素の取り出しによって生じる非文法性の説明に様々な提案がなされてきた．

(1) *Of which car did [the driver/picture ___ cause a scandal]?

(Chomsky (2008: 147))

Chomsky (2008) は位相理論（Phase Theory）の枠組みの中で，(1) の非文法性の説明を試みている．その説明によると，(1) は主節の CP 位相では次の (2) のような形をしている．

(2)　[$_{CP}$ C$_{[EF]}$ [$_{TP}$ the (driver, picture) of which car [$_{T'}$ T (did)
　　　　　　　　(a)　　　　　　　　　　　　　　　　↑
　　　　　　　　　　　　[$_{v*P}$ the (driver, picture) of which car [$_{v*'}$ v*-caused [$_{VP}$ …]]]]
　　　　　　　　(b)　　　　　　　　　　　　　　↑

(2) では v*P の指定部にあった主語 the (driver, picture) of which car は，そのコピーを残しながら TP 指定部に移動を受けている．EF(Edge Feature) を持つ補文標識 C は (a) に示すように TP 指定部にある of which car と，(b) に示すように v*P の指定部にある of which car にアクセスし，of which car をその指定部に誘引（attract）しようとする．Chomsky (2008) によると TP 指定部からの of which car の移動は (3) の不活性条件 (Inactivity Condition; 以下，IC) に違反し，非文となる．

(3)　不活性条件
　　　A 連鎖は，その解釈不能な素性に値が与えられると，更なる統語計算

にとって不可視になる.

TP に A 移動をした the driver of which car は TP 指定部で解釈不能な素性（この場合，格素性）に値が与えられ，不可視となる．一方，v*P 指定部からの of which car の移動に関しては，Chomsky は，v*P に埋め込まれた要素の取出しにはコストがかかるという局所性条件 (Locality Condition) によって，v*P からの取り出しを排除する．この説明は (1) に見られるような，主語からの取り出しはうまく説明をしているようだが，この説明ではうまく説明がつかない文法的な，主語からの部分摘出の現象が存在する．

本論文の構成は以下の通りである．第 2 節では，文法的な主語からの部分摘出の例を示し，現状の分析ではその文法性をうまく説明できないことを示す．第 3 節では代案を示し，第 4 節では代案の展開を示す．第 5 節はこの論文の結論である．

2. 主語条件の反例

前節で概観した Chomsky (2008) の位相理論によると，全ての主語からの部分摘出は非文法性を生じると予測する．しかし，他の構文を検討すると，主語からの部分摘出が必ずしも非文法性を生ずるとは限らない．次の (4) を見てみよう．

(4) a. Of which major is it important for the students to take a course in physics?[1]
   b. Of which major is it important [$_{CP}$ for [$_{TP}$ the students of which major [$_{T'}$ to [$_{v*P}$ the students of which major [$_{v*'}$ v*-take [$_{VP}$ a course in physics]]]]]

ここで補文標識 for が [EF] を持つと仮定すると，この [EF] は (2) と同様に TP と v*P の指定部にある of which major にアクセスし，それを CP 指定部に誘引しようとする．しかし，その文法性は，(1) と同様の派生と構造にかかわらず文法的である．

---

[1] (4) の文法性の判断は Eloise Pearson 氏，Michael Farquharson 氏による．

3. 代案

本節では (4) の文法性を説明する代案を提案する．3.1 節では代案の基礎となる Tonoike (2008) の転出 (Excorporation) 分析を概観する．そして 3.2 節で (4) の文法性を説明する代案を提案する．

3.1. 転出分析

Tonoike (2008) に従い，英語の節の構築に以下の (5) を想定する．

(5) a. 補文標識 C と時制要素 T，軽動詞 v* と動詞 V はそれぞれ C-T, v*-V の語彙複合体として辞書から取り出される．
b. v*-V がその補部と併合 (merge) した後，v* は転出し，すでに構築された VP と併合し，v* の投射を形成し，それに外項が併合する．
c. C-T は v*P と併合し，T の投射を形成した後，C は転出し TP に併合し CP を形成する．

(5) を念頭に置き，英語の疑問文 (6) がどのように派生されるかを検討する．

(6) Which course did you take?

(6) の派生の初期段階 (7) では，v*-V(take) の複合体とその補部 which course が併合し VP を形成する．

(7)   VP

v*[EF]-take[ACC]   which course[...]

ここで V(take) と v* はそれぞれ格素性 ([ACC]) と [EF] を持ち，その補部の which course は値が与えられていない格素性 [...] を持つと想定する．[2] (7) の派生の段階では，V(take) はその補部の which course に対格 ([ACC]) を付与する．[3] それと同時に [EF] を持つ v* は wh 句 which course を認定する

---

[2] この分析では，位相主要部 (C, v*) からの素性の継承 (feature inheritance) は想定しない．

[3] 英語では名詞句の格は，格を付与する主要部との併合 (Merge) によって付与されると想定する．3.2 節の (14) を参照．従って，動詞の補部の名詞句は動詞と併合されて格が与えられる．Chomsky (2008) で仮定されている目的語の VP 指定部への移動分析は採用しない．

(identify). しかし，この段階では wh 句は VP 指定部には移動しない．なぜならば VP 指定部は wh 句の着地点ではないからである．(7) で V(take) が持つ選択素性などの語彙特性は満たされたところで，以下の (8) に見るように v* は音形を持つ V(take) を伴いながら，VP より転出し (excooporate) VP に併合し，v* の投射を形成し，外項の主語が v* の投射の指定部に併合する．[4, 5]

(8)

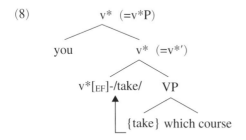

次に which course は，v* が持つ [EF] によって v*P の指定部に移動する．

(9) [$_{v*P}$ /which course/ [$_{v*'}$ you [$_{v*'}$ v*$_{[EF]}$-/take/ [$_{VP}$ {take}{which course}]]]]

(9) の wh 移動は (3) の IC に違反しているように見える．ここでは，位相主要部 (C, v*) による wh 句の認定 (identification) と名詞句が持つ格の値の付与が同時に起こる場合は，IC の違反は起こっていないと仮定する．

派生の次の段階では，C-T(did) が v*P に併合し T の投射を形成する．さらに主語がその指定部に移動をする．

(10) [$_{TP}$ /you/ [$_{T'}$ C$_{[EF]}$-T (did) [$_{v*P}$ /which course/ [$_{v*'}$ {you} [$_{v*'}$ v*-/take/ [$_{VP...}$]

(10) の構造より，C が音形を持つ T(did) を伴い転出し，TP に併合し C の投射を形成する．そして，さらに C が持つ [EF] によって，which course が CP の指定部へ移動を受け，派生が収束する．

---

[4] 本稿では Tonoike (2008) の顕在的統語論仮説 (Overt Syntax Hypothesis) を採用し，v* は単独で移動を受けず，音形を持つ V(take) と共に移動する，と仮定する．

[5] (9) での /.../ と {...} はそれぞれ「音形」と「意味」を意味している．

(11) [_{CP} /which course/[_{C'}C_{[EF]}-T/did/ [_{TP} /you/[_{T'} C-T {did}[_{v*P} /which course/

これが転出分析の概要である．次節では，この転出分析によってどのように (4) の文法性が説明されるかを検討する．

3.2. 代案

(4) の文法性の説明に入る前に，(12) に見られる不定詞補文標識 for によって導かれる不定詞補文の派生と構造について検討をする．

(12) It is important for them to take a course in physics.

補文標識 for で導かれる不定詞補文の派生について，以下の (13) を想定する．

(13) a. 補文標識 for で導かれる語彙主語を持つ英語の不定詞補文では，空の補文標識 C と for と to は C-for-to の複合体として辞書 (lexicon) から引き出される．
b. この複合体はすでに構築された構造から転出し，併合する．
c. 不定詞補文標識の for は T(ense) に属し to は M(odal) に属する．[6]

さらに，英語の格付与に関して，Tonoike (1999), Bošković (2007) に従い，以下の (14) を想定する．

(14) 英語では，格は格付与能力を持つ主要部との併合によって付与される．

(12) の派生の初期段階 (15) では，3.1 節で見た方法で v* の投射が形成され，格の値が未指定の不定詞主語 them_{[...]} がその指定部に併合されている．

(15) [_{v*P} them_{[...]} [_{v*} v*-/take/ [_{VP} {take} a course in physics]]]

(13) の想定に従い，(15) の構造に C-[_{T} for_{[ACC]}]-[_{M} to] が併合して M(odal) P を形成し (16a)，C-[_{T} for_{[ACC]}] が MP より転出して MP に併合し TP を形成する (16b)．

---

[6] M 及び MP (Modal Phrase) に関しては，Nomura (2006) を参照．

(16) a.　[$_{MP}$ C-[$_T$ for$_{[ACC]}$]-[$_M$ to] [$_{v*P}$ them$_{[…]}$ [$_{v*'}$ v*-take [$_{VP}$ …]]]
　　b.　[$_{TP}$ C-[$_T$ for$_{[ACC]}$] [$_{MP}$　　[$_M$ to] [$_{v*P}$ them$_{[…]}$ [$_{v*'}$ v*-take

派生が (16b) まで進むと，不定詞主語 them は (14) に従って格付与主要部の T と併合し，この位置 (TP 指定部) で対格 ([ACC]) の値を付与される．

(17)　[$_{TP}$ /them$_{[ACC]}$/ C-[$_T$ for$_{[ACC]}$] [$_{MP}$ [$_M$ to] [$_{v*P}$ {them} [$_{v*'}$ v*-take

さらに C は (18) に見られるように，音形のある for を伴って，TP より転出し，TP に併合して CP を形成する．

(18)　[$_{CP}$ C-[$_T$ for] [$_{TP}$ /them$_{[ACC]}$/ [$_{T'}$　[$_{MP}$ [$_M$ to] [$_{v*P}$ {them} [$_{v*'}$ v*-take

これが for で導かれる不定詞主語を持つ補文の派生と構造である．(13) で提唱する不定詞補文の派生と構造の意義を一つ挙げるとするならば，不定詞主語の格付与のメカニズムが定形節の主格の付与と平行に扱うことができるという点である．よく知られているように，定形節においては v*P の指定部に生成された主語は，主格を求めて TP の指定部へ移動をする．

(19) a.　They will take a course in physics.
　　b.　[$_{TP}$ /they$_{[NOM]}$/ [$_{T'}$ T$_{[NOM]}$-will [$_{MP}$ [$_{v*P}$ {they} [$_{v*}$ [$_{VP}$ take a course …

(13) では従来の分析とは異なり，不定詞主語に目的格を与える for を T に生成しているために，(19) と平行に扱うことができる．

　ここで，(13) による不定詞補文の派生と構造を念頭に置き，(4)（以下 (20) として再録）がどのように派生されるか検討しよう．

(20)　Of which major is it important for the students to take a course in physics?

まず派生が以下の (21) まで進んだと仮定しよう．(21) では不定詞主語が v*P の指定部に生成され，C-[$_T$ for] は MP より転出し，MP に併合し TP を形成している．なお，[$_T$ for] は格素性 [ACC] を持ち，C は [EF] を持っている．

(21) [$_{TP}$ C$_{[EF]}$-[$_T$ for$_{[ACC]}$][$_{MP}$ to [$_{v*P}$ the$_{[...]}$ students of which major] [$_{v*}$ v*-take

この段階で，C が持つ [EF] は wh 句 of which major を認定する，と同時に不定詞主語は格を求めて T の指定部に併合し，対格を付与される．

(22) [$_{TP}$ the$_{[ACC]}$ students of which major C$_{[EF]}$-[$_T$ for$_{[ACC]}$] [$_{MP}$ to [$_{v*P}$ t

さらに，派生が進み C$_{[EF]}$-[$_T$ for$_{[ACC]}$] が TP より転出し，TP に併合して CP を形成する．

(23) [$_{CP}$ C$_{[EF]}$-for [$_{TP}$ /the students of which major/ [$_{T'}$ [$_{MP}$ to [$_{v*P}$ t

ここで C が持つ [EF] は，(21) の派生の段階で認定した wh 句を CP 指定部に誘引し，(24) が派生される．

(24) [$_{CP}$ of which major [$_{C'}$ C$_{[EF]}$-for [$_{TP}$ /the students ___ / [$_{T'}$ [$_{MP}$ t

さらに主節の CP が形成され of which major がその指定部に移動すると (20) が派生されることになる．

ここで問題になるのは (24) における wh 移動である．不定詞主語 the students of which major は TP の指定部で格を付与されているので，不定詞主語は統語計算（ここでは wh 移動）にとって不可視のはずである．つまり (24) の wh 移動は IC（不活性条件）の違反となり (24)（=(20)）は排除されることになる．しかし，(21) の派生の段階で見たように，C が持つ [EF] による wh 句の認定と不定詞主語の移動は同時起こっている．このように格付与と wh 句の認定が同時に起こっている場合は，(9) で見た派生と同様に，格を与えられた要素からの wh 移動は可能なのである．[7]

これまでのところ，転出分析が不定詞主語からの部分摘出がどのように派生されるかを見てきた．次節ではこの分析がもたらす可能性を検討する．

---

[7] 顕在的統語論仮説の観点から，v*P 指定部にある意味素性だけで構成される {the student of which major} からの，wh 移動の可能性はない．

4. 展開

以下に示す (25) の例文は，(a) はこれまで扱った不定詞主語からの部分摘出の例で文法的な文であるが，(b) は全体摘出——いわゆる for trace 効果——の例で，非文法的な文である．

(25) a. Of which major is it important for the students to take a course in physics?
b. *Who$_i$ is it important for t_i to take a course in physics?

3.2 節で見たように，不定詞補文の TP が形成された段階で C が持つ [EF] による wh 句の認定と，格付与による移動が同時に起これば IC を破ることなく wh 移動ができるのならば，(25b) も文法的な文になるはずである．これに関しては，TP への移動を受けた名詞句の構造の違いに文法性の差を帰することができる．以下の (26) の構造を見てみよう．部分摘出を受ける名詞句の構造は (26a)，全体摘出を受ける名詞句の構造は (26b) であり，格素性は D に与えられている．

(26) a. [$_{DP}$ [$_D$ the$_{[ACC]}$] [$_{NP}$ student [$_{PP}$ of which major]]]
b. [$_{DP}$ [$_D$ who$_{[ACC]}$]]

ここで，格素性が与えられた D のみが，たとえ格付与と wh 句の認定が同時に起こったとしてもさらなる統語計算にとって不可視であるとすれば，(25) の文法性の差は説明ができる．つまり (25a) (=(26a)) では D(the) が統語計算にとって不可視であるが，PP の of which car は可視状態なので wh 移動が可能である．一方 (25b) (=(26b)) では D すなわち who が格付与され不可視であり，wh 移動が不可能である．言い変えれば，(25b) は IC 違反として排除することができるのである．[8]

さらに，(25) の文法性の説明は次の (27) の文法性の違いの説明にも拡張可能である．

(27) a. Of which car is it likely [(that) the (driver, picture)[t caused a scandal]]? (Kobayashi (2011: 42))

---

[8] (6) における V の目的語の移動が問題になるかもしれないが，(3) の IC が非単一 A 連鎖 (non-trivial A-chain) を対象にすると仮定すれば，(6) も同様に扱うことができる．

b. *What is it likely that t caused a scandal?

ここで，従属節では補文標識の that と T は複合体として辞書から取り出されると仮定する．となると，(27) は派生の初期段階で (28) のような構造をしていると考えられる．

　(28) a.　[$_{TP}$ that$_{[EF]}$-T$_{[NOM]}$ [$_{v*P}$ the$_{[...]}$ driver of which car [v*-caused
　　　 b.　[$_{TP}$ that$_{[EF]}$-T$_{[NOM]}$ [$_{v*P}$ what$_{[...]}$ [v*-caused

この段階で that が持つ [EF] が wh 句を認定する．それと同時に v*P の指定部にある名詞句が TP 指定部に移動し [NOM] が付与される．さらに，that-T が TP より転出し，TP に併合して CP を形成する．

　(29) a.　[$_{CP}$ that$_{[EF]}$-T [$_{TP}$ [$_{DP}$ [$_D$ the$_{[NOM]}$] driver of which car] ~~that-T~~ [$_{v*P}$
　　　 b.　[$_{CP}$ that$_{[EF]}$-T [$_{TP}$ [$_{DP}$ [$_D$ who$_{[NOM]}$]] ~~that-T~~ [$_{v*P}$

この段階で，(29a) の that が持つ [EF] は wh 句にアクセスし，of which car をその指定部に IC を破ることなく誘引することができる．一方，(29b) では who は格を与えられ不可視状態になっている．従って，who を CP の指定部に誘引することはできない．言い変えれば，(27b) に見られるような that 痕跡効果は IC 違反に帰することができる．

　ここで問題になるのは，空の C による that 痕跡効果の解消である．

　(30)　Who$_i$ do you think t_i came?

(27b) のような that 痕跡効果が IC に帰されるとするならば，(30) も同様に IC によって排除される可能性がある．なぜならば，who は従属節内で主格を与えられているからである．これに関しては，以下の (31) のような派生と構造を想定すれば説明がつく．まず，(31a) では空の C と T が複合体として辞書から取り出され，v*P と併合し主語 who がその指定部に移動し格素性に値が与えられている．さらに (31b) のように主節の v*P が形成されると，v* が /who/ にアクセスしその指定部へ誘引しようとする．

　(31) a.　[$_{CP/TP}$ /who$_{[NOM]}$/ [C$_{[EF]}$-T$_{[NOM]}$ [$_{v*P}$ {who$_{[...]}$} came]]]
　　　 b.　[$_{v*P}$ v*-think [$_{VP}$ [$_{CP}$ /who$_{[NOM]}$/ [C$_{[EF]}$-T$_{[NOM]}$ [$_{v*P}$ {who$_{[...]}$} came]]]

ここで注目すべき点は，(31a) では C-T の複合体は v*P から転出，併合して TP を形成した後は，これ以上の転出・併合を繰り返さない点である．なぜな

らばCもTも音形を持たないため「顕在的統語論」の観点より，そのような移動は排除される．となると，(31a) の一番上の投射は TP であると同時に，CP でもあるのである．[9] そして，派生が (31b) まで進むと，主節の v^* が who を見る際には，それは CP 指定部に位置している．言い換えれば who は A′連鎖の主要部 (head) であり，IC は受けないということになるのである．

5. 結論

この論文では，for で導かれる不定詞主語からの wh 句の部分摘出が可能であることを指摘し，その文法性を Tonoike (2008) による転出分析と，従来，補文標識として扱われていた for を時制要素 (T) として扱うという分析によって，説明可能であることを示した．[10] この分析は for-to 効果を IC 違反に還元可能であることも示し，その分析をさらに that 痕跡効果まで拡張した．

参考文献

Bošković, Željiko (2007) "On the Locality and Motivation of Move and Agree: An Even More Minimal Theory," *Linguistic Inquiry* 38, 589–644.

Chomsky, Noam (2008) "On Phases," *Foundational Issues in Linguistic Theory: Essays in Honor of Jean-Roger Vergnaud*, ed. by Robert Fredin, Carlos P. Otero and Maria Luisa Zubizarreta, 133–166, MIT Press, Cambridge, MA.

Kobayashi, Keiichiro (2011) "Effects of Pied-piping on Extraction from Subject in English," *Kagaku/Ningen* 40, 31–57.

Nomura, Tadao (2006) *ModalP and Subjunctive Present*, Hituzi Syobo, Tokyo.

Tonoike, Shigeo (1999) "Agreement as Dislocated Morphological Features," *Metropolitan Linguistics* 19, 1–21.

Tonoike, Shigeo (2008) "The General Minimalist Framework," ms., University of Hawaii.

---

[9] 主語が疑問詞の場合の節のラベルが CP/TP の二面性があることに関しては Tonoike (2008) を参照．

[10] (1) の文の非文法性の説明については，次の文法的な (i) によって排除される可能性がある．

　　(i)　[$_{CP/TP}$ A driver of which car [$_{v*P}$ caused the accident]]?

ことばに見る対称性：
サリンジャー・村上春樹・川端康成のカートグラフィー

遠藤　喜雄

神田外語大学

0.　はじめに

外池（1988）では，下に見るように日本語と英語の統語要素が階層的な対称性を持つことが，多様な事例を基に検証されている．

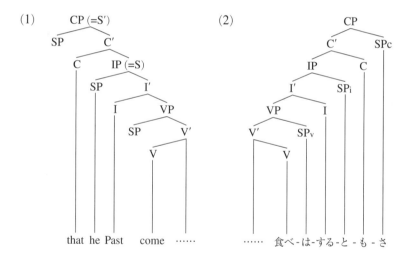

本稿では，このことばに見る対称性をより広い観点から考察する．具体的には，サリンジャーが The Catcher in the Rye のテキストに埋め込んだ意味の2重性を村上春樹が翻訳した際に，対称性に着目していることを見る．そして，そこに見る対称性が，日本語の反転現象や英語の picture noun にも働くことを見ながら，最近 Collins and Postal（2013）で提唱されている imposter という概念と軸を同じくすることを示唆する．

本稿は次のように構成されている．まず，対称性の概念とその基本的な性質

を導入する．次に，サリンジャーの The Catcher in the Ryle を取り上げ，表面的なテキストとその背後にある作者のメッセージからなる2重性を見ながら，それを対称性の観点から考察する．具体的には，村上春樹による同書の翻訳を見ながら，Salinger の隠されたメッセージを読み解く作業がカタカナ語の対称性により達成されていることを見る．そして，これと同種の対称性を，川端康成の文体に見る反転現象や英語の picture noun を見ながら論じ，その派生が，Moro (2010) の考えとカートグラフィーの相互作用によることを見る．最後に，本稿の議論が現代の理論言語学に示唆する点を述べる．

2. 対称性

　対称性 (symmetry) とは，数学の用語で，概略，「入れ替えても変わらない性質」を意味する．例えば，人間の右の腕と左の腕は，入れ替えても全体が同じに見えるので，そこには対称性がある．ここで，対称性は，絶対的な概念ではなく，相対的な概念である点に注意しよう．例えば，風船に描かれた絵は，その風船を膨らました場合，同一ではないが，相似性を持つ．その意味で，ここにもある程度の対称性が見られ，それは膨張対称性と呼ばれる．冒頭で紹介した日英語の統語構造の場合，同じ意味を表わす要素は，音形は入れ替えが出来ないが，同じ構造関係にある統語範疇の要素を入れ替えても意味が大きく異なることはない．その意味で，ある程度の対称性が観察される．一方，数学においては，2×3 と 3×2 は6を生み出すという点で，対称性を持つ．これはブール代数に見る対称性で，日本語でも「乗るなら飲む-な」の「なら」の前後を入れ替えて「飲むなら乗る-な」としても，ほぼ同じ意味を表わす．その意味で，ここにも，ある種の対称性がある．[1]

3. The Catcher in the Rye における多重性

　以上の対称性の概念を念頭において，翻訳における対称性をサリンジャーの作品を見ながら考察しよう．仁田 (2004) や竹内 (2005) が詳細に論じるように，サリンジャーの小説は，表面的な文章の背後に，作者のメッセージが隠さ

---

[1] ブール代数と言語の関係については，Endo (2007: 34-38) を参照．そこでは，等位構造から抜き出しの操作が不可能なのは，A and B の間に入れ替えが可能な対称性の性質がある場合に限られることが述べられている．

れている多重構造を持つ．例えば，The Catcher in the Rye において，主人公のホールデンはイノセンスを敬愛しており，そのイノセンスに関わる作者のメッセージが，青い色の服や物を通して読者に伝えられている．

The Catcher in the Rye は，何人もの手により日本語に翻訳されており，最も新しい翻訳は，村上春樹の「キャッチャー・イン・ザ・ライ」である．この村上の翻訳には，カタカナ語を多用するという特徴がある．村上は，村上・柴田 (2003) の対談において，彼がカタカナ語を多用した理由について述べている．理由のひとつは，カタカナ語が多用される現代の語感に，同作品を近づけたいという願いがある．例えば，野崎孝は村上より前に，同作品を「ライ麦畑で捕まえて」というタイトルで翻訳し，そこでは，heavy smoker の訳語として，「すごいタバコのみ」という日本語を用いている．一方，村上は，「ヘビー・スモーカー」という日本語を用いた．これは，現代の日本の社会では「タバコをのむ」という表現がすでにほとんど用いられていない状況を反映している．このような具体的な名称に加えて，村上は，彼がブラックボックスと呼ぶ効果を求めて，抽象的な概念をカタカナ語で翻訳している．ここで，ブラックボックスとは，読者の注意を引いて，その中身について読者にその解釈を委ねることを意味している．これは，翻訳論において，柳父 (1976, 2003) が「カセット効果」と呼ぶ用語に対応している．ここでカセットとは，フランス語の cassette で，宝石箱を意味する．そのきらびやかな見かけは，読者の注意を引き，その中に何か素敵な物が入っているのでは，という期待を読者に抱かせる効果を指している．このカセット効果により，村上は，サリンジャーが伝えようとしている隠されたメッセージを表わす表現に読者の注意を引くために，そのようなメッセージに関わる用語にカタカナ語を用いた．

Sato (2014) は，同作品の point という用語に，このカセット効果を見い出した．例えば，この物語の主人公が通うプレップスクールでは，スピーチの授業があり，学生がスピーチでポイントから外れたことを言うと，他の学生から非難が浴びせられる．そして，主人公ホールデンは，このようなポイントから外れたスピーチを絶賛している．ここで，point には2つの意味がある．1つ目の意味は，スピーチにおいて求められる表面上の「要点」という意味．2つ目は，「点数」という意味で，社会的規範に沿うことで与えられる点数という意味である．サリンジャーは，要点から外れたスピーチが魅力的なのは，はかない社会的な規範から遠ざかることで，イノセンスに代表されるより大きな存在に繋がることができるためというメッセージを伝えようとしている．そのため，主人公のホールデンは，ポイントから外れたスピーチを絶賛するので

ある．

4. 村上春樹の翻訳に見る対称性

　村上は，このサリンジャーの隠された意味を，ポイントというカタカナ語を用いることにより捉えた．これは，村上が翻訳を行った際に「ポイント」が「要点」と「点数」の2つの意味がほぼ同じ割合で用いられている日本における言語状況により可能となった．逆に言えば，それより前の時代に，「ポイント」というカタカナ語を用いても，それは「要点」という意味しか持たなかったので，「点数」にまつわるサリンジャーのメッセージは伝えわらなかった．

　つまり，村上が翻訳を行った時代には，ポイントというカタカナ語が「要点」と「点数」の両方を同じ程度の割合で意味することができたために，表面的な語とサリンジャーの隠されたメッセージという二重性を伝えることが可能となった．Sato は，村上が翻訳を行った時代にポイントというカタカナ語が「要点」と「点数」の両方を同程度の割合で使用されていることを，朝日新聞のデータベースを用いて検証した．それによると，野崎が同書を翻訳した時代には，「ポイント」という語を朝日新聞のデータベースで検索しても，ほとんどすべてが「要点」の意味で用いられており，多義性は見られなかった．少し詳しく言うと，まずカタカナ語の「ポイント」は「要点」の意味で用いられ，バブル期を境にして，「ポイント」が「点数」の意味で用いられることが多くなり，村上が翻訳を行う時代になると，朝日新聞のデータベースで，ポイントという用語は，要点と点数の意味が同じくらいの割合で生じることとなった．つまり，村上が翻訳を行った時代には，「ポイント」という語が，一方の意味で用いれば，同時にもう一方の意味も喚起される土壌が整っていたため，サリンジャーの意図した意味の二重性を表現することが可能となった．

　さて，ここで，ポイントという語の「要点」と「点数」の意味を，対称性の観点から見よう．ひとつの時代に，「ポイント」という語が，ほぼ同じくらいの割合で「要点」と「点数」の意味する力を持つ均衡した状態にある場合，「ポイント」という語の2つの意味には対称性がある．この均衡状態にある「ポイント」という語の意味の対称性のおかげで，サリンジャーの意図する二重のテキスト構造を表現することが可能となっている．ここでの対称性とは，「要点」と「点数」のどちらの意味にも用いることができるという意味での，対称性を意味する．

　次に，この「要点」と「点数」の2つの意味を言語学的な観点からを見よう．

上で見たサリンジャーの当該作品のスピーチの場面では，この「ポイント」という語は，表面上は，「要点」の意味がスピーチの行われる状況で前景 (foreground) として用いられて，「点数」の意味は隠されたメッセージとして背景 (background) となっている．しかし，サリンジャーのメッセージを伝えるレベルに目を転じると，「点数」と「要点」の 2 つの意味の関係が逆転し，「要点」の意味は背景化され，「点数」の意味の方がサリンジャーのメッセージとして前景となる．この前景・背景の反転が，テキストの重層構造を生み出している．

5. 川端康成の文章に見る反転効果

　これと似た言語現象が，日本語の反転現象に見られる．反転現象とは，「A の B」という表現において，A と B を入れ替えて，「B の A」とすることで，ある種の修辞効果を生み出す現象である．小松原 (2013) は，「一升瓶の酒」という表現における「の」の前後の単語を入れ替えて，「酒の一升瓶」とする現象を取り上げて，その成立条件を検討している．[2] この事例においては，意味と音形の両方を入れ替えることが出来るという点で高い対称性がある．しかし，そこには「A の B」と「B の A」とでは，異なる修辞的な効果が見られるため，完全な対称性はない．ここでの修辞的効果とは，前景 (foreground) と背景 (background) に関わる修辞的な効果で，小松原は，この前景と背景の修辞効果を，次に見る川端康成の「伊豆の踊り子」の一節に見いだしている．

(3) この静けさが何であろうかを闇を通して，見ようとした．踊子の今夜が汚されるのであろうかと悩ましかった．

ここで，「踊子の今夜」という表現に注目しよう．この表現は，「汚される」という述語との関係でいえば，汚される対象は，「今夜」ではなく「踊子」なので，本来ならば，「今夜の踊子」とされるべきである．しかし，上の文章では，「踊子」が背景化され，「今夜」が際立ちを持つ要素として前景化されるという修辞的効果を狙って，反転が生じている．小松原は，この修辞的効果における対称性については言及していないが，この反転が可能となるのは，「A の B」において，A と B の表す意味が対称性を持ち，A か B のどちらかが前景となり，残りが背景になっているのが典型的である．

---

[2] 反転現象の成立条件の文献については，小松原 (2013) を参照のこと．

6. 対称性を解消する派生

では，この対称性を持つ表現が修辞的効果を求めて，前景化や背景化される具体的な派生を見よう．Moro（2000）によれば，自然言語は対称的な構造を許さず，少なくとも派生の最終段階では対称性を解消する必要があるとする．上に見た反転現象も同じように考えることが出来る．つまり，「A の B」という表現の派生は，以下の (4) に見るように，まず，A と B が対称的な構造を持つ小節（small clause）の構造を持ち，その対称性を解消するために A か B の一方が移動する．

(4) … [A B]=>
    … [foreground [background …[A   B] ….

Chomsky が述べるように，移動は，文の談話やスコープの関わる位置に生じるが，本稿では，これが名詞句内の談話構造にも関わると考える．実際，伝統文法（特に機能主義的な文法）では，名詞句の A's B と B of A が異なる情報構造を持つことがしばしば述べられており，本稿の立場はこれと同一線上にある．さて，ここでの A や B の移動の着地点には，前景や背景の情報が関与する位置である．（移動が前景や背景の情報を付与するために生じるという考えは，カートグラフィー研究での探求されており，例えば，Mathieu（2004）を参照．）

7. Picture noun に見る構造的な対称性

前節で見た川端康成の文章に見る反転効果と幾分似た現象は，次に見る英語の絵画名詞（picture noun）に見られる．

(5) John saw [pictures of Mary].

ここで，括弧で囲まれた表現は，名詞句という単位を形成している．これ全体が名詞句であることを決めているのは，その主要部である pictures であるので，統語的には，pictures が名詞句の主要部となる．さて，この名詞句の主要部 pictures は，形式的には，saw の目的語である．しかし，John が見たのは，pictures という「物」であると同時に，そこに映っている「被写体」の Mary

でもある点に注意しよう．つまり，この文において，John が見たのは，pictures という物というよりは，被写体の Mary である．その意味で，Mary は前景化されている．実際，この文を日本語にした場合，Mary は，「見る」の目的語として，「を」でマークすることが出来る．（この点については，Endo (1995: 53-55) や Endo (2007: 156-160) を参照のこと）

(6) ジョンはメアリーを写真で見た．vs. メアリーの写真を見た．

つまり，(5) においては，pictures と Mary はともに，動詞の目的語として働くことが可能となっており，目的語の機能に関して，置き換えが可能な関係を持つ．その意味で，(5) における picture と Mary には，対称性がある．

これと同様の振る舞いをする名詞表現として，以下を挙げることが出来る．

(6′) メアリーの写真を撮る ↔ メアリーを写真に撮る
　　　メアリーの物語を書く／読む ↔ メアリーを物語に書く／
　　　　　　　　　　　　　　　　　メアリー（のこと）を物語で読む

Chomsky (1977) は，see pictures of Mary という表現に対して，picture と Mary が共に saw と構造的に姉妹の関係を持つ (7a) の構造を提案した．

(7) a. 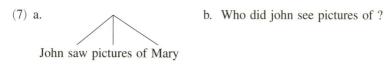　　b. Who did john see pictures of ?

Chomsky がこのような構造を設定したのは，通例の場合，(8) に見るように，名詞句はその中から要素の摘出を阻止するという点で，障壁の機能を持つが，(7b) に見る picture noun はそのような障壁の効果を持たないからである．

(8)

動詞が see の場合に，(7b) で who の摘出が可能であるのは，摘出される要素が名詞の中にはないためである．

ここで，(7a) の構造に着目しよう．この構造においては，pictures と Mary は，動詞 saw に対して，同じ姉妹の関係を持つという意味で，構造的な対称性を持つ．一方，要素の摘出を許さない次に見る通例の名詞は，このような対称性を持つ構造ではなく，名詞句の中に，Mary が埋め込まれる構造を持つと Chomsky は想定する．

(9)
John destroyed pictures of Mary

ここでは，名詞句の中心となる pictures とそれに後続する要素 of Mary は，後者が名詞句の中にあるため，動詞と姉妹の関係にはなく，構造的な対称性は見られない．

8. 言語理論における示唆：imposters

以上，ことばに見る対称性の現象をみた．この現象は，最新の理論言語学に何を示唆するのだろうか．ひとつに，Collins and Postal (2012) の imposter がある．Imposter とは，次の例に見るように，指示内容が話し手 (=I) や聞き手 (=you) であるところを，Your Majesty などの普通名詞により表現する現象を意味する．ここで Your Majesty が you を意味することは，再帰代名詞の yourself が使用可能なことからも検証される．

(10) Your Majesty should praise yourself/herself.

ここでは，Your Majesty と you が入れ替え可能な点で対称性が存在している．2つの言語形式が1つの意味を表す点で，imposter は本論の最初で見た翻訳におけるカタカナ語と同じ関係にある．カタカナの場合，和語で表現可能な事例を，カタカナ語で表現するという随意的な操作 (optional operation) が働いている．一方，すぐ上で見た imposter の場合，you というところを，あえて Your Majesty で表現するという随意的な操作が働いている．Fox (2000) や Reinhart (2006) は，この随意的な操作に次の原則が働くとした．

(11) An optional operation creates a new semantic effect.

つまり，本稿で見た対称性には，すべて，随意的な操作が働いた結果，新たな意味効果が生み出されている．そして，そこで生み出される前景・背景という意味効果は，統語構造で表わされる．カートグラフィー研究では，これを統語化 (syntacticize) と呼ぶ．

9. まとめ

本稿では，外池により議論された日本語と英語の構造的な線対称の関係を足がかりにして，サリンジャーの The Catcher in the Ryle の隠されたメッセージを村上春樹がカタカナ語の使用により達成していることを見た．次に，同種の対称性が川端康成の文章に見る反転現象や picture noun にあることに着目し，その派生が Moro (2010) の対称性についての考えと前景・背景を統語構造で表わすカートグラフィーの考えとの相互作用から導き出されることを示唆した．最後に，本稿の理論的な示唆として，imposter を考察した．

参考文献

Chomsky, Noam (1977) "On Wh-Movement," *Formal Syntax*, ed. by Peter Culicover, Thomas Wasow and Adrian Akmajian, 71-132, Academic Press, New York.

Collins, Chris and Paul M. Postal (2013) *Imposters: A Study of Pronominal Agreement*, MIT Press, Cambridge, MA.

Endo, Yoshio (1995) "Extraction, Negation and Quantification," *Minimalism and Linguistic Theory*, ed. by Shosuke Haraguchi and Michio Funaki, 53-66, Hituzi Syobo, Tokyo.

Endo, Yoshio (2007) *Locality and Information Structure*, John Benjamins, Amsterdam/Philadelphia.

Fox, Danny (2000) *Economy and Semantic Interpretation*, MIT Press, Cambridge, MA.

小松原哲太 (2013)「日本語における連体修飾関係の反転現象」『日本語文法』第13巻2号, 27-53.

Mathieu, Eric (2004) "Discontinuity and Discourse Structure: Stranded Nominals as Asserted Background Topics," *ZAS Papers in Linguistics* 35, ed. by Benjamin Shaer, Werner Frey and Claudia Maienborn, 315-345.

村上春樹 (2003)『キャッチャー・イン・ザ・ライ』白水社, 東京.

村上春樹・柴田元幸 (2003)『翻訳夜話2 サリンジャー戦記』文春新書, 東京.

Moro, Andrea (2000) *Dynamic Antisymmetry*, MIT Press, Cambridge, MA.

Noonan, Máire (2010) "À to *zu*," *Mapping Spatial PPs*, ed. by Guglielmo Cinque and Luigi Rizzi, 161-195, Oxford University Press, Oxford.

新田玲子 (2004)『サリンジャーなんかこわくない』大阪教育図書, 大阪.

野崎孝 (1964)『ライ麦畑でつかまえて』白水社, 東京.

Reinhart, Tanya (2006) *Interface Strategies*, MIT Press, Cambridge, MA.

Salinger, Jerome David (1951) *The Catcher in the Rye*, Little, Brown and Company,

Boston.

Sato, Kota (2014) *On the Chronological and Sociological Perspectives of the Katakana Loanword in Translation – Some Qualitative and Quantitative Studies of 'The Catcher in the Rye,* MA Thesis, Kanda University of International Studies.

竹内康浩 (2005)「ライ麦畑のミステリー」せりか書房,東京.

外池滋生 (1988)「日英語比較統語論〈上〉」月刊『言語』5月号,82-88.

柳父章 (1978)『翻訳文化を考える』法政大学出版局,東京.

ドイツ語における非能格動詞の非対格化

保阪　靖人

日本大学

1. はじめに

Perlmutter (1978), Bruzio (1986) において提唱された非対格仮説については，さまざまなアプローチによる研究がなされている．ドイツ語に関してはGrewendorf (1989) などの研究において，非対格動詞の統語特性についての議論が重ねられてきた．[1]

非対格動詞の重要な統語的特性の一つと考えられているのは，完了形の助動詞の選択である．現代英語では完了形は［have + 過去分詞］で形成されるが，ヨーロッパの言語には，HAVE タイプと BE タイプの選択がある．例えば，次のドイツ語の例では，lesen (読む) は，HAVE タイプ (*haben*), fahren (乗り物で行く) は，BE タイプ (*sein*) が選択されている．[2]

(1) a. Ich habe　　das Buch gelesen.
　　　I 　HAVE　the book　read.
　　　'I have read the book.'
　b. Ich bin mit　dem Fahrrad zur　Post　　gefahren.
　　　I　BE with　the　bicycle　to-the post office gone
　　　'I have been to the post office by bicycle.'

本論文では，ドイツ語の非能格動詞 (HAVE タイプ) が，BE タイプに移行する現象について扱う．この移行は，この現象がイタリア語や，フランス語などの言語と比較してもかなり特徴的であると考えられるからである．

---

[1] Grewendorf (1989) についての批判的検討については，保阪 (2013) を参照のこと．
[2] 選択された助動詞のタイプが have であれば，HAVE, be であれば，BE とグロスには記すことにする．

移動を表す動詞を Sorace (2004: 246f.) は，完了性 (telicity) を統語的，あるいは語彙的に表すかどうかに関して，次の4つの動詞のタイプを区別している．[3]

(2) A: arrive のように完了性を持ち，終点のある移動を表す動詞．
   B: rise のように方向があり，終点のない移動を表す動詞．
   C: run のように完了性がなく，文脈から終点が表示可能な動詞．
   D: stroll のように完了性がなく，文脈によって終点を示すことができない動詞．

フランス語とイタリア語の助動詞の選択は次の通りである．[4]

(3)

	Aタイプ	Bタイプ	Cタイプ	Dタイプ
イタリア語	be	be	be/have	have
フランス語	be	be/have	have	have

興味深いのは，CとDのタイプである．つまり完了性がない動詞においても，文脈によっては BE タイプの完了形が選択される場合がイタリア語には見られる．[5]

(4) a. Giovanna è   corsa/?*ha   corso al   supermercato.
       Giovanna BE run / HAVE run   to-the supermarket
    b. Paul ha   corso più velocemente di   tutti.[6]
       Paul HAVE run   faster   than everyone-else

同じ「走る」(correre) という動詞に対して，移動先が表現されている場合には BE タイプ，運動としてのみは HAVE タイプの助動詞が使用される．しかしながら，同じ運動タイプでも「泳ぐ」(nuotare) 場合には移動先が明示されている場合でも，HAVE タイプが BE タイプになることがない．これは次の節で見るように，ドイツ語とは大きく異なる．[7]

---

[3] Sorace は Donaido の論文を引いているが，残念ながら未見である．
[4] Sorace (2004: 247) の Table 9.1. を一部記載を変えて掲載してある．HAVE は have タイプの助動詞を選択すること，BE は be タイプの助動詞選択を表す．
[5] Sorace (2004: 261).
[6] Sorace (2004: 261).
[7] ibid.

(5) a. Paola ha   nuotato/?*è nutota a stile libero.
       Paola HAVE swum/BE   swum   freestyle
    b. Paola ha   nuotato/?*è nuotata fino all'altra sponda.
       Paola HAVE swum/BE   swum to the other shore

2. ドイツ語の揺れる助動詞選択

　従来のドイツ語文法の決まりでは，前節の (5) とは対照的に，ドイツ語では (5a) パターンは HAVE タイプ，(5b) のパターンは BE タイプとされていた．しかしながら，岡本 (2006) が指摘しているように，「泳ぐ」(schwimmen) は，現在ほぼ BE タイプに移行したと思われる．つまり，schwimmen が非能格的に使用される場合には have/be 共に使用容認可能である．[8]

　このように二つのタイプがあることに対しては，次の二つの動詞の記述構造が想定される．Schwimmen に関しては (6b) に統一されつつあるということである．[9]

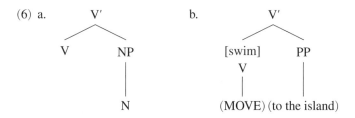

　(6a) は，動詞の目的語である N が V に編入されて，形成されるような laugh, sneeze などのタイプの語彙投射を表している．非能格動詞の基本形がこのパターンであるとすると，「泳ぐ」schwimmen という動詞は一種の他動詞〈do swimming〉が基本であり，次のような編入によって schwimmen が形成されると考えられる．[10]

---

[8] Duden (2007) の haben の項目より．

[9] (8a) は，Hale and Keyser (1993: 54)，(8b) は，Hale and Keyser (1993: 89f.) の提案を一部修正している．

[10] Hale and Keyser (1993: 55)．

(7)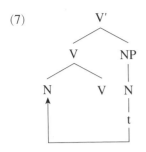

この (7a) の構造を想定するメリットは，ドイツ語では「対格目的語を伴う動詞は HAVE タイプである」ということがこの初期構造から説明出来ることである．特に重要なのは，状態の変化を表す場合には BE タイプの助動詞を選択するが，状態の変化を表していても，再帰動詞の場合には HAVE タイプを選択しなければならないことである．これはロマンス系言語と対照的である．

(8) a. Der Ast ist gebrochen.
 the branch BE broken.
 'The branch has broken.'
 b. Die Tür hat sich geöffnet.
 the door HAVE oneself opened.
 'The door has opened.'
 c. La porta si è aperta.
 the door oneself BE opened
 'The door has opened.'

(8) では，(a) が「折れた」，(b) は「開いた」，(c) はイタリア語で「開いた」であり，どれも状態の変化を表している．ドイツ語は対格目的語（再帰代名詞目的語）を必要とする動詞，つまり他動詞は HAVE タイプであるので，意味的に非対格的であっても (8b) のように BE タイプは選択されない．それに対してイタリア語は (8c) のように BE タイプとなる．つまりドイツ語の助動詞選択は統語的に制約を受けている．

次に BE タイプの (6b) に移ろう．この構造が示しているのは，「島に移動した」，ということであり，その移動の仕方が [swim]，つまり「泳ぎながら」ということになる．動詞が「移動の解釈」が可能であると，ドイツ語では BE タイプが選択される．ドイツ語にこの傾向が強いことは次のオランダ語との比

較からも観察出来る。[11]

(9) a. John heeft　urenlang　　　　op de　tafel gedanst.（オランダ語）
　　　　John HAVE lasing-for-hours on the　table　danced
　　b. John hat stundenlang auf dem Tisch getanzt.（ドイツ語）
　　　'John AUX been dancing on the table for hours.'

この例では「踊る」という動作がテーブルの上という場所に限定されているので，非能格的解釈を受けて HAVE タイプの助動詞が選択されている．それに対して，次のように移動の方向を示す要素が共起すると，(6b) の構造が設定され，BE タイプが選択される。[12]

(10) a. John is　in twee　seconden de　kamer in　gedanst.
　　　　　　　　　　　　　　　　　　　　　　　　（オランダ語）
　　　　John BE in two　seconds　the room　into danced
　　b. John ist in zwei Sekunden ins Zimmer getanzt.（ドイツ語）
　　　'John AUX danced into the room in two seconds.'

しかしながら，この「移動の方向」というのはドイツ語の方がオランダ語よりも解釈が広い．次の例を見てみよう。[13]

(11) a. John heeft　urenlang　　　door　de　zaal　rondgedanst.
　　　　　　　　　　　　　　　　　　　　　　　　（オランダ語）
　　　　John HAVE lasing-for-hours through the saloon round-danced
　　b. John ist stundenlang durch den Saal herumgetanzt.（ドイツ語）
　　　'John AUX been dancing around the room for hours.'

(11) の例からも分かるように，「踊り回る」という場合には，ドイツ語は BE タイプとなる。[14] ドイツ語の非能格動詞は，オランダ語と比べても非対格に移行しやすいことが分かる．この移行の容易さは，移動が想定出来ない動詞の場

---

[11] Randall, van Hout, Weissenborn and Baayen (2004: 334) より．オランダ語，ドイツ語は同じグロスとなるので，2つ目は省略してある．
[12] ibid.: 335. 注の 10 と同様に2つ目のグロスは省略してある．
[13] ibid.
[14] これは durch/door ［英語：through］によって移動が少しだけでも表現されているために，ドイツ語ではこのようになっていると考えられるが，Randall, van Hout, Weissenborn and Baayen (2004) はこのことについて言及していない．

3. 移動を表さない動詞の非対格化

前節で取り上げた schwimmen は，動作自体が動作主によるコントロール可能であり，その場合でも主語に動作主性を想定することができるが，そうでない場合はどうであろうか．

(12) a. Die Frau　　 *ist/hat in der Wohnung　getorkelt.
　　　　 the woman　 HAVE　 in the flat$_{DAT}$　 tottered
　　　　 'The woman tottered in the flat.'
　　 b. Die Frau　　 ist/*hat in die Wohnung　getorkelt.
　　　　 the woman BE　　 in the flat$_{ACC}$　　tottered
　　　　 'The woman tottered into the flat.'

(13) a. Der Zug *ist/hat im　　 Bahnhof　 gerumpelt.
　　　　 the train　HAVE in the station$_{DAT}$ rattled
　　　　 'The train rattled in the station.'
　　 b. Der Zug ist in den Bahnhof　 gerumpelt.
　　　　 the train BE in the station$_{ACC}$ rattled
　　　　 'The train rattled into the station.'

(12) は自分で動作がコントロール出来ない動詞の例，(13) は，いわゆる音放出動詞 (emission verb) の例である．これらの例から見ても，ドイツ語の助動詞選択は，BE タイプに移行しやすいことが分かる．

4. ドイツ語の移動先を表す表現の特殊性について

ではなぜドイツ語では (12b) や (13b) が BE タイプなのだろうか．これはドイツ語の動詞の意味構造が他のヨーロッパ言語と比べて特殊なわけでなく，ドイツ語の前置詞句表現が特別なステータスを持つからであると考えられる．大矢 (2008) が Engelberg (2000) に基づいて議論していることを参考にして，この二つの関係を検討してみよう．Engelberg (2000) は，for an hour に該当する表現が，ドイツ語には二種類あることを指摘している．一つは結果状態が含まれる für eine Stunde (for an hour) であり，もう一つは，結果状態が含

まれない eine Stunde lang (an hour long) である．次の例を見てみよう．[15]

(14) a. Die Arbeiter besitzten die Fabrik für eine Stunde.
        the workers owned   the factory for an   hour
     b. Die Polizei sperrte die Straße für eine Stunde.
        the police blocked the street for an   hour.
     c.??Sie aß den Apfel für eine Stunde.
          she ate the apple for an   hour
     d.??Sie putzte den Flur für eine Stunde.
          she polished the floor for an   hour.

(14c, d) の容認度が低いのは，それぞれの動作に結果状態が含まれていないからである．これらの例は eine Stunde lang を用いれば，容認可能となる．

(15) a. Sie aß den Apfel eine Stunde lang.
     b. Sie putzte den Flur eine Stunde lang.

大矢 (2008: 95) は，さらに次の例文を提示する．

(16) Taro rannte für 5 Minuten zum   Bahnhof, (und danach ging er
     Taro ran   for 5 minutes to-the station and then   went he
     in die Stadt).
     in the city.
     'Taro ran to the station for 5 minutes and then went to the city.'

先ほどの議論から，この (16) における für 5 Minuten (for five minutes) は「駅へ走り，そこに 5 分間滞在した」という解釈を持ちうる．つまりドイツ語の移動先を表す PP には，[BECOME BE-AT][16] という表示機能があるからこそ，独自の振る舞いをすることが分かる．[17] このような特性があるために，(14b) のような emission verb[18] においても動詞が移動を表し，非対格化され

---

[15] Engelberg (2000: 82).

[16] 大矢 (2008: 97).

[17] なお，大矢 (2008: 97) では，このような結果状態を含む副詞表現は日本語でも可能であるが，「太郎は 5 分間学校に行った．」のように，「行く・来る・帰る・戻る」などの本来的な移動動詞に限られると述べている．

[18] 大矢 (2008: 98) には次のような例が挙げられている：brausen (roar), donnern (thunder), klappern (rattle), klatschen (slap), poltern (crash), plätschern (splash) etc.

るのである．

5. まとめ

本稿では，ドイツ語の動詞が容易に非対格化することのメカニズムについてHale and Keyser (1993) のシンプルな枠組みを出発点とした．(6a) の非能格動詞の初期構造によって，非能格動詞が HAVE タイプであることを明らかにしてくれる．(6a) と並んで (6b) の構造がドイツ語では容易に得られるが，それは動詞の持つアスペクトなどの意味構造だけではなくて，動詞と結びつけられる方向の表現が持つ独自の意味合いも関わっている．その点でドイツ語での HAVE/BE 選択は主語の有生性と無関係である．それに対して以下のようにイタリア語では主語の有生性が重要な役割を果たしている．[19]

(17) a. Il   pilota ha/?è   atterrato sulla pista di emergenza.
       the pilot   HAVE/BE landed   on-the runway of emergency
   b. L' elicottero è/?ha   atterrato sul   gratetto del
      the helicopter BE/HAVE landed   on-the roof   of-the
      grattacielo.
      skyscraper

それぞれの言語が持つ要因をさらに分析することによって，助動詞選択における普遍性と個別の言語の特性をこれからも明らかにしていきたい．

参考文献

Alexiadou, Artemis, Elena Anagnostopoulou and Martin Everaert, eds. (2004) *The Unaccusativity Puzzle: Explorations of the Syntax-Lexicon Interface*, Oxford University Press, Oxford.

Burzio, Luigi (1986) *Italian Syntax: A Government-Binding Approach*, Foris, Dordrecht.

Duden (2007) *Richtiges und gutes Deutsch*, 6.Aufl. Dudenverlag [CD-ROM], Mannheim

Grewendorf, Günther (1989) *Ergativity in German*, Foris, Dordrecht.

Hale, Kenneth and Samuel Jay Keyser (1993) "On Argument Structure and the Lexi-

---

[19] Sorace (2004: 261).

cal Expression of Syntactic Relations," *The View from Building 20: Essays in Gnguistics in Honor of Sylvain Bromberger,* ed. by K. Hale and S. J. Keyser, 53-109, MIT Press, Cambridge, MA.

保阪靖人 (2013)「ドイツ語における非対格動詞の統語的性質について」『ドイツ文学論集』第34号, 49-78, 日本大学文理学部ドイツ文学科.

Keller, Frank and Antonella Sorace (2003) "Gradient Auxiliary Selection and Impersonal Passivization in German: An Experimental Investigation," *Journal of Linguistics* 39:1, 57-108.

大矢俊明 (2008)『ドイツ語再帰構文の対照言語学的研究』ひつじ書房, 東京.

Perlmutter, David (1978) "Impersonal Passives and the Unaccusative Hypothesis," *Proceedings of the Berkeley Linguistics Society* 4, 157-189.

Randall, Janet, Angeliek van Hout, Jürgen Weissenborn and Harald Baayen (2004) "Acquiring Unaccusativity: A Cross-Linguistic Look," *The Unaccusativity Puzzle: Explorations of the Syntax-Lexicon Interface*, ed. by Alexiadou et al., 332-353, Oxford University Press, Oxford.

Sorace, Antonella (2004) "Gradience at the Lexicon – Syntax Interface: Evidence from Auxiliary Selection and Implications for Unaccusativity," *The Unaccusativity Puzzle: Explorations of the Syntax-Lexicon Interface*, ed. by Alexiadou et al., 243-268, Oxford University Press, Oxford.

Eタイプ代名詞と「その」

伊藤 達也
首都大学東京

1. はじめに

Elbourne (2005) は，Eタイプ代名詞は補部のNPを削除された定冠詞であると論じている．(1) に示されるように，補部のNPが削除された定冠詞はitなどとして発音されることになる．このように考えると，(2a) のロバ文 (donkey sentence) と (2b) は同じLFを持つことになるため，解釈が同じになることが説明される．

(1)   the ~~donkey~~

   it

(2) a.   Every famer who owns a donkey beats it.
   b.   Every famer who owns a donkey beats the donkey.

Elbourneの分析は冠詞のない日本語にどのように取りこまれるべきなのだろうか．本稿は日本語のEタイプ代名詞の基本的な特性を観察し，それを取り扱うための分析を試みる．

2. 観察

代名詞には指示代名詞や束縛代名詞としての用法に加え，Eタイプ代名詞としての用法が認められている．Eタイプ代名詞は量化表現を先行詞とするが，それによって束縛されはしない．

(3)   指示代名詞
    太郎が踊りだした．そして，{pro／彼は} 歌いもした．

(4) 束縛代名詞
すべての絵が {pro／それを} 描いた人によって紹介された．
(5) E タイプ代名詞
a. 一人の学生が踊りだした．そして，{pro／*彼は} 歌いもした．
b. 太郎が一つのりんごを買ってきた．そして，次郎が {pro／それを} 食べた．

(5) の代名詞は指示代名詞ではありえない．指示代名詞は先行詞と同じものを指す．しかし，(5) では先行詞の「一人の学生」や「一つのりんご」は量化表現であり，そもそも何も指さない．(しかし，(3) では先行詞「太郎」は固有名詞であり，太郎という個体を指している．そして，代名詞も同じ個体を指している．) (5) の代名詞は束縛代名詞でもありえない．(5) では，先行詞の「一人の学生」や「一つのりんご」は代名詞とは別の節にあるので，代名詞を c 統御しておらず，したがって，代名詞を束縛していない．(しかし，(4) では先行詞の「すべての絵」は代名詞を c 統御しているので，代名詞を束縛している．)

(5) の例からは，「彼」が E タイプ代名詞として働くことができないことがわかる．[1] Hoji (1989) は，「彼」が許されない環境では「あの」も許されないことを観察している．

(6) a. 昨日山田さんに会いました．彼いつも元気ですね．
b. 昨日山田さんという人に会いました．*彼，道に迷って困っていたので，助けてあげました．　　　　　　　　　　(Hoji (1991))
(7) a. 昨日山田さんに会いました．あの (*その) 人いつも元気ですね．
b. 昨日山田さんという人に会いました．その (*あの) 人，道に迷って

---

[1] (5a) の「彼」は (9-14a′) の「彼」よりも容認可能性が高いように思われる．Heim and Kratzer (1998: 294) は，(i) のような例の he が二つの方法で分析されうると論じている．
 (i) Only one congressman admires Kennedy. He is very junior.
一つの分析によると，he は E タイプ代名詞である．もう一つの分析によると，he は指示代名詞であり，したがって，自由変項である．この自由変項には，文脈がその値としてケネディーを称賛する議員を与える．(5a) の「彼」も後者の方法で解釈することができるように思われる．しかし，(9-14a′) の「彼」はこの方法では解釈することができない．そうすると，(9a) の「彼」は指示代名詞として分析されることによって，容認されると考えることができる．(i) のような例における代名詞に複数の分析を認めることは非経済的に見えるかもしれないが，Heim and Kratzer はそれには問題がないと論じている．問題がないどころか，日本語の「彼」は二つの分析が必要であることを示しているのかもしれない．

困っていたので,助けてあげました.　　　　　　　　(Kuno (1973))

そして,「あの」は,Kuno (1973) によると,話し手と聞き手の両方が指示されるものを知っていると話し手が知っているときにのみ使われる.「あの」と「彼」が同じ規則によって制限されているなら,「彼」も話し手と聞き手の両方が指示されるものを知っていると話し手が知っているときにのみ使われると言うことができるかもしれない.

Eタイプ代名詞の見方の一つは,それを確定表現の代用と考えることである.「その」は指示詞と考えられているが,「その」がどの程度まで the と同じ働きをするか見てみよう.(3) のEタイプ代名詞は「その」によって修飾された名詞で置き換えることができる.また,この文脈のもとでは,裸名詞は「その」によって修飾されていなくても同じように解釈されうる.

(8) a. 一人の学生が踊りだした.{その学生は/学生は} 歌いもした.
　　b. 太郎が一つのりんごを買ってきた.そして,次郎が {そのりんごを/りんごを} 食べた.

Eタイプ代名詞という用語は考案者である Evans (1982) が意図していたよりも広い範囲の例をカバーするようになっている.[2] 以下の例では,代名詞は指示代名詞や束縛代名詞ではありえない.

(9)　donkey sentence
　　a. 一人の弁護士を雇ったすべての人が {pro/弁護士を} 代わりに出廷させた.
　　a′. 一人の弁護士を雇ったすべての人が {*彼に/その弁護士を} 代わりに出廷させた.
　　b. 一つのりんごを買ったすべての人が {pro/りんごを} デザートに食べた.
　　b′. 一つのりんごを買ったすべての人が {それを/そのりんごを} デザートに食べた.

(9b) と (9b′) では,誰を選ぶかに応じて,代名詞が異なったりんごを表す.

---

[2] 代名詞の分析は,一部には,先行詞が何であるかによる.日本語の裸名詞がどのように取り扱われるべきかについては研究者の間で一致した見解がないので,それが先行詞になるような例は挙げたくなかったが,いくつかの例では量化表現が不自然に聞こえるため,裸名詞を先行詞として使わざるをえなかった.

(10) fish sentence
   a. 太郎は一人の秘書を雇いたがっている．そして，彼は {pro／秘書に} 手伝いをさせるつもりだ．
   a′. 太郎は一人の秘書を雇いたがっている．そして，彼は {*彼女に／*その秘書に} 手伝いをさせるつもりだ．
   b. 太郎は一つのりんごを欲しがっている．彼は {pro／りんごを} デザートに食べるつもりだ．
   b′. 太郎は一つのりんごを欲しがっている．彼は {それを／そのりんごを} デザートに食べるつもりだ．

(10a) と (10a′) には，「一人の秘書」が「雇いたがっている」よりも狭い作用域を取る解釈が可能である．この解釈のもとでは，具体的な秘書は存在しさえしないかもしれない．それにもかかわらず，「一人の秘書」は代名詞の先行詞として働いている．

(11) 他の量化表現に従属
   a. すべてのチームには一人の外国人選手が所属しているが，いくつかのチームでは {pro／外国人選手が} キャプテンを務めている．
   a′. すべてのチームには一人の外国人選手が所属しているが，いくつかのチームでは {*彼が／その外国人選手が} キャプテンを務めている．
   b. すべてのビルに一つのエレベーターがある．しかし，いくつかのビルでは {pro／エレベーターが} 故障している．
   b′. すべてのビルに一つのエレベーターがある．しかし，いくつかのビルでは {それが／そのエレベーターが} 故障している．

(11a) と (11a′) では，どのチームを選ぶかに応じて，代名詞が異なった外国人選手を表す．これまでの例では，pro だけでなく「それ」も許された．しかし，以下の例からは，「それ」が許されなくなる．

(12) paycheck sentence
   a. 太郎は母親を連れてきた．しかし，花子は {pro／母親を} 連れてこなかった．
   a′. 太郎は母親を連れてきた．しかし，花子は {*彼女を／*その母親を} 連れてこなかった．
   b. 太郎は借金のかたに車を売った．次郎も {pro／車を} 売った．

b′. 太郎は借金のかたに車を売った．次郎も{*それを／*その車を}売った．

(12b) では，pro がゆるい同一性のもとに認可されている．裸名詞「車」も許されるが，この文脈では次郎の車を表すと解釈される．

(13) Bach-Peters sentence
  a. {pro／自分が欲しがっていた賞品を} もらう努力をしたすべての学生が自分が欲しがっていた賞品をもらった．
  b. {*それを／*自分が欲しがっていたその賞品を} もらう努力をしたすべての学生が自分が欲しがっていた賞品をもらった．

(13a) では，二つの代名詞がお互いを含む句を先行詞としている．[3] pro は E タイプ代名詞として働いているが，これの先行詞は「自分が欲しがっていた賞品」である．その中には代名詞「自分」が含まれている．「自分」は束縛代名詞として働いていると考えられるが，これの先行詞は「pro もらう努力をしたすべての学生」である．そして，その中には E タイプ代名詞が含まれている．pro と同じ環境にある「自分が欲しがっていた賞品」は定の解釈を受けると思われる．

(14) bathroom sentence
  a. 彼には通訳がついていないか，もしくは，{pro／通訳が} 席をはずしているかだ．
  a′. 彼には通訳がついていないか，もしくは，{*彼が／*その通訳が} 席をはずしているかだ．
  b. 太郎は弁当を持ってこなかったか，もしくは，すでに {pro／弁当を} 食べてしまったかだ．
  b′. 太郎は弁当を持ってこなかったか，もしくは，すでに {*それを／*その弁当を} 食べてしまったかだ．

---

[3] (13) では，「自分」のかわりに，pro が現れてもよい．
  (i) pro もらう努力をしたすべての学生が pro 欲しがっていた賞品をもらった．
二つの pro は先行詞の中にお互いを含んでいる．したがって，Oku (1998) などが提案するコピー分析は，先行詞のコピーを永久に繰り返さなければならず，この文を派生できないかもしれない．pro の素性について議論する紙幅がないので，本稿は pro を他の方法によっては派生できない基本的な要素としてみなしている．

(14b) の裸名詞「弁当」はこの文脈では何らかの方法で，太郎が持ってきた弁当を表すと解釈される．

以上の例から，(15) のようなことが言える．

(15) a. 「彼」は E タイプ代名詞として働くことができない．
   b. pro は E タイプ代名詞として働くことができる．また，同じ環境に「それ」が許される場合がある．
   c. pro と裸名詞が生起する環境は同じである．また「それ」と「その」によって修飾された名詞が生起する環境も同じである．

(15a) に加えて，Saito and Hoji (1983) などは，「彼」は束縛代名詞として働くこともできないと論じている．Kuroda (1965) が指摘したように，日本語の「彼」は指示代名詞，束縛代名詞，E タイプ代名詞として働くことができる英語の人称代名詞とは性質が大きく異なるように思われる．

(15b) については，すでに Kurafuji (1999) によって指摘されている．彼によると，pro には E タイプ代名詞として解釈されるオプションと動的に束縛されるオプションがあるが，「それ」には動的に束縛されるオプションしかない．（動的な束縛については，Chierchia (1992) などを参照．）また，彼は Chierchia にしたがって，paycheck sentence や bathroom sentence では代名詞が E タイプ代名詞として解釈されなければならないと考えている．[4]

(15c) は興味深い事実である．次節では，この事実を取り扱うための分析を提案する．

3. 分析

前節では，pro が E タイプ代名詞として働くことができるとこと，そして，裸名詞も定の解釈を受けることによって同じ環境に現れられることを見た．また，「それ」が許される場合には，「その」によって修飾された名詞も許されることを見た．

まず，「その」には二つの異形態があり，一方には音形があるが (/その/)，もう一方には音形がない (/φ/) と考えてみよう．

---

[4] 本稿では，Bach-Peters sentence においても「それ」が許されないことを見た．しかし，この構文で「それ」が許されない理由と Bach-Peters sentence や bathroom sentence で「それ」が許されない理由が同じかどうかについては議論の余地があるかもしれない．

(16) {その}

　　/その/　　/ϕ/

　また,/その/と/ϕ/の範疇は決定詞であり,補部にNPを取ると考えよう.そして,補部のNPが削除されると,前者はPFで「それ」として発音され,後者はproになると考えることにしよう.このように考えると,/その/で修飾された名詞と/ϕ/で修飾された名詞がそれぞれどのような環境で生起するかを指定することができれば,「それ」とproがどのような環境で生起するかについては何も言う必要がない.

　しかしながら,この考え方には問題がある.まず,/その/と/ϕ/が同じ語の異形態であるなら,一方には動的に束縛されるオプションしかないのに,もう一方にはEタイプ代名詞として解釈されるオプションと動的に束縛されるオプションの両方があると考えることは不自然である.さらに,日本語のように機能範疇が不活発であると考えられている言語に空の決定詞を認める動機は強くない.

　空の決定詞を認めなくてすむ代案は,Partee(1987)にしたがって,名詞の解釈がタイプ変換によって変わると考えることである.日本語の裸名詞の解釈のデフォールトは集合であり,タイプ変換によってそれが(特定の)個体に変わると考えよう.たとえば,(17a)の第2文の「りんご」はりんごの集合({x| x is an apple})を表している.この集合は存在閉鎖される.(第1文の「りんご」も同様.)一方で(17b)の第2文の「りんご」はタイプ変換を受け,特定のりんご($\iota x.\ apple(x)$)を(この文脈では,太郎が買ってきたりんごを)表している.(第1文の「りんご」は集合を表し,それは存在閉鎖される.)また,Tomioka(2003)にしたがって,proの解釈も同様にタイプ変換によって,集合から個体に変わると考えよう.実際,(17a, b)のproは対応する裸名詞と同様に解釈されうる.

(17) a. 太郎がりんごを食べた.次郎も{りんごを/pro}食べた.
　　 b. 太郎がりんごを買ってきた.そして,次郎が{りんごを/pro}食べた.

　そして,音形があろうと(裸名詞)なかろうと(pro),日本語の名詞が個体を表すとき,その名詞は英語の定名詞が個体を表すときと同様に解釈されると考えよう.前節の例を見れば,これは実際そのようである.このように考えれ

ば，proと裸名詞が同じ環境に現れうるという事実を捉えることができる．また，Eタイプ代名詞が定名詞の代用であるなら，proがEタイプ代名詞として働くという事実も捉えることができる．

「その」は動的に束縛されなければならないので，「その」によって修飾された名詞はEタイプ代名詞を要求する構文（paycheck sentenceとbath room sentenceに加えて，もしかするとBach-Peters sentenceも）からは排除される．「その」で修飾された名詞にNP削除を適用することによって「それ」を派生するという考えは保持してもよい．そうすれば，「その」によって修飾された名詞と「それ」が同じ環境に現れるという事実を捉えることができる．

4. おわりに

Elbourneは，英語のEタイプ代名詞を補部のNPが削除された定冠詞として分析した．そうすると，Eタイプ代名詞が定名詞と同じ環境に生起することが捉えられる．本稿は，定の解釈を受ける日本語の裸名詞は英語の定名詞と同じように解釈されると提案した．したがって，日本語の裸名詞は定の解釈を受けることによってEタイプ代名詞が生起する環境に現れることができる．また，そのような名詞の代用として使われる（したがって，定の解釈を受ける）proがEタイプ代名詞として働くと論じた．

参考文献

Chierchia, Gennaro (1992) "Anaphora and Dynamic Binding," *Linguistics and Philosophy* 15, 111–183.

Elbourne, Paul (2000) "E-type Anaphoras as Definite Pronouns," *Natural Language Semantics* 9, 241–288.

Evans, Gareth (1982) "Pronouns," *Linguistics Inquiry* 11, 337–362.

Heim, Irene and Angelika Kratzer (1998) *Semantics in Generative Grammar*, Blackwell, Oxford.

Hoji, Hajime (1991) "*Kare*," *Interdisciplinary Approaches to Language: Essays in Honor of Prof. S.-Y. Kuroda*, ed. by Carol Georgopoulos and Roberta Ishihara, 287–304, Reidel, Dordrecht.

Kuno, Susumu (1973) *The Structure of the Japanese Language*, MIT Press, Cambridge, MA.

Kurafuji, Takeo (1999) *Japanese Pronouns in Dynamic Semantics: The Null-Overt*

Contrast, Doctoral dissertation, Rutgers University.
Kuroda, Shige-yuki (1965) *Generative Grammatical Studies in the Japanese Language*, Doctoral disseratiation, MIT.
Oku, Satoshi (1998) *A Theory of Selection and Reconstruction in the Minimalist Perspective*, Doctoral dissertation, University of Connecticut.
Partee, (1987) "Noun Phrase Interpretation and Type-Shifting Principles," *Studies in Discourse Representation Theory and the Theory of Generalized Quantifiers*, ed. by Groenendijk et al., 115-143, Foris, Dordrecht.
Saito, Mamoru and Hajime Hoji (1983) "Weak Crossover and Move α in Japanese," *Natural Language and Linguistic Theory* 1, 245-259.
Tomioka, Satoshi (2003) "The Semantics of Japanese Null Pronouns and Its Cross-Linguistic Implications," *The Interfaces: Deriving and Interpreting Omitted Structures*, ed. by Kerstin Schwabe and Susanne Winkler, 321-339, John Benjamins, Amsterdam.

Tangled Up in HOME*
—A Functional Approach—

Matazo Izutani
Tokyo Medical and Dental University

1. Introduction

There are basically two different forms of Japanese verbs: a plain form and a polite (*masu*) form. The plain form is used in informal situations (such as when talking with friends) and the *masu* form in formal situations (such as when talking with strangers), as in (1), below.

(1) a. Asita Tookyoo-e ikimasu. (polite form; e.g., as said to your neighbor)
b. Asita Tookyoo-e iku. (plain form; e.g., as said to your friend)
'I'm going to Tokyo tomorrow.

Verbs can appear in either the polite (*ikimasu* 'go') or plain (*iku* 'go') form in a main clause as in (1). However, the situation is drastically changed when a verb appears in the subordinate clause, as in (2) and (3).

(2) a.??[Kaze-o hikimasita] kara, hayaku nemasu.
b. [Kaze-o hiita] kara, hayaku nemasu.
(3) a. *[Kaze-o hikimasita] kara, hayaku neru.
b. [Kaze-o hiita] kara, hayaku neru.
'I'll go to bed early because I've caught a cold.'

The clause preceding *kara* ('because') is subordinate to the main clause in these sentences. The main clause has the same form: the polite *nemasu*

---

* I am deeply indebted to Morikawa Masahiro (Nagoya University of Foreign Studies) for his comments on an earlier version of this paper and to the late Kevin Cleary (TMDU) for suggesting stylistic improvements.

('sleep') in (2) and the plain *neru* ('sleep') in (3), respectively, while the subordinate clause has the polite form *hikimasita* ('caught') in the (a) sentences and the plain form *hiita* ('caught') in the (b) sentences. With respect to the subordinate clause, the polite form is not allowed in (2a) and (3a). The unacceptability cannot be attributed to the difference in form (polite/plain) between the main and subordinate clauses, considering the acceptability of the (b) sentences. Thus, the question must be asked: Why are (2a) and (3a) not allowed?

Next, look at sentences in (4) and (5).

- (4) a. ?*[Kaze-o hikimasita] node, hayaku nemasu.
  - b. [Kaze-o hiita] node, hayaku nemasu.
- (5) a. *[Kaze-o hikimasita] node, hayaku neru.
  - b. [Kaze-o hiita] node, hayaku neru.

  'I'll go to bed early because I've caught a cold.'

The sentences in (4) and (5) are produced by replacing the *kara* in (2) and (3) with *node* ('because'). The level of acceptability of the constructed sentences does not change between (3a) and (5a), while it decreases in (4a) when compared to (2a). Further, (4a) becomes much worse when the conjunction *toki* ('if/when') is used in place of *node*, as in (6a).

- (6) a. *[Kaze-o hikimasita] toki (-ni-wa), hayaku nemasu.
  - b. [Kaze-o hiita] toki (-ni-wa), hayaku nemasu.
- (7) a. *[Kaze-o hikimasita] toki (-ni-wa), hayaku neru.
  - b. [Kaze-o hiita] toki (-ni-wa), hayaku neru.

  'I'd go to bed early if I caught a cold.'

Why is it that the (a) sentences in (2)-(7) with the subordinate *kara* clause, *node* clause, and *toki* clause containing the polite (*masu*) form are all unacceptable? In this paper, we try to give an answer to the above question, by recourse to the semantico-discoursal notions of 'Hearer-Oriented Modality Expressions' (HOMEs) and the subjectivity/objectivity dichotomy, proposed in Izutani (2007).

The organization of this paper is as follows. Section 2 briefly introduces the analysis of the use of polite/plain form in the noun complement clause by Izutani (2007). In section 3, his analysis is extended to the subordinate clauses in (2)-(7). Consequences of the present analysis discussed in section 3 will be briefly touched upon in section 4. The paper is summarized in section 5.

2. HOMEs and Subjectivity/Objectivity

According to Nitta (1991), a sentence is composed of proposition and modality as in (8a), where the proposition is enclosed by modality elements in a manner illustrated in (8b).

(8) a. A sentence or clause = Proposition + Modality
    b.   Modality [Proposition]   (Nitta (1991: 17))

The proposition contains logical elements such as the subject, object NPs, and the predicate that contributes to the core or logical meaning of a sentence. Hence, these NPs can be considered an objective entity. In contrast, modality expresses a speaker's mental attitude regarding the proposition, and thus is a subjective entity. For example, the proposition *Mary-ga asita kuru* 'Mary comes tomorrow' is sandwiched by the modality expressions *osoraku* (the adverb 'perhaps') and *kamosirenai* (the auxiliary verb 'may') in (9a), and the proposition *Mary-ga asita konai* 'Mary does not come tomorrow' is enclosed by the modality expressions *tabun* (the adverb 'probably') and *(ni-)tigainai* (the auxiliary verb 'must') in (9b).

(9) a. Osoraku [Mary-ga asita kuru] kamosirenai.
      'Perhaps, Mary may come tomorrow.'
      [Proposition: Mary-ga kuru; Modality: osoraku, kamosirenai]
  b. Tabun [Mary-ga asita konai] ni-tigainai.
      'Mary probably must not come tomorrow.'
      [Proposition: Mary-ga konai; Modality: tabun, (ni-) tigainai]

With these examples in mind, let us look at the following sentences:

(10) a. *John-wa [$_{NP}$ [$_{IP}$ *t* kinoo koko-ni kimasita] zyosei]-o aisiteimasu.[1]

---

[1] The categorial status of clauses is represented as IP throughout the paper.

b. John-wa [$_{NP}$ [$_{IP}$ t kinoo koko-ni kita] zyosei]-o aisiteimasu.
   'John loves a woman who came here yesterday.'
(11) a. *[$_{NP}$ [$_{IP}$ John-ga nani-o simasita ka]]-ga wakaranai desu.²
   b. [$_{NP}$ [$_{IP}$ John-ga nani-o sita ka]]-ga wakaranai desu.
      'I don't know what John did.'
(12) a. *[$_{NP}$ [$_{IP}$ John-ga sono otya-o nomimasita kadooka]]-ga mondai desu.
   b. [$_{NP}$ [$_{IP}$ John-ga sono otya-o nonda kadooka]]-ga mondai desu.
      'Whether or not John drank that tea is a problem.'
(13) a. *John-ga [$_{IP}$ kinoo Mary-ga kimasita]-to iimasita.
   b. John-ga [$_{IP}$ kinoo Mary-ga kita]-to iimasita.
      'John said that Mary came yesterday.'

In sentences (10)-(13), the main clauses have the polite form *masu* (verb) or *desu* (copula), and the object NPs or subject NPs have an embedded clause. The object NP has a relative clause in (10), and the subject NP contains a *wh*-question clause in (11) and a *kadooka* ('whether') clause in (12), respectively. The clause in (13) is complement to the verb. The (a) sentences with the polite *masu* form are unacceptable, while the (b) sentences with the plain form are acceptable. In general terms, acceptability can be stated as a function of modality as a semantic constraint on NPs and embedded (relative/complement) clauses, as in (14).

(14) Semantic constraints on NPs and embedded (relative/complement) clauses: Modality expressions (*masu* and *desu*) that presuppose the existence of hearers cannot be used in NPs or embedded (relative/complement) clauses.³

The modality expressions *masu* and *desu* that presuppose the existence of hearers are referred to as Hearer-Oriented Modality Expressions (HOMEs). Following Izutani (2007), let us assume that elements contained in the prop-

---

² The *wh*-question and *kadooka* clauses are analyzed as NP here, but not CP as traditionally and widely believed in the literature. For the NP analysis of *wh*-question and *kadooka* clauses, see Izutani (2008).

³ Teramura (1976: 68-71) mentions that the polite verbal form cannot appear in the noun modification (i.e., in the clause headed by a noun), though he does not refer to hearer-oriented modal expressions (HOMEs) used here.

osition (objective entity) must also be objective. In (10a), the object NP (objective entity) contains the subjective HOME *masu* in the relative clause, violating (14). Since subjectivity and objectivity contradict each other, (14) can be paraphrased, as stated in (15).

(15) Ban on clash of reason (BOCOR): Objective entities (such as propositions, NPs, and embedded clauses) are incompatible with subjective HOMEs.

The subjective *masu* form contained in the objective NP in (10a) is in violation of the BOCOR in (15), and (10a) is judged unacceptable. In contrast, the relative clause of (10b) has the plain form *kita* ('came'), not the HOME *kimasita* ('came'), in harmony with (15), and hence (10b) is judged acceptable.

The contrast in (11) and (12) can be explained analogously. Since the clauses marked by the grammatical particles *ga* and *o* function as the subject and object in a sentence, they are categorially identified as an NP (Izutani (2008)). The *wh*-question clause embedded in the subject NP (objective entity) has the subjective HOME *simasita* ('did') in (11a) in violation of (15). In (11b), the embedded *wh*-question does not contain the HOME, but the plain form *sita* ('did'), hence, (11b) does not violate (15). In (12), since the *kadooka* ('whether') clause functions as the subject marked by *ga* and forms an NP, (12a) is banned by (15) from having the subjective HOME *nomimasita* ('drank'). In contrast, the clause in (12b) does not violate (15) and hence (12b) is judged acceptable. In (13a), the embedded clause contains the HOME *kimasita* ('came') in violation of (15), while it does not in (13b). In the next section, we will check to see if the system with (15) that was posed as explaining the acceptability of sentences in (10)-(13) can be applied to sentences in (2)-(7).

3. Discussion

First look at the sentences in (2) and (3). The subordinate clauses in these sentences do not contain NP structures. Since (2a) and (3a) are unacceptable, the subordinate *kara* clause must be objective. This proposition is not implausible. Since the underlying reason, whatever it may be, is the result of objective thinking, it too must be objective. Thus, the *kara* clause providing reason to the main clause is objective. As a result, (2a) and (3a) are excluded by (15) because the objective *kara* clause contains the subjective HOME *hikimasita*. Accordingly, subordinate clauses should be included in (14) and (15).

Let us now turn to the sentences with *node* ('because') in (4) and (5). The conjunction *node* can be analyzed as *no* plus *de* with *no* as a noun forming an NP and *de* as a particle/postposition, as illustrated in (16) and (17).

(16) a.?*[$_{PP}$ [$_{NP}$ [$_{IP}$ Kaze-o hikimasita] no]-de], hayaku nemasu. (= (4))
     b. [$_{PP}$ [$_{NP}$ [$_{IP}$ Kaze-o hiita] no]-de], hayaku nemasu.
(17) a. *[$_{PP}$ [$_{NP}$ [$_{IP}$ Kaze-o hikimasita] no]-de], hayaku neru. (= (5))
     b. [$_{PP}$ [$_{NP}$ [$_{IP}$ Kaze-o hiita] no]-de], hayaku neru.
       'I'll go to bed early because I've caught a cold.'

The unacceptability of (16a) and (17a) obtains straightforwardly, for the subjective HOME *hikimasita* contained in the objective NP headed by *no* violates (15). (16a) and (17a) are alternatively excluded by (15) even when the *node* clause is analyzed as a subordinate clause with *node* as a conjunction (i.e., without forming NP). The (b) sentences are acceptable because they do not involve an HOME in the relevant NPs or subordinate clauses. At this point, one may want to say that the sentences in (2a) and (16a) do not sound as bad as they are judged to be here. However, when compared to the sentences in (18B), they are revealed as being very marginal or almost unacceptable.

(18) A: Doo-site sonnani hayaku neru no desu ka.
        'Why do you go to bed so early?'
     B1: Kaze-o hikimasita kara. 'Because I caught a cold.'
     B2: Kaze-o hikimasita node. 'Because I caught a cold.'

Both replies in (18B) are perfect: (14) and (15) do not come into play because the *kara* and *node* clauses function as main clauses. For speakers who accept (2a) and (16a), it might be the case that the force of the politeness discourse in the main clause 'overrides' the grammar (i.e., functions as a semantic constraint) in (14) and (15). For example, if the speaker wanted to be 'super' polite to his hearer, he might be tempted to use the polite form in the subordinate clause as well, as in (2a), with the discourse force taking precedence over the grammar, leading to a withholding of the unacceptability.[4]

Let us finally consider the sentences in (6) and (7), repeated here as (19) and (20).

(19) a. *[$_{NP}$ [$_{IP}$ Kaze-o hikimasita] toki](-ni-wa), hayaku nemasu. (= (6))
    b. [$_{NP}$ [$_{IP}$ Kaze-o hiita] toki] (-ni-wa), hayaku nemasu.
(20) a. *[$_{NP}$ [$_{IP}$ Kaze-o hikimasita] toki] (-ni-wa), hayaku neru. (= (7))
    b. [$_{NP}$ [$_{IP}$ Kaze-o hiita] toki] (-ni-wa), hayaku neru.
    'I'd go to bed early if I caught a cold.'

The unacceptability of (19a) and (20a) is attributable to (15): the *toki* clause forming NP (objective entity) contains the subjective HOME *hikimasita,* in violation of (15). These sentences are also ruled out by (15) when the *toki* clause is analyzed as a subordinate clause with *toki* as a conjunction in the same way as (16a) and (17a).

4. Consequences

A special verbal form, namely the 'quasi-nominal phrase' (*zyuntaiku*), consists of the adnominal form (*rentaikei*) (or attributive form, to use Miyagawa's (2012) terminology) without a following noun. This form was used normally in classical Japanese, but its use in modern Japanese is limited to

---

[4] Concerning the discourse force with the *kara*/*node* clauses, Masahiro Morikawa (personal communication) pointed out that types of the main clause (request or command) affect the choice of the verbal form (plain or polite) in the subordinate clause, noting the contrasts in (i) and (ii), below.
    (i) Ima {?iku/ikimasu} {kara/ node}, moosukosi matteite kudasai. (Request)
    (ii) Ima {iku/*ikimasu} {kara/ node}, moosukosi mati nasai. (Command)
    'Please wait/Wait a little more, for I'm leaving now.'
The discourse force of politeness overriding grammar is vividly manifested in (i) and (ii), above. Since the main clause uses a polite request type with *kudasai* ('please'), the polite *ikimasu* ('leave') fits better than the expected plain *iku* on discourse demand. In (ii), a command type, the plain *iku* ('leave') is preferred as a result of the discourse force over the polite *ikimasu,* which is banned by the semantic constraint in (15).

poetry and certain idiomatic expressions, as shown in (21).

(21) a. [Hana-mo arasi-mo humikoete yuku]-ga [otoko-no ikiru] miti.
'(The way of) overcoming both happiness and hardships is man's way.'
(Poem: *Tabino Yokaze* 'Night winds on the road' by Yaso Saizyoo)
b. [Yama-no hatake-no kuwanomi-o kokago-ni tunda]-wa itu-no hi ka.
'When was it that I picked the mountain berries in the basket?'
(Poem: *Aka Tonbo* 'A red dragon fly' by Koosaku Yamada)
c. [Tosa-no Kooti-no Harimayabasi-de boosan kanzasi kau]-o mita.
'I saw a monk buy a floral hairpin at Harimaya bridge in Kochi, Tosa.'
(*Yosakoibushi*: Traditional folklore of Kochi prefecture)

Verbs such as *yuku* ('go'), *tunda* ('picked') and *kau* ('buy') in (21) are in the attributive form. This form of a verb was used in classical Japanese and went out of use with the advent of the following nominal element *no* (Tsai (2011: 41)). Clauses containing an attributive verb are assumed to be categorially *taigen* 'nominal' (i.e., *meisi* 'noun') by researchers of both the *kokubungaku* ('Japanese Literature') camp and the non-*kokubungaku* camp because the attributive form in (21) is marked by particles such as *ga, o*, and *wa*. The system suggested in (14) and (15) confirms this assumption. The system predicts that replacing the relevant verbal forms with the polite forms (HOMEs) makes the sentences in (21) ungrammatical. This supposition is borne out, as shown in (22), below.

(22) a. *[Hana-mo arasi-mo humikoete yukimasu]-ga [otoko-no ikiru] miti.
b. *[Yama-no hatake-no kuwanomi-o kokago-ni tumimasita]-wa itu-no hi ka.
c. *[Tosa-no Kooti-no Harimayabasi-de boosan kanzasi kaimasu]-o mita.

The ungrammaticality of sentences with the polite verbal forms in (22) in turn suggests that the clause (IP) with the attributive verb projects up to NP. The architecture of the relevant clause is schematically illustrated in (23).

(23) a. [$_{NP}$ [$_{IP}$ attributive verb] e]-particle (=ga/o) ..... ⟶
   b. [$_{NP}$ [$_{IP}$ attributive verb]no]-particle (=ga/o) .....

The historical fact that diachronically a clause with the attributive form of a verb was later replaced by the same clause with the following *no* indicates that the position taken over by the *no* once was occupied by an empty head *e* of an NP, as shown in (23).[5]

Another consequence concerns *no* construction. Consider the sentences in (24), below.

(24) a. [$_{NP}$ [$_{IP}$ Asita Kyooto-e iku]-no] da! 'I'm going to Kyoto tomorrow!'
   b. *[$_{NP}$ [$_{IP}$ Asita Kyooto-e ikimasu]-no] da!
   c. [$_{NP}$ Kazi/Zisin] da! 'Fire!/Quake!'

Thu unacceptability of (24b) with the *masu* form (*ikimasu* 'go') indicates that the clause headed by *no* is categorially an NP, which is the same as *kazi* ('fire') / *zisin* ('quake') in (24c). From this observation it can be said that the *no da* construction consists solely of an NP (which by itself constitutes proposition) and a copula *da* functioning as a modal, as schematically illustrated in (25). As a corollary of the objective NP being a proposition, the clause (IP) contained in it cannot have the *masu* form by (14) and (15).

(25) *No da* construction:

   [$_{Proposition}$ [$_{NP}$ [$_{IP}$] no]] [$_{Modality}$ da][6] (Cf. (8))

---

[5] In his analysis of case-marking in Old Japanese (OJ), Miyagawa (2012: 294) considers the direct object containing the attributive verb *hukuru* ('fall') in (i) below, for example, as a CP, not an NP (as assumed here).
   (i) [$_{CP}$ yo no hukuru] o matu
       'to wait until the night falls'
Example (i) with the attributive verb *hukuru* has exactly the same structure as (23a). Though he does not show how the overt *o* is assigned to the object (CP) in (i), Miyagawa would presumably have to stipulate that it is assigned morphologically by the conclusive verb (*matu*) to CP as well as NP, with the abstract case banned from being assigned to CP by his initial stipulation that the abstract case can only be assigned to NP. Though Miyagawa's case-marking system is a serious attempt to explain direct objects in OJ, it is not, as just noted, without problems, which we will not pursue here.

[6] *Da* is considered to express modality in the literature (Nitta (1991), Noda (1997), Morikawa (2006)). For a comprehensive analysis of *da* of *noda* construction and its structure similar to the one given in (25), see Morikawa (2009: 61).

5. Concluding Remarks

We argued that the polite form of a verb (the *masu* form) cannot appear in the subordinate clauses in (2)-(7) by recourse to the semantico-discoursal constraints in (14) and (15), by which it is proposed that the *masu* form cannot appear in the embedded clauses in (10)-(13).

Since the polite forms (HOMEs) can appear only in the main clause, only the main clause is a subjective entity and all other clauses discussed here are objective entities (i.e., proposition). Thus, the criterion used to identify whether or not a given clause is a proposition is as follows: If a clause is immediately dominated by the nominal element (i.e., a non-null head noun, pronominal *no*, or empty nominal *e*), then it is proposition.

References

Izutani, Matazo (2007) "Semantic Constraints on NPs in Japanese," *Journal of International Students Education* 12, 59-66.

Izutani, Matazo (2008) "*Wh*-phrases Creating NPs," *Tokyo Medical and Dental University Journal of Letters* 38, 19-53.

Miyagawa, Shigeru (2012) *Case, Argument Structure, and Word Order*, Routledge, New York.

Morikawa, Masahiro (2006) "*Another Function of Da and Desu in Japanese*," *Nagoya University of Foreign Studies Journal of Foreign Languages* 30, 17-31.

Morikawa, Masahiro (2009) *Gimonbun to Da* (Interrogative Sentences and *Da*), Hituzi Syobo, Tokyo.

Nitta, Yoshio (1991) *Nihongo no Modality to Ninsyoo* (Modality and Person in Japanese), Hituzi Syobo, Tokyo.

Noda, Harumi (1997) *No(da) no Kinoo* (Functions of *Noda*), Kurosio, Tokyo.

Teramura, Hideo (1976) "Rentaisyuusyoku no Sintakusu to Imi—Sono 2 (Syntax and Semantics of Noun Modification 2)," *Nihongo/Nihonbunka* 5, 29-78.

Tsai, Hsin Yin (2011) "The Attributive Form, Quasi-nominal Form, and *No*- Pronominalization in *Ukiyoburo* (1809-13)," *Nihon University Bungaku Kenkyuu Ronsyuu* 34, 41-54.

On the Core Ideas of Generative Grammar
—Then and Now*

Ruriko Kawashima
Meiji Gakuin University

Hisatsugu Kitahara
Keio University

1. Introduction

30 years have passed since we sat in the introductory course on generative grammar taught by Professor Shigeo Tonoike. We are grateful to Professor Tonoike for introducing to us the core ideas of generative grammar. They were fascinating then, and remain so today. In this paper, we would like to revisit some of these core ideas from a current perspective, and discuss recent developments in minimalist inquiries.

2. Assumptions

The field of generative grammar is roughly 60 years old, and although there have been many changes over this time, a few things have remained constant. First, we recognize that at the core of language, there must be some generative procedure, a recursive combinatorial operation. Second, we look at language as a biological object (meaning we are interested in an actual linguistic system inside our brain, not some other system outside).

This biological object, namely the human language faculty, or Universal Grammar (UG), must have evolved (that is why we have it), and there are two factual assumptions about UG. One is that UG emerged suddenly, and the other is that UG has not changed since then (meaning there is no known difference regarding the human language faculty today). If so, whatever

---

* We would like to thank Noam Chomsky, Samuel D. Epstein, Roger Martin, Masayuki Oishi, Mamoru Saito, T. Daniel Seely, and Shigeo Tonoike for valuable comments and helpful discussion. All remaining errors are, of course, our own.

happened to yield UG must be very simple (see Chomsky (2013b) for relevant discussion).

Given this much, the thrust of theoretical work (apart from the minimal condition of trying to achieve some kind of descriptive adequacy for a variety of languages) is to simplify UG. There are two good reasons. One reason is just normal science, eliminating stipulations and seeking deeper explanations. But because of the biological context mentioned above, there is another reason. We want to simplify UG because every stipulated property of UG is a potential barrier to the development of an eventual account of the sudden emergence of UG.

If one decides to engage in such a research program for linguistic theory, he or she will face the following question. What would a simple linguistic system in the human brain look like? The strong minimalist thesis (SMT) takes the computational system for human language to be a "perfect system," meeting the interface conditions in a way that satisfies third factor principles (see among others, Chomsky (1995, 2005)).

Under SMT, the combinatorial operation of the generative procedure, which generates hierarchical structures, is expected to be very simple. Presumably, the simplest possible formulation is a set-formation device that takes α and β, and forms $\{\alpha, \beta\}$, which has come to be called Merge. So, the "perfect system" must have this simplest combinatorial operation (and ideally, only this one), and by hypothesis, we expect iterative (recursive) application of Merge to interact with a third factor principle of efficient computation, called Minimal Computation, a notion which (although not totally clear by any means) plausibly involves notions like "less search is better than more search."

To the extent that SMT holds, the "perfect system" is one that meets the interface conditions, and one that consists of just Merge (an operation) and Minimal Computation (a third factor principle). That is ideal, but the system is interesting only if we can get significant results out of it. So, we ask the following question. What results can we get from this third factor compliant, Merge-based system for human language?

With this question, let us consider phrase structure, which has been studied extensively. There were four important properties of phrase structures, discussed in early generative grammar: (i) composition, (ii) order, (iii) projection, and (iv) displacement. The first three belonged to the component of phrase structure grammar, and the last one to the component of transformational grammar.

In the 1980's, each component of grammar was radically simplified. X-bar theory was a step forward. It eliminated many stipulations, but it added a new stipulation that requires all structures to be endocentric (which we will discuss in detail below). As for the transformational component, only one rule survived: Move α—the simplest possible formulation of the transformational rule in the sense of Lasnik and Saito (1992).

In "Problems of Projection" (POP), Chomsky (2013a) has developed a quite different system. First, following earlier work (e.g. Chomsky (2005)), order arises only as part of the process of externalization; hence, it is ancillary to the core linguistic system. Second, composition and displacement fall within Merge. That is, Merge and Move are unified; they are two possible instantiations of the single operation Merge. Finally, projection (or labeling) is no longer stipulated in this system.

3. Merge and Labeling

In POP, Merge is defined as a set-formation device that takes two syntactic objects (SOs), α and β, and forms a new SO, a two-membered set $\{\alpha, \beta\}$.

(1) Merge $(\alpha, \beta) \rightarrow \{\alpha, \beta\}$

Merge, defined in this simplest form, applies freely as long as it conforms to third factor principles such as the inclusiveness condition which states that "no new objects are added in the course of computation apart from arrangements of lexical properties" (Chomsky (1995)), and the no-tampering condition (NTC), according to which "Merge of X and Y leaves the two SOs unchanged" (Chomsky (2008)).

Merge is free to apply or not apply. There are two possible applications of Merge. Suppose X is merged to Y (introducing the asymmetry only for expository purposes). Then, either X originates external to Y, call it External Merge (EM); or X originates internal to Y, call it Internal Merge (IM). Given NTC, IM yields two copies of X: one external to Y and the other within Y. There is no need to stipulate a rule of formation of copies (or remerge), and Chomsky's (1993) copy theory of movement follows from "just IM applying in the optimal way, satisfying NTC" (Chomsky (2007)). It would require stipulation to bar either type of application of Merge.

Notice, Merge does not encode a label. There is no labeled categorial node above α, and β. The categorial status of the set {α, β} is representationally unidentified. For a syntactic object to be interpreted, however, it is necessary to know what kind of object it is (e.g., nominal, verbal, etc.). Chomsky (2013a) takes labeling to be the process of finding the relevant information of {α, β} generated by Merge. He proposes that such labeling is "just minimal search, presumably appropriating a third factor principle, as in Agree and other operations."

To understand how the labeling analysis works, let us examine the following two cases, discussed in POP. Suppose SO = {H, XP}, H a head and XP not a head. Then minimal search will select H as the label, and the usual procedures of interpretation at the interface can proceed. For example, take SO = {v*, {V, α}}. Here, minimal search finds v* as the label of SO since v* is unambiguously identifiable.

Now suppose SO = {XP, YP}, neither XP nor YP a head. This time minimal search is ambiguous, finding both the head X of XP and the head Y of YP, and this ambiguity is not tolerated. For example, take SO = {{n, β}, {v*, {V, α}}}. Here, minimal search is ambiguous, finding n and v*; left as is, labeling fails and Full Interpretation is violated at the interface levels.

To resolve this labeling problem, Chomsky (2013a) suggests the following two strategies: (A) modify SO so that there is only one visible head, and (B) X and Y are identical in a relevant respect, providing the same label, which can be taken as the label of the SO. These two strategies work as follows.

First, consider SO = {{n, β}, {v*, {V, α}}} again. Suppose that T enters this derivation, and the v*P-internal subject {n, β} moves to Spec-T, yielding SO' = {{n, β}, {T, {{n, β}, {v*, {V, α}}}}} (the notion "Spec" is used here only for expository purposes). Chomsky (2013a) argues that this application of Merge renders the lower copy of {n, β} inside SO invisible to minimal search. He proposes that γ is taken to be in domain D if and only if every occurrence of γ is a term of D. Given this definition, after {n, β} moves to Spec-T, minimal search finds v* unambiguously and identifies it as the label of SO, because it is the only "visible" head inside SO.

Turning now to SO' = {{n, β}, {T, {{n, β}, {v*, {V, α}}}}}, notice this is again a potentially problematic structure for label-identification, but this time some prominent shared features appear on the two relevant heads n and T, namely phi features, and Chomsky (2013a) proposes that minimal search identifies the phi features shared by these two heads as the label of SO'.

4. Subject-Raising and Successive Cyclic *Wh*-movement

Chomsky (2013a) argues that the labeling analysis captures the core properties of movement without any additional stipulations. He presents three distinct cases to support the labeling analysis of movement.

First, he shows that the raising of the subject from a v*P-internal position follows without any reference to EPP (which has been taken by many to be a problematic principle). Consider (2a, b):

(2) a. [$_\gamma$ [the boy] [$_\beta$ T$_{phi}$ [$_\alpha$ *t* [v* [likes [the dog]]]]]]
 b. *[$_\beta$ T$_{phi}$ [$_\alpha$ [the boy] [v* [likes [the dog]]]]]

In (2a), the subject undergoes movement, and both the label of α and the label of γ are identifiable; they are v* and phi, respectively, whereas in (2b), the subject remains in situ, and the label of α is not identifiable (since there is no prominent shared feature on the two relevant heads in α). The "obligatory exit" of the subject from a v*P-internal position is thus accounted for by a labeling failure; there is no need to appeal to EPP.

Second, Chomsky argues that the fact that a *wh*-phrase cannot remain in an intermediate position follows without making any *ad hoc* stipulations. Consider (3a, b):

(3) a. [$_\gamma$ [in which Texas city] [$_\beta$ C$_Q$ [$_{TP}$ they think [$_\alpha$ *t* [C [$_{TP}$ the man was assassinated *t*]]]]]]
 b. *[$_\beta$ C$_Q$ [$_{TP}$ they think [$_\alpha$ [in which Texas city] [C [$_{TP}$ the man was assassinated *t*]]]]]

In (3a), the *wh*-phrase undergoes successive-cyclic movement, and both the label of α and the label of γ are identifiable; they are C and Q, respectively, whereas in (3b), the *wh*-phrase remains in the intermediate position, and the label of α is not identifiable (since there is no prominent shared feature on the two relevant heads in α). The "obligatory exit" of the *wh*-phrase from an intermediate position is thus accounted for by a labeling failure.

Third, Chomsky shows that the same reasoning can explain why a *wh*-phrase in "quiz show contexts," although it can remain in situ, cannot raise to an intermeidate position, as illustrated in (4a, b):

(4) a. they thought [$_\alpha$ C [the man was assassinated [in which Texas city]]]
    b. *they thought [$_\beta$ [in which Texas city] [$_\alpha$ C [$_{TP}$ the man was assassinated *t*]]]

In (4a), the *wh*-phrase remains in situ, and the label of α is identifiable as C. By contrast, in (4b), the *wh*-phrase raises to form the embedded clause β and remains there, and the label of β is not identifiable (since there is no prominent shared feature on the two relevant heads in β).

It is important to note that in each deviant case, minimal search fails to label SO, because SO is the form of {XP, YP}, and there is no prominent feature (phi, Q), shared by X and Y.

5. The "Last Resort" Character of A-movement

Epstein, Kitahara and Seely (2014) argue that the labeling analysis of intermediate landing sites can be naturally extended to the "last resort" character of A-movement (see also Goto (2013)). Consider (5a, b):

(5) a. There is likely [$_\alpha$ to be a man in the room]
    b. *There is likely [$_\beta$ [a man] [$_\alpha$ to be *t* in the room]]

In (5a), the noun phrase *[a man]* remains in situ, and the label of α is identifiable as T. By contrast, in (5b), the noun phrase *[a man]* raises to form the embedded clause β and remains there, and the label of β is not identifiable (since there is no prominent shared feature on the two relevant heads in β). There is no need to stipulate Merge-over-Move to account for the contrast in (5a, b).

Under unified Merge, we can strengthen this conclusion. If EM and IM are just two possible instantiations of one and the same operation, it is not clear whether Merge-over-Move is formulable in the first place. If it is not formulable, then data such as (6a, b) can be generated freely, as desired.

(6) a. There is a possibility [$_{CP}$ that [$_\alpha$ [a man] will be t in the room]]
   b. A possibility is [$_{CP}$ that [$_\alpha$ [there] will be a man in the room]]

In (6a), the noun phrase *[a man]* raises to form the embedded clause α, and the label of α is identifiable as phi. In (6b), the expletive is merged to form the embedded clause α, and the label of α is identifiable as phi. Notice, dispensing with Merge-over-Move, data such as (6a, b) can no longer be used to motivate notions such as lexical array (LA) or subarray (SA).

Summarizing, in previous work (e.g. Chomsky (2000)), data such as (5a, b) and (6a, b) motivated the postulation of (7a-d):

(7) a. Move as the composite operation that combines Merge and Agree
   b. lexical array LA
   c. lexical subarray SA (extracted from LA)
   d. Merge over Move (deducibly from (7a))

Epstein, Kitahara and Seely (2014) argue that (7a) loses its conceptual and empirical support, and (7b-d) lose their original empirical motivation. Data such as (5a, b) receive a principled explanation, one that is unified in a key respect with the corresponding cases of successive cyclic *wh*-movement, discussed in POP.

Note that the elimination of SA and LA has an important consequence. That is, unlike Chomsky (2000, 2001), we are no longer able to define a phase of the derivation as a syntactic object derived from an SA, extracted from LA. Epstein, Kitahara and Seely (2012, 2014) argue that there are no phases as such, but they demonstrate that strict cyclic derivation still follows (see also Chomsky (2013a)).

6. The Return of Unvalued Q: A New Analysis

As demonstrated above, the labeling analysis alone explains the "obligatory exit" of the subject from a v*P-internal position, the "obligatory exit" of the *wh*-phrase from an intermediate position, the "obligatory *wh*-in-situ" character of A'-movement in the quiz show context, and the "last resort" character of A-movement in the *expletive* construction. The labeling analysis also predicts that a category that undergoes movement ultimately lands where the two relevant heads—the head of a "moving" category and the head of a "hosting" category—share some prominent features. But what counts as a shared prominent feature?

In POP, Chomsky (2013a) discusses the two sets of shared prominent features: phi for subject N and predicate T, and Q for *wh*-expression and interrogative C_Q. But when extending the labeling analysis to copular constructions (e.g., XP copula {XP, YP}, see Moro (2000)), Chomsky (2013a) notes "[m]ere matching of most prominent features does not suffice" and suggests "[w]hat is required is not just matching but actual agreement, a stronger relation, which holds in the indirect question and subject-predicate examples but not small clauses."

Following this suggestion, we propose that valuation is involved in the label-identification of {XP, YP}; specifically, valuation must hold between the two relevant heads of {XP, YP}, namely the head X of XP and the head Y of YP. For the subject-predicate case, it is generally accepted that unvalued phi on T gets valued by inherently valued phi on N. But what about the *wh*-question case?

Important evidence that valuation holds between a *wh*-expression and an interrogative C_Q comes from Japanese. Saito (2013) argues that a *wh*-expression is an operator without specific quantificational force; its quantificational force gets valued by its associated particle, as illustrated in data such as (8a, b):

(8) a. Taroo-wa [[Hanako-ga   nani-o   tabeta] ka] sitteiru
        Taroo-Top Hanako-Nom what-Acc ate   Q   know
        'Taroo knows what Hanako ate.'
    b. [[Nani-o   tabeta hito]   mo]   manzokusita
        what-Acc ate   person also was.satsified
        'For every x, x a thing, the person that ate x was satsified.'

Saito proposes that in (8a), the disjunctive meaning of the particle *ka* turns the *wh*-expression *nani* 'what' into a *wh*-quantifier, whereas in (8b), the conjunctive meaning of *mo* turns the *wh*-expression *nani* 'what' into a universal quantifier (see also Tonoike (2014) for a different approach to the relation between a *wh*-expression and its associated particle).

If we extend Saito's analysis of (8a, b) to English data, we expect valuation to hold between a *wh*-expression and an interrogative C_Q here as well, i.e., unvalued Q(uantifier) on *wh*-expression gets valued by some inherent property on interrogative C_Q. If this analysis is tenable, we can characterize the so-called "shared prominent features" in terms of valuation. Under this proposal, labeling of subject-predicate involves valuation of phi between subject N and predicate T, and labeling of *wh*-question involves valuation of Q between *wh*-expression and interrogative C_Q.

The valuation-based analysis of labeling is consistent with Chomsky's (2013a) suggestion, but it goes against Chomsky's (2007, 2008) analysis of valuation, in which the unvalued features postulated to implement *wh*-movement (e.g., [uQ], [uWh], see Chomsky (2000)) are eliminated. Chomsky (2008) notes that "[w]e need not postulate an uninterpretable feature that induces movement, and can thus overcome a long-standing problem about crash at the lower phase levels in successive-cyclic movement." So, this long-standing problem comes back if we extend Saito's analysis of (8a, b) to English data.

Consider the sentence *which dog does the boy like*, in particular the relevant aspects of the v*P phase in (9a, b):

(9) a. [$_\alpha$ [the boy] [v* [like [which dog]]]]
 b. [$_\beta$ [which dog] [$_\alpha$ [the boy] [v* [likes [which dog]]]]]

In mapping (9a) to (9b), the *wh*-expression *[which dog]* moves out of the phase-head-complement (PHC) domain *[like [which dog]]*, and then this PHC domain gets transferred. The long-standing problem, noted by Chomsky (2008), is that this transferred domain contains the lower copy of the *wh*-expression bearing unvalued Q. If unvalued features are intolerable for the interface systems, then the presence of unvalued Q in the transferred domain should induce crash—a serious problem, contrary to fact.

One possible solution to this problem, we would like to suggest, is to extend Chomsky's (2013a) invisibility analysis to the PHC domain. Recall that the labeling analysis takes γ to be in domain D if and only if every occurrence of γ is a term of D. Given this definition, minimal search won't be able to find the *wh*-expression inside the PHC domain, because the higher occurrence of the *wh*-expression is not a term of the PHC domain. Thus, the lower copy of the *wh*-expression, whose head bears unvalued Q, does not pose a problem at this point of the derivation. This proposal entails that the interpretation of the *wh*-expression is in effect postponed until the highest copy of the *wh*-expression gets transferred.

We do not know how far this proposal will take us, but in our view, there are good reasons to believe more developments will come, with surprising results.

References

Chomsky, Noam (1993) "A Minimalist Program for Linguistic Theory," *The View from Building 20: Essays in Linguistics in Honor of Sylvain Bromberger*, ed. by Kenneth Hale and Samuel Jay Keyser, 1–52, MIT Press, Cambridge, MA. [Reprinted in *The Minimalist Program,* Noam Chomsky, 1995, 167–217, MIT Press, Cambridge, MA.]

Chomsky, Noam (1995) *The Minimalist Program,* MIT Press, Cambridge, MA.

Chomsky, Noam (2000) "Minimalist Inquiries: The Framework," *Step by Step: Essays on Minimalist Syntax in Honor of Howard Lasnik,* ed. by Roger Martin, David Michaels and Juan Uriagereka, 89–155, MIT Press, Cambridge, MA.

Chomsky, Noam (2001) "Derivation by Phase," *Ken Hale: A Life in Language,* ed. by Michael Kenstowicz, 1–52, MIT Press, Cambridge, MA.

Chomsky, Noam (2005) "Three Factors in Language Design," *Linguistic Inquiry* 36, 1–22.

Chomsky, Noam (2007) "Approaching UG from Below," *Interfaces + Recursion = Language?,* ed. by Uli Sauerland and Hans-Martin Gärtner, 1–29, Mouton de Gruyter, Berlin.

Chomsky, Noam (2008) "On Phases," *Foundational Issues in Linguistic Theory: Essays in Honor of Jean-Roger Vergnaud,* ed. by Robert Freidin, Carlos P. Otero and Maria Luisa Zubizarreta, 133–166, MIT Press, Cambridge, MA.

Chomsky, Noam (2013a) "Problems of Projection," *Lingua* 130, 33–49.

Chomsky, Noam (2013b) "What Kind of Creatures Are We? Lecture I: What Is Language?" *The Journal of Philosophy,* Volume CX, No. 12, 645–662. December 2013.

Epstein, Samuel D., Hisatsugu Kitahara and T. Daniel Seely (2012) "Structure Building That Can't Be!" *Ways of Structure Building,* ed. by Myriam Uribe-Etexebarria and Vidal Valmala, 253–270, Oxford University Press, Oxford.

Epstein, Samuel D., Hisatsugu Kitahara and T. Daniel Seely (2014) "Labeling by Minimal Search—Implications for Successive Cyclic A-movement and the Conception of the Postulate Phase," *Linguistic Inquiry* 45, 463-481.

Goto, Nobu (2013) "Labeling and Scrambling in Japanese," *Tohoku: Essays and Studies in English Language and Literature* 46, 39-73.

Lasnik, Howard, and Mamoru Saito (1992) *Move α: Conditions on Its Application and Output,* MIT Press, Cambrdige, MA.

Moro, Andrea (2000) *Dynamic Antisymmetry,* MIT Press, Cambrdige, MA.

Saito, Mamoru (2013) "Japanese Wh-Phrases as Unvalued Operators," unpublished manuscript, Nanzan University.

Tonoike, Shigeo (2014) "Gimonshi to Ka to Mo (Indeterminates and Their Associated Particles Ka and Mo)," unpublished manuscript, Aoyama Gakuin University.

A Note on Binding Phenomena in Null Operator Constructions

Hirohisa Kiguchi

Miyagi Gakuin Women's University

1. Introduction

Lasnik and Stowell (1991) point out that tough-constructions as well as parasitic gap constructions are free from WCO-effects, both of which have been assumed to involve null operator movement to the CP or the PP.

(1) a. The Yankees$_1$ are [$_{AP}$ tough [$_{CP}$ Op$_1$ [$_{IP}$ to beat t_1]]]
 b. Who$_1$ did you stay with t_1 [$_{PP}$ Op$_1$ before his$_1$ wife had spoken to t_1]?

The sentences in (1) have a typical WCO-configuration (2); the variable which the movement of a null operator generates, is the antecedent of the bound pronoun on its left.

(2) *Op$_1$ .... Pronoun$_1$ ... Variable$_1$

Nevertheless this construction is free from WCO-effects, allowing the intended bound variable reading. Lasnik and Stowell (1991) call weakest crossover these phenomena in which the constructions with null operators are free from WCO-effects.

2. Lasnik and Stowell's (1991) Analysis

On analyzing weakest crossover phenomena, Lasnik and Stowell (1991) attempt to relate these phenomena to epithets. They observe that epithets void WCO-effects.

(3) a. All of Bill's$_1$ friends say his$_1$ mother loves the guy$_1$.

b. Some tenant in every apartment building$_1$ has asked its$_1$ owner to repair the place$_1$.

They analyze that the trace in weakest crossover constructions is not a variable but a phonologically null epithet. They claim that this is why WCO-effects fail to show up in the case that the binder of the pronoun and the trace is a null operator. Furthermore this approach solves a problem with Principle C effects in parasitic gap constructions.

(4) a. *Who$_1$ t_1 gossiped about you despite your having vouched for pg$_1$.
 b. *Which man$_1$ t_1 looked at you after Mary had spoken to pg$_1$.

In the sentences above, the wh-trace in the matrix clause is the subject, which c-commands a parasitic gap in the adjunct. This configuration is formally equivalent to SCO (strong crossover)-effects. A typical SCO configuration is one where a trace left by A'-movement is A-bound by a coreferential NP as in (5). (e.g. Lasnik and Stowell (1991), Safir (1996))

(5) a. *Who$_1$ did you say he$_1$ made you visit t_1.
 b. *Whoever$_1$ John$_1$ said Mary saw t_1 is sick.

Chomsky (1981, 1986) treats SCO-effects as a violation of Principle C. Variables, i.e. the traces of A'-movement in a Case-position (e.g. Chomsky (1986), Safir (1996)) are regarded as r-expressions in terms of Principle C, which prevents an r-expression from being A-bound. Rather, parasitic gaps should be treated as an r-expression. Recall that unlike a trace of a wh-phrase or a quantified NP, a trace of a null operator does not induce WCO-effects, which motivates Lasnik and Stowell (1991) to posit a null epithet in place of a variable for a trace in weakest crossover configurations. Furthermore, Lasnik and Stowell (1991) show that epithets are subject to Principle C.

(6) a. *John$_1$ denied that the man$_1$ was too busy to see me.
 b. *Bill$_1$ thinks that Mary told me to visit the guy$_1$.

However, one simple but serious problem remains; if a null epithet is sensitive to Principle C, then why can tough-constructions exist without being subject to Principle C?

(7) a. The Yankees$_1$ are tough to beat t_1
    b. Which team$_1$ t_1 is tough to beat t_1?

In tough-constructions like (7), the trace would be a null epithet, which is sensitive to Principle C. Since the subject appears to bind it, these constructions should always be ruled out. In face of this puzzle, Chomsky (1986) assumes that a null operator blocks Principle C from being applied when it is in between the name and its variable, defining Principle C as below:

(8) Principle C:
    (a) An r-expression must be A-free in the domain of its operator.
    (b) An r-expression must be A-free.
    The first applies to variables, the second to non variables.

However, this assumption only generates another puzzle. Given Principle C as formulated in (8), it becomes mysterious why parasitic gaps are sensitive to principle C, as we have seen above.

Lasnik and Stowell (1991) argue that tough-constructions are exceptionally invisible to Principle C. Noticing that the null operator must be A-bound in tough-constructions, in order for the rule of Predication to identify the content of a null operator, they suggest the principle below:

(9) If an A-position X A-binds a category Y as a result of Predication, then Condition C does not apply to A-binding of Y by X.

This principle is construction-specific. Obviously, it is desirable to exclude any specific principle, which is designed merely to distinguish tough-constructions from parasitic gap constructions in terms of Principle C.

3. Hornstein's (2001) Null Operator-Constructions without a Null Operator

At this point, we have the following tasks: (i) To explain why WCO-effects are void in tough-constructions and parasitic gap constructions without introducing a novel item. (ii) To explain why Principle C arises in parasitic gap constructions but not in tough-constructions without an ad hoc principle.

Hornstein (2001) proposes an analysis of these null operator-constructions without positing the presence of a null operator. Nunes (2001, 2004) analyzes parasitic gap constructions with sideward movement, instead of null operator movement. Nunes (2001, 2004) argues that if movement is the interaction of the distinct operations, Copy and Merge as Chomsky (1995) assumes, then sideward movement is theoretically possible and empirically motivated. The derivation of parasitic gap constructions with Nunes' analysis, which Hornsetin (2001) adopts, is illustrated below.

(10) Nunes (2001, 2004) and Hornstein's (2001) parasitic gaps
    a. Which book did you read t before Fred reviewed t?
    b. [Fred T [reviewed which book]]
    c. [before [which book$_1$ [Fred T [reviewed which book$_1$]]]]
    d. [read [which book$_1$]] [before [which book$_1$ [Fred T [reviewed which book$_1$]]]]]
    e. [[you [read which book$_1$]] [before which book$_1$ Fred T reviewed which book$_1$]]
    f. Which book$_1$ [you T [[you [read which book$_1$]] [before[which book$_1$ [Fred T [reviewed which book$_1$]]]]]
    g. Which book$_1$ did [you T [[~~you~~ [read ~~which book~~$_1$]] [before [~~which book~~$_1$ [Fred T [reviewed ~~which book~~$_1$]]]]]

In (10b), the adjunct clause is built up. The wh-element moves to Spec CP within the adjunct in (10c). In (10d), the wh-elememt sideward moves to the post verbal position to satisfy the selectional/thematic properties of *read*. The main clause and the adjunct merge in (10e). Then the wh-element moves to Spec CP in (10f). As a result, the uninterpretable wh-feature on the wh-element and the uniterpretable Q-feature on the matrix C are checked. Finally, in (10g), the deletion of copies takes place. Given this derivation with sideward movement, parasitic gap constructions can be generated without null operator movement.

Hornstein (2001) extends the analysis with sideward movement to other null operator constructions, one of which is tough-constructions. Given that the infinitival clauses in tough-constructions are adjuncts, Hornstein (2001) analyzes tough-constructions as follows.

(11) a. Moby Dick is easy to read t.
     b. [to read [Moby Dick]]

c. [$_{CP}$ Moby Dick$_1$ [to read Moby Dick$_1$]]]
  d. [[Moby Dick$_1$] easy] [$_{CP}$ Moby Dick$_1$ [to read Moby Dick$_1$]]]
  e. [Moby Dick$_1$ is [[Moby Dick$_1$] easy]] [$_{CP}$ Moby Dick$_1$ [to read Moby Dick$_1$]]]
  f. [$_{IP/IP}$ [Moby Dick$_1$ is [[Moby Dick$_1$] easy]] [$_{CP}$ Moby Dick$_1$ [to read Moby Dick$_1$]]]]
  g. [$_{IP/IP}$ [Moby Dick$_1$ is [[~~Moby Dick~~$_1$] easy]] [$_{CP}$ ~~Moby Dick~~$_1$ [to read ~~Moby Dick~~$_1$]]]]

In (11b), the adjunct CP is built up. In (11c), *Moby Dick* moves to Spec CP within the adjunct. In (11d), *Moby Dick* sideward moves to the specifier of adjective phrase or a small clause. In (11e), *Moby Dick* moves to the specifier of IP in order to check Nominative Case. In (11f), the two sub trees merge. In (11g), the deletion of copies takes place.

Given Hornstein's analysis, weakest crossover sentences possess the final status of the derivation as shown in (12b) for the case of parasitic gap constructions and (13b) for the case of tough-constructions.

(12) a. Who$_1$ did you stay with t_1 before his$_1$ wife had spoken to t_1?
   b. Who$_1$ [you T [[you [stay with who$_1$]] [before [$_{CP}$ who$_1$ [his$_1$ wife T [had spoken to who$_1$]]]]
(13) a. Who$_1$ t_1 is easy for us to get his$_1$ mother to talk to t_1?
   b. Who$_1$ [[who$_1$ is [who$_1$ easy]] [$_{CP}$ who$_1$ for his$_1$ mother [to talk to who$_1$]]]

Given these analyses of parasitic gaps and tough-constructions, weakest crossover sentences have the trace/copy of *who* in the specifier of the embedded CP (indicated as who$_1$), namely an intermediate wh-trace, instead of a null operator.

(14) ... who$_1$ ... Pronoun$_1$ ... Variable$_1$ ...

If this trace/copy of *who* in the null operator position is an intermediate wh-trace, it should delete at LF as Stowell (1981), Lasnik and Saito (1992), Chomsky (1995) among others argue. As one way of implementation, Hornstein (2001) proposes a minimalist approach to delete immediate traces/copies at LF. The intermediate trace in Hornstein's (2001) derivation of parasitic gap constructions and tough-constructions, i.e. the problematic wh-element in (12b) and (13b) should disappear given the SCA (=Scope Correspondence Axiom) introduced by Hornstein (2001: 85). Assuming that there exists an algorithm for assigning expressions in an LF phrase marker a scope order, Hornstein (2001) argues that if LCA (Linear Corresponding Axiom) forces all copies but one to be deleted at PF as Nunes (2001, 2004) claims, the same thing must happen at the LF side. The SCA forces at most one copy of an expression to survive at the C-I interface to allow expressions to have fixed and coherent scopes. That is, copies unnecessary for scopal relations are deleted at LF. Assuming that an expression E cannot scope over itself (=irreflexivity) and if α scopes over β and β scopes over γ, then α scopes over γ (=transitivity), he argues that the expression cannot be assigned a scope as its multiple copies survive at C-I interface because these multiple copies cause the violation of irreflexivity and transitivity.

In weakest crossover sentences in (12, 13), the operation, which the SCA requires erases the copies of *who* except the one in the matrix CP which checks off all of its uninterpretable features, at LF. But the Case marked copies, which are left by A'-movement, serves as variables (=x) in (15, 16). This means that the copy, *who*, which sits in Spec CP in the adjunct, i.e. the null operator position, has to be deleted at LF. If this copy and the one in the matrix CP both survived at LF, a copy of *who* would take scope over itself, a violation of irrreflexivity.

(15) Parasitic gaps
Who [you T [$_{vP/vP}$ [you [stay with x]] [before [who [his wife T [had spoken to x]]]]

(16) Tough-constructions
Who [[x is [who easy]] [CP who for us [to get his mother to talk to x]]]

Given the SCA, the only copies of a wh-element that survive at LF are the ones which enter into operator-variable relation. The rests of copies are deleted.

Then, consider the representations in (15) and (16). Now we have constructions similar to the one in which A-movement obviates WCO-effects:

(17) a. Everyone$_1$ seemed to his$_1$ mother to t_1 be charming?
    b. Every boy$_1$ is expected by his teacher to be encouraged t_1 by the teacher.

At LF, these sentences are represented as (18a, b) where quantifier raising generates the configuration in which a variable is in between the operator and the bound pronoun, thereby obviating WCO-effects.

(18) a. [$_{IP}$ everyone$_1$ [$_{IP}$ t_1 seemed to his$_1$ mother to t_1 be charming]]
    b. [$_{IP}$ every boy$_1$ [$_{IP}$ t_1 is expected by his$_1$ mother to be encouraged t_1 by the teacher]]
(19) Op$_1$ ... Variable$_1$ ... Pronoun$_1$ ...

Notice that we have a variable between the operator and the pronoun in weakest crossover configurations. The traces in (20) are variables, because they are copies in a Case position generated by A'-movement. Hence they are not deleted at LF.

(20) a. [$_{CP}$ Who$_1$ did [$_{IP}$ you stay with t_1 before his$_1$ wife had spoken to t_1]]
    b. [$_{CP}$ Who$_1$ [$_{IP}$ t_1 is easy for us to get his$_1$ mother to talk to t_1]]
(21) Op$_1$ ... Variable$_1$ ... Pronoun$_1$ ...

That is, given Hornstein's (2001) analysis, weakest crossover phenomena can be reduced to another instance of the obviation of WCO-effects by (sideward) A-movement, together with the SCA.

5. No Principle C in Tough-Constructions

Another remaining task is to explain why tough-constructions are free from Principle C effects whereas parasitic gaps are not. My suggestion is that where an adjunct is attached makes a difference. Hornstein (2001) claims that in tough-constructions, the adjunct is attached to IP.

(22)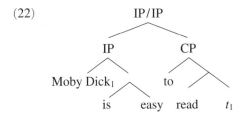

The reading of a tough-construction like that in (23a) whose derivation is illustrated in (23b), is roughly as follows: As far as one's reading Moby Dick is concerned, Moby Dick is easy.

(23) a. Moby Dick$_1$ is easy to read t_1.
 b. [$_{IP/IP}$ [$_{IP}$ Moby Dick is easy] [$_{CP}$ Moby Dick to read Moby Dick]]

According to Hornstein (2001), "the adjunct acts adverbially." It is a scene setter like the adverb. The copies of *Moby Dick* inside the adjunct, as in the derivation shown in (23b), form a species of topic structure that describes in what way ease is being evaluated; "it's with respect to reading it that Moby Dick is easy, not necessarily with respect to memorizing it." Given this type of analysis, there is no c-command relation between the subject of the tough-constructions and the variable. Hence, principle C should not be invoked.

On the other hand, if the adjunct PP is adjoined to a verb phrase in parasitic gap constructions as usually assumed, we expect parasitic gaps to be sensitive to Principle C as the wh-trace in the matrix subject binds the parasitic gap.

(24) *Which book$_1$ t_1 was read by you before Fred reviewed pg$_1$

(25)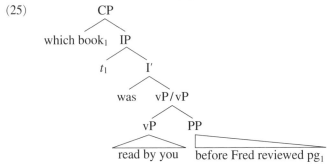

6. On Licensing Bound Pronoun in Weakest Crossover Constructions

The important difference between the attested cases of obviation of WCO-effects like raising constructions and passive constructions on the one hand, and weakest crossover constructions on the other, is that the a variable at issue should not c-command the pronoun in weakest crossover. If the position of the variable were high enough to c-command the pronoun, it would c-command the trace in the adjunct only to induce Principle C. However, as is well known, the licensing of bound pronouns does not require c-command. Consider the following examples:

(26) a. Everybody$_1$'s mother kissed him$_1$.
 b. Elaine gave a picture of no comedian$_1$ to his$_1$ mother.

In (26a, b) sentences the bound pronoun is licensed by its binder, which is further embedded in the element which c-commands it. Thus if the adjunct in tough-constructions is adjoined to IP as Hornstein (2001) assumes, the hierarchical relation between the antecedent and the bound pronoun is similar to the one in (26a).

(27) Nobody$_1$ should be easy to persuade his$_1$ mother to vouch for.

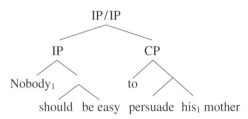

(28) Everybody$_1$'s mother kissed him$_1$.

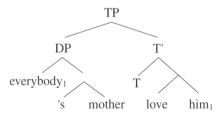

Thus, there is no serious tension between bound pronoun licensing and Principle C in terms of c-command. In short, given Hornstein's (2001) alternative analysis of tough-constructions and parasitic gap constructions with sideward movement, weakest crossover is explained without adding a novelty like null epithets or any construction specific principle concerning Principle C as in Lasnik and Stowell's (1991) original solution for these phenomena.

7. Conclusion

To sum up, given Hornstein's (2001) approach, we reach the following conclusions: (i) Null operators can be dispensed with. (ii) Null epithets can be dispensed with; and weakest crossover is reduced to the fact that A-movement cancels WCO-effects. (iii) Ad hoc exception to Principle C can be dispensed with. Principle C can be simply stated as below:

(29) Principle C: An r-expression must be A-free.

References

Chomsky, Noam (1981) *Lecture of Government and Binding*, Foris, Dordrecht.
Chomsky, Noam (1986) *Knowledge of Language: Its Nature, Origin and Use*, Praeger, New York.
Chomsky, Noam (1995) *The Minimalist Program*, MIT Press, Cambridge, MA.
Hornstein, Norbert (2001) *Move! A Minimalist Theory of Construal,* Blackwell, Oxford.
Lasnik, Howard and Tim Stowell (1991) "Weakest Crossover," *Linguistic Inquiry* 22, 687-720.
Lasnik, Howard and Mamoru Saito (1992) *Move α: Conditions on Its Application and Output*, MIT Press, Cambridge, MA.
Nunes, Jairo (2001) "Sideward Movement," *Linguistic Inquiry* 32, 303-344.
Nunes, Jairo (2004) *Linearization of Chains and Sideward Movement*, MIT Press, Cambridge, MA.
Safir, Ken (1996) "Derivation, Representation, and Resumption: The Domain of Weak Crossover," *Linguistic Inquiry* 27, 313-339.
Stowell, Tim (1981) *The Origins of Phrase Structure*, Doctoral dissertation, MIT.

言語の語順と思考の順序*
―インターフェイス条件の実証的研究にむけて―

小泉　政利

東北大学

1. はじめに

　文を理解（聞く，読む）したり産出（話す，書く）したりする際に，動詞（V）の位置に関わらず主語（S）が目的語（O）に先行する語順（SO 語順＝ SOV, SVO, VSO）のほうが，目的語が主語に先行する語順（OS 語順＝ OSV, OVS, VOS）よりも母語話者に好まれる傾向（SO 語順選好）があることが，日本語やフィンランド語など多くの言語について報告されている．SO 語順はなぜ好まれるのであろうか？　思考の様式と関係しているのだろうか？　そもそも SO 語順選好はどの言語にもみられる普遍的な性質なのだろうか？　著者らの研究グループは，科学研究費補助金を得て過去 5 年間このような問いに関連する研究プロジェクトを実施してきた．本稿ではその成果の一部を概観する．紙幅の都合で説明が簡略的過ぎる部分もあるが，興味をもたれた方は参考文献リストにある原著論文にあたって頂ければ幸いである．

2. SO 語順選好

　SO 語順選好は言語の様々な側面にみられる．本稿では，その中から主に次の 3 つの側面について考察する．

　(1)　**基本語順における SO 語順選好**：　世界の言語の大多数が SO 語順の

＊ 本研究は日本学術振興会から，基盤研究（S）「OS 型言語の文処理メカニズムに関するフィールド言語認知脳科学的研究」ならびに挑戦的萌芽研究「「思考の順序」と「言語の語順」との関係を解明する新たな研究手法の開発」の 2 件の科学研究費補助金の助成を受けて行われたものです．本研究を行うにあたり，外池滋生先生には大変お世話になりました．30 年間の御学恩と合わせて，ここに感謝の意を表します．

いずれかを基本語順に持っている.
(2) **文産出における SO 語順選好**: 語順が比較的自由な個別言語において，SO 語順のほうが OS 語順よりも使用頻度が高い.
(3) **文理解における SO 語順選好**: 語順が比較的自由な個別言語において，SO 語順のほうが OS 語順よりも文理解の際の処理負荷が低い.

現在，地球上で7千以上の言語が使われているという．それらを各言語の基本語順によって分類するとおおよそ次のような割合になる：SOV 41%, SVO 35%, VSO 6.9%, OSV 0.3%, OVS 0.8%, VOS 1.8% (Dryer (2011))．主語が目的語に先行する SO 語順を基本語順にもつ SO 言語の割合が，その逆の OS 語順を基本語順にもつ OS 言語の割合よりも圧倒的に高い．これは，「グリーンバーグの普遍性1」と呼ばれる，言語の普遍性に関する最も有名な一般化である (Greenberg (1966))．本稿ではこれを，**基本語順における SO 語順選好**と呼ぶ (1)．基本語順における SO 語順選好は，音声言語だけでなく手話言語にもみられる．

このように大多数の言語は SO 語順のいずれかを基本語順にしているが，どの言語においても（程度の違いこそあれ）基本語順以外の語順も文法的に許される．例えば，日本語では SOV 語順が基本語順であるが OSV 語順の文も使われている．また，フィンランド語では，基本語順である SVO だけでなく，S と V と O の論理的に可能な6通りの配列順序全てが文法的である．

しかし，文法的な語順がすべて同程度に使用されるわけではない．先行研究で報告されている個別言語の語順毎の産出頻度のデータを見ると，SO 語順のほうが OS 語順よりも使用頻度が高い．例えば，日本語では SOV 語順の文が OSV 語順の文よりもはるかに多く産出されている (SOV 97.3% vs. OSV 2.8%, Koizumi et al. (2014))．また，フィンランド語では SVO 語順の文が他動詞文全体の約72%を占め，2番目に多い OVS 語順の文 (17%) の数倍にのぼる (Kaiser and Trueswell (2004))．このように個々の言語において SO 語順の使用頻度が高い傾向を**文産出における SO 語順選好**と呼ぼう (2)．

SO 語順選好は文理解の側面にもみられる．これまでの文理解に関する研究によると，どの言語でも SO 語順のほうが OS 語順よりも文処理の負荷が低い．例えば，日本語では SOV 語順の文のほうが，対応する OSV 語順の文よりも，より速く正確に理解され，惹起される脳活動も低い (Tamaoka et al. (2005), Kim et al.(2009))．フィンランド語でも，SVO 語順のほうが OVS 語順よりも処理負荷が低い (Kaiser and Trueswell (2004))．このように SO

語順のほうが OS 語順よりも処理負荷が低い傾向を**文理解における SO 語順選好**と呼ぶ (3).

次節以降で，これら 3 種類の SO 語順選好について，それらを生み出す要因ならびに相互の関係について考察する．

3. 基本語順

上で述べたように，世界の諸言語の基本語順として SO 語順のほうが OS 語順よりも圧倒的に好まれている．なかでも SOV 語順を基本語順にもつ言語が一番多い．どうしてこのような著しい偏りがあるのであろうか？ この問いに関連する興味深い研究がある．ゴールデンメドウら (Goldin-Meadow et al. (2008)) は，4 つの異なる言語（中国語，英語，スペイン語，トルコ語）の話者に，出来事を言語で表現する課題と，ジェスチャーで表現する課題を行ってもらった．その結果，言語課題では各話者の母語の基本語順が一番多く用いられた（中国語，英語，スペイン語は SVO，トルコ語は SOV）．ところが，ジェスチャー課題ではどの言語の話者も大多数のジェスチャーを（言語で言えば他動詞能動文の SOV 語順に相当する）「行為者・対象・行為」の順序で行った．この結果から，ゴールデンメドウらは，人間が言語を用いずに出来事を把握する場合の自然な順序は母語の語順によらず「行為者・対象・行為」であり，新しい言語が生まれる場合にはこの思考の自然な順序に対応する SOV 語順が基本語順に採用されるのだ，と提案している．

4. 思考の順序

それでは，なぜ，非言語的思考において「行為者・対象」の順序が好まれるのであろうか？ これに関しては，大きく 2 つの可能性が考えられる．一つは，観点 (perspective) や概念接近可能性 (conceptual accessibility) のような普遍的な認知特性の影響である（＝普遍認知説）(MacWhinney (1977), Bock and Warren (1985))．概念接近可能性というのは，記憶から概念情報を取り出す際の取り出しやすさのことである．概念の種類によって概念接近可能性が異なり，たとえば無生物（「ボート」など）よりも有生物（「少年」など）のほうが概念接近可能性が高い．このような普遍認知的な要因が働いて，対象よりも行為者のほうがよりはやく記憶から取り出されて，それが非言語的思考の「行為者・対象」という順序を生み出しているという可能性がある．もう一つ考え

られるのは,「行為者・対象」という思考の順序が言語の基本語順を反映しているという可能性である（＝個別文法説）．Goldin-Meadow et al. (2008) などのジェスチャー研究で対象にされているのは（動詞の位置は異なるが）すべて SO 言語の話者である．SO 言語の話者が非言語的思考においても言語の基本語順に合わせて「行為者・対象」という順序を用いたとしても不思議ではない（cf. 話すための思考 "Thinking for Speaking", Slobin (1996)）．これら 2 つの仮説は,SO 言語の話者に対しては,非言語的思考で「行為者・対象」順序を好むという同じ予測をする．しかし,OS 言語の話者に対しては予測が異なる．普遍認知説が正しければ,OS 言語の話者も主に「行為者・対象」順序を用いるはずだが,個別文法説が正しければ,OS 言語の話者は「対象・行為者」順序をより頻繁に用いるはずである．

そこでこれらの予測を検証するために,VOS を統語的基本語順にもつカクチケル語（グアテマラで話されているマヤ諸語の 1 つ）の母語話者を対象にジェスチャー産出実験を行った (Sakai et al. (2012))．この実験では,実験参加者に図 1 のような絵を呈示し,そこに描かれている出来事を言葉を使わずにジェスチャーだけで表現してもらった．その結果,8 割以上のジェスチャーが「行為者・対象」順序であり,カクチケル語の統語的基本語順 VOS に対応する「行為・対象・行為者」順序のジェスチャーはほとんど産出されなかった．この結果は普遍認知説の予測と一致し,人間が非言語的に事象を把握する際には母語の語順に関わらず普遍的に「行為者・対象」順序が好まれることを示唆している．

図 1: ジェスチャー産出実験で呈示された絵の例

5. 文産出

それでは,「行為者・対象」順序で把握された事象をカクチケル語のような

OS言語で表現する場合には，どのような語順が用いられるのであろうか？第2節で述べたように，これまで多くの言語でSO語順のほうがOS語順よりも産出頻度が高いことが明らかになっている．しかし，これまでの研究は全てSO言語を対象に行われてきた．OS言語であるカクチケル語の文産出においてもSO語順のほうが好まれるのであろうか？これに関しても思考の順序の場合と同様に，大きく2つの可能性が考えられる．一つは，観点や概念接近可能性のような普遍的な認知特性を反映した思考の順序が主に文産出における語順の選択を決定するという可能性である（＝普遍認知説）．普遍認知説が正しければ，OS言語であるカクチケル語でもSO語順のほうがOS語順よりも使用頻度が高いはずである．もう一つの可能性は，その言語の基本語順が文産出の際に最も好まれるという可能性である（＝個別文法説）．個別文法説は，カクチケル語ではOS語順の1つであるVOS語順の文が産出頻度が一番高いと予測する．

どちらの説が正しいのか（より正確には，どちらの要因がより強く働いているのか）を確かめるためにカクチケル語の文産出実験を行った（Kubo et al. (2012)）．この実験では，上記の図1のような絵をカクチケル語母語話者に見てもらい，絵に描かれている出来事を言葉（カクチケル語）で表現してもらった．その結果，産出された文の68％がSVO語順であり，VOS語順の文は22％にすぎなかった．これは，文を産出する際の語順には，統語的基本語順よりも思考の順序のほうがより強く影響を与えることを示唆しており，普遍認知説が支持された．

6. 文理解

このようにOS言語であるカクチケル語においてもSO語順（の1つであるSVO語順）のほうがOS語順（の1つであり統語的基本語順であるVOS語順）よりも産出頻度が高い．それでは，カクチケル語の文理解においてはどちらの語順が好まれるのであろうか．普遍的な認知特性の影響でSVO語順のほうが処理負荷が低い（＝普遍認知説）のであろうか？それとも，統語的基本語順であるVOS語順のほうが処理負荷が低い（＝個別文法説）のであろうか？

この疑問に答えるために，カクチケル語話者を対象に文理解実験を実施した（Koizumi et al. (2014)）．この実験では，実験参加者に（4）のような文法的な他動詞文を聞いてもらい，文の内容が意味的に自然かどうかを判断し，自然

な場合はYESのボタンを,不自然な場合はNOのボタンを押す,という文正誤判断課題を用いた.文のはじめからボタンを押すまでの時間を反応時間として測定し,文処理負荷の指標とした.

(4) a. *Xuchöy　　　　　　ri　chäj　　ri　ajanel*　　　　[VOS]
　　CP-Abs3sg-Erg3sg-cut the pine tree the carpenter
　　'The carpenter cut the pine tree.'
　b. *Xuchöy　　　　　　ri　ajanel　　ri　chäj*　　　　[VSO]
　　CP-Abs3sg-Erg3sg-cut the carpenter the pine tree
　c. *Ri　ajanel　xuchöy　　　　　　ri　chäj*　　　　　[SVO]
　　the carpenter CP-Abs3sg-Erg3sg-cut the pine tree

その結果,意味的に自然な文に対する反応時間はVOS語順の文が他の2つの語順の文よりも統計的に有意に短く,VSOとSVOの間には有意差がなかった.これはカクチケル語では統語的基本語順であるVOS語順が最も処理負荷が低い語順であることを示しており,個別文法説が支持された.つまり,先行研究で報告されているSO語順選好は普遍的なものではなく,文理解の際の処理負荷には観点や概念接近可能性のような普遍認知的要因よりも個別言語の統語的要因がより大きな影響を与えることが示唆された.

Koizumi et al. (2014) で用いられた刺激文は,主語に人間,目的語に無生物をもつ,いわゆる非可逆文であるが,主語も目的語も有生物(人間や動物)である可逆文の場合にも同様の結果になることがその後の研究で確認された (Kiyama et al. (2013)).また,脳波を用いた研究では,VOS語順に対してSVO語順のときに第三文節 (VOSのSとSVOのO) でP600と呼ばれる成分が観察された (Yasunaga et al. (submitted)).これはSVO語順が統語的移動を含む派生語順であり処理負荷が高いとする分析と整合的である.

7. 理解と産出

心理言語学の文献では一般に次の3要因が文理解の際の処理負荷に影響を与える主たる要因であると考えられている:統語的複雑さ,文脈,使用頻度.これらの観点からみて,統語的基本語順は一般に派生語順よりも処理負荷が低い.まず,各個別言語の統語的基本語順は,定義上,その言語で文法的な他の語順よりも単純な統語構造に対応しており,それゆえ作業記憶への負荷が小さく理解しやすい (Gibson (2000), Marantz (2005), Tamaoka et al. (2005)).

次に，統語的基本語順は様々な文脈で使われるが，派生語順は特定の文脈を要求するため，文脈の要件が満たされない場合には処理負荷が高くなる（Kaiser and Trueswell (2004)）．最後に，統語的基本語順は派生語順よりも産出頻度が高い傾向がある．他の条件が同じならば，使用頻度の高い構文ほどより速く正確に処理される．そのため，統語的基本語順は派生語順よりも処理が容易になる（Trueswell, Tanenhaus and Kello (1993)）．

例えば，日本語では，統語的基本語順である SOV のほうが派生語順である OSV よりも単純な統語構造に対応し，文脈の制限が緩く，使用頻度が高い．すなわち，日本語では，これら 3 要因がすべて SOV 語順の文を OSV 語順の文よりも理解しやすくすることに貢献している（Koizumi et al. (2014)）．他の SO 言語でも同様のことがなりたつ．

それでは OS 言語であるカクチケル語ではどうであろうか？ カクチケル語では VOS が統語的基本語順であり，他の語順よりも単純な統語構造に対応している．また，VOS が中立的な文脈で使えるのに対して，SVO は主語が主題や焦点として解釈されやすく使用文脈に制限がある（García Matzar and Rodríguez Guaján (1997)）．これら 2 つの要因は VOS を SVO よりも理解しやすくする方向に働いている．一方，使用頻度は VOS よりも SVO のほうが数倍高く，SVO の処理負荷を下げる方向に働いている．おそらく，カクチケル語では，統語と文脈の影響のほうが使用頻度の影響よりも大きいため，VOS のほうが SVO よりも文理解の際の処理負荷が低くなっていると思われる．

8. 基底の語順

本稿ではここまで，音声（手話の場合は手指の運動など）に反映された表面的な語順に着目して語順選好について考察してきた．従来の生成文法理論では文法の統語部門内に語順を決定する仕組み（例えば主要部パラメータ）が存在すると考えられていた．この立場をとるとすれば，本稿でいう「語順」を統語部門内での「語順」と同一視して問題ない．一方，ミニマリスト・プログラムと呼ばれる最近の生成文法の研究では，狭い意味での言語機能（faculty of language – narrow sense, FLN）の中では統語構造を構成する要素間の線形順序は決まっておらず階層関係だけが規定されているとする作業仮説が採用されることが多い．その場合は，FLN 内の階層関係と音声化された言語表現の線形順序とを対応付ける何らかの仕組み（例えば Kayne (1994) の Linear Correspondence Axiom）が必要になる．

統語構造に線形順序を認めるか認めないかに関わらず，ミニマリスト・プログラムでいう外的併合だけで作られた構造（つまり内的併合を含まない「基底の構造」）には厳しい制約が課せられており，音声化する際にSVOに対応する構造しか許されないとする説（e.g. Kayne (1994)）やSOVに対応する表象しか生成されないとする説（e.g. Fukui and Takano (1998)）が提案されている．SVOにしてもSOVにしてもSO語順であることに変わりはない．だとすると，「基底の構造」にもある意味でSO語順選好が見られることになる．もし仮にFLNの外的併合がSO語順に対応する構造しか生成しない性質をもつとしたら，それはなぜであろうか？ チョムスキーは一連の論文で「FLNは概念・意図システムや知覚・運動システムなどの運用システムによって課せられたインターフェイス条件（interface conditions）の最適解である可能性（Strong Minimalist Thesis, SMT）」を追求している（e.g. Chomsky (2013: 38)）．ここで，この見通しに従い，本稿でのこれまでの議論を踏まえて次の仮説を提案したい．すなわち，(i) 非言語的思考における「行為者・対象」選好はFLNに課されるインターフェイス条件のひとつである．(ii) このインターフェイス条件を満たすためにFLNは外的併合でSO語順に対応する構造を生成する性質を持つにいたった．すなわち，FLNの「SO語順選好」は，インターフェイス条件（特に概念・意図システムの行為者・対象順序選好）への最適解（の一部）である．

9. おわりに

　人間が非言語的に事象を把握する際には，観点や概念接近可能性などの要因により，「行為者」の処理が「対象」の処理に先行する．文産出においては，非言語的思考が逐次的に言語処理の入力になるので，SO言語だけでなくOS言語においても「行為者・対象」順序に対応するSO語順の使用頻度が高くなる．いっぽう，文理解の際の語順による処理負荷の違いは主に統語表象の複雑さに起因するため，統語的基本語順の文がそれ以外の語順の文よりも処理負荷が低くなる．そのため，SO言語では，「産出頻度の高い語順」と「理解の際の処理負荷が低い語順」がともにSO語順になり，一致する．しかし，OS言語ではこの両者が一致せず，処理負荷が高いSO語順が高頻度で用いられる．もしFLNの外的併合がSO語順に対応する構造しか生成しないとしたら，それは非言語的思考における行為者・対象順序選好がインターフェイス条件としてFLNに課せられた結果かもしれない．

参考文献

Bock, J. Kathryn and Richard K. Warren (1985) "Conceptual Accessibility and Syntactic Structure in Sentence Formulation," *Cognition* 21, 47-67.

Chomsky, Noam (2013) "Problems of Projection," *Lingua* 130, 33-49.

Dryer, Matthew S. (2011) "Order of Subject, Object and Verb," *The World Atlas of Language Structures Online*, ed. by Matthew S. Dryer and Martin Haspelmath, Chapter 81, Max Planck Digital Library, Munich.

Fukui, Naoki and Yuji Takano (1998) "Symmetry in Syntax: Merge and Demerge," *Journal of East Asian Linguistics* 7, 27-86.

García Matzar, Lolmay Pedro and Pakal B'alam José Obispo Rodríguez Guaján (1997) *Rukemik ri Kaqchikel chi': Gramática kaqchikel*, Cholsamaj, Guatemala.

Gibson, Edward (2000) "Dependency Locality Theory: A Distance-Based Theory of Linguistic Complexity," *Image, Language, Brain: Papers from the First Mind Articulation Project Symposium*, ed. by Alec Marantz, Yasushi Miyashita and Wayne O' Neil, 95-126, MIT Press, Cambridge, MA.

Goldin-Meadow, Susan, Wing Chee So, Asli Özyürek and Carolyn Mylander (2008) "The Natural Order of Events: How Speakers of Different Languages Represent Events Nonverbally," *Proceedings of the National Academy of Sciences of the United States of America* 105, 9163-9168.

Greenberg, Joseph H. (1966) "Some Universals of Language with Particular Reference to the Order of Meaningful Elements," *Universals of Language*, ed. by Joseph H. Greenberg, 73-113, MIT Press, Cambridge, MA.

Kaiser, Elsi and John C. Trueswell (2004) "The Role of Discourse Context in the Processing of a Flexible Word-Order Language," *Cognition* 94, 113-147.

Kayne, Richard S. (1994) *The Antisymmetry of Syntax*, MIT Press, Cambridge, MA.

Kim, jungho, Masatoshi, Koizumi, Naho Ikuta, Yuichiro Fukumitsu, Naoki Kimura, Kazumi Iwata, Jobu Watanabe, Satoru Yokoyama, Shigeru Sato, Kaoru Horie and Ryuta Kawashima (2009) "Scrambling effects on the processing of Japanese sentences: An fMRI study," *Journal of Neurolinguistics* 22, 151-166.

Kiyama, Sachiko, Katsuo Tamaoka, Jungho Kim and Masatoshi Koizumi (2013) "Effect of Animacy on Word Order Processing in Kaqchikel Maya," *Open Journal of Modern Linguistics* 3, 203-207.

Koizumi, Masatoshi, Yoshiho Yasugi, Katsuo Tamaoka, Sachiko Kiyama, Jungho Kim, Juan Esteban Ajsivinac Sian and Pedro Oscar García Matzar (2014) "On the (Non-)Universality of the Preference for Subject-Object Word Order in Sentence Comprehension: A Sentence Processing Study in Kaqchikel Maya," *Language* 90, 722-736.

Kudo, Takuya, Hajime Ono, Mikihiro Tanaka, Masatoshi Koizumi and Hiromu Sakai

(2012) "How Does Animacy Affect Word Order in a VOS Language?" 25th Annual CUNY Conference on Human Sentence Processing.

MacWhinney, Brian (1977) "Starting Points," *Language* 53, 152–168.

Marantz, Alec (2005) "Generative Linguistics within the Cognitive Neuroscience of Language," *The Linguistic Review* 22, 429–445.

Sakai, Hiromu, Takuya Kubo, Hajime Ono, Manami Sato and Masatoshi Koizumi (2012) "Does Word Order Influence Non-Verbal Event Description by Speakers of OS Language?" 34th Annual Meeting of the Cognitive Science Society.

Slobin, Dan I. (1996) "From "Thought and Language" to "Thinking for Speaking"," *Rethinking Linguistic Relativity*, ed. by John J. Gumperz and Stephen C. Levinson, 70–96, Cambridge University Press, Cambridge.

Tamaoka, Katsuo, Hiromu Sakai, Jun-ichiro Kawahara, Yayoi Miyaoka, Hyunjung Lim and Masatoshi Koizumi (2005) "Priority Information Used for the Processing of Japanese Sentences: Thematic Roles, Case Particles or Grammatical Functions?" *Journal of Psycholinguistic Research* 34, 273–324.

Trueswell, John C., Michael K. Tanenhaus and Christopher Kello (1993) "Verb-Specific Constraints in Sentence Processing: Separating Effects of Lexical Preference from Garden-Paths," *Journal of Experimental Psychology: Learning, Memory and Cognition* 19, 528–553.

Yasunaga, Daichi, Masataka Yano, Yoshiho Yasugi and Masatoshi Koizumi (submitted) "Is the subject-before-object preference universal? An ERP study in the Kaqchikel Mayan language."

Syntax for Semantics: An Assessment

Eric McCready

Aoyama Gakuin University

1. Introduction and Anecdote

The reason for choosing the present topic for my contribution to this volume is, in some sense, not fully academic, but instead partly personal. Before getting into the meat of my topic, therefore, I would like to indicate what motivated this choice, and simultaneously introduce the theme of this essay.

At Aoyama Gakuin University, we have several yearly faculty parties. These are pleasant occasions at which the faculty members can socialize over drinks and food. They are a nice contribution to the collegial atmosphere of the department, but, like all such parties, they come with a danger: given the presence of alcohol, it is always possible that the attendees drink too much and embarrass themselves. Fortunately, to my knowledge, this has never happened, but it cannot be denied that as the parties progress the talk flows more freely, and topics that might not otherwise have been broached enter the conversation.

Neither Shigeo Tonoike nor myself were exceptions to this generalization. One topic that has often come up between us is the relationship between syntax and semantics. After a few drinks, Professor Tonoike (hereafter referred to as ST) would often say to me (facetiously, of course—I think) that there is no real need for semantics: the field could just as well get by with syntax. Of course I was outraged, every time (also somewhat facetiously). How could anyone be so unreasonable? Or so I would think, unavoidably given my own theoretical predilections. But over the course of these years I have spent quite a bit of time thinking about this idea, which I will call the "syntax as semantics" view. It can be thought of in different ways, strong and weak, each of which requires different formal realizations. The remainder of this paper is devoted to exploring these possible views, their formal counterparts, and their corresponding problems; at the end of the paper, I will indicate which of them I take ST to have had in mind in our conversations.

2. The Strong View

On the strong conception of syntax as semantics, there is nothing in the grammar that can be characterized as "semantics" at all: there just is no meaning component at all. The role of the meaning component is played by the syntax.

Exactly what this amounts to depends on what we allow in the syntax. At its most bare, we could think of the syntax as consisting of nothing but tree structures, plus the words or lexical elements that are their leaves; a slightly more liberal conception would allow for category labels on the nonterminal nodes. There are many other possible variations, some of which I will turn to in a moment; first, though, I want to consider whether the bare tree structures just described (with or without node labels) could serve as a substitute for the semantic component of the grammar. I should also note before going on that I won't consider syntactic theories like LFG which introduce substantial semantic information at any level of representation in the syntax (through e.g. the PRED attribute in LFG f-structures: Bresnan (2002)), but restrict attention to more traditional tree structures.

Before being able to address this question, it is necessary to clarify what the semantic component is supposed to do. Without knowing its intended function, it is impossible to say how adequate tree structures can be in fulfilling it. The usual line here is that the semantic component should model our knowledge of linguistic meaning. As is well known, it is not easy to find theory-independent abstract characterizations of meanings and knowledge of them: but a theory of semantics should, at least, do the following: it should (i) assign truth conditions to all sentences of a language and (ii) allow a characterization of the semantic relations that hold between sentences of a language (e.g. entailments, contradictions, etc.). Here, of course, I am making the usual assumption that linguistic meanings are adequately characterized by truth conditions, and also restricting attention to those strings that can be characterized as grammatical (thus the statement about "sentences"). A third criterion is, perhaps, optional, since it is more of a methodological principle, but I will assume it: (iii) the theory ought to be compositional in the sense of Frege, so that the meanings of complex expressions depend on the meanings of the expressions which compose it, and on how they are combined (Janssen (1997)).

Can these two criteria be fulfilled by a bare theory of phrase structure? It might seem obvious that it can't. How could truth conditions, after all, be characterized by trees? But perhaps this is too fast. If we start with the second criterion, about semantic relations, maybe there is a way to use trees to analyze meanings after all.

Let's consider a way to characterize entailments strictly through the use of trees. We can start with the most basic entailment, that stemming from identity: A entails A, by definition. So we might say that any tree T entails an identical tree T. We would also like to say that any tree T entails any T' which is identical to it except for semantically irrelevant bits such as the inclusion of semantically contentless intermediate nodes: for instance, a tree labeled NP with daughter N should look identical to a tree of the form NP with daughter N' and further daughter N from the perspective of the semantic component (cf. the "nonbranching nodes" rule of Heim and Kratzer (1998)). We can define a notion of equivalence class for trees along these lines, though I won't make it explicit here, and say that a tree T entails all T' such that T' is in the equivalence class of trees with respect to T.

The notion of entailment here is a bit opaque, for we cannot make any reference to meaning. Since we are working with the strong view, there is no meaning component, and all of semantics must be carried out through trees and trees only. With respect to entailment, then, what is needed is a proof-theoretic approach (e.g. Troelstra and Schwichtenberg (2000)). If our resources consist only of trees, we need to define a notion of proof according to which it is possible to determine which trees can be derived from other trees.

Presumably this can be done, but it won't be particularly straightforward, especially since the notion of derivation in question can't be stated independently of the leaves of the trees. Ultimately, just as the traditional semantic approaches would have it, the lexical content available makes a big difference in the semantic relations between sentences. To see this, consider as simple a case as a futurate transitive sentence with an definite object "the N" and whether such a sentence (or the equivalence class of trees associated with that sentence) entails an existential sentence of the form "There is a NP". (Of course, the above sentences should be supplemented with tree structures, which I omit here as I can make my point without them.) Plainly, the answer is neither positive nor negative for the general case: "John will kick the ball" entails "There is a ball", while "John will build the house" does not entail that there is a (physically realized) house (as is well known: see von Stechow (2001), McCready (2006)). The lesson is that entailment can't be defined without reference to the terminal elements, i.e. the lexical items themselves. But this is almost a reductio: it means that a new proof rule is needed for every terminal element. In what sense could the resulting system be viewed as explanatory?

Perhaps the situation is not quite so bad. One partial fix would be to define classes of terminal elements which behave in certain ways in proofs. Still, one has the feeling that explanatory power is being lost. On a semantic approach, it is possible to find commonalities to the meaning of terms which naturally separates them into classes, but, here, the classification is purely external, since from the perspective of syntax we only have similar looking terminal elements. We thus have to stipulate classes of lexical items on the basis of semantic behavior, but without making genuine reference to semantics. All this looks pretty bad.

Could enriching the syntactic representations improve the situation? The answer probably depends on the exact nature of the enrichment. It would be possible in principle to add purely semantic features to the trees: for instance, the tree associated with "is not a dog" (I won't give a specific structure here as my interest here is not in syntactic issues) could be augmented with a "negation feature" which would not be present in the tree for "is a dog"; this feature in turn could be viewed as percolating up from the minimal subtree associated with the negation (where the notion of minimal subtree is defined in the obvious way). This move would allow a (relatively) clean and straightforward way to define many of the kinds of semantic relations needed, and further would be more or less compositional, for all features would be derived from some term or construction. Still, I think it goes against the spirit of the project: since we want the functions of semantics to be carried out by syntax, introducing semantic features looks like just a way to put meanings in through the back door, so to speak.

I will therefore limit my attention to more purely syntactic features, basically just the phi-features assumed by Minimalism (e.g. Chomsky (1995)) and also appearing in somewhat different guise in lexicalist theories like LFG or HPSG (Bresnan (2002), Pollard and Sag (1994)). However, it doesn't take much effort to see that such features won't help much for current purposes. Phi-features contain information about such semantically relevant things as number and gender, and about things like case which are not usually directly useful to semantics; but the problem currently at issue is how to guarantee the availability of inferences about semantic relations in the general case, and phi-features certainly cannot do that.

All this said, there is a prior problem which I have been avoiding. Consider the first criterion I adduced above for a theory which wants to cover semantic data, that it must account for truth conditions. Obviously a purely syntactic theory has no way to to do that. There is no mapping between uninterpreted trees and truth conditions: trees only represent structure, and truth conditions require reference to content. If one wants to uphold the traditional formal semantic program, on which (knowledge of) meanings are represented by (knowledge of) truth conditions, then the strong view already fails; but, as we have seen, even if one is willing to give up the traditional picture, the strong view already has other serious problems in trying to account for the core data of sentential semantic relations (not to mention lexical semantics, which it obviously cannot even address). I conclude that the strong view is pretty much a non-starter. But, fortunately, we have another option available.

3. The Weak View

The strong view amounts to the claim that all semantic aspects of language only involve uninterpreted trees. The weak view is derived from allowing trees to be interpreted. Still, though, the relevant interpretation is not to result in an additional level of semantic *representation*. As with the strong view, the only things living in the semantics are tree structures. In essence, then, we have a kind of direct interpretation of trees, which are now viewed as the only available representation language. Such a view is actually quite natural given that many linguists working in the tradition of generative grammar have proposed the existence of a syntactic level of logical form called LF (potentially distinct from surface structure). One can then simply take LF to be the relevant semantic representation and not derive any further representation from it.

How does such a view (in the abstract) stack up against the criteria given in the previous section? It is plainly compositional, for all interpretation is done on the basis of the leaves and the structures which are built on them; further, unlike the strong view, it is possible to derive truth conditions for sentences. If lexical items are given some sort of interpretation, and we have the resource of tree structures with the corresponding underlying notion of composition, then sentence-level truth conditions should be available. Of course, this is not fully trivial: we are restricted here by the lack of a distinct level of logical form, meaning that it is somewhat unclear what the relevant notion of composition should look like. Still, we can directly define rules which assign interpretations to different sorts of subtrees; for interpretation itself, we are left with possibilities like direct model-theoretic interpretation (without the mediation of an underlying logic) or even a kind of direct "world-checking" in the Heim and Kratzer style. Finally, it is obviously possible to derive semantic relations in this theory, given that the trees are indeed interpreted; entailment (etc.) can simply be defined at the model-theoretic level, or whatever means is used to provide an interpretation for the trees. Thus, all the criteria I proposed are satisfied.

The weak view, then, appears to be feasible. It only remains to ask how useful it is. Let me now return to Shigeo Tonoike. After several conversations with him about this subject, ST's position on these matters became clear to me (to the best of my recollection; as I said above, most of our conversations on this particular topic took place at departmental parties, where I too had probably had more than one glass of beer). He appears to support a version of the weak view. Of course, the fact that he is a syntactician probably influences his desire to eliminate purely semantic levels of representation. And indeed, from the perspective of (many of) the problems in semantics which interest pure syntacticians such as issues of scope, it is natural to think that using something like LF in the syntactic sense is sufficient to represent meaning relations. But should we choose to support this weak view? Let me give my opinion as a semanticist.

The weak view is nice in the sense that one level of representation has been eliminated, that intermediate to syntax and model-theoretic interpretation. It is, however, quite restrictive: for instance, another criterion that many researchers wish their semantic theories to satisfy is that they should make available a simple and economical notion of inference. In this weak view, inference must be defined either over trees or in the model theory (or whatever). The former won't work for much the same reasons I discussed above in the context of the strong view; the latter does work, as I already mentioned, but could be inconvenient in some cases where one might want a proof-theoretic concept of inference. Of course, given that lexical objects can be interpreted at a model-theoretic level, it is of course possible to define syntactic 'rules of proof' over trees much like what we find for proof systems in logic, at least given that we allow ourselves to make use of equivalence classes of trees or possibly simplified representations or 'normal forms'. In any case, though, the weak view allows for the possibility of a theoretically adequate semantics.

It still remains to ask whether it is worth supporting. The utility of this view seems to depend on how much importance one assigns to the existence of a logical language mediating between the structure and the model theory. I personally find such representational levels to be quite useful: consider, for instance, the work that has been done in discourse representation theory and related frameworks (Kamp and Reyle (1993)) in the analysis of semantic phenomena that cross sentential boundaries. While such work is certainly feasible at the purely model-theoretic level, it is definitely convenient to have a way to represent it; if we were restricted to syntax in talking about the interpretation, it would be much more difficult to conduct analysis at this level. The same holds for many other phenomena. I therefore conclude that even the weak view is too strong.

4. Conclusion

This paper has sketched several versions of the "syntax-as-semantics" thesis. I showed that these versions could be separated into essentially two types: a strong view, where semantics just is syntax and nothing more, and a weak view, where the only semantic representation language allowed is syntax itself. The first view was shown to be untenable, and the second I argued to be unnecessarily strict from the perspective of the whole range of semantic analysis. Of course, the reason for this conclusion is likely just my own theoretical predilections: as a semanticist, I see no special reason to give primacy to syntactic representations, and feel that the added complexity of analysis required by limiting representation to syntactic forms outweighs any possible gains in theoretical simplicity from doing so.

References

Bresnan, Joan (2002) *Lexical-Functional Syntax*, Blackwell, Oxford.
Chomsky, Noam (1995) *The Minimalist Program*, MIT Press, Cambridge, MA.
Heim, Irene and Angelika Kratzer (1998) *Semantics in Generative Grammar*, Blackwell, Oxford.
Janssen, T. M. V. (1997) "Compositionality," *Handbook of Logic and Language*, ed. by Johan van Benthem and Alice ter Meulen, 417–474, Elsevier, Amsterdam.
Kamp, Hans and Uwe Reyle (1993) *From Discourse to Logic*, Kluwer, Dordrecht.
McCready, Eric (2006) "Created Objects, Coherence and Anaphora," *Journal of Semantics* 23:3, 251–279.
Pollard, Carl and Ivan Sag (1994) *Head-Driven Phrase Structure Grammar*, University of Chicago Press, Chicago.
von Stechow, Arnim (2001) "Temporally Opaque Arguments in Verbs of Creation," *Semantic Interfaces: Reference, Anaphora and Aspect*, ed. by Carlo Cecchetto, Gennaro Chierchia and Maria Teresa Guasti, 278–319, CSLI Publications, Stanford.
Troelstra, A. S. and H. Schwichtenberg (2000) *Basic Proof Theory*, Cambridge University Press, Cambridge.

「腑に落ちない」の二重性が'腑に落ちる'今日*

森川　正博
名古屋外国語大学名誉教授

1. はじめに

　否定辞「ない」が添加された述語には，その構造が特定しにくいものがある．その例として，イディオムの動詞慣用句「腑に落ちない」がある．

　(1)　私には彼の説明が<u>腑に落ちない</u>．

「ない」は形容詞と同じ活用をする．その「ない」を含む「腑に落ちない」は，動詞慣用句「腑に落ちる」と「ない」が統語で併合したものなのか，全体で形容詞として働く語彙項目なのか，あるいはその両方が関わるものなのかに関しては議論の余地がある．

　当該のイディオムが統語で形成されるとする見解は，岸本 (2010) が否定の作用域に関する議論を用いて出している．[1] 本稿では語彙部門も視野に入れた見解を取る．具体的には，語彙部門で形成された動詞も含めて，広く認識を表すことができる動詞／動詞慣用句（"認識動詞／認識動詞慣用句"）と「ない」の連鎖を考察対象として，その構造を明らかにする．そうすることで，語彙と統語の両部門が関わった二重構造の連鎖があることを示す．

2. 認識動詞と「ない」の連鎖

2.1. 観察

　認識動詞は，否定辞「ない」との連鎖に関して，2種類に分類できる．その

＊ 本稿執筆の段階で，有益なコメントをいただいた高野泰邦氏（長崎大学），泉谷双蔵氏（東京医科歯科大学）に謝意を表したい．なお本稿は，森川 (2014) を縮小，加筆したものである．
[1] 岸本 (2010) の論評は，紙幅の都合上，森川 (2014) を見られたい．

ことは，述語としての動詞や形容詞の統語上の特徴を示す岸本 (2010) の3つのテストに，「ない」を一律に組み込むことで示すことができる．まず，動詞と形容詞とを分別するテスト①，②とその例文を見てみよう．[2]

 テスト①： 「ほしい（と思う）」によって導かれる補文には，形容詞節は許されないが動詞節は許される．

 テスト②： 否定される述語が動詞の場合にのみ，「ないでいる」という否定形を作ることができる．[3]

(2) a. 私は [あの人 {に／が} 来て] ほしいと思う．[4]
 b. *私は [あの人 {に／が} かわいくて] ほしいと思う．
 c. 私は [あの人 {に／? が} その料理を食べて] ほしいと思っている．

(3) a. 太郎はりんごを食べないでいる．
 b. *太郎が {おもしろくないでいる／おもしろくなくている}．

(2a) の補文内の主語をマークする助詞は，岸本 (2010) は「が」を用いているが，やや自然さに欠ける．特に，動詞が他動詞の場合，(2c) のようにその文の容認度が少し低下するように思われるため，本稿では助詞「に」を用いていく（注4も参照のこと）．テスト①，②は，節内の述語が (2a), (3a) の動詞「来る／食べる」を許し，(2b), (3b) の形容詞「かわいい／おもしろい」を許さないことを示す．

(2a), (3a) では行為を表す動詞を用いたが，(4a, b) で示す状態（変化）を表す動詞「開ける／開く／始める」や，(5a-c) で示す認識動詞「諒とする／察する／聞き分ける」を用いることもできる．

 (4) a. 私は [{あの人にドアを開けて／ドアが開いて}] ほしいと思っている．

---

 [2] テスト②に関しては，岸本は益岡・田窪 (1989) を採用している．
 [3] 「ないでいる」形の主語の意味役割は，「*風が吹かないでいる．」のように，動作主以外は許されない．
 [4] (2a) の文の「あの人」は，「ほしい」補文内の主語位置で助詞「が」にマークされている．一方，それが「に」でマークされた場合は，(i) のように述語「ほしい」の取る項の位置にあるが，補文内にある空主語 PRO を介して，意味上，補文内の主語とも解釈されると考えられる．
 (i) [私は [あの人に$_i$ [PRO$_i$ 来て] ほしい]]
なお，(ii) のような表現が自然であることから，助詞「が」を含む (2a) の文が非文法的とは言えない．
 (ii) [高梨選手が出てほしい] 冬季オリンピック

b. 太郎はまだスピーチを始めないでいる．
(5) a. 私は [彼の意向を諒として] ほしい．
b. 太郎は私の気持ちを察しないでいる．
c. 私は [太郎によく聞き分けて] ほしいと思っている．

また，テスト①において補文内に否定辞「ない」を含むと，(6a, b) で示すように行為・状態（変化）を表す動詞は許されるが，認識動詞は許されるものと許されないものが出てくる．(7)，(8) の例文を見られたい．

(6) a. 私は [あの人に {ここで本を読まないで／すぐにドアを開けないで}] ほしいと思っている．
b. 私は [ドアが風で開かないで] ほしいと思っている．
(7) a. 私は 花子に彼の意向を諒としないでほしいと思った．
b. そんなことまで悟らないでほしい．
(8) a. *私は花子にその提案に頷けないでほしいと思った．
b. *そんなに簡単に聞き分けないでほしい．

(7) で示したように，「諒とする」「悟る」などの認識動詞は，「ほしい」の補文内で否定辞「ない」と共起できる．この種の動詞を "認識動詞 A 類" と呼ぶことにする．一方 (8) で示したように，「頷ける」「聞き分ける」などの動詞は，「ほしい」の補文内で否定辞「ない」と共起できない．この種の動詞を "認識動詞 B 類" と呼ぶことにする．ちなみに，後者の動詞は，「頷く＋れる（可能）」「聞く＋分ける」のように，語彙部門で結合した動詞である．そのことは，影山 (1993) が用いた統語操作の 1 つである受身化が，例えば「聞き分ける」に適用できないこと（「*聞かれ分ける」）から明らかである．

テスト②においては，(9a-d) で示すように，認識動詞 A 類，B 類，共に「ないでいる」の否定形を作ることができる．

(9) a. 花子は彼の意向を諒としないでいる．（A 類）
b. 太郎は私の気持ちを察しないでいる．（A 類）
c. 花子はその提案に頷けないでいる．（B 類）
d. 太郎は説明を聞いた後でも，割り切れないでいた．（B 類）

最後に，形容詞に関するテスト③とその例文 (10a, b) を見てみよう．

テスト③： 「思う」によって導かれる小節には，形容詞節しか現れない．

(10) a. *ジョンは [この本を売れなく] 思った.[5]
　　 b. 　ジョンは [この本をおもしろく] 思った. 　　　　（岸本 (2010: 35)）
(10′) b. 　ジョンは [この本をおもしろくなく] 思った.

(10a) で示したように，「思う」の取る小節が，動詞に否定辞「ない」が後接する動詞節であれば，文は非文法的となる．一方，その小節が (10b) のように形容詞節であれば，文は文法的となる．もちろん，(10′b) で示したように，形容詞節には「ない」が付くこともできる．注意を要するのは，小節が形容詞節の場合，否定辞「ない」の有無に左右されず文は文法的となる点である．
　ここで，この「思う」が取る小節内に，(7)，(8) で用いた認識動詞に「ない」を付けた述語を入れると，その文法性の判断に違いが生じる．

(11) a. *花子が彼の意向を諒としなく思っている.
　　 b. *花子がそんなことまで悟らなく思っている.
(12) a. 　私はその提案に今も頷けなく思っている.
　　 b. 　私はその子供を聞き分けなく思った.

「思う」の小節内には，(11) で示したように「認識動詞 A 類 +「ない」」は許されないが，(12) で示したように「認識動詞 B 類 +「ない」」は許される．
　以上をまとめると，表 (14) のようになる．なお，(13) に認識動詞の例を示したが，B 類に分類される動詞の数はそう多くないと思われる.[6]

(13)　認識動詞：
　　　A 類：　諒とする，悟る，察する，分かる，受け取る，取る，納得する，知る，読む，読める，掴む，心得る，飲み込む，消化する，把握する，理解する，会得する，承知する，了解する，…
　　　B 類：　割り切れる，頷ける，聞き分ける，解せる，煮え切る，…[7]

---

[5] 時制を持たない小節内では，主語は助詞「が」ではなく「を」でマークされる (Takezawa (1987) 参照).

[6] (13) の認識動詞において，一見，可能の「られ」が B 類と関わるように見える．しかし，A 類に「読める」があることから（例文 (i) 参照），動詞と「(ら) れ」の連鎖が必ずしも B 類に分類されるとは限らない．
　(i) *太郎は [花子の気持ちを読めなく] 思っている.

[7] 非認識動詞でも B 類と同じ振る舞いをする動詞の数は少ないと思われる．
　(i) a. *私は彼が対戦相手を侮れないでほしい.
　　　b. 　私はいまだ彼を侮れないでいる.

(14)　表（述語「認識動詞＋「ない」」の文法性）

「ない」を含む述語＼認識動詞	A 類	B 類
述語 I：「V+ないでほしい」（cf. テスト①）	◯	×
述語 II：「V+ないでいる」（テスト②）	◯	◯
述語 III：「V+なく思う」（cf. テスト③）	×	◯

2.2. 考察と提案

表（14）から次の3点のことが言える．まず第1に，認識動詞A類と「ない」の連鎖は，述語IとIIから動詞性を保持しており，また述語IIIから形容詞節を構成するものではないことが明らかである．

第2に，認識動詞B類と「ない」の連鎖は，述語IIから形容詞ではなく動詞の特徴を持つと言える（例（9c-d））．しかし，述語Iから，なぜ認識動詞B類が「ないでほしい」形を取れないのかという疑問が生じる（例文（8））．一般的に，「ほしい」補文内では，「*太郎に歩けてほしい」のように可能動詞「（ら）れ」が添加されることはない（泉谷氏（私信）による）．従って，(8a)は排除される．また，B類の認識動詞の用法に限っては，「「ほしい」の補文では肯定形のみ生起できる」という意味上の制約が存在すると仮定することで，上述の疑問は解消する．その制約を設ける根拠は，2点ある．まず第1に，(8′b)のように述語「ほしい」に否定辞「ない」を付けることによって補文内の肯定形が許され，(8b)と同じ解釈が得られることにある．

(8′) b.　そんなに簡単に聞き分けてほしくない．

第2の根拠は，(15a)で示すように否定辞「ない」を常に取る「煮え切る」が，(15b)の「ほしい」の補文内では許されないという事実にある．

(15) a.　太郎の態度が｛煮え切らなかった／*煮え切った｝．
　　 b.＊私は [太郎の態度が煮え切らないで] ほしいと思った．

表（14）に関して言える第3番目の点は，認識動詞B類と「ない」の連鎖は述語IIから動詞性を保持するが（例文（9c-d）），述語IIIから動詞性を保持していない（例文（12））という矛盾である．この矛盾を解明するために，一般

---

　　c.　私は彼を侮れなく思っている．

的に動詞は統語部門で併合されても，B 類の認識動詞に限っては語彙部門でも否定辞「ない」と結合できて形容詞（"派生形容詞"）が派生すると，本稿では提案する．言い換えると，「B 類の認識動詞＋「ない」」が統語で併合した結果の連鎖と，語彙項目としての連鎖とが同一表現となる．具体的には，(9c-d) の「頷けない」「割り切れない」は「頷ける」「割り切れる」が統語で「ない」と併合したものである一方，(12a-b) の「頷けなく」「聞き分けなく」は語彙部門で形成された派生形容詞である．また，否定形で用いる「煮え切る」についても，(16a, b) で示すように，同じことが言える．

(16) a. 彼は（いまだに）態度が煮え切らないでいる．（下線部＝動詞）
　　 b. 私は [太郎の態度を煮え切らなく] 思った．（下線部＝派生形容詞）

なお，認識動詞に限らず普通の動詞に「ない」が付くという語彙部門での現象は，特異なことではない．Kishimoto (2008: 399) は，「やりきれない」「くだらない」「つまらない」「動じない」など，多くの例をリストにしている．

以上，本節では述語「認識動詞＋「ない」」の特徴を考察した結果，動詞性を維持する認識動詞 A 類と，動詞性と形容詞性を併せ持った B 類とに分けた．そして，認識動詞 B 類と「ない」の連鎖は語彙部門と統語部門，それぞれで異なる構造を持つと提案することで，その述語構造の二重性を説明した．

3. 認識動詞慣用句＋「ない」

前節で考察した述語「認識動詞＋「ない」」に見られる現象は，興味深いことに，イディオムにも見つけることができる．まず，認識動詞 A 類と動詞性において同じ振る舞いをする次の認識動詞慣用句を含む例文を見てみよう．

(17) a. 私は太郎がなんだかんだ言って辻褄を合わさないでほしいと思った．
　　 b. その人はあえて辻褄を合わさないでいた．
　　 c. *私はあの人を無理に辻褄を合わさなく思った．
(18) a. 私は太郎がそのお粗末な説明には合点がいかないでほしいと思う．
　　 b. 太郎はまだその説明に合点がいかないでいる．
　　 c. *太郎はその説明に合点がいかなく思った．

「辻褄を合わさない」「合点がいかない」は (17a-c)，(18a-c) で示したように動詞性を保持しているため，否定辞「ない」は統語で併合されたものとみなせ

る．このタイプのイディオムを"認識動詞慣用句 A 類"と呼ぶことにする．

次に，動詞性・形容詞性に関する表（14）の認識動詞 B 類と照合しながら，「ほしい」補文として「メアリーに彼の言うことが腑に落ちない」を持つ例文（19a）を見てみよう．その「メアリーに」は補文の要素であるが，もし述語「ほしい」の取る項とみなしても，この文は非文法的である（注4も参照）．また，現代日本語では，（20）が示すように，「腑に落ちる」には否定辞「ない」が一般的に後接する．[8]

(19) a. *私は [メアリーに彼の言うことが腑に落ちないで] ほしいと思う．
    b. 　彼は（いまだに）その発言が腑に落ちないでいる．
    c.(?)メアリーは [彼の行動を腑に落ちなく] 思った．

(岸本 (2010: 35-36))

(20) *私には，彼の説明が腑に落ちた．

(19a) の否定辞「ない」を (21) のように述語「ほしい」に付けると，文は文法的となり，認識動詞 B 類と同じ意味制約（2.2 節参照）が作用する．

(21) 　私は [メアリーに彼の言うことが腑に落ちて] ほしくないと思う．

また例文（19a-c）から，「腑に落ちる」は B 類の認識動詞と同じパターンを示しているので，"認識動詞慣用句 B 類"と呼ぶことにする．

そうすると，「腑に落ちない」には，2つの構造があると予測できる．その1つは，上述の意味制約と，「ないでいる」形が作れる（例文（19b））ことから，動詞性を保持した動詞慣用句「腑に落ちる」が，統語で「ない」と併合した構造である．もう1つの「腑に落ちない」の構造は，形容詞として機能するという例文（19c）の事実から統語上，単一のものである．つまり，認識動詞慣用句「腑に落ちる」が，語彙部門で「ない」と結合し，派生形容詞となったものである．この構造上の二重性はまさに，前節で提案したことである．よって，

---

[8] 「腑に落ちない」の肯定形は，明治，昭和の時代では用いられている．
　　…（略）…明治時代の徳冨蘆花の小説「思出の記」の中で肯定形で使われていた場面がありました．[…四ヶ月經てば，學校の様子も大略腑に落ちて，僕も先づ關西學院生となり了（すま）したのであつた．]…（略）
　　　「「腑（ふ）に落ちる」とは？－トクする日本語──NHK アナウンスルーム」
　　　www.nhk.or.jp/kininaru-blog/130237.html
　　「大西質店へ行けと言った意味などが──．ちた」〈織田作之助・わが町〉
　　　Goo 辞書 (dictionary.goo.ne.jp)

(19a) の非文法性についても,「ほしい」が取る補文内では認識動詞慣用句「腑に落ちる」が否定形を取れないことと,「腑に落ちない」が派生形容詞であること, という異なる2つの説明が必要とされる.

なお, 否定形で用いられる認識動詞慣用句B類の「腑に落ちる」は, (21) で見たように, あるいは (22) で示すように,「ない」と必ずしも隣接する必要はない. ただし, その認識動詞慣用句B類と「ない」は, (22)-(23) で示すように, 同じ時制節内になければならない.

(22) その十分でない説明に, 腑に落ち{もしなかった／ていない}.
(23) *[私は, [太郎の行動が腑に落ちると] は思っていない].

以上, 認識動詞と並行して, 認識動詞慣用句もA類とB類に分類できるとし, B類については語彙部門と統語部門で派生するという二重構造を支持する議論を提出した.

4. 語彙項目としての「腑に落ちない」

本節では,「腑に落ちない」が語彙項目とも認められる更なる証拠を, 接尾辞「さ」を用いて提示していく.「さ」は, 次の例が示すように, 語彙部門で形容詞 (A)／形容動詞 (AN) の語幹について名詞 (N) を作る.

(24) a. [A 深い] ― [N 深さ], [A 面白い] ― [N 面白さ]
　　　b. [AN 穏やかな] ― [N 穏やかさ], [AN 活発な] ― [N 活発さ]

また, 希望を表す形容詞述語「たい」の語幹にも, (25) で示すように, それと結合する要素が動詞であれば「さ」を添加できる. しかし, (26a, b) で示すように,「さ」は「たい」の補文に動詞句 (VP) を取った形容詞節には添加できない. なお (27) は,「たい」が動詞句を補文に取れることを示している.

(25) [V 見] たい ― [N 見たさ], [V 書き] たい ― [N 書きたさ]
(26) a. 東京には, スカイツリー [N 見たさ] に多くの人が行く.
　　　b.?*東京には, [N [AP [VP スカイツリーを見] た] さ] に多くの人が行く.
(27) 多くの人が, [[VP スカイツリーを見] たい] と思っている.

つまり, 形容詞述語「たい」は, 統語部門で動詞句と併合する用法もあるが, 接尾辞「さ」と結合した「たさ」は語彙部門で生じた結果だと言える.

ここで, 語彙特性としての「さ」の添加を, 述語「認識動詞＋「ない」」で見

てみよう．「さ」の添加は (28a, b) で示すように，リスト (13) の認識動詞 A 類と「ない」の連鎖には許されないが，認識動詞 B 類と「ない」の連鎖には許される．同様のことが，認識動詞慣用句 (29a, b) でも言え，B 類の「腑に落ちない」の「腑に落ちなさ」は語彙部門で形成されたものである．

(28) a. 認識動詞 A 類 +「ない」+「さ」：
　　　　 *諒としなさ，*悟らなさ，*察しなさ，*分からなさ，…
　　 b. 認識動詞 B 類 +「ない」+「さ」：
　　　　 割り切れなさ，頷けなさ，聞き分けなさ，煮え切らなさ，…
(29) a. 認識動詞慣用句 A 類 +「ない」+「さ」：
　　　　 *辻褄を合わせなさ，*合点がいかなさ，…
　　 b. 認識動詞慣用句 B 類 +「ない」+「さ」：
　　　　 腑に落ちなさ

以上，「さ」の添加に関する事実から，認識動詞慣用句 B 類と「ない」の連鎖は，語彙項目にもなり得ることを明らかにした．

5. まとめ

本稿では，否定辞「ない」との連鎖において，一般的な動詞には見られない認識動詞（慣用句）の振る舞いを考察した．認識動詞（慣用句）と「ない」の連鎖は，動詞性のみを保持する A 類の場合は統語部門において併合して形成されたものだが，動詞性と形容詞性の両方を持つ B 類の場合は語彙部門で結合した一語彙項目でもあり得ると主張した．それを支持する議論として，岸本 (2010) の用いたイディオム「腑に落ちない」に，接尾辞「さ」を添加できるという事実から，それが語彙部門で形成されたことを示した．

認識動詞（慣用句）A 類と B 類は統語部門で区別できることは示したが，語彙部門で区別できるのかどうかについては，今後の課題となろう．

参考文献

影山太郎 (1993)『文法と語形成』ひつじ書房，東京．
Kishimoto, Hideki (2008) "On the Variability of Negative Scope in Japanese," *Journal of Linguistics* 44, 379-435.
岸本秀樹 (2010)「否定辞移動と否定の作用域」『否定と言語理論』，加藤泰彦・今仁生

美・吉村あき子(編), 27-50, 開拓社, 東京.
益岡隆志・田窪行則 (1989)『基礎日本語文法』くろしお出版, 東京.
森川正博 (2014)「イディオム「腑に落ちない」の構造をめぐって――語彙部門と統語部門の狭間――」『名古屋外国語大学外国語学部紀要』46 号, 83-101, 名古屋外国語大学.
Takezawa, Koichi (1987) *A Configurational Approach to Case-marking in Japanese*, Doctoral dissertation, University of Washington.

www.nhk.or.jp/kininaru-blog/130237.html
Goo 辞書 (dictionary.goo.ne.jp)

A Note on *Teki*-modifiers in Japanese*

Chigusa Morita

Mejiro University

1. Introduction

In Japanese, the suffix *-teki* attaches to nominal stems and derives nominal adjectives with the following meanings.[1, 2]

(1) a. The qualitative meaning: 'similar to, like'

---

* I am grateful to Tomokazu Takehisa and Akira Watanabe for helpful comments and suggestions. I am also thankful to Miki Obata for judgment on some data. Needless to say, all remaining errors are mine.

[1] Japanese has several morphological types of "adjectives." One is sometimes called "canonical" adjectives, which seem to inflect without a copula verb. Another is referred to as nominal adjectives, whose stem is followed by the morphemes such as *-na* and *-da* to inflect, as in (i). (ii) shows that *teki*-modifiers exhibit the same morphological patterns as nominal adjectives.
  (i) Nominal adjectives
       a. kiree-na   heya   b. Heya-ga   kiree-da.
          clean-NA   room   room-Nom   clean-DA
          'a/the clean room'   'The room is clean.'
  (ii) Adjectives suffixed with the morpheme *-teki*
       a. kensetu-teki-na   iken   b. Iken-ga   kensetu-teki-da.
          construction-TEKI-NA   opinion   opinion-Top construction-TEKI-DA
          'a constructive opinion'   'The opinion is constructive.'

[2] The suffix *-teki* usually attaches to Sino-Japanese nouns, but not to native nouns. Recently it has been observed that the suffix *-teki* attaches to native nouns (e.g., *kimoti-teki* (feeling-TEKI) 'mentally,' *watasi-teki* (I-TEKI) 'in my opinion'). It has also been observed that *-teki* attaches to constituents larger than a stem, as in (i).
  (i) [josi-goruhukai-no   daiitininsya]-teki   jinbutu
      Women-golf.world-Gen   best.person -TEKI   person
      'one of the best person in Women's Golf'
I do not deal with these issues in this paper.

e.g., *titioya-teki* (father-TEKI) 'paternalistic,' *kikai-teki* (machine-TEKI) 'mechanical'
b. The relational meaning: 'having the property of, being in the state of related to, in terms of'
e.g., *genjitu-teki* (reality-TEKI) 'realistic,' *ongaku-teki* (music-TEKI) 'musical' (cf. Takahashi (2009), Mochizuki (2010))

Nominal adjectives suffixed with *-teki* (*teki*-modifiers, henceforth), however, exhibit some different behaviors from other nominal adjectives. First, most nominal adjectives need to be followed by the morpheme *-na* when they modify a noun. *Teki*-modifiers, on the other hand, do not necessarily require *-na* in the prenominal position.

(2) a. kirei*(-na)   hana   b. kanpeki*(-na) engi
    beautiful(-NA) flower   perfect(-NA) performance
    'a/the beautiful flower'   'a/the perfect performance'
(3) a. bungaku-teki(-na)   hyoogen   b. heiwa-teki(-na)   kaiketu
    literature-TEKI(-NA) expression   peace-TEKI(-NA) solution
    'a/the literary expression'   'a/the peaceful solution'

Second, Kageyama (1993) observes a similar difference between *teki*-modifiers and other nominal adjectives in coordinate constructions. While nominal adjectives in the first conjunct require the morpheme *-na*, *teki*-modifiers can appear without it.[3]

---

[3] Kageyama (1993) also gives other examples of coordinate structures where a nominal adjective and a *teki*-modifier appear as the predicate of the first conjunct, as in (ia) and (ib), respectively.
  (i) a. Taro-wa   odayaka?(-de)   Jiro-wa   kaikatu-da.
       Taro-Top gentle(-DE)   Jiro-Top lively-DA.
       'Taro has a gentle personality, and Jiro has a lively character.'
    b. Taro-wa   sekkyoku-teki(-de)   Jiro-wa syookyoku-teki-da.
       Taro-Top positiveness-TEKI(-DE) Jiro-Top passiveness-DA
       'Taro has a positive personality, and Jiro has a passive personality.'
He mentions that the morpheme *-de* in (ia) cannot be deleted, while the one in (ib) can. In my judgment, however, both nominal adjectives and *teki*-modifiers do not have to be followed by the morpheme *-de*, which I suppose is an allomorph of the predicative copula *-na*.

(4) a. Taro-wa hogaraka??(-na) Jiro-wa sunao-na josee-to
   Taro-Top cheerful(-NA) Jiro-Top obedient-NA woman-with
   kekkon-si-ta.[4]
   marry-do-Past
   'Taro got married with a cheerful woman, and Jiro got married with an obedient woman.'
 b. Taro-wa katee-teki?(-na) Jiro-wa riti-teki(-na)
   Taro-Top home-TEKI(-NA) Jiro-Top intellect-TEKI(-NA)
   josee-to   kekkon-si-ta.
   woman-with marry-do-Past
   'Taro got married with a domestic woman, and Jiro got married with an intellectual woman.'

In this paper, I claim that there are two types of the morpheme -*teki* in Japanese; one is the morpheme that derives a nominal adjective from a nominal stem, and the other is a "dissociated" morpheme, which is phonologically inserted to license Case of the modifying noun. The organization of this paper is as follows. Section 2 shows several differences between *teki*-modifiers followed by -*na* and the ones without -*na*. Given that these differences result from their structural differences, section 3 proposes two kinds of structures for *teki*-modifiers. The last section is a brief summary.

2. Some Properties of *Teki*-modifiers

As observed in (3), *teki*-modifiers are not necessarily followed by the morpheme -*na* in the prenominal position. Several differences, however, have been observed between *teki*-modifiers followed by -*na* and the ones that directly combine with the modified nouns. First, Kageyama (1993) observes that degree adverbs such as *taihen* 'very,' *hijooni* 'very' and *kiwamete* 'extremely' can only modify *teki*-modifiers followed by -*na*.[5]

---

[4] Takahashi (2009) claims that (4a) is grammatical even if the morpheme -*na* does not follow the nominal adjective in the first conjunct. Although it is not completely ungrammatical, I consider that it is much less acceptable than other examples. Tomokazu Takehisa (p.c.) points out that this may be due to the garden-path effect.

[5] *Teki*-modifiers can be modified by the degree modifier *tyoo-* 'super, ultra' even if they

(5) a. taihen kiroku-teki*(-na)   atusa
       very   record-TEKI(-NA)   heat
       'the very record-breaking heat'
    b. hijooni sekkyoku-teki*(-na)   sien
       very   positiveness-TEKI(-NA) support
       'very positive support'
    c. kiwamete seeji-teki*(-na)   hatugen
       exteremly politics-TEKI(-NA) statement
       'an/the extremely political statement'

Second, Kageyama (1993) points out that *teki*-modifiers followed by *-na* and the ones without *-na* behave differently in terms of their lexical integrity. The examples in (6) show that an element can intervene between a *teki*-modifier followed by *-na* and a modified noun. In (7), however, no intervening element is allowed between a *teki*-modifier without *-na* and the noun.

(6) a. akarui   syakoo-teki-na   seekaku
       cheerful sociability-TEKI-NA personality
       'the cheerful, sociable personality'
    b. kenkoo-teki-na   akarui   seekaku
       sociability-TEKI-NA cheerful personality
       'the sociable, cheerful personality'
(7) a. akarui   syakoo-teki   seekaku
       cheerful sociable-TEKI   personality
       'the cheerful, sociable personality'
    b. *syakoo-teki   akarui   seekaku
       sociable-TEKI cheerful personality
       'the sociable, cheerful personality'

Third, Takahashi (2009) observes that a semantic difference may arise by attachment of the morpheme *-na* to *teki*-modifiers. Consider *dansee-teki(-na)* (male-TEKI(-NA)) 'manly, mannish,' for example.

---

are not followed by the morpheme *-na* (e.g., tyoo-sekkyoku-teki sien 'very positive support'). The modifier *tyoo-* attaches to both nouns and adjectives.

(8) a. dansee-teki-na   koodoo   b. dansee-teki   koodoo
       male-TEKI-NA behavior   male-TEKI   behavior
       '(women's) mannish behavior'   '(men's) manly behavior'

Takahashi (2009) mentions that (8a) tends to refer to "women's" mannish-looking behavior, while (8b) tends to refer to "men's" manly behavior.[6] In other words, *teki*-modifiers followed by the morpheme *-na* tend to have the qualitative meaning, while *teki*-modifiers without *-na* tend to have the relational meaning.

The differences between *teki*-modifiers followed by the morpheme *-na* and those without *-na* are summarized as follows. First, degree adverbs can modify *teki*-modifiers followed by *-na*, but they cannot modify the ones without *-na*. Second, an element can intervene between a *teki*-modifier followed by *-na* and a modified noun, but no intervening element is allowed between the one without *-na* and the noun. Third, *teki*-modifiers followed by *-na* tend to have the qualitative meaning, while the ones without *-na* tend to have the relational meaning.

3. Morphological Structures of *Teki*-modifiers

The previous section has shown that the two kinds of interpretations of *teki*-modifiers are closely related to their morphology; there is a tendency that *teki*-modifiers followed by *-na* have the qualitative interpretation, while the ones without *-na* have the relational interpretation.

Given that the semantic difference results from their structural differences, I propose that there are two types of morphological structures for *teki*-modifiers, each of which contains a different morpheme *-teki*.

3.1. The Morpheme *-Teki* as a Denominal Adjectivizer

It has been observed in section 2 that *teki*-modifiers have the following properties when they are followed by the morpheme *-na*: (1) they tend to have the qualitative interpretation; (2) they can accept modification by de-

---

[6] Tomokazu Takehisa (p.c.) points out that the interpretation of (8b) is a subset of the interpretation of (8a). That is, the interpretation of (8a) is more specific than the one of (8b).

gree adverbs. These properties suggest that *teki*-modifiers followed by *-na* are denominal "adjectives."

In the framework of Distributed Morphology (Marantz (2001)), a root is category-neutral, and category-defining functional heads such as *n*, *v*, and *a* combine with a root to derive a noun, verb, and adjective, respectively. Given that *teki*-modifiers are derived by attachment of the functional head *a* to a nominal stem, I suppose that the morpheme *-teki* is an overt realization of the *a* head. The internal structure of *dansee-teki-na* 'manly, mannish,' for example, is illustrated in (9).[7]

(9) [PredP [DegP totemo [aP [nP dansee] -teki]] -na] josee
　　　　　　　　very　　　　male　　-a　　-Pred　woman
'a/the very mannish-looking woman'

I assume that prenominal adjectives in Japanese are (reduced) relative clauses. With a slight revision of Nishiyama's (1999) analysis, I claim that the extended projection of *a*P (i.e., DegP) is selected by the functional category Pred(icative) P(hrase), whose head is overtly realized as /na/ (Morita (2010, 2011)). The PredP, which projects above DegP, forms a (reduced) relative clause and modifies the following noun.

3.2.　*-Teki* as a Case-licensing Element

When *teki*-modifiers are not followed by the predicative copula *-na*, they exhibit the following properties: (1) they cannot accept modification by degree adverbs; (2) an element cannot intervene between the *teki*-modifier and a modified noun; (3) they tend to have the relational interpretation.

First, *teki*-modifiers cannot be modified by degree adverbs when the copula *-na* does not attach to these adjectives. Assuming that DegP is the extended projection of *a*P, this fact seems to suggest that *teki*-modifiers do not form *a*P when they are not followed by the copula *-na*.

Second, an element cannot intervene between a *teki*-modifier without the copula *-na* and a modified noun. This lexical integrity effect shows that a *teki*-modifier and a noun form a compound when the morpheme *-na* does

---

[7] I suppose, following Cinque (2010), that modifiers are merged in the specifier position of the functional category FP, whose head takes the modified noun as its complement.

not follow the modifier. *Teki*-modifiers followed by -*na*, on the other hand, are phrasal modifiers and do not form a compound with the modified noun; other modifiers can appear between these adjectives and the noun, and they can accept modification by degree adverbs.

Third, *teki*-modifiers tend to have the relational interpretation when they are not followed by -*na*. It has been pointed out that relational adjectives behave semantically like nouns, although they exhibit the adjectival morphology (Fábregas (2007)). In Morita (2012), developing Fábregas' (2007) analysis of Spanish relational adjectives, I have proposed that relational "adjectives" are "nominal" syntactically as well as semantically. Given that *teki*-modifiers are also nominal modifiers when they are not followed by -*na*, it follows that the morpheme -*teki* is not the overt realization of the functional head *a* to derive an adjective.

From these observations, I suppose *teki*-modifiers form an N-N compound with the following noun when they are not followed by the copula -*na*; -*na* is phonologically inserted to satisfy Case of the head noun.[8] Harley (2009) proposes that an N-N compound has the internal structure where the modifying noun and the head noun's root are in a sisterhood relationship, as in (10a).

(10) a. [$_{nP}$ *n* [$_{\sqrt{P}}$ √SHOES [$_{nP}$ *n* [$_{\sqrt{P}}$ √NURSE]]]]
  b. [$_{nP}$ [$_{\sqrt{}}$ [$_n$ [√NURSE-*n*-√SHOES]-*n* [$_{\sqrt{P}}$ t$_{\sqrt{SHOES}}$ [$_{nP}$ t$_n$ [$_{\sqrt{P}}$ t$_{\sqrt{NURSE}}$]]]]]]

Harley (2009) claims that the complement of the head noun is created by merging the root √NURSE with its own *n* head. The complex √NURSE-*n* undergoes head movement into the root √SHOES, merges with the root of the head noun, and then incorporates with the *n* head of the modified noun, as illustrated in (10b). Harley (2009) assumes that this incorporation is driven by a Case-related feature; if incorporation does not take place, some kind of case-licensing element is required.

Given that relational *teki*-modifiers have the same internal structure as N-N compounds in English, the internal structure of *dansee-teki koodoo*

---

[8] Following Harley (2009), I consider a compound to be "a morphologically complex form identified as word-sized by its syntactic and phonological behavior and which contains two or more roots (Harley (2009: 130))."

(male-TEKI behavior) 'manly behavior,' for example, is given in (11a). Notice that Japanese is a head-final language.

(11) a. [$_{nP}$ [$_{vP}$ [$_{nP}$ [$_{vP}$ √MALE] n] √BEHAVIOR] n]
  b. [$_{nP}$ [$_{vP}$ [$_{nP}$ [$_{vP}$ t$_{√MALE}$] n-√MALE] t$_{√BEHAVIOR}$] n-√BEHAVIOR]
               ↑
            /teki/-insertion

The root of the modified noun √MALE incorporates into the n head, and the structure merges with the head noun's root √BEHAVIOR. Unlike English N-N compounds, however, I suppose that the complex head n-√MALE does not incorporate into the root √BEHAVIOR, which merges into its own n head; instead of head movement of n-√MALE into the root √BEHAVIOR, I assume that a last resort insertion of -*teki* occurs to satisfy the Case needs of the modifying noun. The lack of head movement of the complement into the head noun's root means that the relationship between the modifying noun and the head noun is not so close in Japanese as in English.

This analysis gives an explanation for the fact that a *teki*-modifier cannot be modified by degree adverbs when it is not followed by the copula -*na*; the *teki*-modifier forms a root compound, the part of which is not allowed to undergo syntactic operations such as movement, deletion and modification by the principle of lexical integrity (cf. Anderson (1992)).

Last, let us consider the difference between *teki*-modifiers and other nominal adjectives, as observed in (4). In coordinate constructions, a nominal adjective in the first conjunct must be followed by the predicative copula -*na*, while a *teki*-modifier does not require it. I suppose that the copula -*na* does not follow a *teki*-modifier in the first conjunct only if the *teki*-modifier forms an N-N compound with the modified noun, which appears adjacent to the *teki*-modifier but is phonologically deleted. Consider the following example.

(12) Taro-wa hijooni katee-teki*(-na) Jiro-wa hijooni
   Taro-Top very home-TEKI(-Pred) Jiro-Top very
   riti-teki*(-na)   josee-to kekkon-si-ta.
   intellect-TEKI(-Pred) woman-with marry-do-Past
   'Taro got married with a very domestic woman, and Jiro got married

with a very intellectual woman.'

The example in (12) shows that the *teki*-modifier in the first conjunct requires the copula -*na* in order to accept modification by a degree modifier. That is, the *teki*-modifier in the first conjunct forms an N-N compound when it is not followed by the copula -*na*. But this assumption seems to be untenable, since it is generally impossible to delete the head noun phonologically or extract it from a root compound. Notice, however, that the relationship between the *teki*-modifier and the head noun in an N-N compound is not close in Japanese because incorporation of the complement into the head noun's root does not take place. I suppose that the phonological insertion of /teki/ makes it possible for the *teki*-modifier to occur separately from the head noun.

4. Concluding Remarks

It has been assumed that the morpheme -*teki* in Japanese is the suffix to combine with a nominal stem and derives a nominal adjective. In this paper, however, I proposed that there are two types of the morpheme -*teki*. One is the overt realization of the functional head *a*, which derives a nominal adjective from a nominal stem. The other is a "dissociated" morpheme, which is phonologically inserted to license the modifying noun's Case. Although this account gives an explanation for morphological, syntactic and semantic properties of *teki*-modifiers, there still remain some problems to be explored, and further research is required.

References

Anderson, Stephen (1992) *A-morphous Morphology*, Cambridge University Press, Cambridge.

Cinque, Guglielmo (2010) *The Syntax of Adjectives*, MIT Press, Cambridge, MA and London.

Fábregas, Antonio (2007) "The Internal Syntactic Structure of Relational Adjectives," *Probus* 19, 1–36.

Harley, Heidi (2009) "Compounding in Distributed Morphology," *The Oxford Handbook of Compounding*, ed. by Rochelle Lieber and Pavel Stekauer, 129–144, Oxford University Press, Oxford.

Kageyama, Taro (1993) *Bunpoo to Gokeesee* (Grammar and Word Formation), Hituzi Syobo, Tokyo.

Marantz, Alec (2001) "Words," ms., MIT.

Mochizuki, Michiko (2010) "A Study of 'na' Adjective with Suffix 'teki' and JSL Teaching: Native and Non-Native Compared," *Journal of Foreign Language Studies* vol. 2, 1-12, Kansai University, Osaka.

Morita, Chigusa (2010) "The Internal Structure of Adjectives in Japanese," *Linguistic Research* 26, 105-117, The University of Tokyo English Linguistics Association.

Morita, Chigusa (2011) "Three Types of Direct Modification APs," *Linguistic Research* 27, 89-102, The University of Tokyo English Linguistics Association.

Morita, Chigusa (2012) "Some Adjectives Are Nouns, Some Nouns Are Adjectives," *JELS* 29, 281-287, English Linguistic Society of Japan.

Nishiyama, Kunio (1999) "Adjectives and the Copulas in Japanese," *Journal of East Asian Linguistics* 8, 183-222.

Takahashi, Katsutada (2009) *Hasee Keitairon* (Derivational Morphology), Eihosha, Tokyo.

数量詞の逆スコープ解釈

中栄　欽一

青山学院大学

1. はじめに

　Someone loves everyone. のように複数の数量詞を含む文は someone が広いスコープを持つ解釈（順スコープ）と反対に everyone が広いスコープを持つ解釈（逆スコープ）が得られ多義性が生じる．この現象は生成文法の標準的な分析では quantifier raising（QR）および c 統御により説明される．QR による移動の範囲は顕在的な移動と同じと考えられるため，数量詞が複合名詞句の島や付加部の島の中にある場合，「島の制約」により，その数量詞は島を超えて広いスコープを取ることができない．しかし indefinites（不定名詞句）の中には他の数量詞が従うこの制約に従わず島を超えてスコープを取るものがある．この不定名詞句が取るスコープの特徴について色々な立場から説明がなされているが，本稿はそのうち Fodor and Sag（1982）ならびに Ruys and Winter（2011），Ruys（2006）の主張を検討してその問題点を指摘し，代案として中栄（2011）で提案した参照点構造による説明をおこなう．

2. 不定名詞句が取るスコープの特徴

2.1. 複合名詞句の島のスコープ

　まず数量詞が関係節の中に埋め込まれている複合名詞句の島の例をみる．

(1)　Someone who inhabits every midwestern city participated.

Ruys and Winter（2011）は，(1) は複合名詞句の島の制約により逆スコープ解釈ができないが every midwestern city を単数不定名詞句である a/some midwestern city に置き換えて Everyone who inhabits a/some midwestern city participated. とすると逆スコープ解釈が可能となると主張している．この

257

ような逆スコープ解釈は a, some だけでなく three midwestern cities のような数詞を伴う複数不定名詞句でも可能である.

2.2. 付加部の島のスコープ

下記例文に関し Ruys and Winter (2011) は次のように述べている.

(2) If a friend of mine from Texas had died in the fire, I would have inherited a fortune.　　　　　　　　　　　　(Fodor and Sag (1982))

不定名詞句を数量詞として扱う標準的分析では, 数量詞は付加部の島に制約され if-clause をこえてスコープを取ることができないため, この解釈は次のようになる. If any one of my friends from Texas dies, I inherit a fortune. つまり a friend of mine from Texas はテキサス出身の友人であれば誰でもよい. しかし (2) の a friend of mine はその人の財産を相続することができる特定な友人である. この解釈を得るには島の制約にかかわらず a friend of mine は if-clause を超えてスコープを取ると考えなければならない. (2) における a friend of mine を a certain friend/some fiend/some friends/three friends of mine などの不定名詞句に置き換えても同様に if-clause を超えてスコープを取ることができる. したがって QR で説明するためには不定名詞句にだけ例外, すなわち 'island—free QR' を認めなければならない. しかし 'island—free QR' には scope と distribution に関連して次のような問題点があると Ruys and Winter (2011) は指摘している.

(3) If three relatives of mine die, I will inherit a house.

上記例文の three relatives of mine の解釈は「3 人の specific な親戚」である. この解釈を QR で得るためには不定名詞句を if-clause の外に引き上げなくてはならないが 'island—free QR' を適用してこの移動ができたとしても, three relatives のような名詞句は分散解釈ができるので any one of three relatives という解釈を許す. しかし (3) は If they all die, I inherit a house. という意味であり分散解釈はできない. すなわち, three relatives of mine が if-clause の島の外にスコープを取れるとしても, この名詞句に許される分散性は島の外に出られないとしなければならない. したがって QR に island—free を認めるだけでは例文 (3) を説明できない.

3. 不定名詞句のスコープに関する理論

このように不定名詞句は他の数量詞と比べ，自由なスコープを取るように見える．この不定名詞句の持つ例外性について多くの理論があるが，このうち Fodor and Sag (1982) と Ruys and Winter (2011), Ruys (2006) の提案を検討する．Fodor and Sag (1982) は次のような説明をしている．不定名詞句は内在的に多義性をもっている．一つは数量詞の性質でローカルにスコープを取るが島を超えられない．もう一つは指示詞としての機能で（名前のような表現），そのような表現はスコープに対し反応が鈍く，あたかも広いスコープを取るような印象をあたえる．この立場によれば (2) における a friend of mine は a certain friend of mine あるいは that friend of mine という解釈になる．これに対して Ruys and Winter (2011), Ruys (2006) は以下のような例文を示し反論している．Most linguists have looked at every analysis that solves some problem. この文は some problem の中間位置での逆スコープ解釈が可能である (most > some > every). しかし Fodor and Sag (1982) の主張に従えば，不定名詞句を数量詞と考えると島から抜け出せないし，指示表現であるとするならばスコープに反応が鈍いから文全体に対し広いスコープをとるような印象を与える解釈は得られても，中間位置でのスコープ解釈はできないはずである．したがって不定名詞句は数量詞，指示詞の二面性を持つという主張は成り立たない．不定名詞句の解釈には，島の制約に関係なく説明ができるメカニズムが必要である．しかもそれは分散解釈を許さないものでなければならない．この2点を満たすものとして Ruys (2006) は choice function (Tanya Reinhart (1997)) に基づく分析を主張している．choice function の詳しい説明は省略するが，例文 (2) の例では choice function を a friend of mine のセットに適用すると，そのセットの値として，セットの中からメンバーを一つ選ぶことができる．その結果 a friend of mine は a certain friend from Texas と捉えることができるため，広いスコープが得られるというもので，QR のような統語的操作を使わずに形式意味論に基づく意味構造から説明している．すなわち島の条件に違反するスコープ・メカニズムを必要としないことがポイントである．以上不定名詞句の持つ例外性に関する理論を紹介したが，これらの理論の特徴は不定名詞句のスコープ・メカニズムについて他の数量詞とは別のメカニズムを立てている点である．本稿は不定名詞句の特徴を認知言語学のアプローチである参照点構造を用いて分析し，この分析によればスコープの振る舞いに関して不定名詞句もその他の数量詞も同じメカニズムで説明できること

を主張するものである．

4. 参照点構造による説明
4.1. 参照点構造とは
　参照点は Langacker（1993）の用語である．認知的にあまり prominence（際立ち）が高くない事物を探すときに，人はまずそれよりも際立ちが高い事物にアクセスし，それを手がかりにして目当ての事物にたどり着くことができる．参照点とは，このような人間の基本的な認知能力における「際立ちの高い手がかり」を指して言う．この手がかりが「参照点」，目当ての事物が「ターゲット」，参照点によってアクセスすることができる概念的領域が「ドミニオン（支配領域）」と呼ばれる．

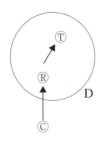

Ⓣ：ターゲット
Ⓡ：参照点
Ⓒ：Conceptualizer（概念主体）
D：ドミニオン（支配領域）
→：心的接触

　この能力を言語面へ適用することにより数量詞が複数含まれ多義性が生じる文の命題（ターゲット）の解釈メカニズムを得ることができる．

4.2. 複合名詞句の島
　文中である数量詞が specific（特定）なものを指していると認識されると，他方の数量詞よりも際立ちが高く参照点となる．この時もう一方の数量詞は不定なものを指す関係にある．参照点となる方の数量詞はターゲットにいたる手がかりだから必ず特定されたものである．不定なものでは手がかりになりえない（両方が特定，あるいは不定のものを指す場合はスコープが生じない）．例文（4）で逆スコープ解釈が得られるプロセスは次のとおりである．

　(4)　Everyone who inhabits a midwestern city participated.

ある特定な midwestern city を話題にしているコンテキストがあると，a midwestern city は際立ちが高く参照点となる.[1] a midwestern city が参照点として機能すると，これを手がかりとしてアクセス可能なドミニオン（a midwestern city に関する知識領域）が想定され，その領域内で文の命題（ターゲット）が解釈される．すなわち命題 everyone who inhabits a midwestern city participated は参照点 a midwestern city に関して成り立っている．これは，参照点 a midwestern city が文中のトピック（clause-internal topic）として働いていることを意味し as for a midwestern city, everyone who inhabits there participated と解釈される．この心的接触の流れにより a midwestern city（特定）が広いスコープを持つ解釈が得られる．参照点構造による分析は移動を伴わないため，島の条件に違反するスコープ・メカニズムを必要としない．なお Ruys and Winter (2011) は例文 (4) の a midwestern city を every midwestern city に入れ替えた例文 (1) Someone who inhabits every midwestern city participated. では複合名詞句の島の制約により逆スコープが得られないと主張している．しかし著者が英語母語話者の一人に確かめたところ，この例文でも逆スコープの解釈ができるとの回答であった．また次の例文でも逆スコープ（every doctor > two patients）の存在が知られている．

(5) I telephoned the two patients that every doctor will examine.
(Alexiadou et al. (2000), Bianchi (1995: 123-124))

この例文に関しては Alexiadou et al. (2000) は QR による説明ではなく，関係代名詞における主要部（先行詞）の繰り上げ分析の立場から（wh 移動），two patients は examine の目的語の位置から繰り上がったので元位置では every doctor から c 統御されており，every doctor > two patients の解釈ができるという説明をしている．[2] 一方，I telephoned two patients that every doctor will examine. では two が決定詞とみなされ，繰り上がる主要部は patients だけなので逆スコープ解釈はないと主張している．しかしこの文を少し変えて I telephoned two senators that every city elected. とすると逆スコープが可能とする英語母語話者がいる．したがって不定名詞句は複合名詞句の島の制約に従わず自由なスコープをとれるが，every NP は関係節の島の外に出ることがで

---

[1] 「特定」という意味は名前まで特定されている必要はない．ある specific な都市，a certain city という意味である．
[2] 主要部繰り上げ・決定詞補部分析では two patients は CP の指定部にあり，その CP は決定詞 the の補部であるとの仮定に基づいている．

きないという主張は常に成り立つわけではない．著者は不定名詞句も every-one のような全称数量詞もスコープ・メカニズムは基本的に同一と考える．例文 (4) においては a midwestern city，その置き換え例では every midwestern city に関して特定解釈ができれば参照点になり逆スコープが得られる．ただし不定名詞句は逆スコープ解釈が比較的容易であるのに対し every NP の場合は逆スコープ解釈ができないとする人も存在し，その受容度にバラツキがある．その理由については次のように考える．例文 (4) における a midwestern city はコンテキストがあれば容易に特定の都市を指していると受け取ることが可能である．これに対し every midwestern city では，より複雑なコンテキストを必要とする．例えば midwestern city 共通の問題に関する集会に全ての midwestern city から（あの都市からも，この都市からも）もれなく参加者があったことを強調するようなコンテキストが必要である．すなわちコンテキストがなくても特定解釈可能な文に対しコンテキストを必要とする文や，より複雑なコンテキストを必要とする文は逆スコープの受容度が落ちると考えられる．これが逆スコープ解釈の受容度に差が生じる理由と考えられる．この点については 6 章でさらに分析する．

4.3. 付加部の島

先にあげた例文 (2) If a friend of mine from Texas had died in the fire, I would have inherited a fortune. を例にとると，テキサス出身のある友人が死んだら自分が遺産を相続するというコンテキストがある場合は，a friend of mine は特定 (specific) な人物であるため際立ちが高く参照点となる．a friend of mine が参照点になると文の命題（ターゲット）は参照点のドミニオン（知識領域）のなかで解釈される．文の命題が a friend of mine に関して成り立つということは，a friend of mine は clause-internal topic として機能していることを意味する (as for a friend of mine from Texas, if he had died in the fire ...)．このため a friend of mine は if-clause よりも広いスコープをとることができる．このようなコンテキストがない場合は a friend of mine の際立ちは高くないため参照点にはならない．この場合 a friend of mine は限定された人物ではなく単に any friend of mine from Texas と理解され，テキサス出身の友人なら誰でもよいという解釈が得られる．以上のように付加部の島においても参照点構造による説明は移動を伴わないため島の条件に違反するスコープ・メカニズムを必要としない．

5. distribution と scope の関係について

先に紹介したように Ruys (2006), Ruys and Winter (2011) は数詞を伴った不定名詞句は島を超えて広いスコープを取れるが，それが持つ分散性は島を超えることができないと主張し，この複数不定名詞句がもつ特徴は choice function を用いれば説明できるとしている．しかし「数詞を伴った不定名詞句が持つ分散性は島を超えることができない」という彼らの指摘自体に疑問がある．確かに例文 (3) If three relatives of mine die, I will inherit a house. では，一軒の家に関係者が 3 人いるのだから「3 人全員が死んだら」という意味であって「3 人のうち誰か 1 人死んだら」という解釈はできない．しかし，たとえば (3) を次のように変えれば，分散解釈の可能性はかなり増す．If three relatives of mine die, I will inherit each of their houses. 3 人の親戚が私にそれぞれの家を相続させる旨のコンテキストがあれば，1 人死ぬごとにその人の家を相続することになる．3 軒の家を相続するのに全員が死ぬまで待たなければならないことはない．さらに，If three relatives of mine wear a yellow tie in the convention, it will be easier to find them. においては 3 人がそれぞれ黄色いネクタイを締めるのであって，3 人が同じ 1 本のネクタイを締めるという解釈はない．したがって distributive reading ができるか否かは不定名詞句の特徴というより文の意味が分散解釈を許すか否かに依存すると思われる．参照点構造による分析では three relatives of mine がコンテキスト等の存在により，際立ちが高く参照点になれるかどうかが問題であって，分散性の有無は単に文の意味で決定されると考える．

6. どのような数量詞が逆スコープを取りやすいか

先に述べたように文中である数量詞が参照点となるためには，その数量詞が特定なものを指していると認識される必要がある．そのためには一般にコンテキストの存在が必要である．コンテキストが与えられていないときは，聴者がコンテキストを想定できることが必要である．例えば John met every man who inhabits *midwestern cities*. のように数詞を伴わない複数名詞句 (bare plural) は逆スコープを取らない．a midwestern city のような単数可算名詞句は具体的なある都市，あるいは a certain/particular city として想定することができる．また three midwestern cities のような数詞を伴った複数名詞句もコンテキストが存在すれば，話題に上がった 3 つの特定の都市を思い浮かべ

ることができる．それに対して数詞を持たない単なる複数名詞句は対象が単に複数ということで漠然としており，個々の構成要素は全体の集積の中に埋没してしまう．つまり対象の都市が幾つかの a certain/particular city であるイメージがわきづらい．このように特定化が容易ではなく参照点になりにくいことが逆スコープを取れない理由である．さらに人により逆スコープの受容度に差が生じるのは，特定された存在を思い浮かべることができるかどうかに差があるためと考えられる．この点に関し Hayashishita (2013) の次の研究が参考になる．[3] 3人の審査員がそれぞれ全てのアブストラクトを査読するというコンテキストの下で (6) の発話がなされたとする．

(6) a. Three reviewers read *Abstract #1 and Abstract #2*. (A and B)
    b. Three reviewers read *every abstract*. (universal quantifier)
    c. Three reviewers read *many abstracts*. (many NP)
    d. Three reviewers read *two abstracts*. (a bare numeral NP)
    e. Three reviewers read *exactly two abstracts*.
                                                                         (modified numeral NP)
    f. Three reviewers read *more than two abstracts*.
                                                                          (modified numeral NP)

上記の目的語の数量詞の際立ちには次のような差がある．(6a) では目的語の不定名詞句は初めから特定な存在 Abstract #1 と Abstract #2 である．したがって際立ちが高く容易に参照点になりうる．(6b) 3人の審査員が一つづつ全部のアブストラクトを査読するというコンテキストがあるので，every abstract を構成する個々のアブストラクトに焦点が当たって際立ちが高く参照点になる．個々のアブストラクトは specific な存在である．(6d) 聴者はアブストラクトの内容を具体的に知らなくても，ある2つのアブストラクトが3人の審査員に査読されたということが分かっている場合には，two abstracts は特定された存在であり参照点になることができる．(6c) many abstracts は漠然としておりこのままでは特定された存在にはなりにくい．したがって例えば

---

[3] Hayashishita (2013) は逆スコープの成立要因として次の二つを挙げている．(1) 逆スコープ解釈は，Computational System の働き（文レベルの要因）のみによって生じるのではなく，談話レベルの情報が関係する複合的な現象なのであり，また，広いスコープを取っている方の数量表現は一般量化子ではなく単体個体群の総和 (a sum of singular-individuals) と分析されるべきである．(2) 逆スコープの対象目的語表現 α が解釈されるときは，α の外延 (extension) とみなされる唯一つの個体が存在する．

現時点で6つのアブストラクトが3人の審査員に査読されたとわかっており、6つは例年に比べ多いという共通認識があれば、この6つのアブストラクトはspecificな存在であり（6d）と同様に参照点となる。(6e) 3人の審査員に査読されたアブストラクトは「数少ない、多分2つか3つだ」という代わりに「丁度3つだけだ」という発話になるコンテキストがあればこれが参照点になりえる。(6f) 3人の審査員に査読されたアブストラクトは3つであるが、「3つのアブストラクトを査読した」という代りに「2つ以上のアブストラクトを査読した」という発話が意味をなすコンテキストが必要。たとえば審査期間の初期で2つを査読するのが目標とされている時期にそのノルマ達成を強調するようなときである。すなわち逆スコープ解釈にはコンテキストの存在が必要で、その受容度はコンテキストが単純なほど高い。またコンテキストをどの程度想定出来るかどうかは人により異なる。これが同じ文を取り上げても逆スコープの存在について意見が割れる原因である。[4]

最後に参照点構造に基づく分析の特徴をまとめる。(1) 参照点構造に基づく分析はsyntacticな分析ではなくsemanticな分析である。数量詞は文の構造のなかでin-situで解釈される。移動を伴わないのでQR分析で生じる問題は生じない。(2) 不定名詞句も他の数量詞句も統一した説明ができる。参照点構造による説明では文中の際立ちの高さだけが参照点を決定する要因であるため、不定名詞句を特殊な存在と扱い、それだけに適用するメカニズムは必要としない。(3) ただし逆スコープの受容度は数量詞ならびに人により異なる。対象の数量詞が高い際立ちを得るには、コンテキストの下でspecificな存在を想起させる必要があるが、それに差があるためと考えられる。(4) 広いスコープを取る数量詞は必ず特定解釈を受けることがストレートに説明できる。なぜならその数量詞は参照点となっているからである。不定なものでは参照点になりえない。参照点は必ずspecificな存在である。

参考文献

Alexiadou, Artemis, Paul Law, André Meinunger and Chris Wilder, eds. (2000) *The Syntax of Relative Clauses*, John Benjamins, Amsterdam and Philadelphia.

---

[4] (6)の例文、およびコンテキストが複雑になるに従い逆スコープの受容度が下がるという指摘はHayashishita (2013)を採用。逆スコープの受容度に差を生じさせる理由の説明はHayashishita (2013)の説明とは異なる。またコンテキストの例示も著者が補足したものである。

Fodor, Janet D. and Ivan Sag (1982) "Referential and Quantificational Indefinites," *Linguistics and Philosophy* 5, 355-398.

Hayashishita, J.-R. (2013) "On the Nature of Inverse Scope Readings,"『言語研究』第143号, 29-68.

Langacker, Ronald (1993) "Reference-Point Constructions," *Cognitive Linguistics* 4:1, 1-38.

中栄欽一 (2011)「参照点構造による数量詞の多義性の説明」『東京大学言語学論集』第31号, 165-186.

Reinhart, Tanya (1997) "Quantifier Scope: How Labour is Divided between QR and Choice Functions," *Linguistics and Philosophy* 20, 335-397.

Ruys, Eddy G. (2006) "Unexpected Wide-Scope Phenomena," *The Blackwell Companion to Syntax*, Vol. V, ed. by Martin Everaet and Henk van Riemsdijk, 175-228, Blackwell, Malden.

Ruys, Eddy G. and Yoad Winter (2011) "Quantifier Scope in Formal Linguistics," *Handbook of Philosophical Logic*, 2nd ed., Vol. 16, ed. by Dov Gabbay, 159-226, Kluwer, Dordrecht, Boston, and London.

統語的機能構造について*

中澤　和夫
青山学院大学

1. はじめに

　我々にとって，文には構造がある，というのは自明のこととしてよい．しかし，我々は一体，文に対してどのような構造を仮定しているのだろうか．統語構造，意味構造，情報構造，そして機能構造などもある．つまり，これは諸家によって様々な仮定，すなわち，それぞれ解明したい文法現象あるいは言語現象にふさわしい構造を仮定している，と言ってよいと思われる．例えば，文構造（sentence structure）に関する分析に伴う術語なりキーワードを順不同に列挙するなら，まず (1) のようなものが思い浮かぶ．

(1) a. NP—AUX—VP
　　b. Agent—Action—Patient—Manner—Locative—...
　　c. Old Information—New Information
　　d. Modality and Proposition

しかし，さらに Theme—Rheme, や Topic—Comment, Focus—Presupposition, Performative Analysis, Empathy, Trajector—Landmark などの術語も文構造の分析に用いられる．これらはあくまで一例であるが，一瞥して明らかなのは，文構造の分析の仕方には様々な可能性があるということである．

　小論では，これから見て行く事実を扱うために，新しい記述上の単位が必要であることを論じたい．それは，いわば「統語的機能」を担う単位であって，換言するなら統語構造にも関わりがあり，機能的にも意味がある，という単位

---

* 本稿の一部は青山英語英文学研究会（ALL）にて口頭発表した．コメントを下さった外池滋生氏はじめ参会者に，例文をチェックして下さった Eric McCready 氏に，また文献の教示を下さった野村忠央氏に感謝申し上げる．

である．これを裏返して言うなら，ここで言う「統語的機能」は，純粋に統語構造のみによっては定義できず，また純粋に意味や機能のみからも定義できない，という概念である．そのような概念を含む構造を，ここでは，統語的機能構造 (syntactic functional structure) と呼ぶことにする．

2. 統語的機能構造

　このような統語的機能を含む構造，すなわち統語的機能構造とは，具体的には，どのようなものであるのか．実は，筆者は既にいくつかの事例研究において，そのような概念が必要であると考えられることを論じている．それらには，例えば，述詞 (predicative) (中澤 (1988)，Nakazawa (2003) 参照),[1] 節導入詞 (clause introducer) (中澤 (1999, 2006b)，Nakazawa (2006c) 参照)，修飾部 (modifier) (中澤 (2006a, 2014) 参照) などがある．これらの事例研究で取り上げた言語現象の分析が言語学的に有意義な規則性を捉えているならば，その限りにおいて，述詞なり節導入詞なり修飾部なりが，言語学的に有意味な概念であると言ってよいと思われる．

　そして小論では，筆者は，ある一群の事実を分析するには，モダリティ (modality: MOD) という，また別の統語的機能単位が必要であるということを論じたい．以下，MOD を措定する動機づけを中心に，説明される事実群，こうした分析が持つ文法理論上の含意，といった事柄について述べる．[2]

3. MOD を含む統語的機能構造

3.1. 事実群と格理論による分析

　まず，次のような事実群がある．

(2) a. John believes that Mary is a genius.
　　b. John believes Mary to be a genius.
　　c. Mary is believed to be a genius.
　　d. It is believed that Mary is a genius. (= We believe that Mary is a genius.)

---

[1] 述詞を文法理論の中で扱うべきと最初に論じたのは梶田 (1990) である．
[2] 小論の MOD は統語的機能を担う．他の様々な「モダリティ」については，例えば中右 (1994)，澤田 (2006) 参照．

(3) a. John said that Mary is/was a genius.
   b. *John said Mary to be a genius.
   c. Mary is said to be a genius.
   d. It is said that Mary is a genius. (= I hear that Mary is a genius.)
(4) a. *John rumored that Mary is/was a genius.
   b. *John rumored Mary to be a genius.
   c. Mary is rumored to be a genius.
   d. It is rumored that Mary is a genius. (= Rumor has it that Mary is a genius.)
(5) a. John murmured that Mary was a genius.
   b. *John murmured Mary to be a genius.
   c. *Mary is murmured to be a genius.
   d. It is murmured that Mary is a genius.
(6) a. John mumbled that Mary was a genius.
   b. *John mumbled Mary to be a genius.
   c. *Mary is mumbled to be a genius.
   d. *It was mumbled that Mary was a genius.
(7) a. John muttered that Mary was a genius.
   b. *John muttered Mary to be a genius.
   c. *Mary is muttered to be a genius.
   d. *It was muttered that Mary was a genius.
(8) a. John whispered that Mary was a genius.
   b. *John whispered Mary to be a genius.
   c. Mary is whispered to be a genius.
   d. It was whispered that Mary was a genius.

一般に，格理論に基づく分析では，主動詞 believe を持つ (2b) は例外的格付与が成り立つので文法的であるが，動詞 say は例外的格付与を認めないので (3b) は非文法的とされる．そこで，(3b) で格を与えられなかった Mary は主語の位置に移動して格を得て，その結果が文法的な (3c) ということになる．

しかし，(4) から (8) の例を見ると，格理論による分析は一気に破綻するのではないか，と思われる．確かに，動詞 rumor は (4b) に見るように例外的格付与をしないので (4c) は文法的になる．しかし，動詞 murmur, mumble, mutter は，それぞれ (5b), (6b), (7b) に見るように例外的格付与

をしないにも拘わらず，それぞれの (c) 文は非文法的である．さらに，動詞 whisper は，(8b) からして例外的格付与をしないのだが，この場合は (8c) の通り文法的になる．動詞 say や rumor, murmur, mumble, mutter そして whisper は，いずれもいわゆる発言動詞（verbs of speaking）であるが，皆，例外的格付与を認めない．しかしながら，格なし名詞句は主語位置への移動が可であったり不可であったりする．このような恣意性は，格理論ではどのように記述し分けるのであろうか．あるいは，(2) から (8) の (d) 文を見ると，それぞれの主節動詞において，例外的格付与の可能性と，仮主語受身構文（つまり，it be Ven that S）の可能性は，全く整合性がない．これはどう扱うのだろうか．

格理論は様々な補助仮説を伴った精密化が可能であろうが，少なくとも，主節動詞が不定詞節の主語に格を与えるか与えないかの違いだけで前掲の事実を記述し尽くすということはできない，としてよいと思われる．

3.2. MOD を含む分析

筆者は，ひとつの文に対する文構造とは単体あるいは一枚岩のものとは考えず，統語構造もあれば意味構造や情報構造もあり，さらに統語的機能範疇を含む文構造もある，と考える．そして，統語的機能範疇 MOD を含む文構造は，概略，次のようなものと仮定する．

 (9) NP MOD VP

これだけを見ると，普通の文の統語構造 [NP AUX VP] となんら変わるところがない，と思われるかもしれない．しかし，重要な点は，その殆ど変わらない，ということと，MOD を含むことにある．

MOD の特徴は，意味的には主に認識的あるいは根源的な法性を表わし，統語的位置としては主語と不定詞動詞句の間に生起する，ということである．これは，つまり典型的には法助動詞の意味機能そして統語的位置である．しかし，注意されたいのは，MOD に該当するのは法助動詞のみならず，他の語類（あるいは語連結）も MOD の働きをするということである．(3c) を例にとると，これは下記 (10) のような統語的機能構造を持つ．

 (10) [$_{NP}$ Mary] [$_{MOD}$ is said] [$_{VP}$ to be a genius]

[is said] という語連結は，統語範疇としては法助動詞ではない．それにも拘わらず，発話者は，[Mary be a genius] という命題について，これが100パー

セント真であるとは言っておらず，あくまで伝聞によるものであることを伝えている．この意味で，[is said] は全く自然に MOD の機能を担っている．

また，ある語（連結）が法性を表わすなら，それはすべて MOD である訳ではないことにも注意されたい．例えば，[I hear that] や perhaps などは十分に法性の意味を持つものであるが，MOD ではない．なぜなら，これらは主語と不定詞動詞句の間に立つという統語的条件を満たさないからである．

では，同じ発言動詞の be Ven を持ちながら，何故 (3c) そして (4c), (8c) の場合は良く，(5c), (6c), (7c) は駄目なのであろうか．その理由は，発言動詞には大別すると，相手を想定する場合とそうでない場合があることにある．つまり，相手に向かって言葉を発する場合（素性 [+public] がある場合）と，相手に伝える意図がなくして言葉を発する場合（[−public] がある場合）がある．動詞 say や rumor そして whisper は [+public] を持ち，murmur や mumble, mutter は [−public] を持つ．素性 [+public] を持つ動詞は相手に向かって何かを言っている訳だから，その動詞の受身形 (be Ven) は，その「言われた」内容を伝える，つまりこれは伝聞の法性を含む．それに対して，素性 [−public] を持つ動詞は相手に向かってものを言っている訳ではないから，その動詞の受身形 (be Ven) を使っても，そもそも「言われ」ていない内容を「伝える」ことはできない．すなわち (5c), (6c), (7c) の be Ven は伝聞の意を表わさない．したがって，(5c), (6c), (7c) の MOD には法性がないので，これらは適格でない．それに対して，(3c), (4c), (8c) の場合は，話者が [Mary be a genius] という命題に対して 100 パーセント真であるとは言ってないので，MOD には法性がある．こうした理由で，一方では (3c), (4c), (8c) の，そして他方では (5c), (6c), (7c) の，文法性に違いが現れるのである．前者は文法的で後者は非文法的である．

なお，(2c) が文法的であるのは次の理由によるものと思われる．つまり，実は (2c) は多義であって，ひとつの解釈は，話者が [Mary be a genius] なる命題を真とは認識していない場合．もう一つは，所与の事態あるいは状況をただ客観的に描写しているという場合．前者の場合は [is believed] が MOD として機能しているゆえ，この文は文法的になる．後者の場合は，(2c) は (2b) を単に受身形に移して，法性を含まぬ直説法で表現しているだけの文である．

本節の最後に，(2) から (8) の (d) 文，すなわち仮主語受身構文について触れておく．(2d), (3d), (4d) は，統語的操作としては文主語を持つ受身文の主語が外置された形としてよいが，それぞれは括弧内に示したパラフレー

ズ³ で表わされた意味を持つ．すなわち，(2d) は，単に法性を含まない直説法での命題表現，(3d) は，it is said that（または I hear that）が，MOD ではないものの，法性を表わし，(4d) は，it is rumored that（または rumor has it that）が，MOD ではないものの，法性を表わしている．同様に，(8d) も，it was whispered that が MOD ではないものの法性を表わしている．なお，この (8d) が法性を持つことは，COD¹¹ が be whispered を be rumoured と語釈している (s.v. whisper) ことからも窺われる．

問題があるように見えるのは (5d), (6d), (7d) である．動詞 murmur, mumble, mutter は能動形では等しく that 節を取るものの，仮主語受身構文では文法性が分かれる．これには各語の語彙的意味が深く関わっているものと思われる．次の COD¹¹ の語義を見てみよう（いずれも各見出し語参照）．

(11) a. murmur: v. say something in a murmur
  　　　　　　　n. a quietly spoken utterance
　　 b. mumble: say something indistinctly and quietly
　　 c. mutter: say in a barely audible voice

これらの動詞はいずれも [–public] な語彙特性を持っているとみなされるのであるが，さらに詳しく見ると，明瞭な違いがあることに気付く．動詞 murmur の発言内容は聞き取れるものだが，mumble と mutter の発言内容は，そもそもはっきりとは「聞き取れない」ものなのである．すると，that 節の命題内容を仮主語受身構文で伝達するに，be murmured の形でなら伝え得るが（「何々が低い声で聞こえた」の意），be mumbled/muttered の形では，そもそも聞こえなかったものを伝えるという非常に奇妙なことを表わしていることになる（敢えて言うなら「*何々がよく聞こえなかったが聞こえた」の意）．(5d), (6d), (7d) 間の文法性の違いはこのような要因によると思われる．⁴

---

　³ パラフレーズとは，元の文と構造的にあるいは文法規則上，関係づけられた文であるとは限らない．同じ意味での，文字通り，言換えである．

　⁴ なお，同じ [is murmured] でも機能が違うことに注意されたい．(5c) における [is murmured] は統語的位置からも MOD の筈が法性を欠くので非文法的．次に，(5d) における [it is murmured that] は伝聞という法性を含んでおらず，単に「何々が低い声で聞こえた」という所与の状況の客観描写ゆえ，文法的．なお，[be muttered] でさえ，「何々という不明瞭な言葉が発せられた」という客観描写なら，頗る自然である．下記 (i) は (7c, d) とは全く異なる構文である．

　　(i) This was muttered apprehensively to himself.　　　　　　　　　(BNC)

3.3. AUX の拡張としての MOD

前節 3.2 節で，MOD は AUX と似ている旨を述べた．それは次のような文法理論上の仕組みに由来する．筆者はかねてより，文法の拡張には (12) のような様式があり，それには A と B の二つの下位類があると主張してきた (Nakazawa (1997, 2002, 2004) 参照)．さらに，筆者は文法の記述様式は (13a) でなく (13b) であると主張してきた．詳細は中澤 (2007) 参照．

(12) Mode of Extension

    Type A: If an item *a* of the category X is in the structure S, then an item *b* of the same category X is in the structure S.

    Type B: If an item *a* of the category X is in the structure S, then an item *b* of the category X' is in the structure S, where *b* in X' is the counterpart of *a* in X. (Nakazawa (2002: 39))

(13) a. If X, then Y.
    b. If Y, then X. (X は当該言語現象に対する文法記述または文法拡張のモデルに関する記述，Y は当該言語現象自体の記述)

すると，例えば (14b) の [is certain/sure/likely] や (14c) の [is supposed/considered/expected/believed/said] が MOD 解釈を持つとするなら，必ず (14a) のような主語と不定詞動詞句の間にも同様に，MOD 解釈を持つ要素が存在していなければならないが，実際それらは具体的には [must/may/can/should] である．これを (12) の Type A のフォーマットに合わせて述べたのが (15) である．

(14) a. Mary must/may/can/should be a genius.
    b. Mary is certain/sure/likely to be a genius.
    c. Mary is supposed/considered/expected/believed/said to be a genius.

(15) If an item [*is certain*] of the category MOD is in the structure NP_VP, then an item [*must*] of the same category MOD is in the structure NP_VP.

このような拡張の様式に基づいているゆえ，徒に恣意的にではなく，MOD は AUX に「似ている」のである．

4. allege 型動詞の「奇妙な」パラダイム

　動詞 allege そしてそれに加えて assure や assert などの動詞には非常に興味深い事実群があることがつとに知られているが、[5] ここでは統語的機能単位 MOD を措定することによって新たな分析の見通しが得られると思われることを示したい．

(16) a. *I alleged John to be a fool.
　　 b. John, I alleged to be a fool.
　　 c. John is alleged to be a fool.
(17) a. *I assure you John to be the best candidate.
　　 b. ?John, I assure you to be the best candidate.　　(Lasnik (2008: 37))
(18) a. *I assert Joe to be a genius.
　　 b. Joe, I assert to be a genius.
　　 c. Joe is asserted to be a genius.

　上の (16) から (18) の例で重要なのは，いずれも不定詞動詞句の主語に例外的格付与が働かないので格を欠くにも拘らず，それが話題化によって文頭の位置（$\overline{\text{A}}$ 位置）に移動可能になっていることである．なお，3 節で論じたように，この名詞句は受身の主語位置（A 位置）にはもちろん移動可能である（(17a) は二重目的語構文ゆえ，そもそも John は受身の主語にはならない）．

　これを格理論の枠組で説明するには様々な補助仮説が必要となると思われる．しかし，統語的機能単位 MOD を措定すると，例えば (16b) は，(19a, b) のような統語的機能構造があるので，(20) のような統語的機能構造を持つことになる．

(19) a.　[$_{NP}$ John] [$_{MOD}$ must] [$_{VP}$ be a fool].
　　 b.　[$_{NP}$ John] [$_{MOD}$ is likely] [$_{VP}$ to be a fool].
(20)　　[$_{NP}$ John] [$_{MOD}$ I alleged] [$_{VP}$ to be a fool].

　(20) における [I alleged] は，意味的にも法性を持ち，統語的にも NP＿VP

---

[5] 動詞 allege その他に関する諸事実・諸分析については Postal (1974, 1993), Tonoike (1997), 長谷川 (2003), Gen'ey (2003), 現影 (2008, 2009), Lasnik (2008) およびそこで言及されている文献を参照されたい．

に位置しているので，十分に MOD たり得るのである．[6] さらに，(21), (22) のような談話の流れは，格理論では説明が難しいと思われるが，遂行分析に法性を組み合わせた (23) や (24) の統語的機能構造を考えれば，この省略現象は，普通の動詞句削除と同じ手続きとみなせる．

(21) a. John, I alleged to be a fool.
  b. Mary did [allege John to be a fool] too.　　　(Lasnik (2008: 34))
(22) ?John, I assure you to be the best candidate. Mary will too.
　　　　　　　　　　　　　　　　　　　　　　　　(Lasnik (2008: 37))
(23) a. I ASSERTED [$_{NP}$ John] [$_{MOD}$ MUST (I alleged)] [$_{VP}$ to be a fool].
  b. MARY ASSERTED [$_{NP}$ John] [$_{MOD}$ MUST] [$_{VP}$ to be a fool] too.
　→ Mary did too.
(24) I (WILL) SAY [$_{NP}$ John] [$_{MOD}$ MUST (I assure you)] [$_{VP}$ to be the best candidate].
  MARY WILL SAY [$_{NP}$ John] [$_{MOD}$ MUST (I assure you)] [$_{VP}$ to be the best candidate] too.
　→ Mary will too.

統語的機能単位 MOD を措定することによって，一見奇妙な本節の事実は非常に自然な記述ができることを見た．

5. 別の問題

統語的機能単位 MOD が直接関わるものではないので小論では扱わないが，allege 型動詞に係わる問題はまだある．それらを簡単に記しておきたい．

(25) I alleged *John/?him to be a fool.　　(Lasnik (2008: 37))
(26) They alleged to be pimps—all of the Parisians who the CIA had hired in Nice.　　(Postal (1974: 305))
(27) a. Which Hollywood actress had alleged to have had sex with an en-

---

[6] 下の例は Heim and Kratzer (1998) の地の文であるが，[$_{MOD}$ we take it] が自然に主語と動詞句の間，すなわち MOD 位置，に入っている例である．(なお，(i) は，(2) という樹形図の説明文で，(2) には助動詞の do が挿入されている．)

　(i) The interpretation of (2) is straightforward ("do", we take it, is vacuous).
　　　　　　　　　　　　　　　　　　　　(Heim and Kratzer (1998: 216))

tire football team which included John Wayne?　　　　　(BNC)
　b. These pictures inside a local hospital allege to show children who've been injured in airborne chemical attacks.　(COCA)
　c. The young women who allege to have been involved with Willie Smith say that they didn't come forward before because of the prominence of his family.　　　　　　　　　　　　(COCA)

(25) に見るように，不定詞動詞句の主語が完全名詞（句）の場合は不可だが，代名詞の場合はかなり良くなる．(26) に見るように，問題の名詞句が「重い」と重名詞句転移が可能である．(27) に見るように，allege は want 型の補部を取ることがある．以上 3 種の問題については，別の機会に論じたい．

6.　結論

6.1.　文法理論における語彙

　文法で記述に用いられる語彙は文法理論で規定されていると考えると，それには統語範疇や意味範疇，それに情報構造に関する術語などが含まれるが，それに加えて統語的機能範疇も含まれると考えられる．

6.2.　文法理論における記述形式

　文法理論で規定している文法の拡張様式には 3.3 節の (12) の形式のものがあり，[7] 文法の記述様式は (13b) の形式であると考えられる．

参考文献

Chiba, Shuji et al., eds. (2003) *Empirical and Theoretical Investigations into Language*, Kaitakusha, Tokyo.
Freiden, Robert, Carlos P. Otero and Maria Luisa Zubizarreta, eds. (2008) *Foundational Issues in Linguistic Theory*, MIT Press, Cambridge, MA.
Gen'ey, Hideaki (2003) "The Syntactic Behavior of *Allege*-Type Verbs," Chiba et al. (eds.), 160-173.
現影秀昭 (2008)「定性効果と派生目的語制約」『紀要』（人間学部篇）第 8 号, 13-27,

---

[7] 文法の拡張において，例えば McCawley (1998: 756ff.) の言う patch その他はその様式に関して何等明示的には述べていないが，これは (12) の様式で述べ直すことができるように思われる．

埼玉学園大学.

現影秀昭 (2009)「情報構造と派生目的語制約」『紀要』（人間学部篇）第 9 号, 29-42, 埼玉学園大学.

語学教育研究所 (編) (2003)『市河賞 36 年の軌跡』開拓社, 東京.

長谷川欣佑 (2003)「目的語への繰り上げと意味的拒否反応」語学教育研究所 (編), 193-201.

Heim, Irene and Angelika Kratzer (1998) *Semantics in Generative Grammar*, Blackwell, Oxford.

池谷彰 (編) (1990)『英語の実証的研究に基づく文法理論の比較研究』, 東京学芸大学.

梶田優 (1990)「範疇, 意味, 文法関係──述語名詞表現とその『関係詞化』」池谷 (編), 60-73.

Lasnik, Howard (2008) "On the Development of Case Theory: Triumphs and Challenges," Freiden et al. (eds.), 17-41.

McCawley, James (1998) *The Syntactic Phenomena of English*, 2nd ed., University of Chicago Press, Chicago.

中右実 (1994)『認知意味論の原理』大修館書店, 東京.

中澤和夫 (1988)「述詞の位置の前置詞句」『英語教育』37 巻 3 号, 70-72; 4 号, 70-72.

Nakazawa, Kazuo (1997) "A Note on the Logic of Linguistic Description: A Case of *Kilometer* in American English," Ukaji et al. (eds.), 19-26.

中澤和夫 (1999)「モデルの研究」『紀要』41 号, 125-134, 青山学院大学文学部.

Nakazawa, Kazuo (2002) "Epenthesis and a Mode of Extension,"『紀要』44 号, 39-46, 青山学院大学文学部.

Nakazawa, Kazuo (2003) "Syntax, Semantics and In-Between: In Defense of Predicative," Chiba et al. (eds.), 510-523.

Nakazawa, Kazuo (2004) "Grammatical Naturalization and a Mode of Extension," *TES* 22, 273-278.

中澤和夫 (2006a)「3 語複合語のリズムと修飾部という概念」『第 78 回 Proceedings』, 29-31, 日本英文学会.

中澤和夫 (2006b)「最上級に導かれる関係節」『英語語法文法研究』13 号, 111-126.

Nakazawa, Kazuo (2006c) "The Genesis of English Head-Internal Relative Clauses: A Dynamic View," *English Linguistics* 23:2, 380-402.

中澤和夫 (2007)「構文拡張の要件」『英語青年』152 巻 12 号, 747-749.

中澤和夫 (2014)「限定修飾について」『英語語法文法研究』21 号, 5-26.

Postal, Paul M. (1974) *On Raising*, MIT Press, Cambridge, MA.

Postal, Paul M. (1993) "Some Defective Paradigms," *Linguistic Inquiry* 24:2, 347-364.

澤田治美 (2006)『モダリティ』開拓社, 東京.

Tonoike, Shigeo (1997) "Defective Paradigms and Case Theory," Ukaji et al. (eds.),

587-597.
Ukaji, Masatomo et al., eds. (1997) *Studies in English Linguistics*, Taishukan, Tokyo.

電子コーパス

BNC: The British National Corpus (via Shogakukan Corpus Network)
COCA: Corpus of Contemporary American English

辞　書

COD[11]: *Concise Oxford English Dictionary*, eleventh edition, revised, Oxford University Press (2008).

文法の発達過程における削除現象

根本　貴行
東京家政大学

1. はじめに

　子供の文法の発達過程において，それぞれの言語環境が異なるばかりか経験可能な言語データが欠如しているにもかかわらず，同じ発達段階を経，類似した発話エラーが観察されていることは一般に知られている．故に，言語は模倣や周囲からの強化などにより個人的な能力だけで獲得されるのではなく，先天的で生得的な機能が多く関与していると考えられる．説明的妥当性を理論の基盤としてきている生成文法は，文法が発達していく過程を説明できるものでなければならない．

　本論では，英語母語話者に動詞句削除現象が現れる段階において，削除がどのような操作により生じるのかを考察していきたい．

　削除現象の扱いに関しては，Williams (1977) 以来行われてきている，先行詞の内容を LF でコピーし削除箇所を解釈する分析と，Chomsky (1995) などが仮定しているように，一度文全体を派生し，先行文との同一箇所を PF で削除する分析がある．本論では，Chung, Ladsaw and McClosky (1995) によるコピー分析と，Merchant (2001, 2008) による PF 削除分析を概観し，文法発達における削除現象の発現時期を予測する際に後者が支持されることを述べる．

　また同時に，文法の発達途上の各段階において幼児が利用できる文構造がどのようなものであるかを概観していきたい．Deprez and Pierce (1993) や Lust (1999, 2006) は，子供は文法発達の初期段階から大人と同じ文構造を持ち，機能範疇を含めて利用可能であると主張している．一方 Radford (1990) は，発達の初期段階では機能範疇を利用できず，語彙範疇のみで文や句が作られると主張している．前者を強い連続性仮説，後者を弱い連続性仮説と呼ぶが，本論では強い連続性仮説を仮定しながら動詞句削除を中心に，削除現象を

見ていくことにする．

2. 削除現象の発現

英語において動詞句削除現象は発達の早い幼児で 22 か月頃から観察される．(1) は CHILDES データベースに見られる動詞句削除の例である．

(1) a. Laura did. (Brownwald 1-10-20)
    b. Santa did. (Cameron 1-11-17)
    c. I do. (Alex 2-3-28)

(1) のいずれの発話も do や did はコンテクストから判断すると本動詞ではなく，また発話の前に大人による動詞句削除表現は見られず，自発的な発話である．(1) で挙げた幼児には，動詞句削除が現れる段階の特徴として，主語と動詞の一致が行われている文 (2a, c) と空主語文 (2b, d) が混在して観察される．[1]

(2) a. There he is. (Brownwald 1-10-19)
    b. Want my salt, please. (Brownwald 1-10-23)
    c. I didn't do this. (Cameron 1-11-17)
    d. Want to do that. (Cameron 1-11-17)

またこの時期までには代名詞の使用が頻繁に見られ，wh 疑問文は型通りのものに限定される．削除現象の一例として挙げられる間接疑問縮約 (Sluicing) は，24 か月前後では全く観察されない．

3. 利用可能な文構造

Deprez and Pirece (1993) や Lust (1999, 2006) は，文法発達のかなり早い段階から機能範疇をはじめとして，大人と同じ文構造が利用可能だと考えている．22 か月前後に多く観察される否定辞が文頭に現れる否定文 (3a) は (3b) のように分析される．

(3) a. No I see truck. (Deprez and Pierce (1993))
    b. [$_{CP}$ [$_{TP}$ [$_{NegP}$ No [$_{VP}$ I see truck]]]]

---

[1] Hyams (1986) によると，空主語文は 2 歳半くらいまで観察される現象である．

(3b) において，主語は T による統率で格付与されるため，TP 指定部へ移動せず VP 内に留まる．文法が発達するにつれて，NP (もしくは DP) に φ 素性が備わり屈折辞が使用可能となると，VP 内の主語は T との照合のため TP 指定部まで上昇し，「主語—否定辞—動詞」の語順が生成される．

Deprez and Pirece (1993) によると，動詞句内の主語に対する統率による格付与は，pro 主語の認可条件と軌を一にする．Koopman and Sportiche (1988) は，空主語言語における pro 主語は機能範疇 I(T) の統率により動詞句内で認可されると述べている．英語において文法の初期段階に見られる空主語が pro であるとすれば，主語は機能範疇 I(T) の統率により格付与されるため，主語が動詞句内に留まる段階でのみ空主語が観察されると考えられる．

2 節で概観した通り，子供により発達の差はあるものの，動詞句削除が発現する段階では，主語—動詞の一致が行われている例と空主語文が混在して観察される．本論では，この段階において，主語が IP(TP) 指定部に上昇する構造と，I(T) の統率による格付与で主語が動詞句内に留まる構造が並行して用いられていると考えてみたい．

一方 Radford (1990) は，文法の発達初期段階における文構造は小節 (Small Clause) であり，幼児は機能範疇を利用することができないと述べている．(4) は Claire 24 か月の発話例である．

(4) a. What kitty doing?
    b. [$_{VP}$ what [$_{VP}$ kitty doing]]   (Radford (1990: 132))

Radford (1990) は主語の前に wh 疑問詞が現れるようになるこの段階でも，時制や動詞の屈折に乏しく，機能範疇を欠いていると分析している．しかし既に述べた通り，動詞句削除が発現する段階では，実際のデータに空主語文と (2a, c) のような主語と動詞が一致している文が混在して観察されるため，部分的もしくは状況に応じて機能範疇 T が使用されている可能性が否めない．

4. LF コピーによる分析から見る削除現象の獲得

初めに Williams (1977) 以来多くの文献で扱われてきた省略現象のコピー分析から見てみよう．Chung, Ladsaw and McClosky (1995) によると，間接疑問縮約 (Sluicing) の派生は，先行文の TP がコピーされ，このコピーが後続文の LF で利用されて意味解釈される．間接疑問縮約では，TP 削除の後残留する wh 疑問詞が島の効果を見せないことが観察されている．

(5) a. They want to hire someone who speaks a Balkan language, but I don't remember which.
   b. *They want to hire someone who speaks a Balkan language, but I don't remember which Balkan language they want to hire someone who speaks t.

(Merchant (2008: 136))

(5a) では，削除されている which 以下の TP は，LF において先行文の TP がコピーされて意味解釈される．削除されず残留している which は従属節 CP 指定部に基底生成しているため，島の効果を見せないと分析される．動詞句削除も間接疑問縮約と同じように先行文のコピーが利用されて，LF で解釈される操作であると仮定してみよう．[2] 2 節で見た通り，母語の発達段階において動詞句削除が発現する段階では，既に代名詞の利用も開始されている．先行文のコピーを後続文で利用することも可能であると考えられるので，代名詞が使用可能な段階では，すでに動詞句削除も発現していることが予測される．

　文法の発達過程において操作がよりシンプルで経済的な操作，もしくは操作数の少ない文法現象から発現するとしよう．Chomsky (2004) は，外的融合はコストがかからず無料の操作であり，また先延ばしの原理 (Chomsky (1995)) に従えば，音声素性を伴う操作より音声素性を伴わない LF における操作の方がより経済的である．これらは同一文に複数の可能な派生が考えられる場合に，派生の経済性を考慮する尺度となる．もしこれが母語の発達についての尺度にもなるとすれば，削除現象はどのように扱われるべきであろうか．

　先延ばしの原理と外的融合における経済性の尺度により，音声素性を伴う代名詞の融合よりも，音声素性を伴わない LF における削除箇所のコピー融合の方がより経済的であると考えられる．故に，先行文のコピーを利用する動詞句削除の発現が音声素性を伴う代名詞の利用よりも早期に発現することが期待され，事実とは異なる予測となる．また，先行文のコピーが幼児にとってより早い段階から利用可能であるとすれば，動詞句削除のみならず間接疑問縮約も同様に早期に発現することが予測される．しかし，2 節で述べたように，間接疑問縮約の発現は動詞句削除に比べ相当に後発の現象である．この点でコピー分析は削除現象に関する母語習得過程を反映しているようには思えない．[3] さら

---

[2] 動詞句削除では島の効果が見られるが，コピー理論におけるこの点の扱いについてはここでは触れない．

[3] 成人による発話が先行文となり間接疑問縮約を発することも予測されるが，実際はそのよ

に，もし間接疑問縮約や動詞句削除がコピーによる派生を経るとすれば，コピー利用の方が代名詞利用より複雑な操作であることを述べなくてはならない．もしそうだとすれば，英語において代名詞やその他の音声を持つ代用表現を用いた派生が，LFにおけるコピーを利用する派生によって阻止されることとなってしまう．

5. PF削除による分析から見る削除現象の獲得

次に動詞句削除のPF削除分析を見てみよう．Merchant (2001) によると，機能範疇にある省略素性 (E feature) により，その補部にある統語要素がPFで音声処理されず出力に至る．

(6) a. John didn't see the teacher but Bill did.
b. ... but [$_{CP}$ [$_{TP}$ Bill [$_{T(E\ feature)}$ did [$_{VP}$ see the teacher]]]]

省略素性が付与されるのは省略素性付与条件 (E-givenness) が満たされる場合であり，概略，先行文に意味的にパラレルな先行詞を持ち，指定部と照合をしている機能範疇に省略素性が付与される．Cに省略素性があればその補部であるTPが削除されて間接疑問縮約が派生され，Tに省略素性が付与されれば (6) のように動詞句削除文が生成されることとなる．(6b) においてVPは意味的にパラレルな先行詞を持ち，Tがdidとの照合関係にあるため省略素性付与条件を満たしている．

文法の発達過程を見てみると，(1) で挙げたどの幼児も動詞句削除を発する以前から代名詞の使用が観察されている．これは先行文を参照して意味的にパラレルな部分を用いる能力が備わっていることを示している．従って，この段階で動詞句削除が発現するために必要な条件は，機能範疇における一致ということになる．この点を観察してみると，(1) で挙げたどの幼児にも，動詞句削除が観察される月齢に達するおよそ2か月程度前には，使用される多くの動詞に形式素性を反映する屈折が見られるようになっている．動詞句削除文を発する段階では機能範疇が備わっており，大人と同じ文構造を利用しているよう

うなデータは見られない．文法の発達途上においてまだ備わっていない文構造は，成人の発話を聞いても文処理することができないとすれば，CPがまだ利用できない段階では，成人の発話を先行文として間接疑問縮約を発することができないことが説明される．Deprez and Pierce (1993) においても，ドイツ語のV2現象の発現時期をもとに，CPが利用開始されるのはIPよりも遅れる可能性があると示唆されている．

に思える．ただし，既に述べたように，この時期には主語を欠いた文も混在しており，TP を構成しつつも照合操作が常に行われているわけではないことが分かる．Alex が動詞句削除を発したダイアログ中には (7) のような発話が観察される．

(7) a. Want that pink one. (Alex 2-3-28)
    b. I did do this. (Alex 2-3-28)

Depreze and Pierce (1993) によれば，(7a) に見られる空主語文の pro 主語は，T による統率によって格付与され，動詞句内に留まっている．興味深いことに，(1) で挙げた幼児が動詞句削除を発する以前から，(8) に示す通り冠詞や属格代名詞が現れるようになっている．

(8) a. I bump my head. (Brownwald 1-8-19)
    b. A prince. / This foots caught.[4] / In the way. / I made a big castle.
        (Cameron 1-9-10)
    c. Give my toast, please. (Brownwald 1-10-20)
    d. A shark. A crab. (Cameron 1-11-17)
    e. I want a blue. (Alex 2-3-28)

Brownwald や Cameron の中で見られる例では，1 歳 8 か月になると，名詞に複数形が現れたり冠詞や属格代名詞が付帯する例が増えてきて，照合される名詞側の形式素性が整ってきていることが伺える．動詞句削除が発現する月齢では，概ね DP の構造が十分使われており，照合操作が行われているように思われる．[5]

強い連続性仮説に従い，動詞句削除を発する Brownwald が 1 歳 10 か月，Cameron が 1 歳 11 か月，Alex が 2 歳 3 か月の段階で，それぞれが大人と同じ文構造が利用可能であるとしよう．この段階では，主語は T による統率か照合のどちらかによって認可されていることになる．しかし動詞句削除は機能範疇における照合操作が条件であるため，空主語がオプションとして存在する

---

  [4] foots に関しては複数形を作る際の過剰生成と思われる．また，D との一致が不十分であると考えられる例でもある．文主語についても，同じ時期に I の代わりに my が用いられる例が観察される．TP や DP の構造は用いられているものの，一致操作自体に未熟さが残ると考えられる．

  [5] Brown (1973) によると，一致が十分発達するのは 2 歳半から 3 歳としている．Brownwald や Cameron の言語発達は標準的なものに比べて早いと言える．

この段階では，(9) のような動詞句削除文は生じないことが予測される．

(9) a. *Did
  b. *[_TP_ φ did [_VP_ I see Mom]]
  c. *[_TP_ φ did [_VP_ pro see Mom]]

事実，動詞句削除が観察される時期には主語を欠く文も混在して見られるが，(9a) で示すような主語を欠く動詞句削除文は少なくともデータの中に現れていない．(9b) は主語が統率により格付与され，動詞句内に留まっているため TP 内で照合が行われず，動詞句削除が認可されない．同じように，(9c) も VP 内に pro 主語が留まっており，TP 内で照合が行われておらず，動詞句削除は認められない．

前節で言及した通り，動詞句削除を発する以前から代名詞の利用が観察されている．PF 削除分析のもとでは，削除文は一度完全な文構造が構成されることから，代名詞の融合よりもコストのかかる派生となるため，代名詞と削除文の発現順序が正しく予測されることとなる．

なお一連の Merchant によるシステムにおいて問題となるのが，フラグメントによる応答文である．Merchant (2004) では，以下のような wh 疑問文における応答をフラグメントとして分析している．フラグメントは島の制約に従い，また束縛条件を遵守する応答となることから，文が一度完全に形成されてから削除操作によって生じると分析されている．

(10) Who did she see?
  a. John.   (Merchant (2004: 673))
  b. [_FP_ John [_F'_ F_(E feature)_ [_TP_ she saw t]]]

(10a) の応答は，(10b) の通り，John が目的語から FP (Focus Phrase) 指定部に移動し，その補部である TP が削除されて派生したものである．機能範疇 F では照合が行われており，省略素性付与条件を満たしている．もし幼児にもこうしたフラグメントが見られるとすれば，その段階で TP より上位の機能範疇が利用可能であることを示すこととなる．実際 (1) で挙げられている幼児には，動詞句削除が現れるよりかなり早い段階から，フラグメントと思われる発話が見られる．

(11) MOT: What is pretty?
    CHI: Flower.   (Brownwald 1-8-19)

(11) の例からも分かる通り，子供の応答には冠詞が付帯しておらず，照合操作が行われているとは考えにくい．この例をフラグメントとして扱うべきか否かは精査しなければならないだろうが，こうした応答は発達途中のかなり早い段階から非常に多く見られる．月齢が上がり，次第に応答文に屈折接辞や冠詞が付帯するようになるが，こうした変化に伴う途上で，ある段階までを削除操作を含まない単語のみによる応答で，屈折接辞が現われ冠詞を伴うようになった段階からフラグメントとして扱うという可能性も考えていかなければならないかもしれない．この段階において，幼児の応答としてはCPまでの構造を理解できている一方で，屈折接辞が不十分で照合操作が完全ではないことが伺える．一致（照合）が生じない段階でも削除操作に基づいたフラグメントが仮定されることをどのようにとらえるべきか考察が必要である．

6. まとめ

　文法の発達には個人差が見られるものの，動詞句削除が現れる段階では，屈折接辞を伴い照合操作が行われている文と空主語文が混在する時期を迎えている．また，幼児は音形を伴う代名詞の使用から始まり，これに後続するかたちで省略現象を用いるようになる．こうした発達のプロセスを示すことが可能であるのは，フラグメントについてはさらなる考察が必要であるものの，派生の経済性の観点からPF削除分析が支持されるであろうということを見た．さらに，文法発達の段階において，機能範疇の存在は必須であると考えられ，強い連続性仮説が支持されることを概観した．

参考文献

Brown, Roger (1973) *A First Language: The Early Stages*, Harvard University Press, Cambridge, MA.

Chomsky, Noam (1995) *The Minimalist Program*, MIT Press, Cambridge, MA.

Chomsky, Noam (2004) "Beyond Explanatory Adequacy," *Structure and Beyond the Cartography of Syntactic Structure*, vol. 3, ed. by Adriana Belleti, 104–131, Oxford University Press, New York.

Chung, Sandra, William Ladsaw and James McClosky (1995) "Sluicing and Logical Form," *Natural Language Semantics* 3, 239–283.

Deprez and Pierce (1993) "Negation and Functional Projections in Early Grammar," *Linguistic Inquiry* 24, 25–67.

Hyams, Nina (1986) *Language Acquisition and the Theory of Parameters*, Reidel, Dordrecht.

Koopman, Hilda, Dominique Sportiche (1991) "The Position of Subjects," *Lingua* 85:3, 211-258.

Lust, Barbara (1999) "Universal Grammar: The Strong Continuity Hypothesis in the First Language Acquisition," *Handbook of Child Language Acquisition*, ed. by William C. Ritchie and Tej K. Bhatia, 111-156, Academic Press, New York.

Lust, Barbara (2006) *Child Language: Acquisition and Growth*, Cambridge University Press, Cambridge.

Merchant, Jason (2001) *The Syntax of Silence: Sluicing, Islands and the Theory of Ellipsis*, Oxford University Press, Oxford.

Merchant, Jason (2004) "Fragments and Ellipsis," *Linguistics and Philosophy* 27, 661-738.

Merchant, Jason (2008) "Variable and Island Repair under Ellipsis," *Topics in Ellipsis*, ed. by Kyle Johnson, 132-153, Cambridge University Press, Cambridge.

Radford, Andrew (1990) *Syntactic Theory and the Acquisition of English Syntax*, Basil Blackwell, Cambridge.

William, Edwin (1977) "Discourse and Logical Form," *Linguistic Inquiry* 8, 101-139.

データベース

CHILDES http://childes.psy.cmu.edu/

The Acquisition of Inversion in Non-Subject *Wh*-Questions by Japanese Learners of English: An Asymmetry between *Why* and Argument *Wh*-Questions*

Miyuki Noji

Joetsu University of Education

1. Introduction

In the L1 acquisition of *wh*-questions, many English-speaking children go through a stage in which correctly-inverted questions co-exist with questions that lack inversion. This phenomenon has been investigated from various points of view: the differences among *wh*-phrases, differences among auxiliaries to be inverted, and the presence or absence of *not* (see Ambridge and Rowland (2006) for the detailed summary of previous studies). One important finding concerning the difference among *wh*-phrases in the rate of subject-auxiliary inversion is that *why* questions display the highest rate of non-inversion (Labov and Labov (1978), De Villiers (1991), Berk (2003)),[1] while there seems to be an asymmetry between argument and adjunct *wh*-questions (Erreich (1984), Stromswold (1990)).

Two different approaches have been proposed to explain the facts. Stromswold (1990) and De Villiers (1991) propose a syntactic account. De Villiers (1991) claims that *why* (as with some other adjunct *wh*-phrases) initially stays in the "IP-adjoined" position and does not move to [Spec, CP] in child grammar, and tries to link this non-adult behavior with an option sanctioned in adult languages (as in French) on the basis of Rizzi's (1990) analysis (see also Thornton (2008)). Another account is based on input frequency (Rowland and Pine (2000, 2003)). It does not assume grammati-

---

* I would like to thank Tetsuya Sano and other TPL members for their helpful comments. Thanks also go to Ivan Brown, who proofread this paper, and the undergraduate students who readily participated in this study.

[1] The results in Ambridge and Rowland (2006) are exceptional in this respect.

cal knowledge such as subject-auxiliary inversion, and takes the position that the acquisition of *wh*-questions is affected by input frequency of lexically specific *wh*-word + auxiliary combinations. That is, the asymmetry is regarded as just reflecting the difference of input frequency.

L2 English learners also have reportedly failed to exhibit the subject-auxiliary inversion at a certain stage of the acquisition of *wh*-questions (e.g., a child Turkish learner in Haznedar (2003), 11-12 years old French learners in Spada and Lightbown (1999), and adult Japanese learners in Sakai (2008)). As illustrated in (1), which are speech data from Erden in Haznedar (2003), auxiliary *be* can remain uninverted, and can drop, while *do* usually does not appear (and the main verb can be overtly inflected) in non-inverted *wh*-questions.

(1) a. What you're saying?
    b. What you doing here?
    c. What I get here?

It may be that L2 learners go through a similar (not fundamentally different) developmental stage as L1 children, where their grammar has a parameter setting of neither L1 nor L2. To explore this possibility, however, it must first be clarified whether L2 learners demonstrating inconsistent inversion show an asymmetry between *why* and argument *wh*-questions regarding the lack of inversion. The purpose of the present study is to offer an answer to this question.

2. Previous L2 Research on Non-Subject *Wh*-Questions

Lee (2008) is the first attempt to show that L2 English learners show such an asymmetry. She conducted a grammaticality judgment task with 41 adult Korean learners as participants, and reports that for the uninverted (i.e., ungrammatical) *wh*-questions, the mean score of *what* (-0.54) was significantly lower than those of *who* (-0.48), *how* (-0.09), and *why* (-0.00),[2] and that significant differences were also found between *who* and *how*, and between *who* and *why*, but not between *how* and *why*. She argues that the

---

[2] The maximal and minimal values of the scale used were +2 and -2 respectively.

asymmetry between arguments and adjuncts supports the generative syntactic approach because it did not accord with the results of an input analysis for Korean learners.

However, the asymmetry found in her study is based on perception data, while the one reported in L1 studies is on production data. They may be essentially the same, but this has not been confirmed. In fact, the participants, who were advanced learners of English, may have past the stage of producing non-inverted *wh*-questions by the time of the investigation.

To collect L2 production data, Yokoyama (2009) administered a translation task to 17 adult Japanese learners of English, and reported an asymmetry between argument and adjunct *wh*-questions. Although the task contained only three test items for each *wh*-phrase, the mean rates of inversion in *what*, *who*, *how*, and *why* questions were 0.61, 0.61, 0.47, and 0.39 respectively. According to Kanai's (2014) later input analysis for Japanese learners, the frequencies of *wh*-questions excluding formulaic expressions such as *how are you?* and those that contain *you* as the subject were as follows: *what* (321) >*how* (97), *why* (90) >*who* (19).[3] These results, which were essentially the same as those in Lee (2008), were reportedly not compatible with Yokoyama's (2009) results.

To summarize, L2 learners seem to accept or produce non-inverted *why* questions more than non-inverted *what* and *who* questions. Furthermore, there may be little difference between *what* and *who* questions without inversion, although *what* questions are much more frequent than *who* questions in L2 input.

The previous findings are limited, but are important in several respects. First, the data on which they are based are from L2 learners whose L1 has no inversion. Both Korean and Japanese, unlike languages such as French, do not show optional inversion in *wh*-questions. Thus, we can exclude the possibility that the asymmetry itself would be affected by L1.

Second, Lee (2008) and Yokoyama (2009) are both experimental studies, where the number and kind of *wh*-phrases and subjects were controlled. Thus their data can be considered as more balanced than naturalistic data, and hence as less affected by noises unrelated to L2 grammar.

---

[3] > stands for 'significantly larger in number.'

However, stronger evidence for the asymmetry is necessary to discuss the question of whether L2 learners structurally distinguish between *why* and arguments in the acquisition of inversion of *wh*-questions.

3. Predictions

The syntactic account and the input frequency account make different predictions concerning the lack of inversion in *why* questions and questions with *what* and *who* in the object (i.e., argument) position. The frequency rank order should be '*why>what, who*' under the former account, while it should be '*who>why>what*' under the latter account. The crucial difference is between *who* and *what*. The syntactic account predicts that the rate of non-inversion in *who* questions would not be significantly different from that in *what* questions, since both of the two *wh*-phrases originate in the complement position of a verb. On the other hand, the input frequency account predicts that the former would be significantly higher than the latter, because inverted *what* questions are more frequent than inverted *who* questions.

4. The Current Study

4.1. Participants

65 Japanese speakers learning English at a university in Niigata, Japan, participated in this study. One had lived in Singapore for three years, and was removed from data. As for the remaining 64 (18–22 years old), no one had experience of staying in a country where English is spoken for more than two weeks. Their mean length of studying English was 8.65 years.

4.2. Task

A self-paced translation task was used to elicit *wh*-questions. It was administered to the participants individually. After two warm-up trials, they orally translated Japanese sentences projected on a computer screen one by one into English, which were audio-recorded and were later transcribed.

The task consisted of 18 test items and 21 fillers, which were presented in a semi-randomized order. Each participant translated the designated part in each item into English as in (2)–(4), where targets are in bold face:

(2) Tasika anata-wa sakihodo made Miki to Ayaka to issho
maybe you-Top a while ago until Miki and Ayaka with
desita yone.
were TagQ
'You were with Miki and Ayaka until a while ago, right?'
Kanojotati-wa kyositu-de nani-o tukutte-ita-no desu ka?
she(Pl)-Top classroom-in what-Acc making were Q
'**What were they making in the classroom?**'

(3) Tasika anata-wa sakihodo made Kate to Airi to issho desita
maybe you-Top a while ago until Kate and Airi with were
yone.
TagQ
'You were with Kate and Airi until a while ago, right?'
Kanojotati-wa ima-de naze waratte-ita-no desu ka?
she(Pl)-Top livingroom-in why raughing were Q
'**Why were they laughing in the living room?**'

(4) Tasika anata-wa sakihodo made Diana to Karen to issho
maybe you-Top a while ago until Diana and Karen with
desita yone.
were TagQ
'You were with Diana and Karen until a while ago, right?'
Kanojotati-wa daidokoro-de dare-o tetudatte-ita-no desu ka?
she(Pl)-Top kitchen-in who-Acc helping were Q
'**Who were they helping in the kitchen?**'

The test items were constructed in such a way that each target sentence would include one of the three *wh*-phrases (*why, what,* and *who*) and one of 6 *do/be* forms (see Appendix 1 for the list of the target sentences).

4.3. Data Analysis

Wh-questions were regarded as inverted if they started with the sequence of *wh*-phrase+auxiliary+subject as in (5), and as non-inverted if they started with a sequence of *wh*-phrase+subject as in (6) (cf.(1)).

(5) a. What does the boy study every day?
b. What are the boy study every day?

(6) a. Why that children are jumping on the bed?
   b. Why the children jumping on the bed?
   c. Why the children jump on the bed?
   d. Why the kids jumped on the bed?

Those in which the presence of an auxiliary in the sequence of *wh*-phrase+auxiliary+subject was not clear were not counted. Furthermore, those containing non-object *what/who* as in (7) were not counted either, while those having *what*+N as in (8) were counted as *what* questions because the fronted *wh*-phrase is originally an object as in other *what* questions.

(7) a. What is the book the children read in the library?
   b. Who is that person Bob introduced?
(8) a. What things did they make at classroom?
   b. What things they often eat?

Repetitions were excluded from the data. As for self-corrections, however, those starting with a *wh*-phrase and lacking inversion either at the beginning as in (9a) or in the rephrased part as in (9b) were regarded as having non-inversion.

(9) a. Why the boy cries ... Why does the boy cry every night?
   b. Who does Nancy ... Who Nancy touch with this glove?

4.4. Results

Out of 64 participants, 23 produced more than one *wh*-question without inversion and more than one *wh*-question with inversion, and were considered as learners having optional inversion.

As for these 23 participants, the mean proportions of non-inverted questions to the total number of inverted and non-inverted questions were 0.53 (SD=0.26) in *why* questions, 0.28 (SD=0.30) in *what* questions, and 0.27 (SD=0.33) in *who* questions (see Appendix 2 for the individual results). A one-way analysis of variance (ANOVA) showed a significant main effect of question type ($F(2, 44)$=9.22, $p<.01$). Further analysis with Bonferroni revealed that the mean non-inversion rate was significantly higher in *why* questions than in *what* and *who* questions, but no significant difference was found between *what* and *who* questions.

These results of *what* and *who* questions made an intriguing contrast with the results concerning *wh*-movement between the two types: 109 (79%) *what* questions out of all trials were judged as involving *wh*-movement (from the object position), while 70 (51%) *who* questions were considered as involving *wh*-movement. A Chi-square analysis revealed that *wh*-movement occurred significantly more frequently in *what* questions, and significantly less frequently in *who* questions ($\chi^2(1, N=276)=22.95, p<.01$).

As for the non-inverted questions, however, closer scrutiny is needed to obtain more reliable results. As is well-known, L2 learners often omit inflection of a verbal element and drop an auxiliary as in (6b) (see Prévost and White (1999, 2000)). Therefore, non-inverted questions without overt inflection such as (6b, c) can be given another interpretation: an auxiliary is phonologically null, is present structurally, and occupies the position of C. Thus such non-inverted questions may have been 'with inversion.' To exclude the possibility and to test whether the asymmetry can be maintained, the number of non-inverted questions with overt inflection such as (6a, d) was calculated. The results are shown in Table 1.

Table 1. Number (%) of Inverted Questions and Non-Inverted Questions

	Inverted	Non-inverted		Total
		With overt inflection	Without overt inflection	
why	62 (47%)	13 (10%)	57 (43%)	132 (100%)
what	85 (75%)	4 (4%)	24 (21%)	113 (100%)
who	52 (72%)	3 (4%)	17 (24%)	72 (100%)

The number of non-inverted questions was largest in *why* questions irrespective of whether they were with overt inflection or not. However, it was small in *what* and *who* questions. A Chi-square analysis revealed that non-inversion occurred significantly more frequently both in *why* questions with overt inflection and in those without overt inflection ($\chi^2(4, N=317)=24.67, p<.01$).

5. Discussion and Conclusion

The results in the previous section indicate that there is an asymmetry between *why* and argument *wh*-questions in L2 as the syntactic account predicts: *why*> *what, who*. Thus the syntactic account is supported: non-inversion occurs more frequently in *why* questions than in *what* and *who* questions because *why* is a sentential adverb, may stay in the original adjunct position for some reason, and hence often fails to move to the sentence-initial position for *wh*-phrases (possibly in [SPEC, CP]). This account, however, amounts to saying that the source of the asymmetry is frequent lack of *wh*-movement in *why* questions.

On the other hand, a difference was found between *what* and *who* questions with respect to the frequency of *wh*-movement. This may reflect L2 input. If so, it would be implausible that only *why* questions are not affected.

In sum, the overall results suggest that the acquisition of *wh*-movement involves various factors, one of which is syntactic and relates to the lack of inversion in *why* questions, and that *wh*-movement triggers T to C movement (i.e., inversion) at a constant rate, at least in *what* and *who* questions, and probably in all *wh*-questions.

In conclusion, L2 learners may go through a similar developmental stage as L1 learners in the acquisition of inversion of *wh*-questions. However, more research will be necessary to address the question of whether it is fundamentally the same.

References

Ambridge, Ben and Caroline F. Rowland (2006) "Comparing Different Accounts of Inversion Errors in Children's Non-Subject *Wh*-Questions: What Experimental Data Can Tell Us?" *Journal of Child Language* 33, 519–557.

Berk, Stephanie (2003) "Why "*Why*" Is Different," *Proceedings of the 27th Boston University Conference on Language Development*, ed. by Barbara Beachley, Amanda Brown and Frances Conlin, 127–137, Cascadilla Press, Somerville, MA.

De Villies, Jill (1991) "Why Questions?" *Papers in the Acquisition of Wh: Proceedings of UMass Roundtable, May 1990*, ed. by Thomas L. Maxfield and Bernadette Plunkett, 155–173, GLSA Publications, Amherst, MA.

Erreich, Anne (1984) "Learning How to Ask: Patterns of Inversion in Yes-No and

Wh-Questions," *Journal of Child Language* 11, 579-592.

Haznedar, Belma (2003) "The Status of Functional Categories in Child Second Language Acquisition: Evidence from the Acquisition of CP," *Second Language Research* 19, 1-41.

Kanai, Takuma (2014) *Nihonjin-Eigo-Gakushusha no Wh-Gimonbun no Kakutoku: Input-Hindo-Setsu no Kensho* (The Acquisition of *Wh*-Questions by Japanese Learners of English: Testing an Input Frequency Approach), Graduation Thesis, Joetsu University of Education.

Labov, Willian and Teresa Labov (1978) "Learning the Syntax of Questions," *Language Development and Mother-Child Interaction*, ed. by Robin N. Campbell and Philip T. Smith, 1-44, Plenum Press, New York.

Lee, Sun-Young (2008) "Argument-Adjunct Asymmetry in the Acquisition of Inversion in *Wh*-Questions by Korean Learners of English," *Language Learning* 58, 625-663.

Prévost, Philippe and Lydia White (1999) "Accounting for Morphological Variation in Second Language Acquisition: Truncation or Missing Inflection?" *The Acquisition of Syntax*, ed. by Marc-Ariel Friedemann and Luigi Rizzi, 202-235, Longman, London.

Prévost, Philippe and Lydia White (2000) "Missing Surface Inflection or Impairment in Second Language Acquisition?: Evidence from Tense and Agreement," *Second Language Research* 16, 103-133.

Rizzi, Luigi (1990) *Relativized Minimality*, MIT Press, Cambridge, MA.

Rowland, Caroline F., and Julian M. Pine (2000) "Subject-Auxiliary Inversion Errors and *Wh*-Question Acquisition: What Children do Know?" *Journal of Child Language* 27, 157-181.

Rowland, Caroline F., and Julian M. Pine (2003) "The Development of Inversion in *Wh*-questions: A Reply to Van Valin," *Journal of Child Language* 30, 197-212.

Sakai, Hideki (2008). "An Analysis of Japanese University Students' Oral Performance in English Using Processability Theory," *System* 36, 534-549.

Spada, Nina and Patsy M. Lightbown (1999) "Instruction, First Language Influence, and Developmental Readiness in Second Language Acquisition," *The Modern Language Journal* 83, 1-22.

Stromswold, Karin (1990) *Learnability and the Acquisition of Auxiliaries*, Unpublished doctoral dissertation, MIT, Cambridge, MA.

Thornton, Rosalind (2008) "Why Continuity," *Natural Language and Linguistic Theory* 26, 107-146.

Yokoyama, Ayumi (2009) *Nihonjin-Eigo-Gakushusha niyoru Gimonbun no Kakutoku: Kou to Fukabu no Kubetsu nitsuite* (The Acquisition of Questions by Japanese Learners of English: On the Argument-Adjunct Distinction), Graduation Thesis,

Joetsu University of Education.

Appendix 1. List of Target Sentences

(1) a. What do they eat often?
 b. Why do they get up early?
 c. Who do they know well?
(2) a. What does the boy study every day?
 b. Why does the boy cry every night?
 c. Who does the boy meet every morning?
(3) a. What did Nancy draw with the pencil?
 b. Why did Nancy run with the shoes?
 c. Who did Nancy touch with the glove?
(4) a. What are the children reading in the library?
 b. Why are the children jumping on the bed?
 c. Who are the children chasing in the park?
(5) a. What is Bob cooking in the kitchen?
 b. Why is Bob swimming in the pool?
 c. Who is Bob introducing in the restaurant?
(6) a. What were they making in the classroom?
 b. Why were they crying in the living room?
 c. Who were they helping in the kitchen?

Appendix 2. Number (%) of Non-Inverted *Wh*-Questions (Individual Results)

Participants	*why*		*what*		*who*	
1	3/6	(50%)	1/6	(17%)	0/3	(0%)
2	6/6	(100%)	1/6	(17%)	1/2	(50%)
3	4/6	(67%)	2/5	(40%)	1/5	(20%)
4	1/2	(50%)	1/3	(33%)	0/0	(0%)
5	6/6	(100%)	2/2	(100%)	2/3	(67%)
6	6/6	(100%)	0/6	(0%)	3/3	(100%)
7	1/6	(17%)	3/6	(50%)	4/4	(100%)
8	3/6	(50%)	0/6	(0%)	0/4	(0%)
9	2/5	(40%)	2/3	(67%)	0/2	(0%)
10	2/6	(33%)	1/5	(20%)	0/5	(0%)
11	2/6	(33%)	0/6	(0%)	0/5	(0%)
12	4/6	(67%)	4/6	(67%)	1/2	(50%)
13	3/5	(60%)	0/3	(0%)	1/2	(50%)
14	2/6	(33%)	0/3	(0%)	0/0	(0%)
15	6/6	(100%)	1/2	(50%)	4/6	(67%)
16	3/6	(50%)	4/6	(67%)	1/2	(50%)
17	2/6	(33%)	0/6	(0%)	0/6	(0%)
18	4/6	(67%)	4/5	(80%)	1/2	(50%)
19	1/6	(17%)	0/6	(0%)	1/6	(17%)
20	2/6	(33%)	0/5	(0%)	0/6	(0%)
21	1/6	(17%)	1/6	(17%)	0/4	(0%)
22	4/6	(67%)	0/5	(0%)	0/0	(0%)
23	2/6	(33%)	1/6	(17%)	0/0	(0%)

On Relatives*

Miyuki Nomura

Hokkaido University of Education

1. Introduction

This paper is an attempt to provide a tentative analysis of the structure of relative clauses in English.

As is well-known, English relatives can be divided broadly into two types: restrictive relatives as in (1a) and nonrestrictive relatives as in (1b).

(1) a. This is the book (that) I bought at the sale.

(Quirk et al. (1985: 1248))

b. My brother, who lives in America, is an engineer. (op. cit.: 1240)

This paper will be mainly concerned with restrictive relative clauses.

2. Some Analyses on Relatives

Many analyses on the structure of relatives have been proposed, but the question of their structure is still controversial. As shown in Yagi (2012), three kinds of analyses on relatives are proposed in the current studies. They are the head external analysis, the head raising analysis, and the matching analysis, as schematized below.

(2) The Head External Analysis
the [book] [which$_i$ John likes ___$_i$]   (Yagi (2012: 51))

---

* I am most grateful to Professor Shigeo Tonoike for allowing me to attend his lectures, especially his intensive course of lectures held at Hokkaido University of Education in 2013, which gave me a crucial insight for this paper. I am also deeply indebted to Michelle La Fay for correcting English in this paper. Needless to say, the remaining errors are mine.

(3) The Head Raising Analysis
   a. the [[book]$_k$ [[which ___$_k$]$_i$ John likes ___$_i$]]
   b. the [[book $_k$ which ___$_k$]$_i$ John likes ___$_i$]]   (ibid.)
(4) The Matching Analysis
   the [book] [[which ~~book~~]$_i$ John likes ___$_i$]   (ibid.)

Under the head external analysis in (2), the head noun is base-generated outside the relative clause. Under the head raising analysis in (3), the head is base-generated within the relative clause, and the *wh*-phrase with the head is moved to the front of the relative clause, and then only the head noun is moved. In (3a), the head is raised outside the *wh*-phrase, whereas the head is moved within the *wh*-phrase in (3b). Under the matching analysis in (4), two head nouns are base-generated both outside the relative clause and inside the relative clause, and the head in the relative clause is deleted under the identity condition.

3. Some Problems

Each of the analyses on relative clauses has both strong points and weak points. There are some data problematic for the analyses of relatives.

3.1. Extraposition from DP

The fact that relative clauses can be extraposed from DPs poses a problem to the head raising analysis as in (3b).

(5) a. A man who was wearing a black cloak entered.
   b. A man entered who was wearing a black cloak.
                                                    (McCawley (1998: 104))

In the case of (3b), the relative pronoun and the sequence following it in the relative clause do not make up a single constituent. The analysis in (3b) cannot explain the applicability of extraposition of relative clauses from DPs. On the other hand, based on the analyses as seen in (2), (3a), and (4), the relative clause makes up a single constituent and therefore it is correctly predicted that the relative clause can undergo extraposition.

3.2. The Case of Antecedents

The case assignment of relative pronouns and head nouns becomes a problem in the head raising analysis.

(6) a. The girl who(m) John married is a nurse.
 b. I know the champion who broke the record.

Taking (6a) as an example, based on the head raising analysis, the head noun and the relative pronoun are base-generated in the object position of the transitive verb, and they are assumed to bear accusative case. However, after they raise to the front of the relative clause and the head noun is placed in front of the relative pronoun, the head noun is in the subject position and is assumed to bear nominative case. Here arises a case conflict. Presumably the head noun in (6a) bears nominative case, though English nouns except pronouns have poor inflection and have no distinction between nominative case and accusative case.

Under the head external analysis and the matching analysis, the head noun is in the subject position in (6a), and it is predicted to have nominative case.

In (6b), under the head raising analysis, the head noun and the relative pronoun are in the subject position and they are assumed to have nominative case, but after being raised to the position following the determiner, the head noun is predicted to have accusative case. Based on the head external analysis and the matching analysis, the head noun is base-generated in the object position and has accusative case.

German nouns inflect more overtly than English ones.

(7) a. Er kennt den Herrn,
 he knows the-masc-sg-acc gentleman-masc-sg-acc
 der in Berlin wohnt.
 that-masc-sg-nom in Berlin lives
 'He knows the gentleman who lives in Berlin.'
 b. *Er kennt den Herr,
 he knows the-masc-sg-acc gentleman-masc-sg-nom
 der in Berlin wohnt.
 that-masc-sg-nom in Berlin lives

In (7), the head noun has accusative case and cannot have nominative case. It can be said that the head is assigned accusative case by the matrix verb and is not assigned nominative case by the T in the relative clause. In other words, the case of the head noun is not determined in the relative clause but in the matrix clause. Under the head raising analysis, where the head noun is base-generated in the relative clause, it is predicted that the head is assigned case within the relative clause, contrary to the fact.

It might be claimed that the ungrammaticality of (7b) is due to the difference of the case between the head noun and its article. However, even if the article has the same case as the head noun has, namely nominative case, the sentence is still ungrammatical.

(8) *Er kennt der   Herr,
    he knows the-masc-sg-nom gentleman-masc-sg-nom
    der   in Berlin wohnt.
    that-masc-sg-nom in Berlin lives

The ungrammaticality of (8) poses a problem for the DP raising analysis of relatives like (9), where the relative clause involves the movement of the DP from the relative clause to the head position.

(9) The DP Raising Analysis
    [$_{DP}$ [$_{DP}$]$_k$ [$_{CP}$ that [$_{DP}$ the gentleman] lives in Berlin]]

3.3. Idioms

The DPs in idiom chunks can be the antecedents of relatives.

(10) a. We made headway.
     b. *(The) headway was satisfactory.
     c. The headway that we made was satisfactory.[1]

(Schachter (1973: 31))

Unlike the usual use of the asterisk with the parentheses, the asterisk used in

---

[1] Emonds (1979: 233) observes that a part of an idiom cannot be the antecedent of the nonrestrictive relative clause.

(i) *The headway, which the student made last week, was phenomenal.

(10b) means that the sentence (10b) is ungrammatical irrespective of whether the parenthesized item *the* exists or not. The noun *headway* cannot be used alone, and must be used as the part of the idiom. Assuming that *headway* must be generated as the object of the verb *made*, the example in (10c) may support the head raising analysis of relatives and may oppose the head external analysis.

It should be noted that *headway* cannot be used with the determiner *the* as in (10b) but that it is used with *the* when it is relativized as in (10c).

3.4. The Article *the* before the Head Noun

Proper nouns are also used with *the* when they are modified by restrictive relative clauses.

(11) a. The Dr Brown I know comes from Australia.[2]
　　 b. Do you mean the Memphis which used to be the capital of Egypt, or the Memphis in Tennessee?　　(Quirk et al. (1985: 290))

The fact that the nouns usually used without articles co-occur with the determiner *the* when they are modified by restrictive relatives shows that the DP raising analysis of relatives like (9) is questionable.

In the case of the relativization of the logical subject of the *there*-construction, the determiner *the* also appears before the antecedent.

(12)　The bugs (that) there were on the windshield were harmless.[3]
　　　　　　　　　　　　　　　　　　　　　　(Carlson (1977: 526))

Normally the logical subject of the *there*-construction cannot be used with the article *the*.

(13) *There were the bugs on the windshield.

---

[2] In the case of nonrestrictive relative clauses, proper nouns are not used with the determiner *the*.
　(i)　Dr Brown, who lives next door, comes from Australia.　(Quirk et al. (1985: 290))

[3] According to Carlson (1977: 526), the relative pronoun in (12) cannot be replaced with the relative pronoun *which*.
　(i)　*The bugs which there were on the windshield were harmless.

3.5. Stacked Relatives

Restrictive relative clauses can be stacked.

(14) The <u>theory of light that Newton proposed</u> that everyone laughed at was more accurate than the <u>one</u> that met with instant acceptance.

(McCawley (1998: 382)) (The underlines are his.)

This fact is difficult to explain assuming the head raising analysis. Taking (14) as an example, based on the head raising analysis, the head noun *theory* alone should be raised both from the first relative clause and from the second relative clause.

However, this case may be dealt with if we assume the NP raising analysis of relatives, where the NP is moved from the relative clause to the head position in the relative construction, as illustrated below.

(15) The NP Raising Analysis

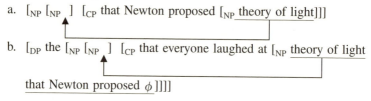

The NP *theory of light* is moved from the first relative clause and merges with the relative clause, and then the NP and the relative clause constitute the NP *theory of light that Newton proposed* ϕ. Next the NP *theory of light that Newton proposed* ϕ is moved from the second relative clause and merges with the relative clause and then the NP and the relative clause constitute the NP *theory of light that Newton proposed* ϕ *that everyone laughed at*.

3.6. Reconstruction Effects

Anaphors can be seen within the antecedents of relative pronouns.

(16) The picture of himself$_i$ that John$_i$ likes best is impressive.

(Aoun and Li (2003: 111))

The head external analysis cannot explain the fact that the anaphor within the antecedent of the relative clause is co-referential with the DP in the relative clause, while the head raising analysis and the matching analysis can.

3.7. Coordination of Antecedents

The antecedents with determiners can be coordinated, as follows.

(17)　the boy and the girl that met in Vienna[4]　　(Jackendoff (1977: 190))

There is a possibility that the determiner *the* and the head noun constitute a unit and that the unit is modified by the relative clause, as schematized below.

(18)　[[$_{DP}$ [$_{DP}$ the boy] and [$_{DP}$ the girl]] [$_{CP}$ that met in Vienna]]

The case in (17) might support the analysis of the relative clause as the adjunct to DP and the DP raising analysis in (9), and it might counter-exemplify the analyses based on the assumption that the head noun and the relative clause constitute a unit, such as in the head raising analysis.

3.8. The Argument for the Analysis of Antecedents as NPs

However, there is sufficient evidence for the analysis of the restrictive relative clause as the adjunct to NP, as shown in McCawley (1998) and Hasegawa (2003).

(19) a. All [[[theorists of gravitation] and [accounts of diffraction]] that have ever been published] are hopelessly inadequate.
　　 b. Most [[linguists who play chess] and [philosophers who play poker]] find this book useful.　　(McCawley (1998: 382))

(20) a. The theory of light that Newton proposed was less successful than the one that Huygen proposed.
　　 b. The theory of light that Newton proposed that everyone laughed at was more accurate than the one that met with instant acceptance.
　　　 (=(14))　　　　　　　　　　(ibid.) (The underlines are his.)

---

[4] It should be noted that (17) is not derived by the application of right node raising or conjunction reduction.

　(i) *the boy that met in Vienna and the girl that met in Vienna

In (19a), the NP *theorists of gravitation* and the NP *accounts of diffraction* are conjoined to form an NP, and the relative clause *that have ever been published* is adjoined to the NP *theorists of gravitation and accounts of diffraction*. The example in (19b) demonstrates that the head noun and the relative clause constitute an NP. Assuming that the pronoun *one* replaces an NP rather than a DP, (20a) shows that the relative clause is adjoined to the NP and (20b) shows that the head noun and the relative clause constitute an NP since they can be replaced with *one*.

The interpretation of restrictive relatives also suggests that the antecedents of relatives are NPs but not DPs. Hasegawa (2003) gives the following examples.

(21) a. Few students I know have beards.
b. the only book D. H. Lawrence wrote that I don't like

(Hasegawa (2003: 110))

Following his interpretation, if the antecedent of the *wh*-relative pronoun in the restrictive relative clause is the DP, the antecedent in (21a) would be *few students*, but (21a) does not imply that I know few students. It means that of the students I know, few have beards. Furthermore, assuming that the antecedent is the DP, the antecedent in (21b) would be *the only book D. H. Lawrence wrote*. However, (21b) does not mean that I don't like the only book D. H. Lawrence wrote, which has the implication that D. H. Lawrence wrote only one book. Considering the interpretation of restrictive relatives, it follows that the antecedents of relatives are not DPs but NPs.

4. The Analyses on Relatives

The behavior of restrictive *wh*-relatives is different from that of *that*-relatives or bare relatives.

(22) a. the boy to whom I talked
b. *the boy to that I talked
c. *the boy to ϕ I talked

(cf. Hasegawa (2003: 108))

The prepositions taking *wh*-relative pronouns as their complements can be pied-piped, whereas the prepositions cannot be moved and must be stranded in the case of the corresponding *that*-relatives and bare relatives.

Observing the difference between *wh*-relatives and *that*-relatives and bare relatives, Hasegawa (2003) assigns different structures to *wh*-relatives and *that*-relatives and bare relatives. He argues that *that*-relatives and bare relatives involve no movement and that a kind of pronominal element referring to the antecedent is deleted *in situ*, and he claims that *wh*-phrases are moved to the initial position of the relative clauses by *wh*-movement in the case of *wh*-relatives.

From the fact that *that*-relatives and bare relatives show different syntactic behavior from that of *wh*-relatives, I assume that *that*-relatives and bare relatives have the same structure and that their structure is different from that of *wh*-relatives. I adopt the head external analysis as in (2) in the case of *wh*-relatives and the NP raising analysis as in (15) in the cases of *that*-relatives and bare relatives.

(23) The Head External Analysis on *wh*-relatives
 [$_{DP}$ the [$_{NP}$ [$_{NP}$ book] [$_{CP}$ [ ] John likes which]]]

(24) The NP Raising Analysis on *that*-relatives and bare relatives
 [$_{DP}$ the [$_{NP}$ [$_{NP}$] [$_{CP}$ [ ](that) Newton proposed [$_{NP}$ theory of light]]]]

I assume that the *wh*-phrase is moved into the initial position in the *wh*-relative clause by *wh*-movement in (23) and that the NP corresponding to the antecedent is moved to [Spec, CP] first and then it is moved to the sister position of the *that*-relative clause or the bare relative clause by sideward movement in (24).

Aoun and Li (2003) observe the differences between *wh*-relatives and *that*-relatives.

(25) a. The headway that Mal made was impressive.
 b.?? The headway which Mal made was impressive.
 (Aoun and Li (2003: 110))
(26) a. The picture of himself$_i$ that John$_i$ likes best is impressive. (=(16))
 b.?*The picture of himself$_i$ which John$_i$ likes best is impressive.
 (op.cit.: 111)

The grammaticality of (25a) and (26a) suggests that the head noun is base-generated within *that*-relative clauses.

Turning back to the examples in (23), the grammaticalness of (22a) is explained on the assumption that *wh*-relatives involve *wh*-movement, which can move not only *wh*-phrases but also the PPs and DPs containing them. The ungrammaticality of (22b) and (22c) is predicted on the assumption that *that*-relatives and bare relatives do not involve *wh*-movement but involve the movement of the antecedent NP. Then it is predicted that the preposition cannot be moved and must be stranded *in situ*.

The analyses in (23) and (24) can deal with the fact about the extraposition of the relative clause from the DP as in (5), since the head noun and the relative clause constitute a single unit. The analyses here also can explain the fact that the relative clauses can be stacked by the movement of NPs schematized in (15) and by the recursiveness of NPs in (23).

The remaining problems are the case agreement of antecedents and the coordination fact of antecedents with articles such as in (17). The case agreement fact is difficult to explain based on the NP raising analysis in (24). Here I suppose tentatively that after the case agreement of the antecedent within the relative clause, the antecedent loses its case when it moves to the specifier position of the CP and moves out of the relative clause, and that it bears case again when it is moved into the head position of the relative clause on the assumption that the case of a DP is determined by the verb or the preposition governing the DP.

As for the coordination of antecedents with articles as seen in (17), it cannot be dealt with by my analysis but it can be dealt with by the analysis of antecedents as DPs. However, relative clauses can take split antecedents.

(27) Tom bought a can-opener and Alice bought a dictionary that were once owned by Leonald Bloomfield.   (McCawley (1982: 100))

This example cannot be explained even by the analysis of antecedents as DPs. I will leave the problem of coordination open.

5. Conclusion

This article has discussed relative clauses. I assigned *wh*-relatives a different structure from that of *that*-relatives *or* bare relatives. I have assumed that the heads of *wh*-relatives are generated outside of the relatives and that *that*-relatives or bare relatives involve the head NP raising. Though the analysis here has some problems to be resolved, I will leave them open for my future research.

References

Aoun, Joseph and Yen-hui Audrey Li (2003) *Essays on the Representational and Derivational Nature of Grammar: The Diversity of Wh-Constructions*, MIT Press, Cambridge, MA.
Carlson, Greg N. (1977) "Amount Relatives," *Language* 53, 520–542.
Emonds, Joseph E. (1979) "Appositive Relatives Have No Properties," *Linguistic Inquiry* 10, 211–243.
Hasegawa, Kinsuke (2003) *Seiseibunpou no Houhou—Eigo-tougoron no Shikumi* (Approaches to Generative Grammar: The Fundamentals of English Syntax), Kenkyusha, Tokyo.
Jackendoff, Ray (1977) $\overline{X}$ *Syntax: A Study of Phrase Structure*, MIT Press, Cambridge, MA.
McCawley, James D. (1982) "Parentheticals and Discontinuous Constituent Structure," *Linguistic Inquiry* 13, 91–106.
McCawley, James D. (1998) *The Syntactic Phenomena of English*, 2nd ed., University of Chicago Press, Chicago.
Quirk, Randolph, Sidney Greenbaum, Geoffrey Leech and Jan Svartvik (1985) *A Comprehensive Grammar of the English Language*, Longman, London.
Schachter, Paul (1973) "Focus and Relativization," *Language* 49, 19–46.
Yagi, Takao (2012) "Kankeisetsu no Head Raising Bunseki ni okeru Hitotsu no Mondaiten: Pied-Piping to Shima no Seiyaku (A Problem with the Head Raising Analysis of Relatives: Pied-Piping and the Island Restriction)," *Eigaku Ronkou* 41, 51–62, Tokyo Gakugei University.

beware の用法及び活用体系に基づく定形性の概念について*

野村　忠央

北海道教育大学旭川校

1. はじめに

　伝統文法では，He *plays* tennis. (3 人称単数直説法現在形) のように，人称，数，法，時制によって動詞が屈折 (inflection) している動詞形態を「定形 (finite form)」，逆に It is difficult for me to *answer* the question. (不定詞形) のように上記要素で屈折しない動詞形態を「非定形 (non-finite form)」と呼ぶ．これらの例を含め，伝統文法では通例，主要な動詞形が以下のように分類される．

(1) a. 定形…直説法 (= 直説法現在形，直説法過去形)，命令法 (形)，仮定法 (= 仮定法過去形，仮定法過去完了形，仮定法現在形)
　　 b. 非定形…不定詞形，動名詞形，分詞形 (= 現在分詞形，過去分詞形)

　ここで，屈折が磨耗した現代英語において問題になるのは，以下のような命令法形 ((2a) 参照) と仮定法現在形 ((2b) 参照) である．

(2) a. *Leave* at once!　　b.　I demanded that John *leave* immediately.

---

* 本稿は日本英語英文学会第 22 回年次大会 (2012 年 3 月 3 日，於：亜細亜大学) での発表内容に少なからず加筆・修正を加えたものである．当日，英和辞書編纂において beware の項を執筆されたご経験のある藤田崇夫氏 (浜松学院大学) を含め，発表内容に有益なコメントをいただいた学会の方々に感謝申し上げる．また，本稿の内容，例文の判断について，英語母語話者の立場から非常に有益なコメントをいただいた Michelle La Fay (北海道大学)，Donald L. Smith (元青山学院大学教授) 両氏に記して感謝申し上げる．また，beware の語源，歴史的な用法についてご教示頂いた山内一芳 (東京都立大学名誉教授)，秋元実治 (青山学院大学名誉教授) 両氏にも併せて謝意を表す．言うを俟たず，残る不備・遺漏は筆者一人に帰せられるべきものである．なお，本研究は平成 23 年度科学研究費補助金基盤研究 (C)「仮定法節と不定詞節の比較による定形性の研究」(課題番号 23520574) の助成を受けている．

すなわち，(2a) の Leave は 2 人称単数命令法（現在）形，(2b) の leave は 3 人称単数仮定法現在形で「定形」ということになるが，どちらも少なくとも形態的には leave の原形（裸不定詞）と同一形態であるのだから，実はどちらも文字通り「原形」すなわち「非定形」だと主張することも可能だからである．

前者の伝統的な見方の解説としては，『英語教育』の Question Box コーナーでの回答に記された以下の記述がわかりやすい（議論の関連部分のみ示す）．

(3) Q. （前略）suggest の後にくる主語＋動詞の文では，その動詞は原形であるはずですが，そうはなっていません．（後略）
Ans.（前略）最後に注記をしておきます．「原形」(root-form) は，suggested, suggesting, suggests などとともに変化形のひとつとしてみた場合（これをパラダイムと言います）の名称です．文中での動詞の形を言う場合は，定形，非定形，直説法（現在形，過去形など），仮定法（現在形，過去形など），命令法などの名称を使うのが普通です．この言い方からすれば，質問者の引用した文中の動詞 takes は「直説法現在形」ということになります．そして，「原形」と言っておられるのは「仮定法現在形」ということになります．

(八木 (2003: 72)，下線筆者)

本論で論ずるが，21 世紀の標準的英文法書の一つである Huddleston and Pullum (2005) も，命令文及び仮定法現在節を定形と捉えている．

これに対し，後者の立場を（主張している内容の自動的な帰結により）採用しているものとして Nomura (2006) が挙げられる．Nomura は，(2a, b) の leave の前には，概略，不可視の命令法・仮定法助動詞が存在しており，leave は文字通り原形だと主張している．本稿では以上の問題意識に立って，活用 (paradigm) において興味深い振る舞いを示す beware の用法について論ずる．

beware は以下の例に代表されるように，命令文が代表的な使用法である．

(4) a. Beware of the dog!　b. Buyer beware!

しかし，本稿ではそれ以外の活用形についても調査し，結論として，「beware は原形（裸不定詞）のみが存在し，定形は存在しない」というのが妥当ですっきりとした動詞活用体系であると主張する．また，その結論は上記，Nomura (2006) の主張を支持することにも繋がることも併せて主張する．

2. インフォーマント・チェックによる beware の用法

動詞 beware は現代英語では欠格動詞（defective verb）として知られるが，*OED* や各種の英語語源辞典を参照すると，古い英語では，定形や動名詞・分詞形も存在したことが記されている．以下は寺澤（編）（1997）からの引用である．

(5) beware v. ((c1200)) (...に) 気をつける，用心する．
◆ ME *be(n) war* ← BE (imper., inf., or pres. subj.) +*war* 'WARE²'.
◇本来は二語からなる動詞句だったが，14C には一語形も現われた．OE *bewarian* to guard, take care of (← BE-+*warian* 'to WARE³') とは別語だが，動詞 *ware* の影響を受けている．1600 年ごろから一語としての動詞の性格を強め <u>bewares, bewared, bewaring などの活用形も用いられたが，今では主として命令文あるいは不定詞，まれに仮定法現在に限られる</u>． （寺澤（編）（1997: 178），下線筆者）

しかし，下線の類の記述が現代英語の用法として正しいかについては，筆者の調査した限り，体系的な調査は見当たらなかった．よって，筆者は今回，全ての活用形についてインフォーマント調査を行った．本節では，まずその結果を，英語語法文法的な留意点と併せて提示したい．[1]

2.1. 命令文の用法

まず beware の典型的な用法とされる命令文であるが，以下の (6) の諸例は全て文法的である．命令文は伝統的に定形文とされることに留意されたい．

(6) a. Beware of the dog!（猛犬注意）(=(4a))
    b. Beware of pickpockets![2]

---

[1] 以下，インフォーマントとなって頂いたお二方（どちらもアメリカ人）について，Michelle La Fay 氏を A 氏，Donald L. Smith 氏を B 氏とそれぞれ記す（例文の文法性・容認性について，OK/* などのように，判断が分かれた場合も，前者が A 氏，後者が B 氏の判断）．また以降の例文で，出典がないものは，各種辞典，文法書などを参考に筆者が作例したものである．

[2] なお，辞書，文法書によっては，下記 (i) の如き他動詞用法も記されているが，本稿の主旨とは外れるので，以下の議論では全て自動詞用法を用いる．
  (i) a. He told me to beware pickpockets.
      b. Beware the avalanche!

c. Beware (of) what you say.
　　d. Beware that you do not wake the baby.
　　e. Beware that you do not fail.
　　f. Beware lest it should fail.
　　g. Beware!
　　h. Buyer beware!（買い物をする者は用心せよ）(=(4b))

但し，beware が想起させる状況はかなり深刻（serious）で，聞き手が脅迫めいた怖ろしさ（scary/intimidating）を感じるため，(6d) は（日本の英和辞典でしばしば見られるが）おかしさを感じさせてしまう（funny）例文である．また，beware が単独で用いられる命令や注意としての (6g) (= Be careful!) や標語的な (6h) は我々日本人が思っている以上に日常生活で用いられる表現である．

2.2. 命令文以外の定形とされている用法

次に，伝統文法で定形文とされているその他の諸用法を概観していく．まず，直説法文の例を以下に挙げる．結果は全く非文法的ということであった．

(7)　a. *{I/You/We/They} always beware of the dog.（3単現以外の現在形）
　　b. *{He/She} always bewares of the dog.（3人称単数現在形）
　　c. *{I/You/He/She/We/They} always bewared of the dog.（過去形）

第2に，法助動詞との共起関係を以下，(8), (9) に示す．

(8)　a. We must beware of committing the same fallacy in the comparison of languages.
　　b. You {must/ought to/should} beware of what you say!
　　c. You {must/ought to/should} beware of how you start in business.
(9)　a. John {will/must/should} certainly beware of the furiously barking dog every day.
　　b. John {*may probably/*might/*could} beware of the dog.

まず，根源的用法については，(8) に示すように，命令文と類似した意味を持つ義務の must や当為の should, ought to と共起する．また，認識的用法につ

---

　　c. Beware the ides of March.（3月15日を警戒せよ）
　　　　　　　　　　　　　　((ic): William Shakespeare, *Julius Caesar*, I. ii. 18)

いては，(9a) に示すように，蓋然性が高い will, must, should とは共起可能だが，(9b) に示すように，確実性が低い may, might, could などとは共起不可能であることがわかった．しかし，これは beware の意味論的な共起関係によるものであり，統語論的に beware は法助動詞と共起できると結論してよい．つまり，法助動詞文は言うまでもなく定形文であるが，通常の直説法文が全く非文法的であるのに対し，こちらは文法的だということである．

次に，仮定法文について考察してみよう．まず，第 3 のグループとして仮定法過去形 ((10a) 参照)，仮定法過去完了形 ((10b) 参照) について挙げると，これも直説法文同様，全く非文法的だということであった．

(10) a. *If you bewared of the dog, you would not get hurt.
   b. *If you had bewared of the dog, you would not have got hurt.

しかし，これに対し，第 4 のグループとして仮定法現在形の諸例を考察してみよう．以下，(11) に用例を示す．

(11) a. They {told/advised/warned} me that I should beware of pickpockets in Tokyo.[3]
   b. It is important that we beware of pickpockets in Tokyo.
   c. They insisted that I beware of the lures of the female spy.

つまり，同じ仮定法でも，仮定法現在節においては beware の使用が文法的であるということである．この事実は注目すべきである．

2.3. 非定形の用法

最後に，beware の非定形の用法に移る．まず，不定詞の用法であるが，調査の結果，基本的にはあらゆる環境で文法的であった．次例 (12) 参照．

---

[3] 興味深いことだが，A 氏も B 氏も (11a) の例文について，(i) のように should を用いない仮定法現在形を用いると，非文になるという判断であった．

(i) */*They {told/advised/warned} me that I *beware* of pickpockets.

この事実は，(11a) の従属節が実は仮定法現在節ではない可能性も示唆するのだが，本論から外れるので，事実の指摘に留めておく．

なお，この (i) の事実は本論に影響を与えない．なぜなら，(11b, c) では明らかに原形が現れているし，例えば，warn などについても，A 氏によれば，以下の (iia, b) などは should の有無に拘わらず文法的だからである．

(ii) a. They warned me that I (should) beware how you got the {money/information}.
   b. The doctor warned me that I (should) beware of the dangers of new medication.

(12) a. To beware what we say is important for us all.（主語）
    b. It is important for us all to beware how we speak.（仮主語構文）
    c. The important thing is to beware what we say.（補語）
    d. {Remember/Don't forget} to beware of the dog.（目的語）
    e. I {advise/order/demand/require/request} you to beware of what you say.（コントロール節の補部）

これに対し，不定詞の名詞的用法と類似の意味を持ちうる動名詞の用法を次に見てみよう．次例 (13) を参照されたい．

(13) a. OK/*Bewaring what we say is important for us all.（主語）
    b. ?/*The important thing is bewaring what we say.（補語）
    c. ??/*I regret not bewaring of the dog.（目的語）
    d. */*{Remember/Don't forget} bewaring of the dog.（目的語）

動名詞については 2 人のインフォーマントで意見が分かれた．要約して言うと，B 氏は動名詞は全て非文法的，A 氏は主語・補語用法はある程度，容認可能だが ((13a, b) 参照)，目的語用法ではかなり容認性が落ちるか非文だということである ((13c, d) 参照)．筆者の私見としては，動名詞用法はほぼ非文法的あるいは容認可能性が低いとしてよいと考える．その主要な理由は，上記 (12) で示したように不定詞では，動名詞の (13) のような容認性の差はなく，文法的であるのに対し，(13) の動名詞では，B 氏は全て非文，A 氏も主語以外の環境では容認性が落ちるからである．[4]

最後に，分詞についてであるが，以下 (14) に示すように，分詞が現れる環境をほぼ全てチェックしてみたが，全く非文法的という結果であった．

(14) a. *John is always bewaring of the dog.（進行形）
    b. *He has always bewared of the dog.（完了形）
    c. *The man always bewaring of the dog is my uncle.
       （現在分詞の形容詞的用法）
    d. *The furiously barking dog bewared by everyone is Bill's.
       （過去分詞の形容詞的用法）
    e. *Mr. Jones finally didn't get hurt at all, bewaring of the furiously

---

[4] そう考えた場合の，A 氏の (13a-c) の容認性については，文法的な不定詞用法の類推によるものと捉えるのが自然だと思われる．

barking dog.（文尾位置の分詞構文）

f. *Not bewaring of the furiously barking dog on his way home, Mr. Jones got seriously hurt.（文頭位置の分詞構文）

以上，本節で示した調査の結果を要約すると，beware は (i) 命令文，不定詞節，仮定法現在節で生起可能だが，(ii) 直説法現在形・過去形，仮定法過去形・過去完了形，動名詞形，分詞形は存在しない，ということになる．

3. 提案

さて本節では，前節での調査結果を踏まえ，beware の活用体系，定形・非定形をどう捉えるかについて提案，議論していきたい．

3.1. 仮定法現在節・命令文の統語構造

ここで，本論に入る前に，Nomura (2006) の提案する，仮定法現在節に現れる動詞が定形ではなく原形動詞であるとする主張の根拠を概観しておく．まず，仮定法現在節には3つの大きな統語的特徴がある．次例を見られたい．

(15) John {demands/demanded} that Susan *leave* immediately.

(16) a. I order that you {not/*do not} go alone.

b. *It is imperative that you {will/can/must/would/could/might} leave on time.

(17) a. I demand that you {not be/*be not} such a fool.

b. His father insisted that John {not smoke/*smoke not/*do not smoke} at home. （以上，Nomura (2006: 161-162) 参照）

まず第1に，「動詞が常に原形」という重要な特徴が挙げられる ((15) 参照)．第2に，仮定法現在節中には「do の支え (*do*-support)」が起こらない ((16a), (17b) 参照)．また，(仮定法代用の法助動詞 should・shall 以外の) 法助動詞も現れない ((16b) 参照)．第3に，否定の語順は標準的・規範的に (have・be も含め)「not+V」であり，「V+not」ではない．また，否定に「do の支え」も用いない ((16a), (17b) 参照) 参照)．以上を踏まえ，Nomura (2006: Chapter 7) はこれらの特徴を整合的に説明するために，以下，(18), (19) の統語構造を仮定する．

(18) I insisted [$_{CP}$ that [$_{IP}$ he I [$_{ModalP}$ M$_\phi$ (not) [$_{VP}$ go there]]]].

(19) a. 仮定法現在節では，ModalP（法助動詞句）主要部に基底生成された（[+Subj(unctive)] と [+Pres] の素性を持つ）不可視の法助動詞 M_ϕ が I の位置に移動し，動詞自身は移動しない．
   b. 仮定法現在の範疇は法助動詞である．但し，may, can, must のような通常の法助動詞が可視的（overt）であるのに対し，この仮定法現在法助動詞 M_ϕ は不可視（covert）である．

これらを仮定すると，上述の3つの統語的特徴は整合的・自動的に説明可能である．すなわち，(i) 仮定法現在が法助動詞の一種だとすれば，後続する動詞がすべて原形であるであるのは当然の帰結である．(ii)「支えの do」や法助動詞が生起しないのは，「法助動詞は共起しない」という一般原則のためである（= 仮定法現在も「支えの do」も法助動詞の一種である）．(iii) 語順がいつも「not+V」なのは，動詞自体はいつも元位置にとどまっているため，基底の語順たる「not+V」が常に反映されるからである，ということである．

同様に，Nomura は命令文も以下（20）に示すような不可視の命令法法助動詞が存在する構造を主張している．それを支えるデータを（21），（22）に示す．

(20)　$[_{CP} [_{IP}$ (You)/pro I $[_{ModalP} M_\phi [_{VP}$ Stand up]]]].
(21) a. *Be not foolish.
   b. *Have not finished the homework before I come back.
(22) a. *Must study hard.　b. *Can swim very fast.
　　　　　　（以上，Nomura (2006: Appendix to Chapter 7) 参照）

(21) のデータは，命令文では，通例「have・be 繰り上げ」があるとされる have 動詞・be 動詞でさえも I の位置には上がらないことを，また，(22) の法助動詞の命令文が存在しないデータは，I の位置には，不可視の命令文法助動詞 M_ϕ の存在により，他の法助動詞が共起不可能であることを示している．[5]

---

[5] ここで読者の中には，命令文には，以下 (i) のように，do や don't が生起するので，やはり命令文中の動詞は定形とみなすべきだと考える向きがあるかもしれない．なぜなら，一般的に，「支えの do」は「時制（つまり定形要素を意味する）が孤立した場合に起こる」とされているからである．
　しかし，筆者は，ここで詳述する余裕はないのだが，簡単に言うと，命令文の do は時制を支えているのではなく，実は「命令法代用助動詞」だと考えている（Nomura (2006: 204) 参照．また，Watanabe (1993) や Nomura (2006) は通常の「支えの do」も「直説法代用助動詞」だと主張している）．そのように考える根拠の一つは，もし命令文の do が時制を支えているなら，以下の (ii) においては，3人称単数の anyone に呼応して，3人称単数現在形たる

3.2. beware の活用体系

さて，beware の用法に話を戻す．伝統的な定形・非定形の分類に従うと，beware は，以下 (23) に示すように，非常に煩雑で，一貫しない活用体系 (paradigm) を持っていることになる．

(23) 伝統的な定形・非定形の分類による beware の活用体系
    a. 定形 → (i) 直説法現在形，直説法過去形，仮定法過去（完了）形は不可，(ii) 命令法形，仮定法現在形は可
    b. 非定形 → (i) 不定詞形は可，(ii) 動名詞形，現在分詞形，過去分詞形は不可

すなわち，定形・非定形のそれぞれに，可能なものと不可能な活用形が存在しているという不自然で煩雑な体系である．しかし，3.1 節での Nomura (2006) の主張に従えば，命令法形，仮定法現在形は実は原形なのであるから，上記 (23) は以下の (24) のように捉え直すことができる．

(24) 本稿の提案 (i)―定形・非定形の分類による beware の活用体系
    a. beware は定形は全て存在しない（→定形 = 直説法現在形，直説法過去形，仮定法過去（完了）形）．
    b. beware は非定形のうち原形のみが存在する（→原形 = 不定詞標識 to の後の原形，法助動詞の後の原形不定詞，仮定法現在助動詞の後の原形，命令法助動詞の後の原形）．よって，動名詞形・分詞形は存在しない．

また，この (24) の提案は理論言語学的な見地に立つと，更に (25) のようにまとめることが可能である．これを本稿の結論として提示したい．

(25) 本稿の提案 (ii)―beware の活用体系
    a. beware は原形（裸不定詞）のみが形態上，存在する
    b. よって，beware は活用体系上，欠格的な動詞であり，接辞転移 (Affix Hopping) が適用されたあらゆる形態（= 全ての直説法形，仮定法過去（完了）形，動名詞形，分詞形）が存在しない．

Doesn't の支えが起こってもいいはずであるが，実際には Don't のみが可能であるという事実があるということである．
  (i) {*Do*/*Don't* (you)} stand up!
  (ii) {Don't/*Doesn't} *anyone* stand up!

3.3. 定形・非定形をどう捉えるか

最後に，定形，非定形をどう捉えるかを論じて，本節を閉じたい．Huddleston and Pullum (2005) は現代英語の優れた記述文法であり，母語話者・非母語話者，両方の学生への英文法の導入を目指しているが，動詞の活用体系についての記述は複雑である．筆者の理解に基づいて Huddleston and Pullum (2005: Chapter 3) の動詞の活用体系をまとめると (26) のようになる．[6]

(26) 　直説法文・法的過去形　　主要形　　　　　　　定形
　　　命令法形　　　　　　　　副次形　単純形　　　定形
　　　仮定法形　　　　　　　　副次形　単純形　　　定形
　　　不定詞形　　　　　　　　副次形　単純形　　　非定形
　　　動名詞分詞形　　　　　　副次形　動名詞分詞形　非定形
　　　過去分詞形　　　　　　　副次形　過去分詞形　　非定形

ごく簡単に，それぞれの用語を説明すると，まず，時制屈折 (= 現在・過去) の区別がある形態を (i) 主要形 (primary form)，ないものを (ii) 副次形 (secondary form) と呼んでいる．そして，その副次形は，(i) いわゆる裸不定詞に相当する単純形 (plain form)，(ii) 伝統的な用語での動名詞と現在分詞を合わせた動名詞分詞形 (gerund-participle) (= 日本の学校文法で -ing 形としてまとめられているものに相当)，そして (iii) 過去分詞形 (past participle) に下位区分される．そして，本稿との関連で話が複雑なのは，動詞の屈折形態の分類ではなく，<u>節タイプ (clause type) の分類としても定形 (finite)，非定形 (non-finite) という用語を用いている</u>と思われることである．

上記を前提に，彼らは「もし動詞が単純形である場合，定形あるいは非定形になってよい：すなわち，(i) 命令節と仮定法節では定形になり，(ii) 不定詞節では非定形になる」という複雑な主張をしている (Huddleston and Pullum (2005: 36) 参照)．しかし，筆者は理論の統一性の観点や本稿での議論の結果から，(そしてまた，彼らの主張も踏まえつつ) 以下の (27) を主張したい．

(27) 　動詞屈折形態としての定形・非定形
　　　a.「原形」と考えられる形態，すなわち，彼らの用語での「単純形」(= 命令法形，仮定法形，不定詞形) は全て「非定形」である．

---

[6] (26) において，「法的過去 (modal preterite)」，「仮定法 (subjunctive)」という用語は，通例，(were (彼らは「非現実法の were (irrealis *were*)」と呼ぶ) 以外の)「仮定法過去形」，「仮定法現在形」と呼ばれているものにそれぞれ相当する．

 b. よって,「主要形」＝定形,「副次形」＝非定形だと結論できる．

(27a, b) はすっきりとした体系であると思われるが,最後に,彼らに従い,節タイプとしての定形(文),非定形(文)にも言及しておく．紙幅の関係からテクニカルな詳細は避けるが,節タイプの定形性について,(28)を提案する．

(28) 節タイプ(clause type)としての定形・非定形[7]
  a. 主格が現れる(認可される)節は定形文である．
  b. 主格以外の格が現れる(認可される)節は非定形文である．
(29) a. Don't {you/*your} sit down. (命令法文＝定形)
  b. I demanded [that {he/*his/*him} leave at once].

              （仮定法現在節＝定形）
  c. I believed [{*he/*his/him} to be happy]. (不定詞節＝非定形)
  d. Would you mind {*I/my/me} opening the window?

                （動名詞節＝非定形）

すなわち,動詞形態が原形か,接辞転移が適用可能かに拘わらず,主格が生起可能な文は定形文,不可能な文は非定形文だと認定できるということである．

4. おわりに

 本稿では,活用体系上,興味深い振る舞いを示す beware を調査した結果,「beware は原形（裸不定詞）のみが存在し,定形は存在しない」というのが妥当ですっきりとした動詞活用体系であると主張した．そして,その結論は,Nomura (2006) の提案する,仮定法現在節や命令文においては不可視の法助動詞 M_ϕ が存在するという主張と合致し,それを支持することにも繋がることを併せて主張した．また,形態上,原形が現れる構文は全て「非定形」であること,また,節タイプ上は,主格が現れる構文が「定形」であると主張した．

---

 [7] 関連して重要なことだが,本稿の立場でも,仮定法現在節・命令文中の不可視の法助動詞自体は定形である,となることに留意されたい．つまり,原形動詞は原形＝非定形であるが,その前に位置する不可視の法助動詞自体は定形であるのである．つまり,八木 (2003) や Huddleston and Pullum (2005) の捉え方は学校文法・伝統文法的な説明としては問題がない（と言っていいかもしれない）が,理論言語学的には,本稿の議論やこの注に記した点で,齟齬あるいは煩雑さが生まれてしまっているのだと結論できる．

参考文献

Huddleston, Rodney and Geoffrey K. Pullum (2005) *A Student's Introduction to English Grammar*, Cambridge University Press, Cambridge.
Nomura, Tadao (2006) *ModalP and Subjunctive Present*, Hituzi Syobo, Tokyo.
寺澤芳雄(編) (1997)『英語語源辞典』研究社，東京．
Watanabe, Akira (1993) *Agr-based Case Theory and Its Interaction with A-bar System*, Doctoral dissertation, MIT.
八木克正 (2003)「suggest that ... の that 節の動詞」『英語教育』11月号，72，大修館書店，東京．

The Hunt for a Label*

Masayuki Oishi

Tohoku Gakuin University

1. Lexicalist Position

One of the alleged merits of the X-bar theory was that it is successful in capturing cross-categorial generalizations with the crucial stipulation of endocentricity, such as internal structure between nominal and sentential expressions. The X-bar theory was claimed to serve to assign one and the same underlying skeletal structure to the expression containing, say a particular verb on the one hand and to that with its derived nominal on the other, with a crucial assumption that these two categories are listed under a single lexical entry. Take a case of a verb *decide* and its derived nominal *decision*. The distinction between *decide* and *decision* is just a matter of phonological realization of a set of features, *DECIDE*, with the selectional properties common to them.

This sense coincides with the general reflection on syntactic aspects of lexical items, or substantive elements. Specifically, it is the idea that syntactically derivable properties are not stated in the lexicon and hence a category label, which is quite syntactic, is automatically determined in syntax. Here "automatic" determination awaits certain clarifications. Thus, earlier work of linguistic theory had claimed that once a category-neutral element DECIDE is inserted under N in the base, it is treated as an N (*decision*), and no transformation (or syntactic operation) can change its category

---

* The paragraphs to follow are meant to constitute a preliminary sketch of my on-going research on labeling in nominal structures (Oishi (in preparation)). I owe Noam Chomsky for detailed discussion and encouragements and Hisatsugu Kitahara for clarifications and comments, whom I thank deeply. Some materials here have been discussed in Oishi (2005, 2011, 2012).

throughout the derivation (hence lexicalist position), and showed that movement operation is applicable within NP as well as S. This is the context where the discussion on the internal structure of derived nominals has entertained theoretical consideration. (See Chomsky (1970/1972, 1986).)

The systems proposed and developed in Chomsky (2007, 2013, 2014) have shed more unified light on such automatic determination, from a perspective of general architecture of language. Specifically, a substantive element is regarded as a syntactic complex (or amalgam) of a categorizer (or categorial specification) K and a root R: <K, R>. The root ("undifferentiated root" in Chomsky's (2007) terminology) is assumed to be common to any relevant categorial alternants, and responsible to the selectional properties. Thus, a verb *decide* is a complex of a categorizer v, and a root DECIDE whereas its nominalized counterpart *decision* is a complex of a categorizer n, and the root DECIDE, each of which selects a sentential complement, and by the same token, we have such alternation as *willing* ~ *willingness* (where lexical alternants are italicized, categories are represented in a lower case, and roots are given in upper case):

(1) a. i. *decide*: [v, DECIDE]
  ii. *decision*: [n, DECIDE]
 b. i. John decided [$_\alpha$ to read the book]
  ii. John's/the/ø decision [$_\alpha$ to read the book]
(2) a. i. *willing*: [a, WILLING]
  ii. *willingness*: [n, WILLING]
 b. i. John is willing [$_\alpha$ to be puzzled]
  ii. John's/the/ø willingness [$_\alpha$ to be puzzled]

Furthermore these inside-materials participate in syntactic derivation, as if they were hunting for a label for Full Interpretation. This analysis falls under a version of lexicalist position in its essential respects while departing from it in assuming that a categorizer and a root to be associated are introduced separately into syntax and end up with an amalgam through derivation, to put it more specifically, that a categorial character of a root is derivationally determined. It inevitably imports reconsideration of characterizing derived nominal structures, some of which I will explore below.

2. Nominal Phrases

To begin, I will review the discussion of the internal structure of nominals suggested in Chomsky (2007), which may be regarded as the initial proposal concerning nominals within the system of labeling and phase. Chomsky employs a factorization of lexical items (substantive elements) along with the theory of labeling and the basic principle of Merge, and furthermore suggests that "the internal structure" of nominal expressions basically "corresponds to verbal phrases," in fact the mechanisms for v*P are plausibly extended to nominal phrases.

Let us consider his proposals on verbal phrases and nominal phrases one by one. In a case of verbal phrases, we will have such a derivation as (3).

(3) {External Argument, {<v*, V>, {Internal Argument, {V_t, Internal Argument$_t$}}}}

A verbal root V and its internal argument (a nominal phrase NP, hence an object NP) are merged (EM). Here a verbal phrase head v* enters, the internal argument NP raises to the SPEC of V, and the root V is then merged with v*, forming an amalgam "{v*, V}". The result is a verbal phrase v*P headed by an invisible head v*, which is a label of this object, and a visible head V. The root V cannot be a label, as assumed in Chomsky (2014), to which we will return directly.

Generalizing this line of characterizing verbal phrases (v*P) to nominal phrases, Chomsky (2007) argues that there are two nominal elements, n* for definite nominals and n for indefinite nominals. Furthermore, definiteness is distinguished by the presence of an element D, and the absence of the element. Accordingly a definite nominal phrase bears D within it whereas an indefinite nominal phrase lacks the element. A head n* takes another head D, which in turn takes an undifferentiated nominal root N as its complement. Now consider a derivation of the simplest possible definite nominal phrase in (4).

(4) a. {the, BOOK}
    b. {n*, {the, BOOK}}
    c. {n*, {BOOK, {the, BOOK$_t$}}}

d. {<n*, the>, {BOOK, {the$_t$, BOOK$_t$}}}

In (4a), "the" = D and its complement N = BOOK, which are merged (EM). Then a nominal phase head n* is merged to yield (4b), where D inherits the features of n* and N raises to the SPEC of D, as in (4c). Now D raises to n*, forming a nominal amalgam of the form <n*, the>, as in (4d). Chomsky then assumes that n* is the head, and label, of the nominal phrase, hence it is n*P rather than DP, and therefore it will bear Case. This derivation is parallel to that of v*P. The same will hold for definite nominal structures with a derived nominal as N.

Indefinite nominal phrases are, in contrast, headed by n with such a root N as its complement. With this minimal mechanisms he exemplifies the derivation of such an indefinite nominal phrase as "author of the book" where "author" is a relational base noun of the kind discussed in Chomsky (1970/1972), different from such a derived nominal as "picture (of NP)". Thus let us see the derivation (5).

(5) a. {n, {AUTHOR, (of) the book}}
   b. {<n, AUTHOR>, {AUTHOR$_t$, (of) the book}}

Here AUTHOR is a nominal root N, and it is already merged with its complement "(of) the book", (5a).[1] This set has been merged further with a nominal head n. The root raises to form a nominal amalgam <n, AUTHOR>, receiving "its nominal character from n." Now the phrase is headed by n; the head will bear Case and enter into selection.

One reasonable aspect of this analysis is that both types of nominal phrases are headed by a nominal, n in indefinite phrases and n* in definite phrases, and hence they are labeled as a nominal rather than D, consistent with the import of Case and selection. The analysis does not seem to be innocent in characterizing the (im-)mobility of a root element N. In particular, it remains to be clarified why a root N stays dangling in the SPEC in

---

[1] Incidentally a preposition *of*, which assigns accusative Case ("who(m) did John see a picture of"), may not have been introduced at this stage of derivation, and it may be inserted automatically by *of*-insertion in the post-nominal genitive context, the characterization of which is irrelevant here, and we will put the issue aside. For the detailed discussion, see Chomsky (1986). For an analysis of (pro)nominal possessors, see Bayer (2014).

the case of definite nominal phrases (as in (4d)) on the one hand and has to move to n in indefinite phrases (as in (5b)) on the other. This asymmetry will naturally follow when put in the system of Chomsky (2014), as we will see directly.

One may oppose to the lack of D in indefinite nominal phrases in arguing that an indefinite article would be a member of determiners and therefore indefinite phrases should have D in the same fashion as definite phrases. The indefinite article, however, might not be an instance of D, contrary to the widely held DP system, and then it could be viewed perhaps as a weak form of the numeral "one", which will then suggest that the familiar category D is a mixture of certain prenominal elements. It should be noted, in this regard, that the assumption of a nominal head for definite phrases seems to fit the intuition that something more nominal than D is involved in selection and Case. If this intuition is on track, then a similar treatment can be made for the definite article "the": namely the definite article can be a weak form of the demonstrative "that". The two articles, viewed along this line, are eventually phrasal (i.e. XP) rather than minimal, which in turn would suggest that an element D is indeed convenient, covering heterogeneous things ranging over demonstratives, numerals, negatives, prenominal genitives (Saxon genitives), but too vague a category to maintain as an independent element in syntax and there might not be such thing as D. Employing the machinery of the amalgam with n* and D would amount to assuming implicitly that definiteness is a part of the features expressed on the nominal head. But it seems to me that definiteness is something added to a nominal phrase by means of placing some element in a position higher than the domain of its head, e.g. in the SPEC. In this sense, we could regard such elements as operators. The situation is also much like a distinction between lexical and syntactic aspects: lexical aspect is something inherent to a predicate whereas syntactic aspect (or the called expanded tense) is something added to VP periphrastically. Furthermore definiteness seems to be one way to express a higher concept of specificity. Then what is involved, we may speculate, would be specificity rather than definiteness. Specificity will be characterized as a part of the features that the nominal heads (n and n*) do not bear along with a categorial specification. Then the articles must be generated somewhere outside nP/n*P. One possible way of getting around the difficulty will be to assume that they are introduced in the same way as, say, an external argument is, with Pair-Merge as a possible option. We will assume the unavailability of D without further argument.

3. Derived Nominals in POP(+) Settings

In the previous sections we have seen briefly that a lexical item (or a substantive element) can be viewed as a syntactic complex (or amalgam) of a category-defining head with nominal character, and a root. These internal constituents are accessible to syntax (much as v* and V in the contemporary theories and abstract verbs such as *cause* assumed, for example, in Chomsky (1970/1972, 2007) and elsewhere). Furthermore, we have also seen the dubious status of D as an independent element, which might be a feature encoded on the head of a nominal phrase. The idea that Chomsky has pursued in discussing nominals appears to be that nominal structures are analogous to verbal structures. It would be an interesting pursuit of the basic properties of language to push this idea to the extent where we can. With this much background, let us proceed to speculate how nominal structures can be characterized under the unified theory of basic structures of language proposed in Chomsky (2013, 2014).

One of the recent claims proposed and developed in Chomsky (2013, 2014) keeps adopting the standard view of substantive elements, but takes a different view of the way a substantive element behaves. Chomsky argues (i) "that substantive elements of the lexicon are roots, unspecified as to category," and (ii) "that ... their category ... derives from merger with a functional element n, v, etc." The first argument implies that the selectional property of an item is indeed one of those that its root inherently has, and therefore, the property is to be attributed to the undifferentiated root, irrespectively of its categorial realization: a version of lexicalist position. Such a root R is invisible to a labeling algorithm LA since it lacks its categorial specification. Recall that for a syntactic object SO to be interpreted, it has to have its label, which tells what kind of object it is (i.e. nominal, verbal, etc.). Labeling is "just minimal search" for the relevant information of SO through finding its head. Then the root R has to become visible somehow derivationally. For R to get visible, it has to be modified by Merge, since it is the only operation available. The modification means a merger with something to form a complex that can label. Since R lacks its categorial specification, it is merged until it gets to a stage where its categorial property is given by something. Chomsky assumes that such specification is provided by an affixal element which is referred to as categorizer K, and that K and R merge to form a complex, which is visible to LA. A categorizer has to be introduced in syntax, not in the lexicon. When R is introduced into syntax by External Merge (EM) (along with its argument), as in (6a) below, it has to be marked as verbal for example by way of merger with the categorizer K in the course of derivation, as in (6b) for example.

(6) a. {K, {R, (Argument)}}
 b. {[K, R], ... {R, (Argument)}}

Chomsky (2014) argues that R alone is universally too weak to label while K, which is affixal, is invisible to LA; and that if R is amalgamated with K, forming a complex with K and R, the complex is labeled as K. And, therefore, R must raise to K. Thus, v* (=K), which is an affix, is invisible to LA. If R (=V) is amalgamated to form the complex of v* and R, [R, v*] in Chomsky's (2014) expression, the complex can label (Chomsky (2014: 9)). This is the only possible structure of what has been referred to as Head-movement or Head-raising, according to the so-called POP(+) system outlined by Chomsky (2014). The complex is not formed by set-Merge (EM or IM), but it is amalgamated by Pair-Merge (or largely Head-adjunction in a classical terminology): we will refer to the complex as <R, K> generally, just for ease of reference.

Then suppose that we have the following system:

(7) Merge:
 a. (Set-)Merge, forming {X, Y}, where X = X, XP, and Y = Y, YP.
 b. (Pair-)Merge, forming <X, Y>, where either is a head.
(8) a. R is visible but too weak to label.
 b. K, affixal, is invisible to LA.
 c. <K, R> can label.

The cross-categorial generalization is not just a mere generalization, but it is something real which is to be spelled out; this has been a long-standing policy of syntax, as expressed in Chomsky (1970/1972). Along with this line, it is reasonably expected that nominal phrases should be quite analogous to verbal phrases (v*P), even to adjectival and prepositional phrases apart from some inevitable differences reducible to its parts, which should be minimal.[2]

Thus let us take a brief look at a case of v*P of the form:

(9) a. $\{V_R, XP\}$
 b. $\{v^*_K, \{V_R, XP\}\}$
 c $\{v^*_K, \{XP, \{V_R, XP_t\}\}\}$
 d. $\{<v^*_K, V_R>, \{XP, \{V_{R_t}, XP_t\}\}\}$
 e. $\{YP, \{<v^*_K, V_R>, \{XP, \{V_{R_t}, XP_t\}\}\}\}$

The substantive element shown as "V_R", in (9a), is a category-neutral, or category-unspecified, "root" that takes, or is externally merged with, its internal (nominal) argument XP, and its "categorial" nature has not been determined at this stage: LA cannot label the set, since it is weak, in accordance with (8a). The set $\{V_R, XP\}$ is then externally merged with v^*_K, a phase head, which functions as a categorizer K: (9b). (Contingent on this merge and the feature inheritance between v^*_K and V_R, the nominal argument XP raises as in (9c).) The phase head v^*_K is invisible to labeling since it is an affixal categorizer, and hence the newly created set is unlabeled yet. Then V_R raises to, or is Pair-Merged with, v^*_K, forming an amalgam of the form $<v^*_K, V_R>$, where v^*_K characterizes the categorial nature of the amalgam as verbal: (9c). In this sense v^*_K is a categorizer. Here recall that the complex or amalgam $<v^*_K, V_R>$ can label the set as $<v^*_K, V_R>$, and therefore it is "$<v^*_K, V_R>$P" or simply v*P in a familiar usage. This implies that the SO "$<v^*_K, V_R>$" is verbal as determined by the complex head with K=v*, and its selectional properties are realized within the phrase as required by V_R. Now the external argument YP is externally merged, forming the set (9e) with "{YP, $<v^*_K, V_R>$P}", which has no label (since it is of the form "{XP, YP}" with no agreeing features). Hence YP is supposed to evacuate the phrase (EPP), which in turn marks the resulting SO, {YP$_t$,

---

[2] For example the escape hatch property of PP as discussed in Riemsdijk (1978) could be incorporated to the framework here, at least with a crucial distinction between "true" and "inserted" Ps, as Chomsky (p. c.) suggests.

$<v^*_K, V_R>P\}$, as "$<v^*_K, V_R>$" (i.e. v*P).

Assume this much technology. Now we are in position to turn to those nominal structures proposed in Chomsky (2007) which we have considered above, translating them in the POP(+) system just reviewed. Suppose that the difference between verbal phrases and nominal phrases is minimal, and it is reduced to the difference in the type of K. First a simplest case:

(10) a. $\{n_K, author_R\}$
 b. $\{<n_K, author_R>, \{author_{Rt}\}\}$
 c. $<n_K, author_R>$

(Set-)Merge defines a structure (10a), which has no label yet. Then the visible but weak root element is (pair-)merged with the affixal nominal categorizer n_K, which forms a pair $<n_K, author_R>$, which is now identifiable; the pair labels the structure (10b): it is NP, in abstraction away from the phasehood of n/n*. Notice here that the pair (10c) could be formed as a singleton directly by merging those two constituents, n_K, $author_R$, skipping stage (10a), implying a classical flavor of "base generation." The amalgam would be embedded in, merged with, another SO, but not with its argument. This formation could be a reasonable option under the conception of free Merge, in such a case as a root is introduced into syntax without selecting any SO. There would be some consequences from this option, but we will put aside this issue.[3]

(11) represents a derivation of a SO with an article, which is an XP, but with a complement.

(11) a. $\{n_K, book_R\}$
 b. $\{<n_K, book_R>, \{book_{Rt}\}\}$
 c. $\{the_{Art}, \{<n_K, book_R>, \{book_{Rt}\}\}\}$
 d. $<the_{Art}, \{<n_K, book_R>, \{book_{Rt}\}\}>$

The root is first set-Merged with a nominal categorizer, (11a), and is then pair-Merged with the categorizer, forming SO (11b); the pair labels the SO as "$<n_K, book_R>$". Here there might be two ways available to introduce an

---

[3] See Kitahara (2014) for such consequences, where he argues that pair-Merge, applied prior to set-Merge, cancels the phasehood of v*.

article, either by set-Merge as in (11c), where the article lies in the SPEC of NP, or by pair-Merge as in (11d), where the phrase is a pair of article and another pair.

Replacing the article with a demonstrative or a Saxon genitive NP, we have the same skeletal structure:

(12) a. {that, {<n_K, book$_R$>, {book$_{Rt}$}}}
    b. <that, {<n_K, book$_R$>, {book$_{Rt}$}}>
(13) a. {John's, {<n_K, book$_R$>, {book$_{Rt}$}}}
    b. <John's, {<n_K, book$_R$>, {book$_{Rt}$}}>

The structures (11d), (12b), (13b) are not of the form <Head, Head>, which has no labelable element within it, since articles, demonstratives, and Saxon genitive NPs are all instances of XP. In the case of v*P, its label is gained by IM of the subject NP out of v*P. But this strategy cannot be at work here in the case of nominals, since those prenominal XPs cannot undergo IM. They have to stay in situ, (14), and will pied-pipe the nominal phrase ("{<n_K, N$_R$>, ...}") when moved, (15):

(14) *that/*the/*John's will read/sell [t, {<n_K, book$_R$>, {book$_{Rt}$} ...}] well
(15) a. which/whose book did John read t
    b. *which/*whose did John read [t, {<n_K, book$_R$>, {book$_{Rt}$} ...}]

This shows that no EPP is generally observed in NPs. Which derivation is the right one, by set-Merge, or by pair-Merge? Recall that the head of the nominal phrase enters into selection by an external element but the SPEC of the phrase does not. Then the label must be that of nominal complex <n_K, N$_R$>, in whichever way the nominal phrase might be formed. What permits the EPP violation in NPs, characterizing it as an island? Suppose that the prenominal specifier of the NP is invisible because it is so weak a phrase, and that the Saxon genitive NP is deeply embedded in, and protected by, some mechanism of assigning the Saxonian affix. Furthermore that the nominal specifier is a part of the amalgam the members of which are not on a par. Even if two members form an amalgam, the two cannot be its head: either of the two, not both (unless they have some agreeing features, perhaps). When Merge forms SO, {α, β}, either of the elements must be its label, or the SO must be modified by further Merge, until it results in asymmetrial relation of head and non-head constituents. In this regard, pair-Merge can be viewed as a step toward gaining such asymmetry. Then the more plausible choice of nominal derivation would be derivation by pair-Merge, which would imply that NP is not a phase.

Assuming this much, we will have a familiar nominalization case of DESTROY, as in (16), which is labeled as "<n_K, DESTROY$_R$>":

(16) <{the enemy's/the}, {<n_K, DESTROY$_R$> {DESTROY$_R$, {(*of*) the city}}}>

Here "the enemy's" lies in the edge of the entire SO, the position often referred to as the subject of NP. The subject position can be filled with various types of categories in nominals, differently from verbal phrases. Thus consider (17), where the agent of "creation" varies depending on such types. The agent is interpreted as the subject of the derived nominal, "Mary's", in (17a). In (17b) it can be either "John" or someone else (e.g. a group of people given in the context). And in (17c) it must be identified with the matrix subject "John". Their relevant structures will look like (18a-c).

(17) a. John dedicated his life to Mary's creation of the computer.
   b. John dedicated his life to the creation of the computer.
   c. John dedicated his life to ø creation of the computer.
(18) a. ... to [nP Mary's [<n_K-CREATE$_R$>, [CREATE$_R$, {PP} ...
   b. ... to [nP the   [<n_K-CREATE$_R$>, [CREATE$_R$, {PP} ...
   c. ... to [nP   [<n_K-CREATE$_R$>, [CREATE$_R$, {PP} ...

The nominal phrase of (18c) cannot be a nominal counterpart of the verbal Equi cases. Since the EPP is violated in NP, (18c) lacks the subject position, which suggests that there will be no such thing as a PRO subject within NP, as argued in Chomsky (1986). The agentive interpretation could be attributed to some implicit argument within the nominal root, much similar to the passive cases. The implicit argument is linked somehow to "Mary's" in (18a), to a pronominal-like article in (18b), and is free in the nominal phase but obligatorily linked to the higher NP. The differences here might relate to the degrees in specificity among prenominal elements and to extractability from NPs. Chomsky (1973) argues that "[s]pecified subjects in

NP's are [+definite]," observing "a three-way gradation of acceptability" concerning with the extractability of a *wh*-phrase from within NP: an indefinite case (19a) is "better than" a definite one (19b), "which is in turn preferable to" a possessive case (19c). Chomsky (1977) also suggests a possibility that specificity may be involved here along with definiteness.

(19) a. Who did you see pictures of
　　 b. Who did you see the pictures of
　　 c. *Who did you see John's pictures of

Chomsky (p.c.) further suggests the relevance of *wh*-in-situ in in these cases, the issue of which I will leave for another occasion.

References

Bayer, Josef (2014) "A Note on Possessor Agreement," ms., University of Konstanz. (In this volume.)

Chomsky, Noam (1970/1972) "Remarks on Nominalization," *Readings in English Transformational Grammar*, ed. by Roderick A. Jacobs and Peter Rosenbaum, Ginn and Co., Waltham, MA. [Also in Noam Chomsky (1972) *Studies in Semantics in Generative Grammar*, Mouton, The Hague.]

Chomsky, Noam (1973) "Conditions on Transformations," *A Festschrift for Morris Halle*, ed. by Stephen R. Anderson and Paul Kiparsky, 232–286, Holt, Rinehart and Winston, New York.

Chomsky, Noam (1977) "On Wh-movement," *Formal Syntax*, ed. by Peter W. Culicover, et al., 71–132, Academic Press, New York.

Chomsky, Noam (1986) *Knowledge of Language: Its Nature, Origin, and Use*, Praeger, New York.

Chomsky, Noam (2007) "Approaching UG from Below," *Interface + Recursion = Language? Chomsky's Minimalism and the View from Syntax-Semantics*, ed. by U. Sauerland and H.-M. Gärtner, 1–29, Mouton de Gruyter, Berlin.

Chomsky, Noam (2013) "Problems of Projection," *Lingua* 130, 33–49.

Chomsky, Noam (2014) "Problems of Projection: Extensions," ms., MIT.

Kitahara, Hisatsugu (2014) Handout (#1, #2, and #3) for discussions. (October 31; November 3.)

Oishi, Masayuki (2005) "Deconstructing PEPS: Evaluation Measure Revisited," A paper read at the Workshop for Henk van Riemsdijk, Tilburg University (Villa De Vier Jaargetijden, Tilburg, December 22).

Oishi, Masayuki (2011) "How much can a label work?" Handout for the Representation of Structure in Grammar: Annesso Cartesiano di Villa Salmi Inaugural Workshop, Annesso Cartesiano, Arezzo, Italy. (July 1-3.)

Oishi, Masayuki (2012) "Merge X and Y, and Z," Handout for The 30th Conference of the ELSJ Workshop (On Merge-Based Generative Procedures: Maximizing Minimum Machinery), Keio University. (November 10.)

Oishi, Masayuki (in preparation) "Labeling in Nominal Structures."

van Riemsdijk, Henk (1978) *A Case Study in Syntactic Markedness: The Binding Nature of Prepositional Phrases*, Foris, Dordrecht.

A Minimalist Sketch of Some Correlations between Word Order and Case

Toshifusa Oka
Fukuoka University of Education

1. Some Universal Correlations

Correlations between word order and case have been one of the most interesting topics, since Greenberg's (1963) epoch-making work. One of his findings is Universal 41: "if in a language the verb follows both the nominal subject and nominal object as the dominant order, the language almost always has a case system." Among accumulated works, see Dryer (2002, 2007) and Müller (2002), for a picture of how things are going. In this paper I will reproduce the essence of Oka (2010), where I proposed a possible way to syntactically address correlations between SOV (the basic Subject-Object-Verb word order, restricting attention to the SVO/SOV distinction), RCS (a morphologically rich case system), and FWO (the property of allowing free or flexible word orders).

As is easily noticed, there is a mismatch between Syntax and Morphology: Syntax is rigid, but Morphology is more arbitrary and irregular. Morphology does not always follow directions that Syntax provides concerning variations and changes. As a result, correlations between Syntax and Morphology only reveal a tendency, which we may understand in terms of statistics. (To see this, recall the null-subject/pro-drop parameter, for example.) However, it is not senseless to try to find a syntactic explanation. Success depends on whether we can construct a falsifiable theory that makes clear predictions.

Let us assume that correlations maximally hold, for the sake of discussion:

(1) SOV = RCS = FWO

a. If SOV, then RCS. b. If RCS, then SOV.
c. If FWO, then RCS. d. If RCS, then FWO.
e. If FWO, then SOV. f. If SOV, then FWO.

Under this idealization, let us start to look for syntactic explanations. In Section 2 through Section 4, I will introduce the mechanism proposed in Oka (2000, 2001, 2004) under Chomsky's (1995, and others) Minimalist Program. And then I will address the correlations in question as far as possible in Section 5 and 6.

2. Inflectional Features

In this section I will outline Oka's (2000, 2001) system of inflectional features, where the notion of Case follows from a more fundamental considerations. Inflectional features are two types: Tense (and Mood) and (lexical as well as grammatical) Aspect are called τ-features, just as Person, Number, and Gender are called φ-features. While φ-features are subject to referential interpretation, τ-features are subject to propositional interpretation. Both types of features must be deleted when they are not properly interpreted. Whether deleted or undeleted, they are morphologically realized on lexical items, following the rules of the particular language.

One of the crucial assumptions I proposed is that instances of Case are nominal realizations of τ-features. Thus, when a Tense feature like [±past], for example, is realized on nominal categories (typically D and N), it is called Nominative Case. (See also Pesetsky and Torrego (2001, 2004) for the essentially same idea.) Similarly, an Aspect feature like [±telic] is realized as Accusative Case. τ-features are realized in two modes just as φ-features are:

(3) a. φ: (i) verbal realization ("loves", "love" ...)
       (ii) nominal realization ("dog", "dogs" ...)
    b. τ: (i) verbal realization ("loved", "love" ...)
       (ii) nominal realization ("he", "him" ...)   —**Case**

Semantically uninterpretable features (e.g. morpho-phonological features) are erased by Transfer to SEM (Semantic Component). Morpho-phonologically uninterpretable features (e.g. semantic features) are erased by Transfer to PHON ((Morpho-)Phonological Component). Syntactically deleted features can be erased by Transfer. Inflectional features are semantic substances that can be interpreted in an appropriate place, and therefore they cannot be directly erased by Transfer to SEM. When they appear in some place where they cannot be properly interpreted, it must be syntactically deleted by Agree so that they can be erased by Transfer, to avoid gibberish. Let us assume a match-and-delete version of Chomsky's Agree operation in Syntax: Agree deletes one and only one of the two matching identical features of Goal and Probe, given the spirit of Recoverability Condition.

Suppose further that ϕ-features and τ-features appear in a set $\{\tau, \phi\}$ on lexical items, such as D, TNS and V. The two elements of $\{\tau, \phi\}$ cannot be properly interpreted on one and the same lexical item at the same time. At least one of them must be deleted. Consider the following derivation:

(4) a. AGREE   TNS   [$_{DP}$ D ...]   V
                    $\{\tau,\phi\}\Longleftrightarrow\{\tau,\phi\}$ $\{\tau,\phi\}$
                    $\{\tau,(\phi)\}$ $\{(\tau),\phi\}$

   b. MOVE [$_{DP}$ D ...]   TNS   V
            $\{(\tau),\phi\}$ $\{\tau,(\phi)\}$ $\{\tau,\phi\}$

   c. AGREE [$_{DP}$ D ...]   TNS   V
             $\{(\tau),\phi\}$ $\{\tau,(\phi)\}\Longleftrightarrow\{\tau,\phi\}$
   [Deleted features are put in parentheses ( ).] $\{(\tau),(\phi)\}$

TNS, D, and V all share the same set $\{\tau, \phi\}$. The τ-feature is morphologically realized as Nominative Case on D, but cannot be properly interpreted there. Similarly, the ϕ-feature cannot be properly interpreted on TNS. Neither feature can be properly interpreted on V. Those improper features must be deleted by Agree.

3. VP-internal Structure

Oka (2004) argues that Subject and Object are first generated inside VP, and then are raised to Spec, TNS (through Spec, v*), and to Spec, v (ASP), respectively. v (ASP) is a lexico-functional head, which contains a τ-feature that is realized as Accusative Case on a nominal category. See Travis (1992, 2010) for Inner Aspect, and Koizumi (1993, 1995) for Split VP Hypothesis. (Oka (2000, 2001) made a different assumption, though, that the external θ-marking property of v* is identified as the τ-feature that is realized as Accusative Case, deriving Burzio's generalization.) The SOV order is illustrated as in (5), where V is combined with functional elements TNS and ASP by Merge, to yield a complex V:

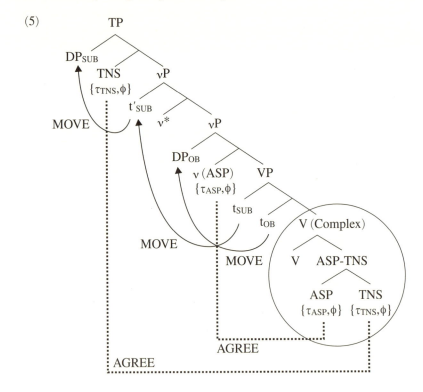

The syntactically complex V is eventually morphologically realized as a single verb After Spell-Out, or Transfer. When Transfer applies, however, the ASP-TNS complex counts as the complement of the lexical V, so that the Complex V appears in the final position under some version of Kayne's (1994) LCA. We can say that all languages are verb-final in the first place, even under his idea of Antisymmetricity. The SVO order are derived from the SOV order by raising the complex V to v*, which is located between Subject and Object at surface. (Note that the raised V can be further raised to TNS, keeping the SVO order.) The SVO/SOV distinction is now reduced to the raising/non-raising of V.

Note that when TNS {τ, φ} and ASP {τ, φ} are combined with V, they cannot be properly interpreted in their positions and therefore must be deleted by Agree, assuming that a hierarchical configuration is needed for propositional interpretation. The duplicates of TNS and ASP in the lexical array (Numeration) are merged in higher positions to be successfully interpreted in the appropriate configuration after their unnecessary φ-features are deleted.

4. Intervention and Free Riding

Returning to Oka's (2000, 2001) system of inflectional features, an intervention effect for Agree is expected to be found when DP intervenes between TNS and V, for example, since {τ, φ} appears on both verbal and nominal categories. Consider the following:

(6) TNS   DP   V
     {τ,φ}   {τ,φ}   {τ,φ}

The application of Agree to TNS and V for {τ, φ} is blocked by the intervening DP under the conventional "closest" requirement. (Note that D itself, the head of DP, cannot probe V in this configuration, because V is not in the complement domain of D.) If DP is Subject, it is moved to Spec, TNS, allowing TNS to probe V successfully, as in (4) above. If DP is Object, V is raised, crossing over DP, to v*, which is located between TNS and DP, so that V gets close enough to be probed by TNS. This yields the SVO order. To keep the SOV order, V must stay in situ and get probed by TNS there to get its {τ, φ} deleted. How is this possible?

The solution I proposed is to suppose that TNS in SOV languages contains the lexical categorial feature [V] (or [+V, -N]). Suppose further that unlike inflectional features, categorial features like [V] do not count as semantic substances, but functions as key instructions for semantic interpretation and morphological realization of the lexical items on which they appear.

Such features cannot be directly erased by Transfer, either, when the lexical items undergo Transfer. However, TNS, as a stand-alone phonetically null element located upstairs, does not require any instructions for morphological realization, unlike V. Thus the [V] of TNS can get deleted by Agree before Transfer. Consider the following:

(7)   TNS   DP   V
       {{τ, ϕ}, [V]}   {τ, ϕ}   {{τ, ϕ}, [V]}

Here TNS probes V for [V] since the intervening DP does not have [V]. This probing establishes the relation between TNS and V for the purpose of Agree. When Agree applies to TNS and V, it does not delete only the [V] of TNS, but also the {τ, ϕ} of V along the way. Namely, {τ, ϕ} can get deleted as free riders.

5. Lexical Languages and Functional Languages

Let us suppose that languages are subject to *Lexicality Parameter [±lexical]*, expecting it to prove deducible from more fundamental considerations as the research proceeds. Languages have lexical categorical features [V] and [N] on their functional heads TNS and D, respectively, if they are valued [+lexical]. Otherwise, they do not. Refer to [+lexical] languages as *lexical languages*, and to the [-lexical] languages as *functional languages*. In lexical languages TNS and D are not purely functional but analogous to lexico-functional categories v and n.

As suggested above, lexical categorical features provide instructions for morphological realization. When [N] appears on D, it allows τ to be realized in a strong form on D, as morphologically rich Case, and further on (A and) N through Concord. Otherwise, it is realized in a weak or null form. Thus, lexical languages, unlike functional ones, are identified with RCS ones.

In functional languages that do not allow TNS to contain [V], the only way to get V's {τ, ϕ} deleted by Agree is to raise V over Object. This raising is triggered by some attracting feature of v^*. For V to be obligatorily raised in Object-less intransitive constructions as well, it will be necessary to assume that both the unergative v^* and its unaccusative counterpart obligatorily contain the attracting feature. A natural property of language will be requirement of *Homogeneity:* Reduce optionality and variation within a language in such a way that for each feature causing a syntactic operation, lexical items keep, as far as possible, from differing from each other with respect to whether they contain that feature or not. Along this line of arguments, functional languages must be SVO ones. Thus, SOV languages must be lexical ones, which reveal RCS. Now (1a) holds: if SOV, then RCS.

How about (1b): if RCS, then SOV? This question is obviously an empirical one. For the sake of discussion, however, let us proceed under the assumption that the answer is positive, and try to see how far Syntax can go with it.

To obtain (1b), lexical languages must be prevented from raising V to v^* to derive the SVO order. What bars V-raising then? We might think of Economy of syntactic derivation: Avoid an unnecessary operation. Or we might think of Economy for the construction of Lexicon: Avoid adding a dispensable feature to Lexicon. Thus the V-attracting feature of v^* should become entirely unavailable in lexical languages.

Alternatively, let us take a more local approach to bar V-raising in lexical languages. Suppose that V-raising is verb incorporation, comparing it to noun incorporation, which is dealt with in terms of derivational rather than inflectional morphology. Whereas cliticization involves movement of a functional element D to C/TNS/ASP (pronominal cliticization), and TNS to C (V1/V2 Phenomena), incorporation involves movement of a lexical element N or V to a lexical element. When a lexico-functional element v^* selects a lexical element for incorporation, it searches for a categorial feature. Suppose that v^* has the selectional feature [__ [±V]], where [+V] = [V] and [-V] = [N], putting aside [±N]. Then noun incorporation and verb incorporation are not distinguishable from each other, because both are triggered by the same selectional feature, which is satisfied by external/internal Merge. Agree is irrelevant here, and no match-and-delete mechanism is operative. Selection for internal Merge, however, requires a Probe-Goal relation just as Agree does, and therefore is not immune from intervention effects produced by the "closest" requirement. Consider the following:

(8)   v*   DP   V
       [__ [±V]] [N]   [V]

DP obligatorily has [N] in lexical languages. Thus, v* cannot select V for incorporation, if it has the selectional feature [__ [±V]]. Verb incorporation will be possible, if, for example, DP is raised to Spec, v* by *wh*-movement or V is intransitive so that DP is missing in the first place. However, this kind of variation would be a vicious one under the light of Homogeneity. Therefore, v* in lexical languages obligatorily lacks such a selectional feature and never attracts V. Given these considerations, (1b) holds: if RCS, then SOV. Since we have seen that (1a) holds, we have SOV = RCS now.

6. Free/Flexible Word Order

Let us refer to FWO in a restricted sense: the SO order can be freely or flexibly reversed by "Scrambling" to derive the OS order. Consider the following possibilities, noting that TNS must probe V for Agree:

(9) a. OB   SUB   **TNS**-----**V**   (OSV from SOV or SVO)
    b. OB   **TNS**-----SUB-----**V**   (OSV from SOV only)
    c. **TNS**-----OB-----SUB-----**V**   (OSV from SOV only)

In (9a) Subject is in Spec, TNS, and nothing intervenes between TNS and V, so that Agree is successfully applied. The OS order should be able to be derived by Scrambling not only from SOV but also from SVO. There is an A/A' issue about Scrambling, however. Oka (1996) argues that when Scrambling shows A'-properties, it is identified with something like English Topicalization, as has been suggested in the literature, and that so-called A-scrambling involves an additional θ-marking by TNS. Suppose that TNS can have a θ-marking-marking property only when it is lexical in some way. In lexical languages TNS, as a lexico-functional element, has [V] and functions more like an instance of v, which generally has a θ-marking property, as is in fact manifested by v*. Scrambling is possible only in lexical languages, restricting the relevant notion to A-scrambling.

Other possibilities proposed in the literature that count as scrambling are the derivations illustrated in (9b, c). In (9b) Object is raised to Spec, TNS, while Subject stays in a $_v$P/VP-internal position. In (9c) Object is in raised to Spec, ASP and Subject stays in a VP-internal position, given the sentential structure illustrated in (5). (This situation used to be referred to as "Object Shift". See Oka (1996) for some differences between Scrambling and Object Shift.) In these derivations Subject (and Object as well, in (9c)) intervenes between TNS and V, so that this derivation is possible only in lexical languages for the already familiar reason. Since lexical languages show RCS, (1c) obtains: if FWO, then RCS.

How about (1d): if RCS, then FWO? Needless to say, it depends on the mechanism of Scrambling. Suppose that Scrambling is costless in the sense that it doesn't require any optionally added attracting feature and just involves an application of (internal) Merge, as has been often suggested in the literature. Then nothing can prevent Scrambling from applying freely in lexical languages. In other words, lexical languages cannot be made to lack Scrambling. As far as we are on the right track, we can say that (1d) holds as well. If (1a–d) hold, then (1e, f) hold. Now it follows in full that SOV = RCS = FWO.

Finally, let us briefly mention VSO languages, to fill a gap. Mainly two possibilities have been proposed in the literature to derive the VSO order:

(10) a. V + C   SUB   **TNS**------------------------t_V
     b.   **V + TNS**--------SUB--------t_V

V is raised to C while Subject is raised to Spec, TNS in (10a), and V is raised to TNS and Subject stays in a $_v$P-internal position in (10b), putting aside the question of exactly how and why V is raised in these derivations. In (10a) Agree successfully applies to TNS and V when V is still downstairs after Subject is raised, so that this derivation is possible both in lexical languages and in functional ones. In (10b), on the other hand, Subject intervenes between TNS and V when V is downstairs, so that only lexical languages allow Agree to apply to TNS and V. (Note that V must undergo Agree before it is extracted from the complement domain of TNS to be raised to TNS.) A prediction is: if V proves to be in the position of TNS in a VSO language, then it should display RCS and FWO. Also, if a VSO language doesn't display RCS or FWO, then V should be in the C position.

References

Chomsky, Noam (1995) *The Minimalist Program,* MIT Press, Cambridge, MA.
Chomsky, Noam (2000) "Minimalist Inquiries: The Framework," *Step by Step: Essays on Minimalist Syntax in Honor of Howard Lasnik,* ed. by R. Martin et al., 89-155, MIT Press, Cambridge, MA.
Chomsky, Noam (2001) "Derivation by Phase," *Ken Hale: A Life in Language,* ed. by M. Kenstowicz, 1-52. MIT Press, Cambridge, MA.
Chomsky, Noam (2008) "On Phases," *Foundational Issues in Linguistic Theory: Essays in Honor of Jean-Roger Vergnaud,* ed. by C. Otero et al., 134-166, MIT Press, Cambridge, MA.
Dryer, Matthew S. (2002) "Case Distinctions, Rich Verb Agreement, and Word Order Type (Comments on Hawkins' paper)," *Theoretical Linguistics* 28:2, 151-158.
Dryer, Matthew S. (2007) "Word Order," *Language Typology and Syntactic Description, Vol. 1, Clause Structure,* ed. by T. Shopen, Cambridge University Press, Cambridge.
Greenberg, Joseph H. (1963) "Some Universals of Grammar with Particular Reference to the Order of Meaningful Elements," *Universals of Language,* ed. by J. Greenberg, 73-113, MIT Press, Cambridge, MA.
Kayne, Richard S. (1994) *The Antisymmetry of Syntax: Linguistic Inquiry Monograph 25,* MIT Press, Cambridge, MA.
Koizumi, Masatoshi (1993) "Object Agreement Phrases and the Split VP Hypothesis," *Case and Agreement I, MIT Working Papers in Linguistics* 18, ed. by J. D. Bobaljik et al., 99-148, MITWPL.
Koizumi, Masatoshi (1995) *Phrase Structure in Minimalist Syntax,* Doctoral dissertation, MIT.
Müller, Gereon (2002) "Free Word Order, Morphological Case, and Sympathy Theory," *Resolving Conflicts in Grammars,* ed. by G. Fanselow and C. Fery, 9-48, Buske (Sonderheft der LinguistischenBerichte), Hamburg.
Oka, Toshifusa (1996) "Scrambling in Japanese and English," *Formal Approaches to Japanese Linguistics 2, MIT Working Papers in Linguistics* 29, 361-388, MITWPL.
Oka, Toshifusa (2000) "Feature Checking and Movement," *Tsukuba English Studies* 19, 1-23, University of Tsukuba.
Oka, Toshifusa (2001) "Feature Checking and Economy of Derivation," *Imi to Katachi no Interface* (Interface of Meaning between Form)*: Festschrift for Dr. Minoru Nakau,* 627-637, Kurosio, Tokyo.
Oka, Toshifusa (2004) "VP-internal Movement," *Tsukuba English Studies 22: A Festschrift in Honor of Minoru Nakau,* 279-294, Tsukuba English Linguistic Society.

Oka, Toshifusa (2010) "SVO vs. SOV, Featuring Case—A Minimalist Scenario," talk given at Tohoku University on October 16, 2010.

Pesetsky, David and EstherTorrego (2001) "T-to-C movement: Causes and Consequences," *Ken Hale: A Life in Language,* ed. by M. Kenstowicz, 355–426, MIT Press, Cambridge, MA.

Pesetsky, David and EstherTorrego (2004) "Tense, Case and the Nature of Syntactic Categories," *The Syntax of Time,* ed. by J. Guéron and J. Lecarme, MIT Press, Cambridge, MA.

Travis, Lisa (1992) "Inner Aspect and the Structure of VP," *Cahiers Linguistique de l'UQAM* 1, 130–146.

Travis, Lisa (2010) *Inner Aspect: The Articulation of VP: Studies in Natural Language and Linguistic Theory 80*, Springer, Dortrecht.

Second Language Acquisition Research and Syllabus Design: The Cognition Hypothesis and Task Sequencing

Peter Robinson

Aoyama Gakuin University

1. Introduction: Time, Acquisition Orders and the Structural Syllabus

In this short paper I am going to talk about some issues in second language (L2) syllabus design, and conclude by describing a solution to the issue of syllabus design I have proposed, the *Cognition Hypothesis*, which has been the basis of an increasing amount of empirical research in recent years. A *syllabus* is the result of decisions about how language teachers and learners can make the best use of their time together. It specifies the *units* of instruction, and the order or *sequence* in which they are presented to learners. *Theoretically*, a decision about L2 syllabus design should be based on research into what the units of language acquisition are, and how they are learned under various psycholinguistic processing conditions, by learners with differing abilities for language processing (Robinson (2009)). In purely *operational* terms, a syllabus is a *schedule* for learning. It specifies the 'what' of learning, and the 'when,' or sequence, in which it is to be learned. It also specifies 'how long,' or how many times, various learning sequences should be presented to learners in instructional programs.

Answers to these critical questions for how to operationally *deliver* instruction—'what' to teach, 'when' to teach it, and for 'how long'—are provided every time a teacher (of any subject matter) conducts a class, for five minutes, an hour, a semester, or longer. Individual *teachers* often answer them, drawing on their own intuitions about the best solution, or on their memory for previously effective solutions. And L2 learning *program designers* often provide teachers with operational answers to them, in the form of a syllabus which aims to co-ordinate teacher and learner activities within and across classes, and across levels of a language learning program.

Second language acquisition (SLA) research is concerned with much more than decision-making about classroom instruction, materials design and assessment. But many areas of SLA research do have theoretical implications for each of these, and so for complementary operational decisions about L2 syllabus design which co-ordinates and articulates them all. For example, a common answer to the question 'what' to teach has been to teach 'units' of language, most often the *grammatical structures* or *patterns* of a language. There are other ways of describing the units of language for instruction. One can identify a list of *words* that need to be learned. Or one can identify a list of *expressions* that are typically used to *do* things in a language, such as 'apologize,' 'invite,' 'disagree,' etc.

The decision to base units of instruction on language thus depends on how we divide up the language to be learned. There is no, one, acknowledged best way to divide language up as 'units' in this way. And so language-based syllabuses differ in what they present to learners, and in what sequence. For example a structural syllabus presents a series of examples that illustrate grammatical rules, such as, in English, the rule for third person agreement. So a basic rule of English morphology is the rule for third person subject verb agreement. Examples illustrating this would be '*I go*,' '*You go*,' '*He/She goes*.' That can be learned, in a sense, almost instantaneously. It is very often presented to learners at the very beginning of English language instruction. But SLA research has shown (see e.g. DeKeyser (2005)) that however easy it is to understand and apply a rule like this in classroom contexts, it is one of the most difficult things about English to control and produce accurately in everyday English conversation. In fact, of the rather small number of grammatical morphemes in English, it appears to be one of the most difficult to learn. Here are some other grammatical morphemes of English.

(1) I *ate* the cake yesterday. (Irregular past tense)
(2) There are two book*s* on the table (Plural *S*)
(3) That is Mary*'s* book (Possessive *S*)
(4) He is runn*ing* to the shop (Progressive *ing*).
(5) I walk*ed* to school (Regular past tense).

It turns out that the order in which they are successfully produced, with consistent accuracy in L2 English speech, is (4) and (2) together, followed by (1), followed by (5) and (3) together. This is what has been called an *acquisition order* for L2 English, which is followed by learners of many different first languages. If you check the order in which these aspects of the structure of English are presented in any textbooks used to learn English, or to teach English from, I think it will be different from the order in which SLA research has shown they are learned. There are many other examples that we know of, concerning the order in which structures of English are learned (such as implicational hierarchies, or late-learned `fragile` features of syntax). But very few of these are accommodated in structural syllabuses, or textbooks that adopt them. So the 3rd person S example I have given is just one indication of a basic problem with structural syllabuses for L2 language learning. They are based on 'third person' (the linguist or teacher's) intuitions about what is difficult for the learner. And these are not always right, as SLA research has shown us.

2. Towards Task-Based Syllabus Design

But there are alternatives to structural, grammatical syllabuses, and much recent SLA research has implications for these task-based approaches to syllabus design too. I will describe these task-based alternatives to structure-based syllabuses, and the very recent SLA research that is relevant to them. But I want first to go back in time, and talk about some previous thoughts on, and proposals for, syllabus design.

In a wide-ranging and insightful chapter called 'The problems and principles of syllabus design' Henry Widdowson talked about two constraints on a language teaching syllabus. On the one hand, he said, a syllabus 'is concerned with both the selection and ordering of what is to be taught' (1990, p. 127). Following this partial definition, a *structural* syllabus is clearly the result of selecting grammatical forms to be taught and then sequencing them in an order that is most effective for instructed L2 learning. In this way the structural syllabus is a way for teachers to set 'goals' for learners, assessed in terms of mastery or successful use of grammatical forms. But Widdowson argued that a syllabus 'is also an instrument of educational policy' (1990, p. 127) and that this reflects 'ideological positions concerning the nature of education in general' (1990, p. 127). He distinguished educational policies that focus on future social role, occupational abilities and 'societal needs', from those that focus on the individual, within any society, and personal 'self-realization'. An example of the former is an educational policy that promotes and invests in the teaching of English for Specific Purposes (ESP). This enables people to learn and use English (or any language) to do specific jobs in a society, like learning English for health-care and nursing purposes. An example of the latter is an educational policy that promotes and invests in the teaching of a language so that the learner may better understand cultural and communicative, as well as purely linguistic differences between themselves and people from other first language (L1) communities. Widdowson's reason for raising this distinction is to make the broad point that proposals for syllabus design 'have always to be referred to sociocultural factors in particular educational settings' (1990, p. 129). Educational systems may differ in whichever focus they promote, and so one choice of syllabus, in one setting, may be different from another choice in a different setting, for these ideological reasons. So Widdowson was talking about external constraints on syllabus implementation, whereas I have been more concerned with psycholinguistic and other cognitive cognitive constraints on learning, and their implications for, in particular, task-based syllabus design.

At about the same time as Henry Widdowson was writing the chapter I have referred to, Christopher Candlin (1987) was writing another influential chapter with implications for the selection and ordering of classroom content, and so for syllabus design. This was called 'Towards task-based language learning'. I will give a fairly long quotation from the first page of Candlin's chapter, in which he argues for:

> '... the introduction of *tasks* as the basis for classroom action .... They serve as a compelling and appropriate means for realizing certain characteristic principles of communicative language teaching and learning, as well as serving as a testing-ground for hypotheses in pragmatics and SLA...task-based language learning is not only a means to enhancing classroom communication and acquisition but also the means to the development of classroom syllabuses' (1987, p. 5).

What Candlin was arguing for was the adoption of 'tasks' as the 'units' of syllabus design, rather than linguistic units such as grammatical structures, functional phrases, or vocabulary lists. And since this early, and stimulating paper many other proposals for task-based language teaching have been made, and a growing amount of SLA research has been done into task-based learning. A task, Candlin said, is 'one of a set of differentiated, sequencable, problem-posing activities involving learners and teachers' (1987, p. 10). In the following section I describe current SLA research into task-based teaching and the 'sequencable' aspect of tasks Candlin identified, and their implications for task-based syllabus design.

3. Task Complexity, Task Characteristics and Task Sequencing

The ability to perform complex tasks, in any domain of thought and endeavor, such as mathematics or music, is inevitably grounded in attempts to perform simple tasks (adding single digit numbers, doing two or five finger exercises). In both unschooled and schooled settings performance on these tasks is supported caregivers, peers, and teachers. Over time, and courses of instruction, from these simple beginnings, tasks are staged to increase in complexity for learners in what are judged to be manageable ways. So after years of instruction, and practice, learners come to be able to do calculus, or play a piano piece by Chopin. These increases in the complexity of learning tasks are of course informed, as much as is possible, by mathematics or music learning theory. Efforts are now under way to similarly inform decisions about increasing L2 task complexity in classrooms, drawing on SLA theory. Some dimensions of task complexity that are being studied for their possible effects on language performance and learning are described below.
Planning time. There have been many studies of how tasks can be made easier for learners by giving them time to plan what they will do or say in the L2 (e.g., Ellis (2005)). This is perhaps the area that has received the most attention by SLA researchers interested in tasks, and it has clear implications for effective pedagogic decision-making. In general, the studies that have been done seem to show that having time to plan a task increases the accuracy, fluency and complexity of learner language.
Single/Dual tasks. Another dimension of task complexity that is similar to

this is the single-dual task dimension. It is much less complex to answer a phone call in the L2, than it is to answer a phone call and monitor a TV screen at the same time, to check the weather, or changes in exchange rates, for example. The latter, dual task, disperses learner attention over a number of L2 stimuli. In some publications (e.g. Robinson (2001a, 2003, 2005, 2007a, 2011a)) I have therefore called +/- planning time, and +/- single tasks 'resource-dispersing' dimensions of task demands. In general tasks made complex on these dimensions all lead to poorer accuracy, fluency and complexity of performance.

Intentional reasoning. In contrast, I think there are dimensions of task complexity which direct learners' attention to the language needed to meet complex task demands. On these 'resource-directing' dimensions I have argued that increasing task complexity should lead to more accurate and complex learner language, over time. However, complex tasks on these dimensions also negatively affect fluency. For example, in L2 English, tasks which require complex reasoning about the intentional states that motivate others to perform actions can be expected to draw heavily on the use of cognitive state terms for reference to other minds—*she suspected, realized* etc.—and in so doing orient learner attention to the complement constructions accompanying them—*suspected that, wonders whether*, etc.—so promoting awareness of, and effort at, complex L2 English syntax (see Robinson (2007b)). I call this the -/+ intentional reasoning demands dimension of complexity.

Spatial reasoning. Another example of resource-directing tasks demands are those tasks which require complex spatial reasoning, and articulation of this in describing how to move, and in what manner, from point A to point E, by way of intermediary landmark points B, C and D, etc. These can be expected to draw heavily on the use of constructions for describing motion events. Such tasks therefore have the potential to promote awareness of lexicalization patterns in L2 English for describing these motion events, in which motion and manner are typically conflated on verbs (e.g. *rushed*) and paths are expressed outside the verb in satellites that conflate a number of motion events (e.g. *rushed out of the house, down the street and into the post office*).

English lexicalization patterns are different from those in Japanese, where motion and path tend to be conflated on verbs, and manner encoded separately (e.g. *isoide haitta*). Consequently, Japanese makes much less use of event conflation in reference to motion that English does. So a task requiring complex spatial reasoning (giving directions from a large map of an unknown area) may prompt Japanese L2 learners of English to revise their preferred ways of referring to motion, in line with English lexicalization patterns (see Cadierno and Robinson (2009); Robinson, Cadierno and Shirai (2009)).

Here-and-Now / There-and-Then. In yet a different conceptual domain, tasks requiring reference to events happening now, in a shared context (Here-and-Now) orient learner attention to morphology for conveying tense and aspect in the present, compared to events requiring much more cognitively demanding reference to events happening elsewhere in time and space (There-and-Then). There-and Then tasks require greater effort at conceptualization (since events are not visually available in a shared context) and greater demands on memory.

One effect of performing tasks on this dimension is to draw learners' attention to the morphological forms and phrases that can be used to refer to the present and the past in English, and these are needed to help them perform the tasks (Robinson (1995); Robinson, Cadierno and Shirai (2009)). The morphology for referring to the past in English is much later acquired by L2 learners than the morphology for referring to the present, so complex tasks may promote learner attention to, and use of it. That is, in this and other cases of increasing the complexity of resource-directing demands of tasks, what I have called the 'Cognition Hypothesis' predicts more 'noticing' of L2 forms, more uptake and incorporation of them, as well as increasing accuracy and complexity of production on complex, compared to simpler task versions.

4. The Cognition Hypothesis of Task-Based Language Learning

Expanding on the ideas described above, for some years now I have been developing and researching the predictions that fall under the scope of what I call the Cognition Hypothesis of task-based learning (e.g. Robinson (2001b, 2005, 2011a)), which claims tasks should be sequenced for learners on the basis of increases in their cognitive complexity alone, and not on linguistic grading, as in traditional structural syllabuses. The fundamental pedagogic claim of the Cognition Hypothesis is that *pedagogic tasks* should be designed and sequenced to increasingly approximate the complex cognitive demands of real world *target tasks*. For example, one target task may be to give directions using an authentic street map to another person while driving quickly through an unknown city. If so, then cognitively simple tasks are designed and performed first in the L2, in which learners have planning time, and use a small map of an already known area. Subsequently, incrementally more complex versions are performed, by first taking away planning time, then by making the map a larger one, and finally by using an authentic map of an unknown area, etc. The idea is basically the same as the procedures guiding educational decision-making and training in many areas of instruction, such as pilot training, or mathematics education, where simple tasks and simulations are performed before more complex ones.

So the Cognition Hypothesis is a *pedagogic claim* about the criteria to be adopted for classifying and sequencing tasks for learners. The Triadic Componential Framework (e.g. Robinson (2001b, 2007a)) describes a taxonomy of task characteristics that can be used to examine the implications of the Cognition Hypothesis for classroom practice and syllabus design. This taxonomy distinguishes between the cognitive demands of pedagogic tasks contributing to differences in their intrinsic *complexity* (e.g. whether the task requires a single step to be performed, or dual, or multiple simultaneous steps, or whether reasoning demands are low or absent, versus high), from the learners' perceptions of task *difficulty*, which are a result of the abilities they bring to the task (e.g. working memory capacity) as well as affective responses (e.g. anxiety). I distinguish both of these from task *conditions*, which are specified in terms of information flow in classroom participation (e.g. one versus two way tasks), and in terms of the grouping of participants (e.g. same versus different gender). This Triadic Componential Framework (TCF) enables the complex classroom learning situation to be analyzed in a manageable way, allowing interactions among these three broad groups of complexity, difficulty and condition factors to be charted. I think it can also be used to operationally guide the design and sequencing of pedagogic tasks in language programs. Underpinning the pedagogic claim of the Cognition

Hypothesis are *five ancillary theoretical claims*.

1) *Output*. The first of these is that increasing the cognitive demands of tasks contributing to their relative complexity along certain dimensions described in the TCF will push learners to greater accuracy and complexity of L2 production in order to meet the consequently greater functional/communicative demands they place on the learner. That is, greater effort at conceptualization will lead learners to develop the L2 linguistic resources they have for expressing such conceptualizations.

2) *Uptake*. The second claim is that cognitively complex tasks promote heightened attention to and memory for input, so increasing learning from the input, and incorporation of forms made salient in the input. So, for example, there should be more uptake of oral recasts on complex, compared to simpler tasks, or more use of written input provided to help learners perform tasks.

3) *Memory*. Related to this the third claim is that on complex tasks there will be longer-term retention of input provided (written prompts, oral feedback, etc.) than on simpler tasks.

4) *Automaticity*. Fourthly, the inherent repetition involved in performing simple to complex sequences will also lead to automaticity and efficient scheduling of the components of complex L2 task performance.

5) *Aptitudes*. Fifthly, and importantly, individual differences in affective and cognitive abilities contributing to perceptions of task difficulty will increasingly differentiate learning and performance as tasks increase in complexity. That is, we know that individual differences in, say, aptitude for mathematics aren't reflected in performance on doing very simple addition problems (e.g. adding 2 and 6). However they are reflected in success at doing complex maths problems, like calculus, or quadratic equations. Similarly aptitudes for task performance will matter most on complex task performance.

While my work on the Cognition Hypothesis, and its five ancillary theoretical claims, has had as a primary motivating goal the development of feasible sequencing criteria for classroom tasks, it is not limited to this either in explanatory scope or in potential practical application. The Cognition Hypothesis is also important to explore for those concerned to develop equivalent forms of language tests (such as versions of standardized proficiency tests, such as TOEFL) and for those concerned to measure gain and achievement resulting from classroom exposure accurately, by using equivalent pre and post test measures of language use. Of particular interest to me is the interaction of difficulty factors, such as aptitude, with the complexity factors manipulated during task design, and the effects of these interactions on performance and learning (Robinson (2013)). Understanding these interactions will be important if we are to be able to make informed decisions about how to match learners to tasks where they have the most chance of being successful. The Cognition Hypothesis, and the TCF for examining its theoretical claims, makes focused, pedagogically useful research into all of these areas possible, and is prompting more and more and more (e.g. Baralt, Gilabert and Robinson (2014); Garcia-Mayo (2007); Housen, Kuiken and Vedder (2012); Robinson (2011b, 2011c)) empirical research into the area of task complexity, sequencing and task-based language instruction, hopefully providing, thereby, an evidentiary (non-intuitive) basis for task-based syllabus design.

References

Baralt, Melissa, Roger Gliabert and Peter Robinson (2014) *Task Sequencing and Instructed Second Language Learning*, Continuum, London.

Cadierno, Teresa and Peter Robinson (2009) "Language Typology, Task Complexity and the Development of L2 Lexicalization Patterns for Describing Motion Events," *Annual Review of Cognitive Linguistics* 6, 245-276.

Candlin, Christopher (1987) "Towards Task-based Language Learning," *Language Learning Tasks*, ed. by Christopher Candlin and Dermot Murphy, 5-22, Prentice Hall, London.

DeKeyser, Robert, ed. (2005) *Grammatical Development in Language Learning*, Wiley-Blackwell, Malden, MA.

Ellis, Rod, ed. (2005) *Planning and Task Performance in a Second Language*, Benjamins, Amsterdam.

Garcia-Mayo, Maria Pilar, ed. (2007) *Investigating Tasks in Formal Language Learning*, Multilingual Matters, Clevedon.

Housen, Alex., Folkert Kuiken and Ineke Vedder, eds. (2012) *Dimensions of L2 Performance and Proficiency: Complexity, Accuracy and Fluency in SLA*, Benjamins, Amsterdam.

Robinson, Peter (1995) "Task Complexity and Second Language Narrative Discourse," *Language Learning* 45, 99-140.

Robinson, Peter (2001a) "Task Complexity, Task Difficulty and Task Production: Exploring Interactions in a Componential Framework," *Applied Linguistics* 22, 27-57.

Robinson, Peter (2001b) "Task Complexity, Cognitive Resources, and Syllabus Design: A Triadic Framework for Examining Task Influences on SLA," *Cognition and Second Language Instruction*, ed. by Peter Robinson, 287-318, Cambridge University Press, Cambridge.

Robinson, Peter (2003) "Attention and Memory during SLA," *Handbook of Second Language Acquisition*, ed. by Catherine Doughty and Michael Long, 631-678, Blackwell, Oxford.

Robinson, Peter (2005) "Cognitive Complexity and Task Sequencing: Exploring Interactions in a Componential Framework for Second Language Task Design," *International Review of Applied Linguistics* 43, 1-33.

Robinson, Peter (2007a) "Criteria for Classifying and Sequencing Pedagogic Tasks," *Investigating Tasks in Formal Language Learning*, ed. by Maria Pilar Garcia-Mayo, 7-27, Multilingual Matters, Clevedon.

Robinson, Peter (2007b) "Task Complexity, Theory of Mind, and Intentional Reasoning: Effects on L2 Speech Production, Interaction, and Perceptions of Task Difficulty," *International Review of Applied Linguistics* 45, 191-213.

Robinson, Peter (2009) "Syllabus Design," *Handbook of Language Teaching*, ed. by Michael Long and Catherine Doughty, 294-310, Blackwell, Oxford.

Robinson, Peter (2011a) "Second Language Task Complexity, the Cognition Hypothesis, Language Learning, and Performance," *Second language Task Complexity: Researching the Cognition Hypothesis of Language Learning and Performance*, ed. by Peter Robinson, 3-38, Benjamins, Amsterdam.

Robinson, Peter, ed. (2011b) *Second Language Task Complexity: Researching the Cognition Hypothesis of Language Learning and Performance*, Benjamins, Amsterdam.

Robinson, Peter, ed. (2011c) *Task-based Language Learning*, Wiley-Blackwell, Malden, MA.

Robinson, Peter (2013) "Aptitude in Second Language Acquisition," *The Encyclopedia of Applied Linguistics,* ed. by Carol Chapelle, 129-133, Wiley-Blackwell, Oxford.

Robinson, Peter, Teresa Cadierno and Yasuhiro Shirai (2009) "Time and Motion: Measuring the Effects of the Conceptual Demands of Tasks on Second Language Speech Production," *Applied Linguistics* 38, 533-554.

Widdowson, Henry (1990) *Aspects of Language Teaching*, Oxford University Press, Oxford.

Another Argument for the Sentential Scope Analysis of a Focus Marker in Child Languages*

Tetsuya Sano

Meiji Gakuin University

1. Introduction

In this paper, I discuss children's interpretations of a focus marker in child languages. An example of a focus marker in English is the word 'only' in (1).

(1) Only John came.

It has been well-known since Crain et al. (1992, 1994) that children interpret a focus marker somewhat differently from adults.

In Crain et al.'s (1992) experiment, a picture as described in (2), as well as others, was shown to a child and a stimulus sentence such as (3) was given for the picture.

(2) picture: a cat is holding a balloon, a bird is holding a balloon and a flag, and a dog is holding a balloon.
(3) stimulus sentence: Only the bird is holding a flag.

Children at age 3-6 often rejected the description in (3), unlike adults, and justified their response by saying 'because the bird is holding a balloon, too.'

As analyzed by Crain et al., this response by children seems to suggest

---

* This is a slightly shortened version of a paper presented at GALANA5. Earlier versions were presented at Tokyo Institute for Advanced Studies of Language and Nanzan University. I would like to thank the audience at those presentations and members of TPL for helpful comments. Thanks also go to Hiroyuki Shimada for helping me in conducting the experiments and to Kevin Varden for giving me comments and suggestions on English writing. Needless to say, all the errors are my own.

that children and adults associate the focus marker with different phrases. In the case of adults, the focus marker in (3) is associated with 'the bird'; it is the phrase c-commanded by 'only.' In the case of children, the focus marker in (3) seems to be associated with 'holding a flag' or 'a flag,' because children often say 'no, the bird is holding a balloon, too,' for the preceding experiment. Why do children interpret 'only' in such a non-adult-like way?

Crain and colleagues have made several proposals on the origin of the children's non-adult-like interpretation of a focus marker. In Crain et al. (1992, 1994), it was proposed that children can take a VP as the scope of a focus marker in the subject position, unlike adults. Thus, for children, the meaning of the sentence (3) would be (4).

(4) The bird is only holding a flag.

More recently, Notely et al. (2009) and Zhou and Crain (2010) have proposed that children can take a sentence as the scope of a focus marker in the subject position, unlike adults, while extending the data coverage to Mandarin. According to them, children may posit a structure such as (3b) for (3), while adults posit a structure such as (3a) for (3).

(3a) Adult: [Only the bird] is holding a flag.
(3b) Child: [Only [the bird is holding a flag]].

In the children's structure (3b), the focus marker 'only' c-commands the rest of the sentence and hence the rest of the sentence is the scope of 'only.' Since a focus marker can be associated with any phrase in its scope, 'only' in (3b) can be associated with the subject NP 'the bird,' the VP 'holding a flag,' or the object NP 'a flag.' According to the experimental data in Crain et al. (1992), it is indeed the case that some children associate 'only' with the subject NP and other children associate it with the VP or the object NP. The structure (3b) can explain this fact. In this paper, I attempt to provide another kind of support for this S-scope analysis.

2. Child Japanese: Setting Up an Issue

My own argument for the S-scope analysis will be based on data from child Japanese. In this section, I review some previous data from child Japanese and point out that the data can be explained in two ways.

A Japanese equivalent for the English focus marker 'only' is the word *dake* in (5).

(5) Tori-dake-ga hata-o motteru.
bird-only-NOM flag-ACC is-holding
'Only the bird is holding a flag.'

(5) is a Japanese equivalent for (3). Note that the focus marker *dake* follows the modified subject NP and it is not in the sentence initial position. Accordingly, it is not possible for *dake* in (5) to take the rest of the sentence as its scope unless some change to the sentence structure is made. Thus, it would be interesting to see if Japanese-speaking children make the non-adult-like interpretation of *dake* like English-speaking children. Would Japanese-speaking children interpret (5) as if *dake* is associated with 'a flag' or 'holding a flag,' like English-speaking children?

In Endo (2004), we can find relevant experimental data. In particular, she provided a situation such as (6) and examined children's responses for a stimulus sentence like (7) with the truth-value judgment task (Crain and McKee (1985), Crain and Thornton (1998)).

(6) Situation: a cow took two bananas; an elephant took an orange and a banana
(7) Zou-dake-ga mikan-o tot-ta.
elephant-only-NOM orange-ACC take-PAST
'Only the elephant took an orange.'

In situation (6), the only participant who took the orange is the elephant. So, the stimulus sentence (7) is true for the situation (6). (8) is the result reported in Endo (2004).

(8) Rejection rates of a sentence such as (7) for a situation such as (6):

G1 (3;6-3;11)	G2 (4;0-4;11)	G3 (5;1-6;3)	Total
4/9	6/10	7/11	17/30 (56.7%)

She examined children aged from 3;6 to 6;3. Overall, in each age range in (8), children rejected the stimulus sentence about half the time, and they justified their answer by saying 'because the elephant took a banana, too.' So, it seems that the non-adult-like interpretation by Japanese-speaking children is equivalent to the one by English-speaking children.

Thus, it seems that Japanese-speaking children often associate the focus marker *dake* in the subject with the VP or the direct object. If we try to extend the S-scope analysis to cover this observation, it is necessary to change the sentential structure so that *dake* can take the rest of the sentence as its scope, because *dake* is not in the sentence-initial position, unlike in the English equivalent sentence. One idea is to raise *dake* from within the subject NP and adjoin it to the whole sentence, as illustrated in (7a), although the resulted structure is a violation of the subject condition (Chomsky (1973)).

(7a) [dake$_i$ [[zou-t_i]-ga   mikan-o   tot-ta]].
 [only$_i$ [elephant-t_i-NOM orange-ACC take-PAST]]

In (7a), *dake* can take the rest of the sentence as its scope, like its English counterpart. The structure (7a) can explain the observation that some children interpret the sentence (7) as if *dake* modifies the object NP or the VP, since the object NP or the VP is in the scope of *dake* in the LF structure (7a).

Alternatively, it is possible to hypothesize that children may directly attach *dake* to the object NP (or the VP) at LF, as illustrated in (7b).

(7b) [[zou-t_i]-ga   [mikan dake$_i$]-o   tot-ta]].
   elephant-t_i-NOM   orange-only$_i$-ACC take-PAST

In (7b), *dake* undergoes lowering. Although this operation may be unexpected by the proper binding condition (Fiengo (1974)), as well as by the subject condition, the LF structure in (7b) seems to be compatible with the observations we have seen so far, including the ones in child English. Below, the analysis illustrated in (7b) is called the direct attachment analysis.

In the rest of this paper, I will compare the two analyses: the S-scope analysis and the direct attachment analysis. On the basis of some observations in child Japanese, I will argue that there is an empirical reason for rejecting the direct attachment analysis and for adopting the S-scope analysis.

3. A Property of S-scope in Adult Japanese: Making Predictions

In this section, I introduce an adult Japanese example in which the focus marker *dake* takes an S-scope. I will then point out that it is possible to compare the two analyses of children's non-adult-like interpretation of a focus marker based on a property of the adult Japanese example.

Kishimoto (2009) observes that Japanese has examples in which the focus marker *dake* takes an S-scope. In example (9), for instance, *dake* at the end takes the preceding rest of the sentence as its scope. It is possible to have a copula *da* after *dake* but it is optional.

(9) John-ga hon-o yon-da-dake (da)
John-NOM book-ACC read-PAST-only (COP)
'It is only the case that John read books.'

Since the sentence preceding *dake* is the scope of *dake*, it is possible to associate *dake* with any phrase contained in the preceding sentence. Thus, *dake* in (9) can be associated with the following four constituents: subject NP *Taro*, the object NP *hon*, the VP *hon o yonda*, and the verb *yonda*. In other words, these four constituents can be the focus of *dake* in (9). This reminds us of what children do with a focus marker according to the S-scope analysis. In discussing this construction, Kishimoto points out something important for our current discussion. He observes that *dake* in (9) can take the whole preceding sentence as the focus. Under this sentential-focus interpretation, example (9) would mean 'John read a book and nothing else happened.' This reading is indeed possible with the Japanese example (9), as observed in Kishimoto (2009). Given this, predictions can be made for the S-scope analysis and the direct attachment analysis for children's non-adult-like focus interpretation.

To be specific, if we give the stimulus sentence (7) for the situation (10), we obtain different predictions for the S-scope analysis and the direct attachment analysis.

(7) Zou-dake-ga mikan-o tot-ta.
elephant-only-NOM orange-ACC take-PAST
'Only the elephant took an orange.'

(10) situation: a cow took a banana; an elephant took an orange

According to the S-scope analysis, the focus marker *dake* takes the rest of the sentence as its scope. Hence, as Kishimoto observes for adult Japanese, it should be possible for Japanese-speaking children to get the sentential focus interpretation, under the S-scope analysis. When a child gets the sentential focus interpretation for (7), the sentence (7) would mean 'The elephant took an orange and nothing else happened.' So, the child who got the sentential focus interpretation for (7) should reject (7) for the situation (10), because there was an extra event, namely, the cow took a banana. In contrast, according to the direct attachment analysis, the stimulus sentence (7) would mean 'The elephant took only an orange.' So, under the direct attachment analysis, a child should accept (7) for the situation (10), because it is indeed the case that the elephant took only an orange in that situation. So, the two analyses make different predictions for the (7)-(10) pair.

Still, a caution is necessary. As we have seen with Kishimoto's example, the sentential focus interpretation is just one possible interpretation for the S-scope analysis. As we have discussed earlier, under the S-scope analysis, a focus marker can be associated with any constituent in the scope. In other words, under the S-scope analysis (7a), a child can interpret (7) as if it means 'Only the elephant took an orange' or 'The elephant took only an orange,' just to mention a few possibilities.

(7a) [dake$_i$ [[zou-t_i]-ga mikan-o tot-ta]].
[only$_i$ [elephant-t_i-NOM orange-ACC take-PAST]]

Under these readings, a child should accept (7) for the situation (10) even if the S-scope analysis is right, because the extra event—the cow took a banana—does not matter for these readings. Thus, the S-scope analysis predicts that a child either rejects or accepts (7) for (10), while the direct attachment analysis predicts that a child always accepts (7) for (10). So, in comparing the two analyses, what we could do is to see if children reject (7) for (10). If it turns out that children indeed reject (7) for (10), the S-scope analysis is supported. If it turns out that children always accept (7) for (10), then the result supports neither the S-scope analysis nor the direct attachment analysis.

4. Relevant Previous Study: Crain et al. (1994)

Before taking up my own experiment, I would like to briefly mention a piece of relevant data in child English in a previous study, Crain et al. (1994).

In an experiment in Crain et al. (1994), 38 children aged 3-6 were examined and 21 of them associated 'only' with the VP in sentences like 'Only the cat is holding a flag.' Out of these 21 children, 6 children were examined further. This follow-up experiment is relevant for the issue discussed in this paper.

For the 6 VP-oriented children, further examination was conducted. In what is called Experiment 2 in Crain et al. (1994), a picture such as (13) was shown to a child and a stimulus sentence such as (14) was given the child for picture (13).

(13) picture: a dinosaur is painting a house, painting a chair, and flying a kite; and also in the same picture, an elephant is painting a car and holding a balloon.

(14) stimulus sentence: Only the dinosaur is painting a house.

The correct answer for this task is 'yes,' but the examined children mostly rejected sentence (14) for picture (13). Three of the examined six children always rejected sentence (14) for the picture (13) on the grounds that the dinosaur is also painting a chair and flying a kite. That is, these 3 children associated 'only' in (14) with the VP 'paining a house.' Because the purpose of Crain et al.'s paper was to show that young children exhibit VP-orientation in interpreting presubject *only*, these 3 children's data support their analysis. The remaining 3 other children's answers are of interest for the issue of this paper. The other 3 children also mostly rejected sentence (14) for picture (13) but they mentioned every other event in the picture for the reason of rejection. Given sentence (14) for picture (13), these children said 'no, because the dinosaur is also painting a chair, and flying a kite, and the elephant is painting a car and holding a balloon.' This data by the other 3 children was not expected under the analysis of Crain et al. (1994) and they speculated that the children were adopting a nonlinguistic strategy in responding.

Now, if we interpret this data from the viewpoint of Kishimoto's observation mentioned earlier, the data may mean something different. Recall Kishimoto's point about the sentential focus interpretation. When a focus marker takes the sentential focus, there should be no event other than the event of the sentence which is focused. When 'only' in sentence (14) takes the sentential focus, there should be no event other than the event that the dinosaur is painting a house, as in 'it is only the case that the dinosaur is painting a house'. If we look at the data of the latter three children from this viewpoint, it seems that those children interpreted sentence (14) with the sentential focus: 'The dinosaur is painting a house, and nothing else is happening.' In the next section, I will try to see if this analysis can hold more generally by examining more children and also by conducting a control test without the focus marker for comparison.

5. Child Japanese: An Experimental Study on the Issue

In order to see if Japanese-speaking children give a sentential focus interpretation for a focus marker in the subject, I examined children's interpretations of a target stimulus sentence such as (16) for a situation such as (15).

(15) situation: an elephant took a tomato; a panda took a carrot.
(16) target stimulus sentence:
Zou-dake-ga tomato-o tot-ta.
elephant-only-NOM tomato-ACC take-PAST
'Only the elephant took a tomato.'

If a child associates the focus marker *dake* with the subject NP, the child should accept the sentence (16) for the situation (15), because the only animal who took a tomato is the elephant in the situation. However, if a child associates the focus marker *dake* with the rest of the sentence, the child should reject the sentence (16) for the situation (15), because there is an extra event other than the event that the elephant took a tomato, that is, the event that the panda took a carrot also happened.

For comparison, I also examined a control stimulus sentence such as (16′) for the same situation (15).

(16′) control stimulus sentence:
  Zou-ga   tomato-o   tot-ta.
  elephant-NOM tomato-ACC   take-PAST
  'The elephant took a tomato.'

Even if a child rejects target sentence (16) for situation (15), it might be the case that the child was just bothered by an extra event because of a consideration of Grice's Maxim of Quantity (Grice (1975)). That is, the child might have just thought that the stimulus sentence (16) is not a complete description and rejected it because of the incompleteness. If so, the child's rejection has nothing to do with the interpretation of a focus marker. To exclude such a possibility, I also examined the control item (16′) for the same situation (15). If a child rejects (16) for (15) because (16) is not a complete description of (15), the child should also reject the control item (16′) for the same situation (15). In contrast, if a child rejects (15) for (16) because the child interprets the focus maker *dake* with the sentential focus interpretation, then the child should accept the control item (16′) for (15) because (16′) does not contain the focus marker *dake*. Thus, if we observe rejection for the (16)-(15) pair but not for the (16′)-(15) pair, the data give support for the S-scope analysis of a focus marker in child Japanese.

The method of the experiment was a kind of the truth-value judgment task (Crain and McKee (1985), Crain and Thornton (1998)). One experimenter shows the child a story with animals and toys. After that, another experimenter, who is playing a role of a puppet, tries to guess what is happening in the picture without looking at it. The child's role is to judge if the puppet's sentence is right or wrong.

Child participants in the experiment were divided into two groups: the target group and the control group. Children in the target group were examined with stimulus sentences with the focus marker *dake*, such as (16), and children in the control group were examined with stimulus sentences without the focus marker *dake*, such as (16′). There were 12 children in the target group (3;10-6;2, mean 4;7) and different 12 children in the control group (4;0-6;4, mean 4;10).

For the control group, a stimulus sentence such as (16′) without a focus marker was given for a situation such as (15). There were two trials such as the (15)-(16′) pair for each of the 12 children in the control group. The rejection rate for the control items was 4.2% (1/24). Thus, in this task, children mostly were not bothered by the extra event (e.g., the panda took a carrot) and they mostly accepted the stimulus sentence for the given story.

For the target group, a stimulus sentence such as (16) with a focus marker *dake* was given for a situation such as (15). As before, there were two trials such as the (15)-(16) pair for each of the 12 children in the target group. The rejection rate for the target items was 41.6% (10/24). When asked for the reason for rejection, these children answered: 'Because the panda took a carrot, too.' Thus, in this task, some children rejected (16) for (15) because of the extra event (e.g. the panda took a carrot).

6. Conclusion

Given the data in the previous section, it seems reasonable to conclude that Japanese-speaking children sometimes assign the sentential-focus interpretation to *dake*. Thus, the results support the S-scope analysis. At the same time, the data are incompatible with the direct attachment analysis. According to the direct attachment analysis, *dake* in (16) is directly attached to the object NP at LF. Thus, (16) would be like 'The elephant took only a tomato' at LF under the direct attachment analysis. If that is the interpretation by the children, they should always accept the sentence in the target condition, because it is true that the elephant took only a tomato in story (15). But the data was to the contrary; children often rejected (16) for (15). The presented data therefore supports the S-scope analysis and goes against the direct attachment analysis.

References

Chomsky, Noam (1973) "Conditions on Transformations," *A Festschrift for Morris Halle*, ed. by Stephen Anderson and Paul Kiparsky, 232-286, Academic Press, New York.

Crain, Stephen and Cecile McKee (1985) "The Acquisition of Structural Restrictions on Anaphora," *Proceedings of NELS 15*, ed. by Stephen Berman, Jae-Woong Choe and Joyce McDonough, 94-110, GLSA Publications, Amherst, MA.

Crain, Stephen, William Philip, Kenneth Drozd, Thomas Roeper and Kazumi Matsuoka (1992) "Only in Child Language," paper presented at the 17th Annual Boston University Conference on Language Development, Boston University, Boston, MA.

Crain, Stephen, Wei-Jia Ni and Laura Conway (1994) "Learning, Parsing, and Modularity," *Perspectives on Sentence Processing*, ed. by Charles Clifton Jr., Lyn Frazier and Keith Rayner, 443-467, Lawrence Erlbaum Associates, Hillsdale, NJ.

Crain, Stephen and Rosalind Thornton (1998) *Investigations in Universal Grammar: A Guide to Experiments on the Acquisition of Syntax and Semantics*, MIT Press, Cambridge, MA.

Endo, Mika (2004) "Developmental Issues on the Interpretation of Focus Particles by Japanese Children," *Proceedings of the 28th Annual Boston University Conference on Language Development*, ed. by Alejna Brugos, Linnea Micciulla and Christine E. Smith, 141-152, Cascadilla Press, Somerville, MA.

Fiengo, Robert (1974) *Semantic Conditions on Surface Structure*, Doctoral dissertation, MIT.

Grice, Paul H. (1975) "Logic and Conversation," *Syntax and Semantics*, Vol. 3, *Speech Acts*, ed. by Peter Cole and Jerry L. Morgan, 41-58, Academic Press, New York.

Kishimoto, Hideki (2009) "Topic Prominency in Japanese," *The Linguistic Review* 26, 465-513.

Notley, Anna, Peng Zhou, Stephen Crain and Rosalind Thornton (2009) "Children's Interpretation of Focus Expressions in English and Mandarin," *Language Acquisition* 16, 240-282.

Zhou, Peng and Stephen Crain (2010) "Focus Identification in Child Mandarin," *Journal of Child Language* 37, 965-1005.

tough 構文の派生について

西前　明

明治学院大学

1. はじめに

(1) は tough 構文 (*tough*-constructions) と呼ばれ，(2) のいわゆる形式主語構文とほぼ同義だとされる．tough 構文の述語は，「難易，快・不快」を表す形容詞 (tough, hard, difficult, easy, impossible, pleasant, comfortable, fun, annoying など) であり，主節の主語が不定詞節内の動詞あるいは前置詞の意味上の目的語となっている．

(1) This knife is easy to cut the ham with.
(2) It is easy to cut the ham with this knife.

tough 構文に含まれる不定詞節を tough 不定詞節 (*tough*-infinitives) と呼ぶことにする．(3) と (4) でそれぞれ見るように，不定詞関係節 (infinitival relatives)，と不定詞目的節 (infinitival purpose clause) では顕在的 wh 関係詞が使えるが，(5) で見るように，tough 不定詞節では使えない．[1]

---

[1] 不定詞目的節については Bach (1982), Jones (1985) などを参照．一般に文献に登場する不定詞目的節は，(ia) のような例であるが，私のインフォーマントは，(ib, c) (=(4)) のように顕在的 wh 関係詞を用いた例も容認した．(id) で見るように，(制限的) 関係節は，代名詞，及び，すでに同定された名詞を修飾しないので，(ib, c) に関係節の解釈はない．(ic) が (ib) に比べて容認度が低いのは，wh 関係詞が人称代名詞を先行詞にとりにくいことによると思われる．

(i) a. (My friend recommended a knife$_i$ to me.) I bought the knife$_i$/it$_i$ [to cut the ham with].
  b. (My friend recommended a knife$_i$ to me.) I bought the knife$_i$ [with which to cut the ham].
  c. (My friend recommended a knife$_i$ to me.) ?I bought it$_i$ [with which to cut the ham].
  d. (My friend recommended a knife$_i$ to me.) *I bought the knife$_i$/it$_i$ [with which I

(3) The knife [with which to cut the ham] is on the table.
(4) (My friend recommended a knife$_i$ to me.) I bought the knife$_i$/?it$_i$ [with which to cut the ham].
(5) *This knife is easy [with which to cut the ham].

また，tough 構文では，(6a, d) で見るように，主節の主語が不定詞の意味上の主語になると非文となる．

(6) a. *John is difficult to read your handwriting.

(McCawley (1988: 101))

b. Your handwriting is difficult to read.
c. It is difficult for John to read your handwriting.
d. *You are easy to cut the ham with this knife.

本稿は，(5) と (6a, d) を排除する方法について考える．

2. tough 不定詞節の派生

tough 不定詞節には，(7) で示す通り，空演算子 Op が関与していると仮定する (Browning (1987) を参照)．

(7) This knife is easy [Op to cut the ham with].

tough 不定詞節の他に，(8) に含まれる不定詞関係節と (9) に含まれる不定詞目的節についても，Op が関与していると仮定する (Browning (1987), Hasegawa (1998) を参照)．

(8) The knife [Op to cut the ham with] is on the table.
(9) (My friend recommended a knife$_i$ to me.) I bought the knife$_i$/it$_i$ [Op to cut the ham with].

空演算子 Op・顕在的 wh 関係詞・不定詞節空補文標識 C_{inf} のそれぞれの演算子関連素性に関して (10) のように指定する．Op が関与する，tough 不定詞節 (7)・不定詞関係節 (8)・不定詞目的節 (9) の派生は (11) のようになり，一方，顕在的 wh 関係詞が関与する，不定詞関係節 (3)・不定詞目的節 (4) の派生は (12) のようになると仮定する．(11) と (12) において，Op と with

---

intended to cut the ham].

which の移動は C_{inf} の演算子関連素性によって引き起こされるものとする。[2]

(10) a. 空演算子 Op = [Op]
b. 顕在的 wh 関係詞 = [Wh$_{rel}$]
c. 不定詞節空補文標識 C_{inf} = [Op] or [[P]+[Wh$_{rel}$]]
(11) [$_{CP}$ [Op([Op])]$_1$ [C([Op])] to cut the ham with t_1]
(12) [$_{CP}$ [with([P]) which([Wh$_{rel}$])]$_1$ [C([[P]+[Wh$_{rel}$]])] to cut the ham t_1]

不定詞関係節でも不定詞目的節でも，(13) で見るように，wh 関係詞が前置詞を随伴しない場合は非文となる．(10c) で指定したように，C_{inf} は演算子関連素性として，[[P]+[Wh$_{rel}$]] はとれるが [Wh$_{rel}$] はとれないとすれば，(13c) の派生は排除できる．

(13) a. *The knife [which to cut the ham with] is on the table.
b. (My friend recommended a knife$_i$ to me.) *I bought the knife$_i$/it$_i$ [which to cut the ham with].
c. *[$_{CP}$ [which([Wh$_{rel}$])]$_1$ [C([[P]+[Wh$_{rel}$]])] to cut the ham with t_1]

ここで，(14) を排除する方法を考える．(14) で示す，tough 不定詞節では顕在的 wh 関係詞が使えないという事実は，tough 不定詞節がもし tough 述語の補部（＝内項）であるなら，tough 述語の語彙記載の中で，(15) のような選択特性を指定することによってとらえることができる．tough 述語としての easy が補部としてとる CP は，(16) であり，(17) ではない．

(14) *This knife is easy [with which to cut the ham]. (=(5))
(15) 補部として，[Op] を持つ C_{inf} を主要部とする CP を選択する．
(16) [$_{CP}$ [Op([Op])]$_1$ [C([Op])] to cut the ham with t_1] (=(11))
(17) [$_{CP}$ [with([P]) which([Wh$_{rel}$])]$_1$ [C([[P]+[Wh$_{rel}$]])] to cut the ham t_1] (=(12))

ここで分裂文をテストとして，(18) の tough 不定詞節を，(19) の標準的に不定詞補部とみなされているもの，および (20) の付加部とされる不定詞目的節と比較してみる．すると，(20b) で見るように，焦点の位置に不定詞目的節は生起できるが，(18b) と (19b) でそれぞれ見るように，tough 不定詞節

---

[2] 補文標識の演算子関連素性によって演算子の移動が引き起こされる，そのメカニズムの詳細については本稿では触れない．

と動詞の不定詞補部はともに生起できないことがわかる．これは tough 不定詞節が補部である可能性を示唆している．

(18) a. This knife is easy [to cut the ham with].
　　 b. *It is [to cut the ham with] that this knife is easy.
(19) a. I decided [to cut the ham with the knife].
　　 b. *It was [to cut the ham with the knife] that I decided.
(20) a. I bought it [to cut the ham with].
　　 b. It was [to cut the ham with] that I bought it.

次に，(21) を排除する方法を考える．すでに述べたように，tough 構文では主節の主語が不定詞の意味上の主語になると非文となる．(21) の tough 不定詞節の派生として，(22) を考えてみる．

(21) *You are easy [to cut the ham with this knife]. (=(6d))
(22) a. [$_{CP}$ [Op([Op])]$_1$ [C([Op])] to t_1 cut the ham with this knife]
　　 b. [$_{CP}$ [C([0])] to PRO cut the ham with this knife]

([0]=「演算子関連素性を持たない」)

まず (22b) は，C_{inf} が [Op] を持っていないので，(15) の選択特性に従えば排除できる．(22a) については，(23) を仮定する必要がある．

(23)　空演算子 Op は格を担う．

空演算子 Op も顕在的 wh 演算子と同じく格を担うと仮定すれば，(22a) は排除される．(22a) には，(24a) と同じく，演算子に格を付与する要素がない．（空格の付与を仮定するなら，Op は PRO と異なり空格は担わないものとする．）

(24) a. *I don't know [who to come].
　　 b. I don't know [what to do].

このようにして，(15) と (23) を仮定すれば，(21) は排除できる．[3,4]

---

[3] 先行詞を意味上の主語とする，不定詞目的節 (ia) と不定詞関係節 (ib) については，tough 構文と異なり，Op を含まない (22b) のような選択肢が選択制限によって排除されることはない，すなわち，(ii) のような構造をとり得る，と仮定する (Browning (1987) を参照)．

　(i) a. We brought him along [to show us the way].　　　　(Jones (1985: 23))
　　 b. The hurricane [to come in a few days] is very huge.

3. for について

不定詞節空補文標識 C_{inf} の演算子関連素性については，すでに (25) のように仮定したが，顕在的補文標識 for については，(26) のように仮定する．すると，(27a) の中括弧で囲んだ部分の構造は，(28) ではなく，(27b) のようになる．

(25) 不定詞節空補文標識 C_{inf} = [Op] or [[P]+[Wh$_{rel}$]]　(=(10c))
(26) 補文標識 for = [0]（=「演算子関連素性を持たない」）
(27) a. This knife is easy {for you to cut the ham with}.
　　 b. [$_{PP}$ for you] [$_{CP}$ [Op([Op])]$_1$ [C([Op])] to PRO cut the ham with t_1]
(28) [$_{CP}$ [Op([Op])]$_1$ [for([*Op])] you to cut the ham with t_1]

　　(ii) a. We brought him$_i$ along [$_{CP}$ C to PRO$_i$ show us the way].
　　　　 b. The hurricane$_i$ [$_{CP}$ C to PRO$_i$ come in a few days] is very huge.
[4] 本稿の説明では，(22a) が排除されるのは，Op が「格」を付与されないからであって，「対格」を付与されないからではない．しかし，Pollard and Sag (1994) が (i) の対立を提出している．本稿の分析に従うと，(ia, b) の tough 不定詞節の派生は，それぞれ (iia, b) のようになる．
　　(i) a. John is easy to believe Mary would kiss.　　(Pollard and Sag (1994: 168))
　　　 b. *John is easy to believe is capable of doing something that stupid.　　(ibid.)
　　(ii) a. [$_{CP}$ [Op([Op])]$_1$ [C([Op])] to believe Mary would kiss t_1]
　　　　 b. [$_{CP}$ [Op([Op])]$_1$ [C([Op])] to believe t_1 is capable of doing something that stupid]
(iib) において Op は (主) 格を付与されているので，本稿のやり方では (iib) を排除することはできない．一つの可能性は，tough 述語の語彙記載の中で，Op が担う格が対格でなければならないことを，例えば (iii) のようにして，指定することである．しかし，(iii) のような指定の仕方が果たして可能なのかは不明である．
　　(iii) 補部として，[[Op]+[accusative]] を持つ（=対格を担う Op の移動を引き起こす）C_{inf} を主要部とする CP を選択する．
しかしこの一方で，Ross (1967) が (iva) のような判断を示している．本稿の分析に従うと，(iva) の tough 不定詞節の派生は (ivb) のようになる．
　　(iv) a. ?*These flowers would be easy for you to say that you had found.
　　　　　　　　　　　　　　　　　　　　　　　　　　　　　　　(Ross (1967: 228))
　　　 b. [$_{CP}$ [Op([Op])]$_1$ [C([Op])] to say that you had found t_1]
Pollard and Sag の (ia) の判断ではなく，Ross の (iva) の判断を採用すれば，(iib) が不適格なのは，Op が対格を担っていないからではなく，tough 不定詞節では何らかの理由で定形節から Op を抜き出すことができないからである，と見ることができる．

(27b) において，for は補文標識ではなく前置詞であり，you を補部として，不定詞節とは独立した前置詞句 PP を成す．不定詞節の補文標識は空の C_{inf} であり，不定詞節の主語は PRO である．(27b) を支持する経験的根拠を以下に与える．

tough 述語が不定詞節とは独立した前置詞句の for 句と共起し得ることを示す証拠として，Jacobson (1992: 275) は (30) と (31) の対立を挙げている．(29a) の Bill は標準的に不定詞節の主語とみなされているが，この構文において，(30) のように for DP を移動させると非文になる．ところが (31) で見るように，tough 構文の for DP は移動できるので，それは独立した前置詞句であるとみなすことができる．

(29) a. It is unlikely for Bill to win.
　　 b. The rock is easy for Bill to move.
(30) a. *For whom is it unlikely to win?　　(Jacobson (1992: 275))
　　 b. *For Bill, it's unlikely to win.　　(ibid.)
(31) a. For whom is the rock easy to move?　　(ibid.)
　　 b. For Bill, the rock is easy to move.　　(ibid.)

tough 不定詞節に顕在的主語は現れないと考えるべき根拠として，Chomsky (1977: 92, 126) が (32) の例を挙げている．

(32) a. The hard work is pleasant for the rich to do.
　　　　　　　　　　　　　　　(Chomsky (1977: 92, 126))
　　 b. *The hard work is pleasant for the rich for poor immigrants to do.
　　　　　　　　　　　　　　　　　　　　　　　　　　(ibid.)
(33)　 It is pleasant [for the rich] [for poor immigrants to do the hard work].　　(ibid.)
(34) a. The hard work is pleasant [for the rich].
　　 b. *The hard work is pleasant [for the rich] [for poor immigrants].

(32b) の tough 構文では，(33) の形式主語構文と異なり，poor immigrants が不定詞節の主語になれないとすれば，(32b) には，不定詞節とは独立した前置詞句の for 句が二つ (for the rich と for poor immigrants) 含まれていることになり，(34b) と同じ理由で不適格なのだと述べることができる．tough 不定詞節に顕在的主語が現れないとすれば，(32) の派生は，(36) ではなく，(35) でなくてはならない．(26) の素性指定はこれを保証する．

(35) a. The hard work is pleasant [for the rich]

   [$_{CP}$ [Op([Op])]$_1$ [C([Op])] to PRO do t_1].

   b. *The hard work is pleasant [for the rich] [for poor immigrants]

   [$_{CP}$ [Op([Op])]$_1$ [C([Op])] to PRO do t_1].

(36) a. The hard work is pleasant

   [$_{CP}$ [Op([Op])]$_1$ [for([*Op])] the rich to do t_1].

   b. The hard work is pleasant [for the rich]

   [$_{CP}$ [Op([Op])]$_1$ [for([*Op])] poor immigrants to do t_1].

以上の経験的根拠に基づいて，tough 不定詞節に顕在的主語は現れない，すなわち，tough 構文に絡む for は補文標識ではなく，不定詞節とは独立した前置詞句を成す前置詞である，と結論する．(26) を仮定すれば，(28) や (36) のような派生は排除される．

4. おわりに

本稿では，tough 構文に含まれる不定詞節が tough 述語の補部（＝内項）であるなら，tough 述語の語彙記載の中で，(37) のような選択特性を指定することによって，(38)-(40) のような文を排除できる，ということを示した．

(37) 補部として，[Op] を持つ C$_{inf}$ を主要部とする CP を選択する．

$(=(15))$

(38) *This knife is easy with which to cut the ham. $(=(14))$

(39) *You are easy to cut the ham with this knife. $(=(21))$

(40) *The hard work is pleasant for the rich for poor immigrants to do.

$(=(32b))$

参考文献

Bach, Emmon W. (1982) "Purpose Clauses and Control," *The Nature of Syntactic Representation*, ed. by Pauline Jacobson and Geoffrey K. Pullum, 35-57, Reidel, Dordrecht.

Browning, Marguerite A. (1987) *Null Operator Constructions*, Doctoral dissertation, MIT. Reproduced by Garland (1991).

Chomsky, Noam (1977) *Essays on Form and Interpretation*, Elsevier North-Holland,

New York.

Hasegawa, Hiroshi (1998) "English Infinitival Relatives as Prepositional Phrases," *English Linguistics* 15, 1-27.

Jacobson, Pauline (1992) "The Lexical Entailment Theory of Control and the *Tough* Construction," *Lexical Matters*, ed. by Ivan A. Sag and Anna Szabolcsi, 268-299, CSLI Publications, Stanford.

Jones, Charles (1985) *Syntax and Thematics of Infinitival Adjuncts,* Doctoral dissertation, University of Massachusetts.

McCawley, James D. (1988) *The Syntactic Phenomena of English,* Vol. 1, University of Chicago Press, Chicago.

Pollard, Carl and Ivan A. Sag (1994) *Head-Driven Phrase Structure Grammar*, University of Chicago Press, Chicago.

Ross, John Robert (1967) *Constraints on Variables in Syntax*, Doctoral dissertation, MIT.

英語の複合名詞再考
―概念結合の観点から―

瀬田　幸人

岡山大学

1. はじめに

英語において beehive や olive oil のように２つの要素が結合して１つの語として機能する名詞は複合名詞と呼ばれる．複合名詞は，上の例のように名詞と名詞で構成される場合もあれば，*pick*pocket, *hot*house, *over*coat の斜体字に見るように，名詞以外の要素（それぞれ動詞，形容詞，前置詞）と名詞で構成される場合もある．複合名詞の意味，とりわけ２つの要素間の関係については，従来から様々な枠組みで論じられてきた．本稿では，２つの名詞で構成される "N+N 複合名詞"（以下，単に複合名詞と呼ぶ）を取り上げて，認知的な観点から複合名詞の構成要素間の関係について検討することにする．

2. 従来の主な提案
2.1. 意味や文法関係による分類に基づく提案

初期の代表的なものとしては Adams（1973）や Levi（1978）がある．Adams（同書）は，構成要素間の関係を "Subject-Verb"（*e.g.* flea-bite）や "Verb-Object"（*e.g.* life insurance）のような文法関係に基づくタイプ，"Composition/Form/Contents"（*e.g.* snowball）のように構成や形に基づくタイプ，broomstick などが含まれる "Associative" のようにパートニミー（partonymy）に基づくタイプ，"Names"（*e.g.* pine tree）のように要素間の関係とは無関係なタイプ，など11のタイプに分類している．瀬田（2006）で指摘したように，この分類には，"Names" のようなタイプは言うまでもなく，kitchen garden のようにどのタイプにも当てはまらないものをまとめて "Other" として分類するなどいくつか問題点がある．

Levi（同書）は，当時の標準理論の枠組みで，基底構造において，CAUSE

(*e.g.* tear gas), HAVE (*e.g.* lemon peel), MAKE (*e.g.* snowball), USE (*e.g.* steam iron), BE (*e.g.* soldier ant), IN (*e.g.* field mouse), FOR (*e.g.* horse doctor), FROM (*e.g.* olive oil), ABOUT (*e.g.* tax law) のような9つの原始述語を設定し，統語操作によって複合名詞を派生しようとしている．瀬田（同書）で指摘したように，この提案にも，例えば snowball のような複合名詞に複数の基底構造を設定するなど原理的な問題がある．

2.2. 論理的な関係に基づく提案

複合名詞の構成要素間の関係を単に列挙するような分類法ではなくて，より包括的な関係として捉えようとしたものに Hatcher (1960) がある．彼女は，(i) Ⓐ = "A is contained in B", (ii) Ⓑ = "B is contained in A", (iii) A → B ("A = Source"), (iv) A ← B ("A = Destination") という4種類の関係を提案している．これらの関係は，いずれも意味範囲が広い包括的な関係として考えられているため，より多くの種類の複合名詞が扱えるという利点はある．例えば，sand-paper などは (i) によって，footstep などは (iii) によってそれぞれ説明されることになる．しかしながら，瀬田（同書）で指摘したように，関係が包括的になればなるほど個々の複合名詞の説明が難しくなり，実際，例えば wineglass や keyhole などの複合名詞については説明が困難となるなど，いくつかの問題点がある．

2.3. 従来の提案の問題点

今までの提案は，上で見たいくつかの提案に代表されるように，広範囲におよぶ複合名詞を対象として，複合名詞の2つの要素の関係を，それぞれの要素の意味に基づいて列挙したり，主語，目的語といった文法関係を用いて説明しようとしたり，それらの両方に基づいて分類しようとするものがほとんどであった．もちろん，限定された包括的な関係のみで説明しようとした Hatcher (同書) のような提案もあり，その試み自体は評価できるが，上で述べたように問題がある．いずれにしても，従来の提案は，いかに多くの複合名詞を余すことなく分類するかということに最大の関心が向けられていたのは確かである．

ここで Devereux and Costello (2005) の実験結果について触れておくことにする．彼らは，Levi（同書）の提案を参考にして，複合名詞の構成要素間の関係として H(ead) ABOUT M(odifier) や M CAUSES H など5つの関係を

設定し，それぞれの関係に広範囲におよぶデータの中から精選した12の複合名詞（およびその意味解釈）を割り当て，合計60個の複合名詞について34名の大学生・院生を対象に実験を行った．この実験は，被験者に30個の複合名詞を示し，例えば dog bed を例に取ると，"a bed where a dog sleeps" という意味と共に，"bed ABOUT dog"，"bed FOR dog" など上述の5つの関係を含む18の関係を提示し，その中から意味解釈として適切だと思うものを Web 上の操作で複数回答させるというものだった．実験結果として重要なのは，例えば job anxiety (= "anxiety about losing a job") に対して，被験者のほとんどが H ABOUT M, H DERIVED FROM M, M CAUSES H の3つの関係を選択したことがあげられるが，これは Levi（同書）に代表されるような細かく分類するというアプローチには問題があり，複合名詞の構成要素間の関係はより包括的な関係で捉えなければならないことを示唆している．

　複合名詞を単なる分類の対象に留めるのではなく，2つの要素の結合がどういう場合に可能であり，どういう場合に可能ではないのか，また2つの要素の結合を支配する何か一般的な原理が存在するのか，という疑問に答えるべく，もっと広い視点からのアプローチが求められている．

3. 認知に基づく提案

　近年，認知の観点から言語現象を捉え直そうとする研究が進んでおり，メタファーやメトニミーなどの比喩表現についても多くの研究があり，興味深い成果をあげている．この節では，メトニミーを支配する原理が複合名詞の要素間にも働くことを提案したい．

3.1. メトニミー

　メトニミーは，「隣接性（contiguity）に基づく比喩」と言われることが多いが，実は，隣接性という概念を巡っては意見が一致しているわけではない．[1] ここでは，隣接性を空間的な近接（spatial nearness）という意味としてではなく，もっと広く2つの要素間の概念的な関係，あるいは連想（association）の意味として捉えることにする．

　さて，後の議論のためにはメトニミーの定義が必要になるが，メトニミーを定義するのはそう簡単なことではない．初期のころは，Lakoff and Johnson

---

[1] Croft (2006: 320), Bierwiaczonek (2013: Chapter 6), Koch (1999: 154) などを参照．

(1980: 36) の "Metonymy […] has primarily a referential function, that is, it allows us to use one entity to *stand for* another" という記述に代表されるように，メトニミーの中心的な機能は，一般に下の (1) の例に見るような指示機能だと考えられていた．[2]

(1) a. We need a couple of *strong bodies* for our team.　(= strong people)
　　b. I've got a new *set of wheels*.　(= car, motorcycle, etc.)

その後の研究によって，メトニミーは，ある事物を別の事物を表すのに用いるという指示の働きではなくて，ある認知領域において1つの概念事物 (conceptual entity) が別の概念事物に心的にアクセスする認知プロセスであるということが次第に明らかになってきた．そこで，本稿では，大枠として Radden and Kövecses (1999: 21) の以下の定義を採用することにする．[3]

(2) Metonymy is a cognitive process in which one conceptual entity, the vehicle, provides mental access to another conceptual entity, the target, within the same idealized cognitive model [ICM].

3.2. メトニミーの原理と複合名詞

Lakoff and Johnson (同書: 38-39) は，メトニミーの概念は無原則ではなくて体系的であるとし，7つの (概念) メトニミーをあげているが，その中の4つを下にあげる．(スモールキャピタルは概念であることを表す．)

(3) a. THE PART FOR THE WHOLE (*e.g.* We don't hire *longhairs*.)
　　b. PRODUCER FOR PRODUCT (*e.g.* He bought a *Ford*.)
　　c. OBJECT USED FOR USER (*e.g.* The *buses* are on strike.)
　　d. THE PLACE FOR THE EVENT (*e.g.* Let's not let Thailand become another *Vietnam*.)

また，Norrick (1981) は，メトニミーの原理 (principle) として19の原理を提案している．以下にその主なものをあげる．

---

[2] Lakoff and Johnson (同書: 36) は，「指示」以外にも「理解」に関係する機能があることに言及している．
[3] メトニミーを概念領域の写像として捉える定義については Barcelona (2003: 246) を参照．なお，理想化認知モデル (idealized cognitive model) は，基本的には Lakoff (1987: Chapter 4) を念頭においている．

(4) a. Cause—effect (1. Cause—effect, 2. Producer—product,
　　　　　3. Natural source—natural product, 4. Instrument—product)
　　b. Acts—major participants (1. Object—act, 2. Instrument—act,
　　　　　3. Agent—act, 4. Agent—instrument)
　　c. Part—whole (1. Part—whole, 2. Act—complex act,
　　　　　3. Central factor—institution)
　　d. Container—content (1. Container—content, 2. Locality—occupant,
　　　　　3. Costume—wearer)
　　e. Possessor—possession (1. Possessor—possession,
　　　　　2. Office holder—office)

さらに比較的最近では，Radden and Kövecses（同書：30-43）が，メトニミーを生み出す関係は大きく Whole ICM（理想化認知モデル）and its part(s) と Parts of an ICM の2つの一般的な概念ゲシュタルト（conceptual configurations）に収斂できるとし，それぞれ7種類と10種類の概念ゲシュタルトを提案し，それに応じた概念メトニミーをいくつか示している．以下では，そのうちの一部を抜き出してあげておく．

(5) 　Whole ICM and its part(s)
　　a. Thing-and-Part ICM
　　　WHOLE THING FOR A PART OF THE THING
　　　(e.g. *The car* needs washing.)
(6) 　Parts of an ICM
　　a. Production ICM
　　　PRODUCER FOR PRODUCT (e.g. I've got a *Ford*. (for 'car'))
　　b. Possession ICM
　　　POSSESSOR FOR POSSESSED (e.g. That's *me*. (for 'my bus'))
　　c. Containment ICM
　　　CONTAINER FOR CONTENTS (e.g. *The bottle* is sour. (for 'milk'))

上述のメトニミーに関する3つの代表的な提案を複合名詞の観点から眺めると，複合名詞の2つの要素間の関係もメトニミーを支配する一般的な原理，あるいはメトニミーも含めたより包括的な上位原理で説明できるのではないか，という予測が立つ．そこで，複合名詞の2つの要素間の関係を支配する認知的な関係として，仮に以下の6つの関係を考えてみよう．

(7) a. Part—Whole, b. Container—Content, c. Cause—Effect
　　d. Act—Participant, e. Location—Event, f. Possessor—Possessed

これらは，Adams（同書）の "Associative" や Levi（同書）の CAUSE や HAVE などを用いた関係，および Hatcher（同書）の "A is contained in B" や "B is contained in A" の関係と類似しているように見えるが，関係の概念は同じではない．上の（2）の定義に見られるように，メトニミーを理想化認知モデル内あるいは概念領域（conceptual domain）内における 2 つの概念事象の関係と捉えているので，(7) の関係も，2 つの概念事象の間の関係と考えたい．[4] ただし，メトニミーが 2 つの下位概念領域（subdomain）[5] の間の概念関係であるのに対して，(7) は 2 つの概念領域（または領域マトリックス（domain matrix））の間の概念関係であると考えている．[6] 言い換えれば，(7) は 2 つの概念領域（つまり理想化認知モデル）の結合を表していると捉えることができる．また，(7) で用いられている語彙は，従来よりも広い概念を表すものと考えている．なお，概念の結合の仕方は文化的な影響を強く受けると思われるため，[7] (7) が認知的な関係として普遍性を持つかどうかは現時点では判断できない．

3.3. 複合名詞と概念結合
3.3.1. 具体的な例

上の (7) がどのように複合名詞の 2 つの要素に作用するか論じる前に，具体例を見ておくことにする．(7a) は，broomstick, doorknob, lemon peel などにおける 2 つの要素の概念結合に関係すると言える．(7b) は，モノが含まれている関係として広く捉えているため，wineglass や sand-paper の他にも

---

[4] Bierwiaczonek（同書：36-38）は，概念どうしの関係として，(i) unassociated separation, (ii) associated separation, (iii) small partial overlap, (iv) large partial overlap, (v) inclusion の 5 つの基本的なタイプをあげているが，これについては別の機会で検討する．

[5] "Subdomain" という概念は Barcelona（同書：222-223）による．彼は，The *ham sandwich* is waiting for his check について，"restaurant domain" の "subdomain" として "a food item" と "the customer" の 2 つを提案している．本稿では，一応この Barcelona の考え方を受け入れることにする．

[6] 2 つの概念領域（領域マトリックス）の間の関係という意味では，1 つの概念領域から別の概念領域への写像であるメタファーと似ている．これに関しては Lakoff（同書：288）や Croft (2003: 177-178) などを参照．

[7] Radden and Kövecses（同書：48-50）は，メトニミーの議論の中で，媒体（vehicle）の選択を支配する認知的な原理の 1 つとして文化的な好み（cultural preferences）をあげている．

field mouse や birdcage などにおける2つの要素の概念結合に関係すると思われる．(7c) は，Producer—Product の関係なども含む広い関係として捉えているため，coffee stain や footstep の他にも steam iron や tear gas，あるいは恐らく silkworm などにおける2つの要素の概念結合に関係する．(7d) は，cow boy の他に horse doctor や soldier ant などにおける2つの要素の概念結合に関係すると考えられる．というのも，後述するように，doctor や soldier にはレキシコン（目的役割（TELIC））において目的・機能に関する語彙情報が記載されていると考えているからである．(7e) は，Location を place や thing なども含む概念として，また Event を activity を含む概念として広く捉えているので，water bird を始め cradle song や keyhole などにおける2つの要素の概念結合に関係すると考えられる．[8] (7f) は，Object–User の関係（この場合の User は人以外のモノも含む概念）も含む広い関係として捉えているため，olive oil や picture book の他にも windmill などにおける2つの要素の概念結合に関係すると思われる．

3.3.2. 概念結合のプロセス

基本的には Pustejovsky(1995)で提案された語彙理論の枠組に基づいた瀬田（同書）の線に沿って，それぞれの語彙（複合名詞の構成要素）の意味内容は，特質構造（Qualia Structure）としてレキシコンに記載されているとする立場をとる．そして，概念結合とは，複合名詞の第2要素（主要部）の語彙情報は引き継がれ，第1要素の語彙情報が新たに第2要素に組み込まれ，新たな概念が形成されるプロセスと考える．具体的には，第2要素の4つの役割[9]に第1要素の情報が組み込まれることになるが，例えば，doorknob の場合は，(7a) の関係が2つの要素に作用し，第2要素の構成役割に第1要素の情報と共に "is part of" のような情報が新たに組み入れられることになる．もちろん，この種の情報は，語彙と語彙の様々な結合の可能性を考えれば，最初からレキシコンに記載されているとするには無理があり，概念結合によって導入されると考えるしかない．

ところで，これについては認知的な立場からの提案もある．例えば，Bier-

---

[8] (7e) は kitchen garden のような複合名詞の2つの要素の概念結合にも関係しているかもしれない．

[9] 形式役割（FORMAL），構成役割（CONSTITUTIVE），目的役割（TELIC），主体役割（AGENTIVE）．詳しくは Pustejovsky（同書：85-104）を参照．

wiaczonek（同書：128-141）は，メンタル・スペース理論の枠組みで，複合語スキーマ（compound schema）という概念を導入して bee sting のような複合名詞の説明を試みているが，語彙情報については単に PROPERTY と大雑把に記述するなど不十分な点が多い．[10]

4. 結語

　本稿では，複合名詞の構成要素間の関係を余すところなく細分化するという従来のアプローチには問題があることを指摘し，人間の認知能力の一つと考えられるメトニミーを支配する原理に注目し，複合名詞の構成要素間の関係を概念どうしの結合関係と捉え，この構成要素の概念結合もメトニミーを支配する原理によって説明可能であることを示した．瀬田（同書）で論じたように，umbrella tree のような複合名詞における構成要素間の関係を説明するには，構成要素の類似性という概念が必要となる．これは，複合名詞を支配する原理にはメタファー的な原理も含まれることを示しているが，さらには，複合名詞の概念結合の本質を捉えるには，メトニミーやメタファーの原理を包括するような上位原理の探求が求められることを示唆している．この非常に興味深い問題については，今後の研究課題としたい．

参考文献

Adams, Valerie (1973) *An Introduction to Modern English Word-Formation*, Longman, London.

Barcelona, Antonio (2003) "Clarifying and Applying the Notions of Metaphor and Metonymy within Cognitive Linguistics: An Update," *Metaphor and Metonymy in Comparison and Contrast*, ed. by René Dirven and Ralf Pörings, 207-277, Mouton de Gruyter, Berlin/New York.

Bierwiaczonek, Bogusław (2013) *Metonymy in Language, Thought and Brain*, Equinox Publishing, Sheffield and Bristol.

Croft, William (2003) "The Role of Domains in the Interpretation of Metaphors and Metonymies," *Metaphor and Metonymy in Comparison and Contrast*, ed. by René Dirven and Ralf Pörings, 161-205, Mouton de Gruyter, Berlin/New York.

---

[10] 本稿の説明は pickpocket や scarecrow のようないわゆる外心的な複合名詞は扱うことができないが，基本的には，レキシコンの語彙情報と (7d) によって説明できると考えている．別のアプローチについては Tuggy (1987) や Bierwiaczonek（同書：140-141）などを参照．

Croft, William (2006) "On Explaining Metonymy: Comment on Peirsman and Geeraerts, 'Metonymy as a Prototypical Category'," *Cognitive Linguistics* 17:3, 317-326.

Devereux, Barry and Fintan Costello (2005) "Investigating the Relations Used in Conceptual Combination," *Artificial Intelligence Review* 24, 489-515.

Hatcher, Anna G. (1960) "An Introduction to the Analysis of English Noun Compounds," *Word* 16, 356-373.

Johnston, Michael and Federica Busa (1999) "Qualia Structure and the Compositional Interpretation of Compounds," *Breadth and Depth of Semantic Lexicons*, ed. by Evelyne Viegas, 167-187, Kluwer, Dordrecht.

Koch, Peter (1999) "Frame and Contiguity: On the Cognitive Bases of Metonymy and Certain Types of Word Formation," *Metonymy in Language and Thought*, ed. by Klaus-Uwe Panther and Günter Radden, 139-167, John Benjamins, Amsterdam/Philadelphia.

Lakoff, George (1987) *Women, Fire and Dangerous Things: What Categories Reveal about the Mind*, University of Chicago Press, Chicago and London.

Lakoff, George and Mark Johnson (1980) *Metaphors We Live By*, University of Chicago Press, Chicago and London.

Langacker, Ronald W. (1987) *Foundations of Cognitive Grammar*, Vol. 1. *Theoretical Prerequisites*, Stanford University Press, Stanford.

Levi, Judith N. (1978) *The Syntax and Semantics of Complex Nominals*, Academic Press, New York.

Nerlich, Brigitte, David D. Clarke and Zazie Todd (1999) " 'Mummy, I like being a sandwich': Metonymy in Language Acquisition," *Metonymy in Language and Thought*, ed. by Klaus-Uwe Panther and Günter Radden, 361-383, John Benjamins, Amsterdam/Philadelphia.

Norrick, Neal R. (1981) *Semiotic Principles in Semantic Theory*, John Benjamins, Amsterdam and Philadelphia.

Pustejovsky, James (1995) *The Generative Lexicon*, MIT Press, Cambridge, MA.

Radden, Günter and Zoltán Kövecses (1999) "Towards a Theory of Metonymy," *Metonymy in Language and Thought*, ed. by Klaus-Uwe Panther and Günter Radden, 17-59, John Benjamins, Amsterdam/Philadelphia.

瀬田幸人 (2006)「英語の複合名詞についての一考察」『言語科学の真髄を求めて』, 鈴木右文・水野佳三・高見健一 (編), 485-498, ひつじ書房, 東京.

Tuggy, David (1987) "*Scarecrow* Nouns, Generalizations, and Cognitive Grammar," *Pacific Linguistics Conference* 3, 307-320. Available on the Internet: http://www-01.sil.org/~tuggyd/Scarecrow/SCARECRO.htm

可能性を表す can, may と必然性を表す must について

島田　守

龍谷大学名誉教授

1. はじめに

　英語法助動詞の多様な意味・用法は，1960年代から1970年代にかけて「根源的（root）」対「認識的（epistemic）」という体系に分類され始めた．その後，この二分法は，Palmer（1990[2]）や澤田（2006）などに見られるように，「事象的モダリティ（event modality）」対「命題的モダリティ（propositional modality）」という対立で捉え直され，それぞれをどのように下位分類するかによって，いくつかの考え方が提案されている．事象的モダリティとは，起こり得る事象に対する指示とか認可といった話者の態度を表すものであり，命題的モダリティとは，命題の真偽に関する話者の判断に関わるものである．

　ここでは紙数の関係で，can と may が表す「可能性（possibility）」と must が表す「必然性（necessity）」を取り上げることにしたい．

2. 可能性と必然性を表す法助動詞の論理的意味体系

　認識論理学（epistemic logic）では，可能性と必然性の間にある同値関係が説明されている．$Poss$ は「可能である」という演算子を，N は「必然である」という演算子を表すことにし，命題は p で，否定は〜で，同値は≡で表すことにする．そこで，可能性と必然性のそれぞれについて，演算子の肯定と否定，命題の肯定と否定を組み合わせると4つの場合が想定でき，可能性と必然性の間には肯定と否定が逆転する次のような「裏返しの同値関係」が成立する．

(1) a.　$Poss(p) \equiv \sim N(\sim p)$
　　b.　$\sim Poss(p) \equiv N(\sim p)$

c. $Poss(\sim p) \equiv \sim N(p)$
   d. $\sim Poss(\sim p) \equiv N(p)$

例えば，(1a) の論理式は，「p は可能である (p is possible)」を意味する $Poss(p)$ と「$\sim p$ は必然でない ($\sim p$ is not necessary)」を意味する $\sim N(\sim p)$ が同値であることを表している．話をわかりやすくするために，可能性を表す法助動詞として may と can を，また，必然性を表す法助動詞として must を取り上げ，命題 p を John is happy. として (1) の同値関係を例示してみよう．なお，法助動詞を用いて表せない論理式の場合には，そのパラフレーズだけを示すことにする．

(2) a. John *may* be happy. ≡ It is not necessary that John is not happy.
   b. John *cannot* be happy. ≡ John *must not* be happy.
   c. John *may not* be happy. ≡ It is not necessary that he is happy.
   d. It is not possible that John is not happy. ≡ John *must* be happy.

さて，(1a-d) の同値関係とそれを例示した (2a-d) から読みとれる法助動詞に関する言語事実は次のようになる．

(1b) の例示である (2b) の場合には，可能性の法助動詞 can を用いた文も必然性の法助動詞 must を用いた文も両方とも文法的であるが，それ以外の3つの場合には，may か must のうちのいずれか1つを用いた文しか許されない．(2a) と (2c) では may を用いた文しか許されないし，(2d) では must を用いた文しか許されないが，いずれにしても，可能性と必然性に関係する4つの場合のすべてを同値関係を利用して法助動詞で表せる仕組みになっている．

(1a) の $\sim N(\sim p)$ と (1d) の $\sim Poss(\sim p)$ のように，演算子の否定と命題の否定が重なる論理式の場合には，(2a) と (2d) から明らかなように，それに対応する法助動詞を用いた文が，通常は，成り立たない．それは，「法助動詞 + not + 本動詞」という連鎖において not は，通常は，一度しか生起できないので，法助動詞を否定する場合か，命題内容を否定する場合かのいずれかに限られることになるためである．(2b) の cannot は，(1b) の $\sim Poss$ に対応する表現であるから，この場合の not は法助動詞を否定している．他方，(2b) の must not と (2c) の may not は，それぞれ，(1b) の $N(\sim p)$，(1c) の $Poss(\sim p)$ に対応した表現なので，not は命題内容を否定している．前者の場合の否定をモダリティ否定，後者の場合の否定を命題否定と呼ぶことにする．

ちなみに，(2b) の must not については，必然性の must には命題否定が起こらなくて，通常は，その交替形である cannot が用いられるとされているが，このことについては 5 節で取り上げることにする．

以上が可能性と必然性を表す法助動詞が持つ論理的な意味体系であるが，この体系を出発点にして，can, may, must それぞれに内在する意味論的な特質を探ってみたい．

3. 可能性を表す can と may

先行研究を概観すると，可能性については，根源的可能性，理論的可能性，事実に基づいた可能性，認識的可能性，状況的可能性など，学者によってさまざまな分類が試みられている．それらの先行研究を Declerck (1991) を軸に取り込むような形で，まとめてみよう．Declerck (1991: 397) は，可能性を「理論的可能性 (theoretical possibility)」と「事実に基づいた可能性 (factual possibility)，即ち，認識的可能性 (epistemic possibility)」の二種類に分類している．

3.1. 理論的可能性

理論的可能性は，非認識的で根源的な可能性で，ある場面・状況の実現が理論的に可能である (= 考えられる) ことを表し，それが実際に行われるかどうかについては言及しない．

(3) Aerosols *can* explode if you do not treat them properly. (=It is theoretically possible for aerosols to explode ...)

(Declerck (1991: 397))

(3) は「殺虫剤用のスプレーは，適切に扱わなければ爆発することがある」という意味を表し，「スプレーの爆発が起こり得る」と，理論的な可能性についてだけ述べていて，実際の爆発については言及していない．理論的可能性の can を用いた文は，It is (theoretically) possible for NP to do とパラフレーズされ，命題内容が実際に起こるとは言っていないので，不定詞節で表されていることに注意したい．

Declerck (1991: 405) は，理論的可能性を表す can のモダリティ否定である cannot を理論的 (= 非認識的) 不可能性 (theoretical (=non-epistemic) impossibility) であるとしている．これは，命題によって表される場面や状況が

現在あるいは未来において実現することが不可能である，という話し手の発話時における確信を表すものである．

    (4) a. I *cannot* give you that information now. (=It is impossible for me to give ...)　　　　　　　　　　　　　　　(Declerck (1991: 405))
        b. I *cannot* see him tonight. (=It is impossible for me to see him tonight.) (present modality, future actualisation)　　　　　　(ibid.)

(4a) と (4b) のパラフレーズに不定詞節が用いられていることが，これらの文が理論的不可能性を表していることを裏付けている．

  ところで，安藤 (2005: 277-279) の可能性の分類には「状況的可能性 (circumstantial possibility)」というものがある．それに属するものの１つに，「主語の行動を妨げるものは外界に存在しない (=nihil obstat) という話し手の判断を表す」ものがあり，It is possible for NP to do でパラフレーズできるものであるとして，次の例を挙げている．

    (5) I *can* see you at any time. (いつでも会いますよ) [都合がつけられる]
　　　　　　　　　　　　　　　　　　　　　　　　　　　(安藤 (2005: 277))

(5) の状況的可能性を表す can は「状況的に見て〜することが可能である，〜することができる」という意味を表している，と思われる．(5) は「差し当たって予定が入っていない状況から判断して，いつでもあなたに会うことができる」と述べているのである．この状況的可能性の can をモダリティ否定したものが，(4) の cannot であると見なせないだろうか．なぜなら，この cannot は「状況的に見て〜することが不可能である，〜できない」という意味を持つ状況的不可能性を表すと言えるからである．だとすると，(5) の can は Declerck (1991) の言う「理論的可能性の can」に組み入れられるべきものと考えられる．

  ちなみに，安藤の言う「状況的可能性」には，(4) や (5) とは異質と思える例も挙げられている．その１つに主語の散発的な行動様式や典型的な振る舞い・状態を表すものがあって，次の (6) を挙げている．

    (6) It *can* be very cold here, even in May.　　　　(安藤 (2005: 277))

(6) は「当地では５月には，普通，だいぶ暖かくなっているはずだが，その５月でさえとても寒いことがある．」という意味を表していて，５月の寒さが散発的であることを示している．同様の議論を澤田 (2006: 233) もしており，

このような can を「散在的（＝分布がまばらである）」で根源的なものとし，散在的な存在を表す can は，非特定的で頻繁にある（起こる）ものではない状況を表す，としている．結論的に言うと，「散発的な状況的可能性の can」と呼ぼうが，「散在的な存在を表す can」と呼ぼうが，(6) の can についても Declerck (1991: 397) は，sometimes とほぼ同じ意味を持つ can であり「理論的可能性を表す can」の下位分類の 1 つとして組み入れている．

3.2. 認識的可能性

Declerck (1991: 397-399) は，事実に基づいた認識的可能性の場合には，話し手は，ある場面・状況がすでに存在していた可能性があるとか，現在存在している可能性があるとか，あるいは，未来において存在する可能性があると述べている，としている．さらに，認識的可能性を表す may は，話者指向的な法副詞である perhaps とほぼ同じ意味を持ち，その文は It is possible that 節でパラフレーズできる，としている．that 節という定形節を用いてパラフレーズしているのは「事実に基づいた認識的可能性」という定義を反映したものである．

(7) His work *may* still improve. (=It is possible that his work will still improve; his work will {perhaps/maybe/possibly} still improve.
(Declerck (1991: 398))

(7) では，話し手は，「彼の仕事がまだ改善する」という状況が未来に実現する可能性があることを発話時点で推量している．未来に実現可能であろうということで that 節中に will が生起しているのである．

Declerck (1991: 406) は，疑問文や否定文に用いられた can も認識的可能性を表すとし，cannot は認識的不可能性（epistemic impossibility）を表すとしている．認識的不可能性では，話し手はある特定の陳述が真ではあり得ない，と述べている．cannot および仮定的で控えめな could not は話し手が現在あるいは未来に関する陳述を却下することを表す．

(8) Jill {*can't/couldn't*} be Laurel's sister. They don't resemble each other a bit. (Declerck (1991: 406))

(8) は認識的不可能性の can't/couldn't を用いた文であるので，It is not possible [=impossible] that 節を用いて (9) のようにパラフレーズできるであろう．(4) で扱った理論的不可能性の cannot のパラフレーズとは違って，不

定詞節を用いていないことに注意したい．

(9) It is impossible that Jill is Laurel's sister.

安藤（2005: 279-280）も，疑問文，否定文に用いられる can を認識的可能性を表すとし，通常肯定平叙文で用いられる認識的可能性の may と相補分布をなす，と述べている．

さらに，Declerck (1991: 400) が言うように，「～だったかもしれない」と，話し手が過去の場面・状況に対して発話時に判断する認識的可能性は「{may/might/could}＋完了形」によって表される．ここで注意したいのは，may やその交替形として仮定的で控え目な might と could は用いることができても，can は用いることができないということである．それは，肯定平叙文で用いられる can は，通常，理論的可能性しか表せないからである．

(10) a. They *may have left* the room in the afternoon. (=It is possible that they left the room in the afternoon.) (Declerck (1991: 400))
b. There's no need to worry yet. He {*could*/*might*} have missed his train and taken the next one. (=It is just possible that he missed his train and took the next one.) (ibid.)

また，「～だったはずはない」という過去の場面・状況の認識的不可能性は「{cannot/could not}＋完了形」によって表される．

(11) He {*can't*/*couldn't*} have seen us yesterday. (=It is not possible that he saw us yesterday.) (Declerck (1991: 406))

4. 必然性を表す must

Declerck (1991: 406-407) は，直接体験によって得られたというよりも，むしろ推論または演繹の結果得られた知識を表す場合を認識的必然性と呼ぶ．must は，話し手が，現在または過去の場面・状況についての唯一可能なあるいは妥当な解釈や説明であると考えているものを表す場合に用いる，としている．

(12) He *must* be stuck in a traffic jam. (=No other explanation of his being late seems possible.) (Declerck (1991: 407))

パラフレーズを参考にして考えると，(12) の話し手は，「彼が遅れている」という発話時の場面・状況を引き起こしている原因を「彼が渋滞に巻き込まれている」ということ以外に考えられない，と思っているのである．このような must の働きを澤田 (2006) は，次のように述べている．

(13) 認識的（必然性の）must は，認識主体（＝話し手）が，現時点（＝発話時点）で入手可能な直接的な証拠に基づいて，p に違いないと「断定 (conclusion)」していることを表す．

(澤田 (2006: 212))

さらに，澤田 (2006: 255) は，認識的必然性を表す must の命題内容条件を「その命題内容は，(単純未来の will で表されるような) 未来の状況であってはならない．」としている．これは，認識的必然性の must には，認識的可能性の may, might, could には適用されない命題内容条件が課されていることを示している．

(14) Don't go near the lion. It {*may*/*might*/*could*/*must} bite you.

(澤田 (2006: 255))

(14) の命題内容は that (if you go near the lion,) it will bite you となり，will を含んだ未来の状況なので，(14) の must は許されない．

5. モダリティ否定の cannot と命題否定の must not

認識的不可能性を表す cannot は，先行文脈中にある認識的必然性を表す must が用いられた文，あるいは，認識的可能性を表す may が用いられた文を否認する場合に用いられることが多い．

(15) A: That man {*must*/*may*} be Tom's father.
 B: Oh, no. He *can't* be. Tom's father is no longer alive.

このような cannot の談話上の働きを，澤田 (2006) は次のように条件づけている．

(16) 既存命題否認の条件：
 話し手は，モダリティ否定の認識的法動詞を用いる際には，証拠 q に基づいて，既存命題（もしくは，主張・想定）p（または〜 p）を否認

したり，p（または～p）とは思えないと主張したりしている．

(澤田 (2006: 273))

さて，2節で，必然性の must には命題否定が起こらなくて，通常は交替形である cannot が用いられるとされている，と述べたが，ここで認識的必然性の must not と認識的不可能性の cannot の使い分けについて取り上げよう．

(17) She walked past me without speaking. She {*cannot/must not*} have seen me.

この例では，cannot も must not も許されるが，話し手の推論プロセスが異なっている．cannot の場合には，(16) の条件が示すように，話し手は「彼女は私を見れば必ず話し掛けてくる．話し掛けずに通り過ぎたことからすると，私を見たということはあり得ない」と主張しているのである．ところが，must not の場合には，事情が変わる．このことに関して澤田 (2006) は次のような条件を提案している．

(18) 否定命題断定の条件：
話し手は，命題否定の認識的法助動詞を用いる際には，「命題 p ならば，証拠 q ということはないはずだ．しかし，実際には，q だ．それゆえ，p ではない」と断定している．

(澤田 (2006: 273))

(18) の条件を援用して (17) を説明すると，話し手は，「彼女が私を見たなら，話し掛けずに通り過ぎることはないはずだ．しかし，実際には，話し掛けずに通り過ぎたので，私を見なかったに違いない」と断定していることになる．(18) は，話し手が must not を用いて否定命題の必然性を述べる場合には，単純に「証拠 q に基づいて p でない」と断定するのではなくて，「p ではない」という結論（＝断定）を引き出すために，その背後に「p ならば q ということはないはずだ」という論理が働いている，ということを指摘しているのである．もしも，(18) のような一捻りした推論プロセスを妥当なものだとすると，must not が用いられる場面や文脈が実際には稀なことも説明できるし，そのために短絡的に「must not は用いられず，その代わりに cannot が用いられる」としてしまう文法書が多いことも説明できるであろう．

6. おわりに

2節で可能性を表すcan, may と必然性を表すmust の論理的同値性を明らかにした後，3.1 節では理論的可能性を表す can と理論的不可能性を表す cannot を扱い，それらが，それぞれ，It is possible for NP to do と It is impossible for NP to do のように命題を不定詞節を用いてパラフレーズできることを示した．さらに，安藤（2005）の「状況的可能性」を表す can や澤田（2006）の「散在的な存在的モダリティ」である can も Declerck（1991）の理論的可能性を表す can の下位分類として組み入れることにした．3.2 節では認識的可能性を表す may と認識的不可能性を表す cannot を取り上げ，前者は It is possible that 節で，また，後者は It is impossible that 節でパラフレーズできることを示した．4節では，認識的必然性を表す must を取り上げ，It is necessary that 節でパラフレーズされ，「その命題内容は（単純未来の will で表されるような）未来の状況であってはならない」という条件が課されていることを示した．5節では，cannot と must not を用いる際の話し手の推論プロセスの違いを，澤田（2006）を援用して，「既存命題の否認」と「否定命題の断定」とした．

以上，先行研究の一部を覚え書き風にまとめただけで，新たな発見も示せないままに紙数が尽きてしまった．can, may とは異なった振る舞いをする could, might や必然性を表す have to も扱う予定であったが，割愛した．多義的で，話し手の主観性との関わりを持つ法助動詞の意味・用法は捉えがたく，未解決な問題も多い．その謎の解明に向けて，小論がささやかなヒントにでもなれば，と願っている．

参考文献

安藤貞雄 (2005)『現代英文法講義』開拓社，東京.

Declerck, Renaat (1991) *A Comprehensive Descriptive Grammar of English*, Kaitakusha, Tokyo.［安井稔(訳)(1994)『現代英文法総論』開拓社，東京.］

Palmer, Frank R. (1990) *Modality and the English Modals*, 2nd ed., Longman, London.

澤田治美 (2006)『モダリティ』開拓社，東京.

ヲ格を伴う移動動詞について

鈴木　泉子

信州豊南短期大学

1. はじめに

　日本語のヲ格は典型的には他動詞の目的語に付与され動作の対象（Theme）の意味役割を担うが，移動を表す動詞と共に用いられ移動の経路（Path）や起点（Source）を担う用法がある。[1]

(1) a. 山田が教室のガラスを割った．
　　 b. 教室のガラスが山田に（よって）割られた．
(2) 　健康維持のため毎日歩くことを医者から勧められた．
(3) a. 田中は週末にレインボーブリッジを歩いた．
　　 b. *レインボーブリッジが週末に田中に（よって）歩かれた．
(4) a. 受験者が控え室を出た．
　　 b. *控え室が受験者に（よって）出られた．

(1a) のヲ格名詞句は動詞「割る」の動作の対象役割を担っており，直接受動文に言い換えることができる（=(1b)）（寺村 (1982: 220) 参照）．それに対し「歩く」はその動作を遂行するのに動作主（Agent）以外の参与者を必要としない自動詞であり，ヲ格名詞句は義務的ではない（=(2)）．また，(3a) のようにヲ格名詞句が現れることもあるが，直接受動文に言い換えることができない（=(3b)）（寺村 (1982: 228-229) 参照）．本稿ではこのような，一見対象役割とは異なる意味役割を担うヲ格名詞句を考察し，両者を共通のものとして分析する可能性を探っていく．

---

[1] 他に「冬休みを楽しく過す」「雨の中を進軍する」といった「時間，状況的用法」も存在するが（岡 (2013: 163)），本稿では考察の対象外とする．

2. 移動動詞の特徴

　寺村（1982: 103）は移動表現を大きく（i）「出どころ（出発点）」（Point of departure）と縁の深いもの，（ii）「通り道（通過点）」（Path）と縁の深いもの，（iii）「到達点（入りどころ）」（Goal）と縁の深いものの3種類に分類している．(i) 類はいわゆる起点を取るタイプで，起点は「（ドコ）ヲ」もしくは「（ドコ）カラ」という形で現れる．本稿では「出る」タイプと呼ぶ．(ii) 類はいわゆる経路を取るタイプで，経路は「（ドコ）ヲ」という形で現れる．本稿では「通る」タイプと呼ぶ．(iii) 類はいわゆる着点を取るタイプで，着点は「（ドコ）ヘ」もしくは「（ドコ）ニ」という形で現れる．ヲ格を伴わないので本稿では立ち入らないことにする．

　「出る」タイプの動詞と共起するヲ格名詞句は起点を表し，ガ格名詞句によって表される移動の主体が人や生物，またはそれになぞらえた物（船，車など）の場合，ヲをカラに言い換え可能である．ただし，起点が観念的な場所，ないし制度や状態として考えられる場合，カラ句への言い換えは不可能である（=(7)）．逆に，人間などの有情物による意識的な動きとは異なり自然現象などの場合，起点をカラ句で表すことはできるがヲ格を用いて表すことは難しい（=(8)）．

(5)　その男が東口ヲ／カラ出る．
(6)　山田がタクシーヲ／カラ降りる．
(7)　3年前に大学ヲ／*カラ卒業した．[2]
(8)　煙が煙突 *ヲ／カラ出る．

「通る」タイプの動詞は共起するヲ格名詞句が通過する場所（経路）を表し，他の助詞を用いた表現に言い換えることができない．

(9)　高速道路が通行止めの為一般道を通って甲府まで行った．
(10)　旧街道を歩くのが私の趣味だ．

　次節では，「出る」タイプ及び「通る」タイプの振る舞いに関する先行研究と

---

[2] 『現代日本語書き言葉均衡コーパス』および検索ツール「NINJAL-LWP for BCCWJ (NLB)」を用いて「大学を卒業する」及び「大学から卒業する」の頻度を調べた結果，「卒業する」全体の1737件中「大学を卒業する」は252件ヒットしたが「大学から卒業する」は0件であった．

して三宅 (2011) を概観し，問題点を指摘する．

3. 三宅 (2011)

　三宅 (2011) は移動動詞とヲ格名詞句の分布について，統語構造における非対格性と語彙概念構造における意味素の編入を用いて説明している．

　まず，前節で見た主語の意図性の有無と「出る」タイプの起点名詞句に付与される格の種類との関連について，Burzio (1986) の一般化を用いて説明する．意図性を持つ主語（動作主）は外項であり，外項を持つ動詞は対格付与能力を持つ．従って「出る」タイプが意図性を持つ主語を伴う場合，対格付与能力を持つ．このため，起点名詞句がヲ格標示される．それに対して，「出る」タイプが意図性を持たない主語を伴う場合，表層の主語は内項として基底生成したものであり，動詞は外項を持たない．従って動詞は対格付与能力を持たず，起点名詞句をヲ格標示することができない．

　外項として統語構造に写像される項に関して三宅 (2011: 124-126) は以下の想定をしている．まず，語彙概念構造に意図的に出来事をコントロールするということを表す CONTROL という意味素を仮定する．CONTROL は意図的な行為者を表す変項 (x) と事象 (EVENT) を取る (=(11))．さらに，(12) の結びつけ規則を仮定し，項構造を介して CONTROL の取る変項が外項として統語構造に投射されると仮定する．

(11)　[$_{EVENT}$ CONTROL x [$_{EVENT}$ …]]
(12)　項構造への結びつけ規則
　　i.　CONTROL に統率された項は，項構造において外項の位置に結びつく
　　ii.　それ以外の項は，内項の位置に結びつく

　さらに，移動を表す意味素として MOVE を導入し，非意図的な移動の場合には (13) の語彙概念構造を，意図的な移動の場合には (14) の語彙概念構造を仮定する．

(13)　[$_{EVENT}$ MOVE x]
(14)　[$_{EVENT}$ CONTROL x [$_{EVENT}$ MOVE x]]

(13) は「煙が出る」のような，非対格動詞としての「出る」の語彙概念構造を表しており，CONTROL が存在しないため外項として統語構造に投射される

項は無く，動詞はヲ格標示することができない．それに対して (14) には CONTROL が存在するため，動詞が潜在的にヲ格標示できる．

意図的な主語を伴う「出る」タイプの取る起点がカラ／ヲ交替することについては，Baker (1988) の編入 (incorporation) を用いて説明する．

(15)　[$_{EVENT}$ CONTROL x [$_{EVENT}$ MOVE x [$_{PATH}$ FROM y]]]
(16)　[$_{EVENT}$ CONTROL x [$_{EVENT}$ MOVE-FROM$_i$ x [$_{PATH}$ t$_i$ y]]]

日本語では前置詞の動詞への編入が形態的に確認できないことから，三宅 (2011: 128) は語彙概念構造において FROM が随意的に編入によって MOVE まで主要部移動していると仮定する．編入が生じなければ FROM はカラとして具現化する．編入が生じた場合，(12) の結びつけ規則により動詞が外項を持つことになる．従って，Burzio の一般化により動詞が対格付与能力を得，FROM(の痕跡) が統率する y 項がヲ格標示される．

「出る」タイプが非意図的な主語を取る場合，語彙概念構造内に CONTROL が存在しないため対格付与能力を持たない．従って，編入が生じなければ y 項はカラ標示されるが，編入が生じると y 項が格標示されなくなるため格交替が生じない．

「通る」タイプの場合，主語が意図性を持つ／持たないに関わらず経路は常にヲ格で標示される ((9), (10) 参照)．この点に関して，三宅 (2011) は「通る」タイプ以外に，Burzio の一般化の例外となる，外項を欠くにもかかわらずヲ格標示できる動詞が有ることを指摘している．

(17) a. 新雪が山頂を覆っている

(三宅 (2011) の (68a), 影山 (1991) より引用)
　　 b. 山頂が *(新雪に) 覆われている
(18)　不合格の知らせが太郎を悲しませた　　　　(三宅 (2011) の (71))

(17a) に関しては，影山 (1991) に基づき次のように論じている．能動文の動作主主語は直接受動文において外項の格下げを伴う為省略できるが，「覆う」「囲む」などの動詞は受動化の際，元の主格名詞句を省略できない．このことは，対応する能動文 (17a) において表層の主語が内項であり，格下げの対象とならないため省略できないとすれば説明できる．

(18) は心理動詞の例であるが，これらの動詞は逆行束縛を許す．

(19)　自分$_i$の学生が山田先生$_i$を悩ませた

(20) *自分ᵢの学生が山田先生ᵢを殴った

動作主主語を取る (20) においては目的語が主語内の照応形を束縛しておらず，その結果「自分」が「山田先生」であるという解釈が生じないが，(19) では，主語は原因を表しており，「自分」が「山田先生」であるという解釈が可能である．この違いは，原因主語が元々内項として VP 内に生起し，派生の過程で「山田先生」が「自分」を束縛する構造が生じるのに対して，動作主主語は VP より上の vP 内に生起するため，派生を通して「山田先生」に束縛されることがないことによると考えれば説明できる．[3]

このように，他に外項を欠くにも関わらずヲ格を付与する動詞があることから，三宅 (2011) は「通る」タイプについても Burzio の一般化の例外として，「覆う」や「悩ませる」同様外項を欠くにもかかわらず対格付与能力を持つと結論づけている．[4]

しかし，仮に三宅 (2011) が言うように「通る」タイプが外項を欠く動詞だと認めると，同じ経路ヲ格を取る (21) のような例はどう説明されるのか．

(21) 田中は人目につかないようわざと裏路地を歩いた．

(21) における「歩く」という行為は故意によるものであり，意図的にコントロールされた出来事である．従って，(11) のように，その語彙概念構造内に CONTROL という意味素を有していると考えられる．従って，(12) の結びつけ規則により外項を有することになる．このことは，「通る」タイプが外項を

---

[3] 詳細な分析に関して三宅 (2011) は Fujita (1993) の分析を紹介するに留めているが，Fujita (1993) では (20) を (i) のように分析している．
  (i) [$_{AgrSP}$ [自分ᵢの学生]ⱼ [[$_{AgrOP}$ 山田先生ᵢ [[$_{VP}$ tⱼ [$_{V'}$ [$_{VP}$ tᵢ 悩ま-せ]]] ... AgrO]] ... AgrS]]
(i) において「自分の学生」は内項として，AgrO よりも下の VP 内に生起し，目的語「山田先生」が AgrOP の指定部に移動することによって，LF で「自分」を含む原因主語名詞句の痕跡 tᵢ を c 統御するため，「山田先生」による「自分」の束縛が可能になる．

[4] Fujita (1993) とは独立に，Hasegawa (2004) も動作主主語他動詞と原因主語他動詞の振る舞いの違いを指摘し，原因項が VP 内に生起すると論じている．さらに，(18)-(19) のように原因項自体が主語位置へ上昇する例に加えて，原因項が VP 内にとどまり，目的語の分離不可能所有者項が主語位置に上昇する (ia) のような例を指摘している．
  (i) a. ドルが戦争で値を上げた．
     b. 戦争がドルの値を上げた．
     c. ドルの値が戦争で上がった．
原因項が主語位置へ上昇する (ib) や対応する非対格動詞「上がる」が用いられている (ic) と比較して分かるように，「ドル」は動作主項というよりは主題項の分離不可能所有者である．

欠くという主張と矛盾する．

　加えて，「出る」タイプについても，ガ格名詞句が意図性を持たないにも関わらず起点をヲ格で標示できる例が存在する．

(22)　煙が煙突を出て，大気中を漂っている
(23)　血は心臓を出て，体中を巡っている

（いずれも，竹林（2007: 74）より）

三宅（2011）に従えば「出る」タイプでヲ格名詞句を伴う場合，必ず語彙概念構造上に CONTROL が存在することになるが，(22) の「煙」や (23) の「血」が意図的に煙突を出たり心臓を出ているとは考え難い．

　さらに，「出る」タイプは一見カラ／ヲ交替を許すようにみえるが，2節で見た通り「カラ」と「ヲ」の一方しか許さない場合や，「カラ」と「ヲ」が共起する場合が存在する．

(24) a.　新宿駅を西口から出る
　　 b. *新宿駅から西口から出る
　　 c. *新宿駅を西口を出る
　　 d. *新宿駅から西口を出る

ヲ格とカラ格がどちらも起点を担っているとすれば，「新宿駅」と「西口」は共起できないはずである．実際，どちらもカラ格もしくはヲ格で標示した (24b, c) は非文である．しかし，(24a) のように「新宿駅」がヲ格で，「西口」がカラ格で標示されると文法的な表現となる．従って，ヲ格名詞句とカラ格名詞句は別の意味役割を担っていると考えられる．ヲ格とカラ格を入れ替えた (24d) が非文なのは，格と意味役割の不一致により意味的に整合性がとれないためと考えられる．このことは，そもそも一見「出る」タイプにおける起点を担うヲ格は単純な格交替により生じるものではないことを意味している．従って，Burzio の一般化によるカラ／ヲ交替という三宅（2011）の分析では，場所を表すヲ格名詞句の分布について説明ができない．

4. 経路としてのヲ格

　「出る」タイプのヲ格名詞句が単なるカラ格からの交替で生じるのではないとすると，この名詞句は何者なのだろうか．加藤（2006）によれば，場所を表

すヲ格には経路格と離格の用法があり，[5] 経路格は移動場所の認知上の形式によって通過域，移動経路，移動領域の3つの下位分類を持つ．経路が有境界性を持ち，その終端部とそこから離れていくことが意識される場合離格と解釈され，当該の場所を移動していくことに焦点が当たる場合に経路格と解釈される．言い換えれば，離格と（通過域等を含む）経路格には明確な境界はないことになる．実際，(25)のヲ格名詞句は路地と大通りの境界に着目すれば起点と解釈できるが，通り抜けられる経路としても解釈可能である．

(25) 細い路地を／から大通りに出ると，小田急線の駅がすぐ近くに見えた
（加藤 (2006) の (68)）

従って，本論では「出る」タイプのヲ格は起点役割と結びついたカラ格との交替によるものではなく，経路役割を担っており，「通る」タイプのヲ格と本質的に同じものであるとの立場を取る．

では，なぜ経路はヲ格によって標示されるのだろうか．ヲ格は典型的には他動詞の目的語に付与される格であり，他動詞の目的語は典型的には直接受動文の主語になることができる．

(26) a. 世界中の人々がハリーポッターシリーズを読んでいる
　　 b. ハリーポッターシリーズは世界中の人々に読まれている
(27) a. 多くのハイカーがこのコースを歩いている
　　 b. このコースは多くのハイカーに歩かれている

「読む」は典型的な活動動詞であり，ヲ格標示された目的語は (26b) が示すように直接受動文の主語になる．それに対してヲ格標示される経路は通常目的語とは見なされず，これらを取る動詞も自動詞に分類されている．しかし，インターネット検索をすると実際に (27b) のような例が少数ながら検出される．また，「読む」同様「歩く」も固有の意味として動作の開始時点および終了時点を含意しないが意図的に開始・終了できるという点で活動動詞と同じアスペクト特性を持ち，目的語等により限定されない限り継続時間表現の「2時間」とは共起できるが時間限定表現の「2時間で」とは共起しない．

(28) 本を2時間／*2時間で読む

---

[5] 加藤 (2006) での「経路格」及び「離格」は意味格であり，ヲ格名詞句の担う用法の1つである．

(29) 湖のまわりを2時間／*2時間で歩く

同時に，「歩く」という行為はその性質上移動を伴うので移動動詞（より正確には移動様態動詞）でもある．影山 (2008, 2010) では経路を伴う移動動詞を通常の活動動詞と区別している．

(30) 活動動詞の語彙概念構造
[x ACT (ON-y)]
(31) 経路を伴う移動動詞の語彙概念構造
[y MOVE [$_{Route}$]]
(32) 着点を伴う移動動詞の語彙概念構造
[[y MOVE [$_{Route}$]] BECOME [y BE AT-z]][6]

影山 (2008) では「足踏みする」は移動を伴わない（為経路を持たない）行為であり (=(33))，活動動詞としているが，影山 (2010) では同様に移動を伴わない「うごめく」を，Route を取らない MOVE としている (=(34))．

(33) *床を足踏みする．（判断は影山 (2008) による）
(34) *多くの若者が裏通りを10メートルうごめいた．
(35) 謎の生物が海底をうごめいている．

だが，「うごめく」が場所をヲ格で標示する例は少なからず見られる (=(35))．「*部屋を飲んだ」「*図書館を読んだ」のように，典型的な活動動詞が単なる活動場所をヲ格で標示できないことを考えると，なぜ「うごめく」の様な移動を伴わない動詞の一部と移動を伴う動詞が同じように場所をヲ格で標示できるのだろうか．

「足踏みする」などの経路を伴わない動詞も「2時間足踏みする」のように継続時間表現と共起できることから活動動詞と同じアスペクト特性を持つ．この点で経路を取る移動動詞と違いがない．「足踏みする」が経路を取らないのはその動きの特徴から来るものであり，言い換えれば，時速0キロメートルで移動していると考えることができる．だとすると「足踏みする」の取るヲ格名

---

[6] 影山 (2008) は「活動→変化→状態」という行為連鎖の変化と状態を繋ぐ推移として BECOME を用いている．なお，CAUSE は活動と変化を繋ぐ使役に対応している．語彙概念構造は最大で以下の構造を持つことになる．
(i) [[x ACT ON-y] CAUSE [[y MOVE [$_{Route}$]] BECOME [y BE AT-z]]]
ACT の x 項は統語構造での外項に，MOVE の y 項は内項に対応する．

詞句は一種の経路と見なすことができる．従って，「出る」タイプと共起する「起点」のヲ格，「通る」タイプと共起する「経路」のヲ格，「足踏みする」などの経路を伴わない移動/活動動詞と共起するヲ格は全て広い意味での「経路」と言える．活動動詞と移動動詞がアスペクトに関して本質的に同じ特性を持ち，(27b) が示すように経路のヲ格が活動動詞の目的語と同じように振る舞うとすれば，移動動詞は活動動詞の一種であり，「経路」は活動動詞の目的語と同じく動作の対象ととらえることができる．従って，本論では，移動動詞は本質的には (30) の語彙概念構造を有し，場所として認識することのできる対象に働きかけることにより動作主の位置変化が含意される場合，その動作が移動と解釈され，y 項が Route と見なされると主張する．その場合，経路が動作の対象として，典型的な活動動詞の目的語同様ヲ格を標示されることが自然に予測される．

5. 今後の課題

本論では，移動動詞と共起するヲ格名詞句が活動動詞の取る対象と本質的に同じであり，一見「起点」「経路」「場所」「対象」といった様々な意味役割を担っているように見えるのは「対象」の捉えられ方によるものであると論じた．しかし，移動動詞の取るヲ格と活動動詞の取るヲ格では直接受動化のされやすさ/されにくさに関して差があることも事実であり，移動と活動の差異について精査していく必要がある．また，「持つ」や「壊す」などヲ格を伴う動詞は移動動詞や活動動詞以外にも多数存在する．ヲ格の認可条件と語彙概念構造との関連についても，今後の課題としたい．

参考文献

Baker, Mark C. (1988) *Incorporation: A Theory of Grammatical Function Changing*, University of Chicago Press, Chicago.
Burzio, Luigi (1986) *Italian Syntax*, Reidel, Dordrecht.
Fujita, Koji (1993) "Object Movement and Binding at LF," *Linguistic Inquiry* 24, 381-388.
影山太郎 (1991)「統語構造と語彙構造のヴォイス変換」『言語理論と日本語教育の相互活性化 (予稿集)』津田日本語教育センター．
影山太郎 (2008)「語彙概念構造 (LCS) 入門」『レキシコンフォーラム No. 4』，影山太郎 (編), 239-264, ひつじ書房, 東京．

影山太郎 (2010)「移動の距離とアスペクト限定」『レキシコンフォーラム No. 5』, 影山太郎 (編), 99-135, ひつじ書房, 東京.
加藤重広 (2006)「対象格と場所格の連続性―格助詞試論 (2) ―」『北海道大学大学院文学研究科紀要』118 巻, 135-182, 北海道大学.
三宅知宏 (2011)『日本語研究のインターフェイス』くろしお出版, 東京.
岡智之 (2013)『場所の言語学』ひつじ書房, 東京.
寺村秀夫 (1982)『日本語のシンタクスと意味 第Ⅰ巻』くろしお出版, 東京.

空所欠落関係節の移動分析*

髙橋　洋平
読売自動車大学校

1. はじめに

　本論文では空所欠落関係節（gapless relative）と呼ばれる構文の一種についてその統語論の考察を行う．空所欠落関係節の特徴として，一般的な関係節構文と異なり，埋め込み節中に空所がなくそのため述部と主要部名詞とが θ 関係を形成していない点が挙げられる．また空所欠落関係節の名で呼ばれる構文が多様であり，構文によって異なる特性を呈するため，構文の一種一種に個別的に取り組むことが要求される．そこで本論文では空所欠落関係節の中でも，(1) のような因果関係に基づく空所欠落関係節（以下，因果空所欠落関係節）に焦点を当てる．この名称は埋め込み節の中で生じた事態の結果，主要部名詞が生じたと考えられることに由来する．

(1) a. 魚が焦げるにおい
　　b. 包丁で切った傷跡
　　c. ジュースを買ったおつり

2. 先行研究の概要

　これまでに多くの研究が問題の構文に対して提示されてきた（井上 (1976)，益岡 (1997)，Tsai (1997)，Murasugi (2000) など参照のこと）．本論文の目的は問題の構文の統語論の考察にあるので，上述の先行研究の中でも統語的アプローチから取り組んでいるもののみを本節で概観したい．

---

* 本論文の執筆にあたり，外池滋生先生に多大なご指導を頂いた．記して感謝申し上げる．

2.1. Murasugi (2000) の分析

Murasugi (2000) では (1) のタイプの空所欠落関係節を pure complex NP と呼称し，以下 (2) のような統語構造を想定している．

(2)　[$_{DP}$ [$_{IP}$ 魚が焦げる] [$_{D'}$ D [$_{NP}$ におい]]]

Murasugi 分析の利点はその構造が非常に単純な点にある．しかしながら，英語のような言語と比較して，どうして日本語の連体修飾表現は修飾部である埋め込み節と被修飾部である主要部名詞句との間で，制約の緩やかな修飾関係を許容するのかという問題が未解決のままである．

2.2. Tsai (1997) のイベント項の関係節化分析

Tsai (1997) は中国語で (1) に相当する構文を取り上げている．[1] Tsai の分析の最も特徴的な部分は Pro というイベント項を仮定している点である．例文 (3a) に対しては (3b) のような内部構造が想定される．

(3) a.　Akiu　tan　gangqin de　　shenyin[2]
　　　　Akiu　play　piano　　PNM sound
　　　　'The sound which (is produced by) Akiu's playing piano'
　　b.　[$_{DP}$ [$_{CP}$ Pro$_i$ [Akiu tan gangqin]]de shengyin$_i$]　(Tsai (1997:(23a)))

以下で論じるように，イベント項を仮定するという案は支持されるように思われるが，Tsai の分析には二つの問題がある．一つは Murasugi 同様，主要部名詞と埋め込み節との制限の緩い関係が何故許可されるのかについて満足のいく説明を提示していない点である．もう一つは，Tsai はイベント項と主要部名詞に同一の指示指標を付与しているものの，どのようにして指示指標がイベント項と主要部名詞との間の意味関係を捉えているのかが不明瞭な点である．さらに言えば，指示指標の使用は Chomsky (1995) の包含性条件 (Inclusiveness Condition) に違反する．

---

[1] Tsai (1997) では gapless relative という呼称ではなく，sloppy relative という呼称を用いている．
[2] 例文中の PNM=pronominalizer である de は後述の修飾部主要部 Mod に相当する．

3. イベント項

　イベント意味論における主要研究者（Higginbotham (1985), Kratzer (1995) など）によると，以下の例 (4b) においてイベント項 e は (i) 存在的に束縛されなければならない．そして，(ii) 例中の yesterday のような空間的・時間的修飾要素によって埋められなければならない．

(4) a. John played the cello yesterday.
　　b. ∃ e[playing (e) & subject (John, e) & object (the cello) & yesterday (4) b.(e)]

Kratzer (1995) はステージレベル述部（stage-level predicate）は，個体レベル述部（individual-level predicate）には存在しない，空間的・時間的なイベント項のための特別な項位置を持つと主張する．これを踏まえて (1a) について再度考えてみよう．(1a) の埋め込み述部は「焦げる」であるが，これは明らかにステージレベル述部に分類されるため，「焦げる」も時間的・空間的なイベント項のための項位置を持っていると考えられる．

　Tsai (1997) は中国語の空所欠落関係節構文の埋め込み節の述部に，状態を表す類の述部が現れえないことを指摘している．この観察は (5) に見られるような因果関係空所欠落関係節にも当てはまるようである．(5) の非文法性は述部「脊椎動物である」ことに由来するとすれば，自然な説明が与えられる．

(5) *魚が脊椎動物であるにおい

また，(1) にイベント項が関与することは thetic/categorical reading の可否からも示唆される．Thetic reading とはその文中で一時的な動作・性質が表されている解釈のことであり，一方 categorical reading とは主語についての総称的な性質について表されている解釈を指す．以下 (6) が示すようにイベント項の使用は categorical reading を促すハ格名詞句が (1) の事例の関係節中の主語として生起できないことからも支持される．

(6) *魚は焦げるにおい

これまでの議論が正しければ，因果空所欠落関係節の中にイベント項を仮定するという扱いは十分に理にかなったものだと考えられる．

4. 提案

4.1. Tonoike (2008) の関係節化の DP 移動分析

前節にて Tsai のイベント項を仮定する分析が評価に値することを見たが，同時に Tsai の分析が現行の極小主義の方針に合致しないことも見た．問題は現行の極小主義に沿う形でどのようにして因果空所欠落関係節を派生するかである．本論文では以下に要約する Tonoike (2008) の関係節化の DP 移動分析を採用する．

(7) a. 述部形成 (Predicate Formation)： 決定詞句 DP を関係節 CP の指定部へと移動する．
 b. L: [$_{CP}$ the book [$_{C'}$ that [$_{TP}$ John bought ~~the book~~]]]
  ……述部形成

(8) a. DP 摘出 (DP Extraction)： 主節中で併合操作を受けるために DP が摘出され一時的に独立した統語対象物となる．なお，元位置にはコピーを残す．[3]
 b. CP 付加 (CP Adjunction)： 関係節 CP が摘出された DP に付加する．
 c. M: [$_{DP}$ the book] ← L: [$_{CP}$ ~~the book~~ [$_{C'}$ that [$_{TP}$ John bought ~~the book~~]]] …CP 付加
  ……DP 摘出

(9) a. DP 併合： 摘出された DP に CP が付加されたものが主節内で併合される．以下の例の中では，主節動詞 *read* の補部として併合される．
 b. N: [$_V$ read] ← M: [$_{DP}$ [$_{DP}$ the book][$_{CP}$ the book [$_{C'}$ that [$_{TP}$ John bought the book]]]]
  …DP 併合

残りの派生は通常通り進行し，(10) のような構造が構築される．

(10) N: [$_{VP}$ read [$_{DP}$ [$_{DP}$ the book] [$_{CP}$ the book [$_{C'}$ that [$_{TP}$ John bought the book]]]]]

---

[3] 元位置には the book の決定詞のコピーが残され，その同一性が先行詞 DP との同一指示を保証する．

4.2. 提案

　Tonoike (2008) に基づいた代案を提示する前に, (1) の意味解釈について論じる必要がある. 以下 (1a) を (11) として再掲する.

(11)　魚が焦げるにおい

(11) の解釈は, 関係節によって描写された出来事の結果においが生じたという事実を含んでいることは明らかである. つまり, この解釈は魚が焦げたという事態の存在を前提としている. このことに留意して, 以下 (12) を想定する.

(12) a. 因果空所欠落関係節は時間的なイベント項 (temporal event argument) TOKI を含んでおり, それが DP 移動分析による関係節化の標的となる.
　　　b. イベント項 TOKI は, 顕在的には日本語の連体助詞「の」に相当する非顕在的な修飾要素 NO (Mod) (cf. Kitagawa and Ross (1982)) によって引き起こされる特徴づけ (characterization) に基づいて, 主要部名詞句と関連付けをされなければならない.

この提案は「魚が焦げるにおい」という表現が「魚が焦げる時のにおい」と同義であることに基づいている.[4] (11) のタイプの空所欠落関係節は一般的に「時の」の挿入を許すため, (11) のように音声的に現れていなかったとしても統語構造内には存在していると考えられる. (12a) は「時」に相当する要素がイベント項として構造内に現れ関係節化の標的となることを捉え, 一方 (12b) は連体助詞「の」に相当する要素がやはり目に見えない形で (11) のタイプの関係節構文に現れ, 主要部名詞句と関係節とを結びつける役割を担っていることを捉えている.

4.3. 時間的イベント項の存在的束縛

　イベント項を用いるという方策に, 顕在的な時間を表す表現「時に」が用いられている以下 (13) が言えないことから, 反論があるかもしれない.

(13) *時に魚が焦げる

(13) が非文となるのは, 奥津 (1977) ですでに指摘されており, 時間を表す

---

[4] ただし井上 (1976) は「時の」という語が加わることにより, 埋め込み節の事態が「特定の出来事」としての意味を失い, 「一般的な意味合い」を帯びると述べている.

要素が不特定のままであることに原因があるとされている．事実，時間的要素「時に」に指示詞「ある」を加えた (14) は文法性が改善される．

(14)　ある時に魚が焦げた

(13) と (14) の文法性の差異は，(11) において時間的イベント項 TOKI が何にも修飾されないそのままの形で，派生に入ってきたわけではないことを示唆する．むしろ，存在的数量詞の役割を担っている非顕在的な指示詞「ある」による修飾を受けた状態で，派生に導入すると考えられる．あるいは，このことを TOKI が派生に導入される際，存在的な特性を [∃] という素性の形で帯びるという形で捉えることとしよう．そして，この素性は関係節化のサインとして機能し，関係節の C 主要部が [∃] を所持する要素を探し出すことを促す．

4.4. 派生

(11) を例に実際に派生がどのように進行するのかを見てみる．(15) は述部形成が (11) に適用された場面を示している．TOKI イベント項は述部形成の結果，関係節 CP の指定部へと移動する．

(15)　L: [[[TOKI$_{[∃]}$ $_{DP}$] 魚が焦げる $_T$ $_{TP}$] C [TOKI $_{DP}$] $_{CP}$]

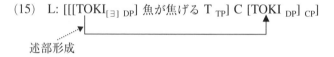
述部形成

次に，DP 摘出が TOKI に適用され，TOKI のコピーが作成される．新しく作成された TOKI のコピーは独立した統語対象物である間に，CP 付加により関係節 CP が付加される．

(16)　L: [[[TOKI$_{[∃]}$ $_{DP}$] 魚が焦げる $_{TP}$] [~~TOKI~~ $_{DP}$] $_{CP}$] ⟶ M: [TOKI $_{DP}$]

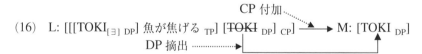

最後に DP 摘出の併合操作が M に適用され，これで関係節化は終わるが，さらに非顕在的な修飾部主要部 Mod である NO の補部へと TOKI を主要部とした DP が併合される．

(17)　M: [[[魚が ~~TOKI$_{[∃]}$~~ 焦げる $_{TP}$] [~~TOKI~~ $_{DP}$] $_{CP}$] [TOKI$_{[∃]}$ $_{DP}$] $_{DP}$]

N: [　　　　NO $_{ModP}$]

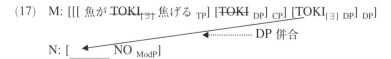

最後に，主要部名詞である「におい」と統語対象物 N とが併合する．

(18) [[[[[魚が TOKI[ヨ] 焦げる TP] [TOKI DP] CP] [TOKI[ヨ] DP] DP] NO ModP] におい NP]

5. 帰結1： なぜ日本語は制限の緩い連体修飾表現を許すのか？

先に，関係節を含む日本語の連体修飾表現は，修飾部である埋め込み節と非修飾部である主要部名詞との間の修飾関係が，非常に制限の緩いことを指摘し，従来の先行研究が何故そのような性質が見られるのか，という問いに対して満足のいく回答を出していないことを指摘した．この問題に対し，本論文では提案した分析の中に現れている非顕在的な Mod の NO が，問題の性質を引き出す鍵となることを主張する．

NO は顕在的な連体助詞「の」に相当すると想定している．この連体助詞「の」を含む名詞句表現については西山 (2003) が詳細な分析を提示している．西山は「NP_1 の NP_2」という表現には全部で五つのタイプが存在すると主張する．[5] その一つ一つについて論じることは紙面の制約上ここでは行わないが，本論文の目的に関連するタイプを一つ引用する．以下に挙げる事例 (19) は，西山で言うところの「タイプ A: NP_1 と関係 R を有する NP_2」に相当する．

(19) 洋子の首飾り　　　　　　　　　　　　　　　（西山 (2003: (28))）

このタイプ A の特徴を簡単に述べると，修飾語に相当する NP_1, つまり (20)

---

[5]「NP_1 の NP_2」という表現については外池 (1990) の議論も一考に値する．外池は「女の先生」という名詞句において，「女の」のような表現は繋動詞（である）が音声的に現れていない縮約関係節であると論じている．また日本語の繋動詞と英語の繋動詞との間に以下のような相違があると述べている．
  (i) 日本語の繋動詞（である）で支えられた述語は何等かの意味で「主語」の特徴づけ (characterization) をしなければならないという緩やかな制限を受けている．（日本語における叙述 (predication) は特徴づけに基づいている．）
  (ii) 英語の繋動詞 be は主語と述語の集合論的一致 (class identification) を要求されていると言える．（英語における叙述は (predication) は集合論的一致 (class identification) に基づいている．）
本論文の提案に含まれている非顕在的な連体助詞 NO が，外池の分析の通り「である」を非顕在的な形で伴う縮約関係節をもたらすとする．すると関係節と主要部名詞は，「である」という述部で支えられることになる．となると (i) が定義するように，関係節と主要部名詞の両者は特徴づけという緩い関係で結び付けられれば良いことになり，どうして関係節と主要部名詞が制限の緩い修飾関係を許すのかという説明が立つことになる．

では「洋子」と主要部である NP_2，すなわち「首飾り」との関係は語用論的な関係により補充されるということである．(20) が許す解釈は「洋子の所有している首飾り」だけでなく，「洋子の手にしている首飾り」であったり，「洋子が買いたがっている首飾り」であったりとコンテクスト次第により如何様にも解釈が可能である．

以上を踏まえた上で，何故 (11) に相当する空所欠落関係節で，関係節と主要部名詞が制限の緩い修飾関係を許可するのか検討してみよう．(11) は (12) の提案に従い，(20) のように非顕在的な時間的イベント項 TOKI と，連体助詞「の」に相当する要素を関係節と主要部の間に内包すると考える．(20) は (11) に西山の分析を適用して，「NP_1 の NP_2」という構造を付与したものである．

(20) 　$\underbrace{\text{魚が焦げる TOKI}}_{NP_1}$ $\underbrace{\text{NO におい}}_{NP_2}$

このように考えると，修飾部である関係節「魚が焦げる TOKI」と非修飾部である主要部「におい」との間は，(11) の話し手及び聞き手の語用論に基づいて修飾関係が構築されることになる．すなわち，空所欠落関係節の修飾関係の制限の緩さとは，話し手および聞き手の有する語用論的知識の程度次第として捉えることが可能となる．

6. 帰結2：因果空所欠落関係節の英語での対応表現について

一般的に，英語には (11) のような表現に相当する構文が存在しないと考えられてきた．しかしながら，これまでの議論が支持されるのであれば，関係副詞 when を含む (21) と，非顕在的な時間的イベント項 TOKI を含む (11) とを関連付けることが可能となるように思われる．

(21) 　the smell of fish when it burns[6]

すると，名詞修飾という点に関して，日本語と英語の間には大きな相違が存在しないことが示唆される．

---

[6] 文法性の判断は Eric McCready 先生によるものである．記して感謝申し上げる．

7. 結びに

この論文では空所欠落関係節の一種,因果関係を表す空所欠落関係節について取り上げ,この種の関係節の派生には時間的なイベント項 TOKI の移動と,非顕在的な修飾主要部 NO の併合が関与していることを提案した.

参考文献

Chomsky, Noam (1995) *The Minimalist Program*, MIT Press, Cambridge, MA.
Higginbotham, James (1985) "On Semantics," *Linguistic Inquiry* 4, 547-593.
井上和子 (1976)『変形文法と日本語 上』大修館書店,東京.
Kitagawa, Chisato and Claudia N. G. Ross (1982) "Prenominal Modification in Chinese and Japanese," *Linguistic Analysis* 9, 19-53.
Kratzer, Angelika (1996) "Stage-level and Individual-level Predicates," *The Generic Book*, ed. by Gregory N. Carlson and Francis Jeffry Pelletier, 125-175, University of Chicago Press, Chicago.
益岡隆志 (1997)「魚が焦げる匂い 因果関係を表す連体修飾表現」『言語』第 26 巻 2 号, 44-49.
Murasugi, Keiko (2000) "Antisymmetry Analysis of Japanese Relative Clauses," *The Syntax of Relative Clauses*, ed. by Artemis Alexiadou, Paul Law, Andre Meinunger and Chris Wilder, 231-264, John Benjamin, Amsterdam.
西山佑司 (2003)『日本語名詞句の意味論と語用論 指示的名詞句と非指示的名詞句』ひつじ書房,東京.
奥津敬一郎 (1977)『生成日本文法論 名詞句の構造』大修館書店,東京.
外池滋生 (1990)「「の」の論理形式 「は,が,も」の論理形式に続いて」『明治学院論叢』467 号, 69-99.
Tonoike, Shigeo (2008) "DP Movement Analysis of Relativization," ms., University of Hawaii and Aoyama Gakuin University.
Tsai, Wei-Tien Dylan (1997) "On the Absence of Island Effects," *Tsing Hua Journal of Chinese Studies* 27, 125-149.

二重目的語／与格構文と「所有」の意味＊

高見　健一

学習院大学

1. はじめに

まず，次の2組の文を見てみよう．

(1) a. I threw John a ball.
　　b. I threw a ball to John.
(2) a. Mary taught Sue French.
　　b. Mary taught French to Sue.

(1a)の二重目的語構文は，話し手が投げたボールがジョンに届き，ジョンはそのボールを受け取っていると解釈されるが，(1b)のtoを用いた構文（以下，「与格構文」と呼ぶ）は，話し手が投げたボールがジョンに届いていないかも知れないし，ジョンがそのボールを受け取っていないかも知れない．同様に，(2a)の二重目的語構文は，メアリーがスーにフランス語を教えた結果，スーはフランス語を学んだ（習得した）ことを表すが，(2b)の与格構文は，メアリーがスーにフランス語を教えたと述べるだけで，スーがフランス語を習得したかどうかまでは分からない．

このような二重目的語構文と与格構文の意味の違いは，Green (1974: 157) をはじめ，Langacker (1987: 39-40, 1991: 358-360), Pinker (1989), Goldberg (1995: 33) 等，多くの研究者によって指摘され，彼らは次に示すように，二重目的語構文は，間接目的語（Y）が「受領者」(recipient) となり，直接目的語（Z）を受け取ったり (RECEIVE)，「所有」(HAVE) したりすることを表すのに対し，与格構文は，目的語（Y）が着点 (goal=Z) の方へ移動する (MOVE/

＊ 本稿の主張は，久野・高見 (2013: 第10章) に基づいており，その内容について多くの議論と重要な助言をいただいた久野暲先生に，ここに記して感謝する次第である．

GO TOWARD) ことのみを表すと主張した.

(3) a. 二重目的語構文： X CAUSES Y to RECEIVE/HAVE Z.
    b. 与格構文： X CAUSES Y to MOVE/GO TOWARD Z.

これに対して近年, Rappaport Hovav and Levin (2008) は,「受領／所有」の意味は, 二重目的語構文か与格構文かという「構文」に依存するのではなく, それらの構文に用いられる「動詞」に全面的に依存すると主張した. そして, give, hand, pass, lend, rent, sell のような「授与動詞」が用いられると, 次の「キャンセル文」が共に不適格であることから分かるように, どちらの構文にも「受領／所有」の解釈があることを示した (p. 146).

(4) a. *John sold Caroline his old car, but she never owned it.
    b. *John sold his old car to Caroline, but she never owned it.

そして, (1a), (2a) の二重目的語構文に観察される「受領／所有」の意味は, 「含意」(entailment) ではなく,「暗意」(implicature) であると述べ, 次のような「キャンセル文」が適格であることを示して (p. 147), 授与動詞以外の動詞が用いられると, どちらの構文にも「受領／所有」の解釈がないと結論づけた.

(5) a. I threw Mary the ball, but she was looking at the birds flying overhead and didn't even notice.
    b. I threw the ball to Mary, but she was looking at the birds flying overhead and didn't even notice.

さて, 上記2つの主張は, 部分的に共に正しいものの, 同時に問題があると考えられる. まず,「受領／所有」の意味が二重目的語構文のみにあるとする (3) の立場では, 例えば send, mail, ship, fax, forward, e-mail のような「送付動詞」の場合に, 与格構文だけでなく, 二重目的語構文にも「受領／所有」の意味がないことを説明することができない.

(6) a. John sent Susan a letter.
    b. John sent a letter to Susan.

(6a, b) は共に, ジョンが送った手紙をスーザンが受け取っているとまでは述べていない. その点で, (6a, b) は (1a, b), (2a, b) とは異なる. 一方, Rappaport Hovav and Levin (2008) の立場では, (1a, b), (2a, b) に見られ

るような意味の違いは,「暗意」ということで捨象されてしまい,意味の考察対象が「含意」のみに限定されて, (1a), (2a) と (1b), (2b) の意味の違いや,その違いが (6a, b) には見られないという事実がなぜなのかを説明することができない.

本稿では,このような観察に基づき,二重目的語構文と与格構文がそれぞれどのような意味を表し, (1a, b), (2a, b) ではなぜ,構文間で「受領／所有」に関して意味の違いが生じるのに, (6a, b) ではそれが生じないのかを明らかにする.また,授与動詞の場合はなぜ,二重目的語構文だけでなく与格構文でも「受領／所有」の意味があるのかを示し,両構文やそこで用いられる動詞と「受領／所有」の関係を明らかにしたい(以下,「受領／所有」は,「所有」のみで統一する).

2. 両構文が表す意味とその違い

(1a, b) や (2a, b) で,二重目的語構文には「所有」の意味があるのに,与格構文にはそれがないのはなぜだろうか.この問題を考えるために,まず次の文を見てみよう.

(7) a. The hunter shot the tiger.
　　b. The hunter shot **at** the tiger.
(8) a. I know him very well.
　　b. I know **of** him, but I've never met him.
(9) a. He swam the river.
　　b. He swam **in** the river.

(7a) では, the tiger が動詞 shot の直接目的語で,動詞と隣接しているが, (7b) では,前置詞 at が間に入り,動詞と the tiger が隣接していない.ここで, (7a) では,ハンターが虎を撃ち,その弾が虎に当たっているが, (7b) では,ハンターが虎を狙って撃っただけで,その弾が虎に当たったかどうかは分からない.つまり,動詞に隣接する目的語の方が,前置詞の目的語より,動詞の表す行為の影響をより強く受けていると言える. (8), (9) も同様である. (8a) は彼のことを直接知っている,面識があるという意味であるが, (8b) は,彼のことを間接的に知っている,彼のことを聞いているという意味であり, (9a) は,彼は川を泳いで渡ったという意味であるが, (9b) は,彼は川(のどこか一部)で泳いだという意味である.したがって,このような例から一般に,

同じ動詞が同じ名詞句と共に他動詞文にも自動詞文にも現れる場合，動詞に隣接する目的語の方が，動詞と離れた前置詞の目的語より，動詞の表す行為の影響をより強く受けていると解釈される．

この点を踏まえて，(1a, b)（以下に再録）を見てみよう．

(1) a. I threw John a ball.
　　b. I threw a ball to John.

John は，(1a) では動詞に隣接しているが，(1b) では動詞から離れ，前置詞 to の目的語である．そのため，(1a) の John の方が (1b) の John より，話し手がボールを投げる影響をより強く受けると考えられる．ある人が別の人にボールを投げた場合，そのボールがまず相手に届くことで，相手はある程度の影響を受け，相手がその届いたボールを受け取る（所有する）ことで，より強い影響を受けると言える．したがって，二重目的語構文と与格構文の表す意味を次のように規定することができる．[1]

(10) a. I threw John a ball.（二重目的語構文）
　　　　X　　　Y　　Z
　　b. 二重目的語構文：X が当該の行為を行って，Y が Z を「所有」するようにする．

(11) a. I threw a ball to John.（与格構文）
　　　　X　　　Z　　　Y
　　b. 与格構文：X が当該の行為を行って，Z が Y に届くようにする．

つまり，(10b)，(11b) に示すように，両構文が表す意味は若干異なっており，この違いは，二重目的語構文では，Y が動詞に隣接しているのに対し，与格構文では，Y が動詞から離れ，到着点を表す前置詞 to の目的語であるという，両構文の形式の違いに起因している．

ここで注意すべきは，両構文は，Y が Z を実際に所有したり，Z が Y に実際に届くということまでは意味せず，主語が当該の行為を行って，そうなるようにするということのみを意味するという点である．実際に所有や到着の意味が生じるかどうかは，動詞の時制や種類，我々の社会常識に大きく依存してい

---

[1] (10b)，(11b) の一般化は，動詞 throw のみに適用するのではなく，両構文に現れるすべての動詞に当てはまる．そして，所有や到着/到達は，ボールのような物理的な場合だけでなく，知識や情報などの抽象的な場合も含む．

る.[2] この点を以下で述べ，これらが (10b)，(11b) の構文の表す意味とどのように関わり合って，所有や到着の意味が生じるかを明らかにしたい．

3. 動詞の意味と語用論的知識

3.1. 授与動詞と伝達動詞

　give, hand（手渡す），pass（手渡す／取る），sell, lend, loan, rent のような「授与動詞」と，tell, show, read のような「伝達動詞」が表す行為は，ある人 (X) と別の人 (Y) がお互い手の届く同じ場所にいてある物 (Z) の「授与」を行ったり，お互いが同じ場所にいて，何か (Z) を言ったり，見せたり，読んだりする行為を表す．この社会常識のために，これらの動詞が過去形で用いられると，二重目的語構文であれ与格構文であれ，Y は Z を（後で述べるような特殊な状況を除けば）必然的に受領し，所有すると解釈される．実際，次のような文では，構文の違いに関係なく，メアリーは花やチケットを受け取っており，メアリーの母親は写真を見ていると解釈される．

(12) a. I **gave** Mary some flowers.
　　 b. I **gave** some flowers to Mary.
(13) a. John **handed** Mary a ticket.
　　 b. John **handed** a ticket to Mary.
(14) a. Mary **showed** her mother the photograph.
　　 b. Mary **showed** the photograph to her mother.

　前節で述べたように，二重目的語構文は，Y が Z の「所有」を示唆し，そして授与動詞や伝達動詞の場合は，当該の行為が，X と Y が同じ場所にいて行われるので，受領や所有を打ち消すような状況が普通頭に浮かばない．つまり，二重目的語構文の持つ (10b) の意味が，授与行為や伝達行為の常識的，一般的理解によって強化され，「所有」の解釈が普通義務的に生じることになる．一方，与格構文は，Z が Y に届くことを示唆するだけで，Y が Z を受け取ることまでは意味しない．したがって，(12)-(14) の (b) で「所有」の解釈

---

[2] これまで本文で観察した例は，動詞がすべて過去形であることに注意されたい．次のように未来表現だと，所有や到着が意図されているだけで，実際にジョンがボールを受け取ったり，ジョンにボールが届くかどうかは分からない．
　(i) I **will** throw John a ball./I **will** throw a ball to John.

が生じるのは，与格構文の意味とは無関係で，X と Y が同じ場所にいるので，X が Y に与えたり，手渡したり，見せたものを Y は普通，受け取ったり見たりしているという常識的知識による．

しかし，二重目的語構文自体は，実際に Y が Z を必ず所有することまでは意味しないので，所有を打ち消して，実際には Y が Z を所有できなかったという状況が考えられないわけではない．例えば，X の売却行為が詐欺だったり，Y が眠っていたというような特殊な状況を想定すれば，「所有」の意味を打ち消すことができる．

(15) a. The man **sold** Lauren a house, but she doesn't actually own it because it was **a scam**.
　　 b. The man **sold** a house to Lauren, but she doesn't actually own it because it was **a scam**.
(16) a. John **read** his daughter a fairy tale, but she **fell asleep** in the middle.
　　 b. John **read** a fairy tale to his daughter, but she **fell asleep** in the middle.

ただ，(15)，(16) のような例は特殊な状況を設定した場合のことであり，両構文のみが示されると，普通はこのような状況が頭に浮かびにくいので，授与動詞や伝達動詞が過去形で用いられると，「所有」の解釈が両構文ともに生じることになる．

ここで，Rappaport Hovav and Levin (2008) は，(4) のような「単純な」状況の不適格キャンセル文と，(5) のような「特殊な」状況の適格キャンセル文を提示し，構文の違いに関係なく，授与動詞は「所有」の解釈があり，それ以外の動詞にはその解釈がないと議論していることに注意されたい．しかし，授与動詞の場合でも，(15a, b) のような適格なキャンセル文は可能であるため，キャンセル文のみで「所有」の解釈があるかどうかを決定づけようとする議論には無理があることが分かる．

3.2. Teach と投与動詞

人が誰かに何かを教える行為は，人が誰かに何かを言ったり，見せたり，読んだりする行為と同様に，ある事柄を別の人に「伝達」する行為なので，teach は，tell, show, read と同様に「伝達動詞」である．そして，teach が表す行為も，伝達動詞（や授与動詞）が表す行為と同様に，授与者と受取人が通例，

同じ場所にいて行われる行為である．それにもかかわらず，teach の場合は，(2a, b) で見たように，二重目的語構文にのみ「所有，習得」の解釈があり，与格構文にはそれがない．これはなぜだろうか．

　それは次の理由による．人が誰かに何かを言ったり，見せたり，読んだりする行為は，それが完了すれば，瞬時に相手が，言われたり，見せられたり，読んでもらったものの「所有者」となるが，人が誰かに何かを教える行為は，相手が教えられたものをすべて所有，習得するとは限らないという，私達の社会常識による．学ぶという行為は，高度な知的活動のため，教えられたものの一部しか習得しなかったり，何も習得できない場合もあり得る．これは，どちらの構文が用いられようと変わりのない事実である．ただ，二重目的語構文には，「Y が Z を習得することができるように，X が Y に Z を教えた」という意味があるため，これを打ち消すような特殊な状況を想定しない限り，X の意図が実際に実現したものとして解釈される．一方，与格構文には，このような習得の意味がないので，「教えられたものが必ずしも習得されたとは限らない」という常識的な解釈が優先されることになる．よって，teach の場合は，(2a, b) で見た違いが生じる．[3]

　同じことは，「投与動詞」と呼ばれる throw, kick, toss, pitch 等が過去形で用いられた場合にも言える．我々は throw が用いられた (1) で，二重目的語構文には「所有」の意味があり，与格構文にはそれがないことを見た．投与動詞が表す行為は，投げたり蹴ったりする人と受け取る人が同じ場所にいて行われるものの，二人が離れている状況で行われる行為である．そのため，投げたり蹴ったりしたものが受け取る人に必ず届くという保証はない．ただ，二重目的語構文には，「Y が Z を受け取ることができるように，X が Y に Z を投げた／蹴った」という意味があるので，これを打ち消すような特殊な状況がない限り，X の意図が実際に実現したものとして解釈される．一方，与格構文にはこのような所有の意味がないので，「投げられた／蹴られたものを必ずしも受け取るとは限らない」という常識的な解釈が強くなる．よって，投与動詞の場合も，(1a, b) で見たように，二重目的語構文と与格構文の間で「所有」に関して違いが生じることになる．

---

[3] 学校教育というような状況で，先生がクラスで多くの生徒に教える場合は，全員がすべてを学ぶということは通例ないという社会常識が優先され，どちらの構文でも「所有」の意味が生じない（久野・高見 (2013) を参照）．

3.3. 送付動詞と将来の所有動詞

それでは，二重目的語構文と与格構文の両方をとる send, mail, forward, e-mail, ship, post, fax, fedex のような「送付動詞」の場合はどうだろうか．これらの動詞で重要な点は，送る人と受け取る人が同じ場所にはいないという点である．そのため，ある人が誰かに何かを送っても，郵便事情が悪かったり，相手が引っ越していたり，機械が故障していたりして，相手に届かない場合が十分あり得ることを我々は社会常識として知っている．その上，送付動詞は，Xの当該行為に，Xのコントロールの外にある第三者の行為（郵便収集，宛先配達など）が介入する．したがって，(6a, b) (=John sent Susan a letter./John sent a letter to Susan.) で見たように，どちらの構文が用いられても所有の意味が生じない．つまり，我々のこの社会常識や語用論的知識が，構文の表す意味に優先し，「所有」の解釈が生じないことになる．[4]

上記の点は，次のような「キャンセル文」がどちらの構文でもまったく自然で適格であることからも裏づけられる．

(17) a. John told me he'd **faxed/e-mailed** me the document, but for some reason I didn't get/receive it.
b. John told me he'd **faxed/e-mailed** the document to me, but for some reason I didn't get/receive it.

二重目的語構文と与格構文をとるさらなる動詞として，promise (〈人に〉…を約束する), offer (〈人に〉…を提供する), leave (〈人に〉財産等を残して死ぬ), assign/allocate (〈人に〉…を割り当てる) など，「将来の所有動詞」と呼ばれるものがある．そして，これらの動詞が過去形で用いられた場合も，次のようにキャンセル文が適格であり，(a) と (b) でその適格性の程度に違いがないことから，どちらの構文が用いられても，「所有」の解釈は生じない．

(18) a. Mary **promised** Sue her pearl necklace, but then she gave it to her old friend instead.
b. Mary **promised** her pearl necklace to Sue, but then she gave it to

---

[4] Write は伝達動詞であるが，tell, show, read 等と異なり，送付動詞と同様に，X と Y が普通，別の場所にいて行われる行為を表す．そのため，ある人が別の人に伝えようと思って何かを書いても，それがその人に届くまでに，その人のコントロールの外にある第三者が介入し，その人に必ず届くとは限らない．この社会的知識が優先し，write の場合は，どちらの構文でも通例，所有の解釈は生じない．

her old friend instead.
- (19) a. He **offered** her a good position, but she refused his offer.
  - b. He **offered** a good position to her, but she refused his offer.

(18a, b) では，メアリーがスーにネックレスをあげると約束しただけで，スーがそのネックレスを必ずもらえるという保証はない．(18a) の二重目的語構文は，メアリーがスーにネックレスをあげると約束して，スーがネックレスの受領者／所有者に将来なるようにするということを表しているが，人に何かをあげると約束しても，その人が必ずそれをもらえる保証はないという社会常識が優先され，どちらの構文でも，所有の解釈が必ずしも生じない．(19a, b) についても同様のことが言える．

4．結び

本稿では，二重目的語構文と与格構文で，従来から指摘されてきた「所有」の意味は，両構文が持つ (10b)，(11b) の意味と，それぞれの動詞が表す行為に対して我々が持っている社会常識，経験的知識との相互作用によって決まることを明らかにした．この点をまとめると以下のようになる．

(20)	二重目的語構文	与格構文
give, hand, pass, sell 等の授与動詞	○	○
tell, show, read 等の伝達動詞	○	○
teach（伝達動詞）	○	×
throw, kick, toss 等の投与動詞	○	×
send, mail, fax, ship 等の送付動詞	×	×
promise, offer, leave 等の将来の所有動詞	×	×

そして本稿では同時に，「所有」の意味が，構文のみで決まるとか，動詞のみで決まるという，これまでの主張が妥当でないことも示した．

参考文献

Goldberg, Adele (1995) *Constructions*, University of Chicago Press, Chicago.
Green, Georgia M. (1974) *Semantics and Syntactic Regularity*, Indiana University Press, Indiana.
久野暲・高見健一 (2013)『謎解きの英文法——省略と倒置』くろしお出版，東京．

Langacker, Ronald (1987) *Foundations of Cognitive Grammar: Theoretical Prerequisites,* Stanford University Press, Stanford.

Langacker, Ronald (1991) *Foundations of Cognitive Grammar: Descriptive Applications,* Stanford University Press, Stanford.

Pinker, Steven (1989) *Learnability and Cognition*, MIT Press, MA.

Rappaport Hovav, Malka and Beth Levin (2008) "The English Dative Alternation: The Case for Verb Sensitivity," *Journal of Linguistics* 44, 129-167.

Anaphora, Deaccenting and Context Incrementation

Christopher Tancredi

Keio University

1. Introduction

In Tancredi (2013) I argued for a reduction of Condition B effects to timing effects of discourse incrementation combined with an analysis of pronouns as anaphoric on individuals or variables in the context. The basic idea pursued in that paper is that pronominal anaphora is a discourse phenomenon whereby a (non-reflexive) pronoun picks up its antecedent not through syntactic mechanisms of anaphora but rather through discourse mechanisms. Discourse anaphora, it was claimed, requires an antecedent to be present in the discourse context at the point where the pronoun is processed. Condition B effects were accounted for as a side effect of the timing by which pieces of a syntactic structure get added to the discourse context, with the minimal chunk that can be added to the discourse context being a phase. Empirical motivation for this claim came from the observation that licensing of deaccenting, a clearly discourse-related process, gives rise to Condition B-like effects as well. Since deaccenting can be licensed independently of coreference and binding, a reduction of deaccenting licensing to binding constraints was seen to be untenable. The reverse reduction, however—of binding constraints to licensing of deaccenting—resulted in an overall simplification of the grammar.

In this paper I will examine the parallelism between pronominal binding and licensing of deaccenting in more detail. Deaccenting will be seen to provide a sharper tool for investigating the timing of discourse incrementation since it can in principle apply to overt expressions of any syntactic category or any semantic type. At the same time, I will show that the binding-deaccenting parallelism breaks down in cases of cataphora: backward binding of a pronoun by an expression that follows it is allowed in a limited range of configurations, but backward deaccenting can never be licensed in those configurations. This suggests that a distinct mechanism is responsible for backward binding. Independent motivation for this suggestion will be seen to come from the fact that cataphora, but not anaphora, can lack number agreement. I will propose that the mechanism involved is a variant of discourse anaphora in which a quantifier is discourse anaphoric on a pronoun rather than the reverse.

2. Binding-Deaccenting Parallelism

In this section I demonstrate the basic parallelism between pronominal binding and licensing of deaccenting. Intended anaphora is indicated by underlining the anaphoric pronoun and bold facing the **intended antecedent**. Intended licensing of deaccenting is indicated by writing the *deaccented expression* in italics and its intended **licenser** in bold face. Using these conventions, the core cases of cross-sentential anaphora and cross-sentential licensing of deaccenting can be indicated as follows:

(1) a. **John / A man** walked into a bar. He sat down.
  b. **A man** walked into a bar. *A man* was sitting there.

In (1a), typically the pronoun would be not only anaphoric on *John/a man* but also deaccented. However, deaccenting is not necessary for the anaphora to hold – it holds just as well if the pronoun is focused, as it could very naturally be if the example were continued *but everyone else in the bar was standing*, showing that anaphora is not dependent on deaccenting. In (1b) deaccenting is seen to not be dependent on coreference, since reuse of an indefinite makes intended coreference an impossibility.

Since both of the examples in (1) involve cross-sentential relations, it is clear that the relations themselves are not purely syntactic in nature. However, both deaccenting and anaphora can be licensed internal to a sentence as well, a fact noted about deaccenting as far back as Tancredi (1992):

(2) a. **John / A man** told Mary that he was smiling.
  b. **A man** told Mary that *a man* was smiling.

And as also noted in Tancredi (1992), in neither case can the licensing be too local:

(3) a. #**John / A man** saw him.
    b. #**A man** saw *a man*.

Examples like these can, of course, be felicitously uttered in a context that provides an appropriate antecedent external to the sentence. Thus, in the context *Many people heard (a) John/(b) a man,* the utterances will be perfectly acceptable, and with *John* used in both the context and in (3a) the pronoun will end up coreferent with both occurrences of *John*. The infelicity of the licensing indicated in (3), however, can be seen clearly by embedding the sentences in a context that lacks such alternative antecedents, one such as: *Entering a mirrored room filled with women,* .... With such a context, the only plausible intended antecedents for the pronoun in (3a) or for licensing the deaccenting of *a man* in (3b) would be the subjects of the sentences these expressions occur in. The infelicity of the examples in such a context shows that the intended antecedents cannot be actual antecedents.

The parallelism seen above extends to a wide range of other cases, as can be seen below. In each case I supply a context that helps to force the intended antecedence or licensing relation. In the (a, b) examples, the relevant relation is too local, making the sentences unacceptable on the intended reading. In the (c, d) examples the intended reading is acceptable.

(4) Yesterday there was a department party.
    a. #Mary showed {**John / a professor**} him.
    b. #Mary showed **a professor** *a professor*.
    c. Mary showed {**John / a professor**} someone sitting close to him.
    d. Mary showed **a professor** someone sitting close to *a professor*.

(5) There will be a school-wide chess competition tomorrow.
    a. #{**John / A student**} believes him to have the best chance of winning.
    b. #**A student** believes *a student* to have the best chance of winning.
    c. {**John / A student**} thinks most people believe him likely to lose.
    d. **Students** think most people believe *students* likely to lose.

(6) Mary is a very irrational person.
  a. #She never considers {**John / a doctor**} him.
  b. #She never considers **a doctor** *a doctor*.
  c. She considers {**John / a doctor**} the source of nasty rumors about him.
  d. She considers **doctors** the source of nasty rumors about *doctors*.

There are additional cases in which deaccenting can be licensed but in which there is no parallel structure in which a pronoun can be bound, for the simple reason that what gets deaccented is of a different semantic type from a pronoun. The following examples fall into this category.

(7) a. John **spoke about** what Bill *spoke about*.
  b. It makes John **happy** to see others *happy*.
  c. A night **when it rains** is better than a day *when it rains*.
  d. **Two** men walked in and sat at *two* tables.
  e. **Interesting** problems often have *interesting* solutions.[1]

However, if we expand the anaphoric expressions we examine beyond personal pronouns, we find that parallel examples involving anaphora can be constructed in many of these cases as well:

(8) a. John **spoke** about what Bill did that about.[2]
  b. It makes John **happy** to see others so.
  c. A night **when it rains** is better than such a day.
  d. **Two** men walked in and sat at as many tables.
  e. (?)**Interesting** problems often have such solutions.

---

[1] The presence of deaccenting is clearest with sentence final expressions, though it can be detected in non-final positions as well, such as in (7d, e). Under the relevant pronunciation, the second occurrences of *two* and *interesting* are reduced to an extent to which *three* and *boring* could not be if substituted.

[2] The parallelism between the (a) and (c) cases in (7) and (8) is not perfect, and (8a) itself is somewhat awkward. (8a) could be made perfect by using only *did* in place of *did that about*, though it is not clear that *did* counts as an anaphoric expression. Indeed, if we accept the arguments of Abe and Tancredi (2014) we would analyze this case as an extreme case of deaccenting, and so the parallelism would be clearly expected but equally irrelevant to connecting deaccenting and anaphora. In the (c) case there seems to be no alternative to placing the anaphoric *such* before the head noun, making for an unavoidable order difference between the anaphora licensing and the deaccenting licensing.

While the underlined expressions in the above examples are not pronominal, they are anaphoric. And while it is difficult to construct examples in which deaccenting of one of these kinds of expressions is not licensed because its intended antecedent is too close, in those cases that can be constructed we find that anaphora is equally blocked in parallel cases:

(9) a. #**Hard** *hard* problems rarely have **easy** *easy* solutions.
    b. #**Hard** such problems rarely have **easy** such solutions.
(10) a. #A **sunny** day *that's sunny* is nicer than a **rainy** night *that's rainy*.
     b. #A **sunny** such day is nicer than a **rainy** such night.

3. Binding-Deaccenting Divergence

The examples in the previous section illustrated a close parallelism between availability of pronoun binding and licensing of deaccenting. The parallelism is not, however, complete. In particular, there are cases of cataphora in English that do not have any deaccenting counterpart. While there is a fair degree of variation in the degree to which people accept cataphora, the following examples at least marginally allow backward binding for some native speakers.[3]

(11) a. His acne bothers **every schoolboy**.
     b. Mary introduced his new teacher to **every student that looked lost**.
     c. His mother **every boy** loves.
     d. His parents are ashamed of **no man who succeeds in life**.
     e. Which of his relatives does **every man** love the most?
     f. It's his mother that **every man** loves the most.

However, structurally parallel examples systematically disallow an expression in the position of the pronoun to be licensed as deaccented by an expression in the position of the quantifier, as seen below.[4]

---

[3] The examples in (11e, f) seem to be more widely accepted than those in (11a–d). I will not attempt to account for this difference in this paper.

[4] In all cases given here it is, irrelevantly, possible for the licensing of deaccenting to go in the opposite (i.e. normal) direction, or for both the italicized expression and the expres-

(12) a. #*A school boy*'s acne bothers **a school boy**.
  b. #Mary introduced *a student's* new teacher to **a student**.
  c. #*New York women's* husbands **New York women** love.
  d. #*Criminals'* parents are ashamed of **criminals**.
  e. #Which of *a New Yorker's* relatives does **a New Yorker** love the most?
  f. #It's *geniuses'* achievements that **geniuses** love the most.

4. Analysis of the Normal Cases of Anaphora and Deaccenting

Licensing of deaccenting is generally accepted to be a discourse phenomenon. Following Schwarzschild (1999), I take deaccenting of an expression to be possible when its interpretation is entailed (module existential F-closure—see Schwarzschild for details) in the local context. Schwarzschild only looked at cases of cross-sentential licensing of deaccenting, and so could implicitly take a very coarse-grained approach to context incrementation, adding whole sentences to the context only after they have been completely processed. If his analysis is to be extended to sentence-internally licensed cases of deaccenting, obviously a more fine-grained analysis of context incrementation is needed. Such a fine-grained analysis is developed in Tancredi (2013) for cases of anaphora and in Abe and Tancredi (2014) for licensing of deaccenting. The common core of these two analyses is that discourse incrementation applies phase by phase, top down, left to right in a sentence, with an expression being semantically interpreted immediately upon being encountered, but added to the discourse context only after it has fulfilled all its syntactic roles. Both pronominal anaphora and deaccenting then relate expressions in a syntactic structure to antecedents in the discourse context, accounting for the parallelism between these two processes.

To see how these assumptions about discourse incrementation help account for the parallel restrictions on deaccenting and anaphora licensing, consider the sentences in (3), repeated here as (13).

---

sion in bold type to be simultaneously deaccented. (Cf. Rooth (1992) for other cases of simultaneous deaccenting.) In this latter case, the licensor is presumably accommodated.

(13) a. #**A man** saw him.
   b. #**A man** saw *a man*.

There are four relevant phases in these sentences: the CP phase, the subject DP phase, the vP phase, and the object DP phase. Top-down, left-to-right processing dictates that these phases be processed in the order given: CP, DP_S, vP, DP_O. Of these, the CP phase can be ignored, adding at most the past tense to the discourse context. The subject DP phase contains a D head *a* and an NP *man*. I assume that *man* has no role to play outside of this phase—whatever features it has are satisfied through agreement with the D head. This allows *man* to be added to the discourse context as soon as the DP_S phase is processed. While the DP as a whole checks its Case within the CP phase, however, it does not have its theta-role checked at this level. On the assumption that both Case and theta-roles are checked through the D head, this means that the D head cannot yet be added to the discourse context. At the vP phase, three overt expressions get added to the discourse context: the subject D, which after having its theta-role checked has no further unchecked features; the verb, which checks its theta-roles with both the subject D and the object D and checks the Case of the object D; and the object D which has both its Case and theta-role checked. Since these expressions all get added to the discourse context together, it is impossible for any of them to act as a discourse antecedent to any of the others. For (13a) this means that neither the subject DP as a whole nor its theta-role can act as an antecedent for the pronoun *him*, making it impossible to generate a bound reading for this pronoun. For (13b) it means that the subject determiner cannot act as an antecedent for deaccenting of the object determiner, making deaccenting of the entire object DP impossible as a consequence.[5]

The acceptable cases of deaccenting and anaphora all involve an antecedent that gets added to the discourse context prior to processing of the pronoun or deaccented expression. To illustrate, consider (2), repeated here as (14).

(14) a. **A man** told Mary that he was smiling.
   b. **A man** told Mary that *a man* was smiling.

---

[5] For more detailed analyses see Tancredi (2013) and Abe and Tancredi (2014).

The processing of these sentences follows that of (13) above, with *man* added to the context at the DP$_S$ phase and *a, told, Mary* and *that* at the vP phase. Since *he* in (14a) and the second occurrence of *a man* in (14b) are not directly syntactically related to the matrix verb, they are not processed at all in the higher vP phase. This means that their intended antecedent *A man* gets added to the discourse context prior to their being processed, making the indicated antecedence relation possible.

4.1. Inapplicability to Cataphora

The analyses of pronominal anaphora and of licensing of deaccenting sketched above make it impossible in principle for a discourse-licensed expression to precede its antecedent. This fits perfectly with observation with respect to deaccenting, but fails with respect to pronominal anaphora. In particular, the analysis sketched has no way to account for the cases of cataphora examined in section 3. To illustrate, consider (11a), repeated here as (15).

(15) His acne bothers **every schoolboy**.

With top-down, left-to-right processing of the sentence, the first word encountered is the pronoun *his*, which by hypothesis needs to be semantically interpreted immediately.[6] Since the quantifier *every school boy* hasn't even been pronounced yet let alone added to the discourse context at this point, there is no way for the pronoun to take the quantifier as a discourse antecedent. If the only way for a pronoun to be bound were for it to be anaphoric on an antecedent in the discourse context, then this sentence together with the rest of the sentences in (11) should disallow a bound variable interpretation for the pronoun. The fact that such an interpretation is at least marginally available shows that some other process must be available for generating bound variable interpretations in these cases.

4.2. Lack of Number Agreement in Cataphora

Independent evidence that something different is going on in the cases of

---

[6] Semantic interpretation is assumed to be immediate and independent of syntactic and discourse timing effects. These effects only affect discourse incrementation.

cataphora in (11) above comes from differences in number agreement. In all those cases of bound variable anaphora for which the analysis in section 4 gives the correct prediction, number agreement between the pronoun and the antecedent is obligatory, as seen below with a few illustrative examples.

(16) a. **Most men** told Mary that {#he was / they were} smiling.
  b. **Most students** think people believe {#him / them} likely to win.
  c. Mary considers **doctors** the source of nasty rumors about {#him / them}.

As observed in Kanazawa, Shimada and Tancredi (2014), however, in cases of cataphora, number agreement is not obligatory. In particular, to the extent to which backward binding is possible with a number-agreeing quantifier, it is equally possible for a singular pronoun to be bound by a plural quantifier in the same configuration, as can be seen by comparing (11) with the examples below.

(17) a. {His / Their} acne bothers **most school boys**.
  b. Mary introduced {his / their} new teacher to **most students that looked lost**.
  c. {His / Their} mother **most boys** love.
  d. {His / Their} parents are ashamed of **few men who succeed in life**.
  e. Which of {his / their} relatives do **most men** love the most?
  f. It's {his / their} mother that **most men** love the most.

5. Analysis of Cataphora

If we are to maintain that pronominal anaphora and licensing of deaccenting are both discourse processes, then the strict linear precedence requirement on licensing of deaccenting makes it clear that the solution to the cataphora problem cannot be to tweak the timing of discourse incrementation. Such a solution would potentially allow for cataphora in (11) and (17) above, but at the cost of wrongly allowing backward licensing of deaccenting in (12). I propose instead to analyze examples of cataphora as involving discourse anaphora of the quantified expression on the pronoun rather than the reverse. Formally this involves interpreting a pronoun as a random variable when it is first encountered and taking anaphora of the quantifier to result in identification of the variable inherent in the quantifier with that assigned to the pronoun. While such identification of variables is in principle possible across sentences, a bound variable interpretation will only result in those cases in which the quantifier can syntactically bind the pronoun, for example through reconstruction of the pronoun to a position in the scope of the quantifier or through raising of the quantifier to a position above the pronoun. Thus the only cases in which such reverse anaphora will even potentially have an interpretive effect are cases where the pronoun and quantifier are in the same sentence.

5.1. Consequences of the Analaysis

Since the analysis proposed is based on anaphora on an expression in the discourse context, the same locality effects that are found with forward binding of pronouns are predicted to occur with backward binding as well. Such effects are indeed found, as can be seen below.

(18) a. #His picture of **every man** appeared in the newspaper.
    b. #He bothers **every man**.

The significance of these observations, however, is unclear given that the configurations involved are all cases of strong crossover and that a separate analysis is still needed for non-local cases of strong crossover like the following.

(19) #He thinks that people respect **every man**.

The analysis also predicts a difference between certain cases of weak crossover involving wh-expressions and parallel cases involving quantifier phrases like the following:

(20) a. #**Who** does his mother love?
    b. ?His mother loves **every man**.

In neither case is the pronoun predicted to be able to be anaphoric on the intended antecedent since in neither case is that antecedent added to the discourse context until its thematic role is discharged, which only occurs after the pronoun is processed. However, the quantifier in (20b) is predicted to be able to be anaphoric on the pronoun in that example since the pronoun is added to the context before the quantifier is interpreted. In the case of (20a), in contrast, the wh-expression is initially processed and hence interpreted before the pronoun gets interpreted, making anaphora of the wh-expression on the pronoun impossible. While (20b) is only marginally acceptable, the distinction between it and (20a) is clear.

6. Discussion

The analysis given in section 5 predicts cases of backward anaphora to be as acceptable as cases of forward anaphora, something that appears not to be the case. In addition, the distinction in acceptability between (11a–d) and (11e, f) is not predicted, and weak crossover cases with quantifiers like (20b) are also wrongly predicted to be perfectly acceptable. The overall degradation in acceptability of these cases suggests that reverse anaphora, i.e. anaphora of a quantified expression on a pronoun, is itself a marginal process, perhaps a post-syntactic fix-up process that overrides standard compositional interpretation.

To the extent to which the proposed analysis of cataphora is plausible, it supports the view that pronominal anaphora and licensing of deaccenting are both processes that involve relating an expression in a sentence to an antecedent in the discourse context. Since in both cases the antecedent can be sentence internal, this view necessitates a fine-grained analysis of context incrementation which allows part of a sentence to be added to the context before the entire sentence has been processed. The analyses of context incrementation developed in Tancredi (2013) and Abe and Tancredi (2014) have this quality, taking the minimal unit of context incrementation to be a phase. Apparent restrictions on antecedence relations fall out on this approach as an epiphenomenon, resulting from the inherent timing relations involved in interpreting expressions and in adding them to the discourse context. Cataphora was seen to be incompatible with such a discourse analysis if analyzed as anaphora of a pronoun on a quantifier that follows it. It was proposed, however, that the anaphoric connection in instances of cataphora is one whereby the quantifier takes the pronoun as an antecedent rather than the other way around. Such an analysis makes it possible to analyze pronominal anaphora as a discourse process that obligatorily takes an antecedent from the discourse context.

While the analysis presented makes crucial reference to top-down, left-to-right processing of syntactic structures, it should not be seen as arguing that syntax itself involves such an ordering. As Chomsky rightfully argues, knowledge of syntax is distinct from the use to which we put that knowledge, and in the analyses presented and examined in this paper it is the use of structures compatible with our syntactic knowledge that is at issue, not our syntactic knowledge of those structures itself. Still, to the extent to which the analysis depends on phase-by-phase processing, it lends indirect support to a syntactic analysis that is based on phases.

References

Abe, Jun, and Christopher Tancredi (2014) "Non-Constituent Deaccenting and Deletion: A Phase-Based Approach," ms., Tohoku Gakuin University and Keio University.

Kanazawa, Makoto, Junri Shimada and Christopher Tancredi (2014) "Singular Pronouns Bound by Plural Quantifiers," *Reports of the Keio Institute of Cultural and Linguistic Studies* 45, 1-53.

Rooth, Mats (1992) "A Theory of Focus Interpretation," *Natural Language Semantics* 1, 75-116.

Schwarzschild, Roger (1999) "Givenness, AvoidF and Other Constraints on the Placement of Accent," *Natural Language Semantics* 7, 141-177.

Tancredi, Christopher (1992) *Deletion, Deaccenting, and Presupposition*, Doctoral dissertation, MIT.

Tancredi, Christopher (2013) "Condition B," *Diagnosing Syntax*, ed. by Lisa Lai-Shen Cheng and Norbert Corver, 371-396, Oxford University Press, Oxford.

Unified Merge into Multidominance*

Takashi Toyoshima
Kyushu Institute of Technology

1. Introduction

In the current mainstream minimalist program (Chomsky (2001, *et seq.*)), syntactic structures are compositionally built bottom-up in an incremental step-by-step fashion by the operation called Merge, which comes in two species: External Merge (EM) and Internal Merge (IM). The latter has previously been regarded as a distinct genus of structure-building operations, called Move. EM and IM are now widely taken as distinct instantiations of a single operation Merge. Yet, there are significant formal disparities between EM and IM that hamper Merge to be straightforwardly recognized as a single genus of operation. This brief note surveys a history and taxonomy of Merge, subjecting them to the minimalist scrutiny, and suggests how the unified Merge should be formulated as a single operation, which leads to multidominance structures as a corollary.

2. Merge and Move: Bare Phrase Structure Perspectives

For phrase structures in the Minimalist Program, Chomsky (1995a, b) proposed the theory of Bare Phrase Structure (BPS) that supplanted representational schemata of the X'-theory. BPS is built up incrementally in the course of a derivation by the two elementary binary operations Merge and Move. In BPS, there are no non-branching projections, and levels of projec-

---

* This work has partially been supported by the Grant-in-Aid for Challenging Exploratory Research #26580086 from the Japan Society for the Promotion of Science, which I gratefully acknowledge here.

tions are taken to be relational properties. A minimal projection, X^0 in the X'-theoretic sense, can be a maximal projection at the same time, equivalent to a non-branching XP in the X'-theoretic terms.

(1) ..., a category that does not project any further is a maximal projection XP, and one that is not a projection at all is a minimal projection X^0; any other is an X', invisible at the interface and for computation. (Chomsky (1995a: 396))

The levels of projections are derivationally determined in their structural configurations so that a maximal projection at a given stage of a derivation may become non-maximal, projecting further at the next stage of the derivation.

Merge combines two separate syntactic objects α and β, and yields a single syntactic object $\gamma = \{\delta, \{\alpha, \beta\}\}$, where δ is the label of γ, projecting either α or β, that indicates whichever is the head of γ (*pace*, *i.a.*, Collins (2001), Citko (2008), Chomsky (2013)). The two syntactic objects to which Merge applies are either two lexical items drawn from the lexicon (numeration/lexical array), two separate complex phrases independently formed in the previous applications of Merge (and/or Move), or one each of such syntactic objects. As any lexical item just drawn out of the lexicon is trivially a root, both of the two syntactic objects Merge operates on are root categories and Merge yields a new root.

A segment projection is distinguished from a category projection by labeling; if α is the head of γ, the former is labeled with an ordered-pair of its head, $\gamma = \{<\alpha, \alpha>, \{\alpha, \beta\}\}$ whereas the latter with simply its head alone, $\gamma = \{\alpha, \{\alpha, \beta\}\}$. Other than being labeled by the ordered-pair of their heads, segment projections, except for the topmost one, are structurally indistinguishable from ordinary intermediate projections, *viz.*, non-minimal, non-maximal, X' projections in the traditional X'-theoretic terms.

Move is taken to be a complex operation, combining Merge + Feature-Checking (+ Generalized Pied-Piping + Copy), and as it involves Merge as its component, Move also takes two syntactic objects as inputs and delivers a single syntactic object. However, the two input syntactic objects are not separate and the output is not always a new root. One of the two input syntactic objects is contained in the other, and either of them can be a non-root or even non-maximal projection. For phrasal movement, the two input syntactic objects are maximal projections, but one of them is not a root. Both "substitution" and "adjunction" yield a new root, but for adjunction, it is a projection of segments, not of a category. Besides, adjunction cannot be driven by the need of Feature-Checking, since a phrase adjoined to a maximal projection XP is not in the checking domain of its head X^0. Chomsky (1995b: 324ff.) suggests that phrasal adjunction, and phenomena attributed to it, such as scrambling, extraposition, VP-fronting, right-node raising, *etc.*, may be relegated to a post-syntactic "stylistic" component, thus outside of the narrow syntax, reflecting their optionality and lack of semantic effects.

For head movement, both of the two input syntactic objects are non-root, non-maximal, minimal projections and they never produce a new root. As the remnants of Chomsky's (1986) X'-theoretic extension of Structure-Preservation to head movement, a head, being X^0, is taken to be able to move only to another head position, *viz.*, X^0 position. As head movement is presumed to be driven by the need of Feature-Checking, for a head to move, its uninterpretable features must be attracted by the matching features of another head. Therefore, there can be no 'empty' head positions into which a head can move as "substitution." That is, head movement is always adjunction to another head.

3. Problems of Adjunction and Segment Projections

Being adjunction, head movement always calls for a segment projection that is non-minimal, non-maximal, as it is still a projection of segments and yet projecting further. Then, no syntactic operation should be able to apply to segmented projections of heads, *e.g.*, head-adjoined complex heads $X_1^0 = [H^0 + X_2^0]$, as they must be "invisible for computation" (1), for Move in particular, just as intermediate projections (X') are (Gärtner (1995)). Accordingly, no head-adjoined complex head $X_1^0 = [H^0 + X_2^0]$ should be able to move further, despite the standard analysis of successive head-to-head adjunction movement of the sort, such as V^0-to-I^0-to-C^0 movement. Being aware of such undesirable consequences, Chomsky (1995b: 245) contrives a novel concept of a maximal zero-level projection X^{0max}, but it is nothing more than the topmost segment projection of a head-adjoined complex head, which is not a derivationally determined relational property of its structural configurations but a mere stipulation.

Head-to-head adjunction has been a headache since the X'-theory, and still is in the current minimalist framework. The adjoined head does not c-command its trace/copy position in the standard first-branching definition of c-command. Head-to-head adjunction does not satisfy the Extension Requirement of Chomsky (1993: 22ff.), a minimalist version of cyclicity. In fact, although Chomsky's (1986) extension of the Structure-Preserving Hypothesis (Emonds (1970)) to head movement has widely been taken for granted, adjunction is structure-changing by nature, as it brings out a new node, be it a segment or a full-fledged category projection.[1] Problems of adjunction and segment projections are more general and not limited to head movement alone. Phrasal adjunction also raises similar concerns.

4. Species of Merge

Chomsky (2000: 101ff.) reinterpreted Move as the combination of Merge + Agree (+ Generalized Pied-Piping + Copy), and Merge that is not part of Move is dubbed Pure Merge (*ibidem*, p. 103).

Keeping the distinction between substitution and adjunction, Chomsky (2000: 133ff.) devises novel species of Merge: Set-Merge and Pair-Merge. The former is a symmetric Merge for substitution that forms an unordered set $\gamma = \{\delta, \{\alpha, \beta\}\}$ of constituents α and β with the label δ whereas the latter is an asymmetric Merge for adjunction that yields $\gamma = \{\delta, <\alpha, \beta>\}$ of an ordered-pair of adjoined constituents α and β with the label δ. However, the congenital problems of adjunction discussed above are not resolved by these innovations.

Converting from the traditional conviction that displacement, *viz.*, movement, is an imperfection of language, to the revelational vision that its absence would rather be, Chomsky (2001) reinterprets Move as a species of Merge, internal Merge (IM), juxtaposing to external Merge (EM) that is Pure Merge, not involving displacement/movement.

---

[1] For a short history of head movement and why head-to-head adjunction cannot simply be a structure-preserving movement, see Toyoshima (2000).

Now extant are the two species of EM, External Set-Merge (ESM) and External Pair-Merge (EPM), and three species of IM that need to be formally distinguished: Internal Set-Merge (ISM) for phrasal "substitution" movement, Internal Pair-Merge (IPMp) for phrasal adjunction movement, and Internal Pair-Merge (IPMh) for head-to-head adjunction movement.[2] That is, there are five species of Merge in total, even though the intention was to consolidate all the structure-building operations into a single operation Merge.

The proliferation of species of Merge stems from recognition of adjunction, whether by "base-generation" or by movement. If there were no adjunction, we would have only two species of Merge: EM and IM. The pivotal question, then, is whether adjunction is real or not.

Formally, ESM can combine a "base-generated" adjunct modifier with a root, without projecting a segment but a distinct category of maximal level that then becomes a 'new' root. This is equivalent to the recursion of X' levels in the traditional X'-theory. As X' projections, *viz.*, intermediate projections, are "invisible for computation" (1), they can never be moved or targeted by movement, just as the non-topmost portion(s) of segment (projection)s cannot.[3]

(2) a.   b.

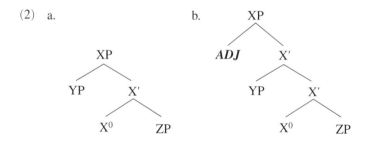

---

[2] Richards (2009) acknowledges IPM as the fourth mode of Merge, arguing that it is naturally implied by Chomsky's (2001) Strong Minimalist Thesis (SMT), but does not discuss the issues of head-to-head adjunction.

[3] Thus, the so-called "tucking-in" movement of, *i.a.*, Richards (1998), if such movement exists, must be able to either "see" an intermediate projection (X') or transpose the moved constituent with the one in the (outermost) specifier, tampering the structure that has already been built. It constitute another (sub)species of Move if sanctioned, violating the Extension Requirement.

Phrasal adjunction movement, by IPMp, can be handled in the same manner, projecting the maximal level, not a segment of the previous root, so that it is no different from phrasal "substitution" movement, by ISM. The targeted root that hosts the "adjunction" simply becomes an intermediate projection X′, after projecting a distinct category of maximal level that then becomes a 'new' root.

Empirically, Chomsky (2001: 18ff.) brings out the anti-reconstruction effect of adjuncts for the Condition C of the Binding Theory and the Adjunct Condition for extraction (*idem* 2008: 146ff.), suggesting that adjunct modifiers may be introduced on a "separate plane," distinct from the "primary plane," where the core predicate-argument structures are built, implicating dimensions higher than two. Instead of counter-cyclic Late-Merge (*i.a.*, Fox and Nissenbaum (1999)) of the relevant adjuncts, they are EPMed cyclically but on a "separate plane." Nevertheless, Oseki (to appear) contends that these two empirical arguments are weak at best, and Pair-Merge should be eliminated from syntax.[4]

More problematic is head-to-head adjunction, which prompted various proposals. Chomsky (2000, *et seq.*), among others, relegates head movement to the PF component, but head movement, such as I^0-to-C^0 movement, does have some semantic effects (*i.a.*, Lechner (2006)). Koopman and Szabolcsi (2000), among others, eliminate head movement, in terms of remnant movement.

In order to bypass the Extension Requirement, Bobaljik and Brown (1997), among others, propose "interarboreal movement" from one tree to another, neither of which contains the other. To the lexical item Y^0 just drawn out of the lexicon, being the root of a trivial tree (3a), X^0 first "interarboreally" moves to adjoin to Y^0, projecting a segment Y_1^0 (3b), and then the head-adjoined complex $Y_1^0 = [X^0 + Y_2^0]$ merges with XP, projecting YP (3c). The Extension Requirement is, in a way, respected, but the problems of segments remain.

---

[4] Oseki's (*op. cit.*) discussion involves the cases of EPM for "base-adjunction" and IPMp for phrasal adjunction movement, but not of IPMh for head-to-head adjunction movement, in our terms.

(3) a. b. c.

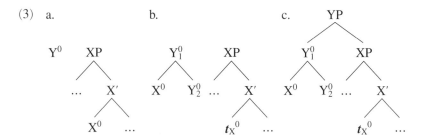

Another approach is to merge the head Y^0 with the root of the containing structure XP by ISM ("substitution"). This approach has two paths to take after ISM. One is to reproject YP from the moved head Y^0 (*i.a.*, Koeneman (2000)).

(4) a. b.

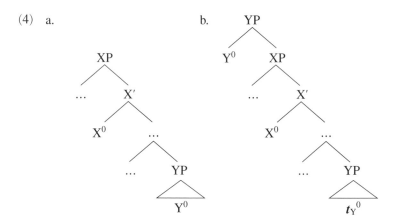

The other path is pursued in Toyoshima (1997, *et seq.*) and followed by many others since (*i.a.*, Fukui and Takano (1998), Matushansky (2006), Vicente (2007)) that a head moves into one of multiple specifiers of XP.

(5) a.   b.

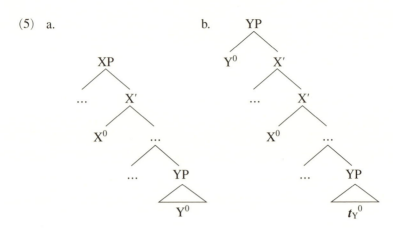

In BPS, multiple specifiers are allowed and nothing, in principle, disallows a head to move into one of the multiple specifiers. See Toyoshima (1997, *et seq.*) and works cited above and therein for detail.

5. The Unified Merge

Given the empirical weakness of phrasal adjunction and the theoretical alternatives to head-to-head adjunction, adjunctions of any kind should be dispensed with, whether "base-adjunction," phrasal adjunction, or head-to-head adjunction, together with segment projections. Then, we are left with two species of (Set-)Merge: E(S)M and I(S)M.

What are the common factors they share? Both EM and IM operate on two syntactic objects and create a new root, assuming no adjunction. At least one of the two syntactic objects must be a root; the other can but need not be a root, and has to be at least a maximal or minimal projection for visibility. We do not specify the relation between the two syntactic objects α and β, whether one is 'internal' or 'external' to the other.

Recapitulating the common factors, we formulate the Unified Merge (UM) as a single operation as follows:

(6) Unified Merge $(\alpha, \beta) \rightarrow \gamma = \{\alpha, \beta\}$
   a. α or β is a root.
   b. α or β is a maximal or minimal projection.
   c. γ is a root.

Taking the labeling function not to be part of the structure-building processes (*i.a.*, Collins (2001), Chomsky (2013)), UM forms a new root γ of an unordered set from two syntactic objects α and β, at least one of which is a root and the other is a maximal or minimal projection (De Vries (2009: 354ff.)). If both of the two syntactic objects are roots, they are separate, thus external to each other by definition, and the operation has been called EM. If one of them is not a root, it has been called IM, but this is misleading. Given no further qualifications, the non-root need not be 'internal' to the other syntactic object whose root is targeted, but can be 'external' to it. This is the situation illustrated in (3a, b) as "interarboreal" movement, modulo head-to-head adjunction. When deployed as phrasal "substitution," it is equivalent to "sideward" movement of, *i.a.*, Nunes (2001).

If no extra machinery is employed to express the "movement" relation, such as copies/traces and chains, it is equivalent to Parallel Merge of Citko (2005) or External Remerge of De Vries (2009), that lead to multidominace structures. With no copy or chain, 'internal' cases of UM, *viz.*, movement, also give rise to multidominance structures (*i.a.* Gärtner (2002), Johnson (2012)).

Oseki (*op. cit.*) eliminates Pair-Merge, *viz.* adjunction, in terms of "two-peaked" structures generated by the Simplest Merge of Epstein, Kitahara and Seely (2012), a kind of multi-rooted structures, which automatically involves multidominance. The Simplest Merge does not have any of the conditions on UM (6a, b, c), so it can operate on two non-roots. That is, it can apply "counter-cyclically," which is the gist of their proposal. Yet, once we allow a "counter-cyclic" application to any pairs of two non-roots, all sorts of multi-rooted or multidominace structures will be over-generated. Whether or not they can all be properly excluded by other general principles awaits further research.

References

Bobaljik, Jonathan and Samuel Brown (1997) "Interarboreal Operations: Head Movement and the Extension Requirement," *Linguistic Inquiry* 2, 345-356.

Chomsky, Noam (1986) *Barriers*, MIT Press, Cambridge, MA.

Chomsky, Noam (1995a) "Bare Phrase Structure," *Government and Binding Theory and the Minimalist Program*, ed. by Gert Webelhuth, 383-439, Blackwell, Oxford.

Chomsky, Noam (1995b) "Categories and Transformations," *The Minimalist Program*, Noam Chomsky, 219-394, MIT Press, Cambridge, MA.

Chomsky, Noam (2000) "Minimalist Inquiries," *Step by Step: Essays on Minimalist Syntax in Honor of Howard Lasnik*, ed. by Roger Martin, David Michaels and Juan Uriagereka, 89-155, MIT Press, Cambridge, MA.

Chomsky, Noam (2001) "Beyond Explanatory Adequacy," *MIT Occasional Papers in Linguistics* 20, 1-28.

Chomsky, Noam (2008) "On Phases," *Foundational Issues in Linguistic Theory: Essays in Honor of Jean-Roger Vergnaud*, ed. by Robert Freidin, Carlos P. Otero and Maria Luisa Zubizarreta, 133-166, MIT Press, Cambridge, MA.

Chomsky, Noam (2013) "Problems of Projections," *Lingua* 130, 33-49.

Citko, Barbara (2005) "On the Nature of Merge: External Merge, Internal Merge, and Parallel Merge," *Linguistic Inquiry* 36, 475-496.

Citko, Barbara (2008) "Missing Labels," *Lingua* 118, 907-944.

Collins, Chris (2001) "Eliminating Labels," *MIT Occasional Papers in Linguistics* 20, 1-25 [*sic*.].

Emonds, Joseph E. (1970) *Root and Structure-Preserving Transformations*, Doctoral dissertation, MIT.

Epstein, Samuel David, Hisatsugu Kitahara and T. Daniel Seely (2012) "Structure Building That Can't Be," *Ways of Structure Building*, ed. by Myriam Uribe-Etxebarria and Vidal Valmala, 257-270, Oxford University Press, Oxford.

Fox, Danny and Jon Nissenbaum (1999) "Extraposition and Scope: A Case for Overt QR," *WCCFL* 18, 132-144.

Fukui, Naoki and Yuji Takano (1998) "Symmetry in Syntax: Merge and Demerge," *Journal of East Asian Linguistics* 7, 27-86.

Gärtner, Hans-Martin (1995). "Has Bare Phrase Structure Theory Superseded X-bar Theory?" *FAS Papers in Linguistics* 4, 22-35.

Gärtner, Hans-Martin (2002) *Generalized Transformations and Beyond: Reflections on Minimalist Syntax*, Akademie Verlag, Berlin.

Johnson, Kyle (2012) "Towards Deriving Differences in How *Wh* Movement and QR are Pronounced," *Lingua* 122, 529-553.

Koeneman, Olaf (2000) *The Flexible Nature of Verb Movement*, Doctoral dissertation, Universiteit Utrecht.

Koopman, Hilda and Anna Szabolcsi (2000) *Verbal Complexes*, MIT Press, Cambridge, MA.

Lechner, Winfried (2006) "An Interpretive Effect of Head Movement," *Phases of*

Interpretation, ed. by Mara Farascarelli, 45-70, Mouton de Gruyter, Berlin.

Matushansky, Ora (2006) "Head-Movement in Linguistic Theory," *Linguistic Inquiry* 37, 69-107.

Nunes, Jairo (2001) "Sideward Movement," *Linguistic Inquiry* 32, 303-344.

Oseki, Yohei (to appear) "Eliminating Pair-Merge," *WCCFL* 32.

Richards, Marc (2009) "Internal Pair-Merge: the Missing Mode of Movement," *Catalan Journal of Linguistics* 8, 55-73.

Richards, Norvin (1998) "Shortest Moves to (Anti-)Superiority," *WCCFL* 16, 335-349.

Toyoshima, Takashi (1997) "'Long' Head Movement, or Wrong 'Head Movement'?" *CLS* 33, 401-416.

Toyoshima, Takashi (2000) *Head-to-Spec Movement and Dynamic Economy*, Doctoral dissertation, Cornell University.

Toyoshima, Takashi (2001a) "Head-to-Spec Movement," *The Minimalist Parameter: Selected Papers from the Open Linguistics Forum, Ottawa, 21-23 March 1997*, ed. by Galina M. Alexandrova and Olga Arnaudova, 115-136, John Benjamins, Philadelphia and Amsterdam.

Toyoshima, Takashi (2001b) "A Neo-Lexicalist Movement Analysis of Incorporation," *WCCFL* 20, 579-592.

Vicente, Luis (2007) *The Syntax of Heads and Phrases*, Doctoral dissertation, Universiteit Leiden.

de Vries, Mark (2009) "On Multidominance and Linearization," *Biolinguistics* 3, 344-403.

文型と項構造に関する一考察

塚田　雅也
青山学院大学

1. はじめに

　日本の学校教育では文型を用いた文法指導がこれまでになされているが，近年では文法の直接的指導ではなく，コミュニケーション重視の指導へとシフトしてきている．しかしそれはあくまでも指導法の部分であって，文法指導を一切しないということではなく，学習指導要領にも文法項目が指導すべき内容に含まれており，ここに文型も含まれている．[1] たしかに文型は学習の上では有益であるが，本稿では，この文型が生成文法における項構造とどのような関連性が見られるのかについてについて考察する．

2. 文型と項構造

　文型として最もなじみ深いものは，Onions (1904) の5文型であろう．多くの文法学習書で扱われているものであるが，これは以下のように分類され

---

[1] 2008（平成20）年3月告示の『中学校学習指導要領』の第9部外国語において，中学校で扱う文法事項の中に文構造が含まれており，次のように記載されている．
　　(a)　主語＋動詞
　　(b)　主語＋動詞＋補語
　　(c)　主語＋動詞＋目的語
　　(d)　主語＋動詞＋目的語＋目的語
　　(e)　主語＋動詞＋目的語＋補語
　このうち，補語として名詞・代名詞・形容詞を，目的語では to-不定詞や how to-不定詞，また that 節を含む場合を扱うようになっている．直接的な文法指導をしない場合でも，文型を扱うことが指定されているため，なんらかの形で文を分類することを学ぶことになる．また辞書等の説明にも文型による意味の区別がなされるため，文型の知識は学習上必要である．

る.[2]

(1) 述部第1型： 述部＝動詞のみ
    述部第2型： 述部＝動詞＋叙述形容詞／名詞／代名詞
    述部第3型： 述部＝動詞＋目的語
    述部第4型： 述部＝動詞＋二重目的語
    述部第5型： 述部＝動詞＋目的語＋叙述形容詞/名詞/代名詞

「叙述形容詞／名詞／代名詞」とは，いわゆる「補語」のことだが，Onions (1904) では「補語」という用語は用いていない．ここでは品詞で明示されていることに留意すべきである．

もちろん，これでは不十分とする考えもある．たとえば，以下の例はどうであろうか．

(2) a. I run in the park.
    b. I run every night.
(3) a. I live in Tokyo.
    b. *I live now.

(2) において，(a) の in the park と (b) の every night はそれぞれ場所と時間を表す副詞的要素であるが，これらは文型を決定する要素には含まれない．一方で (3a) の in Tokyo も場所を表す副詞的要素ではあるが，動詞 live の場合は場所を表す副詞的要素が文法上必要である．(3b) のように時間を表す副詞的要素では非文となるので，あくまでも場所を表す副詞的要素が義務的要素ということになる．すると (3a) の場合には別の文型として分類すべきという考え方は自然である．では，次の場合はどうであろう．

(4) a. I bought some books at the bookstore.
    b. I bought some books yesterday.
(5) I put some books on the table.

(4) では (2) と同様に (a) が場所，(b) が時間を表す副詞的要素を含んでい

---

[2] Onions (1904) では「文型」とは称していない．第1文型に相当するものを first form of the predicate (述部第1型) としていて，文そのものではなく述部の分類をしている．また「補語」には対しては predicative adjective/noun/pronoun (叙述形容詞／名詞／代名詞) という呼称を用いている．

るが，やはり副詞的要素のため文型の分類には影響しない．一方，(5) の場所を表す on the table は義務的要素であるので，この場合も別の文型とすべきだという議論も妥当である．この義務的副詞を A とすると，⟨SV⟩ と ⟨SVA⟩，⟨SVO⟩ と ⟨SVOA⟩ を別の文型とし，7 文型と考えることになり，Quirk et al. (1985) の分類もこれにあたるものである．ただし，あらゆる文を正確に分類しようとすれば，文型の数も必然的に多くなってしまう．これは学習効果の点では望ましくないため，最低限度としての 5 文型であると考えられる．本稿ではどのような文型分類が妥当であるのかを議論するわけではないので，記述的文法の一例として Onions (1904) の 5 文型を扱うこととする．

次に統語理論における項構造 (argument structure) について見てみよう．項構造とは動詞がその補部 (complement) にどのような項 (argument) を取るのかを定めたものである．この点では文型と似るが，文型が 5 つに分類されるのに対し，項構造は動詞ごとに定められる．すなわち分類というよりも辞書的記述であり，生成文法的には語彙目録 (lexicon) に記載される情報で，動詞の数だけ項構造が存在することになる．(3) の live や (5) の put は次のように指定されていることになる．[3]

(6) a. live: [V; ＿＿ PP_{loc}]
    b. put: [V; ＿＿ NP PP_{loc}]

動詞ごとの指定なので当然正確な記述であるが，説明的妥当性のためには一般化が必要であろうし，実際の言語資料と比較すると不十分な部分がある．そこで文型の考え方と項構造の利点・欠点を比較することになるが，この点に関して次項で議論する．

3. 品詞と句構造標識—名詞の考察

品詞とは，言うまでもなく「動詞」や「名詞」などのことであるが，ここではまず，文型をとらえる上での品詞の概念について考える．Onions (1904) の文型分類で必要な品詞は名詞，動詞および形容詞であり，正確に言えばこれらの各品詞の機能を果たす要素である．たとえば that 節は名詞節として主語や目的語になりえるし，群動詞は全体として動詞，分詞も形容詞として補語

---

[3] ここで PP_{loc} と表記したが，時間など他の PP と区別するための便宜的な表記である．

Cになりえる。[4] ここでは最も多くのパターンが考えられる目的語の場合を見てみよう。

Onions (1904) では目的語は「動作の対象」とのみ言及しているが，動作の対象は「人・物・ことがら」であるから，目的語は名詞的性質を持ったもの，すなわち名詞的要素のはずである．具体的には以下のようなものがある．

(7) 名詞的要素[5]
 a. 名詞　　　　　　　　I like cake.
 b. to-不定詞　　　　　　I like to see the movie.
 c. 動名詞　　　　　　　I like seeing the movie.
 d. that 節　　　　　　　I know that he went to America.
 e. 疑問詞節・関係詞節　　I know what he said.

これらの目的語は，(7a) では NP(近年では DP)，(7b-e) では CP と生成文法では考えられるが，一般学習者には理解しにくいであろう．また「目的語は NP または CP」という選択的な点も問題となる．したがって，ここでは次のように指定されていると考えたほうが簡潔である．

(8) [V;　 名詞的要素]

つまり具体的な品詞としてではなく，機能的・概念的な集合を他動詞の補部とするほうが全体像をとらえやすい．(7) の各下線部は代名詞 it にそれぞれ置き換え可能なので，これらが名詞的要素であることは明らかである．Chomsky (1995) 等のミニマリスト・プログラムに見られる Bare Phrase Structure では DP 等を示さないので，この問題が回避されているように見えるが，素性の照合をする際に品詞の概念が必要であろうから，やはり品詞について議論されなくてはならない．言語資料を見るとこの場合のように概念的な要素を含むのは事実である．したがって理論の精緻化と並行して，記述的文法の考え方を取り入れる利点があると思われる．

---

[4] 本稿では議論上，文型の要素としての「補語」と動詞の後続要素としての「補部」がどちらも頻出する．ここでは混乱を避けるために文型の要素としての「補語」については「補語C」と表記する．

[5] CP について，that 節や疑問詞節・関係詞節が CP であることは容易に理解できるが，to-不定詞や動名詞については意味上の主語を PRO とすることで同様に CP と考えられる．
 (i)　to-不定詞　　I like [$_{CP}$ e [$_{TP}$ PRO [$_T$ to see the movie]]].
 (ii)　動名詞　　　I like [$_{CP}$ e [$_{TP}$ PRO [$_T$ seeing the movie]]].

4. 補語の問題

 Onions (1904) で叙述形容詞／名詞／代名詞と呼ばれている補語 C は ⟨SVC⟩ では主格補語として主語の意味を補い，また ⟨SVOC⟩ では目的格補語として目的語の意味を補うものである．まず，⟨SVOC⟩ について考える．

 (9)　John thought him killed in the accident.

ここで killed は補語 C としか考えられない．では，(10) の場合はどうであろうか．

 (10)　He was killed in the accident.

(10) の killed は補語 C ではなく，受動態の一要素と考えるのが学習上一般的であろう．この分詞を補語 C として ⟨SVC⟩ の文型とはみなさないので，(9) と (10) での分詞の扱いの違いで混乱を生じがちである．なお，Onions (1904) ではこの (10) のような場合も，分詞を時制要素の一部ではなく，補語 C に相当する叙述形容詞とし，進行形や受動態の文も ⟨SVC⟩ として扱っている．この点で古い記述的分析ではあるが，この問題をうまくまとめていると言えるし，統一的な説明になっていて興味深いが，指導上の問題については別途議論する必要があるだろう．

5. 二重目的語の問題

 二重目的語も生成文法では大きな問題となっているが，文型の分類上は ⟨SVOO⟩ のように 2 つの目的語が並列しているという事実のみを記述している．また名詞要素全般に目的語 O が可能なので，この点では文型分類は簡潔な説明ができる．

 (11)　Mary bought me a camera.

ここで me は間接目的語 (indirect object), a camera は直接目的語 (direct object) と区別されるが，構造上どちらが上位であるかなどの議論はなされない．ただしあくまでも文型は分類であるので，どの動詞がこの ⟨SVOO⟩ の文型で可能であるのかは，結局は項構造によることになる．

 (12)　buy: [V; __ NP NP]

しかしこれを樹形図などで構造を表記する際など理論上はさまざまな問題が生じるが，本稿の主旨ではないのでここでは触れない．ただしここでも NP とは単なる名詞句ではなく，that 節なども含めたものであることに留意しなくてはならない．

6. 群動詞の扱い

群動詞も文型の分類上，機能的な点で考えるべき問題がある．

(13) John took advantage of her innocence.

この文では，厳密には動詞が took，目的語が advantage であるが，次のような受動文も可能である．

(14) Her innocence was taken advantage of by John.

この変形に関する Chomsky (1957) の変形規則は以下のように記される．

(15) 受動変形
　　構造分析：NP—Aux—V—NP
　　構造変化：$X_1—X_2—X_3—X_4 \rightarrow X_4—X_2+be+en—X_3—by+X_1$
　　　　　　　　　　　　　　　　　　　　　　(Chomsky (1957: 112))

この規則を (13) にあてはめると次のようになる．

(16) [John] [took advantage of] [her innocence].
　　　X_1　　　$X_2—X_3$　　　　　　X_4
　→[Her innocence] [was taken advantage of] [by John].
　　　X_4　　　　　　X_2+be+en—X_3　　　by+X_1

Chomsky (1957) では時制要素が Aux に含まれているので，目に見える形で Aux は存在しない．また en（過去分詞の屈折）の部分は X_3 の動詞と融合して taken となっている．この変形では (13) の群動詞 took advantage of 全体で 1 つの動詞 V，her innocence をその目的語である NP とし，(14) の受動文を作っていることになる．群動詞を生成文法においてどのように構造表記するかはまた別の問題として，実際の言語運用上では群動詞が 1 つの動詞として機能していることは間違いない．このことから，具体的に辞書的な品詞ではなく，動詞に関しても「動詞的である」という機能的な面が実際の文法現象に

反映されていることは興味深く，厳密な品詞ではなく語句の機能の点から文を理解している好例と考えられる．

7. まとめ

記述的文法は理論研究上あまり有益ではないように見えるが，一方では生成文法的にうまく扱えない現象もまとめている点が興味深い．項構造を品詞ではなく，記述的文法に見られるような名詞的要素や動詞的要素という概念的なものにすることで広範な事例を含められる可能性を本稿では示唆した．文型分類と項構造で近似した考え方をしている場合もあり，両者の利点を生かすことで広範な文法事象を考察できる可能性があると考えられる．

参考文献

Chomsky, Noam (1957) *Syntactic Structures*, Mouton, The Hague.
Chomsky, Noam (1995) *The Minimalist Program*, MIT Press, Cambridge, MA.
文部科学省（編）(2008)『中学校学習指導要領』
Onions, Charles T. (1904) *An Advanced English Syntax*, Routledge and Kegan Paul, London. [Revised as Onions, Charles T. (1971) *Modern English Syntax*, ed. by B. D. H. Millar, Routledge and Kegan Paul, London.]
Quirk, Randolph, Sydney Greenbaum, Geoffrey Leech and Jan Svartvik (1985) *A Comprehensive Grammar of the English Language*, Longman, London.

機能性構音障害の音韻体系は「自然」なのか？

上田　功

大阪大学

1. 機能性構音障害の性格

　小論では，機能性構音障害の「自然性」を，非常に特異な音韻体系をもった事例に関する議論を通して考察してみたい．これまで，音韻論における自然性は，自然言語を対象として議論されることが多かったが，本稿では「障害」と呼ばれる音韻体系は，自然言語の音韻体系と比較して不自然なのかという問題に焦点を当てて議論を展開する．

　機能性構音障害とは，聴覚異常，口蓋裂，脳損傷等の器質的な問題に起因しない構音獲得の遅れであり，純然たる言語獲得上の異常とされてきた．以前から，機能性構音障害には体系性があることが指摘されてきたが（上田（1995a），Ueda（2005）），それは誤った調音が規則性をもつという点において議論がなされてきただけで，障害の自然性が議論されることはなかった．そこで次節では，この反例となりうるような，極めて自然性を欠くと思われる，非常に特異な音置換を見せる事例について考察していく．

2. 事例

　次に挙げるのは，機能性構音障害と診断された T.A.（4歳）の発話データである．[1]

(1)　音声形　　　目標形　　　意味
　　 tm.ra　　　 to.ra　　　 トラ
　　 ni.ɰa.tm.ri　ni.ɰa.to.ri　ニワトリ

---

[1] この機能性構音障害児の音韻体系に関しては，Ueda (2013) において，最適性理論による分析を提案しているので参照されたい．

a.sa.ŋa.m	a.sa.ŋa.o	朝顔
ta.km	ta.ko	タコ
m.kaː.saɴ	o.kaː.saɴ	お母さん

この事例においては，母音 [o] が鼻音 [m] によって置換されているのがわかる．普通，日本語においては，母音数が少ないこともあり，母音の構音異常はまれであるので，この事例はきわめて珍しいと言える．現在臨床現場で最も広く用いられている検査法は，Stampe (1969, 1973) によって提唱され，外池 (1976) によって紹介された自然音韻論を基盤とする音韻過程分析 (Natural Process Analysis: NPA) である．音韻過程分析は，伝統的生成音韻論 (Chomsky and Halle (1968)) と同じように，入力と出力の二つの表示を認めるが，記述の前提として，入力表示は常に成人の（それゆえ正しい）形であり，それが幼児の産出した音に写像されたものが出力表示である．この方法で (1) を記述すると次のようになる．[2]

(2)　/o/　→　[m]

(2) の意味するところは，入力表示の /o/ が，出力表示では [m] として，文脈自由に，すなわちすべての位置で具現化するということである．これで「音素」を単位とした音置換は説明されるが，問題は音置換だけにとどまらない．[3] さらに音韻体系全体の検討が必要であり，以下で順を追って論じていく．

3. プロソディー

上記 (2) で示された音韻過程は，/o/ から [m] への音置換のみを表しており，音節等，上位のプロソディーの単位については，何も説明していない．次に，(1) に挙げられたデータから，「トラ」を例にとって，音声形と目標形の音節構造を考える．この際に，音節の形態だけではなく，量も考える必要があ

---

[2] 音韻過程分析に対しては，すでに上田 (1995b, 2013) 等で，理論と臨床の両面にわたって，問題点を指摘してきた．最も大きな問題点は，画一的な入力型が先験的に決められてしまっている点であるが，このケースでは，聴覚的弁別検査等により，正常な入力表示が，ある程度確認されており，この点はクリアしているものとして，議論を進めていく．また自然音韻論の基本的な考え方，特に過程と規則の違いなどに関しては，上記，外池 (1976) の要を得た解説を参照されたい．

[3] なお，自然音韻過程分析では，明示的ではないにせよ，音韻の最小単位を音素と見なしていると考えられる（上田 (2013)）．

るので，(3) では音節の樹状図と分節音，そして分節音がモーラを担っている場合は，その分節音の上に，かっこで μ を印している．

(3)

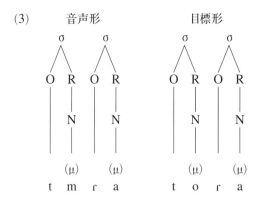

この図からは，次の二つのことがわかる．

(4) 1. 置換されて出現した [m] は音節の核として働いている．
    2. この [m] は，母音と同じようにモーラを担っている．

日本語の [m] は，音節の核にもならず，核位置でモーラを担うこともない．(ただし音声としては，撥音の条件異音として現れることがあり，モーラを担っているが，その場合，尾子音の位置を占めており，核としてウェイトをもつわけではない．) ところが (4) から，この [m] は，プロソディーのレベルでは，この二点において [o] と同じ機能を果たしていることがわかる．このような上位の音韻機能に関して，(2) は何も言うことがない．次に音韻過程分析が最も明示的に現象を説明している分節音レベルの置換の検討に移ろう．

4. 音置換

個々の分節音に関して，[o] と [m] の音韻素性に注目して，その変化を考えてみよう．ごく一般的な階層的素性システム (Dinnsen (1997)) で，[o] と [m] の表示を，必要な素性だけに限定して示すと，それぞれ次のように表示される．なお，両者の間で，指定が異なっている素性には網掛けを施している．[4]

---

[4] 母音の産出にはすべて舌体全体の運動が含まれるので，[o] は Labial だけではなく，Dorsal の指定も受けるが (Hall (2007))，(5) ではここでの議論との関係がないため省略している．

(5)

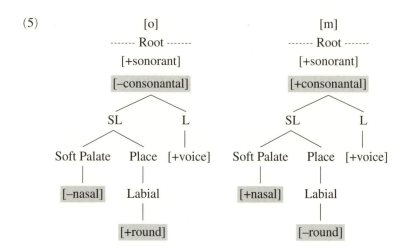

　この音置換で，鍵となるのは，調音位置の Labial「唇」である．[o] は日本語においては唯一の円唇母音であり，[+round] の指定を受ける．上記の素性体系では，[round] と Labial の間には支配／依存関係があり，[+round] であるならば自動的に Labial の指定を受けることになる（[m] のように，逆は真ではない）．この幼児の音韻体系においては，Labial と指定される母音が許されておらず，その代わりとして，同じ Labial の子音を使用しているのである．[5]

5. 逸脱の性格付け

　この音置換に伴う代償は大きい．母音から鼻音への変化には，[nasal] の指定を変えるだけではなく，ルート接点に直結している [consonantal] という，主音類を区別する素性指定を変えねばならない．またその結果として，前節で述べたように，日本語では許されない音節核にモーラを担った鼻音が現れるのである．さらに核が母音から鼻音に変わることで，頭子音との共鳴度の差も小さくなり，音節そのものの適格性も低下することになる．

　しかしながら，次の点も考慮せねばならない．他に Labial の指定を受ける子音には，[p] や [b] があるが，もしこれらを代用していたら，Supralaryngeal 接点の下位の素性である [nasal] の指定は，母音と同じに保てるものの，ルート接点に直結する上位の [consonantal] にとどまらず，さらに [sonorant]

---

[5] 上述したように，詳しい分析については，Ueda (2013) を参照されたい．

の指定まで変更せねばならず，また阻害音が音節核になることで，頭子音との共鳴度の差もさらに小さくなり，音節としての適格性がさらに低下することになる．すなわち，[o] から [m] への置換は，確かに大きな変化を伴っているが，[p] や [b] によって置換されるよりも，払う「犠牲」は少ないと言える．これは母音から鼻音への変化と，母音から阻害音への変化を，階層構造のなかで，指定が変化する素性のルート接点に対する相対的な位置（そして数）を比較するとわかることである．

元来日本語の母音空間において，後舌の中領域には，円唇母音があるだけで，音韻的に対立する非円唇母音があるわけではない．この幼児にとって，[o] を非円唇の [ɤ] で代用することも可能であったはずである．そうすれば，下記の (6) に示すように，もっと小さい変化，すなわち Place から Labial 以下を切り離すことでおさまったはずである．

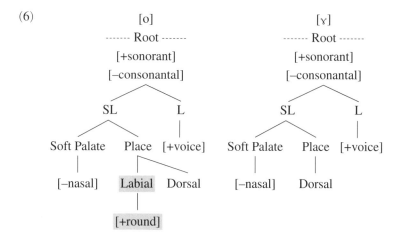

実際，日本語の [o] は，円唇性が弱いという指摘もなされており（Vance (1987)），幼児が非円唇で発音しても，特に不思議ではないし，何より対立する母音がないので，聞き手にはさほど問題なく伝わるであろう．しかしそれは選択されなかった．(5) と (6) を比較すると，この幼児の音韻体系において，何が優先され，何が犠牲にされたかがよくわかる．位置の Labial が優先され，調音方法の [nasal] と，主音を決定する素性の [consonantal] が犠牲になったのである．すなわち，この事例においては，周辺的な素性指定が優先された結果，より上位の，主要な素性指定に齟齬をきたしたと言うことができる．

また (3) で見たように，鼻音が音節核になることによって，日本語の音素

配列は破られるが，頭子音や核等，音節の形自体やモーラの数など，韻律的な構造は保持されていることがわかる．ここで何が優先されて保持され，何が保持されないのかを，以下 (7) にまとめておく．

(7) 保持されるもの： 韻律構造，唇性
　　犠牲になるもの： 音節頭子音と核の共鳴度の差，音素配列，子音性，鼻音性

6. 「障害」の音韻体系の自然性

　本節では，この機能性構音障害の音韻構造の自然性について議論する．構音異常の結果，(7) に「犠牲になるもの」として挙げたうち，特に問題となるのが，音節に関係するものである．まず鼻音が音節核になるというケースは，諸言語に非常に多く見られる．例えば，Clark and Yallop (1990) は次のような例をあげている．

(8) a. 英語
　　　[sʌdn̩]　　sudden　　　[bɹɛdn̩(m̩)bʌtə]　　bread and butter
　　b. ドイツ語
　　　[ha:bm̩]　　have　　　[daŋkn̩]　　thank
　　c. スワヒリ語　　　　　d. ヨルバ語
　　　[m̩tu]　　man　　　　[ń lá]　　big

a. と b. は，基底の弱母音プラス鼻音が弱化によって弱母音が脱落したもので，弱母音付きの異形態をもつ．[6] また c. と d. は語頭であるが，鼻音は独立した音節を形成する．これらはよく知られた数例にすぎないが，共鳴性の高い鼻音や流音が，単独で音節の核を占めることは，よく知られた事実であり，諸言語に散見される．次に音節核の鼻音が阻害音の頭子音と音節を形成する場合であるが，確かに日本語や英語では許されない形式であるが，Dell and Elmedlaoui (1985) には，ベルベル語のイムドラウン・タシュルヒィト方言から次のような例を挙げている．（以下，ピリオドは音節境界を示している．）[7]

---

　[6] これらのケースでは，成節鼻音を形成する際に，モーラをもった弱母音を脱落させ，音節量を犠牲にしていることに注意．
　[7] 以下，ベルベル語の例はいずれも，Prince and Smolensky (2004) に引用されたものである．

(9)　[.tm.zħ.]　　　she jested
　　　[.tzmt.]　　　it (f.) is stifling

これらの例では，いずれも [m] が音節核となり，頭子音は阻害音である．Dell and Elmedlaoui (1985) には，音節頭子音と核の共鳴度の差に関係する例も見られる．

(10)　[.bd.dl.]　　　exchange!
　　　[.ra.tk.ti.]　　she will remember

最初の例では，第 1 音節の [d] が，2 番目の例では，第 2 音節の [k] がそれぞれ核となっている．いずれも阻害音であり，どちらも阻害音の頭子音との間に共鳴度の差はない．これは音節の形としては非常に適格さを欠くものと言えるが，この言語では，音節には頭子音が不可欠であるので，それを優先してこのような音節分けがなされるのである．

　本節では，小論で取り上げた構音障害の最も深刻な問題点である音節形成について述べたが，上記の例に関する限りでは，音節の自然性とは絶対的なものではなく，他の条件との優先順位によって決定されるものと考えられる．

7.　まとめ

　小論で論じてきた機能性構音障害は，特異な事例であっても，いずれかの自然言語に見られる体系をもつことがわかった．その意味ではこの体系は人間の獲得できる音韻体系の枠内に収まっており，それゆえ「自然な体系」であると言えよう．例えば上田 (2008) には，次のように [d] と [ɾ] が交替する機能性構音障害の事例が挙げられている．

(11) a.　音声形　　　目標形　　　意味
　　　 dappa　　　 ɾappa　　　 らっぱ
　　　 demoɴ　　　 ɾemoɴ　　　 レモン
　　　 daɾɯma　　　daɾɯma　　　だるま
　　　 denʃa　　　 denʃa　　　 電車
　　b.　音声形　　　目標形
　　　 ʥiroːʃa　　 ʥidoːʃa　　自動車
　　　 namiɾa　　　namiɾa　　　涙
　　　 gɯroːbɯ　　 gɯroːbɯ　　グローブ

terebi　　　　teɾebi　　　　テレビ

この例では，目標音が /d/ と /r/ どちらであっても，a. の語頭位置においては [d] が，b. の語中位置においては [ɾ] が現れているのがわかる．この音交替は標準的な日本語の体系とは異なり，ために構音の異常とされるが，a. は八丈方言に，b. は新潟県尾崎方言に，それぞれ同じパターンが見られ，また，a. と b. 全体の相補的な分布は，タガログ語にも見られる（Ueda and Davis (2005)）．要するにこの幼児は，他の方言や言語の音韻体系を具現化しているのであり，自然言語に許される体系を有しているという意味では，この音の逸脱は「自然」であると言える．このように，機能性構音障害の体系は人間の言語に可能な文法の枠内に収まっていると考えられる．その意味において，機能性構音障害は自然な音韻体系をもつと考えられる．

参考文献

Chomksy, Noam and Morris Halle (1968) *The Sound Pattern of English*, Harper & Row, New York.
Clark, John and Colin Yallop (1990) *An Introduction to Phonetics and Phonology*, Blackwell, Oxford.
Dell, François and Mohamed Elmedlaoui (1985) "Syllable Consonants in Berber: Some New Evidence," *Journal of African Languages and Linguistics* 10, 1–17.
Dinnsen, Daniel (1997) "Non-segmental Phonologies," *The New Phonologies: Developments in Clinical Linguistics*, ed. by Martin J. Ball and Raymond D. Kent, 77–125, Singular Publishing Group, Inc., San Diego and London.
Hall, Tracy A. (2007) "Segmental Features," *The Cambridge Handbook of Phonology*, ed. by Paul de Lacy, 311–334, Cambridge University Press, Cambridge.
Prince, Alan and Paul Smolensky (2004) *Optimality Theory: Constraint Interaction in Generative Grammar*, Blackwell, Malden, MA.
Stampe, David (1969) "The Acquisition of Phonetic Representation," *CLS* 5, 433–444.
Stampe, David (1973) *A Dissertation on Natural Phonology*, Doctoral dissertation, University of Chicago.
外池滋生 (1976)「自然音韻論とは何か」月刊『言語』第5巻第9号 75–81.
上田功 (1995a)「機能性構音障害における「傾向」と「例外」の言語学的説明を求めて」『言語研究』第106号，74–94.
上田功 (1995b)「機能性構音障害と自然音韻過程音韻分析—音韻論からみたいくつかの問題点」『音声言語医学』第36号 331–337.

Ueda, Isao (2005) "Some Formal and Functional Typological Properties of Developing Phonologies,"『言語研究』127号, 115-139.

上田功 (2008)「音韻理論と構音障害」『音声研究』第 12 巻第 3 号, 3-16.

上田功 (2013)「機能性構音障害の音韻分析——臨床的視点からの考察」『音声研究』第 17 巻第 2 号 21-28.

Ueda, Isao (2013) "Retention of an Irregular Feature Specification as a Source of Functional Misarticulation," *Philologia* 11, 1-10.

Ueda, Isao and Davis, Stuart (2005) "The Developmental Paths in the Acquisition of the Japanese Liquid," *Developmental Paths in Phonological Acquisition: Special Issue of Leiden Papers in Linguistics* 2:1, ed. by Marina Tzakosata, Claatje Levelt and Jeroen van de Weijer, 117-135.

Vance, Timothy, J. (1987) *An Introduction to Japanese Phonology*, State University of New York Press, Albany, NY.

head-last への語順変化は下降リズムが要因

宇佐美　文雄
明治学院大学

1. はじめに

　松本（2006: 214）の統計によると，従属部に対し，主要部が先行する主要部前（head-first）の言語数，そうでない主要部後（head-last）の言語数はほぼ半々である．また，主要部後から主要部前への語順変化が自然であり，これと逆方向の変化は，周辺言語との言語接触などの外的要因による，との見解が一般的である．

　主要部前から主要部後への語順変化は，むしろ，内的要因によるもの，との主張が Donegan and Stampe (1983, 2004) でなされている．主要部前の言語にはなく，主要部後の言語にのみに存在するリズム構造がその語順変化の要因である．

　主要部前から主要部後への語順変化は外的要因とする研究に Hashimoto (1976) を中心とした一連の論考がある．中国語諸方言は，その北に主要部後の言語であるアルタイ諸語，南に主要部前の言語であるタイ諸語を有し，中国語諸方言の分岐（diverge）を「アルタイ語化」と橋本は捉えている．

　小論では，Hashimoto (1976) による地域的推移のデータを，Donegan and Stampe (1983, 2004) によるリズム構造の観点から再分析する．

2. リズム構造

　結論を先に言うと，主要部前から主要部後への語順変化は，主要部後の言語にだけに存在する下降リズムがその要因である．リズム構造を理解するために，はじめに基本事項を略述する．[1]

---

[1] セクション 2 と 3 のリズム構造の考え方および例示は，Donegan and Stampe (2004) に

時間の流れの切り取り方が言語と音楽に共通している．Anacrusis の場合を除いて，卓立した要素から始まり (front-prominent)，同じ程度卓立した要素の前までで 1 区切りになるのが一般的である．この区切り方はビート (beat)，メジャー (measure) いずれの場合にもあてはまる．なお，言語習得の際の幼児の発話に見られる強弱リズム (trochaic) の傾向はこの普遍性を反映している．

Lehiste (1971, 1977) によれば，音節の長さが 1 音節，2 音節，3 音節のように増えても語の長さは変わらないので，stead, steady, steadily のような短い語は，あえて長く・ゆっくり発音する状況でなければ，いずれも 1 ビートで発音される．卓立した第 1 音節は，音楽における，音が長いことを示す付点，♩ = ♪♪ = ♪♪♪で表記される．

elevator, operator のような長い語はそれぞれ 2 ビートで発音される．卓立した第 1 音節から始まる elevator operator という 4 ビートはメジャー 1 つを構成し，音楽における小節 (measure) に対応する．Elevator, operator はそれぞれ半メジャー (half-measure) に収まる．以上を音符で表記すると (1) のようになる．語が半メジャーに収まり，句がメジャーに収まるような，時間との対応づけを普遍的区切りと呼ぶことにする．

(1) 普遍的区切り

$\begin{array}{cccc} 1 & 3 & 2 & 3 \\ \text{♪♪} & \text{♪♪} & \text{♪♪} & \text{♪♪} \\ \text{el.e.} & \text{vat.or} & \text{op.e.} & \text{rat.or} \end{array}$

なお，'elevator operator' の強勢パターンは，第 1 強勢・第 3 強勢・第 2 強勢・第 3 強勢であるが，これは，4 分の 4 拍子の小節が，強拍・弱拍・中強拍・弱拍であることに符合する．

語 Néwton，複合語 Néwtòwn，名詞句 nêw tówn，語の列挙 néw や tówn，などの 4 通りを音符で表記したものを (2) に示す．話し手は意図した 2 つの形態素の凍結度に応じて，リズムのスロットに語・句を落とし込んでいくわけである．この考え方はリズムを構成する強勢を語・句に「付与する」という捉え方とは大きく異なる．

よる．小論の議論に必要な箇所を敷衍しながら提示する．

(2) 2つの形態素の凍結度
 (a) 語

 (b) 複合語

 (c) 名詞句

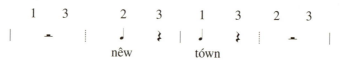

 (d) 語の列挙

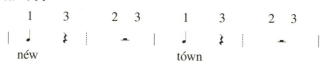

　語・句を，音符によって表示される時間，すなわち，ビート，メジャーにどのように対応づけるかによって，ある言語のリズム構造を特徴づけることができる．語・句の前部（fronts）が主要ビート（main beat）に対応づけられる場合を，下降リズム（falling rhythm），後部（ends）が主要ビートに対応づけられる場合を上昇リズム（rising rhythm）と呼ぶ．古期英語と現代英語の詩，歌を比べると下降リズムと上昇リズムの違いは明確に理解されよう．

　古期英語は下降リズムで，句の前部にある語の前部を卓立させる頭韻詩があり，一方，現代英語は上昇リズムで，句の後部にある語の後部を卓立させる脚韻詩がある．古期英語は下降リズムゆえに，おもに主要部後，現代英語は上昇リズムゆえに，おもに主要部前の語順である．(3)がこの例である．

(3) 下降リズムと上昇リズム

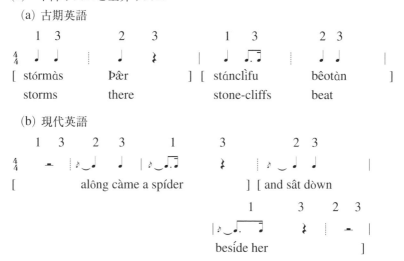

3. 主要部前から主要部後への語順変化

英語史上の主要部前から主要部後への語順変化とは逆方向の変化が，モン・クメール諸語からのムンダ諸語の分岐に観察される.[2]

モン・クメール諸語は主要部前の言語，ムンダ諸語は主要部後の言語である．主要部後の言語にだけに存在する下降リズムが，主要部前から主要部後への語順変化の主要因となった．ムンダ諸語が上昇リズムから下降リズムに変化し，このリズム変化に付随し，主要部前から主要部後への語順変化が生じたのである．

語・句は下降リズムで発話されると普遍的区切りにピッタリ収まる．(4) がこの例である.

---

[2] 周辺言語との言語接触など外的要因によるものとする見解に対する精緻な反論はDonegan and Stampe (2004) を参照のこと．ムンダ諸語とモン・クメール諸語が，文法から音声にいたる言語のすべてのレベルで正反対であるという事実 (Donegan and Stampe (2004: 3) Table 1 を参照) を説明できるのはリズム構造の違いであるとの主張である．

(4) 下降リズム（ムンダ諸語に属するソラ語）

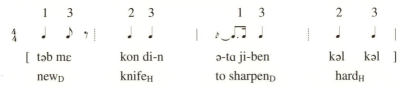

ソラ語で 'A new knife is hard to sharpen.' を発話すると，従属部（dependents）が主要ビートに対応づけられ，2つの句はそれぞれメジャーに，語はそれぞれ半メジャーにぴったりと収まる．

これに対して，語や句が上昇リズムで発話されると，普遍的区切りにピッタリと収まることは決してない．例えば，(5) で示すように，ソラ語の 'A new knife is hard to sharpen.' をクメール語に翻訳したものを上昇リズムで発話した場合などである．従属部の後部を主要ビートに対応づけると，句は1つのメジャーに収まらず，隣接するメジャーにまたがり，2音節語は隣接する半メジャーにまたがる．また休止も多く必要になる．

(5) 上昇リズム（クメール語）

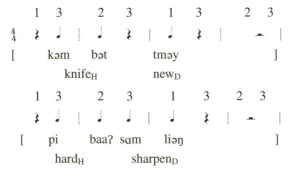

副次音節（minor syllable）を anacrusis にして，後続する音節の左側に付加し，主要音節（major syllable）を後続する休止を埋めるようにゆっくりと発音すると，(6) に示すように，語は半メジャーに収まる．これはモン・クメール諸語の典型である．しかし，このようにしても，句は隣接するメジャーにまたがり1つのメジャーに収まらない．

(6) クメール語（anacrusis をできるだけ活用し，ゆっくりと発音）

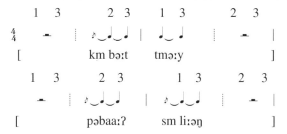

(5) で示した語を半メジャーに収め，句をメジャーに収めるためには，語や句は上昇リズムではなく，下降リズムで発話する必要がある．下降リズムでは，(7) に示すように，語は半メジャーに，句はメジャーに収まる．

(7) クメール語もどき（下降リズムで主要部前の語順）

このようにすると太字で示した主要部が主要ビートに対応づけられる（A *knife*_H that's *new*_D is *hard*_H to *sharpen*_D.）ことになるが，下降リズムでは主要ビートに対応づけられるのは，主要部と比較して卓立のある従属部でなければならない．この不一致を解消するためには，(8) に示すように，主要部前から主要部後へと語順を変化させる必要がある．

(8) クメール語もどき（下降リズムで主要部後の語順）

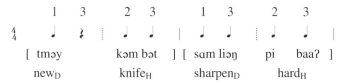

4. Hashimoto (1976) の地域的推移のデータと上昇・下降リズム

中国語諸方言は，その北に，主要部後の言語であるアルタイ諸語，南に，主要部前の言語であるタイ諸語を有している．Hashimoto (1976) は，音韻構造，

形態素構造，統語構造の観点から，諸方言を北方的 (northern; (9) では N)，過渡的 (transitional; (9) では T)，南方的 (southern; (9) では S) に分類している．これら言語的特徴が語族の違いを越え拡散するという視点から，南から北への地域的な推移をたどっている．また，南方的方言から北方的方言への地域的推移は，時間的推移に見られる中国諸方言の分岐を反映したもので，「アルタイ語化」と Hashimoto は捉えている．

Hashimoto (1976) が提示する形態素構造，統語構造のうち名詞句，副詞，比較構文，二重目的語構文について，それぞれで主要部，従属部を分類し，主要部 (H) と従属部 (D) のうち先行するものを (9) の二重線の下段に示す．[3]

(9) 南から北への中国語諸方言 [4]

Dialect	12~18	11	10	9	8	7	6	1~5
Type	N	T	T	T	T	T	T	S
Rhythm	F	F	F	R				R
Noun Phrase	D	D	D	D/H		D	D/H	H
Adverb	D							H
Comparative	D							H
D. Object	D	D	D	D	H	H	H	H

(9) の横軸を見ると，南方 (S) から北方 (N) に至る Dialect 1 から Dialect 18 の地域的推移に沿って，主要部前 (H) から主要部後 (D) へと語順が変化していることが明らかになる．北に，主要部後の言語のアルタイ諸語，南に，主要部前の言語のタイ諸語があり，これらが語順変化に影響を与えたというのが Hashimoto (1976) の主張である．

---

[3] 比較構文で H が先行する例は，kao 'tall$_H$' kuo i 'exceed him$_D$' (Dialect 1, 2)，D が先行する例は，pi ta 'than him$_D$' kao 'tall$_H$' (Dialect 18)．二重目的語構文では，動詞は間接・直接目的語の両者に先行するので，後者の順序を考察．与格が先行する場合を D，直接目的語が先行する場合を H とする．与格を D とする分析は Donegan and Stampe (1983: 338) による．なお，空所はデータが単に入手できなかったことを示す．

[4] Dialect 1: Guangzhou (Yue); Dialect 2: Chaozhou (S.E. Min); Dialect 3: Xiamen (S.E. Min); Dialect 4: Fuzhou (N.E. Min); Dialect 5: Meixian (Hakka); Dialect 6: Nanchang (Gan); Dialect 7: Shuangfeng (Xiang); Dialect 8: Changsha (Xiang); Dialect 9: Wenzhou (S. Wu); Dialect 10: Suzhou (N. Wu); Dialect 11: Shanghai (N. Wu); Dialect 12: Yangzhou (S.E. Mandarin); Dialect 13: Hankou (S.W. Mandarin); Dialect 14: Chengdu (S.W. Mandarin); Dialect 15: Xian (N.W. Mandarin); Dialect 16: Taiyuan (N.W. Mandarin); Dialect 17: Jinan (N. Mandarin); Dialect 18: Beijing (N. Mandarin)

(9) の縦軸を見ると，上昇リズム (R) と主要部前 (H)，および，下降リズム (F) と主要部後 (D) との間に相関関係があることが明らかになる．つまり，主要部前 (H) から主要部後 (D) への語順変化と，上昇リズム (R) から下降リズム (F) への変化との間に相関関係が存在する．Hashimoto (1976) に欠如している視点である．

(9) で示した上昇リズム，下降リズムは，ストレスアクセントの音声的具現3つ，声の高低の変動 (pitch change)，長さ (duration)，強さ (intensity) のうちの，長さを媒介に確定することができる．中国語諸方言 (Dialect 1~18) は，音節中の声の高低やその変動が弁別的特徴をもつ声調言語であり，調連声 (tone sandhi) という，語と語がある程度の凍結度で結びついた時にだけ生じる特有の声調変化が多くの方言で観察される．この声調変化に関与しているのは (10)，(11) のデータで考察するように，音節の長さである．

結論を先に言うと，この声調変化を受けるのは短い音節であり，長い音節ではない．[5] 短い音節では引用形での声調を実現することが困難であることが推察される．調連声が観察される中国語諸方言で，[6] 声調変化を受けない音節が，語・句の前部に位置するのか後部に位置するのかが分かれば，長い音節を仲介として，ストレスアクセントの所在が分かる．ストレスアクセントの位置が主要ビートの位置であるから，語・句の前部にある場合は下降リズム (F)，後部にある場合は上昇リズム (R) ということになる．

上昇リズムに分類される南方的 (S) 諸方言のひとつに福州方言 (Fuzhou: Dialect 4) がある．この方言ではストレスアクセントの位置が語・句の後部にあることが分かる．以下の議論で明らかになるように，声調変化を受けている音節が語・句の前部にあるのがその理由である．

(10)　福州方言 (Fuzhou: Dialect 4)[7]
　　　(a)　(i)　[ku^{52}]　　　'paste'　　　400 msec.

---

[5] Dialect 1: Guangzhou (Yue)，その南に位置するタイ語には調連声が存在しない．両言語には長母音・短母音といった弁別的な長さの対立があるという共通性を持つので，母音の長さが弁別的でることが調連声を生じさせない要因になっているものと推察される．

[6] (9) で示した上昇リズム・下降リズムを確定する際に重要になる，調連声が観察される中国語諸方言についての情報は，Yue-Hashimoto (1987) による．なお，小論で展開している長さを媒介とするストレスアクセントの位置の確定の議論は拙論．

[7] Wright (1983: 37) によるデータ．形態素の右肩の数字は，声の高さを5段階に分けたChao (1930) による表記法．1 は「低」，2 は「半低」，3 は「中」，4 は「半高」，5 は「高」を示す．

(ii) [ku²² tsai²²] 'airplane' 144/366 msec.
(b) (i) [ki⁵²] 'flag' 320 msec.
(ii) [øyŋ²² ki⁵²] 'red flag' 240/304 msec.

(10) の (ii) では形態素が2つ結びついた形が示され調連声が観察される．(a) の形態素 [ku⁵²] は前部に位置すると声調変化を受け，(b) の形態素 [ki⁵²] は後部に位置すると声調変化を受けていないことが分かる．長さを比べてみると，声調変化を受けていない形態素 [ki⁵²] は引用形で 320，連結形で 304 のようにほぼ変化が見られない．これに対して，声調変化を受けた形態素 [ku⁵²] は引用形で 400，連結形で 144 のように半減している．短い音節が声調変化を受けている．

下降リズムに分類される北方的 (N) 諸方言のひとつに北京方言 (Dialect 18: Beijing) がある．この方言ではストレスアクセントの位置が語・句の前部にあることが分かる．以下の議論で明らかになるように，声調変化を受けている音節が語・句の後部にあるのがその理由である．

(11) 北京方言 (Dialect 18: Beijing)⁸

				whole word	first syllable	second syllable
(a)	(i)	[toŋ¹ ɕi¹]	'east and west'	44	20	24
	(ii)	[toŋ¹ ɕɪ]	'thing'	25	15	10
(b)	(i)	[ɕüŋ¹ ti⁴]	'brothers'	44	25	19
	(ii)	[ɕüŋ¹ dɪ]	'younger brother'	23.5	16	7.5

(1/40 seconds)

(11) の (i) と (ii) ともに，同じ形態素が結びついているのであるが，(i) は結びついた2つの形態素全体の意味がそれぞれの形態素の意味の総和であるのに対して，(ii) には意味の特殊化が見られるので，(ii) のほうが凍結度が強いことになる．凍結度の強い (ii) のみに調連声が観察される．(ii) では後部に位置する形態素の声調が失われている．

長さに関して2つのことに気づく．語全体の長さの比が (i) と (ii) でほぼ2対1であること．形態素後部の長さの比が (i) と (ii) でほぼ3対1から2

---

⁸ Cheng (1973: 54-55) によるデータ．形態素の右肩の数字1は「高平板調」，2は「高上昇調」，3は「下降上昇調」，4は「高下降調」を示す．

対 1 であることが分かる．これらのことから，(ii) は 2 ビートで，(2b) に示した英語における複合語に相当し，(i) は 1 ビートで，(2a) に示した英語における語に相当する．福州方言と同じように，北京方言でも短い音節が声調変化を受けている．

5. リズム構造の観点から Hashimoto (1976) の地域的推移のデータを再分析

南方的諸方言（モン・クメール諸語に相当）は主要部前の言語，北方的諸方言（ムンダ諸語に相当）は主要部後の言語である．(4) から (8) で，主要部後の言語にだけに存在する下降リズムが，主要部前から主要部後への語順変化の主要因となることを見た．Hashimoto (1976) が提示する名詞句を取り上げ，北方的諸方言（ムンダ諸語に相当）が上昇リズムから下降リズムに変化し，このリズム変化に付随し，主要部前から主要部後への語順変化が生じたことを以下の (12) から (14) で論じる．

上昇リズムで発話されると，語や句が普遍的区切りにピッタリと収まることは決してない．(12) で示すように，従属部 [kung] を主要ビートに対応づけると，名詞句は 1 つのメジャーに収まらず，隣接するメジャーにまたがる．北方方言では，単音節語よりも 2 音節語になる傾向が強いので，[9] 2 音節語についての考察が必要になる．従属部が 2 音節語で後部に卓立を置く語の場合，この語は隣接するメジャーにまたがることになる．また，主要部が 2 音節語で後部に卓立を置く語の場合，この語は隣接する半メジャーにまたがることになる．北方方言で，2 音節語の後部が卓立を持つ場合は，上昇リズムでの発話で，普遍的区切りにぴったりと収まることはない．

(12) 上昇リズム（(5) に相当）

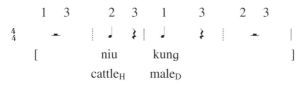

(12) で示した名詞句をメジャーに収めるためには，上昇リズムではなく，下降リズムで発話する必要がある．下降リズムでは，(13) に示すように，名

---

[9] Yue-Hashimoto (1987: 450) による．

詞句はメジャーに，語は半メジャーに収まる．2音節語についての考察も行うと，従属部が2音節語で後部に卓立を置く語の場合，この語は隣接する半メジャーにまたがり，主要部が2音節語で後部に卓立を置く語の場合，この語は隣接するメジャーにまたがることになるが，通例，卓立のない前部は，いずれの場合も (6) で示したように，anacrusis になるものと予想される．

(13) 下降リズムで主要部前の語順（(7) に相当）

(13) のようにすると主要部 [niu] が主要ビートに対応付けられることになるが，下降リズムでは主要ビートに対応づけられるのは，主要部と比べ卓立のある従属部 [kung] でなければならない．この不一致を解消するためには，(14) に示すように，主要部前から主要部後へと語順を変化させる必要がある．

(14) 下降リズムで主要部後の語順（(8) に相当）

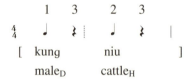

6. おわりに

小論は Hashimoto (1976) を中核とする一連の論考が提供するデータのほんの一部を，Donegan and Stampe (1983, 2004) の枠組みで再分析したものである．再分析を可能にしたのは Yue-Hashimoto (1987) の中国語諸方言の調連声の論考である．

語順変化は言語外にその要因があるとの主張に対し，リズム構造という言語内の要因が関与しているとの Donegan and Stampe の主張を小論は支持している．1991年夏に橋本夫妻の論文に出合い，小論の原型を書き留めた．

参考文献

Chao, Yuen-Ren (1920) "A System of Tone Letters," *Le Maître phonétique* 45, 24-27.

Cheng, Chin-Chuan (1973) *A Synchronic Phonology of Mandarin Chinese*, Mouton, The Hague.

Donegan, Patricia and David Stampe (1983) "Rhythm and the Holistic Organization of Language Structure," *Papers from the Parasession on the Interplay of Phonology, Morphology, and Syntax*, ed. by John F. Richardson et al., 337-353, Chicago Linguistic Society, Chicago.

Donegan, Patricia and David Stampe (2004) "Rhythm and the Synthetic Drift of Munda," *Yearbook of South Asian Languages and Linguistics 2004*, ed. by Rajendra Singh, 3-36.

Hashimoto, Mantaro (1976) "Language Diffusion on the Asian Continent," *Computational Analysis of Asian and African languages* 3, 49-65.

Lehiste, Ilse (1971) "Temporal Organization of Spoken Language," *Form and Substance: Phonetic and Linguistic Papers Presented to Eli Fischer-Jørgensen*, ed. by L. L. Hammerich, Roman Jakobson and Eberhard Zwirner, 159-169, Akademisk Forlag, Copenhagen.

Lehiste, Ilse (1977) "The Timing of Utterances and Linguistic Boundaries," *Journal of the Acoustical Society of America* 51, 2018-2024.

松本克己 (2006)『世界言語への視座』三省堂, 東京.

Wright, Martha (1983) *A Metrical Approach to Tone Sandhi in Chinese Dialects*, Doctoral dissertation, University of Massachusetts.

Yue-Hashimoto, Anne (1987) "Tone Sandhi across Chinese Dialects," *Wang Li Memorial Volume* (English volume), ed. by the Chinese Language Society of Hong Kong, 445-474, Joint Publishing, Hong Kong.

Wh-movement out of DP and Intervention Effect

Masaya Yoshida

Northwestern University

1. Introduction

This short note tries to establish the claim that the condition on wh-movement out of DP with definite determiners, the so-called specificity condition (Bach and Horn (1976), Chomsky (1973), Fiengo and Higginbotham (1981), Mahajan (1992) among many others), is best analyzed as an intervention effect induced by an invisible quantifier generated in the Spec, DP. The specificity effects are illustrated by the pair of examples in (1). In (1a) wh-movement is blocked, unlike in (1b). The crucial difference between (1a) and (1b) is whether or not the DP involves the definite Determiner or possessive genitive DP in Spec, DP position. In the literature, it has been argued that when the DP is 'specific' wh-extraction is blocked.

(1) a. *What did you read the/those/Bill's books about t?
    b. What did you read a book/books about t?

However, in recent literature, it has been reported that even if the DP is headed by the definite determiner, wh-movement is sometimes possible as illustrated in (2) (Davies and Dubinsky (2003), Yoshida (2004) among others).

(2) a. Which city did you witness the enemy's/the destruction of t?
    b. Who did you meet the brother of t?

The contrast between examples like (1) and examples like (2) indicate that it is not the definite determiner that blocks wh-movement out of DP. Rather, wh-movement out of DP is affected by the properties of the head noun. Importantly, it can be shown that when the head noun is pluralized, wh-movement out of 'definite' DP is not possible, as in (3).

(3) a. Which city did you witness the *invasion* of t?
    b.??Which city did you witness the *invasions* of t?

By examining various examples from English, this study aims to show that when wh-movement out of 'definite' DP is blocked, the Spec, DP is occupied by an invisible quantifier. More specifically, it is claimed that when the definite DP shows the maximality effect, the Spec, DP is occupied by an invisible universal quantifier, and this universal quantifier induces intervention effects (Rizzi (1990) among others).

2. Wh-movement out of 'definite' DPs

Davies and Dubinsky (2003) pointed out that the acceptability of wh-movement out of DP is affected by the property of the head noun. They show that when the head noun is an argument-taking, "process" noun, wh-extraction is possible even if the DP is headed by the definite determiner.

(4) Which city did you witness [$_{DP}$ **the enemy's/the** destruction of t]?

The following examples suggest that even if the head noun is a deverbal, argument-taking noun, wh-movement is sometimes not allowed. In (5a), the head noun is pluralized, and the wh-movement is blocked.

(5) a. Which city did you witness the *invasion* of t?
    b.??Which city did you witness the *invasions* of t?

Grimshaw (1990) argues that when a deverbal noun is pluralized, it denotes result of the event rather than the process of the event, and Grimshaw further argues that only the process nouns takes syntactic arguments. Thus, the contrast in (5) suggests that wh-movement out of DP is possible only if the wh-phrase is an argument of the head noun.

However, this type of analysis based only on the argument structure of the head noun faces some problems. When the head noun is an inalienable possession nominal (e.g. the <u>hair</u> of someone) or kinship nouns (e.g. the <u>brother</u> of someone), wh-movement out of DP is possible even if the DP is headed by the definite determiner. However, when the head noun is pluralized wh-movement is blocked. This is illustrated in (6).

(6) a. Who did you cut the hair of t?
    b. Which man did you visit the *brother* of t?
    c. ??Which man did you visit the *brothers* of t?

Thus, the factor that affects wh-movement out of DP is not simply the argument structure of the head noun.

The asymmetry between DPs involving singular nouns and DPs involving plural nouns with respect to wh-movement can be seen in constructions other than overt wh-movement constructions. For example, an NPI is not licensed when it is in the complement position of plural deverbal nouns or plural kinship nouns.

(7) a. *No one witnessed the **invasions** of *any* city.
    b. No one witnessed the **invasion** of *any* city.
    c. *No one visited the **brothers** of *anyone*.
    d. No one visited the brother of *anyone*.

An in-situ wh-phrase in the multiple wh-question construction is also not licensed when the head noun is plural.

(8) a. *Who witnessed the invasions of which city?
    b. Who witnessed the invasion of which city?
    c. *Who visited the brothers of who?
    d. Who visited the brother of who?

3. The Maximality Effect and DP-islands

It has been reported in the literature that a definite DP with a plural head noun shows the so-called Maximality Effect: the plural definite DP is interpreted as the DP with universal quantifier *all*. For example, in the context given in (9), (9a) is false because a definite DP is interpreted as a DP with a universal quantifier *all* as in (9b) (Brisson (1996), Heime (1988) for the detailed discussion of the semantics of definite DPs).

(9) Context: John has five cookies and puts three of them on the table.
    a. #John put the cookies on the table.

b. #John put all the cookies on the table.

In the same way, when a DP with deverbal nouns or kinship nouns is plural, it also shows the maximality effect. In (7a), the head noun denotes multiple events, and the DP induces the maximality interpretation for all of these events. Likewise, in (7c), *the brothers* is interpreted as *all the brothers*.

Based on this interpretive effect, I would like to argue that in these cases where wh-movement is blocked, there is a universal quantifier in the specifier of DP and this universal quantifier is responsible for island effect shown by these DPs. In other words, when a DP shows the maximality effect, that DP hosts the invisible universal quantifier, and the universal quantifier induces the intervention effect (see Rullmann (1995) for the relation between the maximality and island effects).

As reported in the literature, universal quantifiers indeed show the intervention effects. Thus, when a universal quantifier intervenes between the negation and NPI, the NPI is not licensed (Linebarger (1987) among others).

(10) a. *I don't believe that **everyone** bought *anything*.
 b. I don't believe that **John** bought *anything*.

Furthermore, the multiple wh-question is not acceptable when a universal quantifier intervenes between the two wh-phrases. (11a) is degraded compared to (11b) and the pair-list reading is not available in (11a) but is available in (11b).

(11) a. ??Who thinks that **nobody** invited which girl?
 b. Who thinks that John invited which girl?

If we adopt the presence of the invisible strong quantifier, we can capture the parallels between the examples in (10) and (11), and (7) and (8) naturally, i.e., the strong quantifier induces the intervention effect.

Another piece of evidence comes from the so-called *NP-contained ACD* (Kennedy (1997)). The typical example of NP-contained ACD is the following.

(12) a. Beck read a report on every suspect Kollberg did.
 b. Beck read a report on every suspect Kollbert read a report on.

(Kennedy (1997: 680-681))

(12a) is an example of NP-contained ACD, and (12b) is its interpretation. Originally, Kennedy cites these examples in an effort to argue against the A-movement approach to ACD (Hornstein (1995), Lasnik (1999)). He argues that to derive the interpretation of NP-contained ACD, we need an A'-movement operation, namely QR. Kennedy points out that NP-contained ACD is sensitive to the specificity effect, like overt wh-movement. He cites the following pairs of examples.

(13) a. Which orgy did Jill buy a picture of t?
  b. *Which orgy did Jill buy Melvin's/that picture of t?

(Kennedy (1997: 683))

NP-contained ACD shows further similarity to wh-movement, i.e., although deverbal nouns and kinship nouns allow QR like overt wh-movement as in (14), if we replace them with plural head nouns, inducing the maximality effects, the examples are degraded, as in (15).

(14) a. John witnessed the/the barbarian's **invasion** of the same city that Bill did.
  b. John visited the brother of the same guy that Bill did.
(15) a. *John witnessed the/the barbarian's invasions of the same city that Bill did.
  b.??John visited the brothers of the same guy that Bill did.

Again, the presence of the invisible quantifier can capture the parallel easily; the invisible quantifier induces the island effect exactly in the same way as in the cases of overt and covert wh-movement.

Going back to the original observations, we can capture the singular/plural asymmetry seen in (5) and (6) can be naturally accounted for by the invisible quantifier analysis. The quantifier in the Spec, DP induces the intervention effect for overt wh-movement as illustrated in (16). In other words, in these cases, wh-phrase cannot go through Spec, DP position because the invisible quantifier is occupying Spec, DP.

(16)   Which man did you visit [$_{DP}$ ALL [$_{D'}$ the [$_{NP}$ *brothers* of t]]]?

4. Conclusions

This study has shown the following points. First, there are cases where wh-movement out of DP is possible even when the DP is headed by the definite determiner. Second, the factor that affects the acceptability of wh-movement out of definite DPs is not simply argument structure. As Davies and Dubinsky (2003) show, argument structure of the head noun is an important factor, but the argument structure based accounts encounter the problem of the singular/plural differences with respect to possibility of wh-movement out of DP. It has been shown that even if the head noun is an argument-taking noun, when it is pluralized wh-movement is blocked. Based on the observation that definite DPs with plural head nouns show the maximality effect, an analysis of these DPs has been proposed: The invisible universal quantifier is generated in the Spec, DP when the DP shows the maximality effect. Finally, it has been argued that movement out of 'definite' DPs is blocked when an invisible quantifier is generated in the Spec, DP, i.e., the invisible quantifier induces the intervention effects.

References

Bach, Emon and Laurence Horn (1976) "Remarks on "Conditions on Transformation"," *Linguistic Inquiry* 7, 265-361.

Beck, Sigrid (1996) *Wh-constructions and Transparent Logical Form*, Doctoral dissertation, Universität Tübingen.

Brisson, Cristine (1997) "On Definite Plural NP's and the Meaning of *all*," *Semantics and Linguistic Theory VII*.

Chomsky Noam (1973) "Conditions on Transformation," *A Festschrift for Morris Halle*, ed. by Anderson and Kiparsky, 232-286, Holt, Rinehart and Winston, New York.

Davies, William and Stanley Dubinsky (2003) "On Extraction Out of NP," *Natural Language and Linguistic Theory* 21, 1-37.

Fiengo, Robert and James Higginbotham (1980) "Opacity in NP," *Linguistic Analysis* 7, 395-421.

Grimshaw, Jane (1990) *Argument Structure*, MIT Press, Cambridge, MA.

Heim, Irene (1988) *The Semantics of Definite and Indefinite Noun Phrases*, Garland, New York.

Hornstein, Norbert (1995) *Logical Form: From GB to Minimalism*, Blackwell, Oxford.

Kennedy, Christopher (1997) "Antecedent Contained Deletion and the Syntax of Quantification," *Linguistic Inquiry* 28, 662–688.

Lasnik, Howard (1999) *Minimalist Analysis*, Blackwell, Oxford.

Linebarger, Marcia C. (1987) "Negative Polarity and Grammatical Representation," *Linguistics and Philosophy* 10, 325–387.

Mahajan, Anoop (1992) "The Specificity Condition and the CED," *Linguistic Inquiry* 23, 510–516.

Rizzi, Luigi (1990) *Relativised Minimality*, MIT Press, Cambridge, MA.

Rullmann, Hotze (1995) *Maximality in the Semantics of Wh-Constructions*, Doctoral dissertation, University of Massachusetts at Amherst.

Yoshida, Masaya (2004) "The Specificity Condition: PF-Condition or LF-Condition?" *The Proceedings of The 22nd. West Coast Conference on Formal Linguistics (WCCFL 22)*, ed. by G. Garding and M. Tsujimura, 547–560, Cascadilla Press, Somerville, MA.

カクチケル語から見た日本人英語学習者の空主語現象*

遊佐　典昭

宮城学院女子大学

1. はじめに

　日本語は，時制節で空主語（null subject）や空目的語（null object）を許す言語である．母語のこの影響で，日本人英語学習者（Japanese learners of English, JLE）は，英語を産出するさいに主語を省略することが知られている．生成文法理論を基盤とする第二言語獲得研究では，日本語の空主語がスペイン語同様に，空代名詞 *pro* であるという仮説のもと，日本語の [+空主語] から英語の [−空主語] へとパラメータ値を再設定することが可能かどうか議論されてきた．しかし，最近の比較統語論の進展により，日本語空主語はスペイン語空主語とは統語的に大きく異なり，項削除（argument ellipsis）が関わっていることが明らかになってきている．このような分析では，項削除を許す日本語を母語とする JLE は，英語では項削除が許されないことを学習する必要がある．本稿では，まず空主語は φ 素性一致の欠如が引き起こすという Saito (2007) の主張を支持する経験的証拠を，筆者たちが行ったカクチケル語（Kaqchikel）の研究（大滝他 (2011), Otaki et al. (2013)）から紹介する．次に，これらの研究成果に基づき，英語では空主語が許されないことを JLE がどのように獲得するのかを論じる．最後にまとめをする．

2. 空主語と項削除

　日本語を英語から区別する大きな相違の1つに，時制文の主語・目的語が

＊ 本稿に関して，大滝宏一氏から有益なコメントを頂き謝意を表したい．本研究は，日本学術振興会（科学研究費補助金，基盤研究（S）・課題番号23222001，挑戦的萌芽研究・課題番号25580133），および 2014 年宮城学院女子大学特別研究費助成の補助を受けている．

音形的に空 (null) になりうることがある.

(1) a. ケンはりんごを食べた. でも,
 b. マサは＿＿食べなかった.   ［空目的語］
 c. Ken ate an apple, but
 d. #Masa didn't eat ＿＿. (≠ Masa didn't eat an apple.)

(2) a. ケンは [納豆がおいしいと] 思っている. でも,
 b. マサは [＿＿おいしいと] 思っていない.   ［空主語］
 c. Ken thinks that natto is delicious, but
 d. *Masa doesn't think that ＿＿ is delicious.

1980年代頃までの生成文法では，空主語や空目的語を，音形のない一種の代名詞 (*pro*) と考える仮説が採用されていた．代名詞が談話内の要素を指示できるという性質に基づいた空代名詞仮説のもとでは，(1b), (2b) は，(3a, b) のように分析される．ここで, *pro* はそれぞれ「リンゴを」「納豆が」を指す.

(3) a. マサは *pro* 食べなかった.
 b. マサは [*pro* おいしいと] 思っていない.

しかし，空代名詞仮説では説明できない例が存在する (Oku (1998)).

(4) a. メアリーは [自分の論文が採用されると] 思っている.
 b. ジョンも [＿＿採用されると] 思っている.
 c. ジョンも [それが採用されると] 思っている.

空主語を含む (4b) は，「メアリーの論文が採用される」という「厳密な同一読み (strict reading)」と，「ジョンの論文が採用される」という「緩い同一読み (sloppy reading)」の解釈が可能である．ここで空主語が，空代名詞仮説が主張するように *pro* ならば，音形のある顕在的代名詞「それが」で置きかえた (4c) も，(4b) と同様に二通りの解釈が可能なはずである．しかし，(4c) は緩い同一読みを持たず，厳密な同一読みのみを許す．この観察は，(4b) の示す緩い同一読みを捉えるために，空主語を空代名詞 *pro* と考える分析は，経験的に不十分であることを示している．

 Oku (1998) は，(4b) の緩い同一読みを捉えるために，空主語位置には空代名詞 *pro* ではなく，(5) で示すように「自分の論文が」が生じており，これが先行文 (4a) との同一性のもとで削除をうける項削除分析を提案した．

(5) ジョンも [自分の論文が採用されると] 思っている.

この分析では，(5) が「ジョンの論文が採用される」という解釈が可能なので，(4b) で緩い同一読みが許されることが説明できる．ここで重要なのは，緩い同一読みが許容される場合は，項削除が関与しているという点である．

それでは，空主語を許す言語が全て日本語のように項削除，したがって，緩い同一読みを許すのだろうか．次の，スペイン語の例を考えてみよう．

(6) a. María cree [que su propuesta será aceptada] y
　　　Maria believes [that her proposal will-be accepted] and
　　　'Maria$_i$ believes that her$_i$ proposal will be accepted and …'
　b. Juán también cree [que ___ será aceptada]
　　　Juan too believes [that ___ will-be accepted]
　　　Lit. 'Juan also believes that ___ will be accepted.'

(Oku (1998: 305))

埋め込み節に空主語を含む (6b) は，「ファンもマリアの提案が採用されると信じている」という厳密な同一読みを許すが，「ファンも自分（＝ファン）の提案が採択されると信じている」という緩い同一読みを許さない．このような例において緩い同一読みが不可能であることから，Oku (1998) は，スペイン語の空主語は項削除が適用した結果ではなく，空代名詞 *pro* が存在していると提案した．そうすると，自然言語の許す空主語には，少なくとも日本語のように項削除の結果生じたものと，スペイン語のように空代名詞 *pro* の2種類が存在することになる．日本語の空主語は，空代名詞 *pro* とは異なる性質を持つ項削除が関係しているとすると，項削除を許す条件を明らかにすることが，JLE の空主語現象を解明する上で重要となる．

3. 項削除の認可条件

従来の空主語を空代名詞と分析した場合は，*pro* を許す日本語・スペイン語と，*pro* を許容しない英語の相違を説明することが研究課題であった．しかし，空主語には日本語の場合のように項削除が関係している場合があるとする分析では，スペイン語の空主語はなぜ項削除が許されないかが問題となる．

項削除の主な分析は，(a) かき混ぜ規則（自由語順）を持つ言語が項削除を許すとする「自由語順分析」(Oku (1998)) と，(b) 時制 (T) や軽動詞 (*v*)

などの機能範疇と関連要素が義務的一致を起こさない言語が項削除を許すという「無一致分析」(Saito (2007), Şener and Takahashi (2010)) に大別される．日本語は自由語順を許し，機能範疇と主語・目的語の間に義務的な一致が存在しない (Kuroda (1988) など) ので，2つの分析が区別できない．一方，スペイン語は自由語順を許さず，主語と機能範疇は義務的な一致が存在するので，この場合も2つの分析を区別することができない．

Şener and Takahashi (2010) は，トルコ語の分析から項削除の無一致分析を提案している．トルコ語は，かき混ぜ規則，空主語・空目的語を許すので日本語と類似している．また，トルコ語は主語と動詞の一致が存在するが，目的語と動詞の間には存在しない．ここで，トルコ語は，緩い同一読みが空目的語では可能であるが，空主語では不可能である．この事実は，自由語順分析の予測には反するが，無一致分析には合致する．すなわち，トルコ語の空主語は *pro* であるが，空目的語は項削除が関与しているために緩い同一読みを許容する．以上の結果は，自由語順から項削除を導くことが経験的に困難であることを示している．つまり，主語が項削除をうけ空主語を生成するためには，機能範疇との一致が欠如していることが必要である．次節では，項削除の無一致分析をカクチケル語から示した，大滝他 (2011) および Otaki et al. (2013) を紹介する．

3.1. カクチケル語

マヤ諸語の1つカクチケル語は，主にグアテマラ・シティーから西の高原一帯で話されている．カクチケル語は，他のマヤ諸語同様に，主要部標示 (head-marking) 言語である．動詞には主語や目的語との一致が標示されるが，名詞や目的語は無標である．動詞に主語・目的語の文法情報が標示されるので，空主語・空目的語が生産的に用いられる．語順は比較的自由で，VOS を基本語順とするが VSO, SVO などの語順も可能である．カクチケル語は自由語順を許すので，自由語順分析は項削除が可能であることを予測する．一方カクチケル語は主要部標示言語で，動詞が主語・目的語との義務的一致を示すので，無一致分析は項削除を許容しないことを予測する．

それでは，カクチケル語における空目的語の例を見てみよう．[1]

---

[1] ABS: absolutive, ACT: active, AOR: aorist, CLF: classifier, COMP: complementizer, ERG: ergative, FUT: future, IMPF: imperfective, NEG: negation, PEFV: perfective, pl/PL: plural, PRES: present, sg: singular

(7) a. A   Xwan n-Ø-u-na'oj-ij
       CLF   Juan IMPF-3sg.ABS-3sg.ERG-know-ACT
       [chi   xta Mari'y tikir-el n-Ø-u-chäp
       COMP CLF Maria   can   IMPF-3sg.ABS-3sg.ERG-catch
       ri   ru-syan]
       the 3sg.ERG-cat
       'Juan thinks that Maria can catch his cat.'
   b. Chuqa' a   Kalux n-Ø-u-na'oj-ij
       also   CLF Carlos IMPF-3sg.ABS-3sg.ERG-know-ACT
       [chi   ri   xta Mari'y tikir-el n-Ø-u-chäp   ]
       COMP the CLF Maria   can   IMPF-3sg.ABS-3sg.ERG-catch
       Lit. 'Carlos also thinks that Maria can catch ___.'
   c. Chuqa' a   Kalux n-Ø-u-na'oj-ij
       also   CLF Carlos IMPF-3sg.ABS-3sg.ERG-know-ACT
       [chi ri   xta Mari'y tikir-el n-Ø-u-chäp
       COMP the CLF Maria   can   IMPF-3sg.ABS-3sg.ERG-catch
       ri   ru-syan]
       the 3sg.ERG-cat
       Lit. 'Carlos also thinks that Maria can catch his/her cat.'

(7b) の埋め込み文は，厳密な同一読みである「マリアがファンの猫を捕まえられる」のみを許す．一方，(7c) のように空目的語を音形のある名詞句で置き換えると，厳密な同一読みに加えて，緩い同一読みが可能である．すなわち，カクチケル語の空目的語は，項削除を許さないことが分かる．

同様の現象が，空主語の場合にも観察される．

(8) a. A   Xwan n-Ø-u-na'oj-ij
       CLF Juan   IMPF-3sg.ABS-3sg.ERG-know-ACT
       [chi   ri   ru-syan   tikir-el y-e-ru-chäp
       COMP the 3sg.ERG-cat can   IMPF-3pl.ABS-3sg.ERG-catch
       taq ch'oy]
       PL   mouse
       'Juan thinks that his cat can catch mice.'
   b. Chuqa' ri   a   Kalux n-Ø-u-na'oj-ij
       also   the CLF Carlos IMPF-3sg.ABS-3sg.ERG-know-ACT

  [chi tikir-el y-e-ru-chäp   taq ch'oy]
   COMP can IMPF-3pl.ABS-3sg.ERG-catch PL mouse
  Lit. 'Carlos also thinks that ___ can catch mice.'
 c. Chuqa' ri a Kalux n-Ø-u-na'oj-ij
  also the CLF Carlos IMPF-3sg.ABS-3sg.ERG-know-ACT
  [chi ri ru-syan tikir-el y-e-ru-chäp
   COMP the 3sg.ERG-cat can IMPF-3pl.ABS-3sg.ERG-catch
  taq ch'oy]
  PL mouse
  'Carlos also thinks that his cat can catch mice.'

(8b) の空主語は，緩い同一読みを許さない．一方，空主語を顕在的名詞句で置き換えた (8c) は，緩い同一読みが可能である．まとめると，自由語順で動詞が主語・目的語との義務的一致を示すカクチケル語は，空主語・空目的語が，緩い同一読み，すなわち項削除を許さない．この結果は，項削除の分析として，自由語順分析ではなく無一致分析が妥当であることを示している．

4. JLE の空主語現象

　従来の空主語を *pro* と見なす第二言語獲得研究では，[+pro drop] 言語である日本語，スペイン語を母語とする学習者が，英語などの [–pro drop] へパラメータを再設定できるかが大きな問題だった．例えば，[+pro drop] は「顕在的主語と空主語のいずれを使用してもよい」という性質を有し，[–pro drop] は「顕在的主語のみを使える」という性質を有するために，[–pro drop] のパラメータ値を選択したときに生成される文の集合は，[+pro drop] を選択したときに生成される文の集合の部分集合を形成する．このような包含関係がある場合に，[+pro drop] の母語から [–pro drop] の第二言語へ，肯定証拠のみではパラメータの再設定が困難であることが指摘されてきた．しかし，このパラメータは類型論的傾向を示した外延的定義にすぎず，包含関係は言語知識が生み出す外在言語（E-language）の関係であり，脳に存在する生成手続き（generative procedures）である内在言語（I-language）の理論ではない．E-言語は恣意的概念であり，これに基づいて第二言語獲得理論が構築されたとしても，何の理論かさえ定義できない．
　ミニマリストプログラムは言語機能の基本演算を併合（Merge）のみに限定

し，種々の構造関係は併合の帰結として導こうとしている．素性の束である語彙項目を基本単位として併合を再帰的に適用することで階層構造を生み出し，人間言語の基本的特性である離散無限性を創発させる．基本演算である併合は，2つの統語体（syntactic object）に適用してその集合を形成する適用自由な操作であり（Chomsky (2008) 等），ここに言語間差異があるとは想定しにくい．残る可能性は，併合の入力となる語彙項目を構成する素性である．

本稿では，空主語現象に関して次の2点を述べた．(a) 日本語の空主語は，空代名詞 pro ではなく，項削除を適用した結果である．[2] (b) 項削除は，主語と動詞との義務的一致の欠如が関係している．したがって，主語と動詞との義務的一致が存在する英語には，項削除である空主語が存在しない．日本語の空主語を項削除と見なす仮定のもとでは，従来の JLE の空主語研究を再考する必要がある．

まず，ϕ素性一致の欠如が項削除を可能にするならば，英語で空主語を許さないことを JLE が習得するためには，ϕ素性一致の獲得が重要となる．ここで ϕ素性一致とは，機能範疇 T の有している ϕ素性が，主語 NP の ϕ素性値を付与される操作である．Saito (2007) は，Chomsky (2008) の ϕ素性一致メカニズムに基づき，日本語 T は ϕ素性を欠いていることから，日本語に項削除が存在することを示している．一方，英語では，項削除が起こると T の ϕ素性が主語 NP に付与されず派生が破綻し完全解釈原理に違反することを，活性化条件（activation condition）から説明している．

Chomsky (2008) では，主語・動詞一致に関与する値が付与されていない ϕ素性（[uϕ]）は，まず C に導入され T に継承されると考えられている．この素性継承（feature-inheritance）に基づき，Miyagawa (2005) は，英語は一致の ϕ素性が C をから T へ浸透するのに対して，日本語は焦点素性が C から T へ浸透すると仮定している．この仮説のもとでは，JLE が学習すべき点は2つ．1つは，英語では ϕ素性が C から T へ浸透して，T に ϕ素性が存在することを学習する必要がある（Nawata and Tsubokura (2010)）．具体的には T の ϕ素性が関与する主語・動詞一致の知識が確実にならないと，JLE は空主語を誤って産出することを予測する．この分析は，虚辞 it, there を獲得しても主語・動詞一致の知識が不十分な場合は，日本語の空主語を英語に転移して使い続けると予想する．実際，Nawata and Tsubokura (2010) は，

---

[2] スペースの関係で議論できないが，厳密な同一読みを許す空主語も項削除であると仮定する．

JLE が虚辞構文を正しく容認できても空主語を使うことを報告している．英語を母語とする子どもの研究では，動詞の屈折獲得と空主語の使用には相関関係があることが示されている (Sano and Hyams (1994))．しかし，英語の第二言語獲得では，母語獲得とは異なり，顕在的主語と動詞屈折獲得の間には関連性がないことを主張する研究がある (Davies (1996) など)．しかし，Orfitelli and Grüter (2013) は，従来の第二言語獲得研究の不備を指摘し，文法性判断課題は，主語動詞一致とは異なり空主語の知識を捉えるには不適切であることを主張している．この主張が正しければ，空主語と時制の獲得は無関係であるとする第二言語獲得研究は，再考する必要がある．

　これまでの空主語の第二言語獲得研究には，構造的情報への視点が欠けており，空主語の特性を定義せずに行われてきた．JLE に関しては，英語学習の初期段階を超えても依然として空主語を産出することがあることが知られている．英語で顕在的主語の存在を示す肯定的証拠にも関わらず，空主語を使用する要因として，空代名詞を転移しているならば，英語で顕在的主語が義務的であることを獲得することは非常に容易なはずである．空主語が，英語学習の初期段階を超えても生じることを考慮すると，英語の φ 素性の知識が不十分な JLE は，日本語の項削除を用いていると思われる．[3] 宮本 (2012) は，大学生 JLE を被験者とした実験から，JLE の空主語には項削除が関与していることを示している．ここで，英語の空主語を排除するために φ 素性一致を獲得することは，必要条件であるが十分条件ではない．

　JLE の空主語現象にはもう 1 つ重要な点がある．JLE が使用する英語の主語は，日本語の話題構文からの転移で「話題 (topic)」である可能性がある (Kuribara (2004))．JLE は，話題と主語を混同し (9) のような英文を産出することがある．

(9) a. *Konnyaku doesn't get fat.「こんにゃくは太らない」
　　b. *Disneyland cannot bring lunch inside the park.
　　　　「ディズニーランドは園内に昼食を持ち込めない」

このため JLE は，日本語で C から T へ浸透した話題構文に関与する焦点素性 (Miyagawa (2005)) が，英語では使われないことを再学習 (unlearn) する必要がある (Nawata and Tsubokura (2010))．この再学習には，英語の主語

---

　[3] 本稿の分析は，主語と T の一致を示す肯定証拠は三単現の -s から得やすいが，目的語と v の一致を示す肯定証拠は得にくいため，JLE は空主語よりも空目的語のオプションを捨てが

が話題ではないことを示す多量の肯定証拠，あるいは (9) が誤りであることを示す否定証拠が必要である．母語で獲得した素性を取り除くのには困難がともなうために，(9) のような誤りは長年英語を学んでも，時間的制約のある会話などでは産出されてしまう（遊佐 (2012))．また初級レベルに見られる話題を be 動詞と対応させて "*Japan is now is 8 am." (「日本は，今午後 8 時です」) といった誤りも，日本語の話題を示す「は」の影響の強さを示している．[4]

最後に，スペイン語母語話者は日本語母語話者よりも英語の空主語が困難であることが指摘されてきた．空主語を空代名詞と見なす分析では，この相違が上手く説明ができなかった．しかし，φ素性に基づく分析は，母語の T の素性の相違に原因があると考える（宮本 (2012))．スペイン語は，T に豊かなφ素性があり，日本語にはφ素性がない．スペイン語英語学習者は，母語であるスペイン語 T の豊かなφ素性の一部を除去することで，英語 T の貧弱なφ素性に再組織化する必用がある．一方，JLE は，英語 T にφ素性があることを肯定証拠から学ぶだけである．一般に母語の特性を取り除く再学習には困難がともなうために，スペイン語英語学習者が JLE よりも英語の時制文で顕在的主語が義務的であることを学ぶのが困難であることが説明できる．[5]

5. おわりに

本稿では，JLE の空主語現象をφ素性の観点から考察した．この方向性は，φ素性の有無から日英語の相違を捉える日本語生成文法研究と矛盾しない．さらに，φ素性に言及することで空主語を文法内の現象として捉え，母語の転移が空主語現象に関与していることを示した．また JLE の空主語特質を解明するために，日英語と類型論的に異なるカクチケル語を用いた．このことは，JLE にとって無関係に思えるカクチケル語研究が，JLE の I-言語解明および英語教育に貢献しうることを示唆している．

参考文献

Chomsky, Noam (2008) "On Phases," *Foundational Issues in Linguistic Theory*, ed.

たいと予想する（大滝宏一氏の指摘）．
[4] 教室での否定証拠が，日本語の話題構文からの転移を取り除くのに有効かどうかに関しては，白畑 (2012) を参照のこと．
[5] 第二言語獲得における素性転移と素性獲得に関しては，Ishino(2012) を参照のこと．

by Robert Freidin, Carlos P. Otero and Maria Luisa Zubizarreta, 133-166, MIT Press, Cambridge, MA.

Davies, William (1996) "Morphological Uniformity and the Null Subject Parameter in Adult SLA," *Studies in Second Language Acquisition* 18, 475-493.

Ishino, Nao (2012) *Feature Transfer and Feature Learning in Universal Grammar: A Comparative Study of the Syntactic Mechanism for Second Language Acquisition*, Ph.D. thesis, Kwansai Gakuin University.

Kuribara, Chieko (2004) "Misanalysis of Subjects in Japanese English Interlanguage," *Second Language* 3, 69-95.

Kuroda, Sige-Yuki (1988) "Whether We Agree or Not: A Comparative Syntax of English and Japanese," *Linguisticae Investigationes* 12, 1-47.

Miyagawa, Shigeru (2005) "On the EPP," *MITWPL* 49, 201-235.

宮本陽一 (2012)「第二言語における非顕在的な要素に関する一考察」第84回日本英文学会シンポジウム口頭発表.

Nawata, Hiroyuki and Keiko Tsubokura (2010) "On the Resetting of the Subject Parameter by Japanese Learners of English: A Survey of Junior or High School Students," *Second Language Acquisition* 9, 63-82.

Oku, Satoshi (1998) "LF Copy Analysis of Japanese Null Arguments," *Proceedings of CLS* 34, 299-314.

Orfitelli, Robyn and Theres Grüter (2013) "Do Null Subjects Really Transfer?" *Proceedings of GASLA 2013*, 145-154.

大滝宏一・杉崎鉱司・遊佐典昭・小泉政利 (2011)「カクチケル語における項削除の可否について」『日本言語学会第143回大会予稿集』, 28-33.

Otaki, Koichi, Koji Sugisaki, Noriaki Yusa and Masatoshi Koizumi (2013) "The Parameter of Argument Ellipsis: The View from Kaqchikel," *MITWP on Endangered and Less Familiar Languages* 8, 153-162.

Saito, Mamoru (2007) "Notes on East Asian Argument Ellipsis," *Language Research* 43, 203-227, 南山大学.

Sano Tetsuya and Nina Hyams (1994) "Agreement, Finiteness, and the Development of Null Arguments," *NELS* 24, 543-558.

Şener, Serkan and Daiko Takahashi (2010) "Argument Ellipsis in Japanese and Turkish," *MITWPL* 61, 325-339.

白畑知彦 (2012)「第二言語習得における否定証拠の効果：主語卓越構文の習得を題材に」『日英語の構文研究から探る理論言語学の可能性』, 畠山雄二(編), 157-168, 開拓社, 東京.

遊佐典昭 (2012)「生成文法理論からみた第二言語習得研究―日本人英語使用者（学習者）の諸問題」東京言語研究所特別講義, 2012年9月15, 16日.

外池滋生教授　略歴*

1947 年 2 月 24 日　滋賀県生まれ

学　歴

1969 年 3 月　新潟大学人文学部人文学科英文科卒業
1969 年 4 月　東京都立大学大学院人文科学研究科修士課程英文学専攻入学
1971 年 3 月　東京都立大学大学院人文科学研究科修士課程英文学専攻修了（文学修士）
1971 年 4 月　東京都立大学大学院人文科学研究科博士課程英文学専攻入学
1976 年 3 月　東京都立大学大学院人文科学研究科博士課程英文学専攻中途退学
1973 年 9 月　East-West Center の奨学生としてハワイ大学大学院言語学科入学
1976 年 4 月　ハワイ大学大学院言語学科休学
1978 年 4 月　ハワイ大学大学院言語学科復学
1979 年 5 月　ハワイ大学大学院言語学科修了（Ph.D.）
1990 年 8 月　アメリカ合衆国留学　Fulbright 上級研究員として MIT 客員研究員（1992 年 3 月まで）
2007 年 8 月　ハワイ大学言語学科で在外研究（2008 年 9 月まで）

職　歴

1976 年 4 月　明治学院大学文学部英文学科専任講師（1980 年 3 月まで）
1980 年 4 月　明治学院大学文学部英文学科助教授（1988 年 3 月まで）

---

　* 野村忠央さんはじめ読書会メンバーが 2007 年に私の還暦を祝う会を催してくださった．その折に野村さんが略歴と業績一覧をまとめて冊子を作ってくださった．以下の略歴・業績一覧は，その折のものに加筆修正して作成したもので，還暦の折に野村さんがまとめておいてくださらなかったら，私には一からまとめる気力は生まれなかったのではないかと思う．ここに記して野村さんに心からの謝意を表したい．

1988年4月　明治学院大学文学部英文学科教授（2002年3月まで）
1998年4月　明治学院大学国際交流センター長（2000年3月まで）
2002年4月　青山学院大学文学部英米文学科教授（現在に至る）
2010年4月　青山学院大学英米文学科主任（2012年3月まで）

この間，青山学院大学，愛媛大学，学習院大学，九州大学，慶應義塾大学，清泉女子大学，専修大学，東京大学，東北学院大学，日本女子大学，フェリス女学院大学，北海道教育大学，山口大学，立教大学，等で非常勤講師を歴任

学会活動および社会における活動

日本英語学会　　編集委員（1993-1997, 2010-2012），編集副委員長（2010-2011），編集委員長（2011-2012）
　　　　　　　　大会準備委員（1987-1988）
　　　　　　　　評議員（2003-2013）
　　　　　　　　理事（2012-2013）
日本英文学会　　編集委員（1982-1985）
日本言語学会　　大会実行委員長（2003），評議員（2006-2008）
日本語文法学会　編集委員（2001-2004）
国立国語研究所　「日本語疑問文の通時的・対照言語学的研究プロジェクト」共同研究員（2013-現在に至る）

その他，慶応義塾大学言語文化研究所兼任所員，学習院大学人文科学研究所プロジェクト「伝達と認知」研究スタッフ，科学研究費委員会　審査・評価第二部会　人文学・社会学小委員会委員，日米教育交流振興財団評議員，フルブライト同窓会監査役，日本イーストウエストセンター同友会運営委員（会長 2011-2013）等も歴任

外池滋生教授　業績一覧

〈編著書〉

1985　『英語変形文法』（英語学コース [3]），第6章「音韻論」（pp. 137-173）執筆，大修館書店，東京．（今井邦彦編，今井邦彦・瀬田幸人・中島平三・福地　肇と共著）

1986　『英語史』（英語学コース [1]），第6章「アメリカ英語」（pp. 154-169）執筆，大修館書店，東京．（松浪　有編，秋元実治・河井迪男・松浪　有・水鳥喜喬・村上隆太・山内一芳と共著）

1989　『一歩すすんだ英文法』，第5章「名詞句」（pp. 79-105），第6章「分詞構文」（pp. 106-118），第7章「命令文」（pp. 119-128），第13章「ゼロ代用形」（pp. 223-234），第14章「接続詞」（pp. 235-245）執筆，大修館書店，東京．（今井邦彦・中島平三・福地　肇・足立公也と共著）

1991　*Topics in Small Clauses—Proceedings of Tokyo Small Clause Festival*（言語学ワークショップシリーズ (1)），Kurosio, Tokyo．（中島平三と共編）

1994　『言語学への招待』大修館書店，東京．（中島平三と共編著）

1995　*Essentials of Modern English Grammar*, Chapter 10: Embedding, Chapter 11: Embedding into Subject and Complement Position, Chapter 12: Embedding into Adjunct Position, Section 19.2: Double Object Construction and Dative Constructions, Section 19.3: Middle Voice (pp. 103-148, pp. 206-211) 執筆, Kenkyusha, Tokyo．（今井邦彦・中島平三・Christopher D. Tancrediと共著）

1997　*Scrambling* (Linguistics Workshop Series 5), Kurosio, Tokyo．（編著書）

1998　『生成文法』（岩波講座　言語の科学6），「第3章　第2次認知革命」（pp. 97-159）執筆，岩波書店，東京．（田窪行則・稲田俊明・中島平三・福井直樹と共著）

2010a　『英語研究の次世代に向けて—秋元実治教授定年退職記念論文集』ひつじ書房，東京．（吉波弘・中澤和夫・武内信一・川端朋広・野村忠央・山本史歩子と共編著）

2010b　『[入門] ことばの世界』，「第4章　ことばと文法」（pp. 44-55）執筆，大修館書店，東京．（瀬田幸人・保阪靖人・中島平三と共編著）

〈訳　書〉

1977　ドン L. F. ニールセン夫妻共著『意味論展望：歴史・現状・将来の方向』政文堂，東京．(Nilsen, Don L. F. and Alleen Pace Nilsen (1975) *Semantic Theory: A Linguistic Perspective*, Newbury House Publishers, Rowley, MA. の翻訳．) (藤森一明・斎藤興雄と共訳)

1978　P・W・カリカヴァ著『英語シンタクス』開明書院，東京．(Culicover, Peter W. (1976) *Syntax*, Academic Press, New York の翻訳．) (藤森一明・斎藤興雄と共訳)

1993　ノーム・チョムスキー著『障壁理論』研究社，東京．(Chomsky, Noam (1986) *Barriers*, MIT Press, Cambridge, MA. の翻訳．) (大石正幸と監訳，大石正幸・北原久嗣・小泉政利・野地美幸と共訳)

1998　N. チョムスキー著『ミニマリスト・プログラム』翔泳社，東京．(Chomsky, Noam (1995) *The Minimalist Program*, MIT Press, Cambridge, MA. の翻訳．) (大石正幸と監訳，内田　平・大石正幸・川島るり子・菊地　朗・北原久嗣・小泉政利・豊島孝之・保坂靖人・遊佐典昭と共訳)

2000　アンドリュー・ラドフォード著『入門ミニマリスト統語論』研究社，東京．(Radford, Andrew (1997) *Syntax—A Minimalist Introduction*, Cambridge University Press, Cambridge の翻訳．) (泉谷双藏・森川正博と共訳)

2006　アンドリュー・ラドフォード著『新版　入門ミニマリスト統語論』研究社，東京．(Radford, Andrew (2004) *English Syntax—An Introduction*, Cambridge University Press, Cambridge の翻訳) (監訳，泉谷双藏・伊藤達也・江頭浩樹・勝山裕之・西前　明・鈴木泉子・塚田雅也・野村忠央・野村美由紀・森川正博と共訳)

〈辞典分担執筆・事典分担執筆〉

1982　大塚高信・中島文雄監修『新英語学辞典』研究社，東京．(分担執筆)
1986　今井邦彦編『チョムスキー小事典』，「Ⅵ　チョムスキー理論を遡る」(pp. 143-188) 分担執筆，大修館，東京．
1998　松浪　有編集主幹『講談社　キャンパス英和辞典』講談社，東京．(分担執筆)
2002　日本認知科学会編『認知科学辞典』，「S 構造，空範疇，繰上げ，再帰化，使役化，c 統御，受動化，there 構文，生成意味論，tough 構文，同一名詞句削除，統語の制約，標準理論，分裂文，変形規則」分担執筆，共立出版，

東京.

〈書評・文献解題〉

1977a 「『英語の音型』(1967年)」(チョムスキー主要著作解題)『言語』第6巻2号(「特集 チョムスキーの全体像」), 52-54, 大修館書店, 東京.
1977b 「書評:井上和子著『変形文法と日本語』」『言語研究』第71号, 41-55, 日本言語学会.
1978 〈〈BOOK REVIEWS〉〉「『変形文法理論の軌跡』梶田 優著 大修館書店発行, 1977, iv + 394 pp. 1,600円」『英語学』第18号, 107-116, 開拓社, 東京.
1984 (言語圏 α [ことばの書架])「井上和子・小林栄智・R. Linde 編『現代言語学論叢―村木正武教授還暦記念論文集』三修社」『言語』第13巻4号, 139, 大修館書店, 東京.
2007 「チョムスキー『文法理論の諸相』(研究社1970)『日本語学』第26巻5号(特集 日本語学の読書案内―名著を読む―). 163-165, 明治書院.

〈論 文〉
(※断りのないものは単独発表)

1971 "A Note on English Modals (1)," *Metropolitan* 15, 191-219, 東京都立大学英文学会.
1972 「安知魚之楽也」(言語空間 [読者のページ])『言語』第1巻5号, 73, 大修館書店, 東京.
1976a "The Case Ordering Hypothesis," *Papers in Japanese Linguistics* 4, 191-208, Department of Linguistics, University of Southern California, Los Angeles.
1976b "Counter Identity Deletion in Japanese," *Metropolitan Linguistics* 1, 27-43, Linguistic Circle of Tokyo Metropolitan University, Tokyo.
1976c 「自然音韻論とは何か」『言語』第5巻9号, 75-81, 大修館書店, 東京.
1977 "O/Ga Conversion: Ga for Object Marking Reconsidered," *Metropolitan Linguistics* 2, 50-75, Linguistic Circle of Tokyo Metropolitan University, Tokyo.
1978a "Auxiliaries of English and Japanese,"『明治学院論叢』第264号(明治学院百周年記念英米文学語学論集), 221-245, 明治学院大学文経学会.
1978b "On the Causative Construction in Japanese," *Problems in Japanese Syn-*

tax and Semantics, ed. by John Hinds and Irwin Howard, 3-29, Kaitakusha, Tokyo.

1978c （訳者附説）「変形理論による日本語分析」, P・W・カリカヴァ著, 藤森一明・斎藤興雄・外池滋生訳『英語シンタクス』, 405-446, 開明書院, 東京.

1979a *Complementation and Case Particles in Japanese*, Unpublished doctoral dissertation, University of Hawaii.

1979b "*Tough* Verbals as Dative Intransitive Verbals," 『明治学院論叢』第271-272号 英語・英米文学研究, 63-84, 明治学院大学文学会.

1979c "Intra-Subjectivization," *Papers in Japanese Linguistics* 6, 325-339, Department of Linguistics, University of Southern California, Los Angeles, California.

1980 "More on Intra-Subjectivization," *MIT Working Papers in Linguistics* 4, 137-148, Department of Linguistics and Philosophy, MIT, Cambridge, MA.

1981a "On Nasal Vowels," 『明治学院論叢』第309号英語・英米文学第49号, 113-150, 明治学院大学文学会.

1981b "How Things Stand with Reflexives," *Metropolitan Linguistics* 4, 123-136, Linguistic Circle of Tokyo Metropolitan University, Tokyo.

1983a 「誤用の心理言語学」『言語』第12巻3号, 52-60, 大修館書店, 東京.

1983b 「日本語動詞形態論についての覚え書き」『言語文化』創刊号, 92-101, 明治学院大学言語文化研究所.

1983c 「辞書と空範疇——日本語における痕跡」『ソフトウェア文書のための日本語処理の研究』5, 117-132, 情報処理振興事業協会, 東京.

1983d 「態を軸とした動詞分類試案」『ソフトウェア文書のための日本語処理の研究』5, 93-116, 情報処理振興事業協会, 東京.

1983e "Passive and Reciprocal Sentences in Japanese," *Papers from the Kyoto Workshop on Japanese Syntax and Semantics*, 70-74, Kyoto Circle for Japanese Linguistics.

1983f "Multiple Argument Noun Phrase and Case in Japanese and English," *Proceedings of the XIIIth International Congress of Linguists*, 497-502. (John A. Bisazza と共著)

1984a 「言い間違いの言語学的意味」『失語症研究』第4巻1号, 537-541, 日本失語症学会.

1984b "A Note on "Tough" Sentences in Japanese," 『明治学院論叢』第358-360号 英語・英米文学 第57-59号, 275-291, 明治学院大学文学会.

1984c "Reciprocal Sentences and Assume GF in Japanese," *Studies in English Philology and Linguistics in Honor of Dr. Tamotsu Matsunami*, 424-435, Shubun International, Tokyo.

1985 "Determiner PRO and the Structure of NP," *Metropolitan Linguistics* 5, 55-66, Linguistic Circle of Tokyo Metropolitan University, Tokyo.

1986 「IV. 名詞句の解釈」『ソフトウェア文書のための日本語処理の研究』, 263-288, 情報処理振興事業協会.

1987 "Nonlexical Categories in Japanese,"『言語文化』第4号, 83-97, 明治学院大学言語文化研究所.

1988a "Coordinate Structure and Symbiotic Gap,"『言語文化』第5号, 32-40, 明治学院大学言語文化研究所.

1988b 「否定──動詞・名詞の形態論との関わりをめぐって──」『ソフトウェア文書のための日本語処理の研究──9──IPAL(Basic Verbs)』情報処理振興事業協会, 東京.

1988c 「日英語比較統語論〈上〉──日本語に〈冠詞〉はあるが〈主語〉はない──」『言語』第17巻5号, 82-88, 大修館, 東京.

1988d 「日英語比較統語論〈下〉──日本語には統率範疇がない──」『言語』第17巻6号, 79-84, 大修館, 東京.

1989a 「「は, も, が」の論理形式──文文法と談話文法のインターフェイス──」『明治学院論叢』第446号 英語・英米文学 第74号, 51-75, 明治学院大学文学会.

1989b "Small Clause and the Structure of the English Noun Phrase,"『言語文化』第6号, 35-50, 明治学院大学言語文化研究所.

1990 「「の」の論理形式──「「は, が, も」の論理形式に続いて」『明治学院論叢』第467号 英語・英米文学 第78号, 69-99, 明治学院大学文学会.

1991a "Comparative Syntax of English and Japanese: Relating Unrelated Languages," *Current English Linguistics in Japan*, ed. by Heizo Nakajima, 460-506, Mouton de Gruyter, Berlin.

1991b 「日本語の受動文と相互文」『日本語のヴォイスと他動性』, 仁田義雄(編), 83-104, くろしお出版, 東京.

1992a "Proposed Revised Extended X-bar Theory—Specifier Analysis of Semi-Quantifiers and Coordinating Conjunctions—,"『成田義光教授還暦祝賀論文集』, 17-31, 英宝社, 東京.

1992b "Operator Movements in Japanese,"『明治学院論叢』第507号 英語・英米文学 第84号, 79-142, 明治学院大学文学会.

1992c 「最新チョムスキー理論の概要(1)──経済性の諸原理と合法性──」(1. 新

モデルの概要)『英語青年』第138巻5号, 228-232, 研究社, 東京.（大石正幸と共著）

1992d 「最新チョムスキー理論の概要 (2)——経済性の諸原理と合法性——」(2. S構造の消失：合法性と経済性)『英語青年』第138巻6号, 296-298, 研究社, 東京.（大石正幸と共著）

1992e 「最新チョムスキー理論の概要 (3)——経済性の諸原理と合法性——」(3. LF条件によるS構造条件の置き換え)『英語青年』第138巻7号, 341-343, 研究社, 東京.（大石正幸と共著）

1992f 「最新チョムスキー理論の概要 (4)——経済性の諸原理と合法性——」(4. 下接の条件と空範疇原理)『英語青年』第138巻8号, 420-422, 研究社, 東京.（大石正幸と共著）

1992g 「最新チョムスキー理論の概要 (5)——経済性の諸原理と合法性——」(5. 統率と束縛の消失)『英語青年』第138巻9号, 463-466, 研究社, 東京.（大石正幸と共著）

1993a "Two Additional Arguments for the Extended DP Analysis,"『明治学院論叢』第512号 英語英文学 第85号, 9-35, 明治学院大学文学会.

1993b "Wh-Movement Out of and Within the Noun Phrase,"『明治学院論叢』第529号 英語・英米文学 第87号, 25-58, 明治学院大学文学会.

1993c "The Uniform Pro Subject Analysis of Japanese Sentences," *Japanese/Korean Linguistics* 2, ed. by Patricia Clancy, 481-497, Center for the Study of Language and Information, Stanford.[1]

1993d 「ミニマリスト・プログラム：諸問題と展望 (7) 今後の展望——AGRの廃止をめぐって」『英語青年』第139巻7号, 347-349, 研究社, 東京.

1994a 「日本語はOVS言語である」『言語』第23巻3号（特集［入門］Xバー理論 言語の階層性を捉える）, 59-67, 大修館書店, 東京.

1994b 「13. ことばの多様性と普遍性」『言語学への招待』, 中島平三・外池滋生（編）, 154-167, 大修館書店, 東京.

1995a "PRO Expletive: A Case Study from Japanese Existential Sentences,"『明治学院論叢』第552号 英語英米文学 第91号, 19-58, 明治学院大学文学会.

1995b "On Scrambling—Scrambling as a Base-generated Scopal Construction—,"『言語文化』第12号, 25-63, 明治学院大学言語文化研究所.

1995c "On the Benefactive Constructions in Japanese," *Proceedings of TACL Summer Institute of Linguistics 1995*, 191-202.

---

[1] これが原題であるが, 編者の間違いで目次ではProがPROとなっている.

1995d "Japanese as an OVS Language," *Minimalism and Linguistic Theory*, ed. by Shousuke Haraguchi and Michio Funaki, 105-133, Hituzi Syobo, Tokyo.

1996a "Passive Constructions as Evidence for the Left-branching Analysis: A Consequence of the Shortest Link Requirement in Japanese,"『慶応義塾大学言語文化研究所紀要』第28号, 129-146, 慶応義塾大学言語文化研究所.

1996b "A Note on Floating Quantifier," *Metropolitan Linguistics* 16, 1-9, Linguistic Circle of Tokyo Metropolitan University, Tokyo.

1997a "On Scrambling—Scrambling as a Base-generated Scopal Construction," *Scrambling*, ed. by Shigeo Tonoike, 125-159, Kurosio, Tokyo.

1997b "Defective Paradigms and Case Theory," *Studies in English Linguistics—A Festschrift for Akira Ota on the Occasion of His Eightieth Birthday*, ed. by Masatomo Ukaji, Toshio Nakao, Masaru Kajita and Shuji Chiba, 587-597, Taishukan, Tokyo.

1998a "A Binding Asymmetry in Coordinates Structure in Japanese—Evidence for the Left-Branching Analysis—,"『平成9年度 COE 形成基礎研究費成果報告 (2)』(課題番号 08CE1001), 329-340, 神田外語大学言語科学研究科.

1998b "Attract F and Elimination of the LF Component—A Proposed I Model of Grammar—,"『平成9年度 COE 形成基礎研究費成果報告 (2)』(課題番号 08CE1001), 85-110, 神田外語大学言語科学研究科.

1998c 「第2次認知革命」『生成文法』, 田窪行則他, 97-159, 岩波書店.

1999 "Agreement as Dislocated Morphological Features," *Metropolitan Linguistics* 19, 1-21, Linguistic Circle of Tokyo Metropolitan University, Tokyo.

2000a "*Wh*-Movement, Pied-Ping and Related Matters,"『平成11年度 COE 形成基礎研究費研究成果報告 (4)』(課題番号 08CE1001), 211-227, 神田外語大学言語科学研究科.

2000b "An Operator Subject Analysis of Japanese Sentences and Noun Phrases —LF Representation of *Wa, Mo, Ga*, and *No*—," *Keio Studies in Theoretical Linguistics II*, 205-271, 慶応大学言語文化研究所.

2000c "An Operator Subject Analysis of Japanese Sentences and Noun Phrases —LF Representation of *Wa, Mo, Ga*, and *No*," *Syntactic and Functional Explorations: In Honor of Susumu Kuno*, ed. by Ken-ichi Takami, Akio Kamio and John Whitman, 207-248, Kurosio, Tokyo.

2001a "*That*-Trace Effect in the Noun Phrase and the Extended DP Analysis,"『平成 12 年度 COE 形成基礎研究費成果報告 (5)』(課題番号 08CE1001), 125-139, 神田外語大学言語科学研究科.

2001b 「英文科, 英語学, 生成文法」『英語青年』第 147 巻 1 号 (特集 英語学のこれから), 22-24, 研究社, 東京.

2002a 「上代日本語に左方 wh 移動はあったか」『言語』第 31 巻 3 号, 86-91, 大修館, 東京.

2002b 「Chomsky (2001) における 2 つの問題——「音韻部門の移動規則」と EPP 素性——」『英語青年』第 148 巻 5 号 (特集 フェイズと極小主義理論), 279-282, 研究社, 東京.

2002c "Overt Adjuncts and Covert Arguments—A Few Notes on the Structure of Japanese Sentences—,"『英文学思潮』第 75 巻, 133-152, 青山学院大学英文学会.

2003a 「上代日本語に左方 wh 移動はそれでもあったか」『言語』第 32 巻 1 号, 146-152, 大修館書店, 東京.

2003b 「英文解釈と生成文法」『英語青年』第 149 巻 4 号 (特集 英文読解と英語学), 217-219, 研究社, 東京.

2003c "Overt QR—A Case Study from English,"『英文学思潮』第 76 巻, 73-96, 青山学院大学英文学会.

2003d 「係助詞に関するいくつかの推測——文中詞と文末詞のあいだで——」*KLS* 23, 252-260, 関西言語学会.

2003e "Two Subtypes of Nouns in English and Japanese,"『慶應義塾大学言語文化研究所紀要』第 35 号, 85-103, 慶応義塾大学言語文化研究所.

2004a 「上代日本語にこれでも左方 wh 移動はあったか?」『言語』第 33 巻 8 号, 82-92, 大修館書店, 東京.

2004b 「日本語は主語も目的語も (見え) ない——比較統語論の立場からの一つの見方」『国文学 解釈と教材の研究』第 49 巻 7 号 (特集 一読簡単 文章上達術), 50-57, 学燈社, 東京.

2006 「チャモロ語, パラオ語, (上代) 日本語の WH 疑問文」『言語科学の真髄を求めて 中島平三教授還暦記念論文集』, 鈴木右文・水野佳三・高見健一 (編), 432-437, ひつじ書房, 東京.

2007 "Japanese and the Symmetry of Syntax," (Review Article: *Movement and Silence*, by Richard S. Kayne, Oxford University Press, Oxford, 2005,) *English Linguistics* 24:2, 654-683.

2008a "Chapter 1: The General Minimalist Framework," ms., University of Hawaii, Aoyama Gakuin University.

2008b	"Chapter 2: *In-Situ* Operator-Variable Construction—A Proposed Model of Inter-Planar Operator-Variable Constructions—," ms., University of Hawaii, Aoyama Gakuin University.
2008c	"Chapter 3: Merge Theory of Binding," ms., University of Hawaii, Aoyama Gakuin University.
2008d	"Chapter 4: DP Movement Analysis of Relativization," ms., University of Hawaii, Aoyama Gakuin University.
2008e	"Chapter 5: Quantifier Scope and the Japanese Clause Structure," ms., University of Hawaii, Aoyama Gakuin University.
2008f	"Chapter 6: Frozen Scope and Predication," ms., University of Hawaii, Aoyama Gakuin University.
2008g	"Chapter 7: A Left-Branching Analysis of Japanese and Multiple Argument Constructions," ms., University of Hawaii, Aoyama Gakuin University.
2008h	"Chapter 8: Overt QR—A Case Study from English," ms., University of Hawaii, Aoyama Gakuin University.
2009	「ミニマリスト・プログラム」『言語学の領域』,中島平三（編）,135-168,朝倉書店,東京.
2010a	「日英語における話題化について」『英語研究の次世代に向けて―秋元実治教授定年退職記念論文集』,吉波弘他（編）,117-130,ひつじ書房,東京.
2010b	「ことばと文法」『［入門］ことばの世界』,瀬田幸人他（編）,44-55,大修館書店,東京.
2011a	"The Inclusiveness Condition and Operator-Variable Constructions: Definite Determiner as a Variable,"『英文学思潮』第84巻,9-28,青山学院大学英文学会.
2011b	"A Sideward Movement Analysis of Sluicing: A Step toward Elimination of PF Deletion and LF Copying,"『慶応大学言語文化研究所紀要』第42号,101-126,慶応義塾大学言語文化研究所.
2012a	"Frozen Scope and Predication,"『英文学思潮』第85巻,1-27,青山学院大学英文学会.（田口和希と共著）
2012b	"Excorporation and Parametric Variation between English and Japanese," ms., Aoyama Gakuin University.
2013	"A Non-movement Analysis of Operator-Variable Constructions and Its Consequences," *Studies in English Linguistics and Literature* 23, 1-27, Japan Association of English Linguistics and Literature.
2014	「演算子-変項構造とWH疑問文」『日本語疑問文の通時的・対照言語学的

研究　研究報告書 (1)』21-48，国立国語研究所，東京．

〈高等学校教科書編著〉

1988-1993	『MILESTONE English Course 1』啓林館（成田義光他と共著）
1989-1995	『MILESTONE English Course 2』啓林館（成田義光他と共著）
1991-1993	『REVISED MILESTONE English Course 1』啓林館（金田道和他と共著）
1992-1995	『REVISED MILESTONE English Course 2』啓林館（金田道和他と共著）
1994-1997	『MILESTONE English Course 1』啓林館（金田道和他と共著）
1995-1998	『MILESTONE English Course 2』啓林館（金田道和他と共著）
1998-2003	『REVISED MILESTONE English Course 1』啓林館（島田守他と共著）
1999-2004	『REVISED MILESTONE English Course 2』啓林館（島田守他と共著）
2002-2006	『TOMORROW English Course 1』啓林館（島田守他と共著）
2003-2007	『TOMORROW English Course 2』啓林館（島田守他と共著）
2003-2006	『MILESTONE English Course 1』啓林館（島田守他と共著）
2004-2007	『MILESTONE English Course 2』啓林館（島田守他と共著）

〈高等学校準教科書・参考書編著〉

| 1995 | FOCUS『基礎からわかる DISCOVERY English Grammar』啓林館． |
| 1995 | FOCUS『基礎からわかる ディスカバリー高校総合英語』（新課程用）啓林館．（笠井貴征・遊佐典昭・佐藤徹治と共著） |

〈大学英語教科書編著・編注〉

| 1986 | 『スペースシャトル物語』成美堂．(Ride, Sally with Susan Okie (1986) *To Space & Back*, Lothrop, Lee & Shepard, New York の編注．)（斎藤宏・青木　剛と共編注．) |
| 2013 | 『英文法の総復習とワンクラス上の英作文』DTP 出版．（野村忠央・菅野悟・野村美由紀と共著） |

〈TOEIC 問題集編著〉

2006 『英語徹底耳錬！ 新 TOEIC テスト完全対応』実務教育出版．(編著，外池一子・Joseph T. Mckim と共著)
2007 『英語徹底口練！ 発音とリスニングの力を同時に高める本』実務教育出版．(今井邦彦と共著)

〈研究発表・講演〉
(※断りのないものは単独発表)

1970 年 9 月 「Performative Analysis と語法」新潟大学英文学会第 5 回大会，新潟大学．
1972a 年 5 月 "Emphatic Reflexives," 日本英文学会第 44 回大会，南山大学．
1972b 年 9 月 "Emphatic Reflexives," 新潟大学英文学会第 7 回大会，新潟大学．
1973 年 11 月 "Counter Identity Deletion in Japanese," Linguistic Society of Hawaii, A Festival on Korean and Japanese Linguistics, Hawaii.
1975 年 12 月 "Case Ordering Hypothesis," Linguistic Society of America, Winter Meeting, San Francisco.
1977 年 8 月 "On the Causative Constructions in Japanese," Linguistic Society of America, Summer Session, Special Symposium on Problems in Japanese Syntax and Semantics, University of Hawaii, Hawaii.
1979 年 12 月 "More on Intrasubjectivization," *MIT Workshop on Japanese Linguistics*, MIT, Cambridge, MA.
1981 年 5 月 「Substance-based の立場から」日本英文学会第 53 回大会シンポジウム「言語理論は何をなしうるか——音韻論からの展望」，創価大学．
1982 年 8 月 "Multiple Argument Noun Phrases and Case in Japanese and English," The XIIIth International Congress of Linguists, Tokyo. (John A. Bisazza と共著)
1983 年 7 月 「言い間違いの言語学的意味」第 7 回日本失語症研究会学術シンポジウム，日本消防会館ホール，東京．
1984 年 10 月 「日本語の Tough 構文について」第 9 回関西言語学研究会シンポジウム「Tough 構文」，神戸大学．
1985 年 10 月 「名詞句の構造と空範疇：名詞句中の AGR」第 10 回関西言語学会，同志社大学．
1989a 年 11 月 "The Proposed Revised Extended X-bar Theory," 日本英語学会，神戸大学．

1989b 年 12 月　「日本語の受動文と相互文」日本語文法談話会，京都大学．
1990 年 3 月　"Wh-Movement Within and Out of the Noun Phrase," Spring Meeting of the Linguistic Association of Great Britain, St. John's College, Cambridge University, Cambridge.
1991 年 9 月　"Uniform PRO Subject Analysis of Japanese Sentences," Southern California Workshop on Japanese/Korean Linguistics, University of California, Santa Barbara.
1992a 年 6 月　「チョムスキー理論の現状と日本語のケーススタディー」三上文法研究会，学士会館．
1992b 年 9 月　「「が」は主格にあらず」三上文法研究会，学士会館．
1992c 年 11 月　「ミニマリスト・プログラム」日本英語学会第 10 回大会ワークショップ，東京外国語大学．
1992d 年 12 月　「日本語は OVS 言語である」東京地区言語学研究会，慶応大学．
1993 年 5 月　"'That-Trace Effect' in the Noun Phrase and the Extended DP Analysis," 日本英文学会第 65 回大会，東京大学．
1994a 年 7 月　"Japanese as an OVS Language," First Numazu Linguistic Seminar, Numazu, Kanagawa.
1994b 年 7 月　"On Scrambling: Scrambling as a Base-generated Scopal Construction," Tokyo Scrambling Festival, Meiji Gakuin University, Tokyo.
1995a 年 9 月　"On the Benefactive Constructions in Japanese," TACL Summer Institute of Linguistics, Meiji Gakuin University, Tokyo.
1995b 年 11 月　"Two Ways a Language Can Be Head-final," Conference on Final Heads, Tilburg University, Tilburg.
1995c 年 11 月　"PRO Variable and Base-generated Operators," Stuttgart Round Table on Comparative Syntax, Stuttgart University, Stuttgart.
1996 年 9 月　「WH 移動と文法モデル：LF 部門の廃止」COE Workshop，白河．
1997 年 6 月　"Attract F and Elimination of the LF Component—A Proposed I Model of Grammar—," 東京地区言語学研究会，明治学院大学．
1998 年 11 月　"Uninterpretability as Feature Dislocation," COE International Workshop，神田外語大学．
1999a 年 1 月　"Wh-Movement, Pied-Piping, and Related Matters," 東京地区言語学研究会，明治学院大学．
1999b 年 2 月　"Uninterpretability as Feature Dislocation in the Lexicon: A Proposed Syntax of "Checking" and the Structure of Japanese," Korean Generative Grammar Circle, Seoul.
2001 年 11 月　"Phase and Cyclicity," 日本英語学会第 19 回大会シンポジウム

"Phase and Cyclicity" 討論者（高橋大厚・斎藤　衛・長谷川欣佑の発表に対するコメント），東京大学．
2002年10月　「"係り結び"から見えるもの──古い問題への新しい取り組み──」第27回関西言語学会シンポジウム「"係り結び"から見えるもの──古い問題への新しい取り組み──討論者（野村剛史・新里瑠美子・渡辺　明の発表に対するコメント），桃山学院大学．
2003a年6月　「完全 pro 脱落言語としての日本語の分析」日本言語学会第126回大会，青山学院大学．
2003b年12月　「日本語とはどんな言語か──日本語と英語を比較して見えてくるもの」和光大学表現学部文学科企画「日本語を考える」第2回講演会，和光大学．
2004a年6月　「チャモロ語，パラオ語，（上代）日本語の WH 疑問文」日本言語学会第128回大会，東京学芸大学．
2004b年6-7月　「生成文法と古代日本語　係り結びをめぐって」東京大学大学院総合文化研究科　言語情報科学専攻連続講演，東京大学．
2005a年6月　「QR/Scrambling と数量詞作用域と日本語の節構造」日本言語学会第130回大会，国際基督教大学．
2005b年11月　「凍結作用域と題述関係」日本言語学会第131回大会，広島大学．（田口和希と共著）
2005c年11月　「演算子 - 変項構造の元位置2平面分析」("In-Situ Operator-Variable Constructions—A Proposed Model of Inter-Planar Operator-Variable Constructions,") 日本英語学会第23回大会，九州大学．
2006年6月　「日英語の比較から見た言語理論とパラミター」専修大学「21世紀の創造的言語科学を目指して」シンポジウム「言語の普遍性と多様性を捉える」，専修大学．
2007年12月　"Banning Covert Operations—Operator-Variable Constructions in a Minimalist Framework," Tuesday Seminar, Department of Linguistics, University of Hawaii at Manoa.
2008a年2月　"General Theory of Relativization," Tuesday Seminar, Department of Linguistics, University of Hawaii at Manoa.
2008b年4月　"A Minimalist Theory of Binding," Tuesday Seminar, Department of Linguistics, University of Hawaii at Manoa.
2008c年10月　「日英語における左右の（非）対称性について」日本機能言語学会第16回秋期大会特別講演，お茶の水女子大学．
2010a年4月　"A Non-movement Analysis of Operator-Variable Constructions and Its Consequences," 日本英語学会 ELSJ 3rd International Spring Forum

2010, 青山学院大学.

2010b 年 7 月　「ミニマリスト・プログラムと日英語比較統語論」東北大学大学院文学研究科言語学研究室講演会, 東北大学.

2010c 年 11 月　「不活性条件と主要部移動の Excorporation 分析」日本言語学会第 141 回大会, 東北大学.（江頭浩樹と共著）

2012 年 11 月　「Different の内部解釈の Agree 分析と右方節点繰り上げ構造」日本英語学会第 30 回大会, 慶應義塾大学.

2013a 年 8 月　"Organization of Grammar, In-Situ Operator Variable Constructions and Elimination of PF Deletion and LF Copying (along with Many Related Things)" 日本英語英文学会第一回北海道支部大会特別講演.

2013b 年 9 月　「演算子-変項構造と WH 疑問文」「日本語疑問文の通時的・対照言語学的研究」第 1 回研究発表会, 国立国語研究所.

2013c 年 10 月　「英語の省略現象：Sluicing を中心にして」東北学院大学英語英文学研究所学術講演会, 東北学院大学.

2014a 年 3 月　「疑問詞と「か」と「も」」「日本語疑問文の通時的・対照言語学的研究」第 3 回研究発表会, 国立国語研究所.

2014b 年 3 月　「ミニマリスト・プログラムと日英語比較統語論」東京言語研究所集中講義.

2014c 年 6 月　「日英語における多重 WH 構文の扱いと島の制約」「日本語疑問文の通時的・対照言語学的研究」第 4 回研究発表会, 国立国語研究所.

2014d 年 12 月　「私の研究遍歴—The Life of a Rebel Linguist—」第 47 回青山英文学会大会講演, 青山学院大学.

2014e 年 12 月　「Chomsky 2008, 2013 年を巡って」津田塾大学言語文化研究所プロジェクト「英語の共時的および通時的研究の会」第 56 回研究会招待講演, 津田塾大学.

私の研究遍歴
—君子豹変—*

外池　滋生

1. はじめに

　私は天の邪鬼である．そのため，論文を読んで全面的に納得するということは少なく，多くの場合もっと簡潔でエレガントな分析があるのではと考えてしまう．そのような性格が仇となって，論文を読む度ごとに代案を提出したくなり，また，自分の過去の論文についても，例えば口頭発表を行い，それをもとに論文を発表するようなときにも，しばしば，何か新しいことを思いつき，元とは大分違った形になるということがよくある．自分の考えを自分で修正するという点では「君子豹変」を実行してきたと言えそうであるが，他の研究者からの指摘により自説を修正するという点ではそんなに威張れたものでもない．ともあれ，そのような事情で，決定版というものが生まれず，沢山の論文を書いたけれどもまとまった著作がない．
　それではいけないと思い，2007年から2008年にかけて在外研究でハワイ大にいたときには2008a-hを一冊の本にしようと思って書きためたが，まだ出版までには行っていない．この論文集が出版されるころまでには何とか目鼻を付けたいと思っている．[1]

---

　* まず，私の退職を記念して，論文集を編むことを計画して頂いた発起人および編集委員の皆様方，そして，快く寄稿してくださった友人，同僚，研究仲間の皆さんに心よりの感謝を表明したいと思います．この企画を先頭に立って進めてくださった編集委員から，私からも何か書くようにという依頼があり，当初は2007-8年の在外研究中に書きました一連の論文の一つ 2008c の "Merge Theory of Binding" を載せてはどうかという話もありました．しかし，これは英語で書いたものでもあり，また長さの問題もありましたので，代わりに，これまでの研究を振り返り，いくらかなりとも今後に意味を持つだろうと思う私の到達点をまとめておくことにしました．
　[1] それが間に合わなくとも，この論文集が刊行されるまでには，これまでに書いてきた論文で幾らかなりとも今後に影響を残すであろうと思うものについて，2008a-h も含めて，ネット上で検索，閲覧できる形にする予定であるので，本拙稿をお読み頂く際にも参照頂ければ幸

この論文集を機に，これまで，特に過去四半世紀の私の研究の軌跡を振り返っておこうと思う．この間，大体次に示す2つの大きな目標を目指してきたように思う．

(1) a. 日英語鏡像仮説
　　b. 極小主義の精緻化（非極小主義的残滓の除去）

(1a) は 1980 年代後半に到達した仮説の追求であり，(1b) は 1990 年代に入って始まった極小主義から非極小主義的な残滓を取り除くということである．この2つの目標は私の研究の中では互いに支え合って今日まで至っている．(1a) は例えば (2) の例文で比較すると日本語と英語の構造は図式的には (3) のような鏡像関係にあるとする仮説である．

(2) a. (I didn't know) that John criticized Mary
　　b. 花子を太郎が批判したの（を知らなかった）
(3) a. 英語　　　　　　　　　　b. 日本語

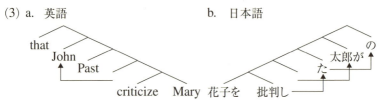

(3a) では John が TP 指定部に移動するのに対して，(3b) では V は v*, T を経由して C まで移動し，その結果 TP 指定部まで主語が移動したとしても (2b) の語順になる．さらに日本語には Scrambling があるため，「太郎が花子を批判した」などの語順も可能になる．このような分析の根拠は後述する．

2. 極小主義の精緻化

　次に列挙するものは現在の極小主義の枠組みに残っているが非極小主義の残滓として除去すべきものであると考えるものである．[2]

いである．
　[2] この他に 1993d では極小主義の当初まだ残っていた Agr を廃止すべきこと，そして 1998b では，部門としての LF は不要であることを指摘した．その指摘に直接影響を受けた訳ではないが，同様の考慮から Chomsky 自身がその後廃止したので，ここでは直接取り扱わないことにする．

(4) a. 非顕在的移動と音声形式部門での消去
　　b. 束縛条件と指示指標
　　c. 演算子−変項構造のための移動
　　d. 継承と主要部移動（拡大条件違反）

2.1. 非顕在的移動と音声形式部門での消去の除去

　May (1977) 以来，音声に影響を与えず，意味構造だけを変化させる非顕在的移動が存在すると広く想定されている．しかし普遍文法理論にとって非顕在的移動は，理論を複雑化するものであり，ないに越したことはない．2003c 以来，移動はすべて顕在的であるとする仮説を提案してきた．

(5)　顕在的統語論仮説（Overt Syntax Hypothesis: OSH）
　　音声（= 形態音韻論的素性）を伴わない移動（= 内部併合）はいかなる形でも存在しない．

移動（= 内部併合）に限るのは，通常の併合（= 外部併合）では，音形を持たない要素の併合を想定する必要があると考えられるからである．
　OSH が成立する普遍文法理論の方が遥かに簡潔な理論であるにも拘らず，非顕在的移動が広く想定されているのはその必要性を示す事実があると考えられているからであるが，顕在的移動を使わなくとも処理することができることを示せば，そのような根拠は崩れる．
　これまでの理論の進展のなかで非顕在的移動を実行する方法は幾つかあった．まず，May (1985) に代表されるような当初の研究は逆 Y 字モデルと呼ばれ，ある時点で音声と意味とが分かれて，LF 部門では意味に対する操作しか行わないということになっていた．しかし，OSH が正しければ LF 部門そのものが存在し得ない．
　その後，現在では LF 部門そのものは廃止されたが，非顕在的移動は移動のコピー理論（Copy Theory of Movement）の一部として残っている．この理論では要素が移動されるとき，それが持つすべての素性のコピーが全体として，移動される位置において併合（Merge）され，低い位置にあるコピーにおいてその音形が消去されると顕在的な移動になり，高い位置のコピーの音形が消去されると非顕在的移動になるというものである．OSH が正しければ，移動のコピー理論はそのままの形では維持できないことになる．そこで，通常の移動のコピー理論に代わって，下の移動の部分コピー理論を提案する．

(6) 移動の部分コピー理論 (Partial Copy Theory of Movement)
　　a. 移動は，そして移動のみが，意味のコピーを残せる．
　　b. 移動は音のコピーは残せない．
　　c. 音を削除する操作は存在しない．

この理論の下では要素 α の移動した結果は，(7) に示す２つの場合しかないことを意味する．/α/ は α の音，{α} は α の意味を表す．

(7) a. /α/ ... {α}　　　音だけの移動
　　b. /α/ {α}$_1$ ... {α}$_2$　音と意味の移動

(7a) では α の音だけが移動されている．(7b) は {α}$_1$ が {α}$_2$ と同一である場合もあるが，{α}$_2$ が {α}$_1$ の一部のコピーであるという可能性もある．これは後述の同一指示の扱いに大きな意味を持つ．これをまとめて UG の原理の一つとして移動の顕在性条件があると想定しておく．

(8) 移動の顕在性条件 (Overtness Condition on Movement: OCM)
　　要素の移動には音という乗り物が必要である．

問題は，OCM（またはその結果として OSH）を維持することができるかどうかである．Heim and Kratzer (1998) が簡潔にまとめているが，非顕在的操作の代表である数量詞繰り上げ (Quantifier Raising: QR) の必要性の証拠とされるのは次の例に見られる数量詞解釈の多義性 (9a)，束縛代名詞の解釈 (9b)，そして先行詞包含削除 (ACD) (9c) の３つの現象が主なものである．

(9) a. Somebody loves everybody.
　　b. Every boy says that Mary talked to him.
　　c. Somebody read every book that Bill did.

(9b) には every boy と him との同一指示の扱いが関与し，(9c) には関係節の分析が関与しているので，それぞれが関係したところで扱うこととして，ここでは (9a) の数量詞作用域の多義性が (8) の下で処理できることを示す．(9a) の派生で (10a) の v*P が形成された段階で，everybody を全体の構造に右方付加すると (10b) の構造が得られる．

(10)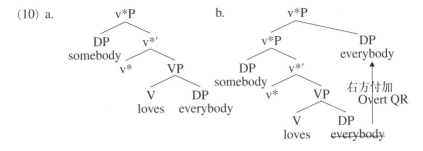

2つの v*P 構造では somebody と everybody の線形順序は同じであるが，c 統御関係は逆転している．これがそれぞれの some>every, every>some の作用域解釈を捉えている．ここで用いている右方付加の移動は音を伴う移動であるので OSH に抵触しない．このことから非顕在的移動の必要性を示す中心的な根拠となっている英語における数量詞の作用域の多義性は，非顕在的操作を想定しなくても記述できることが分かる．(10a, b) ではさらに引き続いて主語の somebody が TP 指定部に移動するが，これは後述するように音だけの移動であると主張する．この右方付加を Overt QR と呼ぶことにする．[3]

この説明は，英語の補部の方向と付加の方向が同じく右であるという事実に依存している．補部の方向が右側であることは論を俟たない．付加が右方向であることも関係節の位置，外置（Extraposition）の方向などで明らかである．このことから (10) で分かるように，例えば目的語は主語に c 統御されていることもあるが，主語を c 統御する可能性もある．これにより OSH が維持できれば，あり得る文法の種類が大幅に減少し，文法理論を大幅に簡素化でき，極小主義をより極小化できることになる．

2.2. 束縛条件と指示指標の除去

極小主義以前は名詞句，より厳密には決定詞句（DP）の指示関係については，束縛条件が次のような事実を捉えていた．

---

[3] 右方付加による作用域の多義性の扱いは次のような例にも有効である．
  (i) I will force you to marry no one.   (Klima (1964), Kayne (1998))
  (ii) She has requested that they read only *Aspects*.   (Kayne (1998))
また，(iii) の例は，音だけの A 移動に意味がただ乗り（Piggy Backing）するというメカニズムにより説明できる．詳しくは 2003c 参照．
  (iii) A hippogryph is likely to be apprehended.   (May (1985))

(11) a　Mary$_i$ hates herself$_i$/*her$_i$
　　 b.　Mary$_i$ thinks that Bill hates her$_i$/*herself$_i$
　　 c.　*She$_i$ thinks that Bill hates Mary$_i$

　これには大きく分けて2つの問題がある．一つは束縛条件が本当に必要であるかという問題で，それに代わるより簡潔な記述が可能であれば束縛条件も除去すべきである．もう一つは，束縛条件で使われている指示指標というものが言語において実在するかという問題である．指示指標は記述的には便利なものであるが，これに概念的必然性があるかは甚だ疑わしい．
　そのような配慮もあって Hornstein (2001) は再帰代名詞と PRO については移動により説明するということを提案し，人称代名詞についても，移動に絡めて処理することを提案した．2008c ではこれをさらに発展させて，次の2点にまとめられる同一指示の理論を提案した．

(12) a.　すべての DP は音形に拘らず定決定詞 D を主要部とする．
　　 b.　DP の指示機能はその主要部の定決定詞のみが担う
　　 c.　DP が移動されるとその後にはその主要部決定詞 D のコピーが残る．

　これを (11) の例にあてはめると，Mary は音声的には顕在化していないが主要部の定決定詞 the を持っていて，(11a, b) の例を少し簡略化すると (13a)，(14a) の構造から派生される (John に付随する定決定詞は省略してある)．

(13) a.　[$_{v*P}$ v*[+refl] [$_{VP}$ hates [the Mary's self]]
　　 b.　[$_{v*P}$ the Mary v*[+refl] [$_{VP}$ hates [the's self]]
(14) a.　[$_{v*P}$ v* [$_{VP}$ thinks [$_{CP}$ that John hates [the Mary]]]
　　 b.　[$_{v*P}$ v* [$_{VP}$ thinks [$_{CP}$ that John hates [the]]] the Mary
　　 c.　[$_{v*P}$ the Mary v* [$_{VP}$ thinks [$_{CP}$ that John hates [the]]]

　(13a) の v* は再帰性を表す [+refl] という素性を持っており，この素性を持つ v* は探索子となって，その c 統御領域に，その主語の位置に併合すべき DP を探して，これを内部併合するという任務を負っている．この場合移動できるのは DP の the Mary であるから，これを主語の位置に内部併合すると後には主要部の the のコピーが残され (13b) の構造が得られる．the's は 's で示すようにその位置で与えられた属格と，Mary との一致で，φ素性 [3rd, Singular, Feminine] を持っていて，そのため the's self は herself という形

で実現される．(13b) の 2 つの the は LF にはそのまま残り，この同一性が Mary と her の同一指示を捉える．[4]

(14a) の場合は，Nunes (2001) の側方移動 (Sideward Movement) を拡大して，従属節にある the Mary を直接下線部に移動することは（位相を越えるため）できないので，一旦 (14b) に示すように，定決定詞のコピーを残して取り出しておいたものを，後に主節の主語の位置に併合すると (14c) が得られる．残された定決定詞 the はそれに与えられている対格と Mary との一致で獲得した ϕ 素性により，her として実現される．ここでも 2 つの the は同じ the のコピーであるから，her と Mary の同一指示は定決定詞の同一性によって捉えられる．(13)，(14) いずれの場合にも the が代名詞に置き換えられるのは，the が付与されている格は解釈不能な素性で，代名詞という音形に置き換えられることにより，格素性が除去されるものと仮定している．

束縛条件 C の違反である (11c) は，併合はもとの構造を大きくしなければならないという拡大条件 (Extension Condition) により，DP を高い位置から低い位置に移動しようがないため，派生の方法がないという事情により自動的に排除される．これにより同一指示を定決定詞の同一性に還元するという最善の (optimal) 形で，束縛条件を除去することができるのである．

2.3. 省略の問題

非顕在的移動も音声的削除もないとなれば，問題になるのがいわゆる省略と呼ばれる現象である．そして意味の同一性は，代名詞などの同一指示の場合同様，移動により残される意味のコピーの同一性に還元するのが最も簡潔な方法である．そうなれば次の (15a) の代名詞の例と (16a) の動詞句削除はいずれも側方移動により処理するのが統一的な扱いということになる．

(15) a. I will talk to the professor if I see him.
    b. to   if I see the professor
                                             the professor の側方移動→
    c. to the professor   if I see {the}
    d. I will talk to the professor, if I see {the}

---

[4] 3 人称男性の場合は hisself, theirselves が形態論的規則により himself, themselves として実現すると想定する．

(16) a. I will talk to the professor if I can.
　　 b. v*　　　　　　　　　　if I can [talk to the professor]
　　　　　　　　　　　　　　　　　　　　　VPの側方移動→
　　 c. v* talk to the professor　　if I can {talk to the professor}
　　 d. I will talk to the professor if I can {talk to the professor}

　(15a) の派生で，the professor は (15b) に示すように従属節中にあり，それが the のコピー {the} を残して主節の to の目的語の位置に側方移動して (15c) が得られ，最終的には (15d) が得られるが，この {the} は him という音形に置き換えられ，(15a) の形になる．
　一方 (16a) の場合は，(16b) で主節の v* が補部の VP を必要としているが，そのために従属節の VP を側方移動することができ，(16c) が得られる．他に必要な操作を加えれば，ここから (16d) を導くことができる．代名詞の場合と異なり，{talk to the professor} には除去すべき解釈不能な素性はないので，音形を与える必要はない．したがって，発音上は (16a) となるが，(16d) がその LF 表示になり，2 つの talk to the professor はコピー同士であるので意味的な同一性はこれにより保証される．(残されたコピーは {talk to the} だけの可能性もある．)
　(17a) の空所化 (Gapping)，(17b) の Sluicing，(17c) の右方節点繰り上げ (Right Node Raising) に見られる省略現象すべてに等位接続が関係している．

(17) a. John ordered beer, and Mary wine.
　　 b. John ordered something, but I forgot what.
　　 c. John loves but Mary hates beer.

このような「省略」現象を扱うためには，等位接続される複数の構成素の一部が共有されている下のような構造を想定することを提案してきた．

(18) a. John order beer　　→ John order beer, and Mary {order} wine
　　　　Mary　　wine
　　 b. John ordered something　→ John ordered something (but
　　　　　　　　　　　what　　　　　I forgot) {John ordered} what
　　 c. John loves beer.　→ John loves {beer} but Mary hates beer
　　　　Mary hates

(18a) は 2 つの v*P が動詞 order を，(18b) では TP が John ordered に相当

する部分を，そして，(18c) では，v*P が目的語の beer を共有している．このままでは線形化できないので，重なった構造を分離して and/but などで等位接続することによって矢印の右側が得られるが，そのときに共有された部分には音形は1つしかないので，音を持たない方は意味のコピー {order}, {John ordered}, {beer} を持ち，これらが意味の同一性を保証している．

2.4. 演算子-変項構造のための移動の除去と包含性条件違反の回避

数量詞の作用域の多義性については非顕在的移動を用いなくても記述できることは上で見た．しかし，数量詞表現は演算子-変項構造 (Operator-Variable Construction) を構成していて，例えば (19a, b) は (19c) のような演算子-変項構造として捉えられるが，その場合の変項をどう導くかが問題である．

(19) a. Every student was there.
    b. All the students were there.
    c. ∀x, x=student, x was there

伝統的な答は QR により残された痕跡を変項として扱うというものであった．さらに Fox (2002) は移動のコピー理論に基づき，QR により (20a) を作り，これに変項 x を加え，2番目の数量詞を定冠詞に変える痕跡転換 (Trace Conversion) と呼ばれる操作により，(21a) を導くという提案をしている．

(20) a. every student [every student was there]
    b. all the students [all the students were there]
(21) a. every student x [the student x was there]
    b. all the students x [the the students x were there]

確かに (19a) は (20a) に見られる演算子と変項の関係をうまく捉えているが，いくつかの深刻な問題がある．変項 x を加えることと数量詞 every/all を the に置き換えることは，派生の途中で新たなものを導入してはならないという包含性条件 (Inclusiveness Condition) に真っ向から違反している．そして，(21b) は2つの the を含んでいて，(19c) に対応する適格な表示とは呼べない．

しかし，問題の解決の手がかりは実は (20b) である．ここには演算子 all と制限子 students に加えて，the が存在している．この the が演算子と組み合わされると変項として働くとすれば，(20b) のままで，演算子-変項構造が元

位置で成り立っていることになる．問題は the のない (20a) であるが，2.2 節ですべての DP が定決定詞を含んでいると仮定した．その仮定が正しければ，(20a, b) は音形を持たない定決定詞 {the} を含んでいることになる．

(22) a. every {the} student was there=every x student was there
b. all the students were there=all x students were there

この定決定詞変項分析を採用すれば，演算子 - 変項構造を作り出すための QR も要らなければ，包含性条件に違反して x や the を導入したりする必要もない．演算子 - 変項構造を構成する要素はすべて元位置に存在しているのである．

こうすると，積み残しにしてきた (23a) として再録する (9b) の問題も解決する．every boy は (23b) に示すように to の目的語として出発する．

(23) a. Every boy says that Mary talked to him
b. [___ v* say [that Mary talked to every {the} boy]]
c. [every {the} boy v* say [that Mary talked to {the}]]
d. every x boy v* says that Mary talked to x

その every {the} boy を側方移動により主節の主語の位置に移動するとき (23c) に示すように，元の位置には定決定詞のコピーが残される．この定決定詞は対格を担っており，boy との一致により獲得した ϕ 素性から，him という代名詞として実現される．他方 (23c) における 2 つの the は同じもののコピーであり，かつ every と結びついているので，(23d) のように同じものを指す変項として解釈される．[5]

2.5. 継承と拡大条件違反の除去

Chomsky (2008) 以降の位相理論 (Phase Theory) では，派生に関わる素性はすべて C と v* の位相主要部 (phase head) にあり，そこから，その補部の T と V に継承され，それによって A′ 移動，A 移動，主要部移動が駆動されるとされている．このうち (24) では，継承と，目的語／主語の A 移動と，

---

[5] この分析では (8a) の v*P の LF は次の 2 つの構造を持つものと分析される．
(i) a. [$_{v*P}$ some-{the}-body [$_{VP}$ loves every-{the}-body]]
b. [$_{v*P}$ [$_{v*P}$ some-{the}-body [$_{VP}$ loves {the}]] everybody]
(ib) が Overt QR を受けた構造で，変項の {the} は θ 位置に残って，右方付加された演算子との間で演算子 - 変項構造を構成している．

find の v* への,そして did の C への主要部移動を示してある.

(24) a. Did they find the picture?

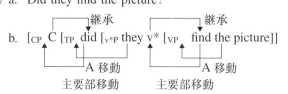

b. [CP C [TP did [v*P they v* [VP find the picture]]]

しかし,これには3つの問題がある.まず,継承は明らかに要素を繰り下げる操作で,位相理論以前には必要なかったものである.さらに主語と目的語のA移動,そしてVとCの主要部移動はいずれも,移動はそれが適用する全構造を拡大しなければならないという拡大条件に抵触している.A移動が適用する段階では既にv*′, C′ が形成されていて,これを拡大する形での移動になっていない.また主要部移動はv*, C への付加であるから,やはりv*′, C′ を拡大していない.

拡大条件は位相内部の操作には該当しないから問題ないという考えがあるようであるが,しかし,そのためには,位相内部を除くという趣旨の規定(stipulation)が必要になるという問題が生じるだけでなく,位相内部であれば繰り下げが起こっても良いことになるが,そのような現象は(継承を除いては)実際には観察されない.そもそも位相主要部に派生を駆動するもの,特に φ 素性があるとするのは,V と目的語,T と主語との間の φ 素性の一致が起こると,同時にそれぞれに対格と主格が与えられてしまい,その結果これらの要素は解釈不能な素性を持たなくなるので,WH 移動などのその後の移動を受けることができなくなるという不活性条件(Inactivity Condition)をかいくぐるためであるが,不活性条件に抵触せず,かつ拡大条件を遵守する方法がある.

それは英語では V, v*, T, C は順次併合されるのではなく, v*-V, C-T という語彙複合体として辞書から取り出され,その複合体から v*, C が転出(Excorporation)すると仮定することである.(24a)の例で示すと次のようになる.

(25) a. [VP v*-find the picture]　　　　　(一致と格付与)転出と併合→
　　　b. [v*′ v*-/find/ [VP {find} the picture]]　　　　　　　　　　主語の併合→
　　　c. [v*P they v*-/find/ [VP {find} the picture]]
　　　　　　　　　　　　　　　　　　Q-did との併合(Q=疑問の C) →
　　　d. [T′ Q-did [v*P they ...]]　　　　主語の移動,一致と主格付与→

e. [$_{TP}$ /they/Q-did [$_{v*P}$ {they} v*-/find/ ...]]　　Q の転出と併合→
f. [$_{CP}$ Q-/did/ [$_{TP}$ /they/ {did} [$_{v*P}$ {they} ...]]]
g. PF: did they find the picture
h. LF: [$_{CP}$ Q [$_{TP}$ did [$_{v*P}$ they v* [$_{VP}$ find the picture]]]]

　まず，一致と格付与は，少なくとも英語では併合のもとで自動的に生じると仮定する．そして，φ素性は v*，C ではなく，V, T が持っていると仮定する．そうすると v*-find と the picture の併合で (25a) が得られるが，この段階で find と the picture の間でφ素性の一致と格付与が成り立つことになる．これにより，v* から V への継承が不要になるばかりでなく，拡大条件違反の目的語の移動も必要なくなる．次に v* は VP を補部として取らなければならない性質を持っているので，転出をして，元の VP と併合されなければならない．しかし，v* はそれ自体としては音形をもたないので，移動操作の一種である転出によって単独で取り出すことは (8) の OCM に違反する．
　しかし，v*-find という複合体には find の音形 /find/ があるので，これを伴えば取り出しが可能になる．後には find の意味 {find} が残る．これが (25b) が表していることである．このように捉えると主要部移動という操作そのものは存在せず，v* の転出に V の音形が随伴するという現象であるということになる．これにより主要部移動が抱えていた理論的な問題はすべて解消する．
　さらに主語の併合 (25c)，C-T の複合体との併合で，(25d) が得られる．(... の部分は VP が転送されたことを表している.) 時制 did は they との間でφ素性の一致と格付与を起こさなければならないが，一致と格付与は併合の下で（のみ）生じるとすれば，they は (25e) に示すように指定部に移動しなければならない．この A 移動は T' において適用して，TP を作るから，拡大条件を遵守している．更に C は TP と併合されなければならない．Q は音形を持たないので単独では転出できないが，did の音形 /did/ を伴えば移動でき，その際に did の意味 {did} が後に残される．これが見かけ上の主要部移動であるが，拡大条件を遵守している．その結果が (25f) であるが，これから音形を持つものだけを引きはがせば (25g) の PF が得られ，その後には (25h) の LF が残る．これにより (25a) の音と意味とが関係づけられたことになる．
　これで節構造の派生にあった非極小主義的な「欠陥」はすべて解決されたが，不活性条件回避の問題が残っている．つまり，v* と C が探索子となって WH 移動を行うときに目標子が一致と格付与を受けていてはならないという点であ

る．この問題も語彙複合と転出に基づく枠組みでは解決されている．(25) の派生で，the picture の位置に which picture がある状況を考えてみよう．v*-find と which picture が併合された段階で，find は which picture と一致し，格を与えるが，同時に v* もそこに存在するので，探索子として WH 要素を探すことができると仮定しよう．そうすれば 2 つの探索子，V と v* は同時に目標子を探し，which picture を見つける．このときにはまだ一致と格付与は行われていないから，which picture は活性的であり，v* による探索は首尾よく実行される．WH 移動は v* が転出してからでないとできないけれども，転出したあとも v* と which picture の間の探索子－目標子の関係が維持されるとすれば，何も問題が生じない．これを節構造の転出理論（Excorporation Theory）と呼ぶことにする．[6]

2.6. 関係節

指示指標とともに束縛条件を除去したことから，関係節の分析にはほぼ一つの可能性しか残らない．決定詞句の同一指示を移動によって生じる決定詞 the のコピーの同一性に還元するなら，次の (26a) の例で，like の目的語の the picture of himself と，発音上現れてはいない painted の目的語とが同一指示的であるという事実を捉えるには 2 つの位置を移動により関係づけるしかない．具体的には次のような派生を想定するのが理にかなっている．

(26) a. Mary likes the picture of himself which John painted
    b. [$_{CP}$ C [$_{TP}$ John painted the picture of himself]]

                                                          WH 移動→
    c. [$_{CP}$ the /picture of himself/ C [$_{TP}$ John painted {the picture of himself}]]   DP 摘出→
    d. [$_{CP}$ the C [$_{TP}$ John painted {the picture of himself}]] [$_{DP}$ the /picture of himself/]
       like   CP 付加→
    e. [$_{DP}$ [$_{DP}$ the /picture of himself/] [$_{CP}$ the C [$_{TP}$ John painted {the picture of himself}]]]
       like   併合→

---

[6] この分析を思いついたのは 2009 を執筆していたハワイ大学在外研究中（2007-2008）であったが，ほぼ同時期に Shimada (2007) が同様の問題意識に立って同様の転出による扱いを提案していたことを 2010c の発表の折に斎藤衛氏 (p.c.) に教えて頂いた．

f. [$_{VP}$ like [$_{DP}$ [$_{DP}$ the$_3$ /picture of himself/] [$_{CP}$ the$_2$ C [$_{TP}$ John painted {the$_1$ picture of himself}]]]]

(26b) が関係節 CP である．関係節を導く C は DP を探してそれを自らの指定部に取り出す使命を持っている．元の位置には音形のないコピーが残る ((26c) 参照)．他に選択しておいた like がその補部を必要としているので，それを (26c) の指定部から側方移動で取り出すと，一旦 (27d) の3つの統語対象物ができる．関係節を導く C は，そこから DP が取り出されると，その DP に付加するという使命も持っていると仮定する ((26e) 参照)．その付加が終わったあとで，DP が like と併合されると (26f) が得られ，後は通常の派生が続く．(26f) には the$_1$, the$_2$, the$_3$ という3つの the があるがいずれも同じ the のコピーである．the$_1$ と the$_3$ が2つの目的語の同一指示を保証している．代名詞化の場合と違って the$_1$ が音形を欠いているのは (,) それが持っていた対格は WH 移動の際に the$_2$ が持っていて，the$_1$ には残っていないために，音形によって取って代わる必要がないからである．他方 the$_2$ が持ち去った対格は，DP 取り出しの際には the$_3$ には引き継がれず，削除されるか，そのまま the$_2$ に残されると仮定する．the$_2$ に残っている場合はその格を除去するため which という音形によって取って代わられる．

これをまとめると関係節化の現象は (27) に図示するように (i) 関係詞化の対象となる DP (またはそれを含むより大きい例えば PP のような構成素) の CP 指定部への取り出し (WH 移動＝述部形成 (Predicate Formation))，(ii) 何らかのθ位置への併合のための側方移動による DP の取り出し (DP 摘出)，そして (iii) その DP への関係節の右方付加 (CP 付加) の3つの操作の組み合わせにより生じるということである (詳しくは未刊であるが 2008d 参照)．

(27)

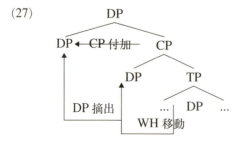

これで，先行詞内在削除の例 (9c) を非顕在的操作を使わずに説明する準備がすべて整ったことになる．(28a) として再録した (9c) は (28b) の2つの

統語構造から出発する．

(28) a. Somebody read every book that Bill did.
   b. [$_{CP}$ that [$_{TP}$ Bill did [$_{VP}$ read every {the} book]]]
      v*   VP の側方移動 + 主語の併合→
   c. [$_{CP}$ that [$_{TP}$ Bill did [$_{VP}$ {read the}]]]
      [$_{v*P}$ somebody v* [$_{VP}$ read every {the} book]]   Overt QR（摘出）→
   d. [$_{CP}$ that [$_{TP}$ Bill did [$_{VP}$ {read the}]]]
      [$_{v*P}$ somebody v* [$_{VP}$ read {the}]]
      [$_{DP}$ every {the} book]   CP 付加→
   e. [$_{DP}$ [$_{DP}$ every {the} book] [$_{CP}$ that [$_{TP}$ Bill did [$_{VP}$ {read the}]]]]
      [$_{v*P}$ somebody v* [$_{VP}$ read {the}]]   Overt QR（付加）→
   f. [[$_{v*P}$ somebody v* [$_{VP}$ read {the}]] [$_{DP}$ [$_{DP}$ every {the} book] [$_{CP}$ that [$_{TP}$ Bill did [$_{VP}$ {read the}]]]]]

(28b) において v* の補部として VP を側方移動すると (28c) が得られるが，このとき目的語の DP のコピーとしては {the} しか残っていないと仮定する．(28c) の CP は関係節で先行詞が取り出されたときと同じ形をしているので，この形で先行詞の DP の every {the} book に付加できるところであるが，(28c) の v*P 内の every {the} book に付加するのは拡大条件に違反する．しかし，この DP は数量詞を含んでいるので Overt QR の適用対象となりうる．Overt QR は付加操作であるが，付加の前に一旦要素を取り出すことになる．それが (28d) に示した段階で，CP はこの DP に拡大条件に違反することなく付加できる．できあがった (28e) の DP は Overt QR の適用途中であったのでそのまま v*P に付加されると (28f) になる．ここにおいて every は some を c 統御している．これにより，(8c) のような ACD の例では関係節を担う目的語の方が主語よりも広い作用域を取ることが自動的に説明される．

3. 日英語鏡像仮説

(3) の日英語鏡像仮説は大方の日本語研究者の想定と異なる点であるが，数量詞作用域の多義性と WH 移動の方向性という 2 つの根拠に基づく．

3.1. 数量詞作用域と節構造

2.1 節で英語の数量詞作用域の多義性が，顕在的移動によって捉えること

ができることを見たが，日本語でも同様のことができる．ただし，日本語ではScrambling が関係していることによって少し複雑になっている．

(29) a. Somebody loves everybody. (=(9a))
b. 誰かがどの人も愛している
c. どの人も誰かが愛している

英語の (29a) が ∃>∀ の解釈と ∀>∃ の解釈の間で多義的であるのに対して，日本語では (29b) は ∃>∀ の解釈の解釈しかない．そして，(29c) は ∃>∀ の解釈と ∀>∃ の解釈の間で多義的である（Kuroda (1970), Kuno (1973), Hoji (1985) 他参照）．この事実に対して QR を想定しての説明は以下の如くである．まず，(29b) が基本語順で，その構造では主語が目的語を c 統御しているのに対して，(29c) の語順は目的語を主語の前に移動する Scrambling によるものである．日本語には硬直性条件 (Rigidity Condition)（Hoji (1985)）というものが働いていて，基本語順の (29b) に対する QR の適用においては，主語と目的語の c 統御関係を変えることはできないのに対して，Scrambling の適用を受けている (29c) では，主語と目的語の c 統御関係は逆転しているので，QR の適用においても，どちらの c 統御関係が生じてもよい．そのため (29b) が一義的で，(29b) は多義的であるというものである．

これには二重の問題がある．一つは，非顕在的操作の問題である．(10) で示したように非顕在的移動を用いずとも (9a) のような英語の例における作用域の多義性を捉えることができるのであるから，日本語で QR が必要であるという独立の根拠が必要である．さらに深刻な問題は，日本語にのみあてはまる硬直性条件の問題である．硬直性条件は明らかに英語では成り立たない．そうすると日本語を習得中の子供にとって日本語に硬直性条件が成り立っているということを示す肯定的証拠がないので，日本語は習得不可能な言語であるということを主張することになる．(29b) が一義的で，(29c) が多義的であるという事実は子供にとって直接観察不可能である．

さて (10) で英語の数量詞作用域の多義性は顕在的な右方移動の Overt QR によって処理できることを見た．これは英語では補部の位置も，付加の位置も共に文末であるという事実に決定的に依存していた．つまり，文末の位置は，通常目的語がそうであるように，文中の最も低い位置であるが，それが右方付加されると同じ文末でも，他より高い位置を占めることができるため，c 統御関係が逆転して，作用域の多義性が生じるというものであった．(3) に示したように日本語が左枝分かれ構造をしており，その結果補部は左端の文頭にある

と仮定すれば，関係節の方向，Scrambling の方向からして，付加も文頭方向であることになり，(10) の分析が日本語でもそのまま使えることになる．以下の v*P 構造を比較してみよう（V-v* 移動は省略してある）．

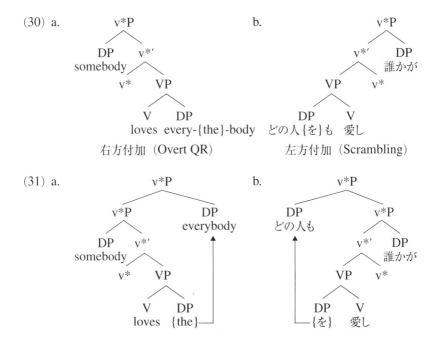

(30a) は英語の v*P 構造，(30b) は日本語の v*P 構造である．後に見るように，日本語では V は v*，T を経由して，C まで移動するため，実際の語順は「どの人も誰かが愛している」となる．これらの構造において主語は目的語を c 統御しているから，∃>∀ の作用域解釈があることが捉えられる．(31) では，英語では右方付加 (=Overt QR) が，日本語では左方付加 (=Scrambling) が適用していて，目的語が主語を c 統御する位置まで繰り上がっている．これにより ∀>∃ の作用域解釈があることが捉えられる．この移動が語順を変えていないことが (29a) と (29c) の作用域解釈の多義性を捉えている．

英語では主語は右方付加を受けることができない（つまり目に見える Scrambling がない）から，これ以上のことは起きないが，日本語では文中の要素を目に見える形で文頭に移動することができる．これを (30b) の主語に適用すると (32) が得られる．

(32)
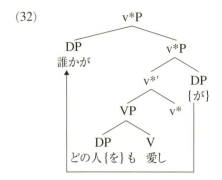

(32) では，主語が目的語を c 統御する関係しかなく，∃>∀ の解釈しかないことが捉えられる．(31b)，(32) の {が}，{を} は Scrambling の結果残された音のない格助詞のコピーであり，このように音のない場合も，「が」，「を」と発音されている場合も，定決定詞変項分析から，格助詞が決定詞として変項の役割を果たしていることになる．また，格助詞が脱落しているとされる場合や，ゼロ代名詞があるとされる場合もすべて，音形のない格助詞が定決定詞として，指示機能を担っていることになる．

この分析では QR のような非顕在的移動も，また硬直性条件などという根拠のない規定も必要とせず，(29a) と (29c) の多義性を同じ付加のメカニズムを用いて説明ができ，また (29b) の一義性という日本語にだけ見られる現象は主語を動かす Scrambling が日本語にはあるが，英語にはないという両言語に独立に観察される相違に帰すことができた．[7]

演算子−変項構造について定決定詞変項分析を採用しているが，日本語では，「誰かが」では，「誰」が制限子，「か」が存在数量詞，そして，格助詞が定決定詞であって，これが変項の働きをしているとすれば英語の場合と並行的に扱うことができる．「どの人も」では定決定詞が見当たらないが，空の対格格助詞 {を} が含まれていて，これが変項として働いていると考える．

このようなエレガントな分析は日本語が (3)，(30) に示すように左枝分かれの構造をしていると想定して初めて可能となる．逆に言えば日本語における数量詞作用域の多義性の事実は (3) の構造を支持する証拠となるのである．[8]

---

[7] この相違はさらに，日本語は格助詞により格関係が明示的であるのに対して，英語では代名詞を除いて格関係が不透明であるという相違に帰すことができる．

[8] 日本語の基本語順が SOV であるとする立場には (1) コーパスにおける語順の中で，SOV の頻度が一番高いことと (2) SOV と OSV の語順の処理時間を比較すると，SOV の処

3.2. WH 移動

(3) の構造が正しければ，日本語では指定部は右側にあることになる．既に (30) で主語は v*P の右端にある指定部を占めていると想定している．主語の他に指定部の位置を示すのは WH 移動である．英語では WH 移動が左方移動であることで指定部が左側にあることは明らかであるが，日本語ではいわゆる疑問詞は文中に留まることができるため，顕在的な WH 移動はないと考えられてきた (Huang (1982), Nishigauchi (1990) 参照).

しかし，次の日本語と英語における対応する事実／現象を考慮すると日本語にも WH 移動があると想定する方が一貫した分析ができることが分かる．[9]

(33) a. A か B か =(either) A or B: か =or=∨
 b. A か B か =(both) A and B: も =and=∧
(34) a. 何処-か =some-where: 何処 =where; か =some=∃
 b. 何処-も =everywhere: 何処 =where; も =every
(35) a. 何処へ行きますか =Where shall we go?
 b. 何処へ行っても =Wherever we (may) go,
 c. 思ったよりか／も簡単だった Cf. smarter than John or/and Mary

まず，(33) の日本語と英語の比較から，「か／も」は選言記号と連言記号という最も基本的な論理連結詞であることが分かり，(34) から，「か／も」が存在数量子と全称数量子というこれも 2 つの最も基本的な演算子であることが分かるが，このことは単なる偶然の一致とは思われない．何らかの意味でこの 2 つは同じ性質を共有しているはずである．このことを念頭に (35) を見てみると，(35a), (35b) の英語の疑問文も譲歩節も，WH 移動を示す．それに相当する日本語ではいわゆる疑問詞の「何処」は移動していないが，代わりに「か／も」がそれぞれの節の右端に生じている．また，(35c) に見るように日本語では比較節の右端にも「か／も」が現れるのに対して，英語でも比較の対象を

理時間の方が短いという 2 つの事実がある．しかし，(1) は談話における情報構造という言語運用の要因によって決定されることであり，かつ，(2) はそのような言語運用上の事実に対して，言語処理装置 (Parser) において，SOV を処理する回路が頻繁に使用され，OSV を処理する回路より「太く」なって (myelination)，その結果処理速度が増すという，これも言語運用上の要因により決定されているためであり，統語構造という言語能力に関わる部分とは別個の問題であると考えられる．

[9] 他に比較構文においても移動が関与している事実があるが，説明の簡素化のために割愛する．

表す表現では than の後に or/and が生じる．この日英語の奇妙な符合も偶然とは思えない．つまり，WH 疑問節，WH 譲歩節と，そして比較節という，WH 移動が関与していると考えられる 3 種類の節に対応する日本語の節ではいずれも「か／も」がそれぞれの節の右端に現れるのである．

　この事実を捉えるのに，まず，(33)-(35) の「か／も」は同じもので，それぞれ選言 ∨，連言 ∧ であるあると仮定することが最も自然である．そうすると (33)，(34) は (36)，(37) に示すように分析できる．

(36) a. {A,B} か ={A,B}∨=A or B（∨=Pick one）　　　→ A か B か
　　 b. {A,B} も ={A,B}∧=A and B（∧=Pick any）　　→ A も B も
(37) a. 何処か ={p₁ ... pₙ}∨={p₁ ... pₙ}=somewhere　　（∨=Pick one）
　　 b. 何処も ={p₁ ... pₙ}∧={p₁ ... pₙ}=every/anywhere　（∧=Pick any）

(36)，(37) においても「か／も」は集合を補部（引数）とする一項述語（関数）∨/∧ である．(37) では A と B という集合の成員は，いわば上下に重なっていて，全体で「か／も」の補部となっているという多重構造をしていると仮定しよう．そのままでは線状化できないので，上下に重なっている構造は引き離されて「A か B か」，「A も B も」となる．その上で，命題内部（TP）において，選言 ∨ は項の集合を入力としてそれに「一つ選べ（Pick one）」という操作を適用して新たな集合を出力として出す関数であり，他方連言 ∧ は項の集合を入力として，これに「どれでも選べ（Pick any）」という操作を適用して新たな（しかし同じ）集合を出力として出す関数である．これが (36a) では or の，(36b) では and の意味を生む．(37) では「何処」は文脈により定義される場所の集合 {p₁ ... pₙ} を表しているから，「か」はその集合のなかから「一つ選び」，「も」はその集合の「どれでも選ぶ」ために存在数量詞，全称数量詞としての働きが導かれる．これにより数量詞は結合子に還元される．

　この説明は WH 移動に拡大することができる．日英語の WH 移動のメカニズムについて，焦点要素 F が関与しているという 2000a での分析を更に精緻化して次のような分析を提案する．「か」，「も」はそれぞれ選言 ∨ と連言 ∧ であり，かつ，焦点素性 F を持っているが，これが疑問／譲歩という発話内行為と結びつくためには C の位置に来なければならないと仮定しよう．他方英語では音形のない選言 ∨ と，連言 ∧ を含む ever が焦点の F と共にやはり文脈により定義される集合を表す where とともに現れる．∧ を担う ever は where に編入されて，wherever となっている．

(38) a. 何処へ F か行きます　　　　shall we go ∨ F where

　　 b. 何処へ F も行って　　　　　we may go F wherever

(39) a. 何処へ F 行きますか　　　　∨F /where/ shall we go {where}
　　 b. 何処へ F 行っても　　　　　F /wher/ever we may go {where}

WH 移動により日本語では「か」と「も」だけが移動し，中に含まれる ∨ と ∧ は C の指定部に移動する．英語では，∨ は音形を持たないので where の音とともに移動する．∧ は ever という音形を持っているが，形態的に where と一体となっているために，wherever として移動する．日本語では F は「何処へ」についているが，これは対比強勢として実現され，英語でも where (ever) についているので対比強勢として実現される．他方 C の位置の ∨ は，主節の疑問文では，当該の命題を成立させる要素を問題の集合の中から「一つ選ぶ」ことを求めているのに対して，∧ は，当該の譲歩の従属節の「何処」where が表す集合の中の「どれでも選ぶ」ことを聞き手に許可し，それでも主節の命題が成り立つことを主張するという意味で，譲歩を表している．このような疑問／譲歩の意味が ∨ と ∧ の意味から自然に導かれ，なぜ C に移動するのかということについても自然な説明が与えられる．

3.3. 日英語の格付与と転出理論

最後に，節構造形成に関して英語と日本語を比較しておきたい．

3.3.1. 転出

(40a) の例は v*-put という v*-V と that-Past という C-T との語彙複合による，2 つの位相（phase）を経て (40b-f) に示す派生をたどる．特に格付与と一致は，V と T との併合のもとに (40b)，(40e) で生じていることが重要である．(40f) が LF 表示で，ここでは，put は「乗る」に相当している．

(40) a. (I didn't know) that John put Mary on the horse.
　　 b. [Mary v*-put on the horse]　→ v* の転出と主語の併合（対格付与）
　　 c. [John v*-/put/ [Mary {put} on the horse]]　　→ that-Past の併合
　　 d. [that-Past [John v*-/put/ [Mary {put} on the horse]]]
　　　　　　　　　　　　　　　　　　　　→主語の A 移動（主格付与）
　　 e. [/John/ that-Past [{John} v*-/put/ [Mary {put} on the horse]]]

　　　　　　　　　　　　　　　　　　　　　　　　　　　→ that の転出
　　f.　[that [/John/ Past [{John} v*-/put/ [Mary {put} on the horse]]]]
　　g.　LF: [that [Past [John v* [Mary put on the horse]]]]

これに対応する (41a) の例の派生が問題であるが，3.1–3.2 節から日本語は左枝分かれ構造をしているという結論を得たこと，日本語では動詞に後続する要素は音声的には一まとまりになっていて，その間に主語などの要素が介在できないという事実を考慮すると「乗－せ－た－の」という V-v*-T-C の語彙複合を含み，これが順次転出するという (41b) 以下の派生をたどると想定するのが最も一貫性があると考えられる．(41b) では補部の「馬に」と指定部＝目的語の「花子を」の併合が終わっている．

(41) a.　馬に花子を太郎が乗せたの（を知らなかった）
　　 b.　[[馬に乗－せ－た－の] 花子を $_{VP}$]
　　　　　　　　　　　　　　　→「せ－た－の」の転出 ＋ 主語の併合
　　 c.　[[馬に {乗} 花子を $_{VP}$] /乗/－せ－た－の 太郎が $_{v*P}$]　→「た－の」の転出
　　 d.　[[馬に {乗} 花子を $_{VP}$] {せ} 太郎が $_{v*P}$] /乗－せ/－た－の$_T$]
　　　　　　　　　　　　　　　　　　　　　　　　　　　→主語の A 移動
　　 e.　[[馬に {乗} 花子を $_{VP}$] {せ} {太郎が} $_{v*P}$] /乗－せ/－た－の$_{T'}$] / 太郎が / $_{TP}$]
　　　　　　　　　　　　　　　　　　　　　　　　　　　→「の」の転出
　　 f.　[[馬に {乗} 花子を $_{VP}$] {せ} {太郎が} $_{v*P}$] {た} $_{T'}$] / 太郎が / $_{TP}$] / 乗－せ－た/－の
　　 g.　PF: 馬に花子を太郎が乗せたの
　　 h.　LF: [[[[馬に乗 $_V$] 花子を $_{VP}$] せ　太郎が $_{v*P}$] た $_{TP}$] の $_{CP}$]

ここで提案する派生において重要なことは語彙複合 X-Y の Y が転出するたびに，X の音 /X/ は /X/-Y という形で Y に随伴されていくが，その意味 {X} は元の位置に残ることである．この随伴の事実は，V, v*, T, C それぞれが音形を持っているから，(5) の OSH からは導けない．これについては，日本語では，V-v*-T-C は音韻的語 (phonological word) というまとまりをなさなければならないという形態論的条件が課されているためであると考えられる．その結果 (41f) が得られるが，これから発音される部分だけを取り出すと (41g) の PF 表示が得られ，その残りが (41h) の LF 表示である．(41h) は (40g) の英語の LF 表示と順序を除いては全く同じ構造をしている．

3.3.2. 格付与

(41) では，主語が v*P の指定部から TP の指定部に移動していることを想定しているが，そのような移動があっても，動詞を含む語彙複合体が C の位置まで移動するために，移動が起こっているかどうかは語順では確認できない．むしろ，併合のもとで格付与が生じる英語と違って，日本語では格付与は格付与子との一致によって認可されるとした方がいくつかの事実をより整合的にとらえることができる．まず，次の例は主語の TP 指定部への移動が義務的でないことを示しているように思われる．

(42) a. [[[{来}誰も] {なかっ}](学生が)] {た}] /来なかった/ の]
    b [[(学生が)[{来}誰も]{なかっ}]] {た}] /来なかった/ の]
(43) a. [[[[{来} {が}] {なかっ}誰も /が/] {た}] /来なかった/ の]
    b. [[/誰もが/ [[{来} {誰も}] {なかっ}] {た}] /来なかった/ の]

「誰も」はいわゆる否定極性項目で，否定（「なかっ」）の作用域の中になければならないから (42) に示すように動詞句の中に留まっている．他方「学生が」は (42a) のように右（恐らくは否定句の指定部）に移動することもできれば，(42b) のように Scrambling で左に移動することもできる．他方「誰もが」は肯定極性項目で (43a) に示すように右側に移動することも可能であるが，Scrambling により (43b) のように左側に移動する可能性もある．(42) では，括弧に入っている「学生が」が同じように否定の作用域の外に出ている．そしてどの場合においても演算子−変項構造は数量詞「も」と格助詞＝定決定詞「が」の間で成り立っている．

格付与については (42) で見たように，「学生が」が「誰も」の右にも左にも現れることを，否定の作用域＝c 統御領域から脱するためのものであるとすると，それに必要な最小の操作は (42a) では否定句の指定部を占め，(42b) では Scrambling で否定句に付加されることである．その結果，「学生が」は，主格を認可する時制「た」に，直接，すなわち間に他の主要部を介在させずに，c 統御されることになる．この直接 c 統御が格の認可の条件であるとすると，それは (43) において，「誰もが」についても成り立っている．

格付与子による直接 c 統御に基づく一致による格認可が日本語の格付与のメカニズムであるとする分析は，次の例に見られるような多重主格構文をも適切に処理することができる．

(44) a. [[[田中の家が] [倒壊し]] た]

b.　[[[田中 D] [[D 家 D] [倒壊し]]] た]

(44a) では，「田中 D」は名詞「家」または D から属格が与えられ，「の」として実現している．(44b) では，「田中 D」が属格を与えられる前に，Scrambling により名詞の c 統御領域から抜け出して，動詞句に付加している．このときに D のコピーを残しているがこれは属格を与えられても音を持たないと仮定しよう．動詞句の外へ出た「田中 D」は時制に直接 c 統御される位置にある．Hiraiwa (2000) などに従って，日本語の時制は何度でも一致できるとすれば，「家 D」とも「田中 D」とも一致し，2つの D はいずれも「が」として実現される．以上が正しければ，英語は併合に基づき格が付与される言語であるのに対して，日本語は一致に基づき格が付与／認可される言語であるということになる．[10]

4. SOV の呪縛――結びに代えて

　日英語鏡像論は 1987 を契機に考え始め 1988c-d, 1991a, 1993c, 1994a, 1995d, 1996a, 1998a, 2000a, b と展開してきたものである．当初指定部が右にあるということは「か」の右方移動を証拠として挙げていたが，主語の位置には言及していなかった．これは日本語が SOV の語順の言語であるという今から思えばドグマと呼んでもよい広く流布している思い込みに縛られてのことであった．日本語が左枝分かれの言語であれば目的語の方が主語より前に来るはずであるが，それでは SOV の語順は説明できない．そこで，(45a) に示すように，日本語では主語でも目的語でもゼロ代名詞で表すことができることをもとに，日本語ではすべての項はゼロ代名詞 pro で，主語や目的語と見えるものは節 =TP に付加された，ゼロ代名詞を束縛する付加部であるという立場を 2002c, 2003a, 2004b で表明してきた．（実は束縛は指示指標で捉える必要があるので，このことだけでも，この分析が維持しがたいことが分かる．）

(45) a.　[$_{TP}$ 山田が $_i$ [$_{TP}$ 田中を $_j$ [$_{TP}$ pro$_j$ pro$_i$ 憎んでいる]]]
　　 b.　[$_{TP}$ 田中を $_j$ [$_{TP}$ 山田が $_i$ [$_{TP}$ pro$_j$ pro$_i$ 憎んでいる]]]

こうすると (45) に示すように語順が自由である Scrambling の現象は付加の

---

[10] 詳しくは 2012b 参照．逆に英語では一致により日本語では併合により格が与えられるとする提案については Saito (2012) 参照．

順番により生じるものであるとする取り扱いが可能になる．この分析を前面に出したのが2003aの日本言語学会での発表であった．このとき金水敏氏から，その発表の司会をしていた上山あゆみ氏が博士論文で扱っている(46b)のような例はうまく扱えないのではないかという指摘があった．

(46) a. [$_{TP}$ 山田が $_i$ [$_{TP}$ 自分の $_i$ 母親を $_j$ [$_{TP}$ pro$_j$ pro$_i$ 憎んでいる]]]
 b. [$_{TP}$ 自分の $_i$ 母親を $_j$ [$_{TP}$ 山田が $_i$ [$_{TP}$ pro$_j$ pro$_i$ 憎んでいる]]]

(46a)では「山田が」が「自分」をc統御しているので問題ないが，(46b)では「山田」が「自分」の先行詞であるという関係が捉えられないのである．

この指摘の他に実は次の例も問題になることに気付いてはいたのである．

(47) a. [$_{TP}$ 一万円も $_j$ [(僕は $_i$) [$_{TP}$ pro$_j$ pro$_i$ 使わなかった]]]
 b. [$_{TP}$ 30人も $_i$ [$_{TP}$ pro$_i$ 来なかった]

「一万円も」，「30人も」が節=TPに付加していると，いずれも否定の作用域の外にあることになるが，「遣った金額が一万円にもならなかった」，「来た人は30人にもならなかった」という解釈があることは，遥か昔に関西言語学会の夏期講座で触れていたことで，問題になると思っていたのであった．

他にも，この分析では，(48b)には∀>∃という解釈しかないという間違った予測をしてしまうという問題もあったが，その段階では2003cで行っていた英語の数量詞の扱いを日本語にあてはめるということはまだ行っていなかったので，この問題には気付かなかったのである．

(48) a. [誰かが $_i$ [どの人も $_j$ [pro$_j$ pro$_i$ 愛している]]]
 b. [どの人も $_j$ [誰かが $_i$ [pro$_j$ pro$_i$ 愛している]]]

金水氏の指摘に対しては，(46a)に対して更にScramblingが適用することを認めればできるというような答をしたと記憶しているが，付加によりScramblingの事実を処理できることが利点であったので，これでは本当の解決になっていないということがその後ずっと頭を離れなかった．

これを契機に(46)-(48)の例の再分析を，2003cの英語の数量詞の分析を日本語に拡大することとあわせて考え始め，そこでようやくSOVドグマの呪縛から解き放たれて，OSVであるという可能性を真剣に考え始め，概略(49)に示すように分析することに思い至ったのである．

(49) a. [[[自分の母親を {憎んで}$_{VP}$] {v*} 山田が $_{v*P}$] /憎んで v*/いる]

(=(46b))
b. [[[一万円も {遣わ}_{VP} {v*}(僕は)_{v*P} /遣わ v*/ なかった]
(=(47a))
c. [[[30人も {来}_{VP} {v}_{v*P} / 来 / v なかった] (=(47b))
d. [[[どの人も {愛して}_{VP} {v*} 誰かが_{v*P} /愛して v*/いる]
(=(48a))

Scramblingにより，(49a)で「山田が」を文頭に出せば(46a)が得られ，(49b, c)で，「一万円も」，「30人も」を否定の外に出せばもう一つの解釈が得られる．そして，(49d)のままであれば∃>∀であるが，「どの人も」をv*Pに付加すれば∀>∃の解釈が得られ，「誰かが」をv*Pに付加すると(48a)の∃>∀の解釈が得られ，その一義性も説明される．

この分析を2005aの日本言語学会で発表し，その後2005cの英語学会，2006のシンポジウムの発表で発展させ，これを2007年の *English Linguistics* 24巻2号に寄稿した "Japanese and the Symmetry of Syntax" というタイトルのKayne (2005)についてのReview Articleの一部として発表したのであった．

振り返ると1987年に考え始めて2005年まで，20年近くにわたってSOVの呪縛のもとにあって，わずか10年ほど前にようやく解き放たれたことになる．この私の研究における大転換は金水氏の質問に端を発したものであったのであるが，この点で氏に大変感謝している．

私のモットーは「君子豹変」である．研究者として仮説を立て，それが正しいことを望むのは人情であるが，抗しがたい反例がある場合は潔く仮説を撤回することが必要である．私が本当の君子であれば，20年近く拘り続けた(45)の分析を，金水氏の指摘に対する返答の段階で気付いて，その場で(49)に示す大転換の必要性を認めていたであろうが，残念ながら，私は君子ではないので，反例が蓄積してから(49)に示す大転換をするのに2年ほどかかってしまった．(その意味では副題は「凡人猫変」とすべきであったか．)それでも昔の考えに拘泥せずに発想を転換できたことを誇りに思うと同時に，今後いつまでもこのような必要性が生じたときに潔く自説を曲げることができることを切に願っている．

参考文献

(外池著の参考文献については業績一覧表を参照)

Chomsky, Noam (2008) "On Phases," *Foundational Issues in Linguistic Theory: Essays in Honor of Jean-Roger Vergnaud*, ed. by Robert Freidin et al., 133-166, MIT Press, Cambridge, MA.

Fox, Danny (2002) "Antecedent-contained Deletion and the Copy Theory of Movement," *Linguistic Inquiry* 33, 63-96.

Heim, Irene and Angelika Kratzer (1998) *Semantics in Generative Grammar*, MIT Press, Cambridge, MA.

Hiraiwa, Ken (2001) "Multiple Agree and the Defective Intervention Constraint in Japanese," *The Proceedings of the MIT-Harvard Joint Conference (HUMIT 2000)* 40, ed. by Ora Matsushansky et al., 67-80, MITWPL, Cambridge, MA.

Hoji, Hajime (1985) *Logical Form Constraints and Configurational Structures in Japanese*, Doctoral dissertation, University of Washington.

Hornstein, Norbert (2001) *Move! A Minimalist Theory of Construal*, Blackwell, Oxford.

Huang, Cheng-Teh James (1982) *Logical Relations in Chinese and the Theory of Grammar*, Doctoral dissertation, MIT.

Kayne, Richard (1998) "Overt vs. Covert Movement," *Syntax* 1, 128-191.

Kayne, Richard (2005) *Movement and Silence*, Oxford University Press, Oxford.

Klima, Edward S. (1964) "Negation in English," *The Structure of Language. Readings in the Philosophy of Language*, ed. by Jerny A. Fodor and Jerrold J. Katz, 246-323, Prentice Hall, Englewood Cliff, NJ.

Kuno, Susumu (1973) *The Structure of the Japanese Language*, MIT Press, Cambridge, MA.

Kuroda, Sige-Yuki (1970) "Remarks on the Notion of Subject with Reference to Words like *also, even,* or *only* Part 2," *Annual Bulletin* 4, 127-152, Research Institute of Logopedics and Phoniatrics, University of Tokyo, Tokyo.

May, Robert (1977) *The Grammar of Quantification*, Doctoral dissertation, MIT.

May, Robert (1985) *Logical Form*, MIT Press, Cambridge, MA.

Nishigauchi, Taisuke (1990) *Quantification in the Theory of Grammar*, Kluwer, Dordrecht.

Nunes, Jairo (2001) *Linearization of Chains and Sideward Movement*, MIT Press, Cambridge, MA.

Saito, Mamoru (2012) "Case Checking/Valuation in Japanese: Move, Agree or Merge?" *Nanzan Linguistics* 8, 109-127.

Shimada, Junri (2007) "Head Movement, Binding Theory and Phrase Structure," ms., MIT.

外池先生との思い出

野村　忠央

1. 外池先生との出会い

　私は，今回，外池滋生先生の退職記念論文集の企画にご賛同頂いた発起人7人の中で一番若く，このようなエッセイを記すのは分不相応であるが，他の方々を代表して，先生との思い出を記させて頂きたい．

　私が2005年に青山学院大学大学院文学研究科英米文学専攻の最初の課程博士号を取得し，その時の副査に外池先生が名前を連ねておられるので（主査は秋元実治先生），私は先生の青学での弟子だと思われるかもしれないが，実は私は公の意味で先生の指導学生であったことは一度もない．[1]

　私は学部時代，英語史を専攻しようと思っていたので，先生のお名前を初めて目にしたのは，1992年に学習院に入学して，大学の書店にあった大修館英語学シリーズ1『英語史』（「アメリカ英語」担当）か，その隣にあったシリーズ3『英語変形文法』（「音韻論」担当），あるいは今井邦彦先生の「英語学概論」の教科書『一歩すすんだ英文法』であろうと思う．その後，先生が初めて明治学院から学習院に非常勤にいらっしゃったのは，大学2年の1993年のことであった．文学部棟のエレベーターで，まだ習ったことのなかった今井先生と一緒になり，「今年は先生の英語学概論が開講されていないので残念です」と立ち話したら，「概論は（澤田治美先生と）隔年で担当していますから，来年，またやりますよ．それから，今年から専門家の外池君に来てもらっていますから（恐らく，MITでの在外研究からお戻りになった年であったのだろう），そちらを取ってみたらいいです」という話をされたことを記憶している．それで，実際に先生の授業を受講できたのは大学3年の「英語学演習」で，[2] よって，私が先生と実際にお会いしたのは，ミニマリスト・プログラムが萌芽し始め

---

[1] 後述，「外池読書会」と呼ばれる研究会の参加メンバーも多くはそのような方々である．
[2] テキストはElizabeth CowperのA Concise Introduction to Syntactic Theory（紫色の本）．

1994年，自分が21才，先生が47才の時ということになる．

そして，私と外池先生がその場で初めてお会いするような方とご一緒すると，「お二人はどういうご関係ですか？」というような話に大抵なる．そうすると必ず先生がされる話なので，（記しづらいのだが）以下のことを記しておくべきだろう．「前期試験の時期になって，ぼくも忙しい時期でもあって，『前期にやったことをまとめなさい』という夏目漱石ばりの問題を出したら，途中で野村君が憤然と立ち上がって，答案用紙に『棄権』と書いて出て行ったんです（学習院には棄権という制度があった）．恐らく『そういう問題を出すのはおかしい』という抗議の気持ちだったんだと思うんですが，今の時代にはそういう野村君のような『侍』はいなくなりました．ちなみに，彼は後期も1回も休まないで授業を受けて，後期試験も受けました．その年は単位を出してあげられなかったんですが，翌年も授業を履修して，[3]今度は正式に単位を出しました．」先生，あの折のこと，申し訳なく，気恥ずかしく思っております....

関連して，家内（野村（旧姓 森）美由紀）のことも一言だけ．私が家内と出会ったのも外池先生の授業の場であった．彼女は私が学部2年の時に，フェリス女学院大学から学習院の大学院に進学してきた．彼女は今，北教大で「英米文学特講」を担当していることからもわかるように，元々，文学にも詳しく，文学を専攻するつもりだったと想像するのだが，フェリスに1年だけ東大退官直前の長谷川欣佑先生が非常勤にお見えだった時に感銘を受け，英語学の道に進むこととなった．その家内が大学院に進学するという話になり，フェリスには生成文法の専門家がいないので外池先生に授業で彼女を指導して欲しいという話になり，先生も「そういう熱心な学生がいるのなら，長谷川先生の後任は務まらないかもしれないが，お引き受けします」ということになった．だが，行ってみると，彼女はフェリスにはおらず，しかし，偶然，教え始めることになった学習院の方に彼女はいたということであった．

2. 外池読書会

私はその後，1996年に青学の大学院に進学したのだが，「今後も生成文法を学んでおくのは大事だ」と考え，学内の谷美奈子先生[4]の授業以外にも外池先生の授業を取りに行こうと決心した．行ったこともない明学の白金キャンパス

---

[3] テキストは Jamal Ouhara の *Introducing Transformational Grammar*.
[4] 偶然ながら，後年2002年，先生は谷先生の後任として青学に着任されることとなる．

に行って，事務の方に「英文学科の外池先生とお会いしたいんですが」，「外池でございますか，少々お待ち下さい」と頼んだ自分は勇気があったと思う．その結果，学部のゼミに出なさいということになって，出させてもらったのだが，テキストが GB 理論のいいまとめになっていると言われて *Minimalist Program* (*MP*) の Chapter 1 を読んでいたのには驚いた．学部3・4年生で *MP* とは，かわいそうだなとも思った．ちなみに，外部の私をコンパに呼んでくれたそのクラスには，大野真機君や渕田美穂さん，私と同じもぐりで（大学卒業後の一般就職先を辞められたという）木口寛久君がおられた．

その後も私は，（大学で正規に開講されていた）先生の「授業」としては，明学の二部の「英文法」で岩波書店の『生成文法』[5]（この頃，青学の博士浪人中だったが，ほぼ毎週に近く，先生は夕飯がてら私を飲みに連れて行って下さったと思う），日本女子大の大学院の授業[6]で Vivian Cook の *Chomsky's Universal Grammar*，今井先生（在外研究時）代理の学習院の大学院の授業で *MP* の Chapter 3 と 4，明学の大学院の授業[7]で長谷川信子編 *Japanese Syntax in Comparative Grammar* や先生の代表的論文の一つ "Japanese as an OVS Language" (1995 年) などを学んだと記憶している．

これに対し，表題の「外池読書会」というのは，多く，上記の「授業」の後，どこかのスペースを借りて，毎週，数時間に亙り（そして，私は遠い北海道の地で参加できなくなってしまったが，今も）続けられている勉強会，読書会である．現在は青学の外池研究室での開催に落ち着いていると思うが，当時は学習院，立教，明学言文研近くの教室など様々な場所を渡り歩き，うまく教室が見当たらない時は，（話し合いなどをしてもよい）高級喫茶店「談話室　滝沢」や池袋駅近くの喫茶店などで読書会をしていたことも思い出される．通常の読書会は 10 人前後が参加していたと思うが，喫茶店の読書会では，先生，西前明さん（発起人），大野君，私の 4 人だけという時代もあった．

ここで外池読書会の特徴を 2 つ記すと，まず，特定の大学に閉じられてい

---

[5] 先生が，「第 1 次認知革命」(GB 理論) の章を執筆された，他の各章の内容も含め，優れた本 (1998 年)．余談ながら，「極小主義理論」については，『言語学の領域〈I〉』(朝倉書店) に簡にして要を得た優れた解説・論考を書かれている (2009 年)．

[6] 女子大だが，青学，明学，法政，津田塾などの 12 大学の大学院で単位互換している「英専協」という便利で有益な制度のために履修できた．恐らく津田塾出身の鈴木泉子さん（発起人）もそのお陰で先生と知り会ったのだと思う．

[7] 先生が明学在職中，齋藤興雄先生の在外研究中に，唯一，大学院を兼担された年で，先生の日本語統語論の授業を受講できたことは幸運であった．

ない，来る者拒まず（言うまでもなく去る者追わず）の開かれた読書会だということが挙げられる．それは，学部生か院生か大学で教鞭を取っている人間かも問わないこと，また，参加者の年齢が下は20代の学生から，上は会社役員を定年し大学院に入り直された，先生よりも年上の坂野収さんや中栄欽一さんなどが参加されていることにも示されている（時に参加されていたドナルド・スミス先生も年上である）．このような多様な人物が集う読書会となった理由は，先生の還暦のお祝いの際，家内が寄せた「大学の垣根を越えて，先生のみもとに，（読書会などの形で）大勢集まりますのは，先生のお人柄とご人徳と存じます」というお祝いのメッセージの通りと思うが，その他にも，先生が明学で大学院を兼担されていなかったこと，[8] また，先生は明学の言文研や国際交流センター長などでもご多忙だったが，依頼される数多くの大学の非常勤を断らず引き受けられていたことなども関係しているのではないかと想像する．つまり，このような偶然の状況がなければ，読書会も例えば，明学の大学院生メンバー中心に閉じて開催されていたかもしれず（仮定法なのでわからないけれども），青学，明学，学習院，都立大，法政，津田塾，東大といった院生が広く参加する読書会にはならなかったのではないかと思う．なお，余談ながら，上記のような事情から，明学の学部時代に先生の授業に感銘を受けて言語学を志した方々で，他大や海外の大学院に進学し，研究者の道に進まれた方も少なくないと想像する．本記念論文集寄稿者に限っても，北原久嗣先生（発起人），遠藤喜雄先生，岡俊房先生，宇佐美文雄先生，江頭浩樹さん（発起人），木口寛久君，吉田正哉君，森田千草さんなどが挙げられる．ちなみに，この論文集の，私ともう一人の編集実働部隊を務めてもらっている江頭さんは，明学の国際学部2年次に初めて先生に会った時，独力で（一時代前の）ジェイコブズ＆ローゼンボーム『基礎英語変形文法』を読んでいた江頭さんに「今の変形文法はもっと華麗に変形する」と言われたことを印象深く覚えているということであった（なお，先生はご記憶にないそうである）．

　次に，外池読書会の第2の特徴として，ハンドアウト発表形式や要旨発表形式ではなく，その難易度に拘らず「精読」を旨とするということが挙げられる．[9] 通例，大学院の授業や研究会では，一人何十ページの分担があたって，

---

[8] 先生に限らず，当時，松本曜先生や佐野哲也先生なども大学院指導教授ではなかったと記憶している．

[9] 長い論文だけではなく，短い記事も精読した．代表選手は先生が大石正幸先生（発起人）と共著で書かれた『英語青年』の連載「最新チョムスキー理論の概要」（1992-93年）などである．この連載はチョムスキーの1991年秋学期の授業を，本記念論文集の寄稿者でもある小泉

そのハンドアウトを作り，完全な理解を前提とした上でのプレゼンテーションが求められるものである（鈴木さんを見ていて津田もそういう厳しさが強くあるんだろうなと感じた覚えがある）．しかし，外池読書会では，毎回数ページの分担について本人なりの「和訳」をしてくることだけが最低条件である．私はこのスタイルでの参加が許されていたからこそ，長年に亘って先生の読書会に参加できたのだと思う．（よって，チョムスキーの最新論文などは半期いっぱい，あるいは通年かかったりすることもしばしばであった．）もちろんハンドアウトを作れば本人も勉強になるし，必死で勉強するからいいに決まっているが（青学の大学院も古英語文献講読以外の授業は当然，そうだった），例えば，外池読書会で全て draft の段階で読んでいたチョムスキーの MP の Chapter 4 (1995 年), "Minimalist Inquiries" (初出 1998 年) (西前さんはこの時から参加されたと思う), "Derivation by Phase" (初出 1999 年), "Beyond Explanatory Adequacy" (初出 2001 年) (江頭さんはこの頃から参加されたと思う) などを，初読の段階で要旨をまとめろと言われても自分には絶対無理である．

　先生は「ヨコのものをタテにするだけでも意味がある」とおっしゃるが，本当にその通りだと思う．だいたいあんな難解なもの，私は一人じゃ絶対読まなかったと思うし，読書会に出ている時は訳してみてもチンプンカンプンということも多かったが（その私の訳を聞いてまわりの方々から「あぁ〜，なるほど」などと聞こえてくるのは不思議な体験だった），しかし，後で何ヶ月か何年か経って，他の論文や本を読んでいたり，あるいは，例えば TEC（理論言語学講座）の長谷川欣佑先生や渡辺明先生が別のトピックの話をなさっていたりする時などに，「あの時のことはこういうことを言っていたのか！」といくつかの点がパーっと結び付く時があるから不思議なものである．昔の漢文素読や『声に出して読む日本語』などでも言われることだが，「わからなくても読んでみる」というのは大切な姿勢だと思う．いつのことだったか，「最近，内容がわからないで読書会に出ています．読書会，やめようかとも迷っています」ということを先生に伝えたことがあったのだが，そうすると「ぼくも昔，太田朗先生の読書会で *Aspects* を読んでいた時，さっぱりわからなかった．でもいつかわかる時が来るから君も頑張って出なさい」と話して下さった．私は先生のこのようなご配慮のおかげで読書会参加を続けることができたし，また他の

政利先生，北原先生，野地美幸先生との研究会での議論も踏まえ，まとめたものだと伺ったことがある．

参加メンバーも私も，上述の外池読書会スタイルの下であったからこそ，本当に多くのことを学べたのではないかと思う．

3. 教育者としての外池先生

　読書会に続いて，先生の教育者としての側面も一言だけ記しておきたい．先生の授業は，概論・講義系の授業でも，演習系の授業でも，上述の如く，基本的に精読を旨とされ，よどみない平板調の日本語，英語で90分びっしり，濃度の濃い授業をされる．また，先生の樹形図を描かれる早さに学生は誰しも圧倒されると思う．[10]

　先生は授業中，学力が低い，勉強ができないという理由で学生を注意されることは決してないが，担当があたった箇所の和訳をやってこないなどの最低限の義務を果たさない学生には非常に厳しい．（言うまでもなく，受講態度が悪い学生に対しても，当然，そのような態度は決して許さないということも耳にしたが，私が受けた授業の中ではそのような学生は見かけなかった．）

　次に，論文指導について記すと，先生を見知っている方はみんなご存知だと思うが，先生は専門的にどんなに難しいことであっても，逆にどんなに初歩的な質問やささいな日常的，時事的な話題であっても，流されたり，馬鹿にされたりすることなく，本気で議論される方である．よって，先生と見解や立場が異なる時は——私も先生と何度か大議論になったが——ちょっと辛いなという経験をされた方々も複数おられると思う．私個人としては，リンカーンのゲティスバーグ演説における government of the people の of の解釈を巡ってとか，博士論文に初めて詳細に書き込んで下さった先生のコメントに，「本当にありがたいことだ．なるほどなるほど」などと思うと同時に，ところどころに散見される厳しい内容に胸が痛くなったことも思い出される．例えば，博論のどこかの章の終わりには「Adjunct 全体の理論を示すべきである」と書かれてあって，青山学院大学図書館や国立国会図書館提出用の修正版の博論を1か月弱で提出する前にどう直せばいいのか途方に暮れた．[11]

---

[10] 私は多くの先生方に生成文法を習う機会があったが，樹形図を描かれる速さでは外池先生と高見健一先生が抜きん出ていたと思う．

[11] ちなみに，外池先生も外部副査の千葉修司先生も私の間違った英語を直して下さって，本当に勉強になった．よってという訳でもないが，自分も現在，学生の卒業論文の英語や査読論文の書式などについて，エネルギーが本当に掛かることだが，気付いた点はできるだけ指摘するように努めている．

しかし，先生に論文指導を受けたことがある人はみんな感じることであろうが，先生は研究者仲間，読書会メンバー，院生，学部生を問わず，論文構想を相談されれば，時間の許す限り，議論に付き合って下さるし（品川へ向かう山手線内で曇ったガラスに指で樹形図を描かれ，指導されていた姿も記憶している），あるいは，ご自身の手柄としてもいいような，なるほどというアイディアをいくつも思い付かれ，惜しげもなく披瀝される．本記念論文集の寄稿者の方々の中にも，先生のアイディアに助けられた方は数多くおられるのではないかと想像する．

4. 研究者としての外池先生

研究者としての外池先生については，今回，先生ご自身の「私の研究遍歴」というエッセイもあるので，書きたいことは多々あるのだが，簡潔に記したい．私なりに先生のご研究をまとめさせて頂ければ，「外池先生は，日本語・英語の両方に対して，鋭い言語直観と言語観察の力をお持ちになり，そして，それらの言語事実を整合的に説明する，大胆奇抜かつアイディアあふれる仮説をいつもご提案なさる」ように思う．また，その根底に力強い英語力が存在することにも多くの人が尊敬の念を抱いていると思う．

先生の前期の一連のご研究としては，私見では例えば，英語では「名詞句の内部構造，抜き出し」に関するもの，日本語では「かきまぜ（Scrambling）」や「日英語鏡像関係」に関するものが挙げられると思うが，個別研究においても，『英語青年』「Agr の廃止をめぐって」（1993 年），EPP 素性の廃止を主張した「Chomsky（2001）における 2 つの問題——「音韻部門の移動規則」と EPP 素性——」（2001 年），『COE 成果報告』"Attract F and Elimination of the LF Component—A Proposed I Model of Grammar—"（1998 年）など，その後のチョムスキーの方向を予言するような重要な論文もいくつもあると思う（海外の研究者が知り得ていないことが残念である）．

また，先生の後期の一連のご研究としては，演算子−変項構造，数量詞，再帰代名詞などを含む，「外池理論による Minimalist 分析」とでも言えるものが挙げられるが，それは先生の爾来からの（そして，恐らくは数ある言語学者の中で唯一の）ご主張である「日本語は英語が SVO 言語であるのと完全な鏡像関係としての OVS 言語である」という仮説に辿り着くものと考えられる．

全ての先生がそうではないが，外池先生のような大家，あるいはそうでなくとも還暦を過ぎられた先生というのは，新しい研究には手を付けず，昔の自分

の研究の貯金のまとめに入られることがしばしばだと思う．しかし，先生は退職間近の今日に至るまで決してそのようなことはなく，チョムスキーや他の研究者から有力な影響力のある仮説が提出されるたびに，その crucial な問題点を指摘し，ご自身なりの，我々がアッと驚くような代案を考え付かれる．チョムスキーがミツ・ロナとの対話で，博士論文でやっていたことを始終やり続けているような研究者は望ましくないという趣旨の発言をしていたと思うが（私はそのような研究者の存在も間違いなく大切だと思うが，しかし），先生はそうではない，チョムスキーが肯定するであろう研究者である．その感を一層強くしたのは，昨年（2013 年）8 月に，日本英語英文学会北海道支部設立大会記念シンポジウムで講演して頂いた時で，久し振りに，66 歳になられた先生の理論全体を伺ったのだが，旧来の外池理論が revise され，随所に新しいアイディアが鏤められていたのは本当に驚き，感心した．日英語鏡像仮説だけ少し記すと，従来，先生は日本語の深層構造の OVS の主語，目的語は見えない pro で，付加部位置にある顕在的な主語，目的語がそれらを c 統御し，同じインデックスがふられるという趣旨の仮説だったのだが，現在では OSV の語順に左方付加（いわゆる「かきまぜ」）が起こることで日本語の諸現象が説明できるという仮説に進化していた（私の理解に誤りがあることを恐れるので，これ以上の詳細は先生の「私の研究遍歴」をご覧頂きたい）．

　これらのことが示しているのは，先生が以前のご自身の仮説に関して，「過ちを改むるに憚ることな」く，「君子豹変す」だということである．この態度は科学者たるに重要な要件であろうが，影響力が大きい人ほど「言うは易く，行うは難し」であろう（例えば，Chomsky が Postal の Raising-to-Object の主張を是認するまで 30 年近い年月が流れたのではないだろうか）．しかし，先生はそれを地で行っている研究者である．一例だけエピソードを記すと，青学で修士の院生であった小澤由紀子さんが there 構文を修士論文のテーマにして，彼女は意味上の主語には部分格が与えられているという立場を採用したのだが，先生はその修論構想を聞いた時に，それはおかしいという議論を非常に強い調子でされた．しかし，それから半年か一年後だったか，酒席で「野村君，there 構文の意味上の主語には be 動詞から partitive が与えられているという仮説は正しいんじゃないかと思う」と聞かされた時は，私もさすがに苦笑しつつ，「先生，それはひどいですよ！」と応じた覚えがある．

　この流れで，しかし，弟子として残念だなあと思うことを一点だけ記すと，先生にはあれだけの業績がありつつ——意外だと思われると思うが——著書としての単著がおありにならない．そして，このことは上記，先生の経験科学者と

しての姿勢と無関係ではないと思う．しかし，昨年の講演を拝聴するに，嬉しいことに，ハワイ大学での在外研究で最新外池理論の核となる諸論文をまとめられたように感じたので，定年後の自由な時間をお使いになられ，ぜひ単著を出版されて，外池理論を世界に問うて欲しいと切に思う．

5. 外池先生のユーモア，いたずら好き

さて，前節までの内容を読んできて下さった読者諸氏には，先生は物事を極めて論理的に考え，合理性を重んずる，[12] 何事にも真面目な研究者としての側面しかないように映るかもしれない．しかし，先生はテニスやゴルフ，囲碁や麻雀などもこよなく愛されるし，実は授業の場面だけでは想像され得ないと思うが，ユーモア溢れた，かなりのいたずら好きでもいらっしゃる．

それこそ，最初に授業でお会いした時には，「この先生は言語学のことしか興味がなく，1分1秒でも無駄にするのが惜しいのだろう」と思っていた．というのは，学習院の2限は10時40分開始なのだが，毎回，授業前の10時35分ぐらいであったであろうかに足早に教室に入って来られ，着くなり，「森君，伊藤君[13]…」などと出席を取り，それが終わるや否や，「今日は123ページの4行目から，野村君」と授業が始まり，90分びっしり授業をやり終えられると，疾風のように，[14] 教室を去って行かれたからである．また，いつであったか，「先生，たまには何か余談をして下さい」とみんなでお願いしたら，「じゃあ，このセクションが終わったら」と言われて，何か先生のご趣味の話か，世俗的な内容の余談が始まるのかと期待していたら，日本語の活用の分析が始まったのであった．

しかし，後から先生と親しくなってからお聞きしたところ，授業はもう10時半には始まっていてご自身は遅刻していると思われていたらしく，また，12時10分を過ぎたら足早に去っていたのは，3限も日本女子大で非常勤があ

---

[12] 余談ながら，その意味で，先生はその思考法が，芸能界からスパッと姿を消された上岡龍太郎氏に似ていると何度か思ったことがある．（先生は幽霊，霊魂，死後の世界，占い，字画なども信じられないが，その点でもお二方は似ていると思う．）いつぞやそのことを尋ねてみたら，やはり先生も上岡氏を尊敬しているとのことだった．

[13] 先生は男女関係なく，学生を「君」で呼ぶ．

[14] 先生のことを「畏友」と称した中島平三先生も『発見の興奮』（大修館書店）の中で「外池さんは大変行動力があり，彼の歩き方や話し方がそうであるように，前へ前へとどんどん進んでいく」と記されていたが，全くその通りである．

り，また，非常勤の方には昼食が出ていたんだそうで，せっかくなのでということで，急いで日本女子大に移動されていたということであった．

　いたずらに関しては枚挙に暇がない．私に関して言うと，例えば，先生やみんなと楽しく飲んで酔っ払った自分が帰宅すると，リュックサックに食べ終わった弁当がまた包装されたものと飲み干したビール瓶の口にティッシュが詰められたものが入っていたりした．翌週，「先生，あの瓶とか一体何なんですか？」とお尋ねすると，「野村君のリュックが汚れないようにティッシュを詰めておいた」という訳のわからないお答えであった．あるいは，明学の学部ゼミのみんなが打ち上げに呼んでくれた時（ちなみに，そのメンバーで寄せ書きをしたベルトを先生に差し上げた覚えがある），2次会に移動する道すがら，信号待ちをしていたところ，私が「先生，天津甘栗，売っていますよ」と何気なく言ったら，急に「買うか」と言われ，その買ったばかりの熱々の天津甘栗を私の背中に入れようとされたり，「2次会のカラオケボックスは持ち込み不可なのでやばいですよ」と言っているのに，灰皿に天津甘栗をいっぱい盛られ，それを店員に注意されると「隠せ，隠せ」と愉快そうに言われたりもしていた．あるいは，読書会後の居酒屋で野球中継がやっていて，確か，根本貴行さんが巨人ファンだと言ったら，アンチ巨人の先生は，「根本君，じゃあ，巨人が負けたら，ここの勘定は全て君が払いなさい」と言われたり（実際に巨人は負け，冗談ながらも根本さんは支払いを迫られていた），帰り道，根本さんの靴の踵を踏むといういたずらを何度も繰り返されたりしていた．明学の読書会の打ち上げでは，その終了間際，お手洗いに立った渕田さんが席に戻って来ると，中華料理屋のテーブルには誰もおらず，彼女が泣きそうな顔になって店を出て来る（みんな店の外で隠れている）ということもあった．

　また，学習院での，毎回，長いチョムスキーの読書会の後，今は壊された目白駅前のコマースというビルにあった中華料理屋によく行ったのだが，ただ飲んでいても面白くないからじゃんけんで負けた人がビールを飲むという罰ゲームをやろうと言い出され，酒を飲まない家内に，「じゃあ，森君は代わりにラー油を飲みなさい」と言われ，彼女は本当にラー油を飲んでいた．それを助けるためか，自分が飲みたいためかわからないのだが，お酒が強い勝山裕之さんは「ぼくが代わりに飲みます」とうれしそうに飲まれていた．

　青学着任後のことも少しだけ記すと，先生の歓迎会を教員や院生で催した折，確か2次会まで行って会計の段になり，幹事の中澤和夫先生（発起人）が「外池先生，今日のところは我々で」という申し出に「いやいや2次会まで全額は申し訳ない」という外交的やりとりを数回繰り返した後，普通は「じゃあ，

今日のところはお言葉に甘えます」で終わると思うのだが，会って間もないであろう中澤先生に，「いいから受け取りなさい！」と，中澤先生のワイシャツと背中の間に1万円札を押し込もうとされていた．また，青学着任後の最初の院生であった田口和希君（嫌いな漬け物を食べさせられるなど，いつも先生にいじられていた）が，打ち上げから渋谷駅までの帰り道，先生をおどかそうと道に隠れていたのだが，それを先んじて察知した先生は知らないお宅の水撒き用のホースだったかの蛇口をひねって，田口君に水しぶきを浴びせていた．この種の話題は事欠かないのだが，この辺でやめておこう．

6. いつまでもご活躍を――結びに代えて

本記念論文集は，予想を遥かに超える多くの方々が執筆をご快諾下さったため，一人当たりのページ数が制限されてしまったことを――寄稿者の方々への感謝の念と共に――心苦しく存じている．よって，先生のことで書きたいことはまだまだあるのだが，私も紙幅を守って，筆を擱きたい．

上述，出会いの頃，「先生は言語学のことしか興味ないのか」と記したが，実は逆で，先生は森羅万象のことに興味がおありだと思う．私との狭い議論だけでも，英語学，言語学に始まり，政治，経済，教育，哲学，果ては5文型論，天皇制などにも及んだ（先生，学部生の頃からの議論ですが，5文型は必要だと思います）．その他，スポーツや科学，[15] 植物などにもご関心深く，要するに，先生は"義務"としてではなく"性分"として「知的好奇心」に溢れており，常に「知の探究」，「真理の探究」を目指しておられるのだと思う．我々弟子たちや本論文集の寄稿者の方々は，（卓越した言語学者としての姿は言うを俟たず）先生のそのような姿に感銘を受け，尊敬の念を抱いていると想像する．

外池先生，どうぞいつまでも，第一線の言語学者，授業をびっしりやりつつも時々，学生にいたずらをしかける先生，ハワイ生活を楽しまれるテニス，ゴルフの愛好家であり続けて下さい．

---

[15] 先生が MP の翻訳を出版された時，記念にサインを求めたら，「反証可能性のないものは科学ではない」と記された．先生の学問に対する姿勢を端的に言い表していると思う．

執筆者一覧

(アルファベット順)

阿部　　潤	東北学院大学・非常勤講師
秋元　実治	青山学院大学・名誉教授
坂野　　収	青山学院大学大学院文学研究科・科目等履修生
Josef Bayer	コンスタンツ大学言語学科・教授
江頭　浩樹	大妻女子大学比較文化学部比較文化学科・准教授
遠藤　喜雄	神田外語大学大学院言語科学研究科・教授
Hubert Haider	ザルツブルク大学言語学科・教授
保阪　靖人	日本大学文理学部ドイツ文学科・教授
今井　邦彦	東京都立大学・名誉教授
伊藤　達也	首都大学東京・非常勤講師
泉谷　双藏	東京医科歯科大学国際交流センター・准教授
川島るり子	明治学院大学・非常勤講師
木口　寛久	宮城学院女子大学学芸学部英文学科・准教授
金水　　敏	大阪大学大学院文学研究科文化表現論専攻日本文学国語学専門分野・教授
北原　久嗣	慶應義塾大学言語文化研究所・教授
小泉　政利	東北大学大学院文学研究科・准教授
久野　　暲	ハーヴァード大学言語学科・名誉教授
Eric McCready	青山学院大学文学部英米文学科・准教授
森川　正博	名古屋外国語大学・名誉教授
森田　千草	目白大学外国語学部英米語学科・専任講師
中栄　欽一	青山学院大学大学院文学研究科・科目等履修生
中島　平三	学習院大学文学部英語英米文化学科・教授
中澤　和夫	青山学院大学文学部英米文学科・教授
根本　貴行	東京家政大学人文学部英語コミュニケーション学科・准教授
西山　佑司	慶應義塾大学・名誉教授
野地　美幸	上越教育大学大学院学校教育研究科言語系（英語）・准教授
野村美由紀	北海道教育大学・非常勤講師

野村　忠央	北海道教育大学教育学部旭川校教員養成課程英語教育専攻・准教授	
大石　正幸	東北学院大学文学部英文学科・教授	
岡　俊房	福岡教育大学教育学部国際共生教育講座・教授	
大塚　祐子	ハワイ大学言語学部・准教授	
Peter Robinson	青山学院大学文学部英米文学科・教授	
西前　明	明治学院大学・非常勤講師	
佐野　哲也	明治学院大学文学部英文学科・教授	
瀬田　幸人	岡山大学大学院教育学研究科社会・言語教育学系英語教育講座・教授	
島田　守	龍谷大学・名誉教授	
Donald L. Smith	北ジョージア大学・非常勤教師, 青山学院大学・元教授	
鈴木　泉子	信州豊南短期大学言語コミュニケーション学科・専任講師	
髙橋　洋平	読売自動車大学校自動車整備学科・非常勤講師	
高見　健一	学習院大学文学部英語英米文化学科・教授	
Christopher Tancredi	慶應義塾大学言語文化研究所・教授	
外池　滋生	青山学院大学文学部英米文学科・教授	
豊島　孝之	九州工業大学大学院情報工学研究院人間科学系／生命体工学研究科人間知能システム専攻・教授	
塚田　雅也	青山学院大学・國學院大学・非常勤講師	
上田　功	大阪大学大学院言語文化研究科言語情報科学講座・教授	
宇佐美文雄	明治学院大学・非常勤講師	
Henk C. van Riemsdijk	ティルブルク大学・名誉教授	
山内　一芳	首都大学東京オープンユニバーシティ・特任教授, 東京都立大学・名誉教授	
吉田　方哉	ノースウェスタン大学言語学科・助教授	
遊佐　典昭	宮城学院女子大学学芸学部英文学科・教授	

より良き代案を絶えず求めて
(In Untiring Pursuit of Better Alternatives)

ISBN978-4-7589-2210-4　C3080

編　者	江頭浩樹・北原久嗣・中澤和夫・野村忠央
	大石正幸・西前　明・鈴木泉子
発行者	武村哲司
印刷所	日之出印刷株式会社

2015 年 3 月 23 日　第 1 版第 1 刷発行Ⓒ

発行所	株式会社　開 拓 社	〒113-0023　東京都文京区向丘 1-5-2 電話　(03) 5842-8900（代表） 振替　00160-8-39587 http://www.kaitakusha.co.jp

JCOPY ＜(社)出版者著作権管理機構 委託出版物＞

本書の無断複写は，著作権法上での例外を除き禁じられています．複写される場合は，そのつど事前に，(社)出版者著作権管理機構（電話 03-3513-6969, FAX 03-3513-6979, e-mail: info@jcopy.or.jp）の許諾を得てください．